Elements of Psychology

❖

ROBERT S. FELDMAN
University of Massachusetts—Amherst

McGraw-Hill, Inc.

New York   St. Louis   San Francisco   Auckland
Bogotá   Caracas   Lisbon   London   Madrid
Mexico   Milan   Montreal   New Delhi   Paris   San Juan
Singapore   Sydney   Tokyo   Toronto

Elements of Psychology

1 2 3 4 5 6 7 8 9 0 VNH VNH 9 0 9 8 7 6 5 4 3 2 1

ISBN 0-07-020562-0

This book was set in Palatino by Waldman Graphics, Inc.
The editors were Christopher Rogers and Margery Luhrs;
the designer was Leon Bolognese;
the production supervisor was Leroy A. Young.
The photo editor was Elsa Peterson.
Von Hoffmann Press, Inc., was printer and binder.

Library of Congress Cataloging-in-Publication Data

Feldman, Robert S. (Robert Stephen), (date).
    Elements of psychology / Robert S. Feldman.
      p.   cm.
    Includes bibliographical references and indexes.
    ISBN 0-07-020562-0
    1. Psychology.   I. Title.
BF121.F33   1992
150—dc20   91-21695

ABOUT THE AUTHOR

Robert S. Feldman is Professor of Psychology at the University of Massachusetts at Amherst. A graduate of Wesleyan University and the University of Wisconsin-Madison, he is a former Fulbright Senior Research Scholar and Lecturer. He is a Fellow of the American Psychological Association and the American Psychological Society and author of more than eighty scientific articles, book chapters, and papers. His research interests include nonverbal behavior and the social psychology of education. He has written or edited eight books, including *Social Psychology: Theories, Research, and Applications* (McGraw-Hill), *The Social Psychology of Education* (Cambridge University Press), and *Fundamentals of Nonverbal Behavior* (Cambridge University Press). His spare time is most often devoted to serious cooking, which he does well, and piano playing, which he doesn't. He lives with his wife, also a psychologist, and three children in a home overlooking the Holyoke mountain range in Amherst, Massachusetts.

TO
Sarah, Josh, and Jon,
and, of course, Kathy

Contents

Preface

The people and events in the world around us defy easy explanation. We see good behavior and bad; we encounter sensible and irrational conduct; and we find cooperation and violent competition among the world's peoples.

Elements of Psychology reflects the efforts of psychologists to understand and explain the myriad forms of behavior that we see in the world. The book provides a broad and concise introduction to psychology. It focuses on the basic building blocks of the field, those essentials that are critical for an understanding of the discipline of psychology. While concentrating on the fundamentals of the discipline, it also makes clear the relevance of psychology to people's everyday lives.

In writing *Elements of Psychology*, I had three overriding goals in mind. First, the book is designed to cover the major areas of the field of psychology, introducing its principal theories, research, and applications. Second, the book is meant to foster an appreciation of the scientific basis of the field, as well as providing an impetus for critical thinking. Finally, the book is intended to be engaging and interesting, a book arousing a reader's natural curiosity about the world. Ultimately, then, *Elements of Psychology* is designed to nurture an appreciation of how psychology can be used to understand the society in which we live.

These three goals, of course, are interdependent. In fact, I would argue that if *Elements of Psychology* is successful in accurately communicating the nature of psychology, understanding and interest regarding the field will follow naturally. To that end, I have lavished considerable attention on the book's writing style. It is intended to provide as close a facsimile to two people sitting down and discussing psychology as can be conveyed with the written word. When I use the word "we," then, I am referring to the two of us—you, the reader, and me, the author.

In addition, this text has special features that highlight the everyday relevance of psychology to the world around you ("Psychology and Society" boxes) and aim to improve the quality of your life ("Informed Consumer of Psychology" sections). It is also a book carefully designed to promote learning. Every chapter presents material in rational, manageable sections. A set of factual and conceptual questions on the information

("Ask Yourself") follows each of these sections. If you thoughtfully answer these questions, you will have a critical head start on mastery and long-term recall of the information.

In sum, *Elements of Psychology* is, as I mention in the first chapter, designed to be user-friendly. It is a book that not only introduces you to the basic content—and promise—of psychology, but it does so in a way that brings alive the excitement of the field. My hope is that your initial exposure to the realm of psychology will forge an ongoing enthusiasm and passion for the discipline—one that lasts a lifetime.

AN OVERVIEW OF ELEMENTS OF PSYCHOLOGY

Elements of Psychology is based on the second edition of the widely used 21-chapter *Understanding Psychology*, a broad and comprehensive introduction to the field of psychology. Like the book from which it is derived, *Elements of Psychology* includes coverage of the traditional topical areas of psychology. It covers, for example, the biological foundations of behavior, sensation and perception, learning, cognition, development, personality, abnormal behavior, and the social psychological foundations of behavior.

Unlike its predecessor, however, *Elements of Psychology* is a considerably briefer volume. It focuses on the essentials of psychology, providing an initial broad introduction to the field. The book also shows how the field's theories and research have an impact on readers' everyday lives.

There is considerable flexibility to the book's organizational structure. Each chapter contains self-contained units, permitting instructors to choose and omit sections according to their syllabus. In addition, the applications material is well integrated throughout even the chapters that cover the most traditional, theoretical topics. Consequently, courses that omit the more applied topical chapters will still be successful in conveying the relevance of psychology to readers.

Overall, then, the book reflects a combination of traditional core topics and contemporary applied subjects, providing a broad, eclectic—and current—view of the field of psychology. It draws from theoretical and applied approaches, and integrates the two with objective presentations of research that illustrate the way in which the science of psychology has evolved and grown. Indeed, the book exemplifies the view that a theory-application dichotomy is a false one. The text does not present applications as devoid of theory, but places them in a theoretical context, grounded in research findings. Likewise, when the text presents theoretical material, it draws practical implications from the theory.

Some examples can illustrate this approach. If you turn to Chapter 3, you will find that it includes the traditional material on hearing in the ear. But the text moves beyond a mere recitation of the various parts of the ear and explanations of hearing and balance; it also explores current work involving an electronic ear implant in the cochlea to help the deaf. Similarly, the development chapter includes a presentation of the classic work on attachment. This material is tied into the question of the effects of child-care arrangements on development. Finally, the chapter on abnormal behavior not only explores the issues of how we identify abnormal behavior, but relates it to the real-life case of a homeless woman who fights—and ultimately defeats—a court order to be placed in a shelter. In each of these instances, the text shows how applications grow out of the theoretical and research base of the field.

*L*EARNING AIDS AND FEATURES OF ELEMENTS OF PSYCHOLOGY

Elements of Psychology is designed with its ultimate consumer—the student—in mind. As you can see from the following full list of elements that are common to every chapter, the book incorporates several major educational features. These features, based on learning and cognitive instructional design theory and research, are meant to make the book an effective learning device and, simultaneously, enticing and engaging:

- *Prologue.* Every chapter starts with an account of a real-life situation that involves major aspects of the topics of the chapter. These scenarios demonstrate the relevance of basic principles and concepts of psychology to actual issues and problems. For example, the chapter on the biology underlying behavior begins with a description of a patient undergoing a controversial operation in which adrenal tissue is implanted in his brain, and the chapter on cognition discusses how the mystery of the Challenger space shuttle explosion is solved.
- *Looking Ahead.* A "Looking Ahead" section follows each prologue. It articulates the key themes and issues and lists a set of questions answered in the chapter.
- *Psychology and Society.* The Psychology and Society boxes illustrate an application of psychological theory and research findings to a real-world problem. For example, the chapter on cognition includes a discussion of eyewitness identification in judicial settings, and the chapter on personality and individual differences introduces material on personality tests that might be encountered when applying for a job.
- *The Informed Consumer of Psychology.* Every chapter includes information designed to make readers more informed consumers of psychological information and knowledge by giving them the ability to evaluate critically what the field of psychology offers. For example, this feature covers treatment of drug and alcohol problems (Chapter 7) and evaluating psychological therapy (Chapter 10).

- *Ask Yourself.* Research clearly indicates the importance of careful organization of textual material, learning material in small chunks, and actively reviewing material. Consequently, each chapter is divided into from three to five sections, each of which concludes with an "Ask Yourself" section. Every "Ask Yourself" section includes a variety of questions to answer, including both those that require recall of factual material and those that test higher-level conceptual understanding of the material.

- *Looking Back.* To simplify the review of the material covered in each chapter and to aid in the synthesis of the information covered, a numbered summary is included at the end of every chapter. The summary emphasizes the key points of the chapter.

- *Key terms and Concepts.* When key terms and concepts are introduced, they are highlighted in bold face type and listed at the end of every chapter (with the page numbers where they were first introduced). Each of these key terms is also included in an end-of-book glossary.

- *A full-color graphic design.* To support the instructional design features of the text, a team of graphic designers has developed a design structure to enhance the written material. The thoughtful design and photos make the text inviting and a book from which it is easy to learn.

ANCILLARY MATERIALS

An extensive ancillary package accompanies *Elements of Psychology*. These materials enhance the value of the text as a teaching and learning tool. The *Study Guide*, by Valerie J. Sasserath and Mark Garrison, comes free to students who purchase the text from us and includes an introductory section on how to study and how to use the *Guide* effectively with the text. There is also an extensive section entitled *A Guide to Critical Thinking*. Following this material are chapters (corresponding to each text chapter) that include chapter outlines and overviews, learning objectives, hundreds of questions in various formats, and application exercises.

The *Test File* offers more than 2,500 multiple-choice and true-false questions that test both factual recall and higher order understanding. The items are keyed to page numbers in the text. This *Test File* was prepared by Louis Banderet of Northeastern University, Dennis Clare of the College of San Mateo, Lynne Kiorpes of New York University, Charles Noble of North Georgia College, and Edward Pflaumer of Loma Linda University. Katherine Vorwerk of the University of Massachusetts was consultant for clarity and construction. The *Test File* is available in a computerized format for use with mainframe and microcomputers.

The *Instructor's Manual* includes chapter overviews, lecture objectives and topics, key terms, discussion topics, "Take a Stand" sections (which outline issues for debate), Psychology in the News topics, demonstrations and projects, essay questions with answers, and an annotated bibliography of audiovisual resources.

An extensive media package accompanies *Elements of Psychology*. The transparency and slide set includes 100 items, and McGraw-Hill provides a catalog of films and videos for book users.

Finally, several software packages accompany this text. These include *PsychWorld*, 2nd ed. (for IBM $3\frac{1}{2}$ and $5\frac{1}{4}$ and Apple); *MacLaboratory*, 2nd ed. (for Macintosh); *Computer Activities for Psychology*, 4th ed. (CAPS IV, for IBM and Apple); *Report Card* (a computerized grade-management program, for IBM and Apple); *Experiments and Personal Applications in Psychology* (for IBM and Apple); and *Statistical Computation Program for Students* (for IBM and Apple).

*A*CKNOWLEDGMENTS

As the following list of reviewers attests, this book involved the efforts of many psychologists. They lent their expertise in evaluating all or part of the manuscript, providing an unusual degree of quality control. Their careful work and thoughtful suggestions have improved the manuscript many times over from its first-draft incarnations. I am grateful to them all for their comments: Patrick T. DeBoli, Nassau Community College; Joyce Webster Dennis, Southern Union State Junior College; Michael Firmin, Baptist Bible College and Seminary; Claudia Graham, Wake Technical Community College; Sheila P. Greenlee, Columbus State Community College; Leon Keys, Ferris State University; Jack Kirschenbaum, Fullerton State University; Rosalyn Mass, Middlesex Community College; Meg Miele, Fashion Institute of Technology; Richard Richter, Lansing Community College; Lawrence C. Shaffer, SUNY Plattsburgh; Lily Shohat, LaGuardia Community College, CUNY; and Floyd Donald Whitehead, Fayetteville Technical Community College.

Many teachers have shaped my thinking. I was introduced to psychology at Wesleyan University, where several committed and inspiring teachers made the excitement and relevance of the field clear to me. By the time I left Wesleyan I could envision no other career except that of psychologist. Although the nature of the University of Wisconsin, where I did my graduate work, could not have been more different from the much smaller Wesleyan, the passion and inspiration were similar. Again, a cadre of excellent teachers molded my thinking and taught me the beauty and science of the discipline of psychology.

My colleagues and students at the University of Massachusetts at Amherst provide ongoing intellectual stimulation, and I thank them for making the university a very fine place to work. Several people also provided extraordinary research and editorial help; they include Carolyn Dash, Richard Fleming, Wendy Copes, Frances Ramos, and the late Kate Cleary.

I am very grateful to both Rhona Robbin and Elisa Adams, whose work as developmental editors shaped the content and form of this book. Their skillful editing and insightful comments improved the volume immeasurably. I've been lucky enough to work with two of the best editors in the publishing field.

Chris Rogers, sponsoring editor, provided the impetus for this book, and I am appreciative of his intelligence and savvy, as well as his friendship. Other people at McGraw-Hill were central to the design and production process; these include Margery Luhrs and David Dunham. I am proud to be a part of this world-class McGraw-Hill team.

Finally, I am, as always, indebted to my family. The love and support of my parents, Leah Brochstein and the late Saul D. Feldman, remain a bedrock of my life. My many nieces and nephews, my brother, my various brothers- and sisters-in-law, Ethel Radler, and Harry Brochstein might all be surprised to know of the influence they have over me. I also remain grateful to my late mother-in-law, Mary Evans Vorwerk, for her encouragement in every sphere of life.

Ultimately, my children, Sarah, Joshua, and Jonathan, and my wife, Katherine, remain the focal point and joy of my life. I thank them, with great love.

Robert S. Feldman

Strategies for Effective Study and Critical Thinking

Elements of Psychology has been written with the reader in mind, and it therefore includes a number of unique features that will help you to maximize your learning of the concepts, theories, facts, and other kinds of information that make up the field of psychology. To take advantage of these features, there are several steps that you should take when reading and studying this book. By following these steps, you will not only get the most out of this book, but you will also develop habits that will help you to study other texts more effectively and to think critically about material you are learning. Among the most important steps to follow:

- Familiarize yourself with the logic of the book's structure. Begin by reading the Table of Contents. It provides an overview of the topics that will be covered and gives a sense of the way the various topics are interrelated. Next, review the Preface, which describes the book's major features. Note how each chapter is divided into three to five self-contained units; these provide logical starting and stopping points for reading and studying. Also note the major highlights of each chapter: a chapter-opening outline, a Prologue, a Looking Ahead section that includes chapter objectives, Ask Yourself questions, and—at the end of every chapter—a Looking Back section and Key Terms and Concepts. Because every chapter is structured in the same way, you are provided with a set of familiar landmarks as you chart your way through new material, allowing you to organize the chapter's content more readily.

- Use a study strategy. Although we are expected to study and ultimately learn a wide array of material throughout our schooling, we are rarely taught any systematic strategies that permit us to study more effectively. Yet, just as we wouldn't expect a physician to learn human anatomy by trial and error, it is the unusual student who is able to stumble upon a truly effective studying strategy.

  Psychologists, however, have devised several excellent (and

proven) techniques for improving study skills, two of which are described here. By employing one of these procedures—known by the initials "SQ3R" and "MURDER"—you can increase your ability to learn and retain information and to think critically, not just in psychology classes but in all academic subjects.

The SQ3R method includes a series of five steps, having the initials S-Q-R-R-R. The first step is to *survey* the material by reading the chapter outlines, chapter headings, figure captions, recaps, and Looking Ahead and Looking Back sections, providing yourself with an overview of the major points of the chapter. The next step—the "Q" in SQ3R—is to *question*. Formulate questions—either aloud or in writing—prior to actually reading a section of the material. For instance, if you had first surveyed this section of the book, you might jot down in the margin, "what do "SQ3R" and "MURDER" stand for?" The reviews that end each section of the chapter are also a good source of questions. But it is important not to rely on them entirely; making up your own questions is critical. Such questioning helps you to focus in on the key points of the chapter, while putting you in an inquisitive frame of mind as well.

It is now time for the next, and most crucial, step: to *read* the material. Read carefully and, even more important, actively and critically. For instance, while you are reading, answer the questions you have asked yourself. You may find yourself coming up with new questions as you read along; that's fine, since it shows you are reading inquisitively and paying attention to the material. Critically evaluate material by considering the implications of what you are reading, thinking about possible exceptions and contradictions, and examining the assumptions that lie behind the assertions made by the author.

The next step—the second "R"—is the most unusual. This "R" stands for *recite*, in which you look up from the book and describe and explain to yourself, or to a friend, the material you have just read and answer the questions you have posed earlier. Do it aloud; this is one time when talking to yourself is nothing to be embarrassed about. The recitation process helps you to clearly identify your degree of understanding of the material you have just read. Moreover, psychological research has shown that communicating material to others (even imaginary others, if you are reciting aloud to yourself and not a friend) aids you in learning it in a different—and deeper—way than material which you do not intend to communicate. Hence, your recitation of the material is a crucial link in the studying process.

The final "R" refers to *review*. Reviewing is a prerequisite to fully learning and remembering material you have studied. Look over the information; reread the Recaps and Looking Back summaries; answer in-text review questions; and use any ancillary materials you may have available. (There is both a traditional and a computerized student study guide available to accompany *Elements of Psychology*.) Reviewing should be an active process, in which you consider how different pieces of information fit together and develop a sense of the overall picture.

An alternative approach to studying—although not altogether dissimilar to SQ3R—is provided by the MURDER system of Dansereau (1978). Despite the unpleasant connotations of its title, the MURDER system is a useful study strategy.

In MURDER, the first step is to establish an appropriate mood for studying by setting goals for a study session and choosing a time and place in which you will not be distracted. Next comes reading for understanding, in which careful attention is paid to the meaning of the material being studied. Recall is an immediate attempt to recall the material from memory, without referring to the text. Digesting the material comes next; you should correct any recall errors, and attempt to organize and store newly learned material in memory.

You should work next on expanding (analyzing and evaluating) new material, and try to apply it to situations that go beyond the applications discussed in the text. By incorporating what you have learned into a larger information network in memory, you will be able to recall it more easily in the future. Finally, the last step is review. Just as with the SQ3R system, MURDER suggests that systematic review of material is a necessary condition for successful studying.

- The last aspect of studying that warrants mention is that *when* and *where* you study are in some ways as important as *how* you study. One of the truisms of the psychological literature is that we learn things better, and are able to recall them longer, when we study material in small chunks over several study sessions, rather than massing our study into one lengthy period. This implies that all-night studying just prior to a test is going to be less effective—and a lot more tiring—then employing a series of steady, regular study sessions.

In addition to carefully timing your studying, you should seek out a special location to study. It doesn't really matter where it is, as long as it has minimal distractions and is a place that you use *only* for studying. Identifying a special "territory" allows you to get in the right mood for study as soon as you begin.

A final comment: By using the proven study strategies presented above, as well as by making use of the pedagogical tools integrated in the text, you will maximize your understanding of the material in this book and you will master techniques that will help you learn and think critically in all your academic endeavors. More importantly, you will optimize your understanding of the field of psychology. It is worth the effort: the excitement, challenge, and promise that psychology holds for you is immense.

Elements of Psychology

———— ❖ ————

1

Introduction to Psychology

❖

PROLOGUE: THE SAN FRANCISCO EARTHQUAKE

The devastation of the San Francisco earthquake produced a wide range of behavior of interest to psychologists.

For most of the people in the San Francisco area, the day began routinely. At 5:04 P.M., however, that routine was abruptly shattered when the ground literally began to shake under people's feet. A major earthquake had started.

The quake brought about the deaths of dozens of people and billions of dollars in property damage. Some people emerged as heroes, digging through tons of rubble in a desperate search to find those buried underneath. Others exhibited a less positive side of human nature, looting homes and stores that were temporarily abandoned by their owners after the quake.

No area resident emerged unscathed from the earthquake. Although the majority of residents were not physically harmed by the quake, most felt anxiety and apprehension that another quake might hit. They received little comfort from geologists, who predicted that the odds were greater than 50 percent that a much worse earthquake would occur at some point within the next three decades.

LOOKING AHEAD

Although its origin was a geological event far beneath the surface of the earth, the San Francisco earthquake raises issues that are primarily psychological in nature. Consider, for example, the ways in which different kinds of psychologists would look at the disaster.

- Psychologists who specialize in the biology underlying behavior would examine changes in the body's internal activity as it prepared to deal with the emergency situation of the disaster.
- Those psychologists who specialize in the study of learning and memory would investigate the kinds of details concerning mishaps that people are most apt to learn about and later recall.
- Psychologists who study people's thinking processes would consider how people view risks and perceive how such risks apply to them personally.
- Developmental psychologists, who study children, might consider how stress brings about an increase in child abuse.
- Health psychologists, who study the relationship between physical and psychological factors, would study the ways in which experiencing the disaster might produce later illness.
- Clinical and counseling psychologists, who provide therapy, would examine how to reduce people's anxiety.
- Social psychologists, who study questions related to interpersonal interaction, would try to understand the reasons behind the helpfulness of some and the aggressiveness of others.

The Common Link among Psychologists: The Study of Behavior and Mental Processes

Although the approaches taken by different psychologists in considering the earthquake are very diverse, the common link among them is that each represents a specialty area within the general area of study called psychology. **Psychology** is the scientific study of behavior and mental processes.

This definition, although clear-cut and accurate, is also deceptively simple. In order to encompass the breadth of the field, "behavior and mental processes" must be understood to mean many things: It includes not just what people do but also their thoughts, their feelings, their perceptions, their reasoning processes, their memories, and even, in one sense, the biological activities that keep their bodies functioning.

When psychologists speak of "studying" behavior and mental processes, their interests are equally broad. To psychologists, it is not

Can the sign language Roger Fouts uses to communicate with the chimp Lucy be similar in sophistication to the language used when human beings converse? As discussed in Chapter 5, the answer is controversial.

enough simply to describe behavior. As with any science—and psychologists clearly consider their discipline a science—psychology attempts to explain, predict, modify, and ultimately improve the lives of people and the world in which they live.

Psychologists seek to achieve these goals through scientific methods. They do not consider it sufficient to rely on intuition, insight, and logic to study behavior; too often, people are simply wrong in their guesses about human behavior (Kohn, 1990).

By using scientific procedures, psychologists are able to find answers to questions about the nature of human behavior that are far more valid than what mere intuition and guesses provide. And what a variety and range of questions psychologists pose. Consider these examples: How do we see colors? What is intelligence? Can abnormal behavior be cured? Is a hypnotic trance the same as sleep? Can aging be delayed? How does stress affect us? What is the best way to study? What is normal sexual behavior?

These questions—whose answers you will know by the time you finish reading this book—provide just a hint of the range of topics that will be presented as we explore the field of psychology. Our discussions will take us across the spectrum of what is known about behavior and mental processes. At times, we will leave the realm of humans and explore animal behavior, since many psychologists study nonhumans in order to determine general laws of behavior that pertain to *all* organisms, and since animal behavior can provide important clues to answering questions about human behavior. But we will always return to the usefulness of psychology in helping to solve the everyday problems that confront all human beings.

In this introductory chapter, we cover a number of topics that are central to an understanding of psychology. We begin by considering the different types of psychologists and the roles they play. Next, we discuss the major approaches and models that are used to guide the work psychologists do. Finally, we examine the research methods psychologists employ in their search for the answers to questions that will help them to better understand behavior.

In covering this introductory material, we also introduce the text itself. This book is intended to provide as close a facsimile to two people sitting down and discussing psychology as one can convey with the written word; when I write "we," I am talking about the two of us—reader and writer. To borrow a phrase from folks who spend much of their time with computers, the book is meant to be "user-friendly."

The text is also designed to make it easier for you to learn the material we discuss. Based on the principles that psychologists who specialize in learning and memory have developed, information is presented in relatively small chunks, with each chapter including from three to five major sections. Each of these sections is followed by a series of "Ask Yourself"

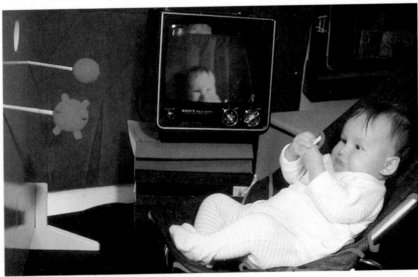

Developmental psychologists conduct sophisticated experiments to study infants and their abilities.

questions relating to the key points of the chapter. Thoughtfully (and faithfully) answering these questions will help you in thoroughly learning, and later recalling, the material.

In sum, after reading this chapter, you will be able to answer the following questions:

- What is psychology and why is it a science?
- What are the different kinds of psychologists?
- What assumptions do psychologists make about the world?
- How do psychologists use theory and research to answer questions of interest?
- What are the different forms of research employed by psychologists?

PSYCHOLOGISTS AT WORK

Wanted: Industrial/Organizational Psychologist. Ph.D. required. Psychologist will work with other psychologists who are responsible for generating accurate job descriptions, developing and administering training programs, designing performance evaluation systems, and developing and implementing a program for the early identification of managerial talent within the company.

♦ ♦ ♦

Wanted: Counseling Psychologist. Ph.D. required, including internship and experience relevant to understanding both college student development and higher education environments. Responsibilities include counseling/therapy with individuals and groups, and consultation with campus units. Innovation in devising new counseling methods and developing new programs is encouraged.

♦ ♦ ♦

Wanted: Psychology Instructor, Community College. Master's degree required. Instructor will teach one to three sections of introductory psychology and two to four classes from interest areas including family relations, child and adult development, educational psychology, personality, social psychology, and experimental psychology. Additional duties will include advising entering and first-year students (American Psychological Association, 1987).

Many people mistakenly believe that almost all psychologists analyze and treat abnormal behavior. However, as the actual job descriptions reprinted above indicate, the range and scope of the field of psychology are much broader than this common misconception would suggest. We can examine the major branches and specialty areas of psychology by describing them in the general order in which they are discussed in this book. Figure 1-1 displays the percentage of psychologists who are engaged in

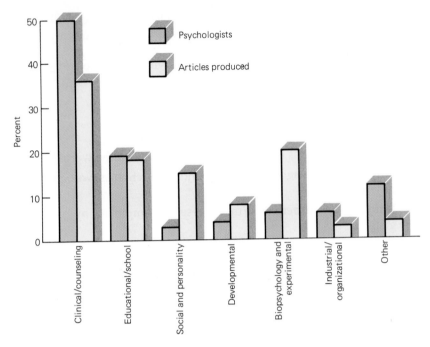

FIGURE 1-1
The major specialties within the field, represented by the percentage of psychologists falling into each catetory and the number of publications produced in each category between 1967 and 1986. (Sources: Stapp, Tucker, & VandenBos, 1985 (table 2), p. 1324; *PsychINFO Training Manual*, 1987.)

each of the major specialty areas. It also shows the proportion of published articles relevant to each area, indicating which of the specialties currently are the heaviest contributors to the psychological research literature.

The Biological Foundations of Psychology: Biopsychologists

In the most fundamental sense, people are biological entities, and some psychologists emphasize how the physiological functions and structures of our body work together with our mind to influence our behavior. **Biopsychology** is the branch of psychology that specializes in the biological bases of behavior. Biopsychologists study a broad range of topics with a focus on the operation of the brain and nervous system. For example, they may investigate the ways in which specific sites in the brain are related to a disorder such as Parkinson's disease (see Chapter 2), or they may attempt to determine how bodily sensations are related to emotion (see Chapter 6).

Sensing, Perceiving, Learning, and Thinking: Experimental Psychologists

If you have ever wondered how acute your vision is, how you experience pain, or how you can most effectively study, you have raised a question that is most appropriately answered by an experimental psychologist. **Experimental psychology** is the branch of psychology that studies the processes of sensing, perceiving, learning, and thinking about the world.

The work of experimental psychologists overlaps that done by biopsychologists, as well as that done in other branches of psychology. Actually, the term "experimental psychologist" is somewhat misleading, since psychologists in every branch use experimental techniques, and experimental psychologists do not limit themselves to only experimental methods.

Several subspecialties have grown out of experimental psychology and have become central parts of the field in their own right. For example, **cognitive psychology** is the branch of psychology that specializes in the study of higher mental processes, including thinking, language, memory, problem solving, knowing, reasoning, judging, and decision making. Covering a wide swath of human behavior, cognitive psychologists have, for instance, identified more efficient ways of remembering and better strategies for solving problems involving logic.

Understanding Change and Individual Differences: Developmental and Personality Psychologists

A baby producing its first smile . . . taking its first step . . . saying its first word. These events, which can be characterized as universal milestones in development, are also singularly special and unique for each person. Developmental psychologists, whose work is discussed in Chapter 8, trace the changes in behavior and in people's underlying capabilities throughout their lives.

Developmental psychology is the branch of psychology that studies how people grow and change throughout the course of their lives. Another branch, **personality psychology,** attempts to explain both consistency and change in a person's behavior over time, as well as the individual traits that differentiate the behavior of one person from another when each confronts the same situation. The major issues relating to the study of personality will be considered in Chapter 9.

Physical and Mental Health: Health, Clinical, and Counseling Psychologists

If you have difficulty getting along with others, continual unhappiness in your life, or a fear that prevents you from carrying out your normal activities, you might consult one of the psychologists who devote their energies to the study of physical or mental health: health psychologists, clinical psychologists, and counseling psychologists.

Health psychology explores the relationship between psychological factors and physical ailments or disease. For instance, health psychologists are interested in how long-term stress (a psychological factor) can affect physical health. They are also concerned with identifying ways of promoting behavior related to good health (such as increased exercise) or discouraging unhealthy behavior such as smoking.

For clinical psychologists, the focus of activity is on the treatment and prevention of psychological disturbance. **Clinical psychology** is the branch of psychology that deals with the study, diagnosis, and treatment of abnormal behavior. Clinical psychologists are trained to diagnose and treat problems ranging from the everyday crises of life—such as grief due to the death of a loved one—to more extreme conditions, such as loss of touch with reality. Some clinical psychologists also conduct research, investigating issues that range from identifying the early signs of psychological disturbance to studying the relationship between how family members communicate with one another and psychological disorder.

As we will see when we discuss abnormal behavior and its treatment in Chapters 10 and 11, the kinds of activities carried out by clinical psychologists are varied indeed. It is the clinical psychologist who administers and scores psychological tests and who provides psychological services in community mental-health centers.

Counseling psychology is the branch of psychology that focuses on educational, social, and career adjustment problems. Almost every college has a counseling center staffed with counseling psychologists, where students can get advice on the kinds of jobs they might be most suited for, on methods of studying effectively, and on strategies for resolving everyday difficulties, from problems with roommates to concerns about a specific professor's grading practices.

Two close relatives of counseling psychology are educational psychology and school psychology. **Educational psychology** considers how the educational process affects students; it is, for instance, concerned with ways of understanding intelligence, developing better teaching techniques, and understanding teacher-student interaction. **School psychology,** in contrast, is the subspecialty devoted to assessing children in elementary and secondary schools who have academic or emotional problems and to developing solutions to such problems.

Many veterans faced psychological difficulties after returning from the war in Vietnam. Clinical and counseling psychologists often used a treatment technique with them that consisted of discussion groups, like this one in Walla Walla, Washington.

Understanding the Social World: Social and Industrial-Organizational Psychologists

None of us lives in isolation; rather, we are all part of a complex network of interrelationships. These networks with other people and with society as a whole are the focus of study for many different kinds of psychologists.

Social psychology, as we will see in Chapter 12, is the study of how people's thoughts, feelings, and actions are affected by others. Social psychologists focus on such diverse topics as understanding human aggression, learning why people form relationships with one another, and determining how we are influenced by advertisements.

Industrial-organizational psychology is concerned with the psychology of the workplace. Such questions as "How do you increase productivity and worker accuracy?" "How can you select the right person for a job?" and "Can an employee's job satisfaction be increased?" are asked by industrial and organizational psychologists.

The Workplace of Psychologists

Given the diversity of roles that psychologists play, it is not surprising that they are employed in a variety of settings. The primary employers are institutions of higher learning: universities, two- and four-year colleges, and medical schools. The next-most-frequent employment settings are hospitals, clinics, community mental-health centers, and counseling centers. A substantial number of psychologists are also employed in private practice. Other settings include human-services organizations, research and consulting firms, and business and industry (Oskamp, 1988).

Why are so many psychologists found in academic settings? The primary reason is that the three major roles played by psychologists in society—teacher, scientist, and professional—are easily carried out in such an environment. Very often professors of psychology are also actively involved in research or in serving clients. Whatever their particular job setting, however, psychologists share a commitment to better both individual lives and society in general, and the topics they explore range from people's inner lives to the psychology of space travel (DeLeon, 1988; Smith, 1990).

ASK YOURSELF

How can the term "psychology" be defined?

What are the major types of psychologists?

Where are psychologists employed?

Why is a scientific approach to understanding why people act the way they do more appropriate than a reliance on common-sense and intuition?

A SCIENCE EVOLVES: THE PAST AND THE FUTURE

Some half-million years ago, primitive peoples assumed that psychological problems were caused by the presence of evil spirits. To allow these spirits to escape, an operation called trephining was performed. Trephining consisted of chipping away at the skull with crude stone instruments until a hole was cut through the bone. Because archeologists have found skulls with signs of healing around the opening, we can assume that patients sometimes survived the cure.

◆ ◆ ◆

The famous Greek physician Hippocrates thought that personality was made up of four temperaments: sanguine (cheerful and active), melancholic (sad), choleric (angry and aggressive), and phlegmatic (calm and passive). These temperaments were influenced by the presence of "humors," or fluids, in the body. For instance, a sanguine person was thought to have more blood than other people.

◆ ◆ ◆

Franz Josef Gall, an eighteenth-century scientist, argued that a trained observer could discern intelligence, moral character, and other basic personality traits from the shape and number of bumps on a person's skull. His theory gave rise to the "science" of phrenology, employed by hundreds of practitioners.

While these "scientific" explanations sound farfetched to us, at one time they represented the most advanced thinking regarding what might be called the psychology of the era. Even without knowing much about modern-day psychology, you can surmise that our understanding of behavior has advanced tremendously since these earlier views were formulated. Yet most of the advances have occurred relatively recently, for, as sciences go, psychology is one of the newcomers on the block.

Although its roots can be traced back to the ancient Greeks and Romans, and though philosophers have argued for several hundred years about some of the same sorts of questions that psychologists grapple with today, the formal beginning of psychology is generally set at 1879. In that year, the first laboratory devoted to the experimental study of psychological phenomena was established in Germany by Wilhelm Wundt; at about the same time, the American William James set up his laboratory in Cambridge, Massachusetts.

Throughout its some 11 decades of formal existence, psychology has led an active life, developing gradually into a true science. As part of this evolution, it has produced a number of conceptual **models**—systems of interrelated ideas and concepts used to explain phenomena—that have guided the work being carried out. Some of these models have been discarded—just as have the views of Hippocrates and Descartes—but others have been developed and elaborated on and provide a set of maps for psychologists to follow.

Each of the models provides a distinct perspective, emphasizing different factors. Just as we may employ not one but many maps to find our

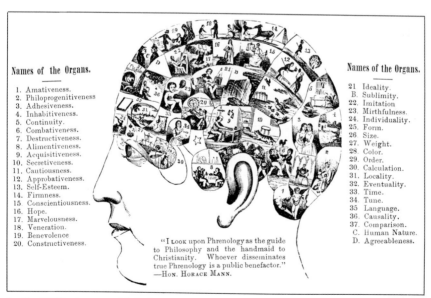

Names of the Organs.

1. Amativeness.
2. Philoprogenitiveness
3. Adhesiveness.
4. Inhabitiveness.
5. Continuity.
6. Combativeness.
7. Destructiveness.
8. Alimentiveness.
9. Acquisitiveness.
10. Secretiveness.
11. Cautiousness.
12. Approbativeness.
13. Self-Esteem.
14. Firmness.
15. Conscientiousness.
16. Hope.
17. Marvelousness.
18. Veneration.
19. Benevolence
20. Constructiveness.

Names of the Organs.

21 Ideality.
B. Sublimity.
22. Imitation
23. Mirthfulness.
24. Individuality.
25. Form.
26 Size.
27. Weight.
28. Color.
29. Order.
30. Calculation.
31. Locality.
32. Eventuality.
33. Time.
34. Tune.
35 Language.
36. Causality.
37. Comparison.
C. Human Nature.
D. Agreeableness.

"I LOOK upon Phrenology as the guide to Philosophy and the handmaid to Christianity. Whoever disseminates true Phrenology is a public benefactor." —Hon. HORACE MANN.

In the 1800s, it was widely believed that phrenology (the study of the contours of an individual's head) could reveal important information about a person.

way around a particular geographical area—one map to show the roads, one the major landmarks, and one the topography of the hills and valleys—psychologists also find that more than one approach may be useful in understanding behavior. Given the range and complexity of behavior, no single model will invariably provide an optimal explanation—but together, the models provide us with a means to explain the extraordinary breadth of behavior.

The Roots of Psychology: Historical Perspectives

When Wilhelm Wundt set up the first psychology laboratory, he was interested in studying the building blocks of the mind. Formally defining psychology as the study of conscious experience, he developed a model that came to be known as structuralism. **Structuralism** focused on the fundamental elements that form the foundation of thinking, consciousness, emotions, and other kinds of mental states and activities.

To come to an understanding of how basic sensations combined into our awareness of the world, Wundt and other structuralists used a procedure called introspection to study the structure of the mind. Using **introspection,** Wundt presented people with a stimulus—such as a bright green object or a sentence printed on a card—and asked them to describe, in their own words and in as much detail as they could manage, what they were experiencing as they were exposed to it. Wundt argued that psychologists could come to understand the structure of the mind through the reports that people made of their reactions.

Wundt's structuralism did not stand the test of time, however, for psychologists became increasingly dissatisfied with the assumption that introspection could unlock the fundamental elements of the mind. For one thing, people had difficulty describing some kinds of inner experiences, such as emotional responses. (For example, the next time you experience anger, try to analyze and explain the primary elements of what you are feeling.) Moreover, breaking down objects into their most basic mental units sometimes seemed to be a most peculiar undertaking. A book, for instance, could not be described by a structuralist as merely a book, but instead had to be broken down into its various components, such as the material on the cover, the colors, the shapes of the letters, and so on. Finally, introspection was not a truly scientific technique; there was little way that an outside observer could verify the accuracy of the introspections that people did make. Such drawbacks led to the evolution of new models, which largely supplanted structuralism.

Interestingly, however, important remnants of structuralism still exist. As we shall see in Chapter 5, the past twenty years have seen a resurgence of interest in people's descriptions of their inner experience. Cognitive psychologists, whose interests center on higher mental processes such as thinking, memory, and problem solving, have devel-

Wilhelm Wundt, in the center of this photo, established the first laboratory to study psychological phenomena in 1879.

oped innovative techniques for understanding people's conscious experience that overcome many of the difficulties inherent in introspection.

The model that largely replaced structuralism in the evolution of psychology was known as functionalism. Rather than focusing on the mind's components, **functionalism** concentrated on what the mind *does*—the functions of mental activity. Functionalists, whose model rose to prominence in the early 1900s, asked what roles behavior played in allowing people to better adapt to their environments. Led by the American psychologist William James, the functionalists, rather than raising the more abstract questions about the processes of mental behavior, examined the ways in which behavior allows people to satisfy their needs. The famous American educator John Dewey took a functionalist approach and from it developed the field of school psychology, theorizing about how students' needs could best be met through the educational system.

Another reaction to structuralism was the development of gestalt psychology in the early 1900s. **Gestalt psychology** is a model of psychology focusing on the study of how perception is organized. Instead of considering the individual parts that make up thinking, gestalt psychologists took the opposite tack, concentrating on how people consider individual elements as units or wholes. Their credo was "The whole is greater than the sum of its parts," meaning that, when considered together, the basic elements that comprise our perception of objects produce something greater and more meaningful than those individual elements alone. As we shall see when we examine perception in Chapter 3, the contributions of gestalt psychologists to the understanding of perception are substantial.

Today, several major models have evolved from the roots of structuralism, functionalism, and gestalt psychology, each of them emphasiz-

TABLE 1-1 COMPARISON OF THE MAJOR MODELS OF PSYCHOLOGY

Model	Conceptual Focus	View of Human Nature	Importance of Mental Processes	Emphasis: Environment or Person
Biological	Biological functions as basis of behavior	Neutral	Moderate	Person
Psychodynamic	Unconscious determinants of behavior	Negative	Maximum (for unconscious)	Person
Cognitive	Nature of thought processes and understanding of world	Neutral	Maximum	Both
Behavioral	Observable behavior	Neutral	Minimum	Environment
Humanistic	Human desire to reach potential	Positive	Maximum	Person

ing different aspects of behavior. These include the biological, psychodynamic, cognitive, behavioral, and humanistic models.

Each of these models varies in a number of critical dimensions, as summarized in Table 1-1. One model may have a basically positive and optimistic view of human nature, focusing on the potential for good in people's behavior, while another may be oriented more toward the negative aspects of human behavior, such as selfishness and aggression. The models may also differ in the degree of emphasis they place on mental processes, with some essentially ignoring thought processes and focusing on observable behavior and others placing primary emphasis on thinking. Finally, some theories consider environmental causes of behavior as predominant, while others base their explanations for behavior more on the nature of the individual.

As we discuss each of the models, keep in mind how they differ in these major dimensions.

Blood, Sweat, and Fears: Biological Approaches

When we get down to the basics, behavior is carried out by living creatures made of skin and guts. According to the **biological model,** the behavior of both people and animals should be considered from the perspective of their biological functioning: how the individual nerve cells are joined together, how the inheritance of certain characteristics from parents and other ancestors influences behavior, how the functioning of the body affects hopes and fears, what behaviors are due to instincts, and so forth. Even more complex kinds of behaviors—emotional responses such as fear, for example—are viewed as having critical biological components by psychologists using the biological model.

Because every behavior can at some level be broken down into its biological components, the biological model has broad appeal. Psychologists who subscribe to this model have contributed important advances in the understanding and betterment of human life, advances that range from suggesting cures for deafness to identifying drugs that help people with severe mental disorders.

Understanding the Inner Person: Psychodynamic Approaches

To many people who have never taken a psychology course, psychology begins and ends with the **psychodynamic model.** Proponents of the psychodynamic perspective believe that behavior is brought about by inner forces over which the individual has little control. Dreams and slips of the tongue are viewed as indications of what a person is truly feeling within a seething caldron of subconscious psychic activity.

The psychodynamic view is intimately linked with one individual: Sigmund Freud. Freud was a Viennese physician in the early 1900s whose ideas about unconscious determinants of behavior had a revolutionary effect on twentieth-century thinking, not just in psychology but in related fields as well. Although many of the basic principles of psychodynamic thinking have been roundly criticized, the model that has grown out of Freud's work has provided a means not only for treating mental disorders but for understanding everyday phenomena such as prejudice and aggression.

Sigmund Freud, a Viennese physician, developed the psychodynamic model in which people's behavior was considered to be determined by unconscious processes.

Understanding Understanding: Cognitive Approaches

The route to understanding behavior leads some psychologists straight into the mind. Evolving in part from structuralism, which, as we noted earlier, was concerned with identifying the various parts of the mind, the **cognitive model** focuses on how people know, understand, and think about the world. The emphasis, though, has shifted away from learning about the structure of the mind itself to learning how people understand and represent the outside world within themselves (Rouse & Morris, 1986).

Psychologists relying on this model ask questions ranging from whether a person can watch television and study a book at the same time (the answer is "probably not") to how people figure out the causes of human behavior. The common element that links cognitive approaches is the emphasis on how people understand the world.

Understanding the Outer Person: Behavioral Approaches

While the biological, psychodynamic, and cognitive approaches look inside the organism to determine the causes of its behavior, the behavioral model takes a very different approach. The **behavioral model** grew out of a rejection of psychology's early emphasis on the inner workings of the mind, suggesting instead that observable behavior should be the focus of the field.

John B. Watson, the first major American psychologist who championed a behavioral approach, was firm in his view that a full understand-

Rejecting psychology's initial emphasis on the inner workings of the mind, John B. Watson proposed a behavioral approach which focused on observable behaviors.

ing of behavior could be obtained by studying and modifying the environment in which people operated. In fact, he believed rather optimistically that by properly controlling a person's environment, any desired sort of behavior could be obtained, as his own words make clear: "Give me a dozen healthy infants, well-formed, and my own specified world to bring them up in and I'll guarantee to take any one at random and train him to become any type of specialist I might select—doctor, lawyer, artist, merchant-chief, and yes, even beggar-man and thief, regardless of his talents, penchants, tendencies, abilities, vocations and race of his ancestors" (Watson, 1925).

As we will see, the behavioral model crops up along every byway of psychology. Along with the influence it has had in the area of learning processes—much of our understanding of how people learn new behaviors is based on the behavioral model—it can also be found in such diverse areas as the treatment of mental disorders, the curbing of aggression, the solution of sexual problems, and even halting drug addiction.

The Special Qualities of Homo Sapiens: Humanistic Approaches

Although it emerged in the 1950s and 1960s, the **humanistic model** is still considered the newest of the major approaches. Rejecting the views that behavior is largely determined by automatic, biological forces or unconscious processes, it suggests instead that people are in control of their lives. Humanistic psychologists maintain that people are naturally inclined to develop toward higher levels of maturity and fulfillment and that, if given the opportunity, they will strive to reach their full potential. The emphasis, then, is on **free will,** the human ability to make decisions about one's life.

More than any other approach, the humanistic model stresses the role of psychology in enriching people's lives and helping them to achieve self-fulfillment. While not as all-encompassing as some of the other general models, the humanistic perspective has had an important influence on the thinking of psychologists, reminding them of their commitment to the individual person and society.

A Final Word About Models

You may be wondering about how the five major models of psychology we have just discussed relate to the different branches of psychology that were presented earlier. The models and branches of psychology actually present two separate and independent ways of approaching the science. Thus a psychologist from any given branch might choose to employ any one, or more, of the major models. (See Table 1-2.) For example, a devel-

TABLE 1-2 MAJOR MODELS OF PSYCHOLOGY AS USED
BY DIFFERENT KINDS OF PSYCHOLOGISTS*

Type of Psychologist	Model				
	Biological	Psychodynamic	Cognitive	Behavioral	Humanistic
Biopsychologist	✔			✔	
Experimental	✔		✔	✔	
Cognitive			✔		
Developmental	✔	✔	✔	✔	✔
Personality	✔	✔	✔	✔	✔
Health	✔		✔	✔	
Clinical	✔	✔	✔	✔	✔
Counseling		✔		✔	✔
Educational			✔	✔	✔
School			✔	✔	✔
Social			✔	✔	✔
Industrial-organizational			✔	✔	

*Models that are used most frequently by a particular type of psychologist are checked.

opmental psychologist might subscribe to a psychodynamic model *or* a behavioral model *or* any of the other models. Although some kinds of psychologists are more or less likely to adhere to a particular model, as the table indicates, in theory at least each of the models is available to any psychologist who chooses to employ it. And don't let the abstract qualities of the models fool you: They each have very practical implications, implications that will concern us throughout this book. (See, for instance, the accompanying Psychology and Society box.)

The Future of Psychology

Where is psychology heading? Although crystal balls looking into the future of scientific disciplines are notoriously cloudy, a few trends can be safely foretold.

- Psychologists will become increasingly specialized. In a field in which practitioners must be experts on such diverse topics as the intricacies of the transmission of electrochemical impulses across nerve endings and the communication patterns of employees in

PSYCHOLOGY AND SOCIETY

Breaking the Cycle of Addiction

At the age of 14, Andrea Schiros had it all. A popular honor student and a cheerleader, she had what seemed to be an ideal life. But when she was suspended from the cheerleading squad for a petty offense, she sought solace in the school's drug culture, and once she began to take drugs, her life went into a tailspin. "I was strung out on coke, acid—everything I could put into my body." Eventually, she ran away from home, and her descent into drugs probably would have been total had it not been for a friend who told her desperate parents where to find her. Two police officers found her in a seedy apartment and brought her to Charter Brook Hospital, a drug rehabilitation center for youths. Although she was hysterical and trying to escape when brought in, Andrea eventually became determined to give up drugs. After seven months of being locked up in the inpatient center, she was allowed to leave the hospital. But her care continues, and she still attends a drug prevention program nightly (Johnson, 1986).

Schiros is one of the lucky ones; she remains free of drugs. Yet thousands of others find it impossible to break the bonds of drug addiction. Even when they are no longer taking drugs, former users are constantly at risk: Everyday sights, smells, and sounds—such as the similarity in appearance between white flour and cocaine—can be enough to bring on a strong craving for drugs.

One obstacle to ending drug abuse is that even after people stop taking an addictive drug, they may experience debilitating physical after-effects as a result of the sudden withdrawal of that drug from their bodies, as psychologists using the biological model have found. Furthermore, even though medicine administered by health-care providers can control physical withdrawal symptoms, users must still move through several distinct psychological stages before they can be considered free of drugs (Gawin & Ellinwood, 1988).

In one new treatment approach, researchers have developed training that is currently being evaluated (O'Brien et al., 1988). Using principles of learning based on the behavioral model, the training process teaches addicts behavior that disrupts behavioral patterns associated with drug use. For instance, former addicts see videos of people using drugs or handling drug paraphernalia. They are shown that users display increased heart rate, reduced skin temperature, and other signals of increased arousal—something about which they are often unaware. Through training, they learn to decrease their physical arousal at the sight of drug stimuli—thereby learning to be less responsive to drugs in future encounters.

But such training does not work by itself. The best results occur in people who receive psychological therapy—typically based on psychodynamic, cognitive, or humanistic models—along with the training. It seems, then, that the optimum combination of therapies includes those based on several of the major models of the field.

Although even a complex mix of different therapies is not sufficient to ensure that a drug addiction is cured, the strategy is a promising one. Furthermore, as the encouraging results of this approach reveal, psychology can provide solutions to complex and urgent societal problems. As we will see throughout this book in other Psychology and Society boxes, the basic principles of the science of psychology are providing both the potential for and the realization of meaningful and significant improvement in the quality of people's lives.

large organizations, no one person can be expected to master the field. It is likely, then, that specialization will increase as psychologists delve into new areas (Altman, 1987; Spence, 1987).

- New models will emerge. As a growing, evolving science, psychology will produce new models to supplant the ones it now has. Moreover, older models may be merged to form new ones. We can be certain, then, that as psychologists accumulate more knowledge they will become increasingly sophisticated in their understanding of behavior and mental processes (Marx & Hillix, 1987).

- Psychological treatment will become more readily available. The number of health-service providers—such as clinical, counseling, and school psychologists—is increasing at a rapid pace; in fact, it is growing more rapidly than any other segment of the field (Howard et al., 1986). As the number of practitioners grows, the services they provide will become more accessible to the general public.

- There will be increasing emphasis on applications of psychological knowledge (Matarazzo, 1987; DeLeon, 1988). The research reported throughout this book is a testament to the fact that the knowledge acquired by psychologists can be applied to the betterment of the human condition.

ASK YOURSELF

What are the major conceptual models of psychology?

How are today's major models of psychology related to the earlier models of structuralism, functionalism, and gestalt psychology?

Where is the field of psychology heading in the future?

Why is a combination of models more effective than the application of any single model alone?

PSYCHOLOGICAL RESEARCH

It took her killer some thirty minutes to finish the job. When Kitty Genovese was first attacked, she managed to free herself and run toward a police call box into which she screamed, "Oh, my God, he stabbed me. Please help me!" In the stillness of the night, her screams were heard by no fewer than thirty-eight neighbors. Windows opened and lights went on. One couple pulled chairs up to the window and turned off the lights so they could see better. Someone yelled, "Let that girl alone." But shouts were not enough to scare off the killer. He chased Kitty, stabbing her eight more times and sexually molesting her before leaving her to die.

And how many of the thirty-eight witnesses came to her aid? Not one.

The Kitty Genovese case remains one of the most horrifying and dismaying examples of "bad Samaritanism." Both the general public and psychologists found it difficult to explain how so many people could stand by without coming to the aid of an innocent victim whose life might well have been saved had there been any active intervention on the part of even one bystander.

Social psychologists in particular puzzled over the problem for many years, and they finally reached a strange conclusion: Kitty Genovese might well have been better off had there been far fewer than thirty-eight people who heard her cries. In fact, had there been just one bystander present, the chances of that person intervening might have been fairly high. For it turns out that the *fewer* witnesses present in a situation such as this one, the better the victim's chances of getting help.

But how could anyone come to such a conclusion? After all, logic and common sense would clearly suggest that more bystanders would mean a greater likelihood that someone would help a person in need. This seeming contradiction—and the way psychologists resolved it—illustrates the crux of a problem central to the field of psychology: the challenge of asking and answering questions of interest.

Asking the Right Questions: Theories and Hypotheses

This challenge has been met through reliance on the joint use of theory and research to guide psychologists in searching for answers to questions that concern them. **Theories** are broad explanations and predictions of phenomena of interest. Because they grow out of the diverse models of psychology that we discussed earlier, theories vary both in their breadth and in terms of the particular levels of explanation that they employ. For example, one theory might seek to explain and predict such a narrow topic as how people communicate the emotion of happiness after receiving good news, whereas a broader theory might purport to explain emotional experience in general.

Although all of us carry around our own theories of human behavior—such as "People are basically good" and "People's behavior is usually motivated by self-interest"—psychologists develop more formal and focused ones (Sternberg, 1985a). For example, social psychologists Bibb Latané and John Darley responded to the Kitty Genovese case by developing a theory based on a phenomenon they called *diffusion of responsibility* (Latané & Darley, 1970). According to their theory, the greater the number of bystanders or witnesses to an event that requires helping, the more the responsibility for helping is felt to be shared by all the bystanders. Because of this sense of shared responsibility, then, the more people present in an emergency situation, the less personally responsible each person feels—and the less likely it is that any single person will come forward to help.

Developing hypotheses. While such a theory makes sense, these psychologists could not stop there. Their next step was to devise a way of testing whether their reasoning was correct. To do this, they needed to derive a hypothesis. **Hypotheses** are predictions stated in a way that allows them to be tested. Just as we have our own broad theories about the world, so do we develop hypotheses about events and behavior (ranging from trivialities, such as why our English professor is such an eccentric, to what is the best way for people to study). Although we rarely test them systematically, we do try to determine whether they are right or not. Perhaps we might try cramming for one exam but studying over a longer period of time for another. By assessing the results, we have created a way to compare the two methods.

Latané and Darley's hypothesis was a straightforward derivation from their more general theory: The more people who witness an emergency situation, the less likely it is that help will be given to a victim. They could, of course, have chosen another hypothesis (for instance, that people with greater skills related to emergency situations will not be affected by the presence of others), but their initial derivative seemed to offer the most direct test of the theory.

There are several reasons why psychologists use theories and hypotheses. For one thing, these postulations allow sense to be made of individual observations, by placing them together within a framework that organizes and summarizes them. In addition, they offer psychologists the opportunity to move beyond facts that are already known about the world and to make deductions about phenomena that have not yet been explained. In this way, theories and hypotheses provide a reasonable guide to the direction that future investigation ought to take.

In sum, then, theories and hypotheses help psychologists ask the right questions. But how do they answer such questions? The answers come from psychological **research**, systematic inquiry aimed at the discovery of new knowledge.

Finding Answers: Psychological Research

Just as we can derive several theories and hypotheses to explain particular phenomenon, so we can use a considerable number of alternate ways to carry out research. The way that is chosen to test the hypothesis is known as operationalization. **Operationalization** refers to the process of taking a hypothesis and translating it into the particular procedures that are used in the experiment. There is no single way to go about this; it depends on logic, the equipment and facilities available, and the ingenuity of the researcher. We will consider several of the major weapons in the psychologist's research arsenal.

Studying one person to learn about many: The case study. When Kitty Genovese's killer was identified, many people found themselves asking what it was in his background that might have led to his behavior. In order to answer this question, a psychologist might conduct a **case study**, an in-depth interview of a single individual. In a case study, psychologists might well include psychological testing, in which a carefully designed set of questions is used to gain some insight into the personality of the person being studied. In using case studies as a research technique, the goal is often not only to learn about the individual, but to use the insights gained to better understand people in general.

Studying the records: Archival research. If you were interested in finding out more about emergency situations in which bystanders did not provide help, you might start by examining historical records. In **archival research**, existing records are examined to confirm a hypothesis. By using newspaper accounts, for example, we might find support for the notion that a decrease in helping behavior accompanies an increase in the number of bystanders.

Studying what is there: Naturalistic observation. Although archival research allows us to test a hypothesis for which data already exist, researchers typically aren't lucky enough to find sufficient appropriate data intact. They often turn instead to naturalistic observation to carry out their research.

In **naturalistic observation**, the investigator simply observes some naturally occurring behavior and does not intervene in the situation. For example, a researcher investigating helping behavior might turn to a high-crime area of a city and observe there the kind of help that is given to victims of crime. The important point about naturalistic observation is that the researcher is passive and simply meticulously records what occurs.

While the advantage of naturalistic observation is obvious—we get a sample of what people do in their "natural habitat"—it also has an important drawback: the inability to control any of the factors of interest. For example, we might find so few naturally occurring instances of helping behavior that we would be unable to draw any conclusions. Because naturalistic observation prevents researchers from making changes in a situation, they must wait until appropriate conditions occur. Similarly, if people know that they are being watched, they may react in such a way that the behavior observed is not truly representative of the group in question.

Asking for answers: Survey research. There is no more straightforward way of finding out what people think, feel, and do than by asking them directly. For this reason, surveys represent an important research method. In **survey research**, people chosen to represent some larger population are asked a series of questions about their behavior, thoughts, or attitudes (Fink & Kosecoff, 1985). Survey methods have become so sophisticated that even using a very small sample is sufficient to infer with great accuracy how a larger group would respond. For instance, sampling just a few thousand voters is sufficient to predict within one or two percentage points who will win a presidential election—if the sample is chosen with care.

Researchers interested in helping behavior might conduct a survey asking people their reasons for not wanting to come forward to help. Similarly, researchers concerned with sexual behaviors have carried out surveys to learn which sexual practices are common and which are not, and to chart the changes in sexual morality that have occurred as time has passed.

Although asking people directly about their behavior in some ways seems like the most straightforward approach to understanding what people do, survey research has several potential drawbacks. For one thing, people may give inaccurate information because of lapses of memory or because they don't want to let the researcher know what they really feel. Moreover, people sometimes make responses they think the researcher wants to hear—or, in just the opposite instance, responses they think the researcher *doesn't* want to hear.

Correlational research. One of the possibilities available to researchers using the survey method as well as the other forms of research we have discussed is to determine the relationship between two behaviors, or between responses to two questions. For instance, we might want to find if people who report that they attend religious services also report that they are more helpful to strangers in emergency situations. If we did find such a relationship, we could say that there was a correlation between attendance at religious services and being helpful in emergencies.

In research that is **correlational**, the relationship between two sets of factors is examined to determine whether they are associated, or "correlated." The strength of a relationship is represented by a mathematical score ranging from +1.0 (a perfect positive relationship, where perfect means that if you know the value of one variable, you can predict the value of the other variable with certainty) to −1.0 (a perfect negative relationship). Although actual correlations are rarely perfect, the closer the correlation is to +1.0 or −1.0, the stronger the relationship. On the other hand, the nearer a correlation is to zero, the weaker the relationship.

Although correlational techniques cannot tell us whether one factor *causes* changes in another, they can indicate whether knowing the value of one factor allows us to predict the value of another variable. We may not be able to tell, then, if attending religious services *causes* people to be helpful in emergencies, but correlational procedures will tell us whether

knowing that specific people attend religious services will help us to predict how they will behave in an emergency situation.

Another example illustrates the critical point that correlations tell us
nothing about cause and effect but only provide a measure of the strength
of a relationship between two factors. For instance, we might find that
children who watch a lot of television programs having aggressive content
are apt to demonstrate a relatively high degree of aggressive behavior,
while those who watch few television shows that portray aggression are
apt to exhibit a relatively low degree of such behavior. However, we cannot say that the aggression is *caused* by the TV viewing, since it is just as
likely to be caused by some other factor. For example, we may learn that
children of low socioeconomic status watch more programs having aggressive content *and* are more aggressive. Factors relating to a family's
socioeconomic status, then, may be the true cause of the children's higher
incidence of aggression. In fact, there may be several factors that underlie
both the aggressive behavior and the television viewing. It is even possible
that people who show high aggressiveness choose to watch shows with
high aggressive content *because* they are aggressive. It is clear, then, that
any number of causal sequences are possible—none of which can be ruled
out by correlational research.

Determining Cause-and-Effect Relationships: Experimental Research

The *only* way that psychologists can establish cause-and-effect relationships through research is by carrying out an experiment. In a formal
experiment, the relationship between two (or more) factors is investigated
by deliberately producing a change in one factor and observing the effect
that change has upon other factors. The change deliberately produced is
called the **experimental manipulation**. Experimental manipulations are
used to detect relationships between **variables**, behaviors, events, or other
characteristics that can change, or vary, in some way.

There are several steps in carrying out an experiment, but the process
typically begins with the development of one or more hypotheses for the
experiment to test. Recall, for example, the hypothesis derived by Latané
and Darley to test their theory of helping behavior: The more people who
witness an emergency situation, the less likely it is that help will be given
to a victim. We can trace the way they developed an experiment to test
this hypothesis.

The first step was to operationalize the hypothesis by translating it
into actual procedures that could be used in an experiment. Operationalizing their hypothesis required that Latané and Darley take into account
the fundamental principle of experimental research that we mentioned
earlier: There must be a manipulation of at least one variable in order to
observe what effects the manipulation has on another variable. But this

manipulation cannot be viewed in isolation; if a cause-and-effect relationship is to be established, the effects of the manipulation must be compared with the effects of no manipulation or a different manipulation.

Experimental research requires, then, that at least two groups be compared with each other. One group will receive some special **treatment**—the manipulation implemented by the experimenter—while another group receives either no treatment or a different treatment. The group receiving the treatment is called the **treatment group**, while the other group is called the **control group**. (In some experiments, however, there are multiple treatment and control groups, each of which is compared with another.)

By employing both a treatment and a control group in an experiment, researchers are able to rule out the effects of factors not associated with the experimental manipulation as a source of any changes seen in the experiment. If we didn't have a control group, we couldn't be sure that some other factor—such as the temperature at the time we were running the experiment or the mere passage of time—wasn't causing the changes observed. Through the use of control groups, then, researchers can be sure that the causes of effects are isolated—and cause-and-effect inferences can be drawn.

To Latané and Darley, a means of operationalizing their hypothesis, based on the requirement of having more than one treatment group, was readily available. They decided they would create a bogus emergency situation which would require the aid of a bystander. As their experimental manipulation, they decided to vary the number of bystanders present. They could have just had an experimental group with, for instance, two people present, and a control group for comparison purposes with just one person present. Instead, they settled on a more complex procedure in which there were three groups that could be compared with one another, consisting of two, three, and six people.

Latané and Darley now had identified what is called the experimenter's **independent variable**, the variable that is manipulated. In this case, it was the number of people present. The next step was to decide how they were going to determine what effect varying the number of bystanders had on participants' behavior. Crucial to every experiment is the **dependent variable**, which is the variable that is measured and is expected to change as a result of changes caused by the experimenter's manipulation. Experiments have, then, both an independent and a dependent variable. (To remember the difference, you might recall that a hypothesis predicts how a dependent variable *depends* on the manipulation of the independent variable.)

How, then, should the dependent measure be operationalized for Latané and Darley's experiment? One way might have been to use a simple "yes"-or-"no" measure of whether a **subject**—as a participant in research is known—helped or didn't help. But the two investigators decided they also wanted a measure that provided a finer-grained analysis of helping behavior, so they assessed the amount of time it took for a subject to provide help.

Latané and Darley now had all the components of an experiment. The independent variable, manipulated by them, was the number of bystanders present in an emergency situation. The dependent variable was whether the bystanders in each of the groups provided help and the amount of time it took for them to do so. *All* true experiments in psychology fit this straightforward model.

The final step: Random assignment of subjects to treatments. To make the experiment a valid test of the hypothesis, the researchers needed to add a final step to the design: properly assigning subjects to a specific treatment group. Why should this step be so important?

The reason becomes clear when we examine various alternative procedures. For example, the experimenters might have considered the possibility of assigning just males to the group with two bystanders, just females to the group with three bystanders, and both males and females to the group with six bystanders. Had they done so, however, it would have become clear that any differences they found in responsive behavior could not be attributed to the group size alone, but might just as well be due to the composition of the group. A more reasonable procedure would be to ensure that each group had the same composition in terms of sex; then they would be able to make comparisons across groups with considerably more accuracy.

Subjects in each of the treatment groups ought to be comparable, and it is easy enough to create similar groups in terms of sex. The problem becomes a bit more tricky, though, when we consider other subject characteristics. How can we ensure that subjects in each treatment group will be equally intelligent, extroverted, cooperative, and so forth, when the list of characteristics—any one of which may be important—is potentially endless?

The solution to the problem is a simple but elegant procedure called **random assignment to condition**. In random assignment, subjects are assigned to different experimental groups, or "conditions," on the basis of chance and chance alone. The experimenter might, for instance, put the names of all potential subjects into a hat and draw names to make assignments to specific groups. The advantage of this technique is that subject characteristics have an equal chance of being distributed across the various groups. By using random assignment, the experimenter can be confident that each of the groups will have approximately the same proportion of intelligent people, cooperative people, extroverted people, males and females, and so on. (For an example of another experiment, see Figure 1-2.)

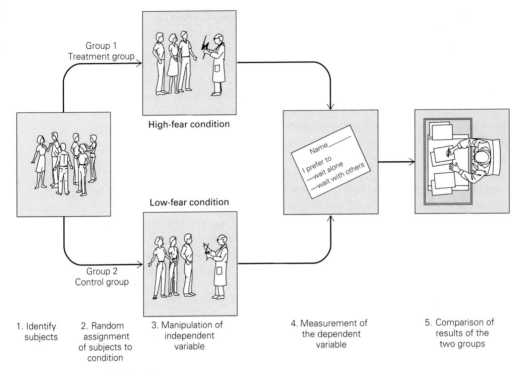

Group 1
Treatment group

High-fear condition

Low-fear condition

Group 2
Control group

Name____
I prefer to
__wait alone
__wait with others

1. Identify
subjects

2. Random
assignment
of subjects to
condition

3. Manipulation of
independent
variable

4. Measurement of
the dependent
variable

5. Comparison of
results of the
two groups

FIGURE 1-2
This depiction of a classic study, on the effects of fear on affiliation with others,
includes the essential elements of an experiment (Schachter, 1959). A group of
people—the subjects of the experiment—were randomly assigned to one of two
groups. Subjects randomly assigned to group 1 were exposed to a treatment, designed to produce high fear, in which they were told that they would be receiving painful shocks as part of the experiment. In comparison, subjects randomly
assigned to group 2, the control group, were in the low-fear condition; they
were told that the shocks they were to receive would be mild, resembling a
slight tingle. The production of high or low fear was the independent variable.
To determine the effects of fear on affiliation, subjects were asked whether they
wished to wait for the start of the experiment either alone or in a room with
several other people. The choice that subjects made was the dependent variable.
(The results? As the experimenter had hypothesized, subjects in the high-fear
condition were considerably more likely to choose to wait with others than
those in the low-fear condition.)

Who should participate? Choosing the appropriate subjects. Latané
and Darley, both college professors, turned to the people who were most
readily accessible to them when they were looking for participants in their
experiment: college students. In fact, this group is used so frequently in
experiments that psychology has sometimes been called the "science of
the behavior of the college sophomore" (Rubenstein, 1982).

The use of college students as subjects has both advantages and drawbacks. The big benefit is their availability: Since most research occurs in

university settings, college students are readily available. Typically, they participate for either extra course credit or a relatively small monetary payment, making the cost to the researcher minimal.

The problem with relying on college students for subjects is that they may not adequately represent the general population. College students tend to be disproportionately white and middle class, more intelligent, and certainly younger and better educated than the rest of the population of the United States. Moreover, their attitudes are likely to be less well formed, and they are apt to be more susceptible to social pressures from authority figures and peers than older adults (Sears, 1986). Given these characteristics, the degree to which we may generalize beyond college students is open to question, and many researchers strive to use subjects who are more representative of the general population.

The issue of subject representativeness becomes even more pronounced when we consider research conducted by psychologists on animals other than humans. If we are concerned that college students are not representative of the population at large, isn't representativeness even more of a problem with research that uses rats, monkeys, gerbils, or pigeons as subjects?

The answer is that the 7 or 8 percent of psychological research that does employ animals has a different focus and is designed to answer different questions from research that uses humans. For example, the shorter life span of animals (rats live an average of two years) allows us to learn about the effects of aging in a much more rapid time frame than if we studied aging directly on humans, with their much longer life. Moreover, the very complexity of human beings may obscure information about fundamental phenomena that can be more plainly identified in animals. Finally, some studies require large numbers of subjects who share similar backgrounds or who have been exposed to particular environments—conditions that could not be met with human beings.

Research using animals as subjects has provided psychologists with information that has profound benefits for humans. For instance, animal research has furnished us with the keys to learning how to detect eye disorders in children early enough to prevent permanent damage, how to communicate more effectively with severely retarded children, and how to reduce chronic pain in people, to name just a few results (American Psychological Association, 1988). In the end, of course, animals are not people, and in any experiment it is important to be aware of the limitations in generalizing beyond the subject group used in a study.

Threats to experiments: Experimenter and subject expectations. You may be thinking that, having chosen college students as subjects, Latané and Darley by this point should have been ready to run their experiment. But they had to take into account a few further considerations to avoid **experimental bias**—factors that distort understanding of how the independent variable affects the dependent variable.

One problem they needed to avoid was **experimenter expectations**, whereby an experimenter unintentionally transmits cues to subjects about the way they are expected to behave in a given experimental condition. The danger is that these expectations will bring about an "appropriate" behavior—one that may not have otherwise occurred. For example, if Latané and Darley had behaved toward subjects in the two-bystander condition as if they expected them to help, but let on that they had low expectations for helping in the six-person bystander condition, such variations in experimenter behavior—no matter how unintentional— might have affected the results.

A related problem is **subject expectations** about what is appropriate behavior. If you have ever been a subject in an experiment, you know that you quickly develop ideas about what is expected of you, and it is typical for people to develop their own hypothesis about what the experimenter hopes to learn from the study. If these expectations influence a subject's behavior, it becomes a cause for concern, since it is no longer the experimental manipulation producing an effect, but rather the subject's expectations.

To guard against the problem of subject expectations biasing the results of an experiment, the experimenter may disguise the true purpose of the experiment. Subjects who are unaware that helping behavior is being studied, for example, are more likely to act in an unbiased manner than if they are told the purpose of the experiment is to study their helping behavior. Latané and Darley decided to tell their subjects, then, that the actual purpose of the experiment was to hold a discussion among college students about their personal problems. In doing so, they expected that their subjects would not suspect the true purpose of the experiment.

In some experiments, it is impossible to hide the actual purpose of the research. In cases such as these, other techniques are available. For example, suppose you were interested in testing the ability of a new drug to alleviate the symptoms of severe depression. If you simply gave the drug to half your subjects and not to the other half, subjects given the drug might report feeling less depressed merely because they knew they were getting a drug. Similarly, the subjects who got nothing might report feeling no better because they knew that they were in a no-treatment control group.

To solve this problem, psychologists typically use a procedure in which subjects in the control group do receive treatment, sometimes in the form of a pill called a placebo. A **placebo** is a "sugar pill," without any significant chemical properties. Because members of both groups are kept in the dark as to whether they are getting a real or a bogus pill, any differences that are found can be attributed to the quality of the drug and not to the possible psychological effects of being administered a pill.

But there is still one more thing that a careful researcher must do in an experiment such as this. In order to overcome the possibility that experimenter expectations will affect the subject, the person who administers the drug shouldn't know whether it is actually the true drug or the placebo. By keeping both the subject and the experimenter who interacts with the subject "blind" as to the nature of the drug that is being administered—a method known as the **double-blind procedure**—researchers can more accurately assess the effects of the drug.

Were Latané and Darley right?: The data answer. By now, you must be wondering whether Latané and Darley were right when they hypothesized that increasing the number of bystanders present in an emergency situation would lower the degree of helping.

According to the results of the experiment they carried out, their hypothesis was right on target. In their test of the hypothesis, they used a laboratory setting in which subjects were told that the purpose of the experiment was to hold a discussion about personal problems associated with college. The discussion was to be held over an intercom in order to avoid the embarrassment of face-to-face contact. This was not, of course, the true purpose of the experiment, but one used to keep subjects' expectations from biasing their behavior. (Consider how they would have been affected if they had been told that their helping behavior in emergencies was being tested. The experimenters could never have gotten an accurate assessment of what the subjects would actually do in an emergency; by definition, emergencies are rarely announced in advance.)

The sizes of the discussion groups were two, three, and six people, which constituted the manipulation of the independent variable of group size. Subjects were randomly assigned to one of these groups upon their arrival at the laboratory.

As the subjects in each group were holding their discussion, they suddenly heard one of the other participants (in reality a trained **confederate** of the experimenters) lapse into what sounded like an epileptic seizure:

> I-er-um-I think I-I need-er-if-if- could-er-er-somebody er-er-er-er-er-er-er give me a little-er give me a little help here because-er-I-er-I'm-er-er-h-h-having a-a-a real problem-er-right now and I-er-if somebody could help me out it would-it-would-er-er s-s-sure be-sure be good ... because-er-there-er-er-a cause I-er-I-uh-I've got a-a one of the-er-sei---er-er-things coming on and-and-and I could really-er-use some help so if somebody would-er-give me a little h-help-uh-er-er-er-er-er c-could somebody-er-er-help-er-us-us-us [choking sounds]. . . .I'm gonna die-er-er-I'm ... gonna die-er-help-er-er-seizure-er- [choking sounds, then silence] (Latané & Darley, 1970, p. 379).

The subjects' behavior was now what counted. The dependent variable was whether subjects helped and the time that elapsed from the start of the "seizure" to the time a subject began trying to help. If six minutes went by without a subject's offering help, the experiment was ended.

As predicted by the hypothesis, the size of the group had a large effect on whether a subject provided help (Latané and Darley, 1970). In the two-person group (in which subjects thought they were alone with the victim), 85 percent of the subjects helped; in the three-person group (the subject, the victim, and one other person), 62 percent helped; and in the six-person group (the subject, victim, and four others), only 31 percent responded. The elapsed-time data showed the same pattern.

Because the results are so straightforward, it seems clear that the original hypothesis was confirmed. However, Latané and Darley could not be sure that the results were truly meaningful until they used formal statistical procedures. Such procedures—which entail several kinds of mathematical calculations—allow a researcher to determine precisely the likelihood that results are meaningful and not merely the outcome of chance.

The Latané and Darley study contains all the elements of an experiment: an independent variable, a dependent variable, random assignment to conditions, and multiple treatment groups. Because it does, we can say with some confidence that group size *caused* changes in the degree of helping behavior.

Of course, one experiment alone does not resolve forever the question of bystander intervention in emergencies. Psychologists require that findings be **replicated**, or repeated, using other procedures in other settings, with other groups of subjects, before full confidence can be placed in the validity of any single experiment. [In this case, the experiment has stood the test of time: In a review of some fifty studies that were carried out in the ten years following their experiment, the finding that an increase in bystanders leads to decreased helping has been replicated in numerous other studies (Latané & Nida, 1981).]

In addition to replicating experimental results, psychologists also need to test the limitations of their theories and hypotheses in order to determine under what specific circumstances they hold and under what conditions they do not apply. It seems unlikely, for instance, that increasing numbers of bystanders *always* results in less helping, and it is therefore critical to understand the conditions in which exceptions to this general rule occur. For example, we might speculate that under conditions of shared outcomes, in which onlookers experience a sense that a victim's difficulties may later affect them in some way, help would be more readily forthcoming (Aronson, 1988). To test this hypothesis—for which, in fact, there is some support—it is necessary to carry out still further experimentation. Like any science, then, psychology increases our understanding in small, incremental steps, with each step building upon previous work.

Knowing What's Right: The Ethics of Research

If you were to put yourself in the place of one of the subjects in the Latané and Darley experiment, how would you feel when you learned that the person who you thought was having a seizure was in reality a confederate of the experimenter?

Although at first you might experience relief that there was no real emergency, you might also feel some resentment that you were deceived by the experimenter. And you might also experience concern that you were placed in an unusual situation in which, depending on how you behaved, you may have had a blow to your self-esteem.

Most psychologists argue that the use of deception is sometimes necessary in order to avoid having subjects influenced by what they think is the study's true purpose. (If you knew the Latané and Darley study was actually concerned with your helping behavior, wouldn't you be tempted to intervene in the emergency?) In order to avoid such behavior, researchers sometimes must use deception.

Because research has the potential to violate the rights of participants, psychologists adhere to a strict set of ethical guidelines aimed at protecting subjects (American Psychological Association, 1990). These guidelines advocate the protection of subjects from physical and mental harm, the right of subjects to privacy regarding their behavior, the assurance that participation in research is completely voluntary, and the necessity of informing the subjects about the nature of procedures prior to participation in the experiment. Although the guidelines do allow the use of deception, the experiment must be reviewed by an independent panel prior to its use—as must all research that uses human beings as subjects (Ceci, Peters, & Plotkin, 1985; Keith-Spiegel & Koocher, 1985; Christensen, 1988).

One of the key ethical principals followed by psychologists is that of **informed consent**. Prior to participating in an experiment, subjects must sign a document affirming that they have been told the basic outlines of the study and are aware of what their participation will involve, what risks the experiment may hold, and the fact that their participation is purely voluntary and may be terminated at any time. The only time informed consent can be dispensed with is in experiments in which the risks are minimal, as in a purely observational study on a street corner or other public location.

It is not just psychologists working with humans who operate under strict ethical constraints; researchers who use animals as subjects have their own set of exacting guidelines to ensure that animals do not suffer. Specifically, they must make every effort to minimize discomfort, illness, and pain, and procedures subjecting animals to distress are used only when an alternative procedure is unavailable and when the goal of research is justified by its prospective value. Moreover, there are federal regulations specifying how animals are to be housed, fed, and maintained.

Because some research with important implications for alleviating human suffering—such as devising techniques for saving mentally disturbed patients who would otherwise starve themselves to death or finding new drugs and procedures to alleviate human pain and depression—cannot be ethically carried out on humans, guidelines permit the use of animals in such cases where the potential benefits clearly outweigh the costs (Gallup & Suarez, 1985; Miller, 1985b; Gill et al., 1989). However, stringent regulations prohibit researchers from inflicting unnecessary pain.

Despite these ethical guidelines, the use of animals for psychological research remains controversial (Goodall, 1987; Holden, 1988; Novak &

Suomi, 1988), with some people calling for a complete ban on the practice. However, most psychologists feel that existing ethical guidelines are sufficiently stringent to provide protection for animals while still allowing valuable animal research to continue.

The Informed Consumer of Psychology: Distinguishing Good Psychology from Bad Psychology

More than any book ever written, *Self-Creation* shows you who you are and reveals the secret to controlling your own life. . . . With it you will discover how to conquer bad habits, solve sexual problems, overcome depression and shyness, deal with infuriating people, be decisive, enhance your career, increase creativity. . . . You created you. Now you can start to reap the boundless benefits of self-confidence, self-reliance, self-determination with *Self-Creation* (excerpted from the back cover; Weinberg, 1979).

"Hello, this is Dr. Joy Browne on WITS," says the agreeable voice on the Boston radio station. "Today we're having an open-line program. You can call in with any problem on any topic." The first call comes from Steve, who opens with "Hi, Dr. Joy," and tells about his fainthearted attempts to reestablish contact with an old flame, now married. Dr. Joy analyzes Steve's problem as "a classic case of approach-avoidance," advises him to stop being "so tentative" and to go ahead and "play it by ear." She asks him to call back to "let me know what happens" (Rice, 1981, p. 39).

From self-help books to talk shows, we are bombarded daily with information about psychology. We are told how to become smarter, happier, and better adjusted by learning psychology's secrets.

Yet the promises are usually empty ones. If things were this easy, we would live in a nation of happy-go-lucky, fully satisfied, and completely fulfilled individuals. Obviously the world is not quite so simple, and the quality of advice supposedly based on psychological truths, provided by self-styled experts—and even by some less-than-reputable psychologists—varies widely. For this reason, there are several points to keep in mind when you evaluate information of a psychological nature.

- There's no free ride. If your problems could be assessed, analyzed, and resolved in five minutes of radio air time, don't you think people would be clogging the phone lines with their calls, rather than spending hundreds of hours in treatment for their problems? The point is that difficult problems require complex solutions, and you should be wary of simple, glib responses on how to resolve major difficulties.
- If advice that is dispensed by psychologists is accepted by a consumer, the consequences of following that advice should be critically monitored, evaluated, and—if necessary—modified to ensure

From advertisements to talk shows, we are bombarded daily with psychology. It is important to distinguish between pop psychology and psychological information that is based on reliable research.

that it is producing desirable effects. In the case of talk-show psychology, this almost never occurs; it is rare that we discover how well the advice that was dispensed in a given case worked. Both the people with the problems *and* the other listeners and viewers may be getting bad advice—but they never have any way of knowing without follow-up.

- No single psychologist or psychological method can solve all problems. The range of difficulties bound up with the human condition is so broad that no person can be an expert in all areas, and any individual or any method that purports to resolve all problems is making an inappropriate claim.

Despite these cautions, the field of psychology has produced a wealth of important information that can be drawn upon for suggestions about every phase of people's lives. One of the major goals of this book is to make you a more informed consumer of psychological knowledge by enhancing your ability to evaluate what psychologists have to offer. Ultimately, this book should provide you with the tools you need to critically evaluate the theories, research, and applications that psychologists have developed. In doing so, you will be able to appreciate the contributions that the field of psychology has made in improving the quality of human life.

ASK YOURSELF

What are theories and hypotheses and how do psychologists use them to guide their research?

How does correlational research examine the relationship between variables?

What are the elements of a formal experiment?

How do experimenter expectations and subject expectations threaten experiments?

Suppose a psychologist studied all the citizens of a town and reported a high positive correlation between height and intelligence. Would the psychologist be correct in concluding that being tall makes people smarter?

LOOKING BACK

1. Although the definition of psychology—the scientific study of behavior and mental processes—is clear-cut, it is also deceivingly simple, since "behavior" encompasses not just what people do, but their thoughts, feelings, perceptions, reasoning, memory, and biological activities.

2. Among the major areas of psychology are biopsychology, experimental, cognitive, developmental, personality, health, clinical, counseling, educational, school, social, and industrial-organizational psychology.

3. Psychologists are employed in a variety of settings. Although the primary employment sites are universities and colleges, many psychologists are found in hospitals, clinics, community mental-health centers, and counseling centers. Many also have practices in which they treat patients privately.

4. The foundations of psychology were established by Wilhelm Wundt in Germany in 1879. Early conceptual models that guided the work of psychologists were structuralism, functionalism, and gestalt theory. Modern-day psychologists rely primarily on five models: the biological, psychodynamic, cognitive, behavioral, and humanistic models.

5. The biological model focuses on the biological functioning of people and animals, reducing behavior to its most basic components. The psychodynamic model takes a very different approach; it suggests that there are powerful, unconscious inner forces about which people have little or no awareness and which are primary determinants of behavior.

6. Cognitive approaches to behavior consider how people know, understand, and think about the world. Growing out of early work on introspection and later work by the gestaltists and functionalists, cognitive models study how people understand and represent the world within themselves.

7. Behavioral models deemphasize internal processes and concentrate instead on observable behavior. They suggest that an understanding and control of a person's environment is sufficient to fully explain and modify behavior.

8. Humanistic models are the newest of the major models of psychology. They emphasize that humans are uniquely inclined toward psychological growth and higher levels of functioning and that human beings will strive to reach their full potential.

9. Research in psychology is guided by theories (broad explanations and predictions of phenomena of interest) and hypotheses (derivations of theories that are predictions stated in a way that allows them to be tested).

10. The case study, archival research, and naturalistic observation rely on correlational studies, which describe associations between various factors but cannot determine cause-and-effect relationships.

11. In a formal experiment, the relationship between factors is investigated by deliberately producing a change—called the experimental manipulation—in one of them and observing the change in the other. The factors that are changed are called variables, behaviors or events that are capable of change and can take on two or more levels. In order to test a hypothesis, it must be operationalized: The abstract concepts of the hypothesis are translated into the actual procedures used in the study.

12. In an experiment, at least two groups must be compared with each other in order to assess cause-and-effect relationships. The group receiving the treatment (the special procedure devised by the experimenter) is the treatment group, while the second group (which receives no treatment) is the control group. There also may be multiple treatment groups, each of which is subjected to a different procedure and can then be compared with the others. The variable that is manipulated is the independent variable; the variable that is measured and expected to change as a result of manipulation of the independent variable is called the dependent variable.

13. In a formal experiment, subjects must be assigned to treatment conditions randomly so that subject characteristics are evenly distributed across the different conditions.

14. The frequent use of college students as subjects has the advantage of easy availability. However, there are drawbacks: Students do not represent the general population well. The use of animals as subjects also has costs in terms of generalizability, although the benefits of using animals in research have been profound.

15. Experiments are subject to a number of threats, or biases. Experimenter bias occurs when an experimenter unintentionally transmits cues to subjects about his or her expectations regarding their behavior in a given experimental condition. Subject expectations can also bias an experiment. To help eliminate bias, researchers use placebos and double-blind procedures.

16. One of the key ethical principals followed by psychologists is informed consent. Subjects must be told, prior to participation, what the basic outline of an experiment is and the risks and potential benefits of their participation. Researchers working with animals must also follow a rigid set of ethical guidelines for the protection of the animals.

Key Terms and Concepts

psychology (p. 2)
biopsychology (p. 6)
experimental psychology (p. 7)
cognitive psychology (p. 7)
developmental psychology (p. 7)
personality psychology (p. 7)
health psychology (p. 8)
clinical psychology (p. 8)

counseling psychology (p. 8)
educational psychology (p. 8)
school psychology (p. 8)
social psychology (p. 9)
industrial-organizational
    psychology (p. 9)
models (p. 11)
structuralism (p. 12)

introspection (p. 12)
functionalism (p. 13)
gestalt psychology (p. 13)
biological model (p. 14)
psychodynamic model (p. 15)
cognitive model (p. 16)
behavioral model (p. 16)
humanistic model (p. 17)
free will (p. 17)
theories (p. 21)
hypotheses (p. 22)
research (p. 22)
operationalization (p. 22)
case study (p. 23)
archival research (p. 23)
naturalistic observation (p. 23)
survey research (p. 24)
correlational research (p. 24)

experiment (p. 25)
experimental manipulation (p. 25)
variables (p. 25)
treatment (p. 26)
treatment group (p. 26)
control group (p. 26)
independent variable (p. 26)
dependent variable (p. 26)
subject (p. 26)
random assignment to condition (p. 27)
experimental bias (p. 29)
experimenter expectations (p. 30)
subject expectations (p. 30)
placebo (p. 30)
double-blind procedure (p. 31)
confederate (p. 31)
replication (p. 32)
informed consent (p. 33)

2

The Biology Underlying Behavior

--- ❖ ---

Prologue: Nelson Martinez ◆ Looking Ahead ◆ The Basics of Behavior: Neurons and the Nervous System ◆ Stringing Neurons Together: The Nervous System ◆ Tying the Nervous System Together: The Brain ◆ Up the Evolutionary Ladder: The Cerebral Cortex ◆ Two Brains or One? The Specialization of the Hemispheres ◆ Looking Back

PROLOGUE: NELSON MARTINEZ

Nelson Martinez holds his wife's hand sixteen hours after undergoing controversial surgery to treat his symptoms of Parkinson's disease.

For fourteen years, Nelson Martinez's life had become increasingly nightmarish. Suffering from Parkinson's disease, he was racked with tremors, could not speak properly, and endured frequent nausea and stiffness—all classic characteristics of the disease. He reached the stage at which he was no longer able to work, drink from a cup, or feed himself, and felt as if he were doomed to spend the rest of his life as an invalid.

After exhausting all standard treatments for Parkinson's disease, Martinez was desperate to stop the progression of the illness. In a last-ditch effort, he turned to an experimental treatment and became the first American to undergo a controversial procedure. During a six-hour operation, researchers implanted eight chunks of tissue from Martinez's left adrenal gland (located near his kidneys) into his brain.

The rationale for the procedure was based on an understanding of the cause of Parkinson's disease, which occurs when there is a deterioration of nerve cells in a region of the brain that produces the chemical dopamine. Because the adrenal gland also produces dopamine, researchers hypothesized that the implantation would provide the brain with sufficient amounts of the chemical to end the symptoms.

39

The operation was painstaking. Peering through a high-powered microscope, a surgeon used tiny stainless steel clips to fasten eight microscopic chunks of tissue, together weighing just over 1 gram, to the surface of the area of the brain that controls body movement. Had the surgeon made a false move, Martinez could have been left completely paralyzed on one side of his body.

The outcome of this high-stakes operation was a success, with the immediate results both dramatic and promising. Just after surgery, Martinez's tremors stopped almost completely, and he lost the stiffness in his body. If his recovery were to follow the predicted course, there would be some setbacks, but ultimately his improvement would be almost total, as his transplanted adrenal gland began to produce a steady output of dopamine. Although his recovery was far from assured—the long-term benefits of the operation are still unproven—his spirits were high: In the words of his wife, "After all these years of suffering, we feel like we've just been reborn" (Rohter, 1987; Lewin, 1988; Lindvall et al., 1990).

LOOKING AHEAD

The results of the operation performed on Nelson Martinez are no less than miraculous. But the greater miracle rests on the object of the surgical procedure: the brain itself. As we shall see in this chapter, the brain, an organ roughly half the size of a loaf of bread, controls our behavior through every waking and sleeping moment. The brain and its pathways extending throughout the body compose the human **nervous system.** Our movements, thoughts, hopes, aspirations, dreams—the very awareness that we are human—are all intimately related to this system.

Because of the importance of the nervous system in controlling behavior, and because human beings at their most basic level are biological entities, psychologists and researchers from other fields as diverse as computer science, zoology, medicine, and physics—experts collectively called **neuroscientists**—have paid special attention to the biological underpinnings of behavior (Osherson, 1990).

Psychologists who specialize in considering the ways in which biological structures and functions of the body affect behavior are known as **biopsychologists.** These specialists seek to answer questions such as these: What are the bases for voluntary and involuntary operation of the body? How are messages communicated from one part of the body to another? What is the physical structure of the brain, and how does this structure affect behavior? Can the causes of psychological disorders be traced to biological factors, and how can such disorders be treated?

These questions and others are addressed in this chapter, which focuses on those biological structures of the body that are most closely related to the interests of biopsychologists. Initially, we discuss nerve cells, called neurons, and the nervous system, which allow messages to travel from one part of the body to another. We will see that through their growing knowledge of neurons and the nervous system, psychologists are increasing their understanding of human behavior and are uncovering important clues in their efforts to cure certain kinds of diseases. The structure and main divisions of the nervous system are then presented, with explanations of how they work to control voluntary and involuntary behaviors and the way the various parts of the nervous system operate together in emergency situations to produce life-saving responses to danger.

Next, we consider the brain itself, examining its major structures and the ways in which these affect behavior. We see how the brain controls movement, the five senses, and our thought processes. We also consider the fascinating notion that the two halves of the brain may operate independently of each other.

As we discuss the biological characteristics that are of interest to biopsychologists, it is important to keep in mind the basic rationale for doing so: Our understanding of human behavior cannot be complete without knowledge of the fundamentals of the brain and the rest of the nervous system. As we shall see, much of our behavior—our moods, motivations, goals, and desires—has a good deal to do with our biological makeup.

In sum, after reading this chapter, you will be able to answer these questions:

- What are the basic elements of the nervous system?
- How does the nervous system communicate electrical and chemical messages from one part to another?
- How can an understanding of the nervous system help us to relieve disease and pain?
- In what way are the structures of the nervous system tied together?
- What are the major parts of the brain, and what are the behaviors for which the parts are responsible?
- In what ways do the two halves of the brain operate independently of each other?

THE BASICS OF BEHAVIOR: NEURONS AND THE NERVOUS SYSTEM

If you have ever watched the precision with which a well-trained athlete or dancer executes a performance, you may have marveled at the complexity—and wondrous abilities—of the human body. But even the most everyday tasks—picking up a pencil, writing, speaking—require a sophisticated sequence of activities that is impressive. For instance, the difference between saying the words "dime" and "time" rests primarily on whether the vocal cords are relaxed or tense during a period lasting no more than one-hundredth of a second. Yet it is a distinction that almost everyone can make with ease.

The nervous system provides the pathways that permit us to carry out such precise activities. To understand how it is able to provide such exacting control over our bodies, we must begin by examining the most basic parts of the nervous system and considering the way in which nerve impulses are transmitted throughout the human body.

Beginning with the Basics: The Neuron

The ability to play the piano, drive a car, or hit a tennis ball depends, at one level, merely on muscle coordination. But if we consider *how* the muscles involved in such activities are activated, we see that there are other, more fundamental processes involved. It is necessary for the body to provide messages to the muscles and to coordinate those messages in order to produce the complex movements that characterize successful physical activity.

Such messages are passed through specialized cells called **neurons,** the basic elements of the nervous system. Their quantity is staggering; it is estimated that there are between 100 billion and 200 billion neurons in the brain alone. Although there are several types of neurons, each has a

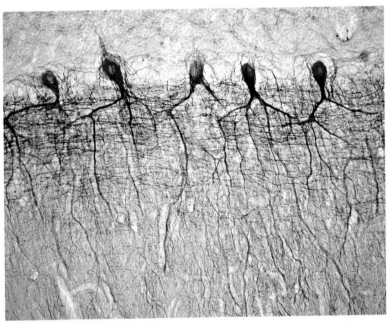

This photograph, made with an electron microscope, shows a group of neurons.

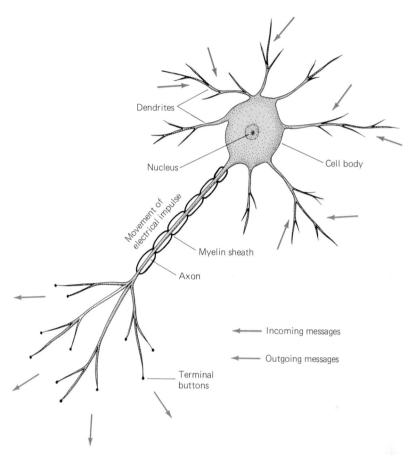

FIGURE 2-1
The primary components of the specialized cell called the neuron, the basic element of the nervous system.

similar basic structure, as illustrated in Figure 2-1 (Levy, Anderson & Lehmkuhle, 1984).

Unique among all the body's cells, neurons have a distinctive feature: the ability to communicate with other cells. As you can see in Figure 2-1, neurons have a cluster of fibers called **dendrites** at one end; it is from these fibers, which look like the twisted branches of a tree, that they receive messages from other neurons. At the opposite end, neurons have a long, slim, tubelike extension called an **axon**, which carries messages destined for other cells through the neuron. The axon is considerably longer than the rest of the neuron; most axons are 1 to 2 inches long, though some may reach 3 feet in length. In contrast, the remainder of the neuron is only a fraction of the size of the axon. Finally, at the end of the axon are small branches called **terminal buttons** through which messages are relayed to other cells.

The messages that travel through the neuron are purely electrical in nature. They generally move across neurons as if they were traveling on a one-way street, following a route that begins with the dendrites, continues into the cell body, and leads ultimately down the tubelike extension, the axon. Dendrites, then, detect messages from other neurons; axons carry signals away from the cell body.

In order to prevent messages from short-circuiting one another, it is necessary for the axons to be insulated in some fashion (analogous to the way electric wires must be insulated). In most axons, this is done with a protective coating known as the **myelin sheath,** made up of a series of specialized cells of fat and protein that wrap themselves around the axon.

The myelin sheath also serves to increase the velocity with which the electric impulses travel through the neurons, with those neurons that carry the most important and urgently required information having the greatest concentrations of myelin. If you touch a hot stove, for example, the information is passed through neurons that contain a relatively large quantity of myelin, speeding the message of pain. In certain diseases, such as multiple sclerosis, the myelin sheath surrounding the axon deteriorates, exposing parts of the axon that are normally covered. The result is a kind of short circuit, producing a disturbance in messages between the brain and muscles and resulting in symptoms such as the inability to walk, vision difficulties, and general muscle impairment.

Although the electric impulse always moves across the neuron in a dendrite-to-cell-body-to-axon sequence, research shows that some substances travel within parts of the neuron in the opposite direction (Schmeck, 1984). For instance, axons allow a reverse flow toward the cell body, whereby chemical substances needed for the nourishment of the cell are brought into the cell nucleus. Certain diseases, such as amyotrophic lateral sclerosis (ALS), or Lou Gehrig's disease (named for its most famous victim), may be caused by the inability of the neuron to transport vital materials in this reverse direction, eventually causing the neuron to figuratively die from starvation. Similarly, rabies is caused by the transmission of the rabies poison by reverse flow along the axon from the terminal buttons.

The movement of material along the dendrite may also be multidirectional: Rather than consistently transmitting information from other neurons to the cell body, a dendrite may occasionally "leak" information intended for its cell body, thereby inadvertently sending messages to other neurons. In fact, some scientists now suspect that such leaks may cause epilepsy, the disorder in which a person suffers from periodic seizures and convulsions. When electric discharges are leaked from dendrites, communicating unintended messages in an uncontrolled manner, furious electric storms are produced in the brain.

The Smoking Gun: Firing the Neuron

Like a gun, a neuron either fires or doesn't fire; there is nothing in between. Pulling harder on the trigger is not going to make the bullet travel faster or more surely. Similarly, neurons follow an **all-or-none law:** They are either on or off; once triggered beyond a certain point, they will fire. When they are off—that is, in a **resting state**—there is a negative electric charge of about -70 millivolts within the neuron (a millivolt is one-thousandth of a volt). This charge is caused by the presence of more negatively charged ions (a type of molecule) within the neuron than outside it. You might think of the neuron as one of the poles of a miniature battery, with the inside of the neuron representing the negative pole and the outside of the neuron the positive pole.

However, when a message arrives from another neuron, the cell walls allow the entry of positively charged ions, which in turn permits the charge within that part of the cell to change momentarily from negative to positive. When the charge reaches a critical level, the "trigger" is pulled, and an electric nerve impulse, known as an **action potential,** then travels down the neuron (see Figure 2-2a).

The action potential moves from one end of the neuron to the other like a flame moves across a fuse toward an explosive. As the impulse moves toward the end of the neuron, the movement of ions causes a sequential change in charge from negative to positive along the cell (see Figure 2-2b). After the passage of the impulse, positive ions are pumped out of the neuron, and the neuron charge returns to negative.

Just after an action potential has passed, the neuron cannot be fired again—it is in its **absolute refractory period.** It is as if the gun has to be reloaded after each shot. Following the absolute refractory period, there is also a **relative refractory period,** in which it is more difficult than usual to fire the neuron. During this period, although an impulse can pass through the neuron, it takes a stronger stimulus to set it off than if the neuron had been given sufficient time to reach its normal resting potential. Eventually, though, the neuron returns to its resting state and is ready to be fired once again.

These complex events occur at speeds that are a function of the size of the axon and the thickness of the myelin sheath. Neurons with small diameters carry impulses at about 2 miles per hour; longer and thicker ones can average speeds of more than 225 miles per hour.

In addition to varying according to how quickly an impulse moves across them, neurons differ in their potential rate of firing. Some neurons have the potential to fire as many as 1000 times per second; others have a maximum potential rate that is much lower. The intensity of a stimulus that provokes a neuron determines how much of this potential rate is reached: A strong stimulus, such as a bright light or loud sound, leads to a higher rate of firing than does a less intense stimulus. Thus, while there

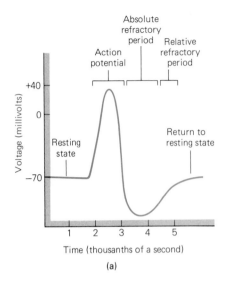

(a)

FIGURE 2-2a
Changes in the electrical charge of a neuron during the passage of an action potential. In its normal resting state, a neuron has a negative charge of around −70 millivolts. When an action potential is triggered, however, the cell charge becomes positive, increasing to about +40 millivolts. Following the passage of the action potential, the charge becomes even more negative than it is in its typical state. It is not until the charge returns to its resting potential that the neuron will be fully ready to be triggered once again.

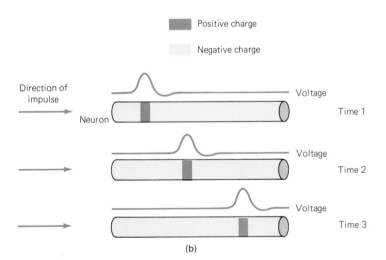

(b)

FIGURE 2-2b
Movement of an action potential across a neuron can be seen in this series of three drawings. Just prior to time 1, positively charged ions enter the cell walls, changing the charge within that part of the cell from negative to positive. The action potential is thus triggered, traveling down the neuron, as illustrated in the changes occurring from time 1 to time 3 (from top to bottom in this drawing). Following the passage of the action potential, positive ions are pumped out of the neuron, restoring its charge to negative. The change in voltage illustrated at the top of the neuron can be seen in greater detail in Figure 2-2a.

are no differences in the strength or speed at which an impulse moves across a given neuron—as the all-or-none law suggests—there is variation in the frequency of impulses, providing a mechanism by which we can distinguish the tickle of a feather from the weight of someone standing on our toe.

The structure, operation, and functions of the neuron illustrate how fundamental biological aspects of the body underlie several primary psychological processes. Our understanding of the way we sense, perceive, and learn about the world would be greatly restricted without the information about the neuron that biopsychologists have acquired.

ASK YOURSELF

What are neurons?

How can you describe the basic structure of all neurons?

How does the all-or-none law affect the firing of neurons?

How do you suppose communication between neurons results in human consciousness?

Bridging the Gap: Where Neuron Meets Neuron

Have you ever put together a radio kit? If you have, you probably remember that the manufacturer supplied you with wires that had to be painstakingly connected to one another or to some other component of the radio; every piece had to be physically connected to something else.

The human body is considerably more sophisticated than a radio, or any other manufactured apparatus, for that matter. It has evolved a neural transmission system that in some parts has no need for a structural connection between its components. Instead, a chemical connection bridges the gap, known as a **synapse**, between two neurons (see Figure 2-3a). When a nerve impulse comes to the end of the axon and reaches a terminal button, the terminal button releases a chemical called a **neurotransmitter.** Neurotransmitters carry specific chemical messages across the synapse to the dendrite (and sometimes the cell body) of a receiver neuron. Although messages travel in electrical form *within* neurons, then, they move *between* neurons through a chemical transmission system.

There are several types of neurotransmitters, and not all receiver neurons are capable of receiving the chemical message carried by every neurotransmitter. In the same way that a jigsaw puzzle piece can fit in only one specific location in a puzzle, so each kind of neurotransmitter has a distinctive configuration that allows it to fit into a specific type of receptor cell on the receiving neuron (see Figure 2-3b). It is only when a neuro-

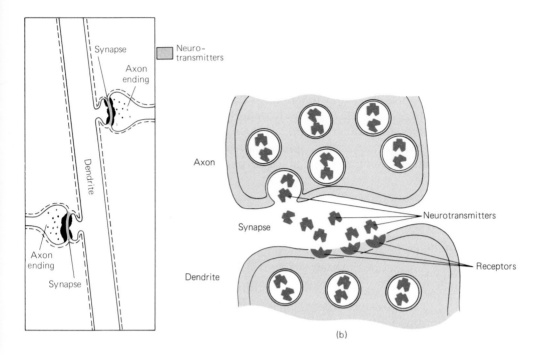

FIGURE 2-3
(a) A synapse is the junction between an axon and a dendrite. The gap between the axon and the dendrite is bridged by chemicals called neurotransmitters.
(b) Just as the pieces of a jigsaw puzzle can fit in only one specific location in a puzzle, each kind of neurotransmitter has a distinctive configuration that allows it to fit into a specific type of receptor cell.

transmitter fits precisely into a receptor cell that successful chemical communication is possible.

If a neurotransmitter does fit into a receiving neuron, the chemical message that arrives with it is basically one of two types: excitatory or inhibitory. **Excitatory messages** make it more likely that a receiving neuron will fire and an action potential will travel down its axons. **Inhibitory messages**, in contrast, do just the opposite; they provide chemical information that prevents or decreases the likelihood that the receiving neuron will fire.

Because the dendrites of a neuron receive many messages simultaneously, some of which are excitatory and some inhibitory, the neuron must integrate the messages in some fashion. It does this through a kind of summation process; if the number of excitatory messages outweighs the number of inhibitory ones, an action potential will occur. On the other hand, if the number of inhibitory messages outweighs the excitatory ones, nothing will happen. The neuron will remain in its resting state.

If neurotransmitters remained at the site of the synapse, effective communication would no longer be possible, since there would be continual stimulation of the receptor cells. Instead, neurotransmitters are either deactivated by enzymes or—more frequently—reabsorbed by the terminal button in an example of chemical thriftiness called **reuptake.** Certain drugs, such as cocaine, inhibit the reuptake of some kinds of neurotransmitters, thereby prolonging their effects and producing a "high."

Varieties of neurotransmitters. So far, some fifty chemicals have been found to act as neurotransmitters, and some experts feel that several hundred may ultimately be identified (Shepherd, 1990). Particular neurotransmitters produce the excitation or inhibition of neurons at different rates and in different concentrations. Furthermore, the effects of a given neurotransmitter vary depending on the portion of the nervous system in which it is produced. The same neurotransmitter, then, can cause a neuron to fire when it is secreted in one part of the brain and can inhibit the firing of neurons when it is produced in another part. (The major neurotransmitters are shown in Table 2-1.)

One of the most common neurotransmitters is **acetylcholine** (or **ACh,** its chemical symbol), which produces contractions of skeletal muscles (Blusztajn & Wurtman, 1983; Kasa, 1986). The venom of the deadly black widow spider causes the continuous release of ACh, eventually killing the victim through muscle spasms. ACh is also related to the drug curare,

TABLE 2-1 MAJOR NEUROTRANSMITTERS

Name	Location	Effects
Acetylcholine (ACh)	Brain, spinal cord, peripheral nervous system, especially some organs of the parasympathetic nervous system	Deficiency: paralysis (curare and botulism), Alzheimer's disease. Excess: violent muscle contraction (black widow spider venom)
Dopamine (DA)	Brain	Deficiency: muscular rigidity and uncontrollable tremors (Parkinson's disease)
Enkephalins and endorphins	Brain, spinal cord	Pain reduction
Gamma-amino butyric acid (GABA)	Brain	Deficiency: mental deterioration (Huntington's chorea)
Norepinephrine (NE)	Brain, some organs of sympathetic nervous system	Deficiency: depression
Serotonin	Brain	Deficiency: depression

used in the poison arrows of South American Indians. Curare blocks reception of ACh, thereby paralyzing the skeletal muscles and ultimately producing death by suffocation, since the victim is unable to breathe. On the brighter side, the study of ACh has helped provide insights into such medical conditions as myasthenia gravis, a disease in which there is a gradual loss of muscle control. Specifically, treatments have been devised in which drugs can be administered to prevent the destruction of ACh by the body, thereby allowing the normal transmission of impulses across the synapses and restoration of muscle control.

Some psychologists now suggest that **Alzheimer's disease,** a progressive degenerative disorder that ultimately produces loss of memory, confusion, and changes in personality, may be related to the production of ACh. For example, evidence is growing that ACh is associated with memory capabilities, and some research now shows that Alzheimer's patients have restricted production of ACh in portions of their brains. If this research is corroborated, it may lead to treatments in which production of ACh (or, in fact, other necessary substances in the brain) can be restored (Wolozin et al., 1986).

Another major neurotransmitter is **dopamine (DA),** which has an inhibitory effect on some neurons and an excitatory effect on others, such as those of the heart. The discovery that certain drugs can have a marked effect on dopamine release has led to the development of effective treatments for a wide variety of physical and mental ailments. For instance, Parkinson's disease, the severe medical condition of Nelson Martinez (whose case was discussed at the start of the chapter) marked by varying degrees of muscular rigidity and shaking, seems to be caused by a deficiency of dopamine in the brain. Drugs have been developed to stimulate the production of dopamine, and they have proved highly effective in reducing the symptoms of Parkinson's in many patients. In extreme cases, such as that of Martinez, production of dopamine has been stimulated by implantation of cells into the brain from other parts of the body.

Researchers have also hypothesized that schizophrenia and some other mental disturbances are affected or perhaps even caused by the overproduction of dopamine (Wong et al., 1986, 1988). Drugs that inhibit dopamine production have been successful in reducing the appearance of abnormal behavior in people diagnosed as schizophrenic—as we will examine further when we consider abnormal behavior and its treatment in Chapters 10 and 11.

A natural high: Endorphins.

Unless he was jogging, David Bartlett was a quiet, unassuming person. Most people who knew him tended to think of him as an introvert. But when he jogged, a noticeable change seemed to come over David. By the time he finished his daily 5- or 6-mile run he was excited, happy—even euphoric at times—and talkative. Anyone who was with David after a run noticed the change. In fact, some of his friends joked about it, saying that he acted as if he were "high" on something he had taken while he was out running.

"Runner's high" may occur from the release of endorphins, or natural painkillers, in the brain.

What happened to David Bartlett when he was jogging? Given our current discussion, you might suspect that his behavior related to a neurotransmitter—an explanation that appears well founded.

The specific neurotransmitter involved is likely to be an endorphin. **Endorphins** are chemicals produced by the body that interact with a particular kind of neuron called an **opiate receptor.** Opiate receptors act to reduce the experience of pain, and in fact many painkilling drugs, such as morphine, are used to activate the opiate receptors. Endorphins are a kind of "natural" morphine produced by the body to reduce pain. For instance, people who are afflicted with diseases that produce long-term, severe pain often develop large concentrations of endorphins in their brains—suggesting an attempt by the body to control the pain (Watkins & Mayer, 1982).

Endorphins like morphine and other opiates may go even further than mere pain reduction: They may also produce the kind of euphoric feelings that jogger David Bartlett experienced after running. It is possible that the amount of exercise and perhaps even the pain involved in a long run stimulate the production of endorphins—ultimately resulting in what has been called a "runner's high" (Hathaway, 1984).

Endorphin release may also explain other phenomena that have long puzzled psychologists, such as the reasons that acupuncture and placebos—pills that contain no actual drugs but that patients *believe* will make them better—are sometimes effective in reducing pain (Bolles & Fanselow, 1982). Specifically, it is possible that acupuncture and placebos both act to release endorphins, thereby bringing about positive results.

The study of endorphins has led biopsychologists to search for neuronal receptors for a variety of drugs. Recently, for instance, researchers identified the neuronal cell that acts as the receptor for the active ingredient in marijuana. Such a discovery has paved the way for the creation of drugs that yield the positive effects of marijuana, such as relief from pain, asthma, and nausea, without any accompanying intoxication. The study of neurotransmitters and the neuronal structure of the body, then, may help biopsychologists develop new, more effective painkillers based on the natural functions of the body (Matsuda et al., 1990).

STRINGING NEURONS TOGETHER: THE NERVOUS SYSTEM

Given the complexity of individual neurons and the neurotransmission process, it should come as no surprise that the structures formed by the neurons are likewise complicated in their own right. However, there is a certain logic—even an elegance—to the human nervous system.

The Near and the Far: Central and Peripheral Nervous Systems

As you can see from Figure 2-4, the nervous system is divided into two main parts: the central nervous system and the peripheral nervous system. The **central nervous system (CNS)** is composed of the brain and spinal cord. The **spinal cord** is a bundle of nerves, about the thickness of a pencil, that leaves the brain and runs down the length of the back. It is the main means for transmitting messages between the brain and the body.

Some simple kinds of behaviors are organized entirely within the spinal cord. A common example is the knee jerk, which occurs when the knee is tapped with a rubber hammer. Such behaviors, called **reflexes,** represent an involuntary response to an incoming stimulus which is "reflected" back out of the body, without the involvement of the brain.

For example, when you touch a hot stove and immediately withdraw your hand, a reflex is at work: Although eventually the brain analyzes the pain, the initial withdrawal is directed only by neurons in the spinal cord. Three sorts of neurons are involved in reflexes: **sensory (afferent) neurons,** which transmit information from the periphery of the body to the central nervous system; **motor (efferent) neurons,** which communicate information from the nervous system to muscles and glands of the body; and **interneurons,** which connect sensory and motor neurons, carrying messages between the two.

The importance of the spinal cord and reflexes is illustrated by the outcome of accidents in which the cord is injured or severed. In one re-

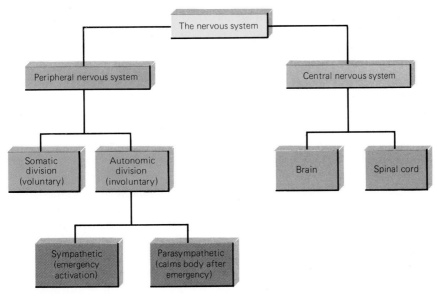

FIGURE 2-4
A schematic diagram of the relationship of the parts of the nervous system.

sulting injury, **paraplegia,** a person is unable to voluntarily move any muscles in the lower half of the body. However, even though the cord is severed, the undamaged area of the spinal cord is still able to produce some simple reflex actions, if stimulated appropriately. For instance, if a paraplegic's knee is tapped lightly, the lower leg will jerk slightly forward. Similarly, in some kinds of spinal cord injuries, people will move their legs in an involuntary response to a pinprick, even though they do not experience the sensation of pain.

The spinal cord is related to other basic biological functions as well. For instance, if a male paraplegic's genitals are stimulated, he is capable of having an erection and ultimately ejaculating. However, with a damaged spinal cord, the paraplegic would not experience the sensations that are normally a part of sexual activity and thus would not be able to perceive his arousal.

As suggested by its name, the **peripheral nervous system** branches out from the spinal cord and brain and reaches the peripheries of the body. Made up of long axons and dendrites, the peripheral nervous system encompasses all parts of the nervous system other than the brain and spinal cord. There are two major divisions, the somatic division and the autonomic division, both of which connect the central nervous system with the sense organs, muscles, glands, and other organs. The **somatic division** specializes in the control of voluntary movements—such as the motion of the eyes to read this sentence or of the hand to turn this page—and the communication of information to and from the sense organs. On the other hand, the **autonomic division** is concerned with the parts of the body that keep us alive—the heart, blood vessels, glands, lungs, and other organs that function involuntarily without our awareness. As you are reading along right now, the autonomic division of the peripheral nervous system is pumping the blood through your body, pushing your lungs in and out, overseeing the digestion of the meal you had a few hours ago, and so on—all without a thought or care on your part.

Emergency! Activating the Autonomic Nervous System

The autonomic division plays a particularly crucial role during emergency situations. Suppose as you are reading you suddenly sense that there is a stranger watching you through the window. As you look up, you see the glint of something that just might be a knife. As confusion races through your mind and fear overcomes your attempts to think rationally, what happens to your body? If you are like most people, you react immediately on a physiological level: Your heart rate increases, you begin to sweat, and you develop goose bumps all over your body.

The physiological changes that occur result from the activation of one part of the autonomic division: the sympathetic division. The **sympathetic division** acts to prepare the body in stressful emergency situations, engaging all the organism's resources to respond to a threat, a response that often takes the form of "fight or flight." In contrast, the **parasympathetic division** acts to calm the body after the emergency situation is resolved. When you find, for instance, that the stranger at the window is actually your roommate who has lost his keys and is climbing in the window to avoid waking you, your parasympathetic division begins to predominate, lowering your heart rate, stopping your sweating, and returning your body to the state it was in prior to your fright. The parasympathetic division also provides a means for the body to maintain storage of energy sources such as nutrients and oxygen. The sympathetic and parasympathetic divisions work together to regulate many functions of the body. For instance, sexual arousal is controlled by the parasympathetic division, while sexual orgasm is a function of the sympathetic division.

ASK YOURSELF

In what way do messages traveling across synapses differ from messages traveling within neurons?

What are neurotransmitters?

How can the major parts of the nervous system be described?

What are the functions of the components of the central nervous system?

What are the components of the peripheral nervous system?

Which part of the nervous system operates in emergency situations?

How does knowledge of the function of neurotransmitters enable biopsychologists to develop treatments for various mental and physical problems?

Why do psychologists need to study the biological underpinnings of behavior?

TYING THE NERVOUS SYSTEM TOGETHER: THE BRAIN

When you come right down to it, it is not a very pretty sight. Soft, spongy, mottled, and pinkish-gray in color, one could hardly say that it possesses much in the way of physical beauty. Despite its physical appearance, however, it ranks as the greatest natural marvel that we know and possesses a beauty and sophistication all its own.

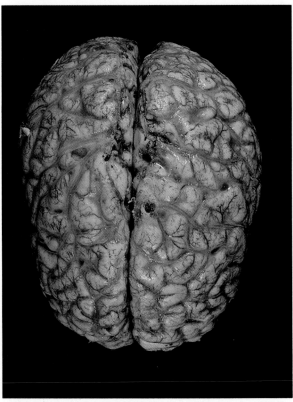

The brain has capabilities far more spectacular than its appearance would lead one to suspect.

The object to which this description applies is, as you might guess, the brain. The brain is responsible for our loftiest thoughts—and our most primitive urges. It is the overseer of the intricate workings of the human body. If one were to attempt to design a computer to mimic the capabilities of the brain, the task would be nearly impossible; in fact, it has proved difficult to even come close (Hellerstein, 1988). Just the sheer quantity of nerve cells in the brain is enough to daunt even the most ambitious computer engineer. Many billions of nerve cells make up a structure weighing just 3 pounds in the average adult. However, it is not the number of cells that is the most astounding thing about the brain but its ability to allow human intellect to flourish as it guides our behavior and thoughts.

Exploring and Mapping the Unknown: Studying the Brain

The brain has always posed a challenge to those wishing to study it. For most of history, it could be examined only after an individual was dead— for only then was it possible to open up the skull and cut into the brain without the risk of causing serious injury. While informative, such a limited procedure could hardly tell us much about the functioning of the healthy brain.

Today, however, the story is different. Probably the most important advances that have been made in the study of the brain use the **brain scan,** a technique by which a picture of the internal workings of the brain can be taken without having to surgically cut into a patient's skull (Turkington, 1985). The main kinds of scanning techniques are described below and illustrated in Figure 2-5.

- The **electroencephalogram (EEG),** records the electrical signals being transmitted inside the brain through electrodes placed on the outside of the skull. Although traditionally the EEG could produce only a graph of electrical wave patterns, new techniques now are able to transform the brain's electrical activity into a pictorial representation of the brain that allows the diagnosis of such problems as epilepsy and learning disabilities.

- The **computerized axial tomography (CAT) scan** uses a computer to construct an image of the brain by combining thousands of separate x-rays taken at slightly different angles. It is extremely useful for showing abnormalities in the structure of the brain, such as swelling and enlargement of certain parts, but does not provide information about brain activity.

- The **nuclear magnetic resonance (NMR) scan** produces a powerful magnetic field to provide a detailed, computer-generated image of brain activity. Although still considered experimental, it is becom-

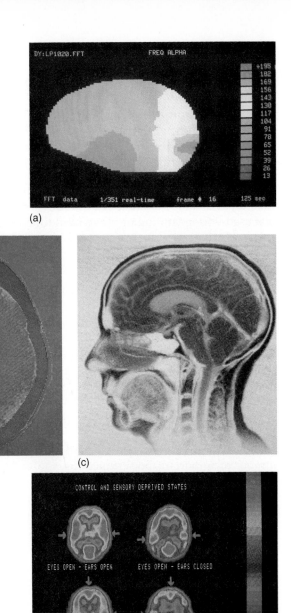
(a)

(b)

(c)

(d)

FIGURE 2-5
Brain scans produced by different techniques. (*a*) A computer-produced EEG image. (*b*) The CAT scan shows the structures of the brain. (*c*) The NMR scan uses a magnetic field to detail the parts of the brain. (*d*) PET scans display the functioning of the brain at a given moment in time and are sensitive to the person's activities. [(a) *Dr. Richard Coppola/NIMH*, (b)*Dan McCoy/Rainbow*, (c) *Courtesy of J. C. Mazziotta and M. E. Phelps, UCLA School of Medicine.*]

ing the scan of choice because of the wealth of detail that can be constructed.

- The **positron emission tomography (PET) scan** indicates how the brain is functioning at a given moment in time. After radioactive sugar is injected into a patient, a computer that measures radiation in the brain displays whether the brain is functioning normally.

Each of these techniques provides exciting possibilities not only for the diagnosis and treatment of brain disease and injuries but also for an increased understanding of the normal functioning of the brain.

Uncovering the "Old Brain": The Central Core

While the capabilities of the human brain far exceed those of the brain of any other species, it is not surprising that the basic functions—such as breathing, eating, and sleeping—that we share with more primitive animals are directed by a relatively primitive part of the brain. A portion of the brain known as the **central core** (see Figure 2-6) is quite similar to that found in all vertebrates (species with backbones). The central core is often referred to as the "old brain" because it is thought to have evolved relatively early in the development of the human species.

If we were to move up the spinal cord from the base of the skull to locate the structures of the central core of the brain, the first part we would come to would be the medulla (see Figure 2-7). The **medulla** controls a number of important body functions, the most important of which are breathing and maintenance of heartbeat. The pons comes next, joining the two halves of the cerebellum, which lies just adjacent to it. Containing large bundles of nerves, the **pons** acts as a transmitter of motor infor-

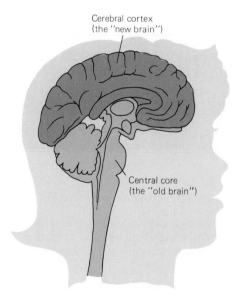

Cerebral cortex
(the "new brain")

Central core
(the "old brain")

FIGURE 2-6
The major divisions of the brain: the central core and the cerebral cortex.

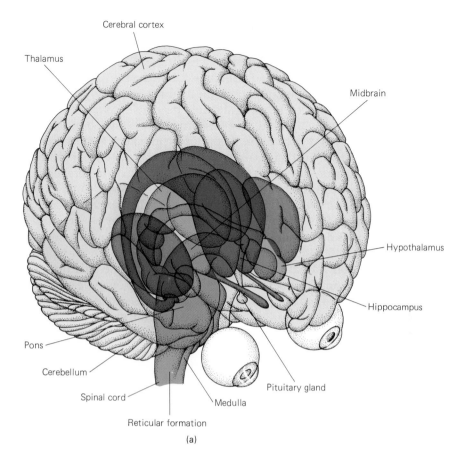

Cerebral cortex

Thalamus

Midbrain

Hypothalamus

Hippocampus

Pons

Cerebellum

Spinal cord

Medulla

Pituitary gland

Reticular formation

(a)

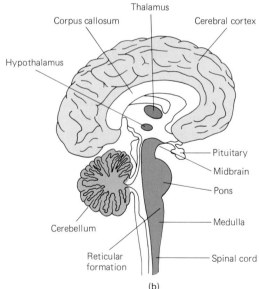

Thalamus

Corpus callosum

Cerebral cortex

Hypothalamus

Pituitary

Midbrain

Pons

Medulla

Cerebellum

Reticular formation

Spinal cord

(b)

FIGURE 2-7
(*a*) A three-dimensional view of the structures within the brain. (Nauta &
Feirtag, 1979.) (*b*) In this view, we can see the inside of a brain that has been cut
in half; we are viewing the inner surface of the right side. (From Thompson,
1967).

59

mation, permitting the coordination of muscles and the integration of movement between the right and left halves of the body.

The **cerebellum** is found just above the medulla and behind the pons. Without the help of the cerebellum we would be unable to walk a straight line without staggering and lurching forward, for it is the job of the cerebellum to control bodily balance. It constantly monitors feedback from the muscles to coordinate their placement, movement, and tension. In fact, drinking too much alcohol seems to depress the activity of the cerebellum, leading to the unsteady gait and movement characteristic of drunkenness.

So far our description of the parts of the brain has suggested that it is made up of a series of individual, well-defined separate structures. However, its parts do not simply follow one another in a sequential order; they are found both within and between other structures. An example of this is the **reticular formation,** which extends from the medulla through the pons. The reticular formation is made up of a group of nerve cells that serves as a kind of guard that immediately activates other parts of the brain to cause a general arousal of the body. If, for example, you are startled by a loud noise, your reticular formation is likely to engage your body in immediate vigilance, prompting a heightened state of awareness to determine whether a response is necessary. In addition, it serves a different function when you are sleeping, seeming to screen out background stimuli to allow you to sleep undisturbed.

The final structures that are part of the "old brain" are the thalamus and the hypothalamus. The **thalamus,** located centrally within the "old brain," acts primarily as a relay station, mostly for messages concerning sensory information (Casey & Morrow, 1983). Messages from the eyes, ears, and skin travel to the thalamus to be communicated upward to higher parts of the brain. The thalamus also integrates information from higher parts of the brain, sorting it out so that it can be sent to the cerebellum and medulla.

The **hypothalamus** is located just below the thalamus. Although tiny—about the size of the tip of a finger—the hypothalamus plays an inordinately important role in the functioning of the body. One of its major functions is to maintain **homeostasis,** a steady internal environment for the body; as we will discuss further in Chapter 6, the hypothalamus helps provide a constant body temperature and monitors the amount of nutrients stored in the cells. A second major function is equally important: It produces and regulates behavior that is important to the basic survival of the species—eating, drinking, sexual behavior, fighting, and nurturance of offspring.

Of Chemicals and Glands: The Endocrine System

As we move upward through the brain, we need to pause a moment to consider the **endocrine system,** a chemical communication network that sends messages throughout the nervous system via the bloodstream. Although not a structure of the brain itself, the endocrine system is intimately tied to the hypothalamus. The job of the endocrine system is to secrete **hormones,** chemicals that circulate through the blood and affect the functioning or growth of other parts of the body (Crapo, 1985; Kravitz, 1988).

Like neurons, endocrines transmit messages throughout the body, although the speed and mode of transmission are quite different. Whereas neural messages are measured in thousandths of a second, hormonal communications may take minutes to reach their destination. Furthermore, neural messages move across neurons in specific lines (as with wires strung along telephone poles), whereas hormones travel throughout the entire body, similar to the way radio waves transmit across the entire landscape. Just as radio waves evoke a response only when a radio is tuned to the correct station, so hormones flowing through the bloodstream activate only those cells that are receptive and "tuned" to the appropriate hormonal message.

The major component of the endocrine system is the **pituitary gland,** found near—and regulated by—the hypothalamus. The pituitary gland is sometimes called the "master gland," because it controls the functioning of the rest of the endocrine system. But the pituitary gland is more than just the taskmaster of other glands; it has important functions in its own right. For instance, hormones secreted by the pituitary gland control growth. Extremely short people—dwarfs—and unusually tall ones—giants—usually have pituitary gland deficiencies. Other endocrine glands affect emotional reactions, sexual urges, and energy levels.

Despite its nickname as the "master gland," the pituitary is actually a servant of the brain, which is ultimately responsible for the endocrine system's functioning. The brain regulates the internal balance of the body, ensuring that homeostasis is maintained through the hypothalamus.

The uncoordinated behavior characteristic of a person who has been drinking occurs because the ingestion of alcohol causes a reduction in the activity of the cerebellum.

Moreover, the road from brain to endocrine system is not strictly a one-way street: Hormones may permanently modify the way in which brain cells are organized. For example, adult sexual behavior is thought to be affected by the production of hormones that modify cells in the hypothalamus.

Passing Beyond the Central Core: The Limbic System

In a bizarre view of the future, some science fiction writers have suggested that people will someday routinely have electrodes implanted in their brains, allowing them to receive tiny shocks that produce the sensation of pleasure by stimulating certain centers of the brain. When they feel upset, people will simply activate their electrodes to achieve an immediate high.

Although farfetched—and ultimately probably unachievable—such a futuristic fantasy is based on fact: The brain does have pleasure centers in an area known as the **limbic system.** Consisting of a series of interrelated structures, the limbic system borders the top of the central core and connects with it and with the cerebral cortex (located in Figure 2-6 roughly at the boundaries between the two colors).

The structures of the limbic system jointly control a variety of basic functions relating to self-preservation—such as eating, aggression, and reproduction—and injury to the limbic system can produce striking changes in behavior. It can turn animals that are usually docile and tame into belligerent savages. Conversely, those that are usually wild and uncontrollable may become meek and obedient (Fanelli, Burright & Donovick, 1983).

Probably the most thought-provoking finding to emerge from the study of the limbic system comes from research that has examined the effects of mild electric shocks to certain parts of the system (Olds & Milner, 1954). In one experiment, rats with an electrode implanted in their limbic systems were given the opportunity to pass an electric current through the electrode by pressing a bar. Even starving rats on their way to food would stop to press the bar as many times as they could. In fact, if allowed to do so, the rats would stimulate their limbic systems literally thousands of times an hour—until they collapsed with fatigue (Routtenberg & Lindy, 1965).

The extraordinarily pleasurable quality of certain kinds of limbic-system stimulation has also been found in humans, who have—usually as part of some treatment of brain dysfunction—received electrical stimulation to certain areas of the limbic system. Although they are at a loss to describe just what it feels like, these people report the experience to be intensely pleasurable—similar in some respects to sexual orgasm.

The limbic system also plays an important role in learning and memory, a finding demonstrated in patients with epilepsy who, in an attempt to stop their seizures, have had portions of the limbic system removed.

Such individuals sometimes have difficulty learning and remembering new information. In one case (discussed again when we focus on memory in Chapter 6) a patient who had undergone surgery was unable to remember where he lived, although he had resided at the same address for eight years. Further, even though the patient was able to carry on animated conversations, he was unable, a few minutes later, to recall what had been discussed (Milner, 1966).

The limbic system, then, is involved in several important functions, including self-preservation, learning, memory, and the experience of pleasure. These functions are hardly unique to humans; in fact, the limbic system is sometimes referred to as the "animal brain" because its structures and functions are so similar to those of other mammals. To find that which is uniquely human, we need to turn to another part of the brain—the cerebral cortex.

*A*SK YOURSELF

Is there a similarity between the central core of the human brain and that of other vertebrates?

What are the parts of the central nervous system from the top of the spinal cord up into the brain?

What does the reticular formation consist of?

How can the thalamus and hypothalamus be differentiated?

What is the endocrine system and how does it function?

Think about the functions of the various parts of the central core. How might damage to each of these parts affect behavior?

Why is the central core called the "old brain"?

*U*P THE EVOLUTIONARY LADDER: THE CEREBRAL CORTEX

As we have moved up the spinal cord and into the brain, our discussion has centered on the areas of the brain that control functions similar to those found in less sophisticated organisms. But where, you may be asking, are the parts of the brain that enable humans to do the things they do best, things that distinguish humankind from all other animals? Those unique features of the human brain—indeed the very capabilities that allow you to come up with such a question in the first place—are embodied in the ability to think and remember. And the central location of these abilities, along with many others, is the **cerebral cortex.**

The cerebral cortex—sometimes called the "new brain" because of its relatively recent evolution—is a mass of deeply folded, rippled, convo-

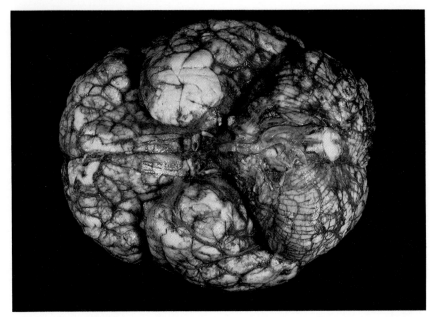

The lobes of the brain.

luted tissue. Although it is only about one-twelfth of an inch thick, if flattened out it would cover a 2½-foot-square area. This physical configuration allows the surface area of the cortex to be considerably greater than if it were more loosely and smoothly packed into the skull. It also allows the neurons within the cortex to be intricately connected to one another, permitting the highest level of integration of neural communication within the brain, and therefore the most sophisticated processing of information.

The cortex has four major sections, called lobes. If we take a side view of the brain, the **frontal lobes** lie at the front center of the cortex, and the **parietal lobes** lie behind them. The **temporal lobes** are found in the lower center of the brain, with the **occipital lobes** lying behind them. These four sets of lobes are physically separated by deep grooves called sulci. Figure 2-8a shows the four areas.

Another way of describing the brain is by considering the functions associated with a given area. Figure 2-8b shows the specialized regions within the lobes related to specific functions and areas of the body. Three major areas have been discovered: the motor area, the sensory and so-matosensory area, and the association area. Although we will discuss them as though they were separate and independent entities, this is something of an oversimplification: In most instances, behavior is influenced simultaneously by several structures and areas within the brain, operating interdependently (Gazzaniga, 1989; Gibbons, 1990).

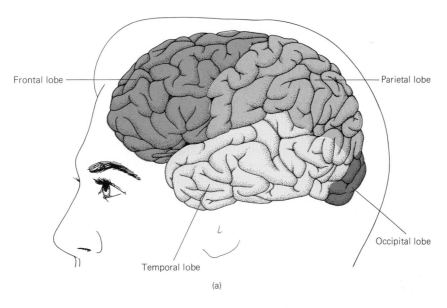

(a)

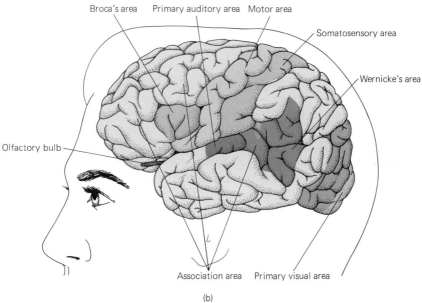

(b)

FIGURE 2-8
The cerebral cortex of the brain. (*a*) The major physical *structures* of the cerebral cortex are called lobes. (*b*) This figure illustrates the *functions* associated with particular areas of the cerebral cortex.

The Motor Area of the Brain

If you look at the frontal lobe in Figure 2-8*b,* you will see a shaded portion labeled the **motor area.** This part of the brain is largely responsible for voluntary movement of particular parts of the body. In fact, every portion of the motor area corresponds to a specific locale within the body. If we were to insert an electrode into a particular part of the motor area of the brain and apply mild electrical stimulation, there would be involuntary movement in the corresponding part of the body (Kertesz, 1983). If we moved to another part of the motor area and stimulated it, a different part of the body would move.

Control of body movements that are relatively large-scale and require little precision—such as movement of a knee or a hip—is centered in a very small space in the motor area. On the other hand, movements that must be precise and delicate—such as facial expressions and the use of the fingers—are controlled by a considerably larger portion of the motor area. In sum, the brain's motor area provides a clear guide to the degree of complexity and the importance of the motor capabilities of specific parts of the body.

The Sensory Area of the Brain

Given the one-to-one correspondence between motor area and body location, it is not surprising to find a similar relationship between specific portions of the brain and the senses. The **sensory area** of the cortex includes three regions: one that corresponds primarily to touch, one relating to sight, and a third relating to sound. The **somatosensory area** encompasses specific locations associated with the ability to perceive touch in a specific area of the body. As with the motor area, the amount of brain tissue related to a specific body part determines the degree of sensitivity of that part: The greater the space within the brain, the more sensitive the part. As you can see from the weird-looking model in Figure 2-9, parts such as the fingers are related to proportionally more space in the somatosensory area and are the most sensitive.

The senses of sound and sight also are represented in specific areas of the cerebral cortex. An auditory area located in the temporal lobe is responsible for the sense of hearing. If the auditory area is stimulated electrically, a person will hear sounds such as clicks or hums. It also appears that particular locations within the auditory area respond to specific pitches.

The visual center in the brain operates analogously to the other sensory areas; stimulation by electrodes produces the experience of flashes of light or colors, suggesting that the raw sensory input of images from the eyes is received in this area of the brain and transformed into meaningful stimuli. The visual area also provides another example of how areas

FIGURE 2-9
If the parts of our bodies reflected proportionally the space that the brain gives to the body parts' sensations, we might look like this strange creature. (British Museum of Natural History.)

of the brain are intimately related to specific areas of the body: Particular areas of the eye are related to a particular part of the brain—with, as you might guess, more space in the brain given to the most sensitive portions of the eye.

The Association Area of the Brain

Twenty-five-year-old Phineas Gage, a railroad employee, was blasting rock one day in 1848 when an accidental explosion punched a 3½-foot-long spike, about an inch in diameter, completely through his skull. The spike entered just under his left cheek, came out the top of his head, and flew into the air. He immediately suffered a series of convulsions, yet a few minutes later was talking with rescuers. In fact, he was able to walk up a long flight of stairs before receiving any medical attention. Amazingly, after a few weeks his wound healed, and he was physically close to his old self again. Mentally, however, there was a difference: Once a careful and hard-working person, Phineas now became enamored with wild schemes and was flighty and often irresponsible. As one of his physicians put it, "Previous to his injury, though untrained in the schools, he possessed a well-balanced mind, and was looked upon by those who knew him as a shrewd, smart businessman, very energetic and persistent in executing all his plans of operation. In this regard his mind was radically changed, so decidedly that his friends and acquaintances said he was 'no longer Gage' " (Harlow, 1869, p. 14).

What had happened to the old Gage? Although there is no way of knowing for sure—science being what it was in the 1800s—we might speculate that the accident may have injured the association area of Gage's cerebral hemisphere.

If you return one last time to our diagram of the cerebral cortex (Figure 2-8*b*), you will find that the motor and sensory areas take up a relatively small portion of the cortex; the remainder contains the association area. The **association area** is generally considered to be the site of higher mental processes such as thinking, language, memory, and speech. Most of our understanding of the association area comes from patients who have suffered some brain injury—from natural causes such as a tumor or a stroke, either of which would block certain blood vessels within the cerebral cortex, or, as in the case of Phineas Gage, from accidental causes. Damage to this area can result in unusual behavioral changes, indicating the importance of the association area to normal functioning.

Consider, for instance, the condition known as **apraxia.** Apraxia occurs when a person is unable to integrate activities in a rational or logical manner. For example, a patient asked to get a soda from the refrigerator might go to the refrigerator and open and close the door repeatedly, or might take bottle after bottle of soda out of the refrigerator, dropping each to the floor. Similarly, a person with apraxia who is asked to open a lock with a key may be unable to do so in response to the request—but, if simply left alone in a locked room, wishing to leave, will unlock the door (Lechtenberg, 1982).

Apraxia is clearly not a muscular problem, since the person is capable of carrying out the individual components of the overall behavior. Moreover, if asked to perform the individual components of a larger behavioral pattern one at a time, a patient is often quite successful. It is only when asked to carry out a sequence of behaviors requiring a degree of planning and foresight that the patient shows deficits. It appears, then, that the association area may act as a kind of "master planner," that is, the organizer of actions.

Other difficulties that arise because of injury to the association area of the brain relate to the use of language. Problems with verbal expression, known as **aphasia,** can take many forms. In **Broca's aphasia** (caused by damage to the part of the brain first identified by a French physician, Paul Broca), speech becomes halting and laborious. The speaker is unable to find the right words—in a kind of tip-of-the-tongue phenomenon that we all experience from time to time—except that in the case of the person with aphasia, it happens almost constantly. Patients with aphasia also speak in "verbal telegrams." A phrase like "I put the book on the table" comes out as "I . . . put . . . book . . . table" (Lechtenberg, 1982).

The Brain Transplant: Solving Old Problems—and Creating New Ones?

The successful operation carried out on Nelson Martinez (described at the beginning of this chapter), in which he received relief from the symptoms of Parkinson's disease by having cells from his adrenal glands transplanted into his brain, raises the possibility of a far more radical procedure in the future: the brain transplant. Although it sounds like something out of a science fiction movie, scientists are taking some tentative first steps toward making such an eerie prospect come true.

In 1976, scientists successfully performed the essential first step in the brain transplant process (White, 1976). They removed the brain of a chimpanzee and kept it alive for more than twenty-four hours by supplying it with oxygen and other essential nutrients. More recent research with Parkinson's patients like Martinez has provided further evidence of the possibilities inherent in brain transplants (Snyder, 1987; Lewin, 1987; Lindvall et al., 1990).

Such work is promising, raising the possibility that damaged areas of the brain may someday be routinely repaired by the introduction of compatible, healthy cells. Similar procedures may prove useful in providing therapy for a variety of problems of the nervous system, including strokes, spinal cord injuries, and brain tumors (Rosenberg et al., 1988). However, the possibility of an actual brain transplant raises a set of psychological and ethical issues that transplants of other organs do not. One issue concerns the distinction between the mind and the body, an ancient philosophical question that we discuss in Chapter 7. If we assume that the mind is separate from the body, whose mind will regulate the recipient's body—the donor's or the recipient's? If we reject the separation of body and mind—as most psychologists do—we have a hard-to-imagine situation: a new mind taking control of the recipient's body.

Brain transplants hold out even more complexities. Because others frequently react to us on the basis of our physical appearance (as we shall see in Chapter 12), a brain inhabiting someone else's body would have to adjust to a whole new set of reactions from others. Who would this new brain-in-a-body be?

While these issues may not be of immediate concern, they must be considered carefully because of their implications. And they may need to be addressed sooner than we think: In the words of neurologist Abraham Lieberman, "Five years ago, when you talked about brain transplantation, you were talking about Boris Karloff and Frankenstein. Today it's no longer science fiction" (Jaroff, 1987, p. 57).

In **Wernicke's aphasia,** named for its discoverer, Carl Wernicke, there are difficulties in understanding the language of others. Found in patients with damage to a particular area of the brain first identified by Wernicke, the disorder produces speech that appears to be fluent—but makes no sense. For instance, one of Wernicke's patients, Philip Gorgan, was asked what brought him to the hospital. He replied, "Boy, I'm sweating, I'm awful nervous, you know, once in a while I get caught up, I can't mention the tarripoi, a month ago, quite a little, I've done a lot well, I impose a lot, while, on the other hand, you know what I mean, I have to run around, look it over, trebbin and all that sort of stuff" (Gardner, 1975, p. 68).

TWO BRAINS OR ONE? THE SPECIALIZATION OF THE HEMISPHERES

The most recent development—at least in evolutionary terms—in the organization and operation of our brain probably occurred in the last million years: a specialization of the functions controlled by the two sides of the brain, which has symmetrical left and right halves.

Specifically, the brain structure can be divided into two roughly similar mirror-image halves—just as we have two arms, two legs, and two lungs. Because of the way nerves are connected from the brain to the rest of the body, these two symmetrical left and right halves, called **hemispheres,** control the side of the body opposite to their location. The left hemisphere of the brain, then, generally controls the right side of the body, and the right hemisphere controls the left side of the body. Thus damage to the right side of the brain is typically indicated by functional difficulties in the left side of the body.

Yet the structural similarity between the two hemispheres of the brain is not reflected in all aspects of its functioning; it appears that certain activities are more likely to occur in one hemisphere than in the other. Early evidence for the functional differences between halves of the brain came from studies of people with aphasia; researchers found that people with the speech difficulties characteristic of aphasia tended to have physical damage to the left hemisphere of the brain. In contrast, physical abnormalities in the right hemisphere of the brain tended to produce far fewer problems with language (Corballis & Beales, 1983). The conclusion? For most people, language is **lateralized,** or located more in one hemisphere than the other—in this case, in the left side of the brain.

It now seems clear that the two hemispheres of the brain specialize in different functions (Hellige, 1990). The left hemisphere concentrates on tasks that require verbal strength, such as speaking, reading, thinking, and reasoning. The right hemisphere has its own strengths, particularly in nonverbal areas such as spatial understanding, recognition of patterns and drawings, music, and emotional expression (see Figure 2-10).

In addition, the way in which information is processed seems somewhat different in each hemisphere: The left hemisphere considers information sequentially, one bit at a time, while the right hemisphere tends to process information globally, considering it as a whole (Gazzaniga, 1983; Springer & Deutsch, 1989). Moreover, there is even evidence suggesting that the two hemispheres develop at slightly different rates during the course of people's lives (Thatcher, Walker & Giudice, 1987; Hahn, 1987).

There is also great variation in the degree and nature of lateralization from one person to another. If, like most people, you are right-handed, the portion of your brain that controls language is probably concentrated on the left side of your brain. By contrast, if you are among the 10 percent of people who are left-handed or are ambidextrous (you use both hands

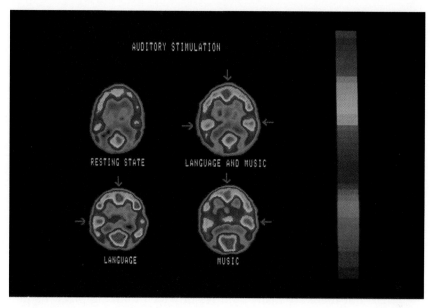

FIGURE 2-10
This series of PET scans shows the activity of the left and right hemispheres while the person is performing various activities. (Courtesy of J. C. Mazziotta and M. E. Phelps, UCLA School of Medicine.)

interchangeably), it is much more likely that the language centers of your brain are located in the right hemisphere or are divided equally between left and right hemispheres (Geschwind & Galaburda, 1985; Gazzaniga, 1985; Beaton, 1986).

It also turns out that males and females show some intriguing sex differences in brain lateralization. Most males tend to show greater lateralization of language in the left hemisphere: For them, language is clearly relegated largely to the left side of the brain. In contrast, women display less lateralization, with language abilities apt to be more evenly divided between the two hemispheres (Gur et al., 1982). Such differences in brain lateralization may account, in part, for the superiority of females often found on some measures of verbal skills, such as the onset and fluency of speech.

You can readily demonstrate which half of someone's brain is processing information by looking at the direction in which the eyes move when the person is thinking of the answer to a question. To try this, ask someone to perform the following tasks and watch to see in what direction his or her eyes move. If the person's eyes move to the right, it suggests that the subject is using the left half of the brain; if they move to the left, it suggests that the individual is using the right half. (This will work only if your subject is right-handed; left-handed people show great variability.)

1. Think of what your mother looked like the last time she got angry with you.
2. Use a sentence with the words "brain" and "behavior."
3. Describe the last sunset you saw.
4. Define the word "lateralization."

Because items 1 and 3 call upon primarily spatial and emotional abilities, most people use right-hemisphere processing and therefore should look toward the left. In contrast, items 2 and 4 call for verbal skills, resulting in left-hemisphere processing; people usually look to the right when responding (Schwartz, Davidson & Maer, 1975).

Is the functioning of one hemisphere more important than that of the other? The fact that language and formal reasoning capabilities are two of the primary functions that distinguish humans from other species might seem to suggest that the left hemisphere is of greater importance. The issue, however, is really a matter of values. In our computerized western culture, a brain that operates in a logical, sequential fashion might be preferred. But there are many cultures in which thinking proceeds in a less direct and less logical fashion and is organized pictorially rather than mathematically and verbally. In cultures such as these, a strong right hemisphere might be preferable (Annett, 1985).

Luckily, none of us has to choose between the two hemispheres of our brains; unless there is brain damage, both halves will be intact and will function together and interdependently (Best, 1985; Kosslyn, 1988). Moreover, people (especially young children) who suffer brain damage to the left side of their brain and lose linguistic capabilities often recover the ability to speak—because the right side of the brain pitches in and takes over some of the functioning of the left side. The brain, then, is remarkably adaptable and can modify its functioning—to some extent at least—in response to adverse circumstances (McConnell, 1985; Beaton, 1986; Kucharski & Hall, 1987).

The differences in hemispheric functioning at least suggest the possibility that there may be individual differences in the strengths of each hemisphere. For example, we might speculate that a talented writer has a brain in which the left side is particularly dominant, while an artist or architect might have more strength in the right hemisphere. What we do best in life, then, may be a function of which side of our brain has the greater strengths.

The Informed Consumer of Psychology: Learning to Control Your Heart—and Brain—through Biofeedback

When her blood pressure rose to unacceptably high levels, Carla Lewitt was first given the option of undergoing a standard treatment with drugs. When she asked whether there was any alternative, her physician suggested an approach that would entail her learning to control her blood pressure voluntarily. Although Carla didn't think she was capable of controlling something she wasn't even aware of, she agreed to give it a try. Within three weeks, her blood pressure had come down to normal levels.

We typically think of our blood pressure, heart, respiration rate, and other bodily functions as being under the control of parts of the brain over which we have no influence. But, as the case above illustrates, psychologists are finding that what were once thought of as entirely involuntary biological responses are proving to be susceptible to voluntary control—and, in the process, they are learning about important treatment techniques for a variety of ailments.

The technique that lowered Carla Lewitt's blood pressure is known as biofeedback. **Biofeedback** is a procedure in which a person learns to control internal physiological processes such as blood pressure, heart rate, respiration speed, skin temperature, sweating, and constriction of certain muscles (Yates, 1980).

How can people learn to control such responses, which are typically considered "involuntary"? They do so through training with electronic devices that provide continuous feedback on the physiological response in question. For instance, a person interested in controlling her blood pressure might be hooked up to an apparatus that constantly monitors and displays her blood pressure. As she consciously thinks about altering the pressure, she receives immediate feedback as to the measure of her success. In this way she can eventually learn to bring her pressure under control. Similarly, if an individual wanted to control headaches through biofeedback, he might have electronic sensors placed on certain muscles in his head and thereby learn to control the constriction and relaxation of those muscles. Then, when he felt a headache coming on, he could relax the relevant muscles and abort the pain.

While the control of physiological processes through the use of biofeedback is not easy to learn, it has been employed with success in a variety of ailments, including emotional problems (such as anxiety, depression, phobias, tension headaches, insomnia, and hyperactivity); medical problems with a psychological component (such as asthma, high blood pressure, ulcers, muscle spasms, and migraine headaches); and physical problems (such as nerve-muscle injuries due to stroke, cerebral palsy, and curvature of the spine).

Given that biofeedback is still experimental, we cannot assume that treatment is going to be successful in every case (Roberts, 1985). What is certain, however, is that learning through biofeedback has opened up a number of exciting possibilities for treating people with physical and psychological problems. Moreover, some psychologists speculate that the use of biofeedback may become a part of everyday life one day in the future.

For instance, one researcher has suggested that students whose minds wander during studying might be hooked up to apparatus that gives them

Psychologists use biofeedback to help patients control internal biological processes.

feedback as to whether they are paying attention to the information they are studying (Ornstein, 1977). If they stop paying attention, the computer will alert them—putting them back on the right track.

ASK YOURSELF

What are the major areas of the cerebral cortex and what do they control?

What skills do the two hemispheres of the brain specialize in?

How does biofeedback operate?

Think about two of your friends. Do they seem to differ in the extent to which their right or left hemispheres dominate? How so?

LOOKING BACK

1. This chapter reviews what biopsychologists (psychologists who specialize in studying the effects of biological structures and functions on behavior) have learned about the human nervous system.

2. Neurons, the most basic elements of the nervous system, allow nerve impulses to

pass from one part of the body to another. Information generally enters a neuron through its dendrite, is passed on to other cells via its axon, and finally exits through its terminal buttons.

3. Most neurons are protected by a coating called the myelin sheath. When a neuron receives a message to fire, it releases an action potential, an electric charge that travels through the cell. Neurons operate according to an all-or-none law: They are either at rest or an action potential is moving through them. There is no in-between state.

4. Once a neuron fires, nerve impulses are carried to other neurons through the production of chemical substances, neurotransmitters, which actually bridge the gaps — known as synapses — between neurons. Neurotransmitters may be either excitatory, telling other neurons to fire, or inhibitory, preventing or decreasing the likelihood of other neurons firing. Among the major neurotransmitters are acetylcholine (ACh) and dopamine. Endorphins, another type of neurotransmitter, are related to the reduction of pain.

5. The nervous system is made up of the central nervous system (the brain and spinal cord) and the peripheral nervous system (the remainder of the nervous system). The peripheral nervous system is made up of the somatic division, which controls voluntary movements and the communication of information to and from the sense organs, and the autonomic division, which controls involuntary functions such as those of the heart, blood vessels, and lungs.

6. The autonomic division of the peripheral nervous system is further subdivided into the sympathetic and parasympathetic divisions. The sympathetic division prepares the body in emergency situations, and the parasympathetic division helps the body return to its typical resting state.

7. The central core of the brain is made up of the medulla (which controls such functions as breathing and the heartbeat), the pons (which coordinates the muscles and the two sides of the body), the cerebellum (which controls balance), the reticular formation (which acts to heighten awareness in emergencies), the thalamus (which communicates messages to and from the brain), and the hypothalamus (which maintains homeostasis, or body equilibrium, and regulates basic survival behaviors). The functions of the central core structures are similar to those found in other vertebrates; this part of the brain is sometimes referred to as the "old brain."

8. The endocrine system secretes hormones, allowing the brain to send messages throughout the body. Its major component is the pituitary gland, which affects growth. The limbic system, found on the border of the "old" and "new" brains, is associated with eating, reproduction, and the experiences of pleasure and pain.

9. The cerebral cortex—the "new brain"— has areas that control voluntary movement (the motor area); the senses (the sensory area); and thinking, reasoning, speech, and memory (the association area). It is divided into two halves, or hemispheres, each of which generally controls the opposite side of the body from that in which it is located. Each hemisphere can be thought of as specialized in the functions it carries out: The left is best at verbal tasks, such as logical reasoning, speaking, and reading; the right is best at nonverbal tasks, such as spatial understanding, pattern recognition, and emotional expression.

10. Biofeedback is a procedure in which a person learns to control internal physiological processes. By controlling what were previously considered involuntary responses, people are able to relieve a wide range of problems.

Key Terms and Concepts

nervous system (p. 40)
neuroscientists (p. 40)
biopsychologists (p. 40)
neurons (p. 42)
dendrites (p. 43)
axon (p. 43)
terminal buttons (p. 44)
myelin sheath (p. 44)
all-or-none law (p. 45)
resting state (p. 45)
action potential (p. 45)
absolute refractory period (p. 45)
relative refractory period (p. 45)
synapse (p. 47)
neurotransmitter (p. 47)
excitatory message (p. 48)
inhibitory message (p. 48)
reuptake (p. 49)
acetylcholine (p. 49)
Alzheimer's disease (p. 50)
dopamine (DA) (p. 50)
endorphins (p. 51)
opiate receptor (p. 51)
central nervous system (CNS) (p. 52)
spinal cord (p. 52)
reflexes (p. 52)
sensory (afferent) neurons (p. 52)
motor (efferent) neurons (p. 52)
interneurons (p. 52)
paraplegia (p. 53)
peripheral nervous system (p. 53)
somatic division (p. 53)
autonomic division (p. 54)
sympathetic division (p. 54)
parasympathetic division (p. 54)
brain scan (p. 56)

electroencephalogram (EEG) (p. 56)
computerized axial tomography (CAT)
scan (p. 56)
nuclear magnetic resonance (NMR) scan
(p. 56)
positron emission tomograph (PET)
scan (p. 58)
central core (p. 58)
medulla (p. 58)
pons (p. 58)
cerebellum (p. 60)
reticular formation (p. 60)
thalamus (p. 60)
hypothalamus (p. 60)
homeostasis (p. 60)
endocrine system (p. 60)
hormones (p. 61)
pituitary gland (p. 61)
limbic system (p. 62)
cerebral cortex (p. 63)
frontal lobes (p. 64)
parietal lobes (p. 64)
temporal lobes (p. 64)
occipital lobes (p. 64)
motor area (p. 66)
sensory area (p. 66)
somatosensory area (p. 66)
association area (p. 68)
apraxia (p. 68)
aphasia (p. 68)
Broca's aphasia (p. 68)
Wernicke's aphasia (p. 69)
hemisphere (p. 70)
lateralization (p. 70)
biofeedback (p. 73)

3

Sensation and Perception

❖

PROLOGUE: GALE SCHOENLEBER

Gale Schoenleber and her daughter.

The pain of childbirth was nothing compared with the headaches Gale Schoenleber experienced for years. A 36-year-old Pennsylvania mother, Schoenleber had her first severe headache when she was 12, and the attacks grew worse over the years. They became so intense that she would go to the hospital for shots of morphine, and during one recent year she spent two months in bed. She lost weight—and she lost self-esteem, unable as she was to live a normal existence.

Schoenleber suffered from migraine headaches, a severe form of headache so painful that sufferers are almost at a loss for words to describe it. Some call migraines ''throbbing,'' ''hammerlike,'' or ''burning.'' Author Joan Didion says they start like a ''pounding terror,'' and the fact ''that no one dies of migraine seems, to someone deep into an attack, an ambiguous blessing.''

For Schoenleber, however, all this changed when she was referred to Seymour Solomon, director of the headache unit at Montefiore Medical Center in New York. Solomon immediately prescribed a change in medicine, placing Shoenleber on a mild tranquilizer and increasing the dosage of a beta blocker, a kind of drug that reduces arousal in certain parts of the nervous system. The result of the new treatment: Schoenleber hasn't had a headache since.

Unfortunately, Schoenleber still has to deal with headaches—those of her 8-year-old daughter, Michele. Migraine headaches run in families, and Michele seems to be developing severe headaches similar to those suffered by her mother for so many years. At least now, however, Schoenleber's freedom from pain allows her to care for her daughter, something she was unable to do before her own successful treatment (Monmaney, 1987).

LOOKING AHEAD

Fortunately, most of us do not suffer the debilitating pain of migraine headaches. Yet the presence of this kind of misery among our fellow human beings clearly illustrates the profound effect our bodily sensations have on our day-to-day behavior.

Pain, of course, is just one of the sensations to which we are sensitive; we respond also to light, sound, tastes, smells, and a variety of other stimulation that comes from the world around us. In this chapter we focus on the areas of psychology concerned with the information our body takes in through its sense organs and the way in which we interpret such information. We will be concerned with **sensation,** the process by which an organism responds to physical stimulation from the environment, as well as **perception,** the sorting out, interpretation, analysis, and integration of stimuli by our sense organs. To a psychologist who is interested in understanding the causes of behavior, sensation and perception are fundamental topics, since our behavior is so much a reflection of how we react to and interpret stimuli from the world around us. Indeed, questions ranging from identifying the fundamentals of vision and hearing, understanding how we know whether sugar or lemon is sweeter, and how we distinguish one person from another all fall into the realms of sensation and perception.

Although perception is clearly an outgrowth of sensation, it is sometimes difficult to distinguish the two. (Indeed, psychologists—and philosophers, as well—have argued for years over the distinction.) The primary difference is that sensation can be thought of as an organism's first encounter with a raw sensory stimulus, while perception is the process by which it is interpreted, analyzed, and integrated with other sensory information. For instance, if we were considering sensation, we might ask how bright a stimulus appears; if we were to consider perception, we might ask whether someone recognizes the stimulus and what its meaning is.

The chapter begins with a discussion of the relationship between the nature of a physical stimulus and the kinds of sensory responses that are made to it. The sensitivity of the senses to various kinds of stimuli is considered, and the degree to which different levels of stimulation can be differentiated from one another is discussed. We will see how the nature of the specific kinds of stimuli to which we, as humans, are capable of responding has important effects on every aspect of our behavior.

The chapter then moves to a discussion of particular senses. It starts with vision, explaining the physical aspects of light and how the eye uses it to see. The structure of the eye is presented, as are the mechanisms by which the eye transforms light into messages that can be used by the brain. Next, the sense of hearing and its relationship to motion and balance are considered as we discuss the ear. Beginning with the physical structure of sound, we trace its movement through the ear and learn how it is modified from a physical stimulus into something usable by the brain. We also discuss some of the remaining senses: smell, taste, and the skin senses, which include touch and the experience of pain.

Next, the chapter discusses a number of issues relating to perception. We begin by discussing the way we organize the stimuli to which our sense organs are exposed in an effort to actively make sense of our environment. Then we consider vision, focusing on how we are able to perceive the world in three dimensions when our retinas are only capable of sensing two-dimensional images. Finally, we discuss visual illusions, which provide us with important clues for understanding our general perceptual mechanisms.

After reading this chapter, then, you will be able to answer questions such as these:

- How keen are the senses?
- What is the relationship between a physical stimulus and the kinds of sensory responses that result from it?
- What are the major senses, and what are the basic mechanisms that underlie their operation?
- What principles underlie our organization of the stimuli to which our sense organs are exposed, allowing us to decipher our environment?
- How are we able to perceive the world in three dimensions?
- How do we sort out auditory stimuli, paying attention to particular stimuli and ignoring others?
- What clues do visual illusions give us about our understanding of general perceptual mechanisms?

*S*ENSING THE WORLD AROUND US

To someone lying on the quiet shore of a lake, the environment may seem serene and tranquil—a silent refuge from the sights and sounds of a clamorous world. Yet to members of nonhuman species, more acute in their natural abilities, the same lake may provide a challenge in sorting out the

This tranquil scene is actually teeming with stimuli, most of which are not perceived by the human sensory system.

many stimuli that are actually present—stimuli that people, because of the limitations of the human body, cannot detect through their senses.

To a dog wandering by, for instance, the lake may unleash an enticing set of smells, a symphony of random sounds, and a bustling scene of swarming insects and other tiny organisms. Furthermore, the area abounds with other forms of physical energy, of which no person or animal, nor any other living organism, has an awareness: radio waves, ultraviolet light, and tones that are extremely high or low in pitch.

To understand how a psychologist might consider such a scene, we first need a basic working vocabulary. In formal terms, if any passing source of physical energy activates a sense organ, the energy is known as a **stimulus**. A stimulus, then, is energy that produces a response in a sense organ. The term sensation is used to describe the process by which an organism responds to the stimulus.

Stimuli vary in both kind and strength. Different kinds of stimuli activate different sense organs. For instance, we can differentiate light stimuli, which activate our sense of sight and allow us to see the colors of a tree in autumn, from sound stimuli, which permit us to hear the sounds of an orchestra through our sense of hearing.

Each sort of stimulus that is capable of activating a sense organ can also be considered in terms of its strength, or **magnitude.** For instance, such questions as how bright a light stimulus needs to be before it is capable of being detected or how much perfume a person must wear before it is noticed by others relate to stimulus magnitude.

The issue of how the magnitude of a stimulus is related to sensory responses falls into a branch of psychology known as psychophysics. **Psychophysics** is the study of the relationship between the physical nature of stimuli and a person's sensory responses to them. Psychophysics played a central role in the development of the field of psychology; many of the first psychologists studied issues related to psychophysics. It is easy to see why: Psychophysics bridges the physical world outside and the psychological world within.

Let There Be Light: Absolute Thresholds

It is obvious that people are not capable of detecting all the physical stimuli that are present in the environment, as noted earlier in our example of the seemingly quiet lake. Just when does a stimulus become strong enough to be detected by our sense organs? The answer to this question requires an understanding of the concept of absolute thresholds. An **absolute threshold** is the smallest amount of physical intensity of a stimulus that must be present for it to be detected. Although we previously compared the sensory capabilities of humans unfavorably with those of dogs, in fact, absolute thresholds in human sensory organs are quite extraordinary. Consider, for instance, these examples of absolute thresholds for the various senses.

- Sight: A candle flame can be seen 30 miles away on a dark, clear night.
- Hearing: The ticking of a watch can be heard 20 feet away under quiet conditions.
- Taste: Sugar can be discerned when 1 teaspoon is dissolved in 2 gallons of water.
- Smell: Perfume can be detected when one drop is present in a three-room apartment.
- Touch: A bee's wing falling from a distance of 1 centimeter can be felt on a cheek (Galanter, 1962).

Such thresholds permit a wide range of sensory stimulation to be detected by the human sensory apparatus. In fact, the capabilities of our senses are so fine-tuned that we might have problems if they were any more sensitive. For instance, if our ears were just slightly more sensitive, we would be able to hear the sound of air molecules in our ears knocking into each other—something that would surely prove distracting and might even prevent us from hearing sounds outside our bodies as well.

Of course, the absolute thresholds we have been discussing are measured under ideal conditions; normally our senses cannot detect stimulation quite so well because of the presence of noise. **Noise,** as de-

The noise in P. J. Clarke's, Chicago, is not just auditory; the crowded conditions produce noise that affects the senses of vision, smell, taste, and touch as well.

fined by psychophysicists, is background stimulation that interferes with the perception of other stimuli. Hence noise refers not just to auditory stimuli, the most obvious example, but also to those stimuli that affect the other senses. Picture a talkative group of people crammed into a small, crowded, smoke-filled room at a party. The din of the crowd makes it hard to hear individual voices, and the smoke makes it difficult to see— and even to taste the food. In this case, the smoke and crowded conditions would be considered "noise," since they are preventing sensation at more discriminating and sensitive levels.

Noise is not the only factor that influences our sensitivity to stimulation; our expectations about whether any stimulus is present, our knowledge about the nature of the stimulus, and our motivation all affect our detection capabilities. For example, a baseball player's ability to visually track a pitch—and ultimately to hit the ball—will be better if the player knows that the pitcher has thrown a curve ball than if the player does not know what kind of pitch to expect. Similarly, the high motivation of a physician to identify abnormalities when listening through a stethoscope is apt to increase the likelihood of detecting stimuli that suggest a problem.

Hence our ability to detect faint stimuli is not just a function of properties of the stimulus; it is also affected by our psychological state. **Signal detection theory** is an outgrowth of psychophysics that seeks to explain the role of psychological factors in producing variations in our ability to identify stimuli (Grieg, 1990).

The theory acknowledges that observers may err in one of two ways: in reporting that a stimulus is present when it is not or in reporting that a stimulus is not present when it actually is. By applying statistical procedures, psychologists using signal detection theory are able to obtain an understanding of how different kinds of decisions—which may involve such factors as observer expectations and motivation—relate to judgments about sensory stimuli in different situations. Statistical methods also allow them to increase the reliability of predictions about what conditions will cause observers to be most accurate in their judgments (Commons, Nevin, & Davison, 1991).

Such findings have immense practical importance, not only in the case of radar operators who are charged with identifying and distinguishing incoming enemy missiles from the radar images of passing birds, but in other areas as well. One arena in which signal detection theory has practical implications is the judicial system. Witnesses who are asked to view a lineup find themselves in a classic signal detection situation, in which misidentification can have grave consequences for an individual (if an innocent person is incorrectly identified as a perpetrator) and for society (if an actual perpetrator is not detected). However, many witnesses have biases stemming from prior expectations about the socioeconomic status and race of criminals, attitudes toward the police and criminal justice system, and other biases that impede accurate judgment.

Using signal detection theory, psychologists have been able to make suggestions to increase the accuracy of witness identification (Buckhout, 1976). For example, it is helpful to tell witnesses viewing a lineup that the prime suspect might not be in the lineup at all. Moreover, justice is better served when the people in the lineup appear equally dissimilar from one another, which seems to reduce the chances of witnesses guessing.

Comparing Apples with Apples: Just Noticeable Differences

Suppose a shopkeeper said you could choose six apples from a barrel, and you wanted to compare them in a number of aspects to see which half-dozen were best—which were bigger, which were redder, which had the fewest blemishes. One approach to this problem would be to systematically compare one apple with another until you were left with a few so similar that you could not tell the difference between them.

Psychologists have discussed this comparison problem in terms of the **difference threshold,** the smallest detectable difference between two stimuli—also known as a **just noticeable difference.** They have found that the stimulus value that constitutes a just noticeable difference depends on the initial intensity of the stimulus. For instance, you may have noticed that the light change which comes in a three-way bulb when you switch from 75 to 100 watts appears greater than when you switch from 100 to 125 watts, even though the wattage increase is the same in both cases. Similarly, when the moon is visible during the late afternoon, it appears relatively dim—yet against a dark night sky, it seems quite bright.

The relationship between changes in the original value of a stimulus and the degree to which the change will be noticed forms one of the basic laws of psychophysics: Weber's law. **Weber's law** states that a just noticeable difference is a constant proportion of the magnitude of an initial stimulus. Therefore, if a 10-pound increase in a 100-pound weight produces a just noticeable difference, it would take a 1000-pound increase to produce a noticeable difference if the initial weight were 10,000 pounds. In both cases, the same proportional increase is necessary to produce a just noticeable difference—1:10 (10:100 = 1000:10,000). (Actually, Weber found the true proportional increase in weight that produces a just noticeable difference to be between 2 and 3 percent.) Similarly, the just noticeable difference distinguishing changes in loudness between sounds is larger for sounds that are initially loud than for sounds that are initially soft—as exemplified by the fact that a person in a quiet room is more apt to be startled by the ringing of a telephone than a person in a room that is already noisy. In order to produce the same amount of reaction in a noisy room, a telephone ring might have to approximate the loudness of cathedral bells.

Weber's law seems to hold for all sensory stimuli, although its predictions are less accurate at extremely high or extremely low levels of stimulation. Moreover, the law helps explain psychological phenomena that lie beyond the realm of the senses. For example, imagine that you own a house you would like to sell for $150,000. You might be satisfied if you received an offer of $145,000 from a potential buyer, even though it was $5000 less than the asking price. On the other hand, if you were selling your car and asking $10,000 for it, an offer of $5000 less than your asking price would probably not make you happy. Although the absolute amount is the same in both cases, the psychological value of the $5000 is very different.

Becoming Accustomed to Stimulation: Sensory Adaptation

> As the circus strongman carries a group of five acrobats across the circus tent, someone asks him if they aren't awfully heavy. He replies, "Not if you've just been carrying an elephant."

This story illustrates the phenomenon of **adaptation,** an adjustment in sensory capacity following prolonged exposure to stimuli. Adaptation occurs as people get used to a stimulus and change their frame of reference. Consequently, they do not respond to the stimulus in the way they did earlier.

One example of adaptation is the decrease in sensitivity that occurs after frequent exposure to a stimulus. If, for example, you were to repeatedly hear a loud tone, it would begin to sound softer after a while. This apparent decline in sensitivity to sensory stimuli is due to the inability of the sensory nerve receptors to constantly fire off messages to the brain. Because these receptor cells are most responsive to *changes* in stimulation, constant stimulation is not effective in producing a reaction. In fact, most receptor cells are incapable of constant firing, and their reaction to unvarying stimulation is a steady decline in the rate at which impulses are communicated.

Adaptation occurs with all the senses. For example, if you were able to stare unblinkingly at the exact same spot on this page for a long period of time—something that is impossible to do because of minute, involuntary movements of the eye—the spot would eventually disappear as the visual neurons lost their ability to fire.

Judgments of sensory stimuli are also affected by the context in which the judgments are made. Carrying five trapeze artists seems like nothing to the strongman who has just carted an elephant around the tent. The reason is that judgments are made not in isolation from other stimuli, but in terms of preceding sensory experience.

Sensory-adaptation phenomena provide another illustration that a person's reaction to sensory stimuli is not always an accurate representation of the physical stimuli that brought it about. This point will become even more apparent as we move from consideration of sensation—which is the direct response of an organism to physical stimuli—and begin to discuss the specific senses of the human body.

*A*SK YOURSELF

What is the distinction between sensation and perception?

What is an absolute threshold and how is it affected by noise?

How is signal detection theory used?

What is Weber's law?

When does sensory adaptation occur?

Think about the words on this page as sensory stimuli. How does sensation process such stimuli, and how does the perception of the words operate on a higher level?

Why is sensory adaptation essential for normal psychological functioning?

THE FIVE + SENSES

As she sat down to Thanksgiving dinner, Rhona reflected on how happy she was to leave dormitory food behind—at least for the long holiday weekend. She was just plain tired of seeing and smelling the same monotonous cafeteria food. Even chewing the stuff was distasteful—it all felt like mush. "In fact," she thought to herself, "if I have to eat toast covered with chipped beef one more time, I may never eat again." But this thought was soon interrupted when she saw her father carry in the turkey on a tray and place it squarely in the center of the table. The noise level, already high from the talking and laughter of the family members, grew still louder. As she picked up her fork, the smell of the turkey reached her and she felt her stomach growl hungrily. With the sight and sound of her family around the table—not to speak of the smell and taste of all that food—she felt more relaxed than she had since she had left for college in the fall. "Ah, home, sweet home," she thought.

Put yourself in this scene and consider how different it might be if any one of your senses were not functioning. What if you were blind and unable to see the faces of your family—or the welcome shape of the succulent turkey? What if you had no sense of hearing and could not listen to the family's talk, or were unable to feel your stomach growl, or smell the dinner, or taste the food? Clearly, an important dimension of the situation would be lacking, and no doubt the dinner would evoke a very different experience for you than it would for someone whose sensory apparatus was intact.

Moreover, the sensations mentioned above barely scratch the surface of sensory experience. Although most of us have been taught at one time or another that there are just five senses—sight, sound, taste, smell, and touch—this enumeration is far too modest, since human sensory capabilities go well beyond the basic five senses. It is well established, for example, that we are sensitive not merely to touch, but to a considerably wider set of stimuli—pain, pressure, temperature, vibration, and more. In addition, the ear is responsive to information that allows us not only to hear but to keep our balance as well. In fact, psychologists now believe that there are at least a dozen distinct senses—all of which are interrelated.

Although all the senses, alone and in combination, play a critical role in determining how we experience the world, most psychological research has focused on vision and hearing—the two sensory modes that are most conspicuous in allowing us to successfully interact with our environment.

The Eyes Have It: Vision

To understand how our sense of vision allows us to view the world, we must first begin outside the body and consider the nature of the stimulus that produces vision—**light.** Although we are all familiar with light, having all our lives basked in the sun or an artificial equivalent, its underlying physical qualities are less apparent.

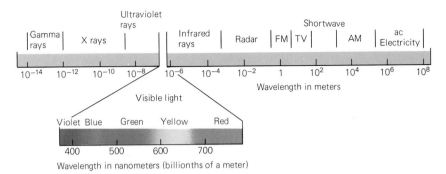

FIGURE 3-1
The visual spectrum—the range of wavelengths to which people are sensitive—represents only a small part of the kinds of wavelengths present in our environments.

The stimuli that register as light in our eyes are actually electromagnetic radiation waves to which our bodies' visual apparatus happens to be sensitive and capable of responding. As you can see in Figure 3-1, electromagnetic radiation is measured in wavelengths, with the size of the wavelength corresponding to different sorts of energy. The range of wavelengths that humans are sensitive to—called the **visual spectrum**—is actually relatively small, but the differences among wavelengths within that spectrum are sufficient to allow us to see a range of all the colors, running from violet at the low end of the visual spectrum to red at the top. Colors, then, are associated with a particular wavelength within the visual spectrum.

Light waves coming from some object outside the body (imagine the light reflected off the face of the Mona Lisa, as in Figure 3-2) first encounter the only organ that is capable of responding to the visual spectrum: the eye. Strangely enough, most of the eye is concerned not with reacting directly to light but with shaping the entering image into something that can be used by the neurons that will serve as messengers. The neurons themselves take up a relatively small percentage of the total eye. In other words, most of the eye is a mechanical device, analogous in many respects to a camera without film, as you can see in Figure 3-2. (It is important to realize, though, the limitations of this analogy: Vision involves processes that are far more complex and sophisticated than any camera is capable of mimicking.)

Illuminating the structure of the eye. The ray of light we are following as it is reflected off the Mona Lisa first travels through the **cornea,** a transparent, protective window that is constantly being washed by tears, keeping it moist and clean. After moving through the cornea, the light traverses the pupil. The **pupil** is a dark hole found in the center of the **iris,** the colored part of the eye, which ranges in humans from a light blue

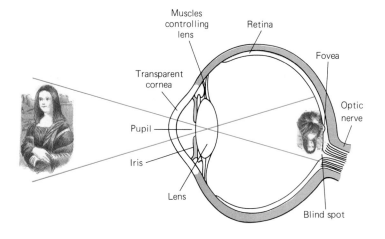

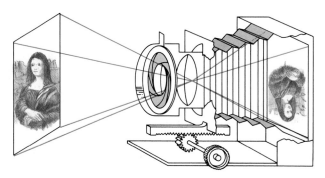

FIGURE 3-2
Although human vision is far more complicated than the most
sophisticated camera, in some ways basic visual processes are
analogous to those used in photography.

to a dark brown. The size of the pupil opening depends on the amount
of light in the environment: The dimmer the surroundings, the more the
pupil opens in order to allow more light to enter.

Why shouldn't the pupil be opened all the way all the time, thereby
allowing the greatest amount of light into the eye? The answer has to do
with the basic physics of light. A small pupil greatly increases the range
of distances at which objects are in focus; with a wide-open pupil, the
range is relatively small, and details are harder to discern. (Camera buffs
know this in terms of the aperture or f-stop setting that they must adjust
on their cameras.) The eye takes advantage of bright light by decreasing
the size of the pupil and thereby becoming more discerning; in dim light
the pupil expands in order to enable us to view the situation better—but
at the expense of visual detail. Perhaps one reason that candlelight dinners

are often thought of as romantic is that the dimness of the light prevents one from seeing the details of a lover's flaws.

Once light passes through the pupil, it enters the **lens,** which is located directly behind the pupil. The lens acts to bend the rays of light coming from the Mona Lisa so that they are properly focused on the rear of the eye. The lens focuses the light by changing its own thickness, a process called **accommodation.** The kind of accommodation that occurs depends on the location of the object in relation to the body. Distant objects require a relatively flat lens; in this case, the muscles controlling the lens relax, allowing the fluid within the eye to flatten the lens. In contrast, close objects are viewed best through a rounded lens. Here, then, the muscles contract, taking tension off the lens—and making it rounder.

Having traveled through the pupil and lens, our image of the Mona Lisa is finally able to reach its ultimate destination in the eye—the **retina**— where the electromagnetic energy of light is converted into messages that the brain can use. It is important to note that—again because of the physics of light—the image has reversed itself as it traveled through the lens, and it reaches the retina upside down (relative to its original position). Although you might think this would cause major difficulties in understanding and moving about the world, it turns out not to be a problem, because the brain rearranges the image back to its proper position. In fact, if we were ever to put on mirrored glasses that righted the image before it reached the brain, we would have a hard time, because everything would look upside down to us—although eventually we would adjust to the new orientation.

The retina is actually a thin layer of nerve cells at the back of the eyeball (see Figure 3-3). There are two kinds of light-sensitive receptor cells found in the retina, and the names they have been given describe their shapes: **rods,** which are long and cylindrical, and **cones,** which are short, thick, and tapered. The rods and cones are distributed unevenly throughout the retina, with the greatest concentration of cones on the part of the retina called the **fovea** (refer back to Figure 3-2). The fovea is a particularly sensitive region of the retina; if you want to focus in on something of particular interest, you will probably center the image from the lens onto the area of the fovea.

The farther away from the fovea, the fewer the number of cones there are on the retina. Conversely, there are no rods in the fovea—but the number increases rapidly toward the edges of the eye. Because the fovea covers only a small portion of the eye, there are fewer cones (about 7 million) than there are rods (about 125 million).

The rods and cones are not only structurally dissimilar, but they play distinctly different roles in vision (Cohen & Lasley, 1986). Cones are primarily responsible for the sharply focused perception of color, particularly in brightly lit situations, while rods are related to vision in dimly lit situations and are largely insensitive to color and to details as sharp as those the cones are capable of recognizing. Rods are used for **peripheral**

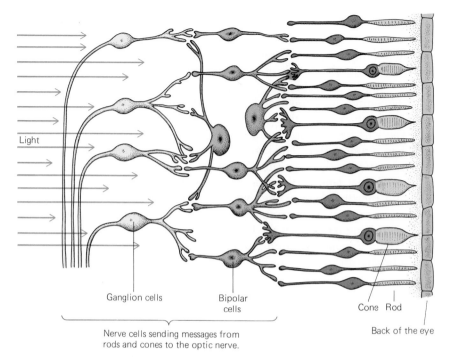

Light

Ganglion cells

Bipolar cells

Cone Rod

Nerve cells sending messages from
rods and cones to the optic nerve.

Back of the eye

FIGURE 3-3
The basic cells of the eye. Light entering the eye travels through the ganglion
and bipolar cells and strikes the light-sensitive rods and cones. The rods and
cones then transmit nerve impulses to the brain via the bipolar and ganglion
cells. (Coren, Porac, & Ward, 1979.)

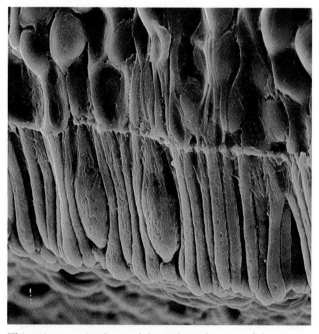

This microscopic photo of the rods and cones of the eye
clearly reveals their distinctive shapes.

vision—seeing objects that are outside the main center of focus—and for night vision. In both cases, the level of detail that can be discerned is far lower when the rods come into play than when the cones are activated— as you know from groping your way across a dark room at night. Although you may just dimly see the outlines of furniture, it is almost impossible to distinguish color and the other details of obstacles in your path. You may also have noticed that you can improve your view of an object at night by looking slightly away from it. The reason? If you shift your gaze off-center, the image from the lens falls not on the relatively night-blind foveal cones but on the more light-sensitive rods.

The distinctive abilities of rods and cones make the eye analogous to a camera that is loaded with two kinds of film. One type is a highly sensitive black-and-white film (the rods); the other type is a somewhat less sensitive color film (the cones).

Shedding light on vision: Sending the message from the eye to the brain. When light energy strikes the rods and cones, it starts the first in a chain of events that transforms light into neural impulses that can be communicated to the brain. In fact, even before the neural message reaches the brain, some initial alteration of the visual information takes place.

When light energy first strikes the retina, what happens is partially dependent on whether it strikes a rod or a cone. Rods contain **rhodopsin,** a complex, reddish-purple substance whose composition changes chemically when energized by light and thereby sets off a reaction. The substance found in cone receptors is different, but the principles are similar: Stimulation of the nerve cells in the eye triggers a neural response that is transmitted to other nerve cells, called bipolar cells and ganglion cells, leading to the brain.

Bipolar cells receive information directly from the rods and cones, and this information is then communicated to the ganglion cells. **Ganglion cells** collect and summarize visual information, which is gathered and moved out of the back of the eyeball through a bundle of ganglion axons called the **optic nerve.**

Because the opening for the optic nerve pushes through the retina, there are no rods or cones in the area, which creates a blind spot. Normally, however, this absence of nerve cells does not interfere with vision, because you automatically compensate for the missing part of your field of vision.

Once beyond the eye itself, the neural signals relating to the image of the Mona Lisa we have been following move through the optic nerve. As the optic nerve leaves the eyeball, its path does not take the most direct route to the part of the brain right behind the eye. Instead, the optic nerves from each eye meet at a point roughly between the two eyes—called the **optic chiasma**—where each optic nerve then splits.

When the optic nerve splits, the nerve impulses coming from the right half of each retina are sent to the right side of the brain, and the impulses arriving from the left half of each retina are sent to the left side of the brain. Because the image on the retina is reversed and upside down, however, those images coming from the right half of the retina are actually included in the field of vision to the left of the person, and images coming from the left half of the retina represent the field of vision to the right of the individual (see Figure 3-4). In this way, our nervous system ultimately produces the phenomenon we discussed first in Chapter 2, in which each half of the brain is associated with the functioning of the opposite side of the body.

One of the most frequent causes of blindness is a restriction of the impulses across the optic nerve. **Glaucoma,** which strikes between 1 and 2 percent of those over age 40, occurs when pressure in the fluid of the eye begins to build up, either because it cannot be properly drained or because it is overproduced. When this first begins to happen, the nerve cells that communicate information about peripheral vision are con-

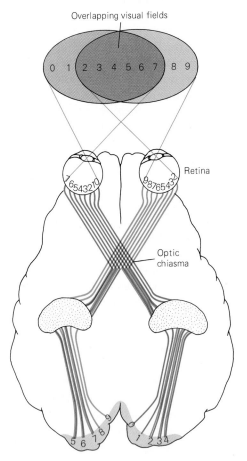

FIGURE 3-4
Because the optic nerve coming from each eye splits at the optic chiasma, the image to a person's right is sent to the left side of the brain, and the image to the person's left is transmitted to the right side of the brain. (Based on Lindsay & Norman, 1977.)

stricted, leading to a decline in the ability to see anything outside a narrow circle directly ahead. This problem is called **tunnel vision.** Eventually, the pressure can become so great that all the nerve cells are contracted, leading to total blindness. However, if detected early enough, glaucoma is highly treatable, either through medication that reduces the pressure in the eye or through surgery.

From light to sight: Processing the visual message. By the time a visual message reaches the brain, it has passed through several stages of processing. One of the initial sites is the ganglion cells. Each ganglion cell gathers information from a group of rods and cones in a particular area of the eye, and compares the amount of light entering the center of that area with the amount of light in the area around it. In some cases, ganglion cells are activated by light in the center (and darkness in the surrounding area). In other cases, the opposite is true: Some ganglion cells are activated when there is darkness in the center and light in the surrounding areas. The ultimate effect of this process is to maximize the detection of variations in light and darkness. The neural image that is passed on to the brain, then, is an enhanced version of the actual visual stimulus outside the body.

The ultimate processing of visual images takes place in the visual cortex of the brain, of course, and it is here that the most complex kinds of processing occur (Hurlbert & Poggio, 1988). Nobel-prize winning psychologists David Hubel and Torsten Wiesel have found that many neurons in the cortex are extraordinarily specialized, being activated only by visual stimuli of a particular shape or pattern—a process known as **feature detection.** For example, some cells are activated only by lines of a particular width, shape, or orientation. Other cells are activated only by moving, as opposed to stationary, stimuli (Hubel & Wiesel, 1979). The specialization of these cells is remarkable.

Researchers have also found that the cells of the visual cortex are organized spatially in a way that represents a visual scene being viewed. In other words, cells that correspond to neighboring areas of the visual field on the retina are located next to each other on the cortex. However, the representation is distorted, with more space on the cortex being devoted to the areas with the most rods and cones. In addition, the brain simultaneously contains not one but several spatial representations of information coming from the visual field. In fact, there appear to be at least ten separate complete representations of the visual world, all of which are integrated by the brain (Merzenich & Kass, 1980).

From light to dark: Adaptation. Have you ever walked into a movie theater on a bright, sunny day and stumbled into your seat, barely being able to see at all? Do you also recall later getting up to buy some popcorn and having no trouble navigating your way up the aisle?

Your initial trouble seeing in the dimly lit theater was due to **light**

adaptation, a phenomenon in which the eye grows insensitive to light that is dimmer than the level to which it has been most recently exposed. In contrast, the fact that you were later able to see relatively well is due to **dark adaptation,** a heightened sensitivity to light that results from being in relative dimness.

The speed at which both dark and light adaptation occur is a function of the rate at which changes occur in the chemical composition of the rods and cones. The cones reach their greatest level of adaptation in just a few minutes, but the rods take close to thirty minutes to reach the maximum level. On the other hand, the cones never reach the level of sensitivity to light that the rods attain, making color vision difficult at low light levels. When rods and cones are considered jointly, though, dark adaptation is complete in a darkened room in about half an hour (Tamura, Nakatani, & Yau, 1989).

The 7-million-color rainbow: Color vision and color blindness. Although the range of wavelengths to which humans are sensitive is relatively narrow, at least in comparison to the entire electromagnetic spectrum, the portion to which we are capable of responding still allows us great flexibility in sensing the world. Nowhere is this clearer than in terms of the colors we can discern: A person with normal color vision is capable of distinguishing no less than 7 million different colors (Bruce & Green, 1984).

Although the variety of colors that people are generally able to distinguish is vast, there are certain individuals whose ability to perceive color is quite limited—the color-blind. Interestingly, the condition of these individuals has provided some of the most important clues for understanding how color vision operates (Nathans et al., 1986).

Look, for a moment, at the photos shown in Figure 3-5. If you cannot see any difference in the series of photos, you probably are one of the 2 percent of men or 2 out of 10,000 women who are color-blind.

For most people who are color-blind, the world looks quite dull: Red fire engines look yellow, green grass looks yellow, and the three colors of a traffic light all look yellow. In fact, in the most common form of color blindness, all red and green objects are seen as yellow. There are other forms of color blindness as well, but they are quite rare. In yellow-blue blindness, people are unable to tell the difference between yellow and blue, and in the most extreme case an individual perceives no color at all: The world to such a person looks something like the picture on a black-and-white television set.

To understand why some of us are color-blind, it is necessary to consider the basics of color vision. There appear to be two processes involved. The first process is based on what has been labeled the **trichromatic theory.** It suggests that there are three kinds of cones in the retina, each

(a)   (b)   (c)   (d)

FIGURE 3-5
(*a*) Six-year-old Paula Vergara playing on a teeter-totter looks like this to someone with normal vision. (*b*) A person with red-green color blindness would see
the scene like this, in hues of blue and yellow. (*c*) A person who is blue-yellow
blind, conversely, would see it in hues of red and green. (*d*) A monochromat, or
a person with total color blindness, would see the scene like this.

of which responds primarily to a specific range of wavelengths. One
is most responsive to blue-violet colors, one to green, and the other to
yellow-red (Brown & Wald, 1964). According to trichromatic theory, perception of color is influenced by the relative strength with which each of
the three kinds of cones is activated. If, for instance, we see a blue sky,
the blue-violet cones are primarily triggered, while the others show less
activity. The trichromatic theory provides a straightforward explanation
of color blindness: It suggests that one of the three cone systems mal-
functions, and colors covered by that range are perceived improperly (Nathans et al., 1989).

However, there are phenomena that the trichromatic theory is less
successful at explaining. For instance, it cannot explain why pairs of colors
can combine to form gray, and it does not explain what happens after you
stare at something like the flag shown in Figure 3-6 for about a minute.
Try this yourself, and then move your eyes to the white space below. You
will see an image of the traditional red, white, and blue American flag.
Where there was yellow, you'll see blue, and where there were green and
black, you'll see red and white.

The phenomenon you have just experienced is called an **afterimage,**
and it occurs because activity in the retina continues even when you are
no longer staring at the original picture. However, it also demonstrates
that the trichromatic theory does not explain color vision completely. Why
should the colors in the afterimage be different from those in the original?

Because trichromatic processes do not provide a full explanation of
color vision, an alternative, the **opponent-process theory,** has been pro-

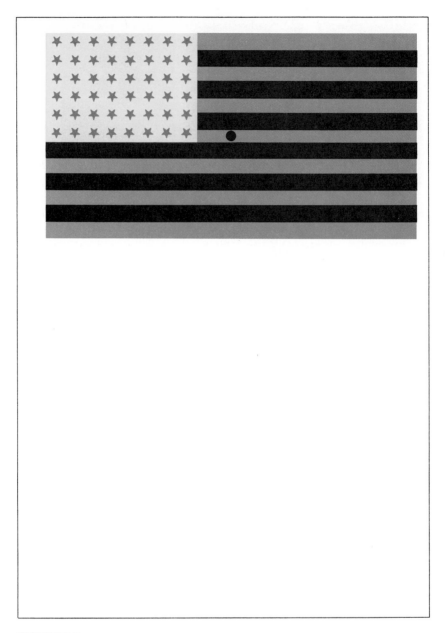

FIGURE 3-6
If you stare at the dot in this flag for about a minute and then look at the white space below it, the afterimage phenomenon will make a traditional red, white, and blue flag appear.

posed. According to the theory, receptor cells are linked in pairs, working in opposition to each other. Specifically, there is a blue-yellow pairing, a red-green pairing, and a black-white pairing. If an object reflects light that contains more blue than yellow, it will stimulate the firing of the blue receptors, simultaneously discouraging or inhibiting the firing of yellow receptors—and the object will appear blue. If, on the other hand, a light contains more yellow than blue, the yellow receptors will be stimulated to fire while the blue ones are inhibited, and the object will appear yellow.

The opponent-process theory allows us to explain afterimages very directly. When we stare at the yellow in the figure, for instance, our receptor cells for the yellow component of the yellow-blue pairing begin to get fatigued and will be less able to respond to yellow stimuli. On the other hand, the blue part of the pair is not tired, since it is not being stimulated. When we look at a white surface, the light reflected off it would normally stimulate both the yellow and the blue receptors equally. But the fatigue of the yellow receptors prevents this; they temporarily do not respond to the yellow, which makes the white light appear to be blue. Since the other colors in the figure do the same thing relative to their specific opponents, the afterimage produces the opponent colors—for a while, at least. Of course, the afterimage lasts only a short time, since the fatigue of the yellow receptors is soon overcome, and the white light begins to be perceived more accurately.

Most psychologists assume that both opponent processes and trichromatic mechanisms are at work in allowing us to see colors, although they operate in different parts of the visual sensing system. It seems most likely that trichromatic processes work within the retina itself, while opponent processes operate at a later state of neuronal connections and processing (Beck, Hope & Rosenfeld, 1983). The ultimate explanation for our color-sensing capabilities still eludes us. We are nevertheless getting an increasingly clear picture that promises to provide psychologists with new applications in such areas as remedying color blindness and devising traffic signals that are effective in reducing accidents (Botstein, 1986; Boynton, 1988; Shapley, 1990).

*A*SK YOURSELF

How many senses are there?

Where does light travel as it moves through the eye, and how does it convert electromagnetic energy into nerve impulses?

What role do the rods and cones play in vision?

What are the two processes involved in color vision?

Does vision entail the simple replication of the physical world, or are visual stimuli transformed by the eye and the brain to

create meaningful representations that may not be exact re-
plicas of the physical world?

Hearing and Moving about the World: The Sense of Sound and Balance

> The blast-off was easy compared with what the astronaut was experiencing
> now: space sickness. The constant nausea and vomiting were enough to make
> him consider calling Mission Control and asking to return to base. Even
> though he had been warned that there was a 50 percent chance that his first
> experience in space would cause such sickness, he wasn't prepared for how
> terribly sick he really felt. How could he live and work on the space station
> for the next three months feeling like this?

Whether or not our mythical astronaut turns his rocket around and
heads back to earth, his experience—which is a major problem for space
travelers—is related to a basic sensory process that is centered in the ear
and its adjacent structure: the sense of motion and balance, which allows
people to navigate their bodies through the world and maintain an upright position without falling. Along with hearing, the process by which
sound waves are translated into understandable and meaningful forms,
the sensing of motion and balance represent the major functions of the
ear.

The site of sound: The ear. While many of us think primarily of the
outer ear when we consider hearing, this part is little more than a reverse
megaphone, designed to collect and bring sounds into the internal portions of the ear, illustrated in Figure 3-7. **Sound** is the movement of air
molecules brought about by the vibration of an object. Sounds travel
through the air in wave patterns similar in shape to those made by a stone
thrown into a still pond.

Once sounds, which arrive in the form of wave vibrations, have been
funneled into the **auditory canal,** a tubelike passage, they reach the
eardrum. The eardrum is aptly named because it operates like a miniature
drum, vibrating when sound waves hit it. The louder the sound, the more
it vibrates. These vibrations are then transmitted into the **middle ear,** a
tiny chamber containing just three bones called, because of their shapes,
the **hammer,** the **anvil,** and the **stirrup.** These bones have one function:
to transmit vibrations to the **oval window,** a thin membrane leading to
the inner ear. Because of their shape, the hammer, anvil, and stirrup do a
particularly effective job not only transmitting vibrations but actually increasing their strength, since they act as a set of levers. Moreover, since
the opening into the middle ear is considerably larger than the opening
out of it, the force of sound waves on the smaller area becomes amplified.
The middle ear, then, acts as a tiny mechanical amplifier, making us aware
of sounds that would otherwise go unnoticed.

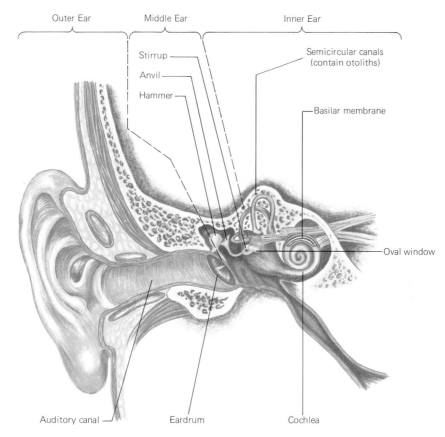

Outer Ear   Middle Ear   Inner Ear

Stirrup

Anvil

Hammer

Semicircular canals
(contain otoliths)

Basilar membrane

Oval window

Auditory canal   Eardrum   Cochlea

FIGURE 3-7
The ear.

The **inner ear** is the portion of the ear that actually changes the sound vibrations into a form that allows them to be transmitted to the brain. It also contains the organs that allow us to locate our position and determine how we are moving through space. When sound enters the inner ear through the oval window, it moves into the **cochlea,** a coiled tube filled with fluid that looks something like a snail. Inside the cochlea is the **basilar membrane,** a structure that runs through the center of the cochlea, dividing it into an upper and a lower chamber (see Figure 3-7). The basilar membrane is covered with **hair cells.** When these hair cells are bent by the vibrations entering the cochlea, a neural message is transmitted to the brain.

Although sound typically enters the cochlea via the oval window, there is an additional method of entry: bone conduction. Because the ear rests on a maze of bones within the skull, the cochlea is able to pick up subtle vibrations that travel across the bones from other parts of the head.

For instance, one of the ways you hear your own voice is through bone conduction, which explains why you sound different to yourself than to other people who hear your voice. (Listen to yourself on a tape recorder sometime to hear what you *really* sound like!) The sound of your voice reaches you both through the air and via bone conduction and therefore sounds richer to you than to everyone else.

The physical aspects of sound. As we mentioned earlier, what we refer to as sound is actually the physical movement of air molecules in regular, wavelike patterns caused by the vibration of an object. Sometimes it is even possible to view these vibrations, as in the case of a stereo speaker that has no enclosure. If you have ever seen one, you know that, at least when the lowest notes are playing, you can see the speaker moving in and out. What is less obvious is what happens next: The speaker pushes air molecules into waves with the same pattern as its movement. These wave patterns soon reach your ear, although their strength has been weakened considerably during their travels. All other stimuli that produce sound work in essentially the same fashion, setting off wave patterns that move through the air to the ear. Air—or some other medium, such as water—is necessary to make the vibrations of objects reach us; there can be no sound in a vacuum.

We are able to see the speaker moving when low notes are played because of a primary characteristic of sound called frequency. **Frequency** is the number of wave crests that occur in a second. With very low frequencies there are relatively few, and therefore slower, up-and-down wave cycles per second—which are visible to the naked eye as vibrations in the speaker. Low frequencies are translated into a sound that is very low in pitch. (**Pitch** is the characteristic that makes sound "high" or "low.") For example, the lowest frequency that humans are capable of hearing is 20 cycles per second. Higher frequencies translate into higher pitch; at this end of the sound spectrum, people can detect sounds with frequencies as high as 20,000 cycles per second.

While sound frequency allows us to enjoy the sounds of the high notes of a piccolo and the bass notes of a tuba, **intensity** is a feature of wave patterns that allows us to distinguish between loud and soft sounds. Intensity refers to the size of the difference between the peaks and valleys of air pressure in a sound wave as it travels through the air. Waves with small peaks and valleys produce soft sounds, while those that are relatively large produce loud sounds.

We are sensitive to a broad range of sound intensity: The loudest sounds we are capable of hearing are about 10 million times as intense as the very weakest sound we can hear. This range is measured in **decibels,** which can be used to place everyday sounds along a continuum (see Figure 3-8). When sounds get higher than 120 decibels, they become painful to the human ear, and long-term exposure to such high levels eventually

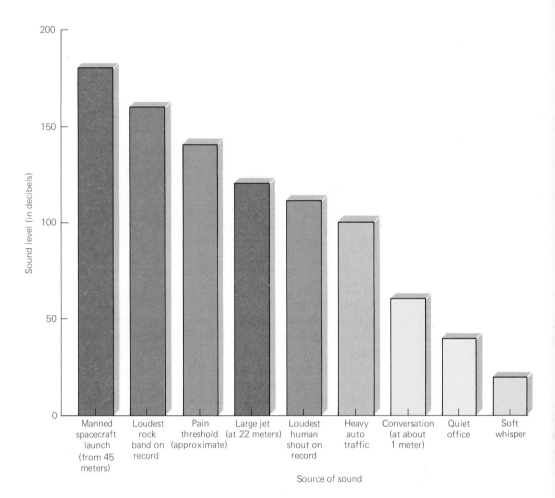

FIGURE 3-8
Illustrations of decibel levels (measures of sound intensity).

leads to a permanent hearing loss—a phenomenon all too familiar to many rock musicians (and some of their fans).

How are our brains able to sort out wavelengths of different frequencies and intensities? One clue comes from studies of the basilar membrane, the area in the cochlea that translates physical vibrations into neural impulses. It turns out that sounds affect different areas of the basilar membrane, depending on the frequency of the wave. The part of the basilar membrane nearest the oval window is most sensitive to high-frequency sounds, while the part nearest the cochlea's inner edge is most sensitive to low-frequency sounds. This finding has led to the **place theory of hearing,** which says that different areas of the basilar membrane respond to different frequencies.

On the other hand, other mechanisms are also involved in hearing. The **frequency theory of hearing** suggests that the entire basilar membrane acts like a microphone, vibrating as a whole in response to a sound. According to the theory, the nerve receptors send out signals that are tied directly to the frequency (the number of wave crests per second) of the sounds to which we are exposed, with the number of nerve impulses being a direct function of the sound's frequency. Thus, the higher the pitch of a sound (and therefore the greater the frequency of its wave crests), the greater the number of nerve impulses that are transmitted up the auditory nerve to the brain.

Most research points to the conclusion that both the place theory and the frequency theory provide accurate descriptions of the processes that underlie hearing, although not at every frequency. Specifically, the place theory seems a better explanation of the sensing of high-frequency sounds, whereas the frequency theory explains what happens when low-frequency sounds are encountered. Sounds with pitch in between seem to incorporate both processes.

After an auditory message leaves the ear, it is transmitted to the auditory cortex of the brain through a complex series of neural interconnections. As the message is transmitted, it is communicated through neurons that respond to specific types of sounds. Within the auditory cortex itself, there are neurons that respond selectively to very specific sorts of sound features, such as clicks or whistles. Moreover, some neurons respond only to a specific pattern of sounds, such as a steady tone but not an intermittent one.

If we were to analyze the configuration of the cells in the auditory cortex, we would find that neighboring cells are responsive to similar frequencies. The auditory cortex, then, provides us with a "map" of sound frequencies, just as the visual cortex furnishes a representation of the visual field. (To learn about the latest attempts at helping people with hearing problems, see the Psychology and Society box.)

Balancing the ups and downs of life. The ear has several other structures that are related more to our sense of balance than to our hearing. The **semicircular canals** of the inner ear consist of three tubes containing fluid that sloshes through them when the head moves, signaling rotational or angular movement to the brain. The pull on our bodies caused by the acceleration of forward, backward, or up-and-down motion, as well as the constant pull of gravity, is sensed by the **otoliths**, tiny, motion-sensitive crystals within the semicircular canals. When we move, these crystals shift like sands on a windy beach. The brain's inexperience in interpreting messages from the weightless otoliths is the cause of the space sickness experienced by the astronaut in our earlier example—a problem that is actually quite common among space travelers.

PSYCHOLOGY AND SOCIETY

Sense Organ Replacements: Electronic Ears for the Deaf and Eyes for the Blind

What appeared to be science fiction just a few years ago is considerably closer to becoming a reality: the replacement of malfunctioning human sense organs with artificial ones.

The greatest step forward has come in the realm of hearing. Because of technological advances, some 60,000 to 200,000 partially deaf people in the United States are now able to hear sounds such as automobile horns and doorbells for the first time. Making this advance possible is an electronic ear implant connected directly to the cochlea.

The device works in some cases of deafness in which the hair cells in the cochlea are damaged and unable to convert vibrations into the electrical impulses that the brain is able to use. A tiny microphone outside the ear is used to pick up sounds, which are then sent to a speech processor worn on a shoulder strap or belt that allows a user to squelch background noise with a button. The electronic signal is then sent from the processor to a transmitter behind the ear and broadcasts a radio wave to a receiver implanted inside the skull. The implanted receiver is directly connected to the cochlea by twenty-two thin wires and emits electrical signals that stimulate the cochlea, sending a message to the brain that sound is being heard (Molotsky, 1984; Clark, 1987).

Although the device does not allow people to pick up words distinctly—users report that the quality of speech is like that of Donald Duck—about half the users of state-of-the-art implants are able to understand familiar voices and speak on the phone. Implants also enable users to detect changes in tone of voice and volume. Moreover, as the technology continues to improve, it is likely that sounds will be made more distinct, perhaps one day approaching the sensitivity of the ear itself.

Technological advances have brought hope to the blind, as well. For example, Bach-Y-Rita (1982) and his colleagues at the Smith-Kettlewell Institute of Visual Science in San Francisco have employed a miniature television camera, which is mounted on spectacle frames worn by a blind person. The picture from the camera is analyzed by a small computer, which translates the picture into 400 dots, varying in darkness. Next, the degree of darkness of each of the spots is transformed into vibrations of varying intensity that are relayed to the blind person's abdomen, with darker spots being represented by more rapid vibrations. With just a small amount of training, blind people are able to "see" and recognize common objects, and eventually they are able to open doors, negotiate their way through halls, and pick up small objects.

The technology is still not as advanced as that employed in ear transplants, since the sensation of sight must be "translated" first into sensations of touch. And neither ear nor eye substitutes have reached the ultimate level of sophistication, in which signals can be fed directly into the brain and perceived as sound or sight. Still, the innovations described here offer real hope to thousands of deaf and blind people now, and the possibility of future improvements is high.

Making Sense of the Other Senses: Smell, Taste, and the Skin Senses

When Audrey Warner returned home after a day's work, she knew that something was wrong the minute she opened her apartment door. The smell of gas—a strong, sickening smell that immediately made her feel weak—permeated the apartment. She left her apartment, ran to the pay phone across the street, and called the gas company. As she was explaining what she smelled, Audrey heard a muffled explosion and then saw flames begin to shoot out of her apartment window. Her life had been saved by her ability to smell the gas.

Although there are few instances in which the sense of smell provides such drama, it is clear that our lives would be considerably less interesting if we could not smell freshly mowed hay, sniff a bouquet of flowers, or enjoy the odor of an apple pie baking. Like our senses of vision and hearing, each of the remaining senses that we now consider—smell, taste, and the skin senses—plays an important role in our lives.

Smell and taste. Although many animals have keener abilities to detect odors than we do—a point reflected by the fact that a greater proportion of their brains is related to the sense of smell than ours is—we are still able to detect a wide range of smells. People can be trained to make sophisticated, complex judgments of smells; there are even professions in which the major task is to continually assess the quality of the odor of a manufactured product.

Results of "sniff tests" have shown that women generally have a better sense of smell than do men and that a nonsmoker's sense of smell is better than a smoker's. In addition, the sense of smell changes with age: Sensitivity to smells is greatest between the ages of 30 and 60, declining from age 60 on. Moreover, a small number of people cannot smell at all. Such a condition may result from a head injury, nasal growths, or sometimes just a bad case of the flu (Doty, 1986; Gilbert & Wysocki, 1987).

For some animals, smells represent an important mode of communication. By releasing **pheromones**, chemicals that produce a reaction in other members of the species, they are able to send such messages as sexual availability. For instance, certain substances in the vaginal secretions of female monkeys contain a chemical that stimulates sexual interest in male monkeys.

Although it seems reasonable that humans might also communicate through the release of pheromones, the evidence is still scanty. Women's vaginal secretions contain chemicals similar to those found in monkeys, but the smells do not seem to be related to sexual activity in humans. On the other hand, the presence of these substances might explain why women who live together for long periods tend to show similarity in the timing of their menstrual cycles (Engen, 1982; 1987). In addition, women are able to identify their babies solely on the basis of smell just a few hours after birth (Porter et al., 1983).

Some researchers suggest that it was the sense of smell that led to the evolution and development of the cerebral cortex of the brain (Bloom & Lazerson, 1988). They base this notion on evidence from the existence of a now-extinct group of shrewlike mammals that roamed the earth at the time of the dinosaurs, some 100 million years ago. The long noses and small eyes of these animals suggest that they used smell as their primary tool of survival. According to this hypothesis, any animal that relied on smell had to develop such higher-order mental capabilities as remembering, planning, and tracking—in contrast to animals that relied solely on visual cues. The hypothesis suggests that animals developed this capability through growth in the part of the brain that was the forerunner of the cerebral cortex.

We know considerably less about the mechanisms underlying smell than we do about those concerning sight and sound. It is clear that the sense of smell comes into play when molecules of a substance enter the nasal passages and meet **olfactory cells**, the receptor cells of the nose. Each of these cells has hairlike structures that stick out into the air and are capable of transforming the passing molecules into nerve impulses that can be used by the brain.

More is understood about the sense of taste, which is intimately related to smell. There are only four fundamental sensations responsible for the myriad tastes that we experience: sweet, sour, salty, and bitter. Every other taste is simply a combination of these four basic qualities.

The receptor cells for taste are located in **taste buds**, which are distributed across the tongue. However, the distribution is uneven, and certain areas of the tongue are more sensitive to certain of the fundamental tastes than are others (Bartoshuk, 1971). As we can see in Figure 3-9, the tip of the tongue is most sensitive to sweetness; in fact, a granule of sugar placed on the rear of the tongue will hardly seem sweet at all. Similarly, only the sides of the tongue are very sensitive to sour tastes, and the rear specializes in bitter tastes.

The different taste areas on the tongue correspond to different locations in the brain. Neurons responding to sour and bitter tastes are located

FIGURE 3-9
Particular portions of the tongue are sensitive
to tastes that are bitter, sour, sweet, or salty.

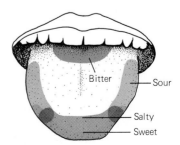

on one end of the area of the cortex corresponding to taste, whereas sweet tastes stimulate neurons on the opposite end of the cortex. In contrast, salty tastes stimulate neurons that are distributed across the entire taste area of the brain (Yamamoto et al., 1981).

Of course, the sense of taste does not operate simply through the tongue, as anyone with a stuffy nose can confirm. The smell, temperature, texture, and even appearance of food all affect our sense of taste. Furthermore, some people are more sensitive to certain tastes than are others, and the ability to taste certain substances runs in some families.

Senses of the skin: Touch, pressure, temperature, and pain. For the Gale Schoenlebers of the world, who suffer from debilitating migraine headaches (described at the beginning of this chapter), pain is the central aspect of life. Yet an inability to experience pain can be just as tragic. Consider the following description of a boy born with an extremely rare inherited defect that made him insensitive to pain:

> His arms and legs are deformed and bent, as though he had suffered from rickets. Several fingers are missing. A large open wound covers one knee, and the smiling lips are bitten raw. He looks, to all the world, like a battered child. . . . His fingers were either crushed or burned because he did not pull his hands away from things that were hot or dangerous. His bones and joints were misshapen because he pounded them too hard when he walked or ran. His knee had ulcerated from crawling over sharp objects that he could not feel. Should he break a bone or dislocate a hip, he would not feel enough to cry out for help (Wallis, 1984, p. 58, p. 60).

Clearly, the consequences of a painfree existence can be devastating. If, for example, you did not experience pain, instead of recoiling when your arm brushed against a hot teapot, you might lean against it, not noticing that you were being severely burned. Similarly, without the warning sign of stomach pain that typically accompanies an inflamed appendix, your appendix might go on to rupture, spreading a fatal infection through your body. Such examples underscore the vital importance of our sense of pain.

In fact, all our **skin senses**—touch, pressure, temperature, and pain— play a critical role in survival, making us aware of potential danger to our bodies. Most of these senses operate through nerve receptor cells located at various depths throughout the skin, although they are not evenly distributed. When we consider receptors sensitive to pressure, for example, some areas—such as the fingertips—have many more cells and are therefore more sensitive to pressure than others—such as the middle of the back (Kreuger, 1989).

Probably the most extensively researched skin sense is pain, and with good reason: People consult physicians and take medication for pain more than for any other symptom or condition. Nearly one-third of the population of the United States has problems with persistent or recurrent pain—and many of these individuals are disabled to the point of being unable to function normally in society.

Until fairly recently, little was understood about the biology and psychology of pain—and even less about how to treat it (Fordyce, 1988; Flor & Turk, 1989). Today, however, the major theory relating to the experience of pain, called the gate-control theory, is providing us with new clues for understanding how we can control pain. The **gate-control theory** suggests that particular nerve receptors lead to specific areas of the brain related to pain (Melzack & Wall, 1965). When these receptors are activated because of some injury or problem with a part of the body, a "gate" to the brain is opened, allowing the sensation of pain to be experienced.

However, another set of neural receptors is able, when stimulated, to close the "gate" to the brain, thereby reducing the experience of pain. The gate may be shut for two different reasons. First, other impulses can overwhelm the nerve pathways to the brain that the pain would otherwise use. In this case, nonpainful stimuli compete with and sometimes displace the neuronal message of pain, thereby shutting off the painful stimulus. This explains why rubbing the skin around an injury helps reduce pain: The competing stimuli from the rubbing may alleviate the painful ones. Similarly, scratching is able to relieve itching (which is technically classified as a kind of pain stimulus).

A second way in which a gate may be activated is through the brain itself. The brain is able to close a gate by sending a message down the spinal cord to an injured area, producing a reduction in or relief from pain. Thus a soldier who is injured in battle may experience no pain (the surprising situation in more than half of all combat injuries), because he experiences such relief at still being alive that his brain sends a signal to the injury site to shut down the pain gate (Sternbach, 1987).

The gate-control theory may explain the effectiveness of **acupuncture**, an ancient Chinese technique in which sharp needles are inserted into various parts of the body. The sensation from the needles may close the gateway to the brain, reducing the experience of pain. It is also possible that the body's own painkillers, the endorphins (discussed in Chapter 2), as well as positive and negative emotions, may play a role in opening and closing the gate (Wall & Melzack, 1984; Warga, 1987).

The Informed Consumer of Psychology: How Do You Spell Relief—from Pain?

You've been hurting for months, perhaps even years. You have tried every home remedy, and your family physician is unable to determine the cause of your pain. As the pain lingers, it begins to affect every aspect of your daily life. Where do you go next?

One place to consider is a comprehensive **pain clinic**. Numbering

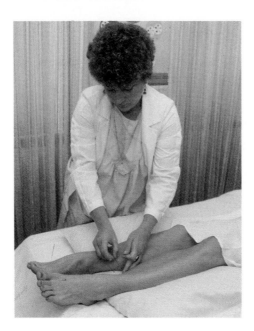

The gate-control theory of pain may explain the effectiveness of acupuncture, in which sharp needles inserted into the skin produce pain relief.

about 150 worldwide, pain clinics are designed for people who suffer from lingering, chronic pain that has resisted previous treatment. They offer a multidisciplinary approach to the relief of pain (Budiansky, 1987; Catalano & Johnson, 1987). In the typical clinic, the patient is first evaluated thoroughly by a team of health practitioners, including physicians, psychologists, and various medical specialists, and then a treatment is prescribed. The major antipain weapons in the arsenal of the pain clinic include:

- Drugs: Drugs remain the most popular treatment in fighting pain. Drugs range from those that treat the source of the pain—such as reducing swelling in painful joints—to those that work on the symptom of the pain.

- Hypnosis: Some 15 to 20 percent of the people who can be hypnotized can achieve a major degree of pain relief.

- Biofeedback: As we discussed in the previous chapter, biofeedback is a process in which people learn to control such "involuntary" functions as heartbeat and respiration. If the pain involves muscles, such as in tension headaches or back pain, biofeedback can be helpful (Dolce & Raczynski, 1985).

- Nerve and brain stimulation: Low-voltage electric current passed through painful parts of the body in a process called **transcutaneous electrical nerve stimulation (TENS)** can sometimes bring pain relief. In extreme cases, electrodes can be surgically implanted into the brain, and a handheld battery pack can stimulate nerve cells to provide direct relief.

- Relaxation techniques: People can be trained to systematically relax their bodies, thereby decreasing the pain caused by tension.
- Surgery: One of the most extreme methods, surgery can be used to cut certain nerve fibers carrying pain messages to the brain. Still, because there is a danger that other functions of the body will be affected, surgery is a treatment of last resort.
- Psychological counseling: In cases where pain cannot be successfully treated (it is important to keep in mind that there are no "miracle cures"), psychological counseling is employed to help a patient cope more effectively with the experience of pain.

ASK YOURSELF

Where are the senses of hearing, motion, and balance located?

What are the major parts of the ear?

What are the physical aspects of sound?

How do the sense of smell, sense of taste, and skin senses function?

How are the processes involved in vision and hearing similar?

Why couldn't we survive without our sense of touch?

MAKING SENSE OF THE WORLD: PERCEPTION

Look for a moment, at the shapes in Figure 3-10. Most of us would report that we saw a figure on a horse in (a), a set of brackets in (b), rows of circles and squares in (c), and an oval and a square intersecting in (d). But are these the only interpretations that could be given? A reasonable person could argue that there are a series of unrelated blotches in (a), ten lines with two protrusions coming off each line in (b), seven columns of alternating circles and squares in (c), and three distinct enclosed areas in (d).

The fact that most of us are apt to interpret the shapes as meaningful wholes illustrates some of the basic processes of perception at work: We try to simplify the complex stimuli presented to us by the environment. If we did not reduce the complex into something understandable, the world would present too much of a challenge for us to function, and—unless we lived as hermits in drab, colorless, silent caves—we would spend all our time just sorting through its myriad stimuli. Ironically, psychologists have found that the process of simplifying the world requires an impressive amount of perceptual effort.

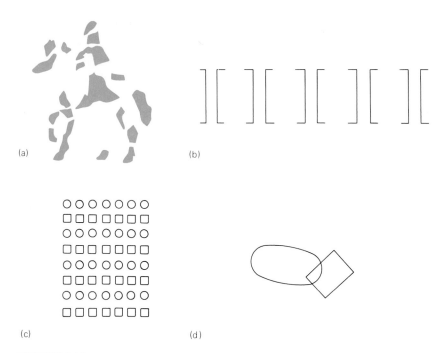

(a)

(b)

(c)

(d)

FIGURE 3-10
Perceptual organization at work. Although the figure in (a) can be seen as a series of unrelated splotches, (b) as lines with protrusions at top and bottom, (c) as columns of alternating circles and squares, and (d) as three separate shapes, most of us see in (a) a horse and rider, in (b) a series of brackets, in (c) rows of circles and squares, and in (d) an overlapping oval and square. [(a) Mednick, Higgins, & Kirschbaum, 1975.)]

Wholes from Parts: The Gestalt Laws of Organization

The basic perceptual processes operate according to a series of principles that describe how we organize bits and pieces of information into meaningful wholes. These are known as **gestalt laws of organization,** set forth in the early 1900s by a group of German psychologists who studied patterns—or **gestalts** (Wertheimer, 1923). They discovered a number of important principles which are valid for visual and auditory stimuli:

- **Closure**—Groupings are usually made in terms of enclosed or complete figures rather than open ones. We tend to ignore the breaks, then, in Figure 3-10a and b and concentrate on the overall forms.
- **Proximity**—Elements that are closer together are grouped together. Because of this, we tend to see pairs of dots rather than a row of single dots in the following:

. .   . .

- **Similarity**—Elements that are similar in appearance are grouped together. We see, then, horizontal rows of circles and squares in (*c*) instead of vertical mixed columns.

- **Simplicity**—In a general sense, the overriding gestalt principle is one of simplicity: When we observe a pattern, we perceive it in the most basic, straight-forward manner that we can (Hochberg, 1978). For example, (*d*) is seen as an interlocking of the simpler two figures, rather than as two separate forms. If we have a choice in interpretations, we generally opt for the simpler one.

Half Full or Half Empty? Figure and Ground

Look at the logo from the movie *Batman* in Figure 3-11. It was designed to be ambiguous, so that sometimes people see a figure of a bat and at other times they see teeth in a gaping mouth.

Chances are that you first saw one but very soon after perceived the other. Most people, in fact, shift back and forth between these two interpretations. The difficulty we face is that because the figure is two-dimensional, the usual means we employ for distinguishing the **figure** (the object being perceived) from the **ground** (the background or spaces within the object) do not work.

The fact that we can look at the same figure in either of two ways illustrates an important point first emphasized by the gestalt psychologists: We do not just passively respond to visual stimuli that happen to

T.M.

FIGURE 3-11
Do you see a bat—or is it teeth and a gaping mouth? Most people can shift their attention back and forth between the two interpretations, illustrating the use of figure and ground cues. (TM indicates a trademark of DC Comics, Inc. © 1989.)

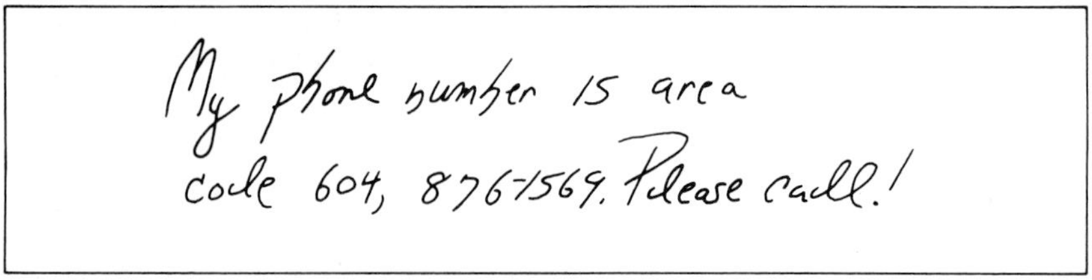

My phone number is area code 604, 876-1569. Please call!

FIGURE 3-12
What does this message say? You probably read it as "My phone number is area code 604, 876-1569. Please call!" If you did, however, you were being affected by the context of the message. Go back and look more carefully at it, and you will notice the word "is" and the number "15" are written identically. You'll also note that the "h" in the word "phone" and "b" in the word "number" are the same, as well as the "d" in the word "code" and the "l" in the word "please." You probably had no trouble in sorting these similarities out, though, because of your prior experience and because of the context that the message provided. (Coren, Porac, & Ward, 1979.)

fall on our retinas. Instead, we actively try to organize and make sense of what we see (see Figure 3-12). Perception, then, is typically a constructive process by which we go beyond the stimuli that are presented to us and attempt to construct a meaningful situation (Haber, 1983; Kienker et al., 1986).

Where 1 + 1 Equals More Than 2: The Whole Is Greater Than the Sum of Its Parts

If someone were to try to convince you that 1 plus 1 equals more than 2, you would think that person needed to brush up on some basic arithmetic. Yet the idea that two objects considered together form a whole that is greater than the simple combination of the objects was a fundamental principle of the gestalt psychologists. They argued—quite convincingly, in fact—that perception of stimuli in our environment goes well beyond the individual elements that we sense and represents an active, constructive process carried out within the brain, where bits and pieces of sensations are put together to make something greater—and more meaningful—than the individual elements separately.

Consider, for instance, Figure 3-13. As you examine the black patches, it is likely that you will perceive the form of a dog. The dog represents a gestalt, or perceptual whole. Although you can see the individual parts that make up the figure, putting each of them together forms something greater than these individual parts. The whole, then, is greater than the sum of the individual elements.

One outgrowth of this active perceptual processing is **perceptual constancy,** a phenomenon in which physical objects are perceived as un-

FIGURE 3-13
Although at first it is difficult to distinguish anything in this drawing, you
probably will eventually be able to discern the figure of a dog (Ronald C.
James, from R. G. Carraher and J. B. Thurston, (1966). Optical illusions in the Visual
Arts. New York: Von Nostrand Reinhold.)

varying and consistent, despite changes in their appearance or in the physical environment. For instance, consider what happens as you finish a conversation with a friend and she begins to walk away from you. As you
watch her walk down the street, the image on your retina becomes smaller
and smaller. Yet you do not think she is shrinking, despite this change in
sensory experience. Instead, because you factor into your thinking the
knowledge that she is also getting farther away, the phenomenon of perceptual constancy compensates for the change in retinal image, and you
ultimately perceive her as the same size no matter how far away she moves.

One of the most dramatic examples of perceptual constancy occurs
with the rising moon. When the moon first appears at night, close to the
horizon, it seems to be huge—considerably larger than when it is high in
the sky later in the evening. You may have thought that the size difference
was caused by the moon's being physically closer to the earth when it
first appears, but in fact this is not the case at all (Reed, 1984; Hershenson,
1989). Instead, the moon appears to be larger when it is close to the horizon because of a breakdown in perceptual constancy (Coren & Aks,
1990). Intervening terrain and objects such as trees convey a greater sense
of distance when the moon is on the horizon; when the moon is higher in
the sky, we see it by itself. To prove this, try looking at the moon when

Various theories have tried to explain the breakdown in perceptual constancy that occurs in the "moon illusion"—the phenomenon of the moon close to the horizon looking so much larger than it looks when higher in the sky.

it is low through a paper-towel tube; the moon will suddenly appear to "shrink" back to normal size.

Perceptual constancy occurs not just with size but with shape and color as well. The image on your retina varies as a plane approaches, flies overhead, and disappears, yet you do not perceive the plane as changing shape. Instead, you perceive it as unchanging, despite the physical variations that occur. Similarly, the soft lighting in a dimly lit restaurant might allow you to notice for the first time that a companion's eyes are an entrancing shade of blue. Yet you probably would not complain the next day when the bright sunlight produced a somewhat different color of blue. In fact, you probably wouldn't even notice the difference: Because of color constancy, you would perceive the blue as the same shade.

Although perceptual constancy aids us in simplifying the world, not all its outcomes are positive ones. For instance, the higher accident rate experienced by drivers of compact cars may be due in part to other drivers' underestimating the closeness of smaller cars, since at a particular distance a small car produces a smaller retinal image than a larger one (Eberts & MacMillan, 1985).

The exact process by which we experience perceptual constancy is not completely understood and has given rise to two competing theories. One explanation—**unconscious inference theory**—suggests that we use our prior experience about the size of an object to make unconscious inferences about its location (Lindsay & Norman, 1977; Rock, 1983). Because we have learned the size of particular stimuli from earlier experience, we compensate for changes in its size on the retina by inferring its location.

In contrast, **ecological theory** suggests that the relationships among different objects in a scene give us clues about their sizes (Gibson, 1979). According to this theory, when a friend walks away from us into the distance, not only is she farther away, but so are the objects she is close to. Therefore, all objects near her are going to produce an image that is proportionally smaller on our retina. Ecological theory suggests that we consider the scene as a whole and that perceptual constancy is brought about by direct perception of all the stimuli in the scene (Bruce & Green, 1990; Landwehr, 1990).

While we cannot say whether unconscious inference theory or ecological theory provides a more complete account of perception, it is clear that perceptual abilities develop early in life (Treisman & Gormican, 1988; Gibson, 1988). Indeed, perception is quite sophisticated even at birth (see Chapter 9), although learning and experience clearly play a critical role in its development.

Translating 2-D To 3-D: Depth Perception

As sophisticated as the retina is, the images that are projected onto it are flat and two-dimensional. Yet the world around us is three-dimensional, and we perceive it that way. How do we make the transformation from 2-D to 3-D?

The ability to view the world in three dimensions and to perceive distance—an ability known as **depth perception**—is due largely to the fact that we have two eyes. Because there is some distance between the eyes, a slightly different image reaches each retina, and the brain integrates them into one composite view. But it does not ignore the difference in images, which is known as **binocular disparity;** the disparity allows the brain to estimate the distance of an object from us.

Generally speaking, the farther away a stimulus is, the less the retinal disparity; and the closer the object, the greater the disparity between the two images. You can see this for yourself. Hold a pencil at arm's length and look at it first with one eye and then with the other. There is little difference between the two views relative to the background. Now bring the pencil just 6 inches away from your face, and try the same thing. This time you will perceive a greater difference between the two views. The fact that the discrepancy between the two eyes varies according to object distance provides you with a means of determining distance: Greater discrepancies are interpreted to mean that an object is closer, while smaller discrepancies are interpreted to mean that an object is farther away.

Filmmakers, whose medium compels them to project images in just two dimensions, have tried to create the illusion of depth perception by using two cameras, spaced slightly apart, to produce slightly different images, each destined for a different eye. In a 3-D movie, the two images are projected simultaneously. This produces a double image, unless special glasses are worn to allow each image to be viewed by the eye for

Moviegoers in the 1950s, such as these people watching *Bwana Devil*, could enjoy a sense of three-dimensionality by wearing specially designed glasses.

which it is intended. The special glasses—familiar to moviegoers since the first 3-D movie, *Bwana Devil*, appeared in 1952—provide a genuine sense of depth. Similar processes are being developed to show 3-D movies on television (Rogers, 1988).

Processes analogous to binocular disparity in the eye give the ear a sense of sound localization—of where a sound is coming from. Because the ears are several inches apart, wave patterns in the air enter each ear at a slightly different time, permitting the brain to use the discrepancy to locate the place from which the sound is originating.

However, it is important to realize that depth or location can be perceived by even a single sense organ. For example, it is not always necessary to use two eyes to perceive depth; certain cues permit us to obtain a sense of depth and distance with just one eye (Burnham, 1983). These cues are known as **monocular cues.** One monocular cue—**motion parallax**—is the change in position of an object on the retina as the head moves from side to side. The brain is able to calculate the distance of the object by the amount of change in the retinal image. Similarly, experience has taught us that if two objects are the same size, the one that makes a smaller image on the retina is farther away than the one that provides a larger image— an example of the monocular cue of **relative size.**

Finally, anyone who has ever seen railroad tracks that seem to join together in the distance knows that distant objects appear to be closer together than nearer ones, a phenomenon called **linear perspective** (see Figure 3-14). People use linear perspective as a monocular cue in esti-

FIGURE 3-14
It appears that the edges of this road come closer together as they move away
from the driver, illustrating the depth cue of linear perspective.

mating distance, allowing the two-dimensional retinal image to register
the three-dimensional world (Bruce & Green, 1990).

As the World Turns: Motion Perception

When a batter tries to hit a pitch, the most important factor is the motion
of the ball. How is a batter able to judge the speed and location of a target
that is moving at some 90 miles per hour?

The answer rests, in part, on several cues that provide us with relevant
information about the perception of motion. For one thing, the perceived
movement of an object across the retina is typically made relative to some
stable, nonmoving background. Moreover, if the stimulus is heading toward us, the image on the retina may expand in size, filling more and
more of the visual field. In such cases, we assume that the stimulus is
approaching—and not that it is an expanding stimulus viewed at a constant distance.

It is not, however, just the movement of images across the retina that
brings about the perception of motion. If it were, we would perceive the
world as moving every time we moved our heads. Instead, one of the
critical things we learn about perception is to factor information about
head and eye movements along with information about changes in the
retinal image.

In some cases, movement is so fast that we are unable to follow it. In those instances, we may be able to anticipate where an object will end up on the basis of our prior experience. For example, computer tracking of baseball pitches has shown that most fast balls thrown in major-league games travel too fast for the eye to follow. Indeed, if a batter tried to follow a fast ball from the moment it left a pitcher's hand, he would lose sight of it by the time it got about five feet from the plate (Bahill & Laritz, 1984). Research suggests that good hitters take their eyes off the ball during the middle of its trip and shift their vision closer to home plate, waiting for the ball's arrival and (hoped-for) impact with the bat. Thus, instead of relying on the raw sensory input from the traveling ball—the process of sensation—they employ perceptual processes, using what they have learned to expect about the way balls travel.

The Direction of Perception: Top-down and Bottom-up Processing

Ca- yo- re-d t-is -en-en-e, w-ic- ha- ev-ry -hi-d l-tt-r m-ss-ng? After a bit of thought, you'll probably be able to figure out that it says, "Can you read this sentence, which has every third letter missing?"

The fact that you are able to recognize such an imprecise stimulus illustrates that perception proceeds along two different avenues, called top-down processing and bottom-up processing. In **top-down processing,** perception is guided by higher-level knowledge, experience, expectations, and motivations. You were able to figure out the meaning of the sentence with the missing letters because of your prior reading experience, and because of the fact that written English contains redundancies: Not every letter of each word is necessary to decode its meaning. Moreover, your expectations played a role in your being able to read the sentence; you were probably expecting a statement that had *something* to do with psychology, and not the lyrics to a U2 song.

Even though top-down processing allows you to fill in the gaps, you would be unable to perceive the meaning of the sentence if you did not use **bottom-up processing,** which consists of recognizing and processing information about the individual components of the stimuli. You would make no headway in your recognition of the sentence without being able to perceive the individual shapes that make up the letters. Some perception, then, occurs at the level of the patterns and features of each of the separate letters.

It should be apparent that both top-down and bottom-up processing occur simultaneously, and interact with each other, in our perception of the world around us. It is bottom-up processing that allows us to process the fundamental characteristics of stimuli, whereas top-down processing allows us to bring our experience to bear on perception. And as we learn more about the complex processes involved in perception, we are developing a better understanding of how our brain continually interprets information from our senses and permits us to make responses appropriate to the environment.

Sorting Out the World: Selective Attention

The scene: a crowded, noisy party. As the woman next to you drones on about her new car, you suddenly hear snatches of conversation from behind you about your friend Terry, who seems to have left the party with another guest. Straining to hear what is being said by the person behind you, you lose track of what the woman is saying about her car—until suddenly you realize she has asked a question that requires a response. Brightly you say, "Pardon me— I didn't hear what you said, with all the noise."

Anyone who has been stuck listening to a bore go on and on about something trivial is probably familiar with situations similar to the one described above. Psychologists interested in perception are also familiar with circumstances such as this one, in which there are many stimuli to pay attention to simultaneously. The psychologist's interest lies primarily in the question of how we are able to sort out and make sense of multiple stimuli.

Selective attention is the perceptual process of choosing which stimulus to pay attention to. We are particularly attentive to stimuli that appear exceptionally bright, large, loud, novel, or high in contrast. We also pay greater attention to stimuli that are particularly meaningful or relevant to our own motivations (Whalen & Liberman, 1987; Posner & Presti, 1987).

Jet pilots face a dizzying array of information, making selective attention a critical process.

BLUE	GREEN
GREEN	ORANGE
PURPLE	ORANGE
GREEN	BLUE
RED	RED
GRAY	GRAY
RED	BLUE
BLUE	PURPLE

FIGURE 3-15
To try the Stroop task, name the colors in which each of these words are printed as quickly as you can, ignoring the word that is spelled out. For most people, the task is frustratingly difficult.

For example, if we feel hungry, we are more apt to be sensitive to food and food-related stimuli.

Advertisers are well aware of the phenomenon of selective attention. For instance, advertisements often include bright contrasts, and television and radio commercials are typically broadcast at higher volumes than the shows they sponsor. Furthermore, television and radio ads are often run at times of the day when people are particularly sensitive to their content (as when food advertisements are shown at the dinner hour).

In some cases, our attention must be divided between two stimuli. For instance, try the task shown in Figure 3-15, in which you are asked to say aloud the color of the ink used in each of the words—not the color the word spells out. Known as the **Stroop task,** the exercise is a frustratingly difficult one because it encompasses the perception of two powerful stimuli, and you are forced to divide your attention between the color and the meaning of the words (Stroop, 1935). Because both are potent stimuli and because, like most people, you are more experienced with reading than with naming colors, your attention is apt to be drawn away from the color of the ink toward the meaning of the words.

In order to study selective attention in the auditory realm, psychologists have developed a procedure called **dichotic listening,** whereby a person wears earphones through which a different message is sent to each ear at the same time. The individual is asked to repeat one of the messages aloud as it comes into one ear—a process known as **shadowing,** since the listener's voice acts as a verbal "shadow" of the message being received.

The question of interest is not so much whether the person is able to shadow the message adequately (most people can do so fairly easily); instead, it revolves around the effects of the message coming into the other ear. It turns out that although the content of the second message typically cannot be recalled, certain characteristics of the message can be remembered (Cherry, 1953). For instance, listeners accurately report whether the speaker was a man or a woman and whether the sex of the speaker changed during the course of the message. About one-third of the time, they can also report hearing whether their names were spoken.

One factor that seems particularly important is the meaningfulness of the message being shadowed. If a message that is being shadowed from one ear suddenly switches to the other, subjects generally "follow" the message to the second ear and begin to shadow from the second ear, even though they have been specifically instructed to shadow only what is being heard in the first ear (see Figure 3-16). Moreover, they are usually not even aware that they have made the switch (Treisman, 1960).

Experiments such as these suggest that although people may fully concentrate on only one message at a time, they still pay attention on some level to other information. This, then, explains our ability to eavesdrop on one conversation at a party but to know when it is time to make a response to someone to whom we are supposedly listening at the same time.

The phenomena involved in selective attention are of particular importance to people whose jobs require the constant monitoring of gauges or dials: pilots, air traffic controllers, nuclear power plant operators, and so on. Ironically, however, research has shown that as the importance of

FIGURE 3-16
A shadowing experiment. Subjects are told to shadow—or repeat—only the message being heard in their right ear, as the two messages shown in the captions are heard simultaneously. Although subjects are unaware that they are doing it, if the message switches to the opposite ear, they will typically begin to shadow the message, despite the experimenter's instructions.

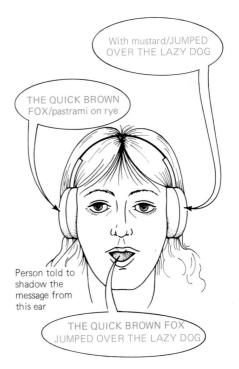

accurately attending to deviations from normal readings increases, people are less successfully able to carry out the task (Wickens, 1984). For example, in the late 1970s the nuclear power plant at Three Mile Island suffered a loss of cooling fluid that ultimately led to the leak of clouds of radioactive steam. At the time, information was available that could have rectified the crisis at an early stage. However, the operators on duty attended only to certain portions of the information, which turned out to be erroneous. Had they been attentive to information that was indicated on other instruments, they would have been able to stop the leakage before serious damage had been done.

In order to increase the accuracy with which people are able to scan and selectively attend to many stimuli simultaneously, psychologists have developed several principles for designing instruments that provide important information (Sanders & McCormick, 1987). Among the major ones are minimizing the number of sources of information, simplifying the display of information, and keeping sources of information physically close to one another. These guidelines have helped to improve the accuracy of perception as well as to reduce stress levels among those workers monitoring the instruments (Wiener & Nagel, 1988).

PERCEPTION IN EVERYDAY LIFE

> For sight follows gracious contours, and unless we flatter its pleasure by proportionate alternations of these parts (so that by adjustment we offset the amount to which it suffers illusions), an uncouth and ungracious aspect will be presented to the spectators.

The phenomenon to which Vitruvius, a Greek architect who lived around 30 B.C., refers in such cultivated language is that people do not always view the world accurately, and that it is important to consider how people's eyes and brains perceive buildings when designing architectural works.

Consider the Parthenon, one of the most famous buildings of ancient Greece. Although it looks true and straight to the eye, it was actually built with a bulge on one side. This protrusion fools viewers into thinking it is straight. If it didn't have that bulge—and quite a few other "tricks" like it, such as columns that incline inward—it would look as if it were crooked and about to fall down.

The fact that the Parthenon appears to be completely upright, with its lines straight and right angles at every corner, is the result of a series of **visual illusions,** physical stimuli that consistently produce errors in perception (Coren & Ward, 1989). As you can see in Figure 3-17a, if the building were completely square it would seem to be sagging, since there is a common visual illusion that makes angles placed above a line give the line the appearance of being bent (as in Figure 3-17b). If this had not been

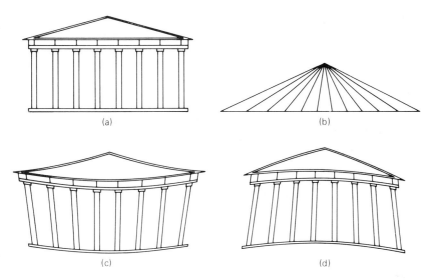

FIGURE 3-17
In building the Parthenon, the Greeks constructed an architectural wonder that looks perfectly straight, with right angles at every corner, as in (*a*). However, the visual illusion illustrated in (*b*) would have made it look as it appears in (*c*) if it actually had been built with true right angles. To compensate for this illusion, the Parthenon was designed to have a slight upward curvature, as shown in (*d*). (Coren, Porac, & Ward, 1979, p. 6.)

compensated for, the Parthenon would have looked as it does in Figure 3-17*c*. Therefore, the Parthenon was built with a slight upward curvature (as in Figure 3-17*d*).

Such perceptual insights did not stop with the Greeks; modern-day architects and designers also take visual distortions into account in their planning. For example, the New Orleans Superdome makes use of several visual tricks: Its seats vary in color throughout the stadium in order to give the appearance, from a distance, that there is always a full house. The carpeting in some of the sloping halls has perpendicular stripes that make people slow their pace by producing the perception that they are moving faster than they actually are. The same illusion is used at toll booths on superhighways: Stripes painted on the pavement in front of the toll booths make drivers feel that they are moving more rapidly than they actually are and cause them to decelerate quickly.

Misperceptions of the Eye: Visual Illusions

The implications of visual illusions go beyond the attractiveness of buildings. For instance, suppose you were an air traffic controller watching a radar screen like the one shown in Figure 3-18*a*. You might be tempted to sit back and relax as the two planes, whose flight paths are indicated

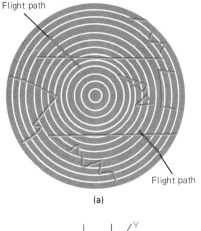

Flight path

Flight path

(a)

FIGURE 3-18a
Put yourself in the shoes of a flight controller and look at the flight paths of the two planes on this radar screen. A first glance suggests that they are headed on different courses and will not hit each other. But now take a ruler and lay it along the two paths. Your career as a flight controller might well be over if you were guiding the two planes and you allowed them to continue without a change in course. (Coren, Porac, & Ward, p. 7.)

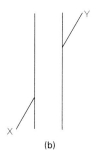

(b)

FIGURE 3-18b
The Poggendorf illusion, in which the two diagonal lines appear (incorrectly) as if they would not meet if extended toward each other.

in the figure, drew closer and closer together. If you did, however, you might end up with an air disaster: Although it looks as if the two planes will miss each other, they are headed for a collision. In fact, investigation has suggested that some 16 percent of all airplane accidents are caused by misperceptions of one sort or another (Kraft & Elworth, 1969; Hurst, 1984; Wiener & Nagel, 1988).

The flight-path illustration provides an example of a well-known visual illusion called the **Poggendorf illusion.** As you can see in Figure 3-18*b*, the Poggendorf illusion, when stripped down to its basics, gives the impression that line X would pass *under* line Y if it were extended through the pipelike figure, instead of heading directly toward line Y as it actually does.

The Poggendorf illusion is just one of many that consistently fool the eye (Perkins, 1983; Greist-Bousquet & Schiffman, 1986). Another is the one illustrated in Figure 3-19 called the **Müller-Lyer illusion.** Although the two lines are the same length, the one with the arrow tips pointing inward (Figure 3-19*a*, top) appears to be longer than the one with the arrow tips pointing outward (Figure 3-19*a*, bottom).

Although all kinds of explanations for visual illusions have been suggested, most concentrate either on the eye's visual sensory apparatus itself or on the interpretation that is given a figure by the brain. Visual expla-

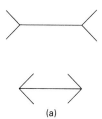

FIGURE 3-19a
The Müller-Lyer illusion, in which the upper horizontal line appears longer than the lower one.

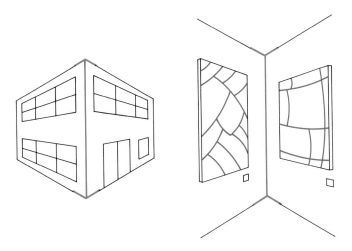

FIGURE 3-19b
An explanation for the Müller-Lyer illusion suggests that the line with arrow points directed out is interpreted as the relatively close end of a rectangular object extended out toward us (as in the building corner), and the line with arrow points directed inward is viewed as the inside corner of a rectangle extending away from us (as in the room corner). Our previous experience with distance cues leads us to assume that the outside corner is closer than the inside corner and that the inside corner must therefore be longer.

nations for the Müller-Lyer illusion suggest, for example, that eye movements are greater when the arrow tips point inward, making us perceive the line as longer than when the arrow tips face outward.

Other evidence suggests that the cause of the illusion rests on the brain's interpretive errors. For instance, one hypothesis assumes that the Müller-Lyer illusion is a result of the meaning we give to each of the lines (Gregory, 1978). When we see the top line in Figure 3-19a, we tend to perceive it as if it were the inside corner of a room extending away from us, as illustrated on the right in Figure 3-19b. On the other hand, when we view the bottom line in Figure 3-19*a*, we perceive it as the relatively close outside corner of a rectangular object such as the building on the left in Figure 3-19*b*. Because previous experience leads us to assume that the outside corner is closer than the inside corner, we make the further assumption that the inside corner must therefore be larger.

Given all the underlying assumptions, it may seem unlikely that this explanation is correct, but in fact there is a good degree of convincing evidence for it. One of the most telling pieces of support comes from cross-cultural studies that show that people raised in areas where there are few right angles—such as the Zulu in Africa—are much less susceptible to the illusion than people who grow up where most things are built using right angles and rectangles (Segall, Campbell & Herskovits, 1966).

Several kinds of cultural factors affect the ways in which we perceive the world. Consider, for example, the drawing in Figure 3-20. Sometimes called the "devil's tuning fork," it is likely to produce a mind-boggling effect, as the center tine of the fork alternates between appearing and disappearing.

Now try to reproduce the drawing on a piece of paper. Chances are that the task is nearly impossible for you—unless you are a member of an African tribe with little experience with western cultures. For such individuals, the task is simple; they have no trouble in reproducing the figure. The reason seems to be that western people automatically interpret the drawing as something that cannot exist in three dimensions, and they are therefore inhibited from reproducing it. The African tribal members, on the other hand, do not make the assumption that the figure is "impossible" and instead view it in two dimensions, which enables them to copy the figure with ease (Deregowski, 1973).

The misinterpretations created by visual illusions are ultimately due, then, to errors in both fundamental visual processing and in the way the brain interprets the information it receives (see Figure 3-21). But visual illusions also illustrate something fundamental about perception that makes them more than mere psychological curiosities: There is a basic connection between our prior knowledge, needs, motivations, and expectations about how the world is put together and the way we perceive it.

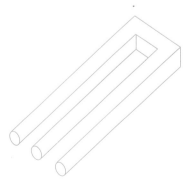

FIGURE 3-20
The "devil's tuning fork" has three prongs . . . or does it have just two?

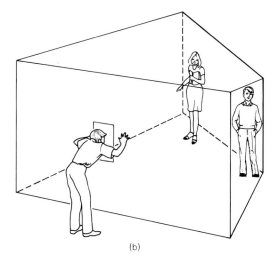

(b)

FIGURE 3-21
Despite the fact that the two people in (*a*) look like a giant and
dwarf, the woman is actually considerably taller than the child.
The reason for their perceived differences in size is that we assume that the room is rectangular, with the back walls at right
angles to the side walls. Actually, the room forms a trapezoid, as
the floorplan (*b*) shows, and the woman seen in (*a*) is standing
considerably further back than the child. Because the images that
reach our retina differ—the image of the woman is considerably
smaller than that of the child—we make the only logical assumption: there is a size discrepancy. In fact, even when we know the
truth about the room, the illusion is compelling and it is hard to
dispel the notion of size discrepancy.

Our view of the world is very much a function, then, of fundamental psychological factors. Furthermore, each of us perceives the environment in a way that is unique and special—a fact that allows each of us to make our own personal contribution to the world.

ASK YOURSELF

What are the major gestalt laws of organization?

How do the unconscious inference and ecological theories compare?

What are visual illusions?

What are the explanations for the most common visual illusions?

What is meant by the phrase "perception is a constructive process"?

What do cross-cultural differences in susceptibility to the Müller-Lyer illusion tell us about the nature of perception and about the impact of experience on perception?

LOOKING BACK

1. This chapter has examined how our senses respond to the world around us. It has focused on sensation, which concerns our initial contact with stimuli (forms of energy that activate a sense organ), and perception, the way in which we experience and respond to such stimuli.

2. The study of sensation has traditionally been investigated by the branch of psychology called psychophysics. Among the major areas of psychophysics is the study of absolute thresholds, the smallest amount of physical intensity of a stimulus that can be detected.

3. Signal detection theory is used to predict success and accuracy of judgments by systematically taking into account the kind of errors made by observers.

4. Difference thresholds relate to the smallest detectable difference between two stimuli, a difference known as a just noticeable difference. According to Weber's law, a just noticeable difference is a con-

stant proportion of the magnitude of an initial stimulus.

5. Sensory adaptation occurs when we become accustomed to a constant stimulus and change our evaluation of it. Repeated exposure to a stimulus results in an apparent decline in sensitivity to it.

6. Vision depends on sensitivity to light, electromagnetic waves that are reflected off objects outside the body. The eye shapes the light into an image that is transformed into nerve impulses and interpreted by the brain.

7. When light first enters the eye, it travels through the cornea and then traverses the pupil. The size of the pupil opening adjusts according to the amount of light entering the eye. Light then enters the lens, which, by a process called accommodation, acts to focus light rays onto the rear of the eye. On the rear of the eye is the retina, which is composed of light-sensitive nerve cells called rods and cones.

8. The visual information gathered by the rods and cones is transferred via bipolar and ganglion cells through the optic nerve, which leads to the optic chiasma—the point where the optic nerve splits. Because of the phenomenon of adaptation, it takes time to adjust to situations that are either measurably lighter or measurably darker than the previous environment.

9. Color vision is described by the trichromatic theory and the opponent-process theory. The trichromatic theory suggests that there are three kinds of cones in the retina, each of which is responsive to a certain range of colors. The opponent-process theory presumes pairs of different types of cells in the eye that work in opposition to each other so that if one is activated, the other is inhibited or prevented from firing.

10. Sound, motion, and balance are centered in the ear. Sounds enter through the outer ear and auditory canal until they reach the eardrum. The vibrations of the eardrum are transmitted into the middle ear, consisting of three bones: the hammer, the anvil, and the stirrup. These bones transmit vibrations to the oval window. In the inner ear, vibrations move into the cochlea, which encloses the basilar membrane. Hair cells on the basilar membrane change the mechanical energy into nerve impulses, which are transmitted to the brain. In addition to processing sound, the ear serves as the site of the organs that sense balance and motion through the semicircular canals and otoliths.

11. Sound has a number of important characteristics. One is frequency, the number of wave crests that occur in a second. Differences in frequency of sound waves are related to sounds of different pitches. Another aspect of sound is intensity, the variations in pressure produced by a wave as it travels through the air. Intensity is measured in decibels. The place theory of hearing and the frequency theory of hearing explain the processes involved with how sounds of varying frequencies and intensities are distinguished.

12. Smell employs the olfactory cells (the receptor cells of the nose), and taste is centered in the taste buds of the tongue. The skin senses are responsible for the experiences of touch, pressure, temperature, and pain. We know the most about pain, which is explained by the gate-control theory. In cases of severe long-term pain, pain clinics can sometimes offer relief.

13. Perception follows the gestalt laws of organization. These laws provide a series of principles by which we organize bits and pieces of information into meaningful wholes, known as gestalts. Among the most important laws are those of closure, proximity, similarity, and simplicity.

14. Work on figure/ground distinctions shows that perception is a constructive process in which people go beyond the stimuli that are physically present and construct a meaningful situation. The gestalt psychologists have demonstrated convincingly that the whole is greater than the sum of its parts.

15. Perceptual constancy permits us to perceive stimuli as unvarying and consistent, despite changes in the environment or the appearance of the objects being perceived. Two competing theories seek to explain constancy effects: unconscious inference theory and ecological theory.

16. Depth perception is the ability to perceive distance and to view the world in three dimensions, even though the images projected on our retinas are two-dimensional. We are able to judge depth and distance as a result of binocular disparity and monocular cues.

17. Motion perception depends on several cues. They include the perceived movement of an object across our retina and information about how the head and eye are moving.

18. Processing of perceptual stimuli occurs in both a top-down and a bottom-up fashion.

19. Selective attention is the perceptual process of choosing which stimulus to pay attention to. Psychologists study attention using a dichotic listening procedure.

20. Visual illusions are physical stimuli that consistently produce errors in perception, causing judgments that do not accurately reflect the physical reality of a stimulus. Among the best-known illusions are the Poggendorf illusion and the Müller-Lyer illusion.

Key Terms and Concepts

sensation (p. 78)
perception (p. 78)
stimulus (p. 80)
magnitude (p. 80)
psychophysics (p. 81)
absolute threshold (p. 81)
noise (p. 81)
signal detection theory (p. 82)
difference threshold (p. 83)
just noticeable difference (p. 83)
Weber's law (p. 84)
adaptation (p. 84)
light (p. 86)
visual spectrum (p. 87)
cornea (p. 87)
pupil (p. 87)
iris (p. 87)
lens (p. 89)
accommodation (p. 89)
retina (p. 89)
rods (p. 89)
cones (p. 89)
fovea (p. 89)
peripheral vision (p. 89)
rhodopsin (p. 91)
bipolar cells (p. 91)
ganglion cells (p. 91)
optic nerve (p. 91)
optic chiasma (p. 91)
glaucoma (p. 92)
tunnel vision (p. 93)
feature detection (p. 93)
light adaptation (p. 93)
dark adaptation (p. 94)
trichromatic theory of color vision (p. 94)
afterimage (p. 95)
opponent-process theory (p. 95)
outer ear (p. 98)
sound (p. 98)
auditory canal (p. 98)

eardrum (p. 98)
middle ear (p. 98)
hammer (p. 98)
anvil (p. 98)
stirrup (p. 98)
oval window (p. 98)
inner ear (p. 99)
cochlea (p. 99)
basilar membrane (p. 99)
hair cells (p. 99)
frequency (p. 100)
pitch (p. 100)
intensity (p. 100)
decibel (p. 100)
place theory of hearing (p. 101)
frequency theory of hearing (p. 102)
semicircular canals (p. 102)
otoliths (p. 102)
pheromones (p. 104)
olfactory cells (p. 105)
taste buds (p. 105)
skin senses (p. 106)
gate-control theory of pain (p. 107)
acupuncture (p. 107)
pain clinic (p. 107)
transcutaneous electrical nerve stimulation (TENS) (p. 108)
gestalt laws of organization (p. 110)
gestalts (p. 110)
closure (p. 110)
proximity (p. 110)
similarity (p. 111)
simplicity (p. 111)
figure/ground (p. 111)
perceptual constancy (p. 112)
unconscious inference theory (p. 114)
ecological theory (p. 114)
depth perception (p. 115)
binocular disparity (p. 115)
monocular cues (p. 116)

4

Learning

---❖---

PROLOGUE: GARY FINKLE (AND JO)

Capuchin monkey Jo helps quadra-plegic Gary Finkle perform many everyday tasks.

Try this: Take the most comfortable chair you own into the pleasantest room in your house, arrange it in a convenient location, and sit down. Don't move. Wait fifteen or twenty minutes for your muscles to loosen up. Relax. Look around; take stock of your surroundings. If any visitors walk in, you can turn your head to greet them but you can't stand or shake hands. You can admire the view out your window, but you can't crack it open for a breath of fresh air if the room becomes stuffy or warm. Wait another hour. Are you bored yet? Hungry? Thirsty? Sorry, but you'll just have to wait until somebody happens by. Don't worry, it shouldn't be too long—probably no more than a couple of hours (Mac-Fadyen, 1987, p. 125).

Welcome to Gary Finkle's world—and that of some 90,000 other Americans who have suffered spinal cord injuries that have left them without feeling or movement below their shoulders. Finkle, though, has an advantage over most of those who have suffered similar accidents: Jo, a female capuchin monkey.

Finkle is one of the first participants in a program called Helping Hands: Simian Aides for the Disabled. The organization trains capuchins to reduce the dependence of the disabled on family and friends and to increase their self-reliance.

Through careful and systematic training, Jo has become Finkle's arms and legs. By using his mouth to control a laser attached to his wheelchair, Finkle is able to direct Jo

132

to turn the pages of a book, take a sandwich out of the refrigerator, turn lights on and off, comb his hair, put a tape into a cassette player, and even wipe up a spill.

Jo's miraculous capabilities did not just happen, of course. They are the result of meticulous training procedures based on basic principles of learning. For example, in one training procedure, Jo was taught to fetch any article to which a laser beam was pointed. She began by learning the subcomponents of the task: first learning to merely look at the beam, then learning to go to the place where the beam was pointed, then touching the object, and so forth, until she mastered the entire task. Whenever she successfully completed an assignment, she was immediately given a re-ward—typically a sip of sticky, strawberry-flavored Nutrament. And if she failed at a task, she received nothing. Through this simple procedure, the inventory of tasks Jo could accomplish was gradually expanded and refined (Blumenthal, 1987; MacFadyen, 1987).

To Gary Finkle, the process by which Jo was able to learn so much is less important than the changes that have occurred in his own life. Her presence has given him the opportunity to maintain a considerable degree of independence, one of the most precious commodities for a disabled person. "I definitely cannot imagine living without her," he says.

*L*OOKING AHEAD

The same procedures that allowed trainers to harness and shape Jo's ca-pabilities to benefit Gary Finkle are at work in each of our lives, as we read a book, drive a car, play poker, study for a test, or perform any of a myriad of other activities central to us. Like Jo, each of us must acquire and then hone our skills and abilities through learning.

A fundamental topic for psychologists, learning underlies many of the diverse areas discussed throughout this book. For example, a psy-chologist studying perception might ask, "How do we learn that people who look small from a distance are just far away and not simply tiny?" A developmental psychologist might inquire, "How do babies learn to distinguish their mothers from other people?" A clinical psychologist might wonder, "Why do some people learn to be afraid when they see a spider?" A social psychologist might ask, "How do we learn to feel that we are in love?" Each of these questions, although drawn from very dif-ferent fields of psychology, can be answered only with reference to learn-ing processes. In fact, learning plays a central role in almost every topic of interest to psychologists.

What do we mean by learning? Although psychologists have identi-fied a number of different types of learning, a general definition encom-passes them all: **Learning** is a relatively permanent change in behavior brought about by experience. What is particularly important about this definition is that it permits us to distinguish between performance changes due to **maturation** (the unfolding of biologically predetermined patterns of behavior due simply to getting older) and those changes brought about by experience. For instance, children become better tennis players as they grow older partially because their strength increases with their size—a maturational phenomenon. Such maturational changes need to be distinguished from improvements due to learning, which are a consequence of practice.

Similarly, we must distinguish between short-term changes in behavior that are due to factors other than learning, such as declines in performance resulting from fatigue or lack of effort, and performance changes that are due to actual learning. For example, if Jennifer Capriati performs poorly in a tennis game because of tension or fatigue, this does not mean that she has not learned to play correctly or has forgotten how to play well.

The distinction between learning and performance is critical, and not always easy to make. Learning is an *inferred* process; we cannot see it happening directly, and we can assume that learning has occurred only by observing changes in performance. This fact makes the learning psychologist's task a difficult one, since there is not always a one-to-one correspondence between learning and performance—as those of us who have done poorly on an exam because we were tired and made careless mistakes can well understand. Poor performance, then, does not necessarily indicate an absence of learning.

In this chapter, we examine basic learning processes in order to answer a number of fundamental questions:

- What are the different forms of learning, and how can we differentiate among them?
- What is the role of reward and punishment in learning?
- What is the role of thinking in learning?
- How can we formally analyze behavior, and how does this lead to techniques for modifying and controlling it?
- What are some practical methods for bringing about behavior change, both in others and in ourselves?

PAVLOV'S DOGS AND THE GOLDEN ARCHES: CLASSICAL CONDITIONING

What do you think of when you catch a glimpse of the golden arches in front of McDonald's? If the mere sight of them makes your stomach rumble a bit and your thoughts turn to hamburgers and french fries, you are displaying a rudimentary form of learning called classical conditioning.

The processes that underlie classical conditioning explain such diverse phenomena as crying at the sight of a bride walking down the aisle at a wedding, fearing the dark, and falling in love with the boy or girl next door. To understand classical conditioning, however, it is necessary to move back in time and place to the early part of the century in Russia.

Canine Conditioning

Ivan Pavlov, a Russian physiologist, never intended to do psychological research. In 1904 he won the Nobel Prize for his work on digestion, testimony to his contribution to that field. Yet Pavlov is remembered not for his physiological research, but for his experiments on basic learning processes—work that he began quite accidentally.

Pavlov had been studying the secretion of stomach acids and salivation in dogs in response to the ingestion of varying amounts and kinds of food. While doing so, he observed a curious phenomenon: Sometimes stomach secretions and salivation would begin when no food had actually been eaten; the mere sight of a food bowl, the individual who normally brought the food, or even the sound of the footsteps of that individual was enough to produce a physiological response in the dogs. Pavlov's genius was his ability to recognize the implications of this rather basic discovery. He saw that the dogs were responding not only on the basis of a biological need (hunger), but also as a result of learning—or, as it came to be called, classical conditioning. In **classical conditioning**, an organism learns a response to a neutral stimulus that normally does not bring about that response.

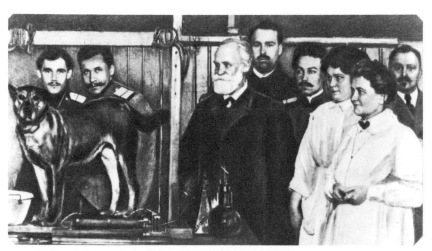

Ivan Pavlov (center, with white beard), a Russian physiologist, was the first to recognize the importance of the learning processes represented in classical conditioning.

To demonstrate and analyze classical conditioning, Pavlov ran a series of experiments (Pavlov, 1927). In one, he attached a tube to the salivary gland of a dog, allowing him to measure precisely the amount of salivation that occurred. He then sounded a tuning fork and, just a few seconds later, presented the dog with meat powder. This pairing, carefully planned so that exactly the same amount of time elapsed between the presentation of the sound and the meat, occurred repeatedly. At first the dog would salivate only when the meat powder itself was presented, but soon it began to salivate at the sound of the tuning fork. In fact, even when Pavlov stopped presenting the meat powder, the dog still salivated after hearing the sound. The dog had been classically conditioned to salivate to the tone.

As you can see in Figure 4-1, the basic processes of classical conditioning underlying Pavlov's discovery are straightforward, although the terminology he chose has a technical ring. Consider first the diagram in Figure 4-1a. Prior to conditioning, we have two unrelated stimuli: the sound of a tuning fork and meat powder. We know that the sound of a tuning fork leads not to salivation but to some irrelevant response such as perking of the ears or, perhaps, a startle reaction. The sound in this case therefore is called the **neutral stimulus** because it has no effect on the response of interest. We also have meat powder, which, because of the biological makeup of the dog, naturally leads to salivation, the particular response that we are interested in conditioning. The meat powder is considered an **unconditioned stimulus**, or **UCS**, because food placed near a dog's mouth automatically causes salivation to occur. The response that the meat powder produces is called an **unconditioned response**, or **UCR**—a response that is not associated with previous learning. Unconditioned responses are natural and innate responses that need no training, and they are always brought about by unconditioned stimuli.

Figure 4-1b illustrates what happens during conditioning. The tuning fork is repeatedly sounded just before presentation of the meat powder. The goal of conditioning is for the tuning fork to develop into a substitute for the unconditioned stimulus (meat powder) and therefore to bring about the same sort of response as the unconditioned stimulus. During this period, salivation gradually increases each time the tuning fork is sounded until the tuning fork alone causes the dog to salivate.

When conditioning is complete, the tuning fork has evolved from a neutral stimulus to what is now called a **conditioned stimulus**, or **CS**. At this time, salivation that occurs as a response to the conditioned stimulus (tuning fork) is considered a **conditioned response**, or **CR**. This situation is depicted in Figure 4-1c. The conditioned stimulus evokes the conditioned response.

The sequence and timing of the presentation of the unconditioned stimulus and the conditioned stimulus is particularly important (Rescorla, 1988). Like a signal light at a railroad crossing that does not operate until after a train has passed by, a neutral stimulus that follows an uncondi-

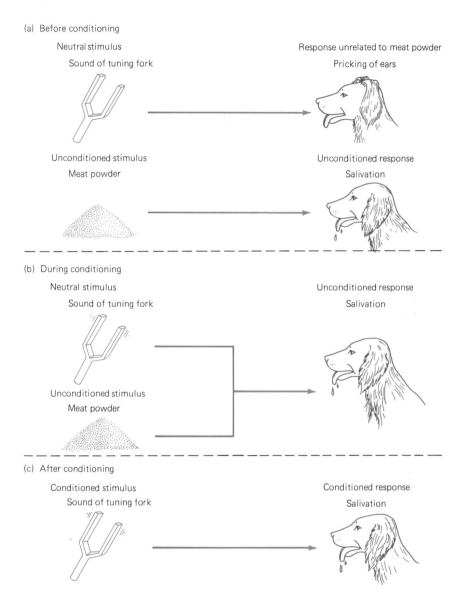

FIGURE 4-1

The basic process of classical conditioning. (*a*) Prior to conditioning, the sound of a tuning fork does not bring about salivation—making the tuning fork a neutral stimulus. On the other hand, meat powder naturally brings about salivation, making the meat powder an unconditioned stimulus and salivation an unconditioned response. (*b*) During conditioning, the tuning fork is sounded just before the presentation of the meat powder. (*c*) Eventually, the sound of the tuning fork alone brings about salivation. We can now say that conditioning has been accomplished: The previously neutral stimulus of the tuning fork is now considered a conditioned stimulus which brings about the conditioned response of salivation.

tioned stimulus has little chance of becoming a conditioned stimulus. On the other hand, just as a warning light works best if it goes on right before a train is about to go by, a neutral stimulus that is presented just before the unconditioned stimulus is most apt to result in successful conditioning. Research has shown, in fact, that conditioning is most effective if the conditioned stimulus precedes the unconditioned stimulus by between a half second and several seconds, depending on what kind of response is being conditioned.

Although the terminology employed by Pavlov to describe classical conditioning may at first seem confusing, the following rules of thumb can help to make the relationships between stimuli and responses easier to understand and remember:

- *Un*conditioned stimuli lead to *un*conditioned responses, and *un*conditioned stimulus–*un*conditioned response pairings are *un*learned and *un*trained.
- Conditioned stimuli lead to conditioned responses, and conditioned stimulus–conditioned response pairings are a consequence of learning and training.
- Unconditioned responses and conditioned responses are similar (such as salivation in the example described above), but the conditioned response is learned, whereas the unconditioned response occurs naturally.

Applying Conditioning Principles to Human Behavior

Although the initial classical conditioning experiments were carried out with animals, the principles that underlie the early work were soon found to explain many aspects of everyday human behavior. Consider someone whose stomach begins to rumble and whose mouth waters at the sight of McDonald's golden arches. The cause of this reaction is classical conditioning: The previously neutral arches have come to be associated with the food inside the restaurant (the unconditioned stimulus), causing the arches to become a conditioned stimulus that brings about the conditioned response of salivation.

Emotional responses are particularly apt to be learned through classical conditioning processes. For instance, how do some of us develop fears of mice, spiders, and other creatures that—if we thought about it much—do not seem intrinsically more ferocious or potentially harmful than a pet dog or cat? In a now-famous experiment designed to show that classical conditioning was at the root of such fears, an 11-month-old infant named Albert, who initially showed no fear of rats, was exposed to a loud noise at the same time that a rat was presented to him (Watson & Rayner, 1920). The noise (the UCS) evoked fear (the UCR); after just a few pairings,

Albert began to show fear of the rat by itself. The rat, then, had become a CS that brought about the CR, fear. Similarly, it is likely that the pairing of the appearance of certain species with the fearful comments of an adult causes children to develop the same fears their parents have.

In adulthood, learning via classical conditioning occurs a bit more subtly. You may come to know that a professor's mood is particularly menacing when her tone of voice changes; in the past you may have seen that the professor uses that tone only when she is about to criticize someone's work. Likewise, you may not go to a dentist as often as you should because of prior associations with dentists and pain. Classical conditioning, then, explains many of the reactions we have to stimuli in the world around us (Klein & Mowrer, 1989a).

Unlearning What You Have Learned: Extinction

As long as you can remember, you have hated broccoli. The very sight of it makes you queasy. Yet your new girlfriend's parents seem to love it, serving it every time you come to visit. Being polite, you feel you must eat a little of it. The first few times it is torture; you feel as if you are about to embarrass yourself by getting sick at the table, but you steel yourself to keep the broccoli down. After a few weeks it becomes easier. In fact, after a couple of months, you are surprised to realize that you no longer feel sick at the thought of eating broccoli.

Your behavior can be explained by one of the basic phenomena of learning: extinction. **Extinction** occurs when a previously conditioned response becomes weaker and eventually disappears. To produce extinction, one needs to end the association between conditioned and unconditioned stimuli. If we had trained a dog to salivate at the sound of a bell, we could bring about extinction by ceasing to provide meat after the bell was sounded. At first the dog would continue to salivate when it heard the bell, but after a few such instances, the amount of salivation would probably decline, and the dog would eventually stop responding to the bell altogether. At that point, we could say that the response had been extinguished. In sum, extinction occurs when the conditioned stimulus is repeatedly presented without the unconditioned stimulus.

As we will describe more fully in Chapter 11, psychologists have treated people with irrational fears or phobias using a form of therapy called **systematic desensitization**, in which the goal is to bring about the extinction of the phobia. For instance, a person who has an intense fear of heights and has been undergoing systematic desensitization therapy might be told to climb to the first floor of a building and look out the window. When he is on the first floor, he uses relaxation procedures he has been taught by the therapist until he feels comfortable at that height. To feel truly relaxed, he may have to repeat this process several times. Next he is told to climb to a somewhat higher floor and do the same thing.

By increasing the height to which he climbs each time—and discovering that there are no negative consequences—he may eventually be able to overcome his fear of high places.

The basic goal of systematic desensitization is to bring about the extinction of the phobia in question. When the treatment begins, the patient demonstrates a conditioned response to the feared object; in our example, for instance, a high place acts as a conditioned stimulus that produces the conditioned response of fear. Each time the person is exposed to the conditioned stimulus (being in a high place) without experiencing negative consequences, the likelihood that the conditioned stimulus will evoke the undesirable response is weakened. Eventually, then, the conditioned response is extinguished.

The Return of the Conditioned Response: Spontaneous Recovery

Once a conditioned response has been extinguished, is it lost forever? Not necessarily. As Pavlov discovered, if he returned to his previously conditioned dog the day after the conditioned behavior had been extinguished and rang a bell, the dog would once again salivate. Similarly a person once "cured" of a phobia may find that the phobia recurs after a long period of absence from the feared object.

This phenomenon is called **spontaneous recovery**—the reappearance of a previously extinguished response after time has elapsed without exposure to the conditioned stimulus. Usually, however, responses that return through spontaneous recovery are weaker than they were initially and can be extinguished more readily than before.

A Rose Is a Rose: Generalization and Discrimination

Despite differences in color and shape, to most of us a rose is a rose is a rose: The pleasure we experience at the beauty, smell, and grace of the flower is similar for different roses. Pavlov noticed an analogous phenomenon: His dogs often salivated not only at the sound of the tuning fork that was used during their original conditioning but at the sound of a bell or a buzzer as well.

Such behavior is the result of stimulus generalization. **Stimulus generalization** takes place when a conditioned response follows a stimulus that is similar to the original conditioned stimulus. The greater the similarity of the two stimuli, the greater the likelihood of stimulus generalization. Baby Albert, who, as we mentioned earlier, was conditioned to be fearful of rats, was later found to be afraid of other furry white things; he was fearful of white rabbits, white fur coats, and even a white Santa Claus mask. On the other hand, according to the principle of stimulus general-

In Watson's work with Little Albert, the boy's conditioned fear of white rats was generalized to include many furry white objects, including the Santa Claus mask worn by Watson in this photo.

ization, it is unlikely that he would be afraid of a black dog, since its color would differentiate it sufficiently from the original fear-evoking stimulus.

The conditioned response that is evoked by the new stimulus is usually not as intense as the original conditioned response, although the more similar the new stimulus is to the old one, the more similar the new response will be. It is unlikely, then, that Albert's fear of the Santa Claus mask was as great as his learned fear of a rat. Still, stimulus generalization permits us to know that we ought to brake at all red lights, even if there are minor variations in size, shape, and shade.

If stimuli are sufficiently distinct from one another so that the presence of one evokes a conditioned response but the other does not, we can say that stimulus discrimination has occurred. In **stimulus discrimination**, an organism learns to differentiate among different stimuli and restricts its responding to one stimulus rather than to others. Without the ability to discriminate between a red and a green traffic light, we would be mowed down by oncoming traffic; and if we could not discriminate a cat from a mountain lion, we might find ourselves in uncomfortable straits on a camping trip.

When a CS Becomes a UCS: Higher-order Conditioning

If you are knocked over a few times by your neighbor's vicious Doberman, Rover, it would not be surprising that merely hearing the dog's name called would produce an unpleasant emotional reaction. This represents an example of higher-order conditioning. **Higher-order conditioning** occurs when a conditioned stimulus that has been established during earlier conditioning is then paired with a neutral stimulus, and the neutral stimulus comes to evoke a conditioned response similar to the original conditioned stimulus. The original conditioned stimulus, in effect, acts as an unconditioned stimulus.

Our example of Rover can illustrate higher-order conditioning. You have learned to associate the sight of vicious Rover, who originally was a neutral stimulus, with rough behavior. The mere sight of Rover, then, has become a conditioned stimulus, which evokes the conditioned response of fear.

Later, however, you realize that every time you see Rover, its owner is calling the dog's name, saying, "Here, Rover." Because of this continual pairing of the name of Rover (which was originally a neutral stimulus) with the sight of Rover (now a conditioned stimulus), you become conditioned to experience a reaction of fear and loathing whenever you hear the name Rover, even though you may be safely inside your house. The name "Rover," then, has become a conditioned stimulus because of its earlier pairing with the conditioned stimulus of the sight of Rover. Higher-order conditioning has occurred: The sound of Rover's name has become a conditioned stimulus evoking a conditioned response.

Theoretically, it ought to be possible to keep producing unlimited higher-order response chains, associating one conditioned stimulus with another, and in fact Pavlov hypothesized that all learning is nothing more than long strings of conditioned responses. However, this notion has not been supported by subsequent research, and it turns out that classical conditioning provides us with only a partial explanation of how people and animals learn.

We turn next to another major model of learning, called operant conditioning, that accounts for people's learning in order to obtain some reward.

ASK YOURSELF

What is learning, and how does it differ from maturation?

How is something learned via classical conditioning?

How can these basic learning processes be described and differentiated: extinction, systematic desensitization, spontaneous recovery, stimulus generalization and discrimination, and higher-order conditioning?

Many people are afraid to swim in the ocean after seeing the movie *Jaws*. Using the principles of classical conditioning, how can you explain such fear?

*T*HE REWARDS OF REINFORCEMENT: OPERANT CONDITIONING

Very good ... What a clever idea ... Far out ... I agree ... Thank you ... Excellent ... This is the best paper you've ever written; you get an A ... You are really getting the hang of it ... I'm impressed ... Let me give you a hug ... You're getting a raise ... Have a cookie ... You look great ... I love you

Few of us would mind having any of the above comments directed at us. But what is particularly noteworthy about them is that each of these simple statements can be used to bring about powerful changes in behavior and to teach the most complex tasks through a process known as operant conditioning. Operant conditioning forms the basis for much of the most important kinds of human, and animal, learning.

Operant conditioning describes learning in which people make responses as a result of positive or negative consequences that are contingent (or dependent) on their responses. Unlike classical conditioning, in which the original responses are the natural, biological outgrowth of the presence of some stimulus such as food, water, or pain, operant conditioning applies to voluntary responses, which an organism performs willfully—in order to produce a desirable outcome. The term "operant" emphasizes this point: The organism *operates* on its environment in order to produce some desirable result. For example, operant conditioning is at work when we learn that working diligently can bring about a raise, or that cleaning our room produces words of praise from our parents, or that studying hard results in good grades.

Like the roots of classical conditioning, the foundations for understanding operant conditioning were laid by work with animals. We turn now to some of that early research, which began with a simple inquiry into the behavior of cats.

Cat-in-a-Box: Thorndike's Law of Effect

If you placed a hungry cat in a cage and then put a small piece of food outside, chances are the cat would eagerly search for a way out of the cage. The cat might first claw at the sides or push against an opening. Suppose, though, that you had rigged things so that the cat could escape by stepping on a small paddle that released the latch to the door of the cage (see Figure 4-2). Eventually, as it moved around the cage, the cat would happen to step on the paddle, the door would open, and the cat would eat the food.

What would happen if you then returned the cat to the box? The next time, it would probably take a little less time for the cat to step on the paddle and escape. After a few trials, the cat would deliberately step on

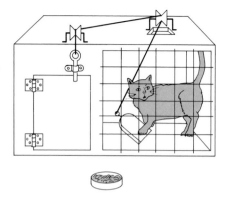

FIGURE 4-2
Edward L. Thorndike devised this puzzle box to study the process by which a cat learns to press a paddle to escape the box and receive food. (Thorndike, 1932)

the paddle as soon as it was placed in the cage. What would have occurred, according to Edward L. Thorndike (1932), who studied this situation extensively, was that the cat would have learned that pressing the paddle was associated with the desirable consequence of getting food. Thorndike summarized that relationship by formulating the **law of effect**, which states that responses that are satisfying are more likely to be repeated, and those that are not satisfying are less likely to be repeated.

Thorndike felt that the law of effect operated as automatically as leaves falling off a tree in autumn. It was not necessary for an organism to understand that there was a link between a response and reward. Instead, he thought that over time and through experience, the organism would form a direct connection between the stimulus and the response without any awareness that the connection existed.

From Cat-in-a-Box to Skinner Box: The Basics of Operant Conditioning

Thorndike's early research formed the foundation for the work of one of the most famous contemporary psychologists, B. F. Skinner, who died in 1990. You may have heard of the Skinner box (shown in one form in Figure 4-3), a chamber with a highly controlled environment used to study operant conditioning processes with laboratory animals. Whereas Thorndike's goal was to get his cats to learn to obtain food by leaving the box, animals in a Skinner box learn to obtain food by operating on their environment within the box. Skinner became interested in specifying how behavior varied as a result of alterations in the environment.

Skinner, whose work goes far beyond perfecting Thorndike's earlier apparatus, is considered the father of a whole generation of psychologists studying operant conditioning. To illustrate Skinner's contribution, let's consider what happens to a pigeon in the typical Skinner box.

Suppose you want to teach a hungry pigeon to peck a key that is located in its box. At first the pigeon will wander around the box, ex-

FIGURE 4-3
A Skinner box, used to study operant conditioning. Laboratory animals learn to press the lever in order to obtain food, which is delivered in the tray.

ploring the environment in a relatively random fashion. At some point, however, it will probably peck the key by chance, and when it does, it will receive a food pellet. The first time this happens, the pigeon will not learn the connection between pecking and receiving food and will continue to explore the box. Sooner or later the pigeon will again peck the key and receive a pellet, and in time the frequency of the pecking response will increase. Eventually, the pigeon will peck the key continually until it satisfies its hunger, thereby demonstrating that it has learned that the receipt of food is contingent on the pecking behavior.

Reinforcing desired behavior. In a situation such as this one, the food is called a reinforcer. A **reinforcer** is any stimulus that increases the probability that a preceding behavior will occur again. Here, food is a reinforcer because it increases the probability that the behavior of pecking the key (formally referred to as the "response" of pecking) will take place. Bonuses, toys, and good grades could also serve as reinforcers, since they strengthen a response that comes before the introduction of the reinforcer. In each case, it is critical that the organism learn that the delivery of the reinforcer is contingent on the response occurring.

Of course, we are not born knowing that 50 cents can buy us a candy bar. Rather, through experience we learn that money is a valuable commodity because of its association with stimuli, such as food, drink, and shelter, that are naturally reinforcing. This fact suggests a distinction that can be drawn regarding whether something is a primary reinforcer or a secondary reinforcer. A **primary reinforcer** satisfies some biological need and works naturally, regardless of a person's prior experience; food for the hungry person, warmth for the cold person, and cessation of pain for a person who is hurting would all be classified as primary reinforcers. A **secondary reinforcer**, in contrast, is a stimulus that becomes reinforcing because of its association with a primary reinforcer. For instance, we know that money is valuable because it allows us to obtain other desirable objects, including primary reinforcers such as food and shelter; money thus becomes a secondary reinforcer.

What makes something a reinforcer is very individualistic. While a Hershey bar may act as a reinforcer for one person, an individual who hates chocolate might find 50 cents much more desirable. The only way we can know if a stimulus is a reinforcer for a given organism is to observe whether the rate of response of a previously occurring behavior increases after the presentation of the stimulus.

Positive reinforcers, negative reinforcers, and punishment. In many respects, reinforcers can be thought of in terms of rewards; both a reinforcer and a reward increase the probability that a preceding response will occur again. But the term "reward" is limited to *positive* occurrences, and this is where it differs from a reinforcer—for it turns out that reinforcers can be positive or negative.

A **positive reinforcer** is a stimulus added to the environment that brings about an increase in a preceding response. If food, water, money, or praise is provided following a response, it is more likely that that response will occur again in the future. The paycheck I get at the end of the month, for example, increases the likelihood that I will work the following month.

In contrast, a **negative reinforcer** refers to a stimulus whose *removal* is reinforcing, leading to an increase in the probability that a preceding response will occur in the future. For example, if you have cold symptoms that are relieved when you take medicine, you are more likely to take the medicine when you experience such symptoms again. Similarly, if the radio is too loud and hurts your ears, you are likely to find that turning it down relieves the situation; lowering the volume is negatively reinforcing and you are more apt to repeat the action in the future. Negative reinforcement, then, teaches the individual that taking an action removes a negative condition that exists in the environment.

It is important to note that negative reinforcement is not the same as punishment. **Punishment** refers to unpleasant or painful stimuli—termed **aversive stimuli**—that are *added* to the environment if a certain behavior occurs; the result is a *decrease* in the probability that that behavior will occur again. In contrast, negative reinforcement is associated with the *removal* of an unpleasant or painful stimulus, which produces an *increase* in the behavior that brought an end to the unpleasant stimulus. If we receive a shock for behaving in a particular fashion, then, we are receiving punishment; but if we are already receiving a shock and do something to stop that shock, the behavior that stops the shock is considered to be negatively reinforced. In the first case, a specific behavior is apt to decrease because of the punishment; in the second, we are likely to increase the behavior because of the negative reinforcement (Azrin & Holt, 1966).

While punishment is typically considered in terms of applying some aversive stimulus—the back of the hand for being disobedient or ten years in jail for committing a crime—it may also consist of the removal of something positive. For instance, when a teenager is told she will no longer be able to use the family car because of her poor grades, or when an employee is informed that he has been demoted with a cut in pay because of poor job evaluations, punishment in the form of the removal of a positive reinforcer is being administered.

The distinctions between the types of punishment, as well as positive and negative reinforcement, may appear confusing at first glance, but the following rules of thumb (and the summary in Table 4-1) can help you to distinguish these concepts from one another:

- Reinforcement is meant to *increase* the behavior preceding it; punishment is meant to *decrease* the behavior preceding it.
- The *application* of a *positive* stimulus is intended to bring about an increase in behavior and is referred to as positive reinforcement; the *removal* of a *positive* stimulus is meant to decrease behavior and is called punishment by removal.
- The *application* of a *negative* stimulus is intended to reduce behavior and is called punishment by application; the *removal* of a *negative* stimulus that results in an increase in behavior is termed negative reinforcement.

TABLE 4-1 TYPES OF REINFORCEMENT AND PUNISHMENT

Nature of Stimulus	Application	Removal or Termination
Positive	*Positive reinforcement* Example: Giving a raise for good performance Result: Increase in frequency of response (good performance)	*Punishment by removal* Example: Removal of favorite toy after misbehavior Result: Decrease in frequency of response (misbehavior)
Negative	*Punishment by application* Example: Giving a spanking following misbehavior Result: Decrease in frequency of response (misbehavior)	*Negative reinforcement* Example: Terminating a headache by taking aspirin Result: Increase in frequency of response (taking aspirin)

Why reinforcement beats punishment: The pros and cons of punishment. Is punishment an effective means of modifying behavior? Punishment often presents the quickest route to changing behavior that, if allowed to continue, might be dangerous to an individual. For instance, we may not have a second chance to warn a child not to run into a busy street, so punishing the first incidence of this behavior might prove to be wise. Moreover, the use of punishment to suppress behavior, even temporarily, provides the opportunity to reinforce a person for behaving in a more desirable way.

There are some instances in which punishment may be the most humane approach to certain deep-seated psychological problems. For example, some children suffer from autism, a rare psychological disorder in which they may abuse themselves, tearing at their skin or banging their heads against the wall, injuring themselves severely in the process. In such cases, punishment in the form of a quick but intense electric shock—sometimes with remarkable results—has been used to prevent self-injurious behavior when all other treatments have failed (Lovaas & Koegel, 1973). Such punishment, however, is used only as a treatment of last resort, keeping the child safe and buying time until positive reinforcement procedures can be initiated.

Several disadvantages make the routine use of punishment questionable. For one thing, it is frequently ineffective, particularly if the punishment is not delivered shortly after the behavior being suppressed occurs

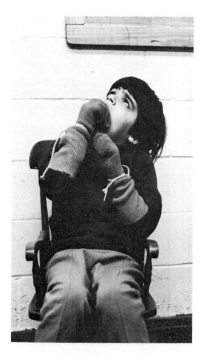

Autistic children must sometimes wear physical restraints to prevent them from injuring themselves when they engage in self-destructive behavior.

or if the individual is able to withdraw from the setting in which the punishment is being given. An employee who is reprimanded by the boss may quit; a teenager who loses the use of the family car may run away from home. In such instances, then, the initial behavior that is being punished may be replaced by one that is even more objectionable.

Even worse, physical punishment may convey to the recipient the idea that physical aggression is permissible and perhaps even desirable. A father who yells and hits his son teaches the son that aggression is an appropriate, adult response, and the son may soon copy his father's behavior and act aggressively toward others. In addition, physical punishment is often administered by people who are themselves angry or enraged. It is unlikely that individuals in such an emotional state will be able to think through what they are doing or to carefully control the degree of punishment they are inflicting.

The use of physical punishment produces the risk that the people administering the punishment will grow to be feared. Furthermore, unless people who are being punished can be made to understand the reasons—that the punishment is meant to change behavior and that it is independent of the punishers' view of them as individuals—punishment may lead to lowered self-esteem.

Finally, punishment does not convey any information about what an alternative, more appropriate behavior might be. In order to be useful in bringing about more desirable behavior in the future, punishment must be paired with specific information about what is being punished, along with information about a more desirable behavior. To punish a child for staring out the window in school may lead her to stare at the floor instead. Unless we teach her the appropriate way to respond, we have just substituted one undesirable behavior for another. If punishment is not combined with reinforcement for alternative behavior that is more appropriate, little will be accomplished. In sum, reinforcing desired behavior is a more appropriate technique for modifying behavior than is using punishment. In the scientific arena, then, reinforcement usually beats punishment (Sulzer-Azaroff & Mayer, 1990).

ASK YOURSELF

How do you describe the learning process known as operant conditioning?

What is a reinforcer, and what is the difference between a positive reinforcer and a negative reinforcer?

How can punishment and negative reinforcement be distinguished?

What are the arguments for and against the use of punishment to produce desired behavior?

> Can you determine that a stimulus will be a reinforcer before trying to see if it works for a particular individual?
>
> Can something be a reinforcer to one person and a punishment to another?

Timing Life's Rewards: Schedules of Reinforcement

The world would be a different place if a cardplayer stopped playing as soon as he was dealt a losing hand, a fisherman stopped fishing as soon as he missed a catch, or a door-to-door salesperson stopped selling at the first house at which she was turned away. The fact that such unreinforced behaviors continue, often with great frequency, illustrates that reinforcement need not be received continually in order for behavior to be learned and maintained. In fact, behavior that is reinforced only occasionally may ultimately be learned better than behavior that is always reinforced.

When we refer to the frequency and timing of reinforcement following desired behavior we are talking about **schedules of reinforcement**. Behavior that is reinforced every time it occurs is said to be on a **continuous reinforcement schedule**; if it is reinforced some but not all of the time, it is on a **partial reinforcement schedule**. Although learning occurs more rapidly under a continuous reinforcement schedule, learned behavior lasts longer after reinforcement stops when it is learned under a partial reinforcement schedule.

Why should partial reinforcement schedules result in stronger, longer-lasting learning than continuous reinforcement schedules? We can answer the question by examining how we might behave when using a soda vending machine compared with a Las Vegas slot machine. When we use a vending machine, prior experience has taught us that the schedule of reinforcement is continuous—every time we put in 75 cents, the reinforcement, a soda, ought to be delivered. In comparison, a slot machine offers a partial reinforcement schedule: We have learned that after putting in 75 cents, most of the time we will not receive anything in return. At the same time, though, we know that we will occasionally win something.

Now suppose that, unbeknownst to us, both the soda vending machine and the slot machine are broken, and neither one is able to dispense anything. It will not be very long before we stop depositing coins into the broken soda machine; probably at most we would try only two or three times before leaving the machine in disgust. But the story would be quite different with the broken slot machine. Here, we would throw in money for a considerably longer time, even though no response would be forthcoming.

In formal terms, we can see the difference between the two reinforcement schedules: Partial reinforcement schedules (such as those provided by slot machines) maintain performance longer than do continuous re-

Because we expect continuous reinforcement from vending machines—e.g., every
time we insert the required coins, we get a
newspaper—we become frustrated very
quickly when the reinforcement is not
forthcoming.

inforcement schedules (such as those established in soda vending machines) before extinction occurs.

Using a **cumulative recorder**, a device that automatically records and
graphs the pattern of responses made in reaction to a particular schedule
(see Figure 4-4), learning psychologists have found that certain kinds of
partial reinforcement schedules produce stronger and lengthier responding before extinction than do others (King & Logue, 1990). Although many
different partial reinforcement schedules have been examined, they can
be most readily classified into two categories: schedules that consider the

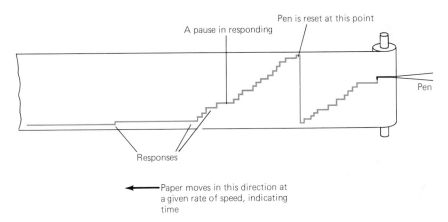

FIGURE 4-4
A cumulative recorder. As the paper slowly unrolls, the pen indicates when a
response has been made by moving a notch upward. Pauses in responding are
indicated by a lack of upward movement of the line. As is the case in this example, it is typical for the time between initial responses to decrease as the organism learns to make the response.

number of responses made before reinforcement is given—called fixed-ratio and variable-ratio schedules—and those that consider the *amount of time* that elapses before reinforcement is provided—called fixed-interval and variable-interval schedules.

Counting responses: Fixed- and variable-ratio schedules. In a **fixed-ratio schedule**, reinforcement is given only after a certain number of responses are made. For instance, a pigeon might receive a food pellet every tenth time it pecked a key; here, the ratio would be 1:10. Similarly, garment workers are generally paid on fixed-ratio schedules: They receive *x* dollars for every ten blouses they sew. Because a greater rate of production means more reinforcement, people on fixed-ratio schedules are apt to work as quickly as possible. Even when rewards are no longer offered, responding comes in bursts—although pauses between bursts become longer and longer until the response peters out entirely (see Figure 4-5).

In a **variable-ratio schedule**, reinforcement occurs after a varying number of responses rather than after a fixed number. Although the specific number of responses necessary to receive reinforcement varies, the number of responses usually hovers around a specific average. Probably the best example of a variable-ratio schedule is that encountered by a door-to-door salesperson. She may make a sale at the third, eighth, ninth, and twentieth houses she visits without being successful at any of the houses in between. Although the number of responses that must be made before making a sale varies, it averages out to a 20 percent success rate. Under these circumstances, you might expect that the salesperson would try to make as many calls as possible in as short a time as possible. This is the case with all variable-ratio schedules; they promote a high rate of response and a high resistance to extinction.

Passing time: Fixed- and variable-interval schedules. In contrast to fixed- and variable-ratio schedules—in which the crucial factor is the number of responses—fixed- and variable-*interval* schedules focus on the amount of *time* that has elapsed since a person or animal was rewarded. One example of a fixed-interval schedule is a weekly paycheck. For people who receive regular, weekly paychecks, it makes little difference how much they produce in a given week—as long as they show up and do *some* work.

Because a **fixed-interval schedule** provides a reinforcement for a response only if a fixed time period has elapsed, overall rates of response are relatively low. This is especially true in the period just after reinforcement when the time before another reinforcement is relatively great. Students' study habits often exemplify this reality: If the periods between exams are relatively long (meaning that the opportunity for reinforcement for good performance is fairly infrequent), students often study minimally or not at all until the day of the exam draws near. Just before the exam,

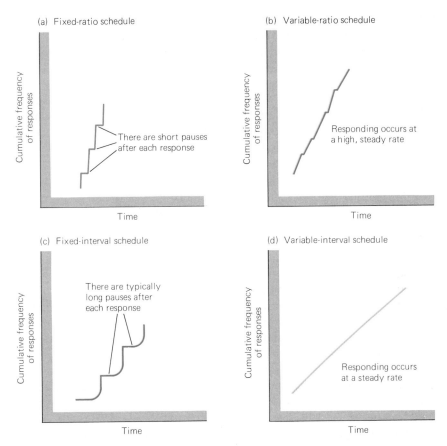

FIGURE 4-5
Typical outcomes of different reinforcement schedules. (*a*) In a fixed-ratio schedule, short pauses occur following each response. Because the more responses,
the more reinforcement, fixed-ratio schedules produce a high rate of responding. (*b*) In a variable-ratio schedule, responding also occurs at a high rate. (*c*) A
fixed interval schedule produces lower rates of responding, especially just after
reinforcement has been presented, since the organism learns that a specified
time period must elapse between reinforcement. (*d*) A variable-interval schedule
produces a fairly steady stream of responses.

however, students begin to cram for it, signaling a rapid increase in the
rate of their studying response (Mawhinney et al., 1971). As you might
expect, just after the exam there is a rapid decline in the rate of responding,
with few people opening a book the day after a test.

One way to decrease the delay in responding that occurs just after
reinforcement, and to maintain the desired behavior more consistently throughout an interval, is to use a **variable-interval schedule**. In a
variable-interval schedule, the time between reinforcements varies around

some average rather than being fixed. For example, a professor who gives surprise quizzes that vary from one every three days to one every three weeks, averaging one every two weeks, is using a variable-interval schedule. Students' study habits would most likely be very different as a result of such an unpredictable schedule than those we observed with a fixed-interval schedule: Students would be apt to study more regularly since they would never know when the next surprise quiz would be coming. Variable-interval schedules, in general, are more likely to produce relatively steady rates of responding than are fixed-interval schedules, with responses that take longer to extinguish after reinforcement ends.

Distinguishing the Right Stimulus from the Wrong: Discrimination and Generalization in Operant Conditioning

It does not take a child long to learn that a red light at an intersection means stop, while a green light indicates that it is permissible to continue. Just as in classical conditioning, then, operant learning involves the phenomena of discrimination and generalization.

The process by which people learn to discriminate stimuli is known as stimulus control training. In **stimulus control training**, an organism is reinforced in the presence of a specific stimulus, but not in its absence. For example, one of the most difficult discriminations many people face is determining when someone's friendliness is not mere friendliness, but a signal of romantic interest. People learn to make the discrimination by observing the presence of certain subtle nonverbal cues—such as increased eye contact and touching—that indicate romantic interest; when such cues are absent, they learn that no romantic interest is indicated. In this case, the nonverbal cue acts as a **discriminative stimulus**, one to which an organism learns to respond during stimulus control training. A discriminative stimulus signals the likelihood that reinforcement will follow a response. For example, if you wait until your roommate is in a good mood before asking to borrow her favorite record, your behavior can be said to be under stimulus control.

Just as in classical conditioning, the phenomenon of stimulus generalization, in which an organism learns a response to one stimulus and then applies it to other stimuli, is also found in operant conditioning. If you have learned that being polite produces the reinforcement of getting your way in a certain situation, you are likely to generalize your response to other situations. Sometimes, though, generalization can have unfortunate consequences, such as when people behave negatively toward all members of a racial group because they have had an unpleasant experience with one member of the racial group.

Superstitious Behavior

Whenever Phil Esposito, a hockey star for eighteen years, drove to a game, he always wore a black tie and always passed through the same tollbooth he had driven through on the way to his last winning game. When he arrived at the site of the game, he would put on the black turtleneck he wore when he became the team's high scorer. He then arranged his wardrobe in a particular order (underwear, pants, skates, and laces), and was sure to include a pack of gum plus one additional stick of gum. Next, he arranged his skating paraphernalia with black tape on the bottom, then white tape, and then his gloves, which he carefully aligned and placed palms up on each side of his hockey stick. As the game was about to start he would say a Hail Mary and the Lord's Prayer and would pray that his team played well and that the game would be free of injuries. *Then* he was ready to play hockey.

While it is easy to scoff at Phil Esposito's elaborate pregame ritual of **superstitious behavior**, such behavior is relatively common among athletes (Zimmer, 1984). In fact, many of us have some superstitions of our own; wearing a special shirt when we take a test or go for a job interview, telling ourselves that if we make all the traffic lights on a certain road we'll have good luck for the rest of the day, or—an old favorite—avoiding a black cat in our path.

Where do such superstitions come from? To learning psychologists, there is a simple answer, having to do with the principles of reinforcement (Justice & Looney, 1990). As we have discussed, behavior that is followed by a reinforcer tends to be strengthened. Occasionally, however, the behavior that occurs prior to the reinforcement is entirely coincidental. Imagine, for instance, that a baseball player hits his bat against the ground three times in a row and then gets a home run. The hit is, of course, coincidental to the batter's hitting the ground, but to the player it may be seen as somehow related. Because the association is made in the player's mind, he may hit the ground three times every time he is at bat in the future. And because he will be at least partially reinforced for this behavior—batters usually get a hit 25 percent of the time—his ground-hitting behavior will probably be maintained.

Superstitious behavior is learned through the coincidental association between an idea, object, or behavior and subsequent reinforcement. Because the number 13 has come to be associated with bad luck, many buildings do not include a thirteenth floor.

PSYCHOLOGY AND SOCIETY

A Pigeon Posse: Saving Lives with Operant Conditioning

Your sailboat has capsized in the Pacific and you have been drifting for three days. Your mouth is dry, your stomach hungers for food, and you don't know how much longer you can hang on to the side of the boat. Suddenly, you see a speck in the sky off in the distance. It gets closer and closer until it is flying directly above, and you can see on it the markings of a Coast Guard rescue helicopter. As it hovers above, you wonder how you will ever be able to repay the pilots of the helicopter who have saved your life.

Actually, if you did thank the pilots for rescuing you, you might well be thanking the wrong species. For in reality you might owe your life to three pigeons caged in the belly of the helicopter.

These pigeons, trained in Sea Hunt, a Navy program currently under development, represent a dramatic example of the use of operant conditioning principles. The director of the Sea Hunt project, James Simmons, has taken ordinary pigeons and, using operant conditioning, trained them to peck a series of keys at the sight of an orange speck in the ocean—such as a downed sailor wearing a life jacket (Cusack, 1984).

The training uses basic shaping procedures: Pigeons are first taught in a Skinner box to peck a key to receive food, and then to peck it only when an orange light is present. Next, the size of the light is decreased so the pigeons learn to peck only when an orange speck of light is present.

(Lasers are used to control with exact precision the size of the light beam.) Finally the pigeons are taken out to sea and taught to peck at the key only when they see an orange stimulus in the ocean. The entire training process takes from six to ten months (Simmons, 1984).

In operation, the Sea Hunt system is simplicity itself. When the pigeons, which are strapped in the belly of a search helicopter (see Figure 4-6), peck a key to indicate the sighting of an orange stimulus, a signal is sent to the pilot. With three trained birds being used simultaneously, each in a separate chamber with a different viewing area, the pilot knows in what direction to orient the search. Because their visual acuity is far superior to that of humans, pigeons can spot a target 90 percent of the time the first time they are over an area—considerably better than the 40 percent success rates of human searchers. Moreover, they are less apt to be affected by sun glare and the problems of concentration and boredom that pilots experience during long searches.

Because the Sea Hunt system is effective, easy to use, reliable, and economical, the Navy is giving serious consideration to routinely using pigeons trained through operant conditioning as part of rescue operations. If you are ever stranded at sea, then, you should not be too surprised if you are saved not by a human search party but by a feathered one.

Do superstitions actually affect subsequent behavior? In fact, they do. According to some psychologists, superstitious behavior allows people to cope with anxiety by providing routines or rituals that can give them a sense of control over a situation (Zimmer, 1984). In this way, wearing a "lucky" shirt helps to calm a person—which, in fact, may lead to better performance when taking a test or during a stressful interview. As you can see, then, your superstitions may shape your subsequent behavior.

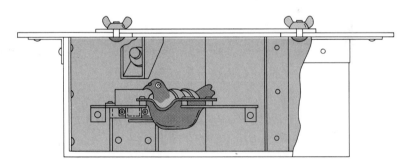

FIGURE 4-6
In the Sea Hunt system, pigeons trained by operant conditioning to identify downed sailors wearing orange life jackets are strapped into the
belly of a search helicopter. When a pigeon spots an appropriate stimulus, it pecks a key, which alerts the helicopter pilot. (Based on Simmons,
1984.)

Reinforcing What Doesn't Come Naturally: Shaping

Consider the difficulty of using operant conditioning to teach people to repair an automobile transmission. If you had to wait until they fixed it perfectly before you provided them with reinforcement, the Model T might be back in style long before they ever mastered the repair.

There are many complex behaviors, ranging from auto repair to zebra hunting, which we would not expect to occur naturally as part of anyone's spontaneous behavior. In cases such as these, in which there otherwise might be no opportunity to provide reinforcement for the particular behavior (since it never occurs in the first place), a procedure known as shaping is used. **Shaping** is the process of teaching a complex behavior by rewarding closer and closer approximations of the desired behavior. In shaping, any behavior that is at all similar to the behavior you want the person to learn is reinforced at first. Later, you reinforce only responses that are closer to the behavior you ultimately want to teach. Finally, you reinforce only the desired response. Each step in shaping, then, moves only slightly beyond the previously learned behavior, permitting the person to link the new step to the behavior learned earlier.

Shaping even allows lower animals to learn complex responses that naturally would never occur, ranging from porpoises trained to jump through hoops and walk on the water with their tails, to pigeons trained to rescue people lost at sea (see the Psychology and Society box). Shaping also underlies the learning of many complex human skills. For instance, the organization of most textbooks is based on the principles of shaping. Typically, material is presented so that new material builds on previously learned concepts or skills. Thus the concept of shaping could not be presented in this chapter until we had discussed the more basic principles of operant learning.

Where Professors Are Programs: Using Programmed Instruction in College Classes

> Chemistry students can mix chemicals to their hearts' delight without risk of explosion. Medical students can perform simulated operations without endangering a patient's life. Physics students can see the path electrons travel in response to different forces (Pollack, 1987, p. D6).

The opportunity to carry out each of these activities comes not from a resourceful and clever classroom teacher but from an inanimate replacement: a computer. According to proponents of the use of computers to teach college students, the increasingly widespread availability of computers and an increase in computer literacy on many college campuses will lead to a revolution in instruction. In this view, computers may be routinely used to supplement human instruction, or to teach courses entirely, in the not-too-distant future.

The use of computers in classrooms is based on a procedure first developed some sixty years ago (Benjamin, 1988). Called programmed instruction or computer-assisted instruction, it represents one of the most common applications of shaping (Cherry, 1983; Skinner, 1984). **Programmed instruction** explicitly uses the principles of learning in the design of instructional material. A student using such material is first asked to type into the computer very simple responses that are printed on the screen; then the student moves on to increasingly complex problems. Correct responses are immediately reinforced, while mistakes evoke a review of previous material. The reinforcement for correct responses may be explicit, in the form of encouragement printed on the screen ("Good," "Great job, Wendy," "Keep it up," and the like), or the user may simply be allowed to move on to the next part of the lesson, which in itself can act as a powerful reinforcer. Each correct response shapes the student's behavior to bring him or her closer to the final desired behavior—mastery of a relatively complex body of material.

The advantages of using programmed instruction are many (Hassett & Dukes, 1986). Computers never become fatigued, and they are available whenever the student is. Sophisticated programs can critically analyze students' patterns of errors and present material in a manner that is specifically suited to the learning capabilities of the student. In addition, the computer is capable of providing sophisticated simulations that permit students to experience situations that would otherwise be physically impossible or excessively expensive. State-of-the-art computers use optical discs—newer versions of the compact discs used for music—to deliver stereo sound, photos, and moving pictures, along with enough written text to fill a small library (Rogers, 1988).

For instance, using one computer program, students can learn physiology by determining how the power exerted by a muscle varies with the muscle's length and the weight of the load it must lift. They can also "participate" in a bicycle race on the video screen, experimenting with the effects of shifting gears to modify the output of certain muscles (Pollack, 1987).

Programmed instruction is not without its critics, however. Some people feel that the excessive use of simulations will not provide students with an understanding of what actually happens in the real world, such as when laboratory experiments go awry. Others feel that the inability of students to ask questions beyond those that have been programmed is too restrictive. Still, most data suggest that carefully designed programmed instruction can be an effective teaching technique (Wilkinson, 1983; Mandl & Lesgold, 1988; Burns, Parlett, & Luckhardt-Redfield, 1990).

Discriminating between Classical and Operant Conditioning

Up to this point, we have been discussing classical and operant conditioning as though they were two entirely distinct approaches. However, these two types of conditioning share several features.

For example, generalization and discrimination processes are found in operant conditioning, just as they are in classical conditioning. A pigeon that has learned to peck a red key to receive food will probably do the same thing to a blue key, illustrating that generalization has occurred. Similarly, discrimination processes are also present in operant conditioning. When a child learns from the reinforcers his parent provides that he ought to stay away from strangers but be polite and friendly to acquaintances, we can see an example of discrimination.

The fact that generalization and discrimination are present in both classical and operant conditioning suggests that the distinction between these two types of learning is not always clear-cut. Consider, for instance, what happens when you are called into the house for dinner. As you hear the call for dinner, you begin to salivate, and the smells of the food get stronger as you walk toward the kitchen. You quickly reach the table and receive your reward for coming: a big helping of roast beef, potatoes, and salad.

Is your behavior the result of classical conditioning or operant conditioning? Actually, it is both. Your salivation reflects classical conditioning; you have learned to associate being called in to dinner with the food that follows it. But the footsteps taking you to the table, which actually allow you to receive the reinforcement of food, reflect a behavioral pattern learned through operant conditioning; you have purposefully responded in a way that gets you a reward.

As you see, the distinction between classical and operant conditioning is not always clear when we consider specific instances of behavior, since both processes are often at work in terms of a particular sequence of behavior. Moreover, even some of the most basic differences between operant and classical conditioning have been called into question. For example, as we discussed in Chapter 2, people are able to learn to control "involuntary" responses, such as blood pressure and heart rate, through biofeedback. What would typically be thought of as a response involving classical conditioning, then, can be viewed in terms of operant conditioning.

Although many questions remain regarding classical and operant conditioning (Rescorla, 1988; Rachlin, 1990; Spear, Miller, & Jagielo, 1990), the two processes are distinct in most of the cases of behavior that psychologists analyze: In classical conditioning, the unconditioned stimulus precedes the response; the response is elicited by the unconditioned stimulus. In operant conditioning, in contrast, the response is made prior to the reinforcement and is therefore performed intentionally—that is, the response is made to obtain the reward. In classical conditioning, then, the response is basically involuntary, whereas in operant conditioning the response is voluntary.

You Can't Teach an Old Dog Difficult Tricks: Biological Constraints on Learning

Keller and Marian Breland were pleased with their idea. As professional animal trainers for the circus, they came up with the notion of having a pig place a wooden disk into a piggy bank. With their experience in training animals through operant conditioning, they thought the task would be easy to teach, given that it was certainly well within the range of the pig's physical capabilities. Yet every time they tried out the procedure, it failed: Upon viewing the disk, the pigs were willing to do nothing but root the wooden disk along the ground. Apparently, the pigs were biologically programmed to push stimuli in the shape of disks along the ground.

Their lack of success with porkers led the Brelands to substitute a raccoon. Although the procedure worked fine with one disk, when two disks were used, the raccoon refused to deposit either of them and instead rubbed the two together, as if it were washing them. Once again, it appeared that the disks evoked biologically innate behaviors that were impossible to supplant with even the most exhaustive training (Breland & Breland, 1961).

The Brelands' difficulties illustrate an important point: Not all behaviors can be trained in all species equally well. Instead, there are **biological constraints**, built-in limitations, in the ability of animals to learn particular behaviors. In some cases, an organism will have a special bent that will aid in its learning a behavior (such as behaviors which involve pecking in pigeons); in other cases, biological constraints will act to prevent or inhibit an organism from learning a behavior. In either instance, it is clear that animals have specialized learning mechanisms which influence how readily both classical and operant conditioning function, and each species is biologically primed to develop particular kinds of associations and to face obstacles in learning others (Klein & Mowter, 1989b).

*A*SK YOURSELF

Does reinforcement need to be constant in order for behavior to be learned and maintained?

What is the difference between fixed-ratio and variable-ratio schedules of reinforcement?

How is reinforcement supplied in fixed-interval and variable-interval schedules?

What are generalization, discrimination, and shaping?

Can learning of complex tasks, such as reading and writing, be explained by principles of operant and classical conditioning?

If a parent responds to a baby crying at night by periodically comforting the infant, what would be the likely result, according to learning theory?

THINKING ABOUT LEARNING THEORY: COGNITIVE APPROACHES TO LEARNING

The criminal in the television movie hits a police officer's head against a brick wall. By knocking the officer out, the criminal manages to escape. He smiles triumphantly and coolly steps on the body as he runs away.

◆ ◆ ◆

An 8-year-old boy, who has seen the movie the previous evening, gets into a fight with his brother. Although in the past the fights have never involved physical violence, this time the boy knocks his brother into a wall and tries to step on him.

The impetus for the boy's new behavior is clear: It is the television movie. But the underlying process that accounts for his conduct cannot easily be explained by either classical or operant conditioning. Knocking people into a wall would not seem to be either an unconditioned or a conditioned response, nor, given the fact that the boy had never had fights of this sort in the past, would he have had the opportunity to be reinforced for such behavior. Instances such as these suggest that some kinds of learning involve higher-order thinking processes in which people's thoughts and memories and the way they process information account for their responses.

Some psychologists have concentrated on the thought processes that underlie learning—an approach known as **cognitive learning theory**. Although psychologists using cognitive learning theory do not deny the importance of classical and operant conditioning, they have developed approaches that focus on the unseen mental processes that occur during the learning process, rather than concentrating solely on external stimuli, responses, and reinforcements.

In its most basic formulation, cognitive learning theory suggests that it is not enough to say that people make responses because there is a hypothetical link between a stimulus and a response due to a past history of reinforcement for the response. Instead, according to this point of view, people—and even animals—develop an *expectation* that they will receive a reinforcer upon making a response.

Evidence for this point of view comes from a famous series of experiments that revealed a type of cognitive learning called **latent learning**. In latent learning, a new behavior is learned but is not demonstrated until reinforcement is provided for displaying it (Tolman & Honzik, 1930). In the studies, the behavior of rats in a maze such as that shown in Figure 4-7a was examined. In one representative experiment, a group of rats was allowed to wander around the maze once a day for seventeen days without ever receiving any reward; understandably, these rats made many errors and spent a relatively long time reaching the end of the maze. A second group, however, was always given food at the end of the maze, and these rats learned to run quickly and directly to the food box, making few errors.

A third group of rats started out in the same situation as the unrewarded rats, but only for the first ten days. On the eleventh day, a critical experimental manipulation was instituted: From that point on, the rats in this group were given food for completing the maze. The results of this manipulation were dramatic, as you can see from the graph in Figure 4-7b. The previously unrewarded rats, who had earlier seemed to wander about aimlessly, showed reductions in running time and declines in error rates that almost immediately matched those of the group that had received rewards from the start.

To cognitive theorists, it seemed clear that the unrewarded rats had learned the layout of the maze early in their explorations; they just never displayed their latent learning until the reinforcement was offered. Instead, the rats seemed to develop a **cognitive map** of the maze—a mental representation of spatial locations and directions.

People, too, develop cognitive maps of their surroundings, based primarily on particular landmarks (Garling, 1989). When they first encounter a new environment, their maps tend to rely on specific paths—such as the directions we might give someone unfamiliar with an area: "Turn right at the stop sign, make a left at the bridge, and then go up the hill." However, as people become more familiar with an area, they develop an overall conception of it and an abstract cognitive map of the area. Using such a map, they are eventually able to take shortcuts as they develop a broad understanding of the area.

Unfortunately, though, our cognitive maps are often riddled with errors, representing simplifications of the actual terrain. We tend to develop maps that ignore curving roads and instead conceive of areas in terms of straight grids of intersecting roadways (Tversky, 1981). Our cognitive maps, then, are imperfect versions of actual maps.

Despite their inadequacies, the possibility that we develop our cognitive maps through latent learning presents something of a problem for strict reinforcement theorists. If we consider the results of Tolman's maze experiment, for instance, it is unclear what the specific reinforcement was that allowed the rats that received no reward to initially learn about the layout of the maze, since there was no obvious reinforcer present. Although we might speculate on the presence of internal reinforcers—such as the fulfillment of the organism's curiosity—such talk leaves behavioral psychologists uneasy. Given their focus on external and environmental

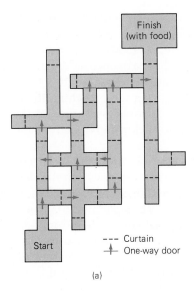

(a)

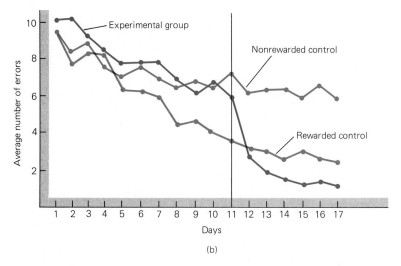

(b)

FIGURE 4-7

(*a*) In an attempt to demonstrate latent learning, rats were allowed to roam through a maze of this sort once a day for seventeen days.

(*b*) Those rats that were never rewarded (the nonrewarded control condition) consistently made the most errors, whereas those that received food at the finish every day (the rewarded control condition) made far fewer errors. But the results also showed latent learning: Rats that were initially unrewarded but began to be rewarded only after the tenth day (the experimental group) showed an immediate reduction in errors and soon matched the error rate of the rats that had been consistently rewarded. According to cognitive learning theorists, the reduction in errors indicates that the rats had developed a cognitive map—a mental representation—of the maze. (Tolman & Honzik, 1930.)

reinforcement, psychologists who rely on operant conditioning explanations of learning are left with a theoretical question that has yet to be resolved satisfactorily.

Learning through Imitation: Observational Learning

Although latent learning suggests how a behavior may be learned but not demonstrated, it does not explain the case of the boy who imitates a response that he has earlier observed in a television movie. In order to account for how a person who has no direct experience in carrying out a particular behavior learns and carries out the behavior, psychologists have proposed another form of cognitive learning: observational learning.

According to psychologist Albert Bandura and colleagues, a major part of human learning consists of **observational learning**, which they define as learning through observing the behavior of another person, a **model** (Bandura, 1977). Bandura and his colleagues demonstrated rather dramatically the ability of models to stimulate learning. In what is now considered a classic experiment, young children saw a movie of an adult wildly hitting a 5-foot-tall inflatable punching toy called a Bobo doll (Bandura, Ross & Ross, 1963). Later the children were given the opportunity to play with the Bobo doll themselves and, sure enough, they displayed the same kind of behavior, in some cases mimicking the aggressive behavior almost identically.

It is not only negative behaviors that are acquired through observational learning. In one experiment, for example, children who were afraid of dogs were exposed to a model—dubbed the Fearless Peer—playing with a dog (Bandura, Grusec & Menlove, 1967). Following exposure, observers were considerably more likely to approach a strange dog than were children who had not viewed the Fearless Peer.

According to Bandura, observational learning takes place in four steps: (1) paying attention and perceiving the most critical features of another person's behavior; (2) remembering the behavior; (3) reproducing

Observational learning has taken place when a child imitates a behavior which she or he has seen someone else display.

the action; and (4) being motivated to learn and carry out the behavior. Instead of learning occurring through trial and error, then, with successes being reinforced and failures punished, many important skills are learned through observational processes.

Observational learning is particularly important in acquiring skills in which shaping is inappropriate. Piloting an airplane and performing brain surgery, for example, would hardly be behaviors that could be learned using trial-and-error methods without grave cost—literally—to those involved in the learning.

Not all behavior that we witness is learned or carried out, of course. One crucial factor that determines whether we later imitate a model depends on the consequences of the model's behavior. If we observe a friend being rewarded for putting more time into her studies by receiving higher grades, we are more likely to model her behavior than if her behavior results in no increase in grades but rather greater fatigue and less social life. Models who are rewarded for behaving in a particular way are more apt to be mimicked than models who receive punishment. Interestingly, though, observing the punishment of a model does not necessarily stop observers from learning the behavior. Observers can still recount the model's behavior—they are just less apt to perform it (Bandura, 1977).

Accepting the Unacceptable: Learned Helplessness

Have you ever heard someone say, "You can't fight city hall"; "No matter how hard I study I'll never pass this course"; or "I'll never learn to play tennis, regardless of how much I practice"? According to psychologist Martin Seligman, each of these statements may represent an example of **learned helplessness**, the learned belief of a person or animal that no control can be exerted over the environment (Seligman, 1975).

Learned helplessness was first demonstrated in experiments in which dogs were exposed to a series of moderately painful but not physically damaging shocks that they could not avoid. Although at first the dogs tried desperately to escape, they eventually accepted the shocks. But the next phase of the experiment was the most revealing: The dogs were placed in a box with two compartments, separated by a low barrier that they could easily jump over. By jumping the barrier, they could avoid any shock administered in the first compartment. In comparison with dogs who had not received shocks previously and who quickly learned to jump into the next compartment, the dogs who had received the inescapable shocks earlier tended to give up rapidly, lie down, and wait for the shock to be over. The conclusion drawn by Seligman was that the dogs had learned to be helpless. They expected that nothing they did would be useful in preventing the shocks and therefore simply accepted them.

People, too, can learn to be helpless (Mineka & Hendersen, 1985). For example, in one experiment, groups of college students were exposed to a loud tone from which they could not escape. When later they were asked to complete a task and were given the opportunity to avoid a loud noise, they made fewer attempts to escape and performed more poorly than a control group of subjects completing the task who had earlier been exposed to a tone from which they could escape. The students had seemingly learned to be helpless in the face of something that, if they had only tried, they could have escaped (Hiroto & Seligman, 1975).

The concept of learned helplessness provides an explanation for several puzzling phenomena. For instance, battered children sometimes do not seek relief even when given the oppportunity and may come to accept their beatings. One explanation is that they have learned helplessness in the face of what they perceive to be inescapable punishment. Similarly, as we will discuss in Chapter 10, learned helplessness may underlie cases of severe human depression in which people come to feel that they are victims of events beyond their control and are helpless in their environment.

The Unresolved Controversy of Cognitive Learning Theory

The degree to which learning is based on unseen internal factors rather than on external factors remains one of the major issues dividing learning theorists today (Amsel, 1988). Both classical conditioning and operant conditioning consider learning in terms of external stimuli and responses—a kind of "black box" analysis in which all that matters are the observable features of the environment, not what goes on inside a person's head. To the cognitive learning theorists, such an analysis misses the mark; what is crucial is the mental activity—in the form of thoughts and expectations—that takes place.

Some psychologists feel that neither approach, by itself, is sufficient to explain all learning. Rather than viewing behavioral and cognitive approaches as contradictory, they see them as addressing learning through differing but complementary approaches. Such a theoretical outlook has allowed psychologists to make important advances in such areas as the treatment of certain kinds of abnormal behavior, as we will see in Chapter 10.

Still, while the controversy surrounding different approaches to learning rages on as a major issue of psychology, tremendous advances are taking place in the practical application of principles derived from the various theories (Glaser, 1990).

The Informed Consumer of Psychology: Behavior Analysis and Behavior Modification Procedures

A couple who had been married for three years began to fight more and more frequently. The issues ranged from the petty, such as who was going to do the dishes, to the more serious, such as the quality of their sex life and whether they found each other interesting. Disturbed about this increasingly unpleasant pattern of interaction, they went to a behavior analyst, a psychologist who specialized in behavior-modification techniques. After interviewing each of them alone and then speaking to them together, he asked them to keep a detailed written record of their interactions over the next two weeks—focusing, in particular, on the events that preceded their arguments.

When they returned two weeks later, he carefully went over the records with them. In doing so, he noticed a pattern that the couple themselves had observed after they had started keeping their records: Each of their arguments had occurred just after one or the other had left some household chore undone. For instance, the wife would go into a fury when she came home from work and found that her husband, a student, had left his dirty lunch dishes on the table and had not even started dinner preparations. The husband would get angry when he found his wife's clothes draped on the only chair in the bedroom; he insisted it was her responsibility to pick up after herself.

Using the data that had been collected, the behavior analyst devised a system for the couple to try out. He asked them to list all of the chores that could possibly arise and assign each one a point value depending on how long it took to complete. Then he had them divide the chores equally and agree in a written contract to fulfill the ones assigned to them. If either failed to carry out one of the assigned chores, he or she would have to place $1 per point in a fund for the other to spend. They also agreed to a program of verbal praise, promising to verbally reward each other for completing a chore.

Although skeptical about the value of such a program, the couple agreed to try it for a month and to keep careful records of the number of arguments they had during this period. To their surprise, the number declined rapidly, and even the more basic issues in their marriage seemed on the way to being resolved.

The case described above illustrates **behavior modification**, a formalized technique for promoting the frequency of desirable behaviors and decreasing the incidence of unwanted ones. Using the basic principles of learning theory, behavior-modification techniques have proved to be helpful in a variety of situations (Wielkiewicz, 1985). Severely retarded people have learned the rudiments of language and, for the first time in their lives, have started dressing and feeding themselves. Behavior modification has also helped people to lose weight, give up smoking, and behave more safely (Cooper, Heron & Heward, 1987).

The variety of techniques used by behavior analysts is as varied as the list of processes that modify behavior—including the use of reinforcement scheduling, shaping, generalization training, discrimination training, and extinction. Behavioral approaches do, however, typically follow a series of similar basic steps in a behavior-change program (Royer & Feldman, 1984). These steps include:

- Identifying goals and target behaviors. The first step is to define "desired behavior." Is it an increase in time spent studying? A decrease in weight? A reduction in the amount of aggression displayed by a child? The goals must be stated in observable terms and lead to specific targets. For instance, a goal might be "to increase study time," while the target behavior would be "to study at least two hours per day on weekdays and an hour on Saturdays."

- Designing a data-recording system and recording preliminary data. In order to determine whether behavior has changed, it is necessary to collect data before any changes are made in the situation. This provides a baseline against which future changes can be measured.

- Selecting a behavior-change strategy. The most crucial step is to select an appropriate strategy. Since all the principles of learning can be employed to bring about behavior change, a "package" of treatments is normally used. This might include the systematic use of positive reinforcement for desired behavior (verbal praise or something more tangible, such as food), as well as a program of extinction for undesirable behavior (ignoring a child who throws a tantrum). Selecting the right reinforcers is critical; you may have to experiment a bit to find out what is important to a given individual.

- Implementing the program. The next step is to institute the program. Probably the most important aspect of program implementation is consistency; if the program is not consistently applied, the chances for success are greatly reduced. It is also important to make sure that you are reinforcing the behavior you want to reinforce. For example, suppose you want a child to spend more time on her homework, but as soon as she sits down to study, she asks for a snack. If you get one for her, you are likely reinforcing her delaying tactic, not her studying. Instead, you might tell her that you will provide her with a snack after a certain time interval has gone by during which she has studied—thereby using the snack as a reinforcement for studying.

- Keeping careful records after the program is implemented. Another crucial task is record keeping; if the target behaviors are not monitored, there is no way of knowing whether the program has actually been successful. Don't rely on your memory, because it is all too easy for memory lapses to occur.

- Evaluating and altering the ongoing program. Finally, the results of the program should be compared with preimplementation data to determine its effectiveness. If successful, the procedures employed can be gradually phased out. For instance, if the program called for reinforcing every instance of picking up one's clothes from the bedroom floor, the reinforcement schedule could be modified to a fixed-ratio schedule in which every third instance was reinforced. On the other hand, if the program had not been successful in bringing about the desired behavior change, consideration of other approaches might be advisable.

ASK YOURSELF

What is the focus of cognitive learning theory?

How does modeling underlie some forms of learning?

What is learned helplessness?

How can behavior modification techniques be used to change your own behavior and the behavior of others?

How would cognitive learning theory account for the fact that child abusers were often abused themselves as children?

How could you use the concept of learned helplessness to understand the problems of the urban poor, and what solutions to the problem of poverty does learned helplessness suggest?

LOOKING BACK

1. Learning, a relatively permanent change in behavior due to experience, is a basic topic of psychology, although it is a process that must be assessed indirectly. (We can only assume that learning has occurred by observing performance, which is susceptible to such factors as fatigue and lack of effort.)

2. One major form of learning is known as classical conditioning. First studied by Ivan Pavlov, classical conditioning occurs when a neutral stimulus—one that brings about no relevant response—is repeatedly paired with a stimulus (called an unconditioned stimulus) that brings about a natural, untrained response. For instance, a neutral stimulus might be a buzzer; an unconditioned stimulus might be a dish of ice cream. The response ice cream might bring about in a hungry person—salivation—is called an unconditioned response; it occurs naturally, owing to the physical makeup of the individual being trained.

3. The actual conditioning occurs when the neutral stimulus is repeatedly presented just before the unconditioned stimulus. After repeated pairings, the neutral stimulus begins to bring about the same response as the unconditioned stimulus. When this occurs, we can say that the neutral stimulus is now a conditioned stimulus, and the response made to it is the conditioned response. For example, after a person has learned to salivate to the sound of the buzzer, we say the buzzer is a conditioned stimulus, and the salivation is a conditioned response.

4. Learning is not always permanent, however. Extinction occurs when a previously learned response weakens and eventually disappears. Extinction provides the basis for systematic desensitization, a treatment designed to decrease people's strong, irrational fears.

5. Stimulus generalization occurs when a conditioned response follows a stimulus that is similar to the original conditioned stimulus. The greater the similarity between the two stimuli, the greater the likelihood of stimulus generalization; the closer the new stimulus to the old one,

the more similar the new response. The converse phenomenon, stimulus discrimination, occurs when an organism learns to respond to one stimulus but not to another.

6. Higher-order conditioning occurs when an established conditioned stimulus is paired with a neutral stimulus, and the new neutral stimulus comes to evoke the same conditioned response as the original conditioned stimulus. The neutral stimulus changes, then, into another conditioned stimulus.

7. A second major form of learning is operant conditioning. According to B. F. Skinner, the major factor underlying learning is the reinforcer—any stimulus that increases the probability that the preceding response will occur again.

8. We can determine whether a stimulus is a reinforcer only by observing its effects upon behavior. If behavior increases, the stimulus is, by definition, a reinforcer. Primary reinforcers involve rewards that are naturally effective without prior exposure because they satisfy a biological need. Secondary reinforcers, in contrast, begin to act as if they were primary reinforcers through frequent pairings with a primary reinforcer.

9. Positive reinforcers are stimuli that are added to the environment and lead to an increase in a preceding response. Negative reinforcers are stimuli whose removal from the environment leads to an increase in the preceding response.

10. Punishment is the administration of an unpleasant stimulus following a response in order to produce a decrease in the incidence of that response. Punishment is also characterized by the removal of a positive reinforcer. In contrast to reinforcement, in which the goal is to increase the incidence of behavior, punishment is meant to decrease or suppress behavior.

11. Schedules and patterns of reinforcement affect the strength and duration of learning. Generally, partial reinforcement schedules—in which reinforcers are not delivered on every trial—produce stronger and longer-lasting learning than do continuous reinforcement schedules.

12. Among the major categories of reinforcement schedules are fixed- and variable-ratio schedules, which are based on the number of responses made, and fixed- and variable-interval schedules, which are based on the time interval that elapses before reinforcement is provided when a desired response occurs.

13. Generalization and discrimination are phenomena that operate in operant conditioning as well as classical conditioning. Generalization occurs when an organism makes the same or a similar response to a new stimulus that it has learned to make in the past to a similar stimulus. Discrimination occurs when the organism responds to one stimulus, but does not respond to a similar (but different) stimulus.

14. Superstitious behavior is the mistaken belief that particular ideas, objects, or behavior will cause certain events to occur, as a result of learning that is based on the coincidental association between a stimulus and subsequent reinforcement.

15. Shaping is a process for teaching complex behaviors by rewarding closer and closer approximations of the desired final behavior. Shaping forms the basis for learning and teaching many everyday skills and is central to presenting complicated information in textbooks and in computerized programmed instruction.

16. There are biological constraints, or built-in limitations, on the ability of an organism to learn. Because of these constraints, certain behaviors will be relatively easy to learn, whereas other behaviors will be either difficult or impossible to learn.

17. Cognitive learning seeks to explain phenomena such as latent learning—in which a new behavior is learned but not performed until reinforcement is provided for its performance—and the apparent development of cognitive maps. Learning also occurs through the observation of the behavior of others, known as models. The

major factor that determines whether a behavior will actually be performed is the nature of reinforcement or punishment a model receives. Learned helplessness, the learned belief of a person or animal that it cannot exert control over the environ- ment, also suggests the importance of cognitive processes in learning.

18. Behavior modification is a method for formally using the principles of learning theory to promote the frequency of desired behaviors and to decrease or eliminate unwanted ones.

Key Terms and Concepts

learning (p. 133)
maturation (p. 134)
classical conditioning (p. 135)
neutral stimulus (p. 136)
unconditioned stimulus (UCS) (p. 136)
unconditioned response (UCR) (p. 136)
conditioned stimulus (CS) (p. 136)
conditioned response (CR) (p. 136)
extinction (p. 139)
systematic desensitization (p. 139)
spontaneous recovery (p. 140)
stimulus generalization (p. 140)
stimulus discrimination (p. 141)
higher-order conditioning (p. 142)
operant conditioning (p. 143)
law of effect (p. 144)
reinforcer (p. 145)
primary reinforcer (p. 145)
secondary reinforcer (p. 146)
positive reinforcer (p. 146)
negative reinforcer (p. 146)
punishment (p. 146)

aversive stimulus (p. 146)
schedules of reinforcement (p. 150)
continuous reinforcement (p. 150)
partial reinforcement (p. 150)
cumulative recorder (p. 151)
fixed-ratio schedule (p. 152)
variable-ratio schedule (p. 152)
fixed-interval schedule (p. 152)
variable-interval schedule (p. 153)
stimulus control training (p. 154)
discriminative stimulus (p. 154)
superstitious behavior (p. 155)
shaping (p. 156)
programmed instruction (p. 159)
biological constraints (p. 161)
cognitive learning theory (p. 162)
latent learning (p. 162)
cognitive map (p. 163)
observational learning (p. 165)
model (p. 165)
learned helplessness (p. 166)
behavior modification (p. 168)

5

Cognition

❖

PROLOGUE: RICHARD FEYNMAN

Physicist Richard Feynman shows how the material which the solid rocket booster O-rings are made of fails in cold weather.

When the *Challenger* space shuttle blew up, killing all the astronauts aboard, it represented more than a human tragedy. To NASA engineers, and the members of a presidential commission appointed to determine the cause of the accident, it also exemplified a scientific puzzle of the most important kind: Without a clear understanding of the reason for the accident, space travel by the United States could not proceed.

To one member of the commission, Nobel-prize winning physicist Richard Feynman, at least part of the answer to the problem was apparent early in the investigation. In a briefing he received soon after being appointed to the commission, Feynman was apprised of a problem with the O-ring seals, which later were judged to be the actual cause of the accident. But Feynman was frustrated in his attempts to pursue the issue. When he tried to obtain information from the NASA bureaucracy about the resiliency of the O-ring rubber at low temperatures, he received only a stack of papers with the answer to a question he didn't ask.

Feynman was ultimately able to obtain the answer to his question in a novel and eye-opening way. In his words, "Later I'm feeling lousy and I'm eating dinner; I look at the table,

173

and there's a glass of ice water. I think,'Damn it, *I* can find out about the rubber *without* sending notes to NASA and getting back a stack of papers; all I've got to do is get a sample of the rubber, stick it in ice water and see how it responds when I squeeze it!' " (Feynman, 1988, p. 30).

After obtaining a piece of rubber from NASA—not an easy task (NASA is very careful with its supplies, and every piece of material is checked and counted and controlled)—Feynman went to a hardware store to purchase screwdrivers, pliers, clamps, and other supplies needed to carry out a small experiment.

The experiment itself was a simple demonstration. To lower the temperature of the rubber, Feynman thrust it into a pitcher of ice water and left it there for a few minutes. When he took it out, it was brittle and broke apart. To observers, his point had been made: At lowered temperatures, the rubber in the O-rings was rendered inadequate for the job of sealing the rocket joints. The cause of the shuttle accident had been demonstrated in a way the world could understand (Feynman, 1988).

*L*OOKING AHEAD

Feynman's simple demonstration produced an understanding of the causes of the shuttle accident in a simple and elegant manner. In addition, it raised many issues that are central to the field of psychology: How do people retrieve information from memory and use it to devise solutions to problems? How is knowledge transformed, elaborated upon, and utilized? How do people think about, understand, and, using language, describe the world?

These questions and others are being addressed largely by **cognitive psychologists**, who specialize in the study of cognition. **Cognition** encompasses the higher mental process of humans, including how people know and understand the world, process information, make judgments and decisions, and describe their knowledge and understanding to others.

In this chapter, we cover the breadth of cognitive psychology. We begin by examining the ways in which information is stored and retrieved, discussing evidence that there are actually three separate types of memory. The problems of retrieving information from memory and the reasons we sometimes forget stored material are considered.

Next, we examine problem solving and discuss various ways to approach problems, generate solutions, and make judgments about the usefulness and accuracy of solutions. Finally, we consider language: its basic characteristics, how it is developed and acquired, and how it relates to thinking.

After reading this chapter, you will be able to answer the following questions:

• What are the different kinds of memory and how do they operate?

- How can we explain forgetting?
- How do people approach and solve problems, and what are the major obstacles to finding solutions?
- How do people use language, and how does it develop?

*M*EMORY'S THREE R'S: RECORDING, RETAINING, AND RETRIEVING INFORMATION

What is memory, and why do we remember certain events and activities and forget others? Psychologists define **memory** as the capacity to record, retain, and retrieve information—the three R's of remembering. Without memory, learning would be impossible; people could not build on past experiences or adapt their knowledge to new situations.

Each of the three parts of the definition of memory—recording, retention, and retrieval—represents a different process in remembering and allows us to systematically consider the point at which memory may fail. For example, suppose, in the middle of a game of Trivial Pursuit, you are asked to name the crime Al Capone was finally imprisoned for in 1931. If you can't, the source of your failure may reside in the initial recording stage; you may never, for instance, have been exposed to the information. In this case, your failure relates to **encoding**, the process by which information is recorded in a form usable by memory.

Even if you were exposed to the information and originally knew of the crime, you may still be unable to recall it because of a failure in the retention process. Memory specialists speak of placing information in **storage**, the location in the memory system in which material is saved. If the material is not stored adequately in the first place, it cannot later be recalled.

Memory depends on one last process: retrieval. In **retrieval**, material in memory storage is located, brought into awareness, and used. Your ineptitude in recalling Capone's conviction, then, may rest on your inability to retrieve the information that you learned earlier. (In case your own memory has failed, Capone was convicted of income tax evasion.)

The Short and Long of It: The Three Stages of Memory

Although the processes of recording, retaining, and retrieving information are necessary for memory to operate successfully, they do not describe the specific manner in which material is entered into our storehouse of memories. Many psychologists studying memory suggest that there are different stages through which information must travel if it is to be remembered.

According to one influential theory, there are three kinds of memory, which vary in terms of their function and the length of time information is retained (Atkinson & Shiffrin, 1968). As shown in Figure 5-1, **sensory memory** refers to the initial, momentary storage of information, lasting only an instant; it is recorded by the person's sensory system as a raw, nonmeaningful stimulus. **Short-term memory** holds information for fifteen to twenty-five seconds; in this phase, the information is stored in terms of its meaning rather than mere sensory stimulation. The third type of memory is **long-term memory**. Here, information is relatively permanent, although it may be difficult to retrieve.

The initial encounter: Sensory memory. A momentary flash of lightening, the sound of a twig snapping, and the sting of a pinprick all represent stimulation of exceedingly brief duration, but they may nonetheless provide important information that can require some response. Such stimuli are initially—and briefly—stored in sensory memory, the first repository of the information that the world presents to us. Actually, the term "sensory memory" encompasses several types of sensory memories, each related to a different source of sensory information. There is an **iconic memory**, which reflects information from our visual system, an **echoic memory**, which stores information coming from the ears, as well as corresponding memories for each of the other senses.

Regardless of the individual subtypes, sensory memory in general is able to store information for only a very short time, and if material does not pass to another form of memory, that information is lost for good. For instance, iconic memory seems to last less than a second, although, if the

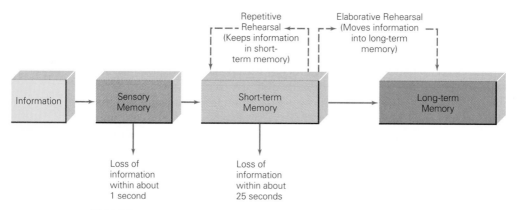

FIGURE 5-1
In this three-stage model of memory, information initially recorded by the person's sensory system enters sensory memory, which momentarily holds the information. It then moves to short-term memory, which stores the information for fifteen to twenty-five seconds. Finally, the information can move into long-term memory, which is relatively permanent. Whether the information moves from short-term to long-term memory depends on the kind and amount of rehearsal of the material that is carried out. (After Atkinson & Shiffrin, 1968.)

initial stimulus is very bright, the image may last a little longer (Long & Beaton, 1982). Echoic memory fades within three or four seconds (Darwin, Turvey & Crowder, 1972). However, despite the brief duration of sensory memory, its precision is high: It is able to store an almost exact replica of each stimulus to which it is exposed.

If the storage capabilities of sensory memory are so limited and information stored within sensory memory so fleeting, it would seem almost impossible to find evidence for its existence; new information would be constantly replacing older information, even before a person could report its presence. Not until psychologist George Sperling (1960) conducted a series of clever and now-classic studies was sensory memory well understood. Sperling briefly exposed people to a series of twelve letters arranged in the following pattern:

F T Y C
K D N L
Y W B M

When exposed to this pattern for just one-twentieth of a second, most people could accurately recall only four or five of the letters. Although they knew that they had seen more, the memory had faded by the time they reported the first few letters. It was possible, then, that the information had initially been accurately stored in sensory memory, but during the time it took to verbalize the first four or five letters the memory of the other letters faded.

To test that possibility, Sperling had a high, medium, or low tone sounded just after a person had been exposed to the full pattern of letters. People were told to report the letters in the highest line if a high tone were sounded, the middle line if the medium tone occurred, or the lowest line at the sound of the low tone. Because the tone occurred after the exposure, people had to rely on their memory to report the correct row.

The results of the study showed very clearly that people had been storing the complete pattern in memory: They were quite accurate in their recollection of the letters in the line that had been indicated by the tone, regardless of whether it was the top, middle, or bottom line. Obviously, *all* the lines they had seen had been stored in sensory memory. Despite its rapid loss, then, the information in sensory memory was an accurate representation of what the people had seen.

By gradually lengthening the time between the presentation of the visual pattern and the tone, Sperling was able to determine with some accuracy the length of time that information existed in sensory memory. The ability to recall a particular row of the pattern when a tone was sounded declined progressively as the period between visual exposure and tone lengthened but leveled off when it reached about one second in duration. The conclusion: The entire visual image was stored in sensory memory for less than a second.

"Well, here I sit, surrounded by my memorabilia, and I can't remember having done a damn thing."

(Drawing by Richter; © 1982 The New Yorker Magazine, Inc.)

In sum, sensory memory operates as a kind of snapshot that stores information—which may be of a visual, auditory, or other sensory nature—for a brief moment in time. But it is as if each snapshot, immediately after being taken, is destroyed and replaced with a new one. Unless the information in the snapshot is transferred to some other type of memory, it is lost.

Our working memory: Short-term memory. Because the information that is stored briefly in our sensory memories consists of representations of raw sensory stimuli, it is not necessarily meaningful to us. In order for us to make sense of it and to allow for the possibility of long-term retention, the information must be transferred to the next stage of memory, short-term memory. Short-term memory, sometimes referred to as working memory, is the memory in which material initially has meaning, although the maximum length of retention is relatively short.

The specific process by which sensory memories are transformed into short-term memories is not yet clear. Some theorists suggest that the information is first translated into graphical representations or images, and others hypothesize that the transfer occurs when the sensory stimuli are changed to words (Baddeley, 1985). What is clear, however, is that unlike sensory memory, which holds a relatively full and detailed—if short-lived—representation of the world, short-term memory has incomplete representational capabilities.

In fact, the specific amount of information that can be held in short-term memory has been identified: seven items, or "chunks," of information, with variations up to plus or minus two chunks. A **chunk** is a meaningful grouping of stimuli that can be stored as a unit in short-term memory. According to George Miller (1956), it could be individual letters, as in the following list:

C T N Q M W N

Each letter here qualifies as a separate chunk, and—as there are seven of them—they are easily held in short-term memory.

But a chunk might also consist of larger categories, such as words or other meaningful units. For example, consider the following list of letters:

TWACIAABCCBSMTVUSAAAA

Clearly, because the list exceeds seven chunks, it is difficult to recall the letters after one exposure. But suppose they were presented to you as follows:

TWA   CIA   ABC   CBS   MTV   USA   AAA

In this case, even though there are still twenty-one letters, it would be possible to store them in memory, since they represent only seven chunks.

Chunks can vary in size from single letters or numbers to categories that are far more complicated, and the specific nature of what constitutes a chunk varies according to one's past experience. You can see this for yourself by trying an experiment that was first carried out comparing expert and inexperienced chess players (deGroot, 1966).

Examine the chessboard on the top of Figure 5-2 for about five seconds, and then, after covering up the board, try to reproduce the position of the pieces on the blank chessboard on the bottom. Unless you are an experienced chess player, you will likely have great difficulty carrying out such a task. Yet chess masters—the kind who win tournaments—do quite well: Ninety percent are able to correctly reproduce it. In comparison, inexperienced chess players typically are able to reproduce only 40 percent of the board properly.

The chess masters do not have superior memories in other respects; they generally test normally on other measures of memory. What they can do better than others is to chunk the board into meaningful units and reproduce the chess pieces by using these units. An analogous skill is found among electronics technicians, who are able to glance at a complicated circuit drawing and recall it without difficulty because of their ability to chunk it into meaningful configurations (Egan & Schwartz, 1979).

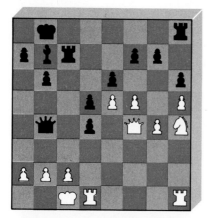

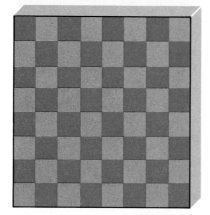

FIGURE 5-2
Look at the top chessboard for about five seconds, and then cover it with your hand. Now try to recreate the chess pieces on the blank board below it. Unless you are an experienced chess player, you will probably have a good deal of difficulty recalling the configuration and types of chess pieces. On the other hand, expert chess players have little difficulty recreating the board on the left. (deGroot, 1966.)

Although it is possible to remember seven or so relatively complicated sets of information entering short-term memory, the information cannot be held there very long. Just how short term is short-term memory? Anyone who has looked up a telephone number at a pay phone, struggled to find coins, and forgotten the number at the sound of the dial tone knows that information in short-term memory does not remain there terribly long. Most psychologists believe that information in short-term memory is lost after fifteen to twenty-five seconds—unless it is transferred to long-term memory.

The transfer of material from short- to long-term memory proceeds largely on the basis of **rehearsal**, the repetition of information that has entered short-term memory. Rehearsal accomplishes two things. First, as long as the information is repeated, it is kept alive in short-term memory. More important, however, rehearsal allows the material to be transferred into long-term memory.

Whether the transfer is made from short- to long-term memory seems to depend largely on the kind of rehearsal that is carried out. If the material is simply repeated over and over again—as we might do with a telephone number while we rush from the phone book to the telephone—it is kept current in short-term memory but it will not necessarily be placed in long-term memory. Instead, as soon as we stop dialing, the number is likely to be replaced by other information and will be completely forgotten.

On the other hand, if the information in short-term memory is rehearsed using a process called elaborative rehearsal, it is much more likely to be transferred into long-term memory (Craik & Lockhart, 1972). **Elaborative rehearsal** occurs when the material is considered and organized in some fashion. The organization might include expanding the information to make it fit into a logical framework, linking it to another memory, turning it into an image, or transforming it in some other way. For example, a list of vegetables to be purchased at a store could be woven together in memory as items being used to prepare an elaborate salad; they could be linked to the items bought on an earlier shopping trip; or they could be thought of in terms of the image of a farm with rows of each item.

By using organizational strategies called mnemonics, we can vastly improve our retention of information. **Mnemonics** (pronounced "nee-MAHN-iks") are formal techniques for organizing material in a way that makes it more likely to be remembered. For instance, when a beginning musician learns that the spaces on the music staff spell the word "FACE" or when we learn the rhyme "Thirty days hath September, April, June, and November; all the rest have . . . ," we are using mnemonics.

The final repository: Long-term memory. Material that makes its way from short-term memory to long-term memory enters a repository of almost unlimited capacity. Like a new book delivered to a library, the information in long-term memory is filed and cataloged so that it can be retrieved when we need it.

Evidence of the existence of long-term memory, as distinct from short-term memory, comes from a number of sources. For example, people with certain kinds of brain injury have no long-term recall of new information following the injury, although people and events in memory prior to the injury remain (Milner, 1966). Because short-term memory following the injury appears to be operative—new material can be recalled for a very brief period—and because information from before the injury is intact, we might infer that there are two distinct memories, one for short-term and one for long-term storage.

Evidence from laboratory experiments is also consistent with the notion of separate short- and long-term memories. For example, in one set of studies people were asked to recall a relatively small amount of information (such as a set of three letters)—but then, to prevent practice of the initial information, were required to recite some extraneous material aloud, such as counting backward by three (Brown, 1958; Peterson & Peterson, 1959). By varying the amount of time between which the initial material was first presented and when its recall was required, investigators found that recall was quite good when the interval was near zero, but it declined rapidly thereafter. In fact, after fifteen seconds had gone by, recall hovered at around 10 percent of the material initially presented.

Apparently, counting backward prevented almost all the initial material from reaching long-term memory. Initial recall was good because it was coming from short-term memory, but these memories were lost at a rapid rate. Eventually, all that could be recalled was the small amount of material that had made its way into long-term storage despite the distractions of counting backward.

Episodic and semantic memories. There are actually two kinds of memories held in long-term memory: episodic and semantic (Tulving, 1983). **Episodic memories** relate to our individual lives, recalling what we have done and the kinds of experiences we have had. When you recall your first date, the time you fell off your bicycle, or what you felt like when you graduated from high school, you are recalling episodic memories. The information in episodic memory is connected with specific times and places. In contrast, **semantic memories** consist of organized knowledge and facts about the world; because of semantic memory, we know that $2 \times 2 = 4$, the earth is round, and "memoree" is misspelled.

Episodic memories can be surprisingly detailed. Consider, for instance, what your response would be if you were asked to identify what you were doing on a specific day two years ago. An impossible task? You might think otherwise as you read the following exchange between a researcher and a subject who was asked, in a memory experiment, what he was doing "on Monday afternoon in the third week of September two years ago."

SUBJECT: Come on. How should I know?

EXPERIMENTER: Just try it anyhow.

SUBJECT: OK. Let's see: Two years ago . . . I would be in high school in Pittsburgh. . . . That would be my senior year. Third week in September—that's just after summer—that would be the fall term. . . . Let me see. I think I had chemistry lab on Mondays. I don't know. I was probably in chemistry lab. Wait a minute—that would be the second week of school. I remember he started off with the atomic table—a big fancy chart. I thought he was crazy trying to make us memorize that thing. You know, I think I can remember sitting. . . (Lindsay & Norman, 1977).

Episodic memory, then, can provide information from events that happened long in the past (Reynolds & Takooshian, 1988). But semantic memory is no less impressive: By calling upon it, all of us are able to dredge up thousands of facts ranging from the date of our birthday to the knowledge that $1 is less than $5. Both individual pieces of information

Looking at photos taken years ago can trigger episodic memories, detailed recollections of past events.

and the rules of logic for deducing other facts are stored in semantic memory.

   Storage in long-term memory. There are several ways in which both
episodic and semantic information is stored in long-term memory. One
of the primary ways is through the **linguistic code**, which relies on language. The linguistic code allows us to store information abstractly without having to rely on a specific image. For instance, we may be able to
recall that someone talking about a sloth is discussing an animal, even
while we are unable to conjure up a specific image of what it looks like.
   An **imaginal code**, in contrast, is memory storage that is based on
visual images. If someone asked you to describe the path you take on the
way from your psychology class to your home or dormitory, you would
likely recall the images you have seen when taking the route in the past.
   The third type of coding in long-term memory is the **motor code**,
storage that is based on memories of physical activities. Your ability to
ride a bicycle is based on motor memories; you probably would be hard-
pressed to recall in verbal terms how you are able to do it. Motor codes
are particularly well remembered. Even after years of never riding a bicycle, you would probably have little trouble remembering how to do it.

Levels of Processing

As an alternative to the notion that the processing of information proceeds
along three sequential stages, some psychologists, in an increasingly influential view, suggest that a single process accounts for how well information is remembered: the way in which material is first perceived and
considered.

The **levels-of-processing** approach emphasizes the degree to which new material is mentally analyzed (Craik & Lockhart, 1972). In contrast to the view that there are sensory, short-term, and long-term memories, levels-of-processing theory suggests that the amount of information processing that occurs when material is initially encountered is central in determining how much of the information is ultimately remembered. According to this approach, the depth of processing during exposure to material—meaning the degree to which it is analyzed and considered—is critical; the greater the intensity of its initial processing, the more likely we are to remember it.

Because we do not pay close attention to much of the information to which we are exposed, only scant mental processing takes place, and we forget it almost immediately. However, information to which we pay more attention is processed more thoroughly. Therefore, it enters memory at a deeper level—and is less apt to be forgotten than information processed at more shallow levels.

The theory goes on to suggest that there are considerable differences in the way information is processed at various levels of memory. At shallow levels, information is processed merely in terms of its physical and sensory aspects; for example, we may pay attention only to the shapes that make up the letters in the word "dog." At an intermediate level of processing, the shapes are translated into meaningful units—in this case, letters of the alphabet. These letters are considered in the context of words, and a specific sound of the word may be attached to the letters.

At the deepest level of processing, information is analyzed in terms of its meaning. It may be seen in a wider context, and associations between the meaning of the information and broader networks of knowledge may be drawn. For instance, we may think of dogs not merely as animals with four legs and a tail, but in terms of their relation to cats and other mammals. We may form an image of our own dog, relating it to our own lives.

According to the levels-of-processing approach, the deeper the initial level of processing of specific information, the longer the information will be retained. The approach suggests, then, that the best way to remember new information is to consider it thoroughly when you are first exposed to it—reflecting on how it relates to information that you currently have.

The levels-of-processing theory considers memory as involving more active mental processes than does the three-stage approach to memory. However, neither model has been able to account for all phenomena relating to memory, and both remain plausible explanations.

ASK YOURSELF

What is memory?

How does sensory memory operate?

What is the capacity of short-term memory?

What is the difference between episodic and semantic long-term memories?

What explanation is provided by the levels-of-processing approach, and how does it differ from the three-stage model of memory?

Imagine a friend is having difficulty memorizing the species of plants for a biology exam. How might you help your friend retain the material?

How might we explain the behavior of a woman who is a genius at mathematics but has great difficulty remembering where she leaves her car keys?

*M*ISPLACED OR LOST FOR GOOD? RECALLING LONG-TERM MEMORIES

Have you ever tried to remember someone's name, absolutely certain that you knew it, but unable to recall it no matter how hard you tried? This not infrequent occurrence—the **tip-of-the-tongue phenomenon**—exemplifies the difficulties that can occur in retrieving information stored in long-term memory (Harris & Morris, 1984).

One reason recall is not perfect is the sheer quantity of recollections

Memory retrieval cues include drawings and photographs, such as these being viewed by Sgt. Mark Tracy of Santa Cruz, California.

that are stored in long-term memory. Although the issue is far from settled, many psychologists have suggested that the material that makes its way there is relatively permanent (Tulving & Psotka, 1971). If they are correct, this suggests that the capacity of long-term memory is vast, given the variety of people's experiences and learning. For instance, if you are like the average college student, your vocabulary includes some 50,000 words, you know hundreds of mathematical "facts," and you are able to conjure up images—such as the way your childhood home looked—with no trouble at all. In fact, simply cataloging all your memories would probably take years of work.

How do we sort through this vast array of material and retrieve specific information at the appropriate time? One of the major ways is through the use of retrieval cues. A **retrieval cue** is a stimulus that allows us to more easily recall information that is located in long-term memory (Tulving & Thompson, 1973). It may be a word, an emotion, a sound; whatever the specific cue, a memory will suddenly come to mind when the retrieval cue is present. For example, the smell of roasting turkey may evoke memories of Thanksgiving or family gatherings.

Retrieval cues guide people through the vast array of information stored in long-term memory in much the same way as the cards in a card catalog guide people through a library. They are particularly important when *recalling* information, as opposed to being asked to *recognize* material stored in memory. In **recall**, a specific piece of information must be retrieved—such as that needed to fill in the blanks or write an essay on a test. In contrast, **recognition** occurs when people are presented with a stimulus and asked whether they have been exposed to it previously, or are asked to identify it from a list of alternatives.

As you might guess, recognition is generally much easier than recall. Suppose, for instance, you witnessed a robbery and were asked to describe the thief—a recall task. Clearly, this would be harder than being shown a police "mug book" and asked to pick out the robber—a recognition problem. The reason that recall is more difficult is that it consists of a series of processes: a search through memory, retrieval of potentially relevant information, and then a decision regarding whether or not the information you have found is accurate. If it appears correct, the search is over, but if it does not, the search must continue. On the other hand, recognition is simpler since it involves fewer steps (Anderson & Bower, 1972). Even recognition, though, is subject to error, as the Psychology and Society box illustrates.

Flashbulb Memories

Ask anyone over the age of 40 what he or she was doing on first hearing that President John F. Kennedy was assassinated, and that person is likely to be able to provide you with a thorough description of his or her activities some thirty years previously.

PSYCHOLOGY AND SOCIETY

Memory on Trial: Witness Fallibility

It is a scene immortalized in scores of old television shows and movies: A lineup is called and a nervous heroine picks out one of five suspects, saying with confidence, "He's the one. I'm certain of it."

Ongoing research on eyewitness memory for details of crimes suggests that most eyewitnesses should be considerably less confident than they often are in their ability to recall either the identity of a suspect or any other details of a crime. Work on eyewitness identification has shown that witnesses are apt to make substantial errors when they try to recall details of criminal activity (Bishop, 1988; Kassin, 1985; Wells & Luus, 1990).

Consider the three faces shown below. As you can see, the men share certain characteristics; they are all wearing glasses and have mustaches and similar hairstyles. Their similarity led to near-tragic consequences when one of them was arrested for several rapes and another for a robbery, all

crimes that the third person had actually committed. The bases of their arrests were the mistaken impressions of eyewitnesses who—before the actual criminal had been found—felt sure that they had identified the right person as the perpetrator.

This case of mistaken identification is not an isolated event, according to research on the topic; eyewitnesses are prone to frequent errors in memory (Wells & Loftus, 1984; Cutler & Penrod, 1988). For instance, viewers of a twelve-second film of a mugging that was shown on a New York City television news program were later given the opportunity to pick out the assailant from a six-person lineup. Of some 2000 viewers who called the station after the program, only 15 percent were able to pick out the right person—a figure just slightly higher than if they had guessed randomly (Buckhout, 1975).

Other research suggests that the mistakes witnesses make show wide variability. For example, one study found that witnesses of staged crimes disagreed by as much as 2 feet in their estimates of the height of a perpe-

In a case of mistaken identification, the men in the photos on the left and right were arrested for crimes actually committed by the man in the center. Both of the innocent men had been identified as guilty in separate lineups by victims of the real criminal.

trator and averaged a difference of 8 inches from his true height. There was a discrepancy from the true age averaging eight years, hair color was recalled incorrectly 83 percent of the time, and about a quarter of all witnesses left out more than half of the details they had actually seen (Gardner, 1933).

Even the specific wording of a question posed to a witness can affect the way in which something is recalled, as a number of experiments illustrate. For example, in one experiment subjects were shown a film of two cars crashing into each other. Some were then asked the question, "About how fast were the cars going when they *smashed* into each other?" They estimated the speed to be an average of 40.8 miles per hour. In contrast, when another group of subjects was asked, "About how fast were the cars going when they *contacted* each other?" the average estimated speed was only 31.8 miles per hour (Loftus & Palmer, 1974).

In sum, the memories of eyewitnesses are far from infallible. Furthermore, it is not just the memory processes of witnesses that determine how fairly justice is meted out, but the memories of jurors as well. In complex cases, jurors must sort through a vast array of information, typically using only their memory of what was presented to them in the courtroom (Hastie, Penrod & Pennington, 1983). In addition, they sometimes are directed to *forget* information to which they have been exposed, when told by a judge to disregard information that may not be legally considered during their deliberations. As you might guess, it is almost impossible for jurors to disregard information that they are directed to forget, especially if they consider the information to be important or relevant to their deliberations (Allen, 1988).

Similarly, it may be easy for you to recall events that took place last New Year's Eve. What makes this possible is a phenomenon known as flashbulb memories. **Flashbulb memories** are memories centered around a specific, important event that are so clear it is as if they represented a snapshot of the event. For example, common flashbulb memories among college students are involvement in a car accident, meeting one's roommate for the first time, and the night of high school graduation (Rubin, 1985). (See Figure 5-3.)

Of course, not every detail of an original scene is recalled in a flashbulb memory (McCloskey et al., 1988). Even though I may remember that I was sitting in Mr. Sharp's tenth-grade geometry class when I heard that President Kennedy was shot, and I remember where my seat was located and what my classmates did, I may not recall what I was wearing or what I had for lunch that day.

Still, flashbulb memories are extraordinary because of the details they do include. An analysis of people's recollections of the Kennedy assassination found that their memories tended to have a number of features in common (Brown & Kulik, 1977). Most contained information regarding where the person heard the news, who told him or her about it, what event was interrupted by the news, the emotions of the informant, the person's own emotions, and some personal details of the event (such as seeing a robin fly by while the information was being given).

Flashbulb memories illustrate a more general phenomenon about memory: Memories that are distinctive are more easily retrieved than

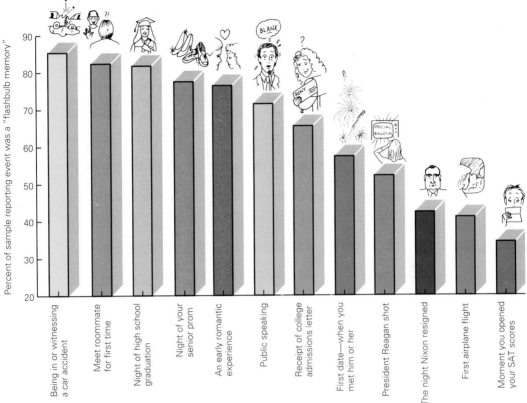

FIGURE 5-3
The most common flashbulb memories of a sample of college students are shown here. (Rubin, 1985.)

those relating to events that are commonplace. We are more likely, for example, to recall a particular number if it appears in a group of twenty words than if it appears in a group of twenty other numbers. The more distinctive a stimulus, then, the more likely we are to recall it later—the **von Restorff effect**, a phenomenon named after its discoverer (von Restorff, 1933).

The von Restorff effect operates in our own lives: We are far better at remembering unusual, atypical events that happen to us than the mundane, routine occurrences that take up most of our time. For instance, in one study, a group of college students were equipped with beepers that went off at random intervals, at which time they wrote down what they were doing. Most of what the students had done was soon forgotten; what was recalled best were distinctive, unusual events, such as a student's first date (Brewer & Dupree, 1983).

Building Memories: Constructive Processes in Memory

Although it is clear that we can have detailed recollections of significant and distinctive events, it is difficult to gauge the accuracy of such memories. In fact, it is apparent that our memories reflect, at least in part, **constructive processes**, processes in which memories are influenced by the meaning that we give to events. When we retrieve information, then, the memory that is produced is affected not just by the direct prior experience we have had with the stimulus, but by our guesses and inferences about its meaning as well.

The notion that memory is based on constructive processes was first put forward by Sir Frederic Bartlett, a British psychologist, who suggested that people tend to remember information in terms of **schemas**, general themes that contain relatively little specific detail (Bartlett, 1932). He argued that such schemas were based on the information provided not just by a stimulus but by our understanding of the situation, our expectations about the situation, and our awareness of the motivation underlying people's behavior.

In a demonstration of the operation of schemas, researchers have employed a process known as **serial reproduction**, in which information from memory is passed sequentially from one person to another. For an example of serial reproduction, briefly look at the cartoon in Figure 5-4,

FIGURE 5-4
When one person views this cartoon and then describes it from memory to a second person, who in turn describes it to a third, and so on—in a process known as serial reproduction—the last person to repeat the contents of the cartoon typically gives a description that differs in important respects from the original. (Allport & Postman, 1958.)

and then try to describe it to someone else without looking back at it. Then ask that person to describe it to another, and repeat the process with still one more person.

If you listen to the last person's report of the contents of the cartoon, you are sure to find that it differs in important respects from the cartoon itself. Many people recall the cartoon as showing a razor in the hand of the black person—obviously an incorrect recollection, given that the razor is held by the white person (Allport & Postman, 1958).

This example, which is drawn from a classic experiment, illustrates the role of expectations in memory. The migration of the razor from the white person's hand to the black person's hand in memory clearly indicates that expectations about the world—reflecting, in this case, the unwarranted prejudice that blacks may be more violent than whites and thus more apt to be holding a razor—have an impact upon how events are recalled.

WHEN MEMORY FAILS: FORGETTING WHAT YOU HAVE REMEMBERED

He could remember, quite literally, nothing—nothing, that is, that had happened since the loss of his temporal lobes and hippocampus during experimental surgery to reduce epileptic seizures. Until that time, his memory had been quite normal. But after the operation he was unable to recall anything for more than a few minutes, and then the memory was seemingly lost forever. He did not remember his address, or the name of the person to whom he was talking. He would read the same magazine over and over again. According to his own description, his life was like waking from a dream and being unable to know where he was or how he got there (Milner, 1966).

The difficulties faced by a person without a normal memory are legion, as exemplified in the case described above of a patient immortalized in the annals of memory research as "H. M." All of us who have experienced even routine instances of forgetting—such as not remembering an acquaintance's name or a fact on a test—understand the serious consequences of memory failure.

The first attempts to study forgetting were made by German psychologist Hermann Ebbinghaus about a hundred years ago. Using himself as his only subject, he memorized lists of three-letter nonsense syllables— meaningless sets of two consonants with a vowel in between, such as FIW and BOZ. By measuring how easy it was to relearn a given list of words after varying periods of time from initial learning had passed, he found that forgetting occurred systematically, as shown in Figure 5-5. As the figure indicates, the most rapid forgetting occurs in the first nine hours, and particularly in the first hour. After nine hours, the rate of forgetting slows and declines little, even after the passage of many days.

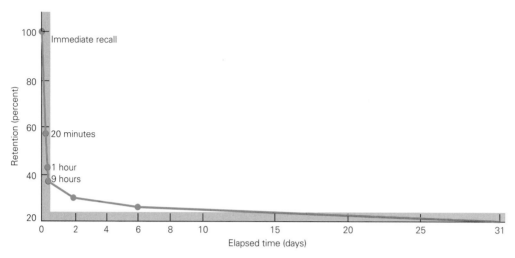

FIGURE 5-5
In his classic work, Ebbinghaus found that the most rapid forgetting occurs in the first nine hours after exposure to new material. However, the rate of forgetting then slows down and declines very little even after many days have passed. (Ebbinghaus, 1885.)

Despite his primitive methods, Ebbinghaus's research had an important influence on subsequent research, and his basic conclusions have been upheld. There is almost always a strong initial decline in memory, followed by a more gradual drop over time. Furthermore, relearning of previously mastered material is almost always faster than starting from scratch, whether the material is academic information or a motor skill such as riding a bike.

Efforts at understanding *why* we forget have produced two major explanations. One theory explains forgetting in terms of a process called **decay**, or the loss of information through its nonuse. The theory assumes that when new material is learned, a **memory trace** or engram—an actual physical change in the brain—occurs. In decay, the trace simply fades away with nothing left behind, because of the mere passage of time.

Although there is some evidence that decay does occur, it does not seem to be the complete solution to the puzzle of forgetting. The difficulty with relying on decay as an explanation is that there is often no relationship between how long ago a person was exposed to information and how well it is recalled. If decay explained all forgetting, we would expect that the longer the time between the initial learning of information and our attempt to recall it, the harder it would be to remember it, since there would be more time for the memory trace to decay. Yet people who take several sequential tests on the same material often recall more of the initial information when taking later tests than they did on earlier tests. If decay were operating, we would expect the opposite to occur (Payne, 1986).

Because decay is not able to fully account for forgetting, memory specialists have proposed an additional mechanism: **interference**. In interference, information in memory displaces or blocks out other information, preventing its recall.

To distinguish between decay and interference, think of the two processes in terms of a row of books on a library shelf. In decay, the old books are constantly crumbling and rotting away, leaving room for new arrivals. Interference processes suggest that new books knock the old ones off the shelf, where they become inaccessible.

Most research suggests that interference is the key process in forgetting. We mainly forget things not because the memory trace has decayed, but because new memories interfere with the retrieval of old ones (Potter, 1990).

The Before and After of Forgetting: Proactive and Retroactive Interference

There are actually two sorts of interference that influence forgetting: proactive and retroactive. In **proactive interference**, information learned earlier interferes with recall of newer material. Suppose, as a student of foreign languages, you first learned French in tenth grade, and then in eleventh grade you took Spanish. When it comes time to take a college achievement test in the twelfth grade in Spanish you may find you have difficulty recalling the Spanish translation of a word because all you can think of is its French equivalent. In contrast, **retroactive interference** refers to difficulty in recall of information because of later exposure to different material. If, for example, you have difficulty on a French achievement test because of your more recent exposure to Spanish, retroactive interference is the culprit (see Figure 5-6). One way of remembering the difference between proactive and retroactive interference is to keep in mind that *pro*active interference moves forward in time—the past interferes with the present—whereas *retro*active interference retrogresses in time, working backward as the present interferes with the past.

Although the concepts of proactive and retroactive interference suggest why material may be forgotten, they do not explain whether forgetting is caused by the actual loss of information or by problems in retrieval of information. Most research suggests that material that has apparently been lost because of interference can eventually be recalled if appropriate stimuli are presented (Tulving & Psotka, 1971), but the question has not been fully answered.

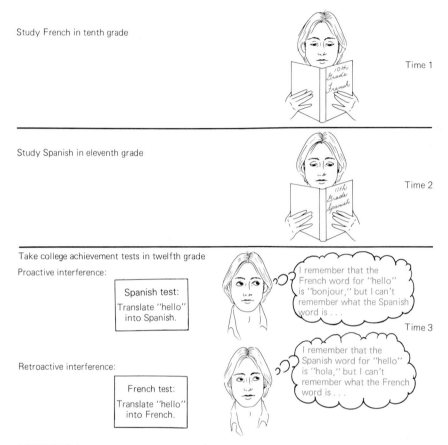

FIGURE 5-6
Proactive interference occurs when material learned earlier interferes with recall of newer material. In this example, exposure to French prior to learning Spanish interferes with performance on a Spanish test. In contrast, retroactive interference exists when material learned after initial exposure to other material interferes with the recall of the first material. In this case, retroactive interference occurs when recall of French is impaired because of later exposure to Spanish.

Afflictions of Forgetting: Memory Dysfunctions

To a casual observer, Harold appears to be a brilliant golfer. He seems to have learned the game perfectly; his shots are almost flawless.

Yet anyone accompanying him on the course is bound to notice some startling incongruities. Although he is immediately able to size up a situation and hit the ball exactly where it should go, he cannot remember where the ball has just landed. At the end of each hole, he forgets the score (Blakeslee, 1985, p. C1).

Harold's problem: he suffers from **Alzheimer's disease**, the illness that counts severe memory problems among its symptoms. Alzheimer's, discussed first in Chapter 2, strikes about 7 percent of people over the age of 65.

In its initial stages, Alzheimer's appears as simple forgetfulness of things like appointments and birthdays. As the disease progresses, memory loss becomes more profound, and even the simplest tasks—such as how to dial a telephone—are forgotten. Ultimately, victims can forget their own names or family members' faces. In addition, physical deterioration sets in, and language abilities may be lost entirely.

Alzheimer's disease is just one of several memory dysfunctions that plague their victims. Another is **amnesia**, memory loss that occurs without other mental difficulties. The classic case—immortalized in many a drama—is a victim who receives a blow to the head and is unable to remember anything from his or her past. In reality, amnesia of this type, known as retrograde amnesia, is quite rare. In **retrograde amnesia**, memory is lost for occurrences prior to a certain event. There is usually a gradual reappearance of lost memory, although it may take as long as several years for a full restoration to occur. In certain cases, some memories are lost forever (Baddeley, 1982).

A second type of amnesia is exemplified by the case of "H. M.," the man we discussed earlier who could remember nothing of his current activities. In **anterograde amnesia**, loss of memory occurs for events following an injury. Information cannot be transferred from short-term to long-term memory, resulting in the inability to remember anything other than what was in long-term storage prior to the accident.

Amnesia is also displayed by people who suffer from **Korsakoff's syndrome**, a disease that afflicts long-term alcoholics who have also had an impaired diet, resulting in a thiamine deficiency. Although many of their intellectual abilities may be intact, they display a strange array of symptoms, including hallucinations; repeating questions, even after being told the answer; and repeating the same story over and over again.

Fortunately, most of us have memories that are intact, and the occasional failures that we do suffer may in fact be preferable to having a perfect memory. Consider, for instance, the case of a man who had total recall. After reading passages of the *Divine Comedy* in Italian—a language he did not speak—he was able to repeat it back from memory even some fifteen years later. He could memorize lists of fifty unrelated words and recall them at will more than a decade later. He could even repeat the same list of words backward, if asked (Luria, 1987).

Such a skill might at first seem to have few drawbacks, but it actually presented quite a problem. The man's memory became a jumble of lists of words, numbers, and names, and when he tried to relax, his mind was filled with images. Even reading was difficult, since every word evoked a flood of thoughts from the past that interfered with his ability to understand the meaning of what he was reading. Partially as a consequence of the man's unusual memory, psychologist A. R. Luria, who studied his case, found him to be a "disorganized and rather dull-witted person" (Luria, 1968, p. 65).

We may be grateful, then, that being somewhat forgetful plays at least some useful role in our lives.

When memory becomes a burden: A woman with total recall would remember every word and every scene of every movie she saw, whether or not she liked the film!

ASK YOURSELF

What is the tip-of-the-tongue phenomenon?

What are retrieval cues and flashbulb memories?

What are constructive processes in memory?

How do decay and interference provide explanations for forgetting?

What are the major memory impairments?

Think about the problems associated with eyewitness testimony combined with what you learned about the constructive nature of memory. What do these ideas suggest about the reliability of eyewitnesses and the potential for prejudice in criminal trials?

COGNITIVE PROCESSES IN PROBLEM SOLVING

According to legend, a group of monks in Vietnam spend a considerable amount of their time attempting to solve a problem called the Tower of Hanoi puzzle. If they are successful in finding a solution, the monks expect that it will bring an end to the world as we know it (Raphael, 1976).

FIGURE 5-7
The goal of the Tower of Hanoi puzzle is to move all three disks from the first post to the last and still preserve the original order of the disks, using the least number of moves possible while following the rules that only one disk at a time can be moved and no disk can cover a smaller one during a move. Try it yourself before you look at the solution, which is listed according to the sequence of moves. (Solution: Move C to 3, B to 2, C to 2, A to 3, C to 1, B to 3, and C to 3.)

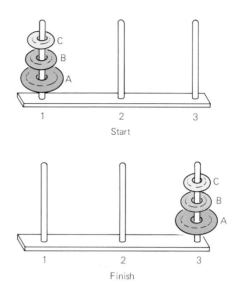

(Happily, there is no need for immediate concern; according to one estimate, the monks' puzzle is so complex that it will take about a trillion years to reach a solution.)

In a simpler version of the puzzle, illustrated in Figure 5-7, there are three posts on which three disks are to be placed in the order shown. The goal of the puzzle is to move all three disks to the third post in the same order, using as few moves as possible. But there are two restrictions: Only one disk can be moved at a time, and no disk can ever cover a smaller one during a move.

Why are cognitive psychologists interested in the Tower of Hanoi problem? The answer is that the way people go about solving this puzzle and simpler ones like it helps illuminate the processes by which people solve more complex problems that they encounter in school and at work. For example, psychologists have found that problem solving typically follows three major steps: preparation for the creation of solutions, production of solutions, and evaluation of solutions that have been generated.

Preparation: Understanding and Diagnosing the Problem

When presented with a problem such as the Tower of Hanoi, most people begin by trying to ensure that they thoroughly understand the problem. If the problem is novel, they will likely pay particular attention to any restrictions placed on coming to a solution and the initial status of the components of the problem. If the problem is familiar, they are apt to spend considerably less time in this stage than if it is completely new to them.

Problems vary from well defined to ill defined (Reitman, 1965). For a well-defined problem—such as a mathematical equation or the solution to a jigsaw puzzle in which no pieces have been lost—both the nature of the problem itself and the information needed to solve the problem are available and clear. Thus, straightforward judgments can be made about whether a potential solution is appropriate. With an ill-defined problem, such as how to increase morale on an assembly line, not only may the specific nature of the problem be unclear, but the information required to solve the problem may be even less obvious.

The clarity of a problem has important effects on the ultimate success of the problem solver. Consider a physician encountering a patient who complains, rather vaguely, that he feels tired. The way in which the physician defines and frames this initial complaint is likely to have an important impact on the physician's ultimate success in solving the problem.

Kinds of problems. Problems typically fall into one of the three categories exemplified in Figure 5-8: arrangement, inducing structure, and transformation (Greeno, 1978). Each requires somewhat different kinds of psychological skills and knowledge to solve.

Arrangement problems require that a group of elements be re-arranged or recombined in a way that will satisfy a certain criterion. There are usually several different possible arrangements that can be made, but only one or a few of the arrangements produce a solution. Anagram problems and jigsaw puzzles represent arrangement problems.

In problems of **inducing structure**, a person must identify the relations that exist among the elements presented and construct a new relationship among them. In such a problem, it is necessary to determine not only the relationships among the elements but the structure and size of the elements involved. In the example shown in Figure 5-8, a person must first determine that the solution requires the numbers to be considered in pairs (14-24-34-44-54-64). It is only after that part of the problem is identified that the solution rule (the first number of each pair increases by one, while the second number remains the same) can be determined.

The Tower of Hanoi puzzle represents still another kind of problem. **Transformation problems** consist of an initial state, a goal state, and a series of methods for changing the initial state into the goal state. In the Tower of Hanoi problem, the initial state is the original configuration; the goal state consists of the three disks on the third peg; and the method consists of the rules for moving the disks.

Whether the problem is one of arrangement, inducing structure, or transformation, the initial stage of understanding and diagnosing is critical in problem solving because it allows us to develop our own cognitive representation of the problem and to place it within a personal frame-

---

A.   ARRANGEMENT PROBLEMS

   ANAGRAMS: Rearrange the letters in each set to make an English word:

      EFCTA
      IAENV
      BODUT
      LIVAN
      IKCTH

B.   PROBLEMS OF INDUCING STRUCTURE

1.   What number comes next in this series?

                        142434445464

2.   Complete the analogy:
     baseball is to bat as tennis is to   a. kick
                                                    b. court
                                                    c. racket

C.   TRANSFORMATION PROBLEMS

   1. HOBBITS AND ORCS: 2. WATER JARS

Three hobbits and three orcs stand   A person has three jars having the
on one side of a river. On their   capacities listed. How can the
side of the river is a boat which   person measure exactly 11 ounces
will hold up to two creatures.   of water?
The problem is to transport all six   Jar A—28 ounces
creatures to the other side of the   Jar B— 7 ounces
river. However, if orcs ever   Jar C— 5 ounces
outnumber hobbits, orcs will eat the
hobbits. How should they get
across?

                        (Solutions are on page 200.)

FIGURE 5-8

The major categories of problems: (a) arrangement, (b) inducing structure, and (c) transformation. (Bourne et al., 1986.)

work. The problem may be divided into subparts, or some information
may be ignored, as we try to simplify the task. Winnowing out the ines-
sential information is often a critical step in problem solving.

Representing and organizing the problem. A crucial aspect of the
initial encounter with a problem is the way in which we represent it to
ourselves and organize the information presented to us. Consider the following problem:

> A man climbs a mountain on Saturday, leaving at daybreak and arriving at
> the top near sundown. He spends the night at the top. The next day, Sunday,
> he leaves at daybreak and heads down the mountain, following the same
> path that he climbed the day before. The question is this: Will there be any
> time during the second day when he will be at exactly the same point on the
> mountain as he was at that time on the first day?

If you try to solve this problem by using algebraic or verbal representations, you will have a good deal of trouble. However, if you represent
the problem with the kind of simple diagram illustrated in Figure 5-9, the
solution becomes apparent.

FIGURE 5-9
Using a graph, it is easy to solve the problem posed at the bottom of page 199. Remember, the goal is not to determine the time, but just to indicate whether an exact time exists. (Anderson, 1980.)

Successful problem solving, then, requires that a person form an appropriate representation and organization of the problem. However, there is no one optimal way of representing and organizing material, since that is dependent on the nature of the problem. Sometimes simply restructuring a problem, from a verbal form to a pictorial or mathematical form for instance, can help point out a direct solution (Mayer, 1982).

Production: Generating Solutions

If a problem is relatively simple, a direct solution may already be stored in long-term memory, and all that is necessary is to retrieve the appropriate information. If the solution cannot be retrieved, or is not known, a process by which possible solutions are generated and compared with information in long- and short-term memory is instigated.

At the most primitive level, solutions to problems can be obtained through trial and error. Thomas Edison was able to invent the light bulb only because he tried thousands of different kinds of material for a filament before he found one that worked (carbon). The difficulty with trial and error is, of course, that some problems are so complicated it would take close to forever to try out every possibility. For example, according to one estimate, there are some 10^{120} possible sequences of chess moves.

Answers to problems posed in Figure 5-8

A. facet, naive, doubt, anvil, thick

B. 1. 7
   2. c

C. 1. Hobbits and Orcs. (Using h = hobbit, o = Orc, F = forward boat move, B = backward boat move; for example, F/2o means move the boat forward with two orcs): F/2o (or F/1h, 1o), B/1o (or B/1h), F/2o, B/1o, F/2h, B/1h, 1o, F/2h, B/1o, F/2o, B/1h (or B/1o), F/1h, 1o (or F/2o).

   2. Fill jar A, empty into jar B once and into jar C twice. What remains in jar A is 11 oz.

In place of trial and error, more complex problem solving requires the use of algorithms and heuristics. An **algorithm** is a set of rules which, if followed, guarantee a solution, even if the reason it works is not understood. For example, you may know that the length of the third side of a right triangle can be found by using the formula $a^2 + b^2 = c^2$. You may not have the foggiest notion why it works, but this algorithm is always accurate and provides you with a solution to a particular problem.

Heuristics, in contrast, are rules of thumb or mental shortcuts that may lead to a solution but are not guaranteed to do so (Groner, Groner & Bischof, 1983). For example, a heuristic that chess players often follow is to gain control of the center of the board. The tactic doesn't guarantee that they will win, but it does increase their chances. Similarly, students may follow the heuristic of preparing for a test by ignoring the assigned textbook reading and studying only their lecture notes—a strategy that may or may not pay off.

Several general heuristics tend to be employed in solving problems that require making judgments or decisions. **Representativeness** is the heuristic in which people determine whether a given example is a member of a particular category by evaluating how representative it is of that category. Suppose, for instance, you are the owner of a fast-food store and you have been robbed many times by people who come into your store looking nervous and shifty. The next time someone who fits this description enters your store, it is likely that—if you employ the representativeness heuristic—you will assume that danger lurks, since your prior experience suggests that the person is likely to be a member of a class of people you have come to know as "thief."

The **availability heuristic** involves judging the probability of an event by how easily the event can be recalled from memory (Tversky & Kahneman, 1974). According to this heuristic, we assume that events we recall easily are likely to have occurred more frequently in the past, and we further assume that the same sort of event is more likely to occur in the future. The availability heuristic explains why, after we hear about an airplane crash, we estimate a greater likelihood of being in a crash ourselves.

Probably the most frequently applied heuristic is a means-ends analysis. In a **means-ends analysis**, a person repeatedly tests for differences between the desired outcome and what currently exists, trying each time to reduce the difference between the possible solution and desired outcome. For example, people using a means-ends analysis to search for the correct sequence of roads to get to a city that they can see in the distance would analyze their solutions in terms of how much closer each individual choice of roadways brings them to the ultimate goal of arriving at the city. Such a strategy is effective, though, only if there is a direct solution to the problem. If the problem is such that indirect steps have to be taken that appear to *increase* the discrepancy between the current state and the solution, means-ends analyses can be counterproductive. In our example, if roadways are laid out in such a way that a person must temporarily move *away* from the city in order to reach it eventually, a means-ends analysis will keep the person from reaching the goal.

In fact, for some problems the converse of a means-ends approach is the most effective: working backward by beginning with the goal and moving toward the starting state. Instead of altering the elements of a problem in a series of steps that move closer and closer to the solution, people can work in the opposite direction, moving away from the goal and aiming to reach the beginning point (Malin, 1979; Bourne et al., 1986).

Subgoals. Another commonly used heuristic is to divide a problem into intermediate steps, or subgoals, and to solve each of those steps. For instance, if you return to the Tower of Hanoi problem, there are several obvious subgoals that could be chosen, such as moving the largest disk to the third post.

If solving a subgoal is part of the ultimate solution to a problem, then identifying subgoals is an appropriate strategy. There are cases, however, in which the formation of subgoals is not all that helpful and may actually take the problem solver longer to find a solution (Reed, 1988; Hayes, 1966). For example, some problems cannot be subdivided. Others are so difficult to subdivide that it takes longer to identify the appropriate subdivisions than to solve the problem by other means. Finally, even when a problem is divided into subgoals, it may be unclear what to do when the subgoal has been reached.

Insight. Some approaches to problem solving focus less on step-by-step processes than on the sudden bursts of comprehension that may come when solving a problem. Just after World War I, German psychologist Wolfgang Köhler examined the learning and problem-solving processes in chimps (Köhler, 1927). In his studies, Köhler exposed chimps to challenging situations in which the elements of the solution were all present; what was necessary was for the chimps to put them together.

For example, in one series of studies, chimps were kept in a cage in which boxes and sticks were strewn about, with a bunch of tantalizing bananas hanging high in the cage out of their reach. Initially, the chimps engaged in a variety of trial-and-error attempts at getting to the bananas: They would throw the stick at the bananas, jump from one of the boxes, or leap wildly from the ground. Frequently, they would seem to give up in frustration, leaving the bananas dangling temptingly overhead. But then, in what seemed like a sudden revelation, they would leave whatever activity they were involved in and stand on a box in order to be able to reach the bananas with a stick. Köhler called the cognitive processes underlying the chimps' behavior **insight**, a sudden awareness of the rela-

(a)   (b)   (c)

In a remarkable display of problem solving, Köhler's chimp Sultan sees a bunch of bananas out of his reach (*a*). He then retrieves several crates sitting in the room (*b*), and stacks them up so that he can reach the bananas (*c*).

tionships among various elements that had previously appeared to be independent of one another.

Although Köhler emphasized the apparent suddenness with which solutions were revealed, subsequent research has shown that prior experience and initial trial-and-error practice in problem solving are prerequisites for producing the appearance of insight (Metcalfe, 1986). One study demonstrated that only chimps who had experience in playing with sticks could successfully solve the problem; inexperienced chimps never made the connection between standing on the box and reaching the bananas (Birch, 1945). Some researchers have suggested that the behavior of the monkeys represented little more than the chaining together of previously learned responses, no different from the way a pigeon learns, by trial and error, to peck a key (Epstein, 1987; Epstein et al., 1984). It is clear that insight depends on previous experience with the elements involved in a problem.

Judgment: Evaluating the Solutions

The final step in problem solving consists of judging the adequacy of a solution. Often, this is a simple matter: If there is a clear solution—as in the Tower of Hanoi problem—we will know immediately whether we have been successful. On the other hand, if the solution is less concrete, or if there is no single correct solution, evaluating solutions becomes more difficult.

If there is more than one solution to a problem, or if the solution criteria are vague, we must decide which solution alternative is best. Unfortunately, we are sometimes quite inaccurate in estimating the quality of our own ideas: there is often little relationship between our own judgments of the quality of our ideas and more objective criteria (Johnson, Parrott & Stratton, 1968).

Theoretically, if the heuristics and information we rely on to make decisions are appropriate and valid, we can make accurate choices among problem solutions. However, as we see next, there are several kinds of obstacles and biases in problem solving that affect the quality of the decisions we make.

OVERCOMING OBSTACLES TO PROBLEM SOLVING

Consider the following problem-solving test (Duncker, 1945): You are presented with a set of tacks, candles, and matches in small boxes, and told your goal is to place three candles at eye level on a nearby door, so that wax will not drip on the floor as the candles burn (see Figure 5-10). How would you approach this challenge?

If you have difficulty solving the problem, you are not alone: Most people are unable to solve it when it is presented in the manner illustrated in the figure, in which the objects are located *inside* the boxes. On the other hand, if the objects were presented *beside* the boxes, just resting on the table, chances are you would solve the problem much more readily—

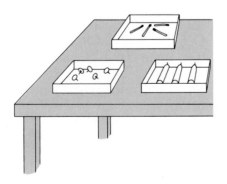

FIGURE 5-10
The problem here is to place three candles at eye level on a nearby door so that the wax will not drip on the floor as the candles burn—using only materials in the figure (tacks, candles, and matches in boxes). For a solution, turn to page 206, Figure 5-11.

which, in case you are wondering, requires tacking up the boxes and then placing the candles on top of them (see Figure 5-11).

The difficulty you probably had in solving the problem stems from its presentation and relates to the fact that you were misled at the initial preparation stage. In fact, significant obstacles to problem solving exist at each of the three major stages. Although cognitive approaches to problem solving suggest that thinking proceeds along fairly rational, logical lines as a person confronts a problem and considers various solutions, there are actually a number of factors acting to hinder the development of creative, appropriate, and accurate solutions.

Preparation Hindrances: Jumping to Conclusions

The reason that most people experience difficulty with the candle problem rests on a phenomenon known as **functional fixedness**, the tendency to think of an object only in terms of its typical use. Functional fixedness occurs because the objects are first presented inside the boxes which are then seen simply as containers for the objects they hold rather than as a potential part of the solution.

Functional fixedness is an example of a broader phenomenon known as **mental set**, the tendency for old patterns of problem solving to persist. This phenomenon was demonstrated in a classic experiment carried out by Abraham Luchins (1946). As you can see in Figure 5-12, the object of the task is to use the jars in each row to measure out the designated amount of liquid. (Try it yourself to get a sense of the importance of mental set before moving on.)

If you have tried the problem, you know that the first five parts are all solved in the same way: Fill the largest jar (B) and from it fill the middle-size jar (A) once and the smallest jar (C) two times. What is left in B is the designated amount. (Stated as a formula, it is $B - A - 2C$.) The demonstration of mental set comes with the sixth part of the problem, a point at which you probably encountered some difficulty. If you are like most people, you tried the formula and were perplexed when it failed. Chances are, in fact, that you missed the simple (but different) solution to the problem, which simply involves subtracting C from A. Interestingly, those people who were given problem six *first* had no difficulty with it at all.

Production Hindrances: Biases in Algorithms and Heuristics

Suppose you encounter a person named Tom who is highly intelligent, neat, and orderly, but lacks true creativity. His writing is rather dull, although it is occasionally enlivened by corny puns and flashes of sci-fi

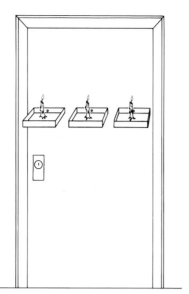

FIGURE 5-11
A solution to the problem posed in Figure 5-10 involves tacking the boxes to the wall and placing the candles on the boxes.

imagination. Being rather self-centered, he does not have much feeling and is not sympathetic to others, but he does have a strong moral sense.

If you were asked whether he is a computer science major or a humanities major, what would you guess? To answer such a question, the first thing you would probably do is to employ the heuristic of representativeness and determine how well the person fits your mental image of "computer science major" or "humanities major." If you are like most people, you'll probably opt for computer science major.

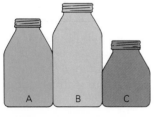

	Given jars with these capacities (in quarts)			Obtain
	A	B	C	
1.	21	127	3	100
2.	14	163	25	99
3.	18	43	10	5
4.	9	42	6	21
5.	20	59	4	31
6.	28	76	3	25

FIGURE 5-12
Try this classic demonstration, which illustrates the importance of mental set in problem solving. The object is to use the jars in each row to measure out the designated amount of liquid. After you figure out the solution for the first five rows, you'll probably have trouble with the sixth row—even though the solution is actually easier. In fact, if you had tried to solve the problem in the sixth row first, you probably would have had no difficulty at all.

However, what if you were to learn that Tom is a member of a class of 100 students, of whom 80 are humanities majors and 20 are computer science majors? Has your guess changed on the basis of this new information?

Your answer is most likely "no." But if you were to follow the laws of logic and probability more precisely, your answer *should* have changed, despite the representativeness heuristic: chances are that any one person from the class would most likely belong to the group of 80 who are humanities majors, regardless of any personality characteristics that that person may display (Kahneman & Tversky, 1973).

Although algorithms and heuristics most frequently help us to solve problems, their use may sometimes backfire. In one of the major obstacles to problem solving, we may apply algorithms and heuristics to situations in which they are not relevant, thereby coming up with incorrect solutions or applying them erroneously. Consider the following information:

> There are two programs in a high school. Boys are a majority (65 percent) in program A and a minority (45 percent) in program B. There are an equal number of classes in each of the two programs. You enter a class at random and observe that 55 percent of the students are boys. What is your best guess: Does the class belong to program A or to program B? (Kahneman & Tversky, 1972, p. 433).

Most people rely on the heuristic of representativeness to come up with the answer that the class belongs to program A—a solution that is incorrect. They assume that just because there are more boys in the class, and there are more boys than girls in program A, this particular class is more likely to represent program A.

However, there are several considerations that lead to a different—and more accurate—conclusion. First, recall that there are equal numbers of classes in the two programs, and therefore any class that one enters is equally likely to be in either program. Moreover, the specific percentage of boys found in the class (55 percent) is halfway between the percentage of boys in program A (65 percent) and the percentage of boys in program B (45 percent). In fact, the most reasonable answer is that it is no more likely for the class to be in either program A or B. In this case, the representativeness heuristic leads people astray.

The availability heuristic, in which judgments of the probability of an event are based on how easily the event can be recalled, is also a potential source of error in problem solving. Suppose you were asked to pick up a dictionary and randomly choose a word with at least three letters. After you have chosen a word, would you think it more likely that the first letter or the third letter of the word would be an "r"?

Most people conclude that the first letter would more likely be an "r," which is erroneous. (The letter "r" actually occurs more frequently as the third letter than the first in the English language.) The reason for the mistaken judgment? It is considerably easier to retrieve words from memory that start with a given letter (run, rats, root) than it is to retrieve words on the basis of their third letter (bar, tart, purse).

As you see, the same heuristics that assist in problem solving can also be misapplied and act as hindrances in finding the correct solution to problems. But it is not only at the production stage that heuristics can hinder problem solving; even during the final judgment stage, the misuse of heuristics can lead to confusion.

Judgment Hindrances: Obstacles to Accurate Evaluation of Solutions

When the nuclear power plant at Three Mile Island in Pennsylvania suffered its initial malfunction in 1979—a disaster that almost led to a nuclear meltdown—the plant operators were faced immediately with solving a problem of the most serious kind. Several monitors indicated contradictory information about the source of the problem: One suggested that the pressure was too high, leading to the danger of an explosion; others indicated that the pressure was too low, which could lead to a meltdown. Although the pressure was in fact too low, the supervisors on duty relied on the one monitor—which was faulty—that suggested the pressure was too high. Once they had made their decision and acted upon it, they ignored the contradictory evidence from the other monitors (Wickens, 1984).

One reason for the operators' mistake is the **confirmation bias**, in which initial hypotheses are favored and contradictory information supporting alternative hypotheses or solutions is ignored. Even when we find evidence that contradicts a solution we have chosen, then, we are apt to stick with our original hypothesis.

There are several reasons for the confirmation bias. One is that it takes cognitive effort to rethink a problem that appears to be already solved, so we are apt to stick with our first solution. Another is that evidence contradicting an initial solution may present something of a threat to our self-esteem, leading us to hold to the solutions that we have come up with first (Fischoff, 1977; Rasmussen, 1981).

Creativity

Despite obstacles to problem solving, people are very adept at coming up with creative solutions to problems. In fact, one of the enduring questions that cognitive psychologists have tried to answer is what factors underlie **creativity**, which is usually defined as the combining of responses or ideas in novel ways (Mumford & Gustafson, 1988).

Although being able to identify the stages of problem solving helps us to understand how people approach and solve problems, it does little to explain why some people come up with better solutions than others. There are several factors, however, that seem to be associated with creativity (Richards et al., 1988).

One factor that is closely related to creativity is divergent thinking. **Divergent thinking** refers to the ability to generate unusual, but still appropriate, responses to problems or questions. This type of thinking contrasts with **convergent thinking**, which produces responses that are based primarily on knowledge and logic. For instance, convergent thinking answers "You read it" to the query "What do you do with a newspaper?" In contrast, "You use it as a dustpan" is a more divergent—and creative—response.

Another ingredient of creativity is **cognitive complexity**, the use of and preference for elaborate, intricate, and complex stimuli and thinking patterns. Similarly, creative people often have a wider range of interests and are more independent and more interested in philosophical or abstract problems than are less creative individuals (Barron, 1969).

One factor that is *not* closely related to creativity is intelligence. In fact, because most tests of intelligence focus on convergent thinking skills—their problems are well defined and have only one acceptable answer—creative people who are divergent thinkers may find themselves at a disadvantage. This may explain why researchers consistently find that creativity is only slightly related to intelligence or school grades, particularly when intelligence is measured using typical intelligence tests (Barron & Harrington, 1981; Sternberg, 1986).

The Informed Consumer of Psychology: Thinking Critically and Creatively

On the basis of the research we have discussed on problem solving, thinking, and creativity, there are several strategies that can help you think more critically and evaluate problems more creatively—whether they be the challenges of everyday life or more academically oriented problems such as finding the correct solution to a question on a test. Suggestions for increasing critical thinking and creativity include (Baron & Sternberg, 1986; Feldman & Schwartzberg, 1990; Hayes, 1989):

- Redefine problems. The boundaries and assumptions you hold can be modified; the problem can be rephrased at a more abstract or more concrete level, depending on how it is initially presented, or it can be divided into separate parts (Rice, 1984).

- Adopt a critical perspective. Rather than passively accepting assumptions or arguments, critically evaluate material by considering

its implications and thinking about possible exceptions and contradictions.

- Use analogies. Analogies not only help us uncover new understanding, they provide alternative frameworks for interpreting facts. One
particularly effective means of coming up with analogies is to look
for them in the animal kingdom when the problem concerns people,
and in physics or chemistry when the problem concerns inanimate
objects.

- Think divergently. Instead of thinking in terms of the most logical
or most common use for an object, consider how it might be of help
if you were forbidden to use it in its usual way.

- Take the perspective of another person, either one who is involved
in the situation or who is a disinterested bystander. In doing so, you
may get a fresh view on the situation.

- Use heuristics. As mentioned earlier, heuristics are rules of thumb
that can help bring about a solution to a problem. If the nature of
the problem is such that it has a single, correct answer, and a heuristic is available—or can be constructed—using the heuristic frequently helps to develop a solution more rapidly and effectively.

- Experiment with different solutions. Don't be afraid to use different
routes to solutions to problems (verbal, mathematical, graphic, even
acting out a situation). Try coming up with every conceivable idea
you can, no matter how wild or bizarre it may seem at first. After
you have come up with a list of solutions, you can go back over
each and try to think of ways of making what at first appeared
impractical seem more feasible.

ASK YOURSELF

What are the three steps people pass through in problem solving?

What are algorithms and heuristics?

How does insight aid in problem solving?

What are the obstacles to successful problem solving?

How is creativity related to divergent thinking and cognitive complexity?

When faced with a difficult problem, why might asking someone
else's advice be helpful?

What is the difference between a good student and a creative
student? Why might the creative student sometimes receive
poorer grades?

COMMUNICATING WITH OTHERS: LANGUAGE

'Twas brillig, and the slithy toves
    Did gyre and gimble in the wabe:
All mimsy were the borogoves,
    And the mome raths outgrabe.

Although few of us have ever come face to face with a tove, we have little difficulty in discerning that in Lewis Carroll's (1872) poem "Jabberwocky," the expression "slithy toves" contains an adjective, "slithy," and the noun it modifies, "toves."

Our ability to make sense out of nonsense, if the nonsense follows typical rules of language, illustrates both the sophistication of human language capabilities and the complexity of the processes that underlie the development and use of language. The way in which people are able to use **language**—the systematic, meaningful arrangement of symbols—clearly represents an important ability, one that is indispensable for communicating with others. But language is not only central to communication, it is closely tied to the very way in which we think about and understand the world, for there is a crucial link between cognition and language. It is not surprising, then, that psychologists have devoted considerable attention to studying the topic of language.

The Language of Language: Grammar

In order to understand how language develops, and its relationship to cognition, we first need to discuss some of the formal elements that constitute language. The basic structure of language rests on **grammar**, the framework of rules that determine how our thoughts can be expressed.

Grammar deals with three major components of language: phonology, syntax, and semantics. **Phonology** refers to the smallest unit of sounds, called **phonemes**, that affect the meaning of speech and the way we use those sounds to produce meaning by placing them into the form of words. For instance, the "a" in "fat" and the "a" in "rake" represent two different phonemes in English.

Although English-speakers use just forty-two basic phonemes to produce words, the basic phonemes of other languages range from as few as fifteen to as many as eighty-five (Akmajian, Demers & Harnish, 1984). The differences in phonemes underlies one reason why people have difficulty in learning other languages: for example, to the Japanese-speaker, whose native language does not have an "r" phoneme, English words such as "roar" present some difficulty.

Syntax refers to the rules that indicate how words and phrases can be combined to form sentences. Every language has intricate rules that guide the order in which words may be strung together to communicate meaning. English-speakers have no difficulty in knowing that "Radio down the turn" is not an appropriate sequence, while "Turn down the radio" is. The importance of appropriate syntax is demonstrated by the changes in meaning that come from the differing order of words in the following three sequences: "John kidnapped the boy," "John, the kidnapped boy," and, "The boy kidnapped John."

The third major component of language is semantics. **Semantics** refers to the rules governing the meaning of words and sentences. Semantic rules allow us to use words to convey the most subtle of nuances. For instance, we are able to make the distinction between "The truck hit Laura" (which we would be likely to say if we had just seen the vehicle hitting Laura) and "Laura was hit by a truck" (which we would probably say if asked why Laura was missing class while she recuperated).

Despite the complexities of language, most of us acquire the basics of grammar without even being aware that we have learned its rules (Rice, 1989). Moreover, even though we might have difficulty explicitly stating the rules of grammar that we employ, our linguistic abilities are so sophisticated that they enable us to utter an infinite number of different statements. We turn now to how such abilities are acquired.

Developing a Way with Words: Language Development

To parents, the sounds of their infant babbling and cooing are music to the ears (except, perhaps, at three o'clock in the morning). These sounds also serve an important function: They mark the first step on the road to the development of language.

Children **babble**—making speechlike but meaningless sounds—from around 3 months to a year. While babbling, they may produce, at one time or another, any of the sounds found in all languages, not just the one to which they are exposed. However, babbling increasingly begins to reflect the specific language that is being spoken in the environment, initially in terms of pitch and tone, and eventually in terms of specific sounds (Reich, 1986).

By the time the child is around a year old, sounds that are not in the language disappear. It is then a short step to the production of actual words. In English, these are typically short words that start with a consonant such as "b," "d," "m," "p," or "t"—helping to explain why "mama" and "dada" are so often among the first words to be said. Of course, even before they produce their first words, children are capable of understanding a fair amount of the language they hear. Language comprehension, then, precedes language production.

After the age of 1 year, children begin to learn more complicated forms of language. They produce two-word combinations, which become the building blocks of sentences, and there is an acceleration in the number of different words they are capable of using. For example, by the age of

2 years, the average child has a vocabulary of more than fifty words. Just six months later, the vocabulary has grown to several hundred. At that time, children can produce short sentences, although they use **telegraphic speech**—sentences that literally sound as if they were part of a telegram, in which words not critical to the message are dropped. Rather than saying, "I showed you the book," a child using telegraphic speech might say, "I show book," and "I am drawing a dog" might become "Drawing dog." As the child gets older, of course, the use of telegraphic speech declines and sentences become increasingly complex.

By the time children are 3 years old, they learn to make plurals by adding "s" to nouns, and they are able to form the past tense by adding "ed" to verbs. This ability also leads to errors, since children tend to apply rules indiscriminately. This phenomenon is known as **overregularization**, whereby children apply rules even when the application results in an error. Thus, although it is correct to say "he walked" for the past tense of "walk," the "ed" rule doesn't work quite so well when children say "he runned" for the past tense of "run."

Much of children's acquisition of the basic rules of language is complete by the time they are 5. However, a full vocabulary and the ability to comprehend and use subtle grammatical rules are not attained until later. For example, if you showed a 5-year-old boy a blindfolded doll and asked, "Is the doll easy or hard to see?" he would have great difficulty answering the question. In fact, if he were asked to make the doll easier to see, he would probably try to take off the doll's blindfold. On the other hand, 9-year-olds have little difficulty understanding the question, realizing that the doll's blindfold has nothing to do with an observer's ability to see the doll (Chomsky, 1969).

The Roots of Language: Understanding Language Acquisition

While anyone who is around children will notice the enormous strides that are made in language development throughout childhood, the reasons for this rapid growth are less obvious. Two major explanations have been put forward: one based on learning theory and the other on innate processes.

The learning-theory approach suggests that language acquisition follows the principles of reinforcement and conditioning we discussed in Chapter 4. For example, a child who utters the word "mama" is hugged and praised by her mother, thereby reinforcing the behavior and making its repetition more likely. This view suggests that children first learn to speak by being rewarded for making sounds that approximate speech. Ultimately, through a process of shaping, language becomes more and more like adult speech (Skinner, 1957).

As children develop, their language becomes increasingly sophisticated. By the age of 5, they are able to communicate in a surprisingly sophisticated fashion, even adjusting the complexity of their speech to match the comprehension level of the listener.

The learning-theory approach is less successful when it comes to explaining the acquisition of language rules. Children are reinforced not only when they use proper language, but also when they respond incorrectly. For example, parents answer "Why the dog won't eat?" as eagerly as they do the correct "Why won't the dog eat?"; both sentences are understood equally well. Learning-theory views thus do not seem to provide the full story of language acquisition.

An alternative model is provided by Noam Chomsky (1968, 1978), who argues that innate mechanisms play an important role in learning a language. He suggests that humans are born with an innate linguistic capability that emerges primarily as a function of maturation. According to his analysis, all the world's languages share a similar underlying structure—what he calls a **universal grammar**—which is based on the structure and functions of the human brain. The brain has a neural system, the **language-acquisition device**, which not only permits the understanding of the structure of a language but also provides people with strategies and techniques for learning the unique characteristics of a native language.

According to this view, then, language is a uniquely human phenomenon brought about by the presence of the language-acquisition device.

Chomsky's view, as you might suspect, is not without its critics, particularly among learning theorists, who contend that the fact that chimpanzees can seemingly be taught the fundamentals of sign language and communicate with humans argues against the innate view (deLuce & Wilder, 1983; Keerdoja, 1985). The issue of how humans acquire language thus remains hotly contested (Rice, 1989).

Does Language Determine Thought—
or Does Thought Determine Language?

When an Eskimo woman peers outside her igloo and sees that it is snowing, she doesn't simply announce, "It's snowing." For Eskimos have at their disposal more than twenty individual words to describe different sorts of snow. This linguistic prowess suggests an important question: Do Eskimos *think* about snow differently than do English-speakers?

The answer to that question is quite controversial. According to the **linguistic-relativity hypothesis**, language shapes and, in fact, may determine the way people of a particular culture perceive and understand the world (Whorf, 1956). According to this view, Eskimos think about snow in a way that is qualitatively different from the way English-speakers think about it, since the range of linguistic categories provided by the Eskimo language permits finer discriminations than the more limited English language.

Let us consider another possibility, however. Suppose that, instead of language being the *cause* of certain ways of thinking about the world, language is a *result* of thinking about and experiencing relevant stimuli in the environment. In this view, thought *produces* language. The only reason Eskimos have more words for "snow" than we do is that snow is considerably more relevant to them than it is to people in most other cultures. According to this point of view, if we were to move to the Arctic Circle (or become ski bums), we would be perfectly capable of differentiating various types of snow. Our language usage might not be particularly eloquent (we might say "deep, crunchy, hard-packing snow that is going to be on the ground all winter"), but we would have no trouble perceiving and thinking about the differences in snow.

By and large, most research has been unsupportive of the linguistic relativity hypothesis (Brown, 1986). It seems most appropriate to conclude that, in general, cognition influences language and not the other way around. On the other hand, language *does* affect thinking and cognition in some ways. For instance, the manner in which information is stored in memory—and how well such information can subsequently be retrieved—is related to language (Cairns & Cairns, 1976). Likewise, the linguistic categories available in a given language affect the way that concepts are formed. Finally, our impressions and memory of others' personality and behavior are affected by the linguistic categories provided us by the language we speak (Hoffman, Lau & Johnson, 1986). Although language does not determine thought, then, it certainly influences it.

ASK YOURSELF

What is grammar?

How does language develop as children age?

What is the distinction between the learning-theory view and Chomsky's explanation for language acquisition?

Does language determine thought or does thought determine language?

If you travel to another country, how might learning the native language help to enrich your experience there, even if English is also spoken by many of the local people?

LOOKING BACK

1. Cognitive psychologists study cognition, which encompasses the higher mental processes. These processes include the way people know and understand the world, process information, make judgments and decisions, and describe their knowledge and understanding to others.

2. Memory is defined by the three R's of remembering; it consists of the capacity to record, retain, and retrieve information. There are three basic kinds of memory storage: sensory memory, short-term memory, and long-term memory.

3. Sensory memory (made up of memories corresponding to each of the sensory systems) is the first place where information about the world is saved, although the memories are very brief. Unless they are transferred to other types of memory, however, sensory memories appear to be lost.

4. Roughly seven (plus or minus two) chunks of information are capable of being transferred and held in short-term memory. Information in short-term memory is held from fifteen to twenty-five seconds and, if not transferred to long-term memory, is lost primarily through interference, as well as through decay.

5. Memories are transferred into long-term storage through rehearsal. The most effective type is elaborative rehearsal, in which the material to be remembered is organized and expanded. Formal techniques for organizing material are called mnemonics. If memories are transferred into long-term memory, they become relatively permanent. Long-term memories are of two types: episodic and semantic.

6. The levels-of-processing approach to memory suggests that the way in which information is initially perceived and analyzed determines the success with which the information is recalled. The deeper the initial processing, the greater the recall of the material.

7. The tip-of-the-tongue phenomenon refers

to the experience of trying in vain to remember information that one is certain one knows. A major way of successfully recalling information is to use retrieval cues, stimuli that permit a search through long-term memory. Flashbulb memories illustrate the point that the more distinctive a memory, the more easily it can be retrieved—a phenomenon called the von Restorff effect.

8. Memory is a constructive process in which we relate memories to the meaning, guesses, and expectations that we give to the events the memory recalls.

9. Even with the use of retrieval cues, some information appears irretrievable, owing to decay or interference. Interference seems to be the major cause of forgetting. There are two sorts of interference: proactive interference and retroactive interference.

10. The major memory dysfunctions include Alzheimer's disease, retrograde amnesia, anterograde amnesia and Korsakoff's syndrome.

11. Problem solving typically follows three major steps: preparation, production of solutions, and evaluation of solutions that have been generated. Preparation begins when people try to understand the problem. In arrangement problems, a group of elements must be rearranged or recombined in a way that will satisfy a certain criterion. In problems of inducing structure, a person must identify the relationships among the elements presented and construct a new relationship among them. Finally, transformation problems consist of an initial state, a goal state, and a series of methods for changing the initial state into the goal state.

12. In the production stage, people try to generate solutions. The solutions to some problems may already be in long-term memory and can be directly retrieved. In addition, some problems may be solved through simple trial-and-error. More complex problems, however, require the use of algorithms and heuristics.

13. One approach to problem solving is ex-

emplified by Köhler's research with chimps, in which the elements of the situation had to be manipulated in a novel fashion in order for the chimps to solve the problem. Köhler called the cognitive processes underlying the chimps' behavior insight, a sudden awareness of the relationships among elements that had previously seemed independent.

14. Several factors hinder effective problem solving. Functional fixedness is an example of a broader phenomenon known as mental set. The inappropriate use of algorithms and heuristics can also act as an obstacle to the production of solutions to problems. Finally, the confirmation bias can hinder the accurate evaluation of solutions to problems.

15. Creativity is the combining of responses or ideas in novel ways. Divergent thinking is the ability to respond with unusual, but still appropriate, responses to problems or questions and is associated with creativity. Cognitive complexity, the use of and preference for elaborate, intricate, and complex stimuli and thinking patterns, is also related to creativity.

16. Language is the systematic, meaningful arrangement of symbols. All languages have a grammar—a framework of rules that determine how our thoughts can be expressed—which encompasses the three major components of language: phonology, syntax, and semantics.

17. Language production, preceded by language comprehension, develops out of babbling (speechlike but meaningless sounds), which leads to the production of actual words. After a year, children use two-word combinations and their vocabulary increases. They first use telegraphic speech, in which words not critical to the message are dropped. By the age of 5, acquisition of language rules is relatively complete.

18. There are two major theories of language acquisition. Learning theorists suggest that language is acquired simply through reinforcement and conditioning. In contrast, Chomsky suggests that there is an

innate language-acquisition device which guides the development of language. The degree to which language is a uniquely human skill remains controversial.

19. The linguistic-relativity hypothesis suggests that language shapes and may determine the way people think about the world. Most evidence suggests that although language does not determine thought, it does affect the way information is stored in memory and how well it can be retrieved.

Key Terms and Concepts

cognitive psychology (p. 174)
cognition (p. 174)
memory (p. 175)
encoding (p. 175)
storage (p. 175)
retrieval (p. 175)
sensory memory (p. 176)
short-term memory (p. 176)
long-term memory (p. 176)
iconic memory (p. 176)
echoic memory (p. 176)
chunk (p. 179)
rehearsal (p. 180)
elaborative rehearsal (p. 181)
mnemonics (p. 181)
episodic memories (p. 182)
semantic memories (p. 182)
linguistic code (p. 183)
imaginal code (p. 183)
motor code (p. 183)
levels-of-processing theory (p. 184)
tip-of-the-tongue phenomena (p. 185)
retrieval cue (p. 186)
recall (p. 186)
recognition (p. 186)
flashbulb memories (p. 188)
von Restorff effect (p. 189)
constructive processes (p. 190)
schemas (p. 190)
serial reproduction (p. 190)
decay (p. 192)
memory trace (p. 192)
interference (p. 193)
proactive interference (p. 193)

retroactive interference (p. 193)
Alzheimer's disease (p. 194)
amnesia (p. 195)
retrograde amnesia (p. 195)
anterograde amnesia (p. 195)
Korsakoff's syndrome (p. 195)
arrangement problems (p. 198)
inducing structure problems (p. 198)
transformation problems (p. 198)
algorithm (p. 201)
heuristic (p. 201)
representativeness heuristic (p. 201)
availability heuristic (p. 201)
means-ends analysis (p. 201)
insight (p. 202)
functional fixedness (p. 205)
mental set (p. 205)
confirmation bias (p. 208)
creativity (p. 208)
divergent thinking (p. 209)
convergent thinking (p. 209)
cognitive complexity (p. 209)
language (p. 211)
grammar (p. 211)
phonology (p. 211)
phonemes (p. 211)
syntax (p. 211)
semantics (p. 212)
babble (p. 212)
telegraphic speech (p. 213)
overregularization (p. 213)
universal grammar (p. 214)
language-acquisition device (p. 214)
linguistic-relativity hypothesis (p. 215)

6

Motivation and Emotion

❖

Prologue: Christine Bergel ◆ Looking Ahead ◆ Conceptions of Motivation ◆ Eat, Drink, and Be Daring: Human Needs and Motivation ◆ Understanding Emotional Experience ◆ Knowing How We Feel: Understanding Our Own Emotions ◆ Expressing Emotions: The Role of Nonverbal Behavior ◆ Looking Back

PROLOGUE: CHRISTINE BERGEL

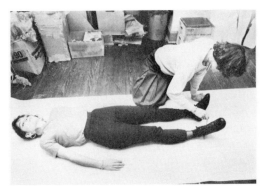

Prior to being photographed, Christine Bergel said she was afraid she would appear too fat. Having her body outline traced gave her an opportunity to view her own silhouette more objectively.

She could be the girl next door. Bright, hard-working, successful and good-looking, 20-year-old Christine Bergel was a standard against whom others compared themselves.

The trouble was that Christine never saw herself in the way others did. She hated how she looked and grew preoccupied with her appearance and weight. To cope with her feelings, Christine secretly began repeated cycles of binging on huge quantities of food and then eliminating the food by vomiting. During her worst times, she would stuff herself and then force herself to throw up three times a day. Obsessed by the thought that she was too fat, she exercised three hours daily. Her constant binging-and-purging cycles were accompanied by deep feelings of guilt and depression over what she recognized as self-destructive behavior.

Christine's problem is called bulimia, and it is shared by some 10 percent of college-age women. It is one of a number of eating disorders that afflict mainly women of college age, although it can be found in others as well. The habitual binging-and-purging cycles of bulimia can lead to digestive-tract problems, rotted teeth, and even

219

heart failure. Other eating disorders may lead people to literally starve themselves to death.

Christine's story, however, has a happy ending. Realizing the seriousness of her problem, Christine checked herself into the Renfrew Center, the first residential treatment facility in the United States designed exclusively for people with eating disorders. After six weeks of treatment, which included individual and group therapy, Christine came to put her eating behavior, and her obsession with her appearance, in perspective. As she says, "Somebody could look at my picture and say, 'Oh, she's pretty. Bulimia didn't do anything to her.' But that's all I was, my looks. It was such a shallow world" (Kohn, 1987).

*L*OOKING AHEAD

Fortunately, few of us have eating behavior problems as severe as those that beset Christine Bergel. In fact, the major question that psychologists face when considering eating is just how we manage to regulate our food intake so effectively. Most of us show only minor variation in weight from one day to another, even though the kind of food we eat and the amount may vary significantly.

Eating behavior is just one aspect of the two central topics of psychology to which we turn our attention in this chapter: motivation and emotion. **Motivation** looks at the factors that direct and energize the behavior of humans and other organisms. Psychologists who study motivation seek to discover the **motives,** or desired goals, that underlie behavior. Such motives may be as fundamental as eating to satisfy the motive of hunger or as inconsequential as taking a walk to obtain exercise. To the psychologist specializing in the study of motivation, the common factor in both behaviors is that underlying motives are assumed to steer the choice of both activities.

The study of motivation, then, consists of identifying why people do the things they do. Psychologists studying motivation ask questions such as these: "Why do people choose particular goals for which to strive?" "What specific motives direct behavior?" "What are the individual differences in motivation that account for the variability in people's behavior?"

Whereas motivation is concerned with the forces that direct future behavior, a second, and related, major area of psychology—emotion—deals with the feelings we experience throughout the course of our lives. The study of emotions focuses on our internal experiences at any given moment. Most of us have felt a variety of emotions: happiness at getting an A on a difficult exam, sadness brought about by the death of a loved one, anger at being unfairly treated. Because emotions not only can motivate our behavior but also can reflect our underlying motivation, they play a broad role in our lives, and the study of emotions has been a critical area for psychologists.

In this chapter, we consider motivation and emotion. We begin by focusing on the major conceptions of motivation, discussing how the different motives and needs people experience jointly affect behavior. We consider both primary motives, those that are biologically based and universal such as hunger and sex, as well as motives that are unique to humans: the need for achievement, the need for affiliation, and the need for power. We then turn to the nature of emotional experience on both a physiological and a cognitive level. We consider the roles and functions that emotions play in people's lives, discussing a number of theories meant to explain how people understand what emotion they are experiencing at a given moment. Finally, the chapter ends with a discussion of how emotions are communicated to others through nonverbal behavior.

After you finish this chapter, then, you will be able to answer questions such as these:

- What are the biological and social factors that underlie eating and sexual behavior?
- How are needs such as the need for achievement, affiliation, and power exhibited?
- What factors lead to the experience of an emotion?
- What are the major emotions and their functions?
- How does nonverbal behavior relate to the expression of emotions?

*C*ONCEPTIONS OF MOTIVATION

Consider the case of 22-year-old Marine Lance Cpl. Karl Bell, who spent forty days in a steep canyon after falling in a freak hiking accident. Avoiding starvation by eating anything he could find, even ants, Bell finally found a way out. He had lost seventy-five pounds, his ankle was fractured, his body was covered with hundreds of cuts, and his clothing was torn to shreds. But he had managed to stay alive, after fighting every day and night to save himself.

What was it that drove Bell on, even in the face of overwhelming odds against survival? Like most questions revolving around motivation, this one has several answers. Clearly, biological aspects of motivation were at work: The need for food, water, and warmth affected Bell's attempts to extricate himself from the canyon. But cognitive factors were also apparent in his belief that he was too young to die. Finally, social factors—his desire to see family and friends—helped keep his will to survive intact.

The complexity of motivation has led to the development of a variety of conceptual approaches to it. Although they vary in the degree to which they encompass biological, cognitive, and social factors, all seek to explain the energy that guides people's behavior in particular directions.

Born to Be Motivated: Instincts

Psychologists first sought to explain motivation in terms of **instincts,** inborn patterns of behavior that are biologically determined. According to instinctive theories of motivation, people and animals are born with preprogrammed sets of behaviors essential to their survival. These instincts provide the energy that channels behavior in appropriate directions. Hence, sex might be explained as a response to an instinct for reproduction, and exploratory behavior might be viewed as motivated by an instinct to examine one's territory.

There are several difficulties with such a conception, however. For one thing, psychologists have been unable to agree on what the primary instincts are. One early psychologist, William McDougall (1908), suggested that there were eighteen, including pugnacity and gregariousness. Others found even more—with one sociologist claiming that there were exactly 5,759. Clearly, such an extensive enumeration provides little more than labels for behavior.

No explanation based on the concept of instincts goes very far in explaining *why* a specific pattern of behavior, and not some other, has appeared in a given individual. Furthermore, the variety and complexity of human behavior, much of which is clearly learned, are difficult to explain if instincts are the primary motivational force. Therefore, conceptions of motivation based on instincts have largely been supplanted by newer theories, although instinctual approaches still play a role in contemporary psychology. For example, in later chapters we will discuss Freud's theories, which suggest that such instinctual drives as sex and aggression largely motivate behavior. Moreover, many animal behaviors clearly have an instinctual basis.

Drive-Reduction Theories of Motivation

In rejecting instinct theory, psychologists first proposed simple **drive-reduction theories** of motivation in its place (Hull, 1943). Drive-reduction theories suggest that when people lack some basic biological requirement such as water, a drive to obtain that requirement (in this case, the thirst drive) is produced.

To understand the approach, we need to begin with the concept of drive. A **drive** is motivational tension, or arousal, that energizes behavior in order to fulfill some need. Many basic kinds of drives, such as hunger, thirst, sleepiness, and sex, are related to biological requirements of the body or of the species as a whole. These are called **primary drives.** Primary drives contrast with **secondary drives,** in which no obvious biological need is being fulfilled. In secondary drives, needs are brought about by prior experience and learning. As we will discuss later, some people have strong needs to achieve academically and in their careers; we can say that their achievement need is a secondary drive motivating their behavior.

We usually try to resolve a primary drive by reducing the need underlying it: After exercising, we may become thirsty and seek out the nearest water fountain. We become hungry after not eating for a few hours and may raid the refrigerator if our next scheduled meal is too far away. If the weather turns cold, we put on extra clothing or raise the setting on the thermostat in order to keep warm.

The reason for such behavior is homeostasis, a basic motivational phenomenon underlying primary drives. **Homeostasis** is the process by which a person or animal tries to maintain some optimal level of internal biological functioning by compensating for deviations from its usual, balanced, internal state. Although not all basic biological behaviors related to motivation fit a homeostatic model—sexual behavior is one example, as we will see later in the chapter—most of the fundamental needs of life, including hunger, thirst, and the need for sleep, can be explained reasonably well by such an approach.

Unfortunately, although drive-reduction theories provide a good explanation of how primary drives motivate behavior, they are inadequate when it comes to explaining behaviors in which the goal is not to reduce a drive, but rather to maintain or even to increase a particular level of excitement or arousal. For example, many of us go out of our way to seek thrills through such activities as riding a roller coaster and steering a raft down the rapids of a river.

Other behaviors seem to be motivated by nothing more than curiosity. Anyone who has rushed to pick up newly delivered mail, or who avidly follows gossip columns in the newspaper, or who yearns to travel to exotic places, knows the importance of curiosity in directing behavior. And it is not just human beings who display behavior indicative of curiosity: Even monkeys will learn to press a bar just to be able to peer into another room, especially if something interesting (such as a toy train moving along a track) can be glimpsed (Butler, 1954). Monkeys will also expend considerable energy solving simple mechanical puzzles, even though their behavior produces no obvious reward (Harlow, Harlow & Meyer, 1950; Mineka & Hendersen, 1985).

Thrill seeking and curiosity are just two kinds of behavior that shed doubt on drive-reduction theories of motivation. In both cases, rather than seeking to reduce an underlying drive, people and animals appear to be motivated to increase their overall level of stimulation and activity. In order to explain this phenomenon, psychologists have suggested several alternatives to drive reduction.

The Search for Stimulation: Arousal Theory

Arousal theories seek to explain behavior in which the goal is the maintenance of or an increase in excitement (Berlyne, 1967; Brehm & Self, 1989). According to **arousal theory,** each of us tries to maintain a certain level of stimulation and activity. As with the drive-reduction model, if our stimulation and activity levels become too high, we try to reduce them. But the arousal model also suggests something quite different from the drive-reduction model: If the levels of stimulation and activity are too low, we will try to *increase* them by seeking stimulation.

Arousal theory provides an explanation for one of the oldest principles of psychology, devised by two psychologists in 1908: the **Yerkes-Dodson law.** According to this law and its later revisions, a particular level of motivational arousal produces optimal performance on a task; more specifically, performance on simple tasks usually benefits from higher levels of arousal than does performance on more complex tasks (Hebb, 1955). It seems as if high arousal gets in the way of successful responses to complex tasks, while promoting better performance on simpler tasks (see Figure 6-1).

On the other hand, both complex and simple tasks suffer when the level of arousal is *too* high. In this case, the arousal is distracting and anxiety-producing, decreasing performance regardless of the difficulty of the task (Covington & Omelich, 1987). In sum, consistent with arousal theory, there is an optimal level of arousal for task performance; arousal that is either too high or too low will result in poorer performance.

Arousal theory has significant applications to a variety of fields. For example, students who are highly anxious while taking tests on complex material may perform well below their ability because of their high level of arousal. In a completely different realm—the baseball field—research has shown that batting performance, which represents a complex task, suffers under conditions of high arousal but is enhanced under conditions of low arousal (Jackson, Buglione & Glenwick, 1988).

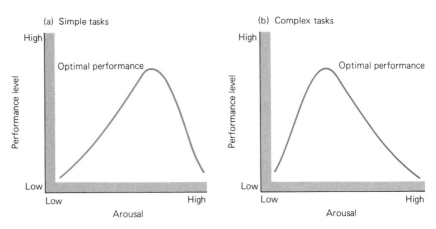

FIGURE 6-1
The Yerkes-Dodson law claims that the optimal performance on a task will come from different levels of arousal, depending on whether the task is simple as seen in (*a*) or complex as seen in (*b*).

Pulling Behavior: Incentive Theory

When a luscious dessert is brought to the table after a filling meal, the attraction we feel has little or nothing to do with internal drives or with the maintenance of arousal. Rather, if we choose to eat the dessert, such behavior is motivated by the external stimulus of the dessert itself, which acts as an anticipated reward. This reward, in motivational terms, is an **incentive.**

Incentive theory attempts to explain why behavior is not always motivated by an internal need such as the desire to reduce drives or to maintain an optimum level of arousal. Instead of focusing on internal factors, incentive theory explains motivation in terms of the nature of the external stimuli—the incentives that direct and energize behavior. In this view, properties of external stimuli largely account for a person's motivation.

Although the theory explains why we may succumb to an incentive (such as an attractive dessert) even though internal cues (such as hunger) are lacking, it seems insufficient to provide a complete explanation of motivation, since organisms seek to fulfill needs even when incentives are not apparent. Because of this, many psychologists feel that the internal drives proposed by drive-reduction theory work in tandem with the external incentives of incentive theory to "push" and "pull" behavior, respectively. Rather than contradicting each other, then, drives *and* incentives may work together in motivating behavior (Hoyenga & Hoyenga, 1984).

The Yin and Yang of Motivation: Opponent-Process Theory

When Chinese philosophers suggested long ago that there were two opposing forces in the universe—the yin and the yang—which influenced human behavior, they were foreshadowing the development of one further model of motivation called opponent-process theory (Solomon & Corbit, 1974). **Opponent-process theory** helps explain the motivation behind such phenomena as drug addiction and the physiological and emotional reactions that occur as a result of extremes of physical danger, as in skydiving.

According to opponent-process theory, stimuli that first produce increases in arousal later produce an opposite, calming reaction in the nervous system, whereas stimuli that first produce decreases in arousal later produce an increase in arousal. Moreover, with each exposure to a stimulus, the original response to the stimulus remains fairly stable or perhaps even declines, while the opponent process—the reaction to the original response—tends to grow in strength.

Let's look at some concrete examples. Suppose a man takes a drug that produces feelings of unusual happiness. According to the theory,

after these initial positive feelings subside, an opponent process will follow, swinging the man toward an opposite of happiness, or depression.
In addition, the theory suggests that the opponent process (depression)
tends to strengthen each time the drug is taken, whereas the initial process
(happiness) tends to weaken. Consequently, the negative reaction will
increase after each drug use, whereas the pleasure derived from the drug
will decline. Ultimately, the man's motivation to increase the positive
process (and avoid the eventual unpleasant opponent process) will lead
him to take a larger quantity of the drug—likely resulting in a pattern of
addiction.

Opponent processes work in the reverse way when the initial experience is negative. Consider a woman about to make her first skydiving
jump from an airplane. Her initial reaction is likely to be one of terror.
But there will also be an opponent process at work: a feeling of euphoria
after the jump is over. Opponent-process theory suggests that each time
she jumps, the original process resulting in terror will grow no stronger
and in fact may even weaken, whereas the opponent process resulting in
euphoria is likely to increase. Ultimately, then, skydiving may become
almost addictive to a skydiver.

In sum, opponent-process theory helps explain why people hold
strong motivation for behavior that on the surface has few benefits. It is
frequently the opponent process, not the initial reaction, that maintains
the motivation to carry out such behavior.

Thinking about Motives: Cognitive Theory

One contemporary approach to motivation focuses on the role of our
thoughts, expectations, and understanding of the world. As we will discuss in detail in Chapter 12, we develop sophisticated explanations for
the causes behind other people's behavior, and these explanations have
an important impact on our own subsequent behavior. In short, each of
us develops our own, personal motivational theories, based on our understanding of the world, in an effort to explain the reasons for others'
behavior.

One central distinction psychologists make is intrinsic versus extrinsic
motivation. **Intrinsic motivation** causes us to participate in an activity for
our own enjoyment, not for any tangible reward that it will bring us. In
contrast, **extrinsic motivation** causes us to do something for a tangible
reward. According to research on the two types of motivation, we are
more apt to persist, work harder, and produce work of higher quality
when motivation for a task is intrinsic rather than extrinsic (Lepper, 1984;
Deci & Ryan, 1985).

Such research suggests the importance of promoting intrinsic motivation and indicates that providing extrinsic rewards may actually un-
dermine the effort and quality of performance. Teachers might think

twice, then, about offering their students an A for a good composition. Instead, the work on intrinsic motivation suggests that better results would come from reminding students about the intrinsic reasons—such as the joys of producing a carefully crafted paper—for good performance.

Ordering Motivational Needs: Maslow's Hierarchy

What do Eleanor Roosevelt, Abraham Lincoln, and Albert Einstein have in common? Quite a bit, according to a model of motivation devised by psychologist Abraham Maslow: Each of them reached and fulfilled the highest levels of motivational needs underlying human behavior.

Maslow's model considers different motivational needs to be ordered in a hierarchy, and it suggests that before more sophisticated, higher-order needs can be met, certain primary needs must be satisfied (Maslow, 1970; 1987). The model can be thought of as a pyramid (see Figure 6-2) in which the more basic needs are at the bottom and the higher-level needs are at the top. In order for a particular need to be activated and thereby guide a person's behavior, the more basic needs in the hierarchy must be met first.

The most basic needs are those described earlier as primary drives: needs for water, food, sleep, sex, and the like. In order to move up the

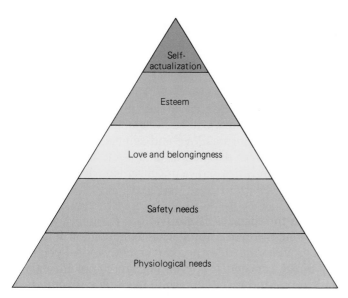

FIGURE 6-2
Maslow's hierarchy shows how our motivation progresses up the pyramid from a basis in the broadest, most fundamental biological needs to higher-order ones. (After Maslow, 1970.)

hierarchy, a person must have these basic physiological needs met. Safety needs come next in the hierarchy; Maslow suggests that people need a safe, secure environment in order to function effectively. Physiological and safety needs compose the lower-order needs.

Only when the basic lower-order needs are met can a person consider fulfilling higher-order needs, consisting of love and belongingness, esteem, and self-actualization. Love and belongingness needs include the need to obtain and give affection and to be a contributing member of some group or society. After these needs are fulfilled, the person strives for esteem. In Maslow's thinking, esteem relates to the need to develop a sense of self-worth by knowing that others are aware of one's competence and value.

Once these four sets of needs are fulfilled—no easy task—the person is ready to strive for the highest-level need, self-actualization. **Self-actualization** is a state of self-fulfillment in which people realize their highest potential. When Maslow first discussed the concept, he used it to describe just a few well-known individuals such as Eleanor Roosevelt, Lincoln, and Einstein. But self-actualization is not limited to the famous. A parent with excellent nurturing skills who raises a family, a teacher who year after year creates an environment that maximizes students' success, and an artist who realizes her creative potential might all be self-actualized. The important thing is that people feel at ease with themselves and satisfied that they are using their talents to the fullest. In a sense, reaching self-actualization produces a decline in the striving and yearning for greater fulfillment that marks most people's lives and instead provides a sense of satisfaction with the current state of affairs.

Although there is very little research to validate the exact ordering of the stages of Maslow's theory (Haymes, Green, & Quinto, 1984), the model is important in two ways: It highlights the complexity of human needs, and it emphasizes the fact that until more basic biological needs are met, people are going to be relatively unconcerned with higher-order needs. If people are hungry, their first interest will be in obtaining food; they will not be concerned with such things as love and self-esteem. The model helps explain why victims of such disasters as famine and war may suffer the breakdown of normal family ties and be unconcerned with the welfare of anyone other than themselves.

A final word about the theories of motivation. Now that we have examined several different theoretical approaches to motivation, it is natural to wonder which provides the fullest account of motivational phenomena. In fact, many of the conceptual approaches are complementary—rather than contradictory—and it is often useful to employ several theories simultaneously in order to understand a particular motivational system. Thus, as we next consider specific motives, such as the needs for food, water, achievement, affiliation, and power, we will draw upon several of the theories in order to gain a full understanding of motivation.

*A*SK YOURSELF

What is the definition of motivation?

What are primary and secondary drives?

How can drive-reduction theory, arousal theory, and opponent-process theory be distinguished?

What are the stages of Maslow's motivational hierarchy?

How much of your time do you spend satisfying primary drives?

Can primary drives and secondary drives be satisfied at the same time by the same behavior?

*E*AT, DRINK AND BE DARING: HUMAN NEEDS AND MOTIVATION

To Bob, doing well in college meant that he would get into a good law school, which he saw as a stepping-stone to a successful future. Consequently, he never let up academically and always tried his best to do well in his courses. But his constant academic striving went well beyond the desire to get into law school; he tried not only to get good grades, but to get *better* grades than his classmates.

In fact, Bob was always trying to be the best at everything he did. He could turn the simplest activity into a competition. Bob couldn't even play poker without acting as if his success at the game were essential. There were, however, some areas in which he didn't compete. He was interested only if he thought he had a fighting chance to succeed; he ignored challenges that were too difficult as well as those that were too easy for him.

What is the motivation behind Bob's consistent striving to achieve? To answer that question, we must begin to consider some of the specific kinds of needs that underlie behavior.

We will examine several of the most important human needs. Because human beings are in a fundamental sense biological creatures, we first consider the primary drives of hunger and sex. But because much of human behavior has no clear biological basis, we will also examine the secondary drives—those uniquely human strivings, based on learned needs and past experience, that help explain behavior such as Bob's.

Eating Your Needs Away: Hunger

With about one quarter of the United States population suffering from **obesity** (defined as being more than 20 percent above the average weight for a person of a given height), losing unwanted weight has become an American obsession. Many people spend untold time, energy, and money attempting to regulate the amount and type of food they eat in order to decrease their weight. Others, with a problem many of us would envy, are concerned with trying to *gain* weight. Yet, in most cases, people who are not monitoring their weight show only minor weight fluctuations in spite of substantial variations in how much they eat and exercise over time. Clearly, then, eating is subject to some form of homeostasis.

Psychologists began their search for an understanding of eating motivation with animals, which are relatively free of the problems of obesity that beset human beings. Most nonhumans, when left in an environment in which food is readily available, do a good job regulating their intake—as anyone knows who makes sure that a dish of food is always available for a pet. Cats, for instance, will eat only until their immediate hunger is satisfied; they leave the remainder, returning to it only when internal cues tell them to eat.

Furthermore, there appear to be internal mechanisms that regulate not only the quantity of food intake, but the kind of food that an animal desires. Hungry rats that have been deprived of particular foods tend to seek out alternatives that contain the specific nutrients their diet is lacking, and laboratory experiments show that animals given the choice of a wide variety of foods in cafeteria-like settings choose a fairly well-balanced diet (Rozin, 1977).

The mechanisms by which organisms know whether they require food or should stop eating are complex ones (Keesey & Powley, 1986). It is not just a matter of an empty stomach causing hunger pangs and a full one alleviating hunger, since people who have had their stomachs removed still experience the sensation of hunger (Inglefinger, 1944). Similarly, laboratory animals tend to eat larger quantities when their food is low in nutrients; in contrast, when given a high-nutrient diet, they lower their food intake—despite the degree to which their stomach is empty or full or the amount of time it takes to eat the food (Harte, Travers & Savich, 1948).

It appears, then, that animals, as well as people, are sensitive to both the amount and the nutritional value of the foods they eat (Barker, Best & Domjan, 1977). One mechanism that helps to regulate food intake is a change in the chemical composition of the blood. For instance, experiments show that when glucose, a kind of sugar, is injected into the blood, hunger decreases, and animals will refuse to eat. On the other hand, when insulin, a hormone that is involved in the conversion of glucose into stored fat, is introduced into the bloodstream, hunger increases (Rodin, 1985).

But what part of the body monitors changes in the blood chemistry relating to eating behavior? One particular structure of the brain, the **hypothalamus,** appears to be primarily responsible for food intake. Injury to the hypothalamus has been shown to cause radical changes in eating behavior, depending upon the site of the injury. For example, rats whose **lateral hypothalamus** is damaged may literally starve to death; they refuse food when offered, and unless they are force-fed they eventually die. Rats with an injury to the **ventromedial hypothalamus** display the opposite problem: extreme overeating. Rats with this injury can increase in weight by as much as 400 percent (see Figure 6-3). Similar phenomena occur in humans who have tumors of the hypothalamus.

Although it is clear that the hypothalamus plays an important role in regulating food intake, the exact mechanism by which it operates is uncertain. Some researchers think it affects an organism's sense or perception of hunger; others hypothesize that it directly regulates the neural connections that control the muscles involved in eating behavior (Stricker & Zigmond, 1976).

One theory suggests that injury to the hypothalamus affects the weight set point by which food intake is regulated (Nisbett, 1972). The **weight set point** is the particular level of weight that the body strives to maintain. Acting as a kind of internal weight thermostat, the hypothalamus calls for either greater or less food intake. According to this explanation, injury to the hypothalamus drastically raises or lowers the set point, and the organism strives to meet its internal goal by increasing or decreasing its food consumption.

Social factors in eating. You have just finished a full meal and are completely stuffed. Suddenly, your host announces with great fanfare that he will be serving his "house specialty" dessert, flaming bananas, and

FIGURE 6-3
Following an operation in which its ventromedial hypothalamus was cut, this obviously pudgy rat tipped the scales at something on the order of four times its normal weight.

that he has spent the better part of the afternoon preparing it. Even though you are full and don't even like bananas, you accept a serving of his dessert and eat it all.

Clearly, internal biological factors are not the full story when it comes to explaining our eating behavior. External social factors, based on societal rules and conventions, and on what we have learned about appropriate eating behavior from our prior experience, also play an important role.

Take, for example, the simple fact that people customarily eat breakfast, lunch, and dinner at approximately the same times every day. Because we are accustomed to eating on schedule every day, we tend to feel hungry as the usual hour approaches—sometimes quite independently of what our internal cues are telling us. Similarly, we tend to take roughly the same amount of food on our plates every day—even though the amount of exercise we may have had, and consequently our need for energy replenishment, varies from day to day. We also tend to prefer particular foods over others; grasshoppers may be a delicacy in certain cultures, but few people in western cultures find them greatly appealing—despite their potentially high nutritional value. In sum, cultural influences and our own individual habits play an important role in determining when, what, and how much we eat (Boaks, Popplewell, & Burton, 1987).

An oversensitivity to external eating cues based on social convention, and a parallel insensitivity to internal hunger cues, is related to obesity in some individuals. Research has shown, for example, that obese people who are placed in a room next to an inviting bowl of crackers are apt to eat considerably more than nonobese people—even though they may have just finished a filling sandwich (Schachter, Goldman & Gordon, 1968). In addition, obese individuals are more apt to scorn and avoid unpleasant-tasting food—even if they have been deprived of food for a period of time—than nonobese individuals, who tend to be less concerned with the taste of the food, suggesting that the obese respond less to internal hunger cues than the nonobese. Finally, the obese are less apt to eat if doing so involves any sort of work: In one experiment obese subjects were less likely to eat nuts that had to be shelled, but ate copious amounts of nuts that already had their shells removed. Nonobese people, in contrast, ate the same amount of nuts, regardless of whether it was necessary to remove the shells (Schachter, 1971).

At the same time that obese people are overly sensitive to external cues, they may be relatively insensitive to internal hunger cues. In fact, there is essentially no correspondence between reports of hunger in obese individuals and the amount of time they have been deprived of food, in contrast to a significant correlation for people of normal weight (Nisbett, 1968). It thus appears that many obese people give undue attention to external cues and are less aware of the internal cues that help nonobese people regulate their eating behavior.

On the other hand, many individuals who are highly reliant on external cues never become obese, and there are quite a few obese people

The appearance of these fat cells, magnified many times, illustrates the outcome of over-eating.

who are relatively unresponsive to external cues (Rodin, 1981). Other factors, then, are clearly at work in determining why some people become obese.

The weight set point, metabolism, and obesity. One suspect that appears to be a plausible cause of obesity is the weight set point. Specifically, it is possible that overweight people have higher set points than people of normal weight. Because their set points are unusually high, their attempts to lose weight by eating less may make them especially sensitive to external, food-related cues and therefore more apt to eat, perpetuating their obesity.

But why may some people's weight set points be higher than others? One factor may be the size and number of fat cells in the body, which rise as a function of weight increase. Because the set-point level may reflect the number of fat cells a person has, any increase in weight, which raises the number of fat cells, may raise the set point. Moreover, any loss of weight after the age of 2 does not decrease the number of fat cells in the body, although it may cause them to shrink in size (Knittle, 1975). Hence, although fat babies are sometimes considered cute, obese children may have acquired so many fat cells that their weight set point is too high— long after they have reached the age at which being chubby or fat is still appealing.

In sum, according to weight-set-point theory, the presence of too many fat cells may result in the set point becoming "stuck" at a higher level than is desirable. Under such circumstances, losing weight becomes a difficult proposition, since one is constantly at odds with one's own internal set point.

Other factors also work against people's efforts to lose weight. For example, there are large differences in people's **metabolism**, the rate at which energy is produced and expanded by the body. Some people, with a high metabolism rate, seem to be able to eat as much as they want without gaining weight, while others, with low metabolism, may eat only half as much and yet gain weight readily. Actually, those who gain weight easily are biologically more efficient: They have the dubious advantage of easily converting food into body tissue. In contrast, those who are able to eat large quantities without gaining weight are inefficient in using the foods they eat; much gets wasted—and they stay thin.

Still other factors may lead to obesity. Children who are given food after becoming upset may learn, through the basic mechanisms of classical and operant conditioning, that eating is associated with consolation, so they may eat whenever they experience difficulties as adults. When parents provide food as the "treatment" for their child's stress, anxiety, and depression, eating may become a learned response to any emotional difficulty, leading to eating behavior that has little or nothing to do with internal hunger cues (Davis, 1986; Herman & Polivy, 1975).

In the most extreme cases, eating behavior can be so disordered that it becomes life threatening, as described in the case of Christine Bergel at the beginning of the chapter. In one major disorder, **anorexia nervosa**, people may refuse to eat, while denying that their behavior and appearance—which can become skeleton-like—are unusual. Some 15 to 20 percent of anorexics literally starve to death.

Anorexia nervosa afflicts mainly females between the ages of 12 and the early twenties, although both men and women of other ages may develop it. People with the disorder tend to come from stable homes, and they typically are successful, attractive, and relatively affluent. Their lives revolve around food: although they eat little themselves, they may cook for others, go shopping for food frequently, or collect cookbooks (Brumberg, 1988).

Christine Bergel suffered from a related problem, **bulimia**, a disorder in which a person binges on incredibly large quantities of food. An entire gallon of ice cream and a whole pie may easily be consumed in a single sitting. Following such a binge, sufferers feel guilt and depression and typically induce vomiting or take laxatives to rid themselves of the food—behavior known as purging. Constant binging-and-purging cycles, and the use of drugs to induce vomiting or diarrhea, may create a chemical imbalance that can lead to heart failure. Typically, though, the weight of a person suffering from bulimia remains normal (Fichter, 1990).

What causes anorexia nervosa or bulimia? Some researchers suspect there is a physiological cause such as a chemical imbalance in the hypothalamus or pituitary gland (Gold et al., 1986). Other psychologists feel that the cause is rooted in societal expectations about the value of slenderness, in social definitions of appropriate eating behavior, or in strained family interactions (Polivy & Herman, 1985). For instance, some evidence suggests that there are clear standards on certain college campuses about "appropriate" binging behavior, and the amount of binging is associated with a woman's popularity (Crandall, 1988). It would not be surprising if anorexia nervosa and bulimia were found to stem from both physiological and social causes, just as eating behavior in general is influenced by a variety of factors (Hsu, 1990; Schlundt & Johnson, 1990).

The Informed Consumer of Psychology: Dieting and Losing Weight Successfully

For many people, dieting represents a losing battle: Most people who diet eventually regain the weight they have lost, so they try again and get caught in a seemingly endless cycle of weight loss and gain. Given what we know about the causes of obesity this is not entirely surprising, since there appear to be so many factors that affect eating behavior and weight.

According to Jules Hirsch, an obesity specialist, there are several things to keep in mind when trying to lose weight (Kolata, 1988):

- There is no easy route to weight control; you will have to make permanent changes in your life in order to lose weight. The most obvious step, cutting down on the amount of food you eat, is just the beginning of a lifetime commitment to changing your eating habits.

- Exercise. When you exercise, you burn fat stored in your body, which is used as fuel for the muscles that are working. As this fat is used, you will probably lose weight. Weight-set-point theory suggests another advantage to moderate exercise: It may lower your set point. Although there is some dispute about just how much exercise is sufficient to actually lower weight (Pi-Sunyer, 1987), most experts recommend at least thirty consecutive minutes of moderate exercise at least three times a week. (If nothing else, the release of endorphins following exercise—discussed in Chapter 2—will make you feel better, even if you don't lose weight.)

- Decrease the influence of external, social stimuli on your eating behavior. There are a number of things you can do to lower your susceptibility to external food cues. For example, you can give yourself smaller portions of food, or you can leave the table before you see what is available for dessert. Don't even buy snack foods such as peanuts or potato chips; if they're not readily available in the kitchen cupboard, you're not apt to eat them. Wrap foods in the refrigerator in aluminum foil so you cannot see the contents. That way, you won't be tantalized by the sight of food every time you open the refrigerator.

- Avoid fad diets. No matter how popular they are at a given time, over the long term extreme diets usually don't work (Charlier, 1988).

Above all, don't feel guilty if you don't succeed in losing weight. The inability to lose weight should not be seen as a major failure in life. Indeed, you are in good company, for some 90 percent of dieters put back the weight they have lost (Bennett & Gurin, 1982). And even a relatively small weight loss is better than none: just a 10 percent drop in body weight may lower the major health risks that are associated with obesity (Brody, 1987).

The Facts of Life: Human Sexual Motivation

You would probably find no argument with the statement that sex is very different from hunger as a motivational drive. Unlike hunger, no one ever died from an unfulfilled sexual need. Similar to hunger, however, sex remains one of our primary motivating forces, fulfilling not only important biological needs but some crucial social ones as well.

Anyone who has seen two dogs mating knows that sexual behavior has a biological basis; their sexual behavior appears to occur spontaneously, without much prompting on the part of others. In fact, a number of genetically controlled factors influence the sexual behavior of animals. For instance, animal behavior is affected by the presence of certain hormones in the blood. Moreover, females are receptive to sexual advances only at certain, relatively limited periods of time during the year.

Human sexual behavior, by comparison, is more complicated, although the underlying biology is not all that different from related species. In males, for example, the **testes** secrete androgen, the male sex hormone, beginning at puberty. Not only does androgen produce secondary sex characteristics, such as the development of body hair and a deepening of the voice; it also increases the sex drive. Although there are long-term changes in the amount of androgen that is produced—with the greatest production occurring just after sexual maturity—its short-term production is fairly constant. Men, therefore, are capable of (and interested in) sexual activities without any regard to biological cycles. Given the proper stimuli leading to arousal, male sexual behavior can occur.

Women show a different, and more complex, pattern. When they reach maturity at puberty, the two **ovaries,** the female reproductive organs, begin to produce estrogen—the female sex hormone. Estrogen, however, is not produced consistently; instead, its production follows a cyclical pattern. The greatest production occurs during **ovulation,** when an egg is released from the ovaries, making the chances of fertilization by a male sperm cell highest. Although in lower animals the period around ovulation is the only time that the female is receptive to sex, human beings are different: Although there are variations in reported sex drive, women are receptive to sex throughout their cycles, depending on the external

People's sexual fantasies can take many forms, as suggested by this painting by surrealist Paul Delvaux. (*Phases of the Moon.* 1939. Oil on canvas, 55 × 63″. Collection, The Museum of Modern Art, New York. Purchase.)

stimuli they encounter in their environment (Hoon, Bruce & Kinchloe, 1982).

Though biological factors "prime" people for sex, it takes more than hormones to motivate and produce sexual behavior. In animals it is the presence of a partner who provides arousing stimuli that leads to sexual activity. Humans are considerably more versatile; not only other people, but nearly any object, sight, smell, sound, or other stimulus can lead to sexual excitement. Because of prior associations, then, people may be turned on sexually by the smell of Chanel No. 5 or Brut, the sight of a bikini brief, or the sound of a favorite song, hummed softly in their ear.

Sexual fantasies also play an important role in producing sexual arousal. Not only do people have fantasies of a sexual nature during their everyday activities, but about 60 percent of all people have fantasies during sexual intercourse. Interestingly, such fantasies often include having sex with someone other than one's partner of the moment.

Men's and women's fantasies differ little from each other in terms of content, as you can see in Figure 6-4. For both sexes, thoughts of being sexually irresistible and of engaging in oral-genital sex are most common (Sue, 1979). It is important to note that fantasies are just that—fantasies—

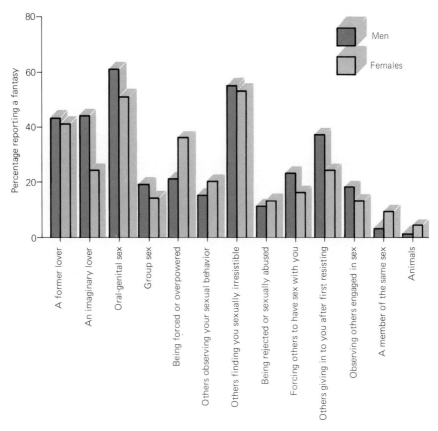

FIGURE 6-4
The kinds of fantasies that men and women have during sexual intercourse are relatively similar. (Sue, 1979.)

and do not represent a desire to fulfill them in the real world. We should not assume from such data that females want to be sexually overpowered, nor should we assume that in every male lurks a potential rapist desirous of forcing sexual overtures on a submissive victim.

The varieties of sexual experience. The variety of human sexual behavior was largely a mystery shrouded in ignorance until the 1930s, when Albert Kinsey, a biologist by training, began a series of surveys on the sexual behavior of Americans that was to span eighteen years.

Kinsey's work, as well as subsequent surveys (e.g., Klassen et al., 1989), has provided us with a fairly complete picture of the kinds of sexual activities and behavior that people typically engage in in private. It is important to keep in mind, though, that such a picture only represents a snapshot in time, as there can be rapid and rather dramatic shifts in sexual practices. An example is the impact of AIDS on sexual behavior, discussed in the Psychology and Society box.

PSYCHOLOGY AND SOCIETY

The Case of AIDS

No factor has had a greater effect on sexual behavior in the last decade than **acquired immune deficiency syndrome,** or **AIDS.** Transmitted only through sexual contact or by exposure to infected blood, AIDS has no cure and is ultimately fatal to those afflicted with it.

Although AIDS began in the United States largely as a disease affecting homosexuals, it has spread to other populations, and in some parts of the world, such as Africa, it primarily affects heterosexuals. In America, it is thought that there are more than 1 million people presently infected with the AIDS virus, all of whom will die unless a cure is found. The worldwide figures are even more daunting: as many as 8 to 10 million individuals are thought to carry the AIDS virus. By the end of this decade, close to 20 million will be infected (Crowley, 1990).

Although some researchers argue the odds of contracting AIDS from any one sexual encounter are not high (Hearst & Hulley, 1988), others dispute this contention (Masters, Johnson & Kolodny, 1988). However, the outcome of getting the ultimately fatal disease is of such magnitude that AIDS has led to several large-scale changes in sexual behavior. People are less likely to engage in "casual" sex with new acquaintances, and the use of condoms during sexual intercourse has increased (Adler, 1985; McKusick, Horstman & Coates, 1985; Bauman & Siegel, 1987; O'Keefe, Nesselhof-Kendall, & Baum, 1990).

The only foolproof method of avoiding AIDS is celibacy—a drastic step that most people find an unrealistic alternative. However, there are ways of reducing the risk of contracting AIDS through what have come to be called "safe sex" practices. Safe sex practices include the following guidelines:

• *Know your sexual partner—well.* Sexual activities are risky with someone whose sex-

The spread of AIDS has led to many forms of educational outreach, such as this discussion group led by Ronald Austin of the New Jersey Department of Health.

ual history is unfamiliar to you. Before entering into a sexual relationship with someone, be aware of his or her background.

• *Avoid the exchange of bodily fluids, particularly semen.* In particular, most experts recommend the avoidance of anal intercourse. The AIDS virus can spread through small tears in the rectum, making anal intercourse without using condoms particularly dangerous.

• *Use condoms.* For those in sexual relationships, condoms are the most reliable means of preventing transmission of the AIDS virus.

• *Consider the benefits of monogamy.* People in long-term, monogamous relationships with partners who have been faithful are at a lower risk of contracting AIDS.

AIDS presents several profound psychological issues (Backer et al., 1988; Namir et al., 1987). First, there is the question of how to treat the psychological distress of victims of the disease, who must face the knowledge that their disease is incurable and invariably fatal—and that society is fearful that they will spread the disease. Second, because a blood test can detect whether a person who does not have the disease yet is a carrier of the virus (and therefore at risk to actually contract AIDS in the future), there is an issue of how to deal with the concerns of people who stand a probability of eventually coming down with the disease (Tross & Hirsch, 1988). Finally, psychologists need to devise methods of reducing the anxiety of people whose fears of catching AIDS lead them to demand that extreme measures be taken against the victims of the disease (going so far, for instance, as calling for a quarantine for those with AIDS). Until a cure is found for the disease, AIDS will continue to present difficult problems that are likely to have a profound impact on sexual behavior.

Masturbation. One of the most widely practiced forms of sexual activity is **masturbation,** or sexual self-stimulation. Some 94 percent of all males and 63 percent of all females have masturbated at least once, and among college students, the frequency ranges from "never" to "several times a day" (Hunt, 1974; Houston, 1981).

Despite the high incidence of masturbation, attitudes toward it still reflect some of the negative views of yesteryear. For instance, one survey found that around 10 percent of the people who masturbated experienced feelings of guilt, and 5 percent of the males and 1 percent of the females considered their behavior perverted (Arafat & Cotton, 1974). Despite these negative attitudes, however, most experts on sex view masturbation not only as a healthy, legitimate—and harmless—sexual activity, but also as a means of learning about one's own sexuality.

Heterosexuality. Despite the frequency of masturbation, there is another sexual activity that is probably even more common: **heterosexuality,** or sexual behavior between a man and a woman. People often believe that the first time they have sexual intercourse represents one of life's major milestones. Although heterosexuality goes well beyond sexual intercourse between men and women (it encompasses kissing, petting, caressing, massaging, and other forms of sex play), the focus of sex researchers has been

While researchers of heterosexual behavior have focused on intercourse, a heterosexual relationship actually consists of a wide variety of other activities.

on the act of intercourse, particularly in term of its first occurrence and its frequency.

Before and after marriage: Premarital sex. Although as recently as the mid-1960s about 80 percent of adult Americans believed that premarital sex was always wrong, by the 1970s a dramatic shift had occurred: Only about one-third felt this way (Reiss, 1980). Even higher rates of approval for premarital sex are found within certain age groups; for example, 80 percent of the males and 68 percent of the females in one poll of college students agreed that sexual intercourse prior to marriage was permissible (Arena, 1984).

Changes in approval of premarital sex were matched by changes in actual rates of premarital sexual activity in the 1970s and early 1980s. In one survey, for example, close to 80 percent of women under the age of 25 said they had experienced premarital intercourse, while just over 20 percent of those over 55 years of age reported having had premarital sexual intercourse (Horn & Bachrach, 1985), and some figures put the proportion of college-age women who had had premarital sexual intercourse at 59 percent (Arena, 1984). Although some statistics suggest that there was a drop in women's sexual activity in the mid-1980s (Gerrard, 1988), overall the general trend over the last two decades has been toward more women engaging in premarital sexual activity.

Males, too, have shown an increase in the rate of premarital sexual intercourse, although the increase has not been as dramatic as it has for females—probably because the rates for males were higher to begin with. For instance, the first surveys carried out in the 1940s showed a rate of 84 percent; recent figures put the figure at closer to 95 percent. Moreover, the average age of males' first sexual experience has also been declining

"Your friend is more than welcome, dear, but we just want you to know that your father and I didn't do anything funny till <u>after</u> we were married."
(Drawing by Modell; © 1972, The New Yorker Magazine, Inc.)

steadily, and some 76 percent of college-age males have already had in-tercourse (Arena, 1984).

Marital sex. To judge by the number of articles about sex in marriage, one would think that sexual behavior was the number-one standard by which marital bliss is measured. Married couples are often concerned that they are having too little sex, too much sex, or the wrong kind of sex.

Although there are many different dimensions against which sex in marriage is measured, one is certainly the frequency of sexual intercourse. What is typical? As with most other types of sexual activities, there is no easy answer to the question, since there are such wide variations in patterns between individuals. We do know that the average frequency for married couples is approximately eight times per month (Westoff, 1974; Blumstein & Schwartz, 1983). In addition, there are differences according to the age of the couple; younger couples tend to have sexual intercourse more frequently than older ones.

It also appears that the frequency of marital sexual intercourse is higher at this point in time than in other recent historical periods. A num-ber of factors account for this increase. Increased availability of birth-control methods (including birth-control pills) and abortion have led cou-

The overall level of satisfaction in marriage is related to sexual satisfaction.

ples to be less concerned about unwanted pregnancies. Moreover, several social changes have likely had an impact. As sex becomes more openly discussed in magazines, books, and even television shows, many married couples have come to feel that the frequency of sex is a critical index of the success of their marriage. Furthermore, as women's roles have changed, and the popular media have reinforced the notion that female sexuality is OK, the likelihood that a wife may initiate sex, rather than waiting for her husband's overture as in the more traditional scenario, has increased (Westoff, 1974).

Homosexuality and bisexuality. Just as there seems to be no genetic or biological reason for heterosexual women to find men's buttocks particularly erotic, humans are not born with an innate attraction to the special characteristics of the opposite sex. We should not find it surprising, then, that some people, **homosexuals,** are sexually attracted to members of their own sex, while others, **bisexuals,** are sexually attracted to people of the same *and* the opposite sex. In fact, the number of people who choose same-sex sexual partners at one time or another is considerable. Estimates suggest that about 20 to 25 percent of males and about 15 percent of females have had at least one homosexual experience during adulthood, and between 5 and 10 percent of both men and women are estimated to be exclusively homosexual during extended periods of their lives (Hunt, 1974; Kinsey, Pomeroy, & Martin, 1948; Fay et al., 1989).

Although people often view homosexuality and heterosexuality as two completely distinct sexual orientations, the issue is not that simple. Pioneering sex researcher Alfred Kinsey acknowledged this when he considered sexual orientation along a scale, with exclusively homosexual at one end and exclusively heterosexual at the other. According to this view, bisexuals belong somewhere in the middle of the scale, with the precise location determined by the person's specific sexual experiences.

Why are people homosexual? Although there are a number of theories, none has proved completely satisfactory. Some approaches are biological in nature, suggesting that there may be a genetic or hormonal reason for the development of homosexuality (Gladue, 1984; Hutchinson, 1978). There is little conclusive evidence for such an approach, however, although it is still possible that there may be some genetic or biological factor that predisposes a person toward homosexuality, if certain environmental conditions are met (Gartell, 1982).

Other theories of homosexuality have focused on the childhood and family background of homosexuals. For instance, Freud felt that homosexuality occurred as a result of inappropriate identification with the opposite-sex parent during development (Freud, 1922/1959). Similarly, other psychoanalysts suggest that the nature of the parent-child relationship can lead to homosexuality, and that homosexuals frequently have overprotective, dominant mothers and passive, ineffective fathers (Bieber, 1962).

The problem with such theories is that there are probably as many homosexuals who were not subjected to the influence of such family dynamics as who were. The evidence does not support explanations which rely on child-bearing practices or on the nature of the family structure (Bell & Weinberg, 1978).

Another explanation for homosexuality rests on learning theory (Masters & Johnson, 1979). According to this view, sexual orientation is learned through rewards and punishments in much the same way that we might learn to prefer swimming over tennis. For example, a young adolescent who had a heterosexual experience whose outcome was unpleasant might learn to link unpleasant associations with the opposite sex. If that same person had a rewarding, pleasant homosexual experience, homosexuality might be incorporated into his or her sexual fantasies. If such fantasies are then used during later sexual activities—such as masturbation—they may be positively reinforced through orgasm, and the association of homosexual behavior and sexual pleasure might eventually cause homosexuality to become the preferred form of sexual behavior.

Although the learning theory explanation is plausible, there are several difficulties which prevent it from being seen as a complete explanation for homosexuality. Because our society tends to hold homosexuality in low esteem, one ought to expect that the punishments involved in homosexual behavior would outweigh the rewards attached to it (Whitam, 1977). Furthermore, children growing up with a homosexual parent statistically are unlikely to become homosexual, thus contradicting the notion that homosexual behavior might be learned from others (Green, 1978).

Given the difficulty in finding a consistent explanation, the majority of researchers reject the notion that any single factor orients a person toward homosexuality, and most suspect that a combination of biological and environmental factors is the cause (Money, 1987). Although we don't know at this point exactly why people become homosexual, one thing is clear: There is no relationship between psychological adjustment and sexual preference (Reiss, 1980). Bisexuals and homosexuals enjoy the same overall degree of mental and physical health as do heterosexuals, and they hold equivalent ranges and types of attitudes about themselves, independent of sexual orientation.

ASK YOURSELF

What are the primary determinants of hunger?

What factors underlie people's eating patterns?

How might you design a weight-loss program that would take into account obese people's oversensitivity to social cues related to eating?

How do biological and social factors prime people for sex?

What are the major forms and frequencies of various sexual behaviors?

Striving for Success: The Need for Achievement

While hunger, thirst, and sex represent the most potent drives in our day-to-day lives, we are also motivated by powerful secondary drives that have no clear biological basis (McClelland, 1985; Geen, 1984). Among the most prominent of these is the need for achievement.

The **need for achievement** is a stable, learned characteristic in which satisfaction is obtained by striving for and attaining a level of excellence (McClelland, Atkinson, Clark & Lowell, 1953). People with a high need for achievement seek out situations in which they can compete against some standard—be it grades, money, or winning at a game—and prove themselves successful. But they are not indiscriminate when it comes to picking their challenges: They tend to avoid situations in which success will come too easily (which would be unchallenging) or those in which success is unlikely. Instead, people high in achievement motivation are apt to choose tasks that are of intermediate difficulty.

In contrast, people with low achievement motivation tend mainly to be motivated by a desire to avoid failure. As a result, they seek out easy tasks, being sure to avoid failure, or they seek out very difficult tasks for which failure has no negative implications, since almost anyone would fail at them. People with a high fear of failure will stay away from tasks of intermediate difficulty, since they may fail where others have been successful (Atkinson & Feather, 1966).

The outcomes of a high need for achievement are generally positive, at least in a success-oriented society such as our own (Heckhausen, Schmalt & Schneider, 1985; Spence, 1985). For instance, people motivated by a high need for achievement are more likely to attend college than their low-achievement counterparts, and once in college they tend to receive higher grades in classes that are related to their future careers (Atkinson & Raynor, 1974). Furthermore, high achievement motivation is associated with future economic and occupational success (McClelland, 1985).

Measuring achievement motivation. How can we measure a person's need for achievement? The technique used most frequently is to administer a **Thematic Apperception Test**, or **TAT**. In the TAT, people are shown a series of ambiguous pictures, such as that in Figure 6-5. They are told to write a story that describes what is happening, who the people are, what led to the situation, what the people are thinking or wanting, and what will happen next. A standard scoring system is then used to determine the amount of achievement imagery in people's stories. For example, someone who writes a story in which the main character is striving to beat an opponent, studying in order to do well at some task, or working hard in order to get a promotion shows clear signs of achievement imagery. It is assumed that the inclusion of such achievement-related imagery indicates an unusually high degree of concern with—and therefore a relatively strong need for—achievement.

Other techniques have been developed for assessing achievement motivation on a societal level (Reuman, Alwin & Veroff, 1984). For example, a good indication of the overall level of achievement motivation in a particular society can be found by assessing achievement imagery in children's stories or folk tales. Researchers who have examined children's reading books for achievement imagery over long periods have found correlations between the amount of imagery in the books and the economic activity in the society over the next few decades (DeCharms & Moeller, 1962). Whether stories incorporating achievement imagery actually influence children or simply reflect growing economic trends cannot be determined, of course. It is clear, though, that children might be learning more from their books than how to read—they may be acquiring the level of achievement motivation that society expects from them.

There has been one major drawback to the work on achievement motivation: The findings have been considerably more consistent for men than for women, and TAT measures of the need for achievement do not correlate with actual achievement for females as strongly as they do for males. One explanation for the discrepancy is that some women view achievement and success with a certain ambivalence (Horner, 1972). According to this explanation, women who have been raised according to the traditional standards of society—in which competition and independ-

FIGURE 6-5
This ambiguous picture is similar to those used in the
Thematic Apperception Test to determine people's
underlying motivation. (© 1943 by the President and Fel-
lows of Harvard College; © 1971 by Henry A. Murray.)

ence are deemed inappropriate for females—might find success in a field
typically dominated by males as anxiety-provoking. Some women, then,
may actually experience a **fear of success**: They are afraid that being successful will have a negative influence on the way others view them and
on their definition of themselves as female.

Although the evidence in support of the fear-of-success explanation
is far from consistent, it does seem as if women who have a high fear of
success do not strive to achieve in areas that are seen as competitive, male-
dominated, or challenging. However, we would expect that as society's
view of appropriate female behavior becomes less constrained, fear of
success ought to be on the decline (Veroff, 1982; Jenkins, 1987).

The work on fear of success provides an illustration of how complex
our motivational structures may be (Gama, 1985). Any particular behavior
may be motivated simultaneously by several underlying needs, and it is

possible that for some of us the need for achievement and the fear of success operate jointly to direct our behavior.

Learning to achieve: The development of achievement motivation. How do people come to be high in the need for achievement? Several factors seem to be at work, beginning at a very early age. For instance, parents whose children turn out to be high in achievement motivation tend to be relatively strict in their feeding schedules—from birth onward—and in their toilet-training practices (McClelland, 1985). Furthermore, parents who set high standards—even when it comes to everyday tasks such as dressing—who are relatively demanding, and who strongly encourage independence produce children high in need for achievement.

Although parental directiveness may make parents seem rather unpleasant, this is not the case: Such parents are also quick to praise their children's success, and they warmly encourage their children in all areas of endeavor. Even if their child fails, these parents do not complain; instead, they urge their children to find areas in which they will be able to succeed.

Striving for Friendship: The Need for Affiliation

Few of us choose to lead our lives as hermits. Why?

One reason is that most people have a **need for affiliation**, a concern with establishing and maintaining relationships with other people. Individuals with a high need for affiliation write TAT stories that emphasize the desire to maintain or reinstate friendships and show concern over being rejected by friends.

People who are higher in affiliation needs are particularly sensitive to relationships with others. They like to work with their friends and may be more likely to pay attention to the social relationships within work settings than to getting the job done. For example, United States presidents whose inaugural addresses were high in affiliation imagery tend to be rated by historians as relatively inactive and ineffective (Winter, 1976). On the other hand, such presidents also seem to avoid war and to sign weapons-control agreements.

Striving for Impact on Others: The Need for Power

If your fantasies include being elected President of the United States, running General Motors, or receiving the Nobel Prize, they may be reflecting a high need for power. The **need for power**, a tendency to seek impact, control, or influence over others, and to be seen as a powerful individual, represents an additional type of motivation (Winter, 1973).

As you might expect, people with a strong need for power are more apt to belong to organizations and seek office than those low in the need for power. They also are apt to be in professions in which their power needs may be fulfilled (such as business management and—you may or may not be surprised—teaching). In addition, they try to show the trappings of power: even in college, they are more apt to collect prestigious possessions, such as stereos and sports cars.

There are some significant sex differences in the display of need for power. Men who are high in power needs tend to show unusually high levels of aggression, be heavy drinkers, be sexually exploitative, and participate more frequently in competitive sports—behaviors that collectively represent somewhat extravagant, flamboyant behavior (Winter, 1973). In contrast, women display their power needs in a more restrained manner, congruent with traditional societal restraints on women's behavior: Women high in a need for power are more apt than men to channel their power needs in a socially responsible manner (such as by showing concern for others or through highly nurturant behavior) (Winter, 1988).

Clearly, needs for power can be fulfilled in several sorts of ways. As with all motives, the way in which a need will be manifested is a combination of people's skills, values, and the specific situations in which they find themselves.

*A*SK YOURSELF

What are the components of need for achievement?

What is the risk-taking behavior of people high and low in need for achievement?

How can the need for affiliation and need for power be described?

How is the expression of various motivational needs shaped by social and cultural norms?

*U*NDERSTANDING EMOTIONAL EXPERIENCE

Karl Andrews held in his hands the envelope he had been waiting for. It could be his ticket to his future: An offer of admission to his first-choice college. But what was it going to say? He knew it could go either way; his grades were pretty good, and he had been involved in some activities; but his SAT scores had been, to put it bluntly, lousy. He felt so nervous—scared really—that his hands shook as he opened the thin envelope (not a good sign, he thought). Here it comes. "Dear Mr. Andrews," it read. "The President and Trustees of the University are pleased to admit you . . . ." That was all he needed. With a whoop of excitement, Karl found himself gleefully jumping up and down. A rush of emotion overcame him as it sank in that he had, in fact, been accepted. He was on his way.

At one time or another, all of us have felt the strong feelings that accompany both very pleasant and very negative experiences. Perhaps it was the thrill of being accepted into college, the joy of being in love, the sorrow over someone's death, or the anguish of inadvertently hurting someone. Moreover, we experience such reactions on a less intense level throughout our daily lives: the pleasure of a friendship, the enjoyment of a movie, or the embarrassment of forgetting to return a borrowed item.

Despite the varied nature of these feelings, there is a common link between them: They all represent emotions. As we discussed earlier, such emotions are an important component in motivating our behavior, and the behavior that results from motivational needs in turn influences our emotions.

While we all know what it is like to experience an emotion, finding a definition acceptable to psychologists has proven to be an elusive task. One reason is that different theories of emotion—which we will discuss later—emphasize different aspects of emotions, and therefore each theory ultimately produces its own definition. Despite these difficulties, though, we can use a general definition: **Emotions** are feelings that generally have both physiological and cognitive elements and that influence behavior.

Consider, for example, how it feels to be happy. First, you obviously experience a feeling that you can differentiate from other emotions. It is likely you also experience some identifiable physical changes in your body: Perhaps your heart rate increases, or—as in our example earlier—you find yourself "jumping for joy." Finally, the emotion probably encompasses cognitive elements; your understanding and evaluation of the meaning of what is happening in your environment prompts your feelings of happiness.

It is also possible, however, to experience an emotion without the presence of cognitive elements. For instance, we may react with fear to an unusual or novel situation (such as coming into contact with a disturbed, unpredictable individual), or we may experience pleasure over sexual excitation without having cognitive awareness or understanding of what it is about the situation that is exciting.

In fact, some psychologists argue that there are entirely separate systems that govern cognitive responses and emotional responses. One current controversy is whether the emotional response takes predominance over the cognitive response or vice versa (Izard, Kagan, & Zajonc, 1989). Some theorists suggest that we first respond to a situation with an emotional reaction, and later try to understand it (Zajonc, 1985). For example, we may enjoy a complex modern symphony without understanding it or knowing why we like it.

In contrast, other theorists suggest that people first develop cognitions about a situation and then react emotionally (Lazarus, 1984). This school of thought suggests that it is necessary for us to first think about and understand a stimulus or situation, relating it to what we already know, before we can react on an emotional level.

Both sides of this debate are supported by research, and the question is far from being resolved (Frijda, 1988; Kemper, 1990). It is possible that the sequence varies from situation to situation, with emotions predominating in some instances and cognitive processes occurring first in others. Whatever the ultimate sequence, however, it is clear that our emotions play a major role in affecting our behavior.

What Emotions Do for Us: Understanding the Functions of Emotions

Imagine what it would be like if you had no emotions—no depths of despair, no depression, no feeling apologetic, but at the same time, no happiness, joy, or love. Obviously life would be much less interesting, even dull, without the experience of emotion.

But do emotions serve any purpose beyond making life interesting? Psychologists have identified a number of important functions that emotions play in our daily lives (Moore & Isen, 1990; Scherer, 1984). Among the most important of those functions are the following:

- Preparing us for action. Emotions act as a link between events in the external environment and behavioral responses that an individual makes. For example, if we saw an angry dog charging toward us, the emotional reaction (fear) would be associated with physiological arousal of the sympathetic division of the autonomic nervous system, which we discussed in Chapter 2. The role of the sympathetic division is to prepare us for emergency action, which presumably would get us moving out of the dog's way—quickly. Emotions, then, are stimuli that aid in the development of effective responses to various situations.

- Shaping our future behavior. Emotions serve to promote learning of information that will assist us in making appropriate responses in the future. For example, the emotional response that occurs when a person experiences something unpleasant—such as the threatening dog—teaches that person to avoid similar circumstances in the future. Similarly, pleasant emotions act as reinforcement for prior behavior and therefore are apt to lead an individual to seek out similar situations in the future. Thus, the feeling of satisfaction that follows giving to a charity is likely to reinforce charitable behavior and make it more likely to occur in the future.

- Helping us to regulate social interaction. As we shall discuss in detail later, the emotions we experience are frequently obvious to observers, as they are communicated through our verbal and nonverbal behaviors. These behaviors can act as a signal to observers, allowing them to better understand what we are experiencing and

The emotion of joy is characterized by positive feelings and thoughts.

predict our future behavior. In turn, this promotes more effective and appropriate social interaction. For instance, a mother who sees the terror on her 2-year-old son's face when he sees a frightening picture in a book is able to comfort and reassure him, thereby helping him to deal with his environment more effectively in the future.

KNOWING HOW WE FEEL: UNDERSTANDING OUR OWN EMOTIONS

I've never been so angry before; I feel my heart pounding, and I'm trembling all over . . . I don't know how I'll get through the performance. I feel like my stomach is filled with butterflies . . . That was quite a mistake I made! My face must be incredibly red . . . When I heard the footsteps in the night I was so frightened that I couldn't catch my breath.

If you examine our language, you will find that there are literally dozens of ways to describe how we feel when we are experiencing an emotion, and that the language we use to describe emotions is, for the most part, based on the physical symptoms that are associated with a particular emotional experience (Koveces, 1987).

Consider, for instance, the experience of fear. Pretend that it is late one New Year's Eve. You are walking down a dark road, and you hear a stranger approaching behind you. It is clear that he is not trying to hurry by but is coming directly toward you. You think of what you will do should the stranger attempt to rob you—or worse, hurt you in some way.

While these thoughts are running through your head, it is almost certain that something rather dramatic will be happening to your body. Among the most likely physiological reactions that may occur, which are associated with activation of the autonomic nervous system (see Chapter 2), are those listed here:

- The rate and depth of your breathing will increase.
- Your heart will speed up, pumping more blood through your circulatory system.
- The pupils of your eyes will open wider, allowing more light to enter and thereby increasing your visual sensitivity.
- Your mouth will become dry as your salivary glands, and in fact your entire digestive system, stop functioning. At the same time, though, your sweat glands may increase their activity, since increased sweating will help you rid yourself of excess heat developed by any emergency activity in which you engage.
- As the muscles just below the surface of your skin contract, your hair may literally stand on end.

Of course, all these physiological changes are likely to occur without your awareness. At the same time, though, the emotional experience accompanying them will be obvious to you: You would most surely report being fearful.

Although it is a relatively straightforward matter to describe the general physical reactions that accompany emotions, the specific role that these physiological responses play in the experience of emotions has proved to be a major puzzle for psychologists. As we shall see, some theorists suggest that there are specific bodily reactions that *cause* us to experience a particular emotion—we experience fear, for instance, *because* our heart is pounding and we are breathing deeply. In contrast, other theorists suggest that the physiological reaction is the *result* of the experience of an emotion. In this view, we experience fear, and this emotional experience causes our heart to pound and our breathing to deepen.

Do Gut Reactions Equal Emotions?
The James-Lange Theory

To William James and Carl Lange, who were among the first researchers to explore the nature of emotions, emotional experience is, very simply, a reaction to instinctive bodily events that occurred as a response to some situation or event in the environment. This view is summarized in James's statement, ". . . we feel sorry because we cry, angry because we strike, afraid because we tremble" (James, 1890).

James and Lange took the view that the instinctive response of crying at a loss leads us to feel sorrow; that striking out at someone who frustrates us results in our feeling anger; that trembling at a menacing threat causes us to feel afraid. They suggested that every major emotion has a particular physiological "gut" reaction of internal organs—called a **visceral experience**—attached to it, and it is this specific pattern of visceral response that leads us to label the emotional experience.

In sum, James and Lange proposed that we experience emotions as a result of physiological changes that produce specific sensations. In turn, these sensations are interpreted by the brain as particular kinds of emotional experiences (see Figure 6-6). This view has come to be called the **James-Lange theory of emotion**.

The James-Lange theory has some serious drawbacks, however. In order for the theory to be correct, visceral changes would have to occur at a relatively rapid pace, since we experience some emotions—such as fear upon hearing a stranger rapidly approaching on a dark night—almost instantaneously. Yet, emotional experiences frequently happen even before many physiological changes have time to be set into motion. Because of the slowness with which some visceral changes take place, it is hard to see how they could be the source of immediate emotional experience.

The James-Lange theory poses another difficulty: Physiological arousal does not invariably produce emotional experience. For example, a person who is jogging has an increased heartbeat and respiration rate, as well as many of the other physiological changes associated with certain emotions. Yet joggers do not typically think of such changes in terms of emotions. There cannot be a one-to-one correspondence, then, between visceral changes and emotional experience, and visceral changes—by themselves—may not be sufficient to produce emotion.

Finally, our internal organs produce relatively limited sensations. It is difficult to imagine how the range of emotions that people are capable of experiencing could be the result of unique visceral changes. Many emotions are actually correlated with relatively similar sorts of visceral changes, a fact that contradicts the James-Lange theory.

Physiological Reactions as the Result of Emotions: The Cannon-Bard Theory

In response to the difficulties inherent in the James-Lange theory, Walter Cannon—and later Philip Bard—suggested an alternative view. In what has come to be known as the **Cannon-Bard theory of emotion**, they proposed the model illustrated in the second part of Figure 6-6 (Cannon, 1929). The major thrust of the theory is to reject the view that physiological arousal alone leads to the perception of emotion. Instead, the theory assumes that both physiological arousal *and* the emotional experience are produced simultaneously by the same nerve impulse, which Cannon and Bard suggested emanates from the brain's thalamus.

According to the theory, after an emotion-inducing stimulus is perceived, the thalamus is the initial site of the emotional response. In turn, the thalamus sends a signal to the viscera, which are then activated, and at the same time communicates a message to the cerebral cortex regarding the nature of the emotion being experienced. Hence, it is not necessary for different emotions to have unique physiological patterns associated with them—as long as the message sent to the cerebral cortex differs according to the specific emotion.

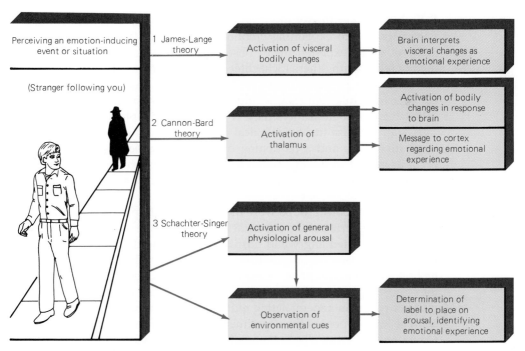

FIGURE 6-6
A comparison of three models of emotion.

The Cannon-Bard theory seems to have been accurate in its rejection of the view that physiological arousal alone accounts for emotions. However, recent research has provided some important modifications to the theory. As you may recall from Chapter 2, it is now understood that the hypothalamus and the limbic system—not the thalamus—play a major role in emotional experience. In addition, the simultaneity of the physiological and emotional responses—a fundamental assumption of the theory—has yet to be conclusively demonstrated (Pribram, 1984). This ambiguity has allowed room for yet another theory of emotions: the Schachter-Singer theory.

Emotions as Labels: The Schachter-Singer Theory

Suppose, as you were being followed down the dark street on New Year's Eve, you noticed a man being followed by a shady figure on the other side of the street. Now assume that instead of reacting with fear, the man begins to laugh and act gleeful. Might the reactions of this other individual be sufficient to lay your fears to rest? Might you, in fact, decide there is nothing to fear, and get into the spirit of the evening by beginning to feel happiness and glee yourself?

According to an explanation that focuses on the role of cognition, the **Schachter-Singer theory of emotion**, this might very well happen. This final approach to explaining emotions emphasizes that we identify the emotion we are experiencing by observing our environment and comparing ourselves with others (Schachter & Singer, 1962).

A classic experiment found evidence for this hypothesis. In the study, subjects were told that they would receive a vitamin injection of a drug called Suproxin. In reality, they were given epinephrine, a drug that causes an increase in physiological arousal, including higher heart and respiration rates and a reddening of the face—responses that typically occur as part of strong emotional responses. Although one group of subjects was informed of the actual effects of the drug, another was kept in the dark.

Subjects in both groups were then individually placed in a situation where a confederate of the experimenter acted in one of two ways. In one condition, he acted angry and hostile, complaining that he would refuse to answer the personal questions on a questionnaire that the experimenter had asked him to complete. In the other condition, his behavior was quite the opposite: He behaved euphorically, flying paper airplanes and tossing wads of paper, in general acting quite happy with the situation.

The key purpose of the experiment was to determine how the subjects would react emotionally to the confederate's behavior. When they were asked to describe their own emotional state at the end of the experiment, subjects who had been told of the effects of the drug were relatively unaffected by the behavior of the confederate: Being informed of the effects of the epinephrine earlier, they thought their physiological arousal was due to the drug and therefore were not faced with the need to find a reason for their arousal. Hence, they reported experiencing relatively little emotion.

On the other hand, subjects who had not been told of the drug's real effects were influenced by the confederate's behavior. Those subjects exposed to the angry confederate reported that they felt angry, while those exposed to the euphoric confederate reported feeling happy. In sum, the results suggest that uninformed subjects turned to the environment and the behavior of others for an explanation of the physiological arousal they were experiencing.

The results of the Schachter-Singer experiment, then, support a cognitive view of emotions, in which emotions are determined jointly by a relatively nonspecific kind of physiological arousal *and* the labeling of the arousal based on cues from the environment (refer back to the third part of Figure 6-6).

The Schachter-Singer theory has led to some interesting experiments coming from many areas of the field of psychology. For example, psychologists interested in the determinants of interpersonal attraction have drawn applications from the theory. In one intriguing and imaginative experiment, an attractive, college-aged woman stood at the end of a swaying 450-foot suspension bridge that spanned a deep canyon. The woman was ostensibly conducting a survey, and she asked men who made it across the bridge a series of questions. She then gave them her telephone number, telling them that if they were interested in the results of the experiment they could contact her in the upcoming week.

In comparison to members of a control group who had completed the questionnaire after strolling across a stable bridge spanning a shallow stream ten feet below, the men who had come across the dangerous bridge showed significant differences in their questionnaire results: sexual imagery was considerably higher. Furthermore, those crossing the dangerous span were significantly more likely to actually call the woman in the upcoming week, suggesting that their attraction to her was higher. The men whose arousal was increased by the dangerous bridge seemed to have searched for a reason for their physiological arousal—and ended up attributing the cause to the attractive woman (Dutton & Aron, 1974). Consistent with the Schachter-Singer theory, then, the men's emotional response was based on a labeling of their arousal.

Unfortunately, evidence gathered to confirm the Schachter-Singer theory has not always been supportive (Reisenzein, 1983; Leventhal & Tomarken, 1986). Even the original experiment has been criticized on methodological grounds and for certain ambiguities in the results. Furthermore, there is evidence that in some cases physiological arousal is not essential for emotional experience to occur and that physiological factors *alone* can account for one's emotional state without any labeling process occurring (Marshall & Zimbardo, 1979; Chwalisz, Diener, & Gallagher, 1988). For example, some drugs invariably produce depression as a side effect no matter what the nature of the situation or the environmental cues present.

On the whole, however, the Schachter-Singer theory of emotions is important because it suggests that, at least under some circumstances, emotional experiences are a joint function of physiological arousal and the labeling of that arousal (Frijda, Kuipers, & terSchure, 1989). When the source of physiological arousal is unclear to us, we may look to our environment to determine just what it is we are experiencing.

Summing Up the Theories of Emotion

At this point, you have good reason to ask why there are so many theories of emotion and, perhaps even more important, which is most accurate. Actually, we have only scratched the surface; there are even more explanatory theories of emotion (Scherer & Ekman, 1984; Frijda, 1988; Izard, 1988).

The explanation as to why there are so many theories and which is the most accurate is actually the same: Emotions are such complex phenomena that no single theory has been able to explain all facets of emotional experience completely satisfactorily. For each of the three major theories there is contradictory evidence of one sort or another, and therefore no theory has proven invariably accurate in its predictions. On the other hand, this is not a cause for despair—or unhappiness, fear, or any other negative emotion. It simply reflects the fact that psychology is an evolving, developing science. Presumably, as more evidence is gathered, the specific answers to questions about the nature of emotions will become more clear.

ASK YOURSELF

How can emotions be defined?

What are the functions of emotions?

How do the major theories of emotion compare and contrast?

Do the major theories of emotion, when taken together, adequately explain all of human emotional experience?

How would you distinguish emotions from cognitions, and are they ever completely separate?

EXPRESSING EMOTIONS: THE ROLE OF NONVERBAL BEHAVIOR

Ancient Sanskrit writings speak of someone who, on making an evasive answer, "rubs the great toe along the ground, and shivers." Shakespeare writes of Macbeth's face as "a place where men may read strange matters." Old torch songs claim "your eyes are the eyes of a woman in love." Such examples demonstrate how nonverbal behavior has long had the reputation of revealing people's emotions. Only recently, though, have psychologists demonstrated the validity of such speculation, finding that nonverbal behavior does represent a major means by which we communicate our emotions.

We now know that nonverbal behavior communicates messages simultaneously across several **channels**, paths along which communications flow. For example, facial expressions, eye contact, body movements, and even less obvious behaviors such as the positioning of the eyebrows can each be conceptualized as separate nonverbal channels of communication. Furthermore, each individual channel is capable of carrying a particular message—which may or may not be related to the message being carried by the other channels. Because facial expressions represent the primary means of communicating emotional states, we will concentrate on them, considering their role in the experience of emotions.

Universality in Emotional Expressivity

Consider, for a moment, the six photos displayed in Figure 6-7. Can you identify the emotions being expressed by the person in each of the photos?

If you are a good judge of facial expressions, you will conclude that six of the basic emotions are displayed: happiness, anger, sadness, surprise, disgust, and fear. These categories are the emotions that emerge in literally hundreds of studies of nonverbal behavior as being consistently distinct and identifiable, even by untrained observers (Wagner, MacDonald & Manstead, 1986).

What is particularly interesting about these six categories is that they are not limited to members of western cultures; they appear to represent the basic emotions expressed universally by members of the human race, regardless of where they have been raised and what learning experiences they have had. This point was demonstrated convincingly by psychologist Paul Ekman, who traveled to New Guinea to study members of an isolated jungle tribe having had almost no contact with westerners (Ekman, Friesen & Ellsworth, 1972). The people of the tribe did not speak or understand English, they had never seen a movie, and they had had very limited experience with Caucasians before Ekman's arrival.

To learn about how the New Guineans used nonverbal behavior in emotional expression, Ekman told them a story involving an emotion and then showed them a set of three faces of westerners, one of which was displaying an emotion appropriate for the story. The task was to choose the face showing the most reasonable expression. The results showed that the New Guineans' responses were quite similar to those of western subjects and New Guinean children showed even greater skill in identifying the appropriate emotion than did the New Guinean adults. Interestingly,

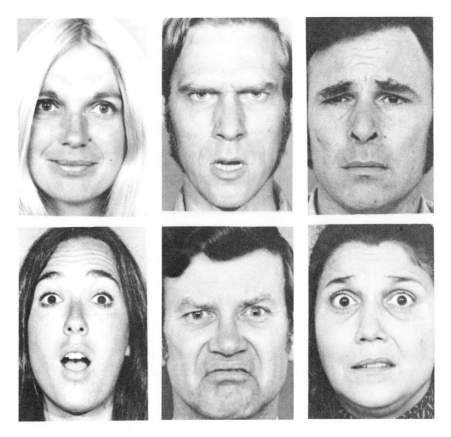

FIGURE 6-7
These photos demonstrate six of the primary emotions: happiness, anger, sadness, surprise, disgust, and fear.

the only difference occurred in identifying fearful faces, which were often confused with surprise by the tribespeople.

In addition to learning whether the New Guinean natives interpreted emotional expression in the same way as westerners did, it was important to find out whether both groups showed similar nonverbal responses. To do this, other natives were told the stories that Ekman had used earlier and were asked to provide a facial expression appropriate to the subject of the story. These expressions were videotaped, and a group of subjects in the United States were asked to look at the faces and identify the emotion being expressed. The results were clear: The western viewers—who had never before seen any New Guineans—were surprisingly accurate in their judgments, with the exception of expressions of fear and surprise.

In sum, convincing evidence exists for universality across cultures in the way basic emotions are displayed and interpreted (Ekman et al., 1987; Aronoff, Barclay & Stevenson, 1988). Because the New Guineans were so isolated, they could not have learned from westerners to recognize or produce similar facial expressions. Instead, their similar abilities and manners of responding emotionally appear to have been present innately. Of course, it is possible to argue that similar experiences in both cultures led to learning of similar types of nonverbal behavior, but this appears unlikely, since the two cultures are so very different. The expression of basic emotions, then, seems to be universal (Zivin, 1985).

What is the mechanism that produces similarity in the expression of basic emotions across cultures? One explanation is based on a hypothesis known as the facial-affect program (Ekman, 1984). The **facial-affect program**—which is assumed to be universally present at birth—is analogous to a computer program that is turned on when a particular emotion is experienced. When set in motion, the "program" activates a set of nerve impulses that make the face display an appropriate expression. Each primary emotion produces a unique set of muscular movements, forming the kind of expressions seen in Figure 6-7. For example, the emotion of happiness is universally displayed by movement of the zygomatic major, a muscle that raises the corners of the mouth—forming what we would call a smile.

Smile, Though You're Feeling Blue: The Facial-Feedback Hypothesis

If you want to feel happy, try smiling.

That is the implication of an intriguing notion known as the **facial-feedback hypothesis.** According to this hypothesis, facial expressions not only *reflect* emotional experience, they also help *determine* how people experience and label emotions (Izard, 1977; 1990). The basic idea is that "wearing" an emotional expression provides muscular feedback to the brain which helps produce an emotion congruent with the expression. For instance, the muscles activated when we smile may send a message to the brain indicating the experience of happiness—even if there is nothing in the environment that would produce that particular emotion. Some theoreticians have gone even further, suggesting that facial expressions are *necessary* for an emotion to be experienced (Rinn, 1984). According to this view, if there is no facial expression present, the emotion cannot be felt.

Support for the facial feedback hypothesis comes from what has become a classic experiment carried out by psychologist Paul Ekman and colleagues (Ekman, Levenson & Friesen, 1983). In the study, professional actors were asked to follow very explicit instructions regarding movements of muscles in their faces (see Figure 6-8). You might try this example yourself:

Raise your brows and pull them together; raise your upper eyelids; now stretch your lips horizontally back toward your ears.

FIGURE 6-8
The instructions given this actor were to (*a*) "raise your brows and pull them together," (*b*) "now raise your upper eyelids," and (*c*) "now also stretch your lips horizontally, back toward your ears." If you follow these directions yourself, it may well result in your experiencing fear. (Ekman, Levenson, & Friesen, 1983.)

After carrying out these directions—which, as you may have guessed, are meant to produce an expression of fear—the actors showed a rise in heart rate and a decline in body temperature, physiological reactions that are characteristic of fear. Overall, facial expressions representative of the primary emotions produced physiological effects similar to those accompanying the emotions in other circumstances.

Although support for the facial-feedback hypothesis is not firm (Matsumoto, 1987), there is sufficient evidence in its favor to suggest that the old lyric "Smile, though you're feeling blue" may not be far from the mark in its suggestion that you will feel better by putting a smile on your face (McCanne & Anderson, 1987; Adelmann & Zajonc, 1989).

ASK YOURSELF

What are the six primary emotions displayed through facial expressions?

What is the facial-affect program?

What is the facial-feedback hypothesis?

How does our environment and culture contribute to our experience and expression of emotions?

LOOKING BACK

1. The topic of motivation considers the factors that direct and energize behavior, whereas the study of emotions focuses on internal experiences. Drive is the motivational tension that energizes behavior in order to fulfill a need. Primary drives relate to basic biological needs; secondary drives are those in which no obvious bio-

logical need is fulfilled. Motivational drives often operate under the principle of homeostasis.

2. A number of broad theories of motivation move beyond explanations that rely on instincts. Drive-reduction theories, though useful for primary drives, are inadequate for explaining behavior in which the goal is not to reduce a drive but to maintain or even increase excitement or arousal. Arousal theory suggests that we try to maintain a particular level of stimulation and activity. Finally, opponent-process theory suggests that opponent forces in the nervous system arise when initial arousal results from some stimulus. If the initial arousal is positive, the opponent forces are negative, and vice versa.

3. Maslow's hierarchy of needs suggests that there are five needs (physiological, safety, love and belongingness, esteem, and self-actualization). Only after the more basic needs are fulfilled is a person able to move toward higher-order needs.

4. Eating behavior is subject to homeostasis, since most people's weight stays within a relatively stable range. Organisms tend to be sensitive to the nutritional value of food they eat, with the hypothalamus being closely related to food intake. In addition to the biological factors that affect eating behavior, social factors also play a role. An oversensitivity to social cues and an insensitivity to internal cues also may be related to obesity. In addition, obesity may be caused by an unusually high weight set point—the weight at which the body attempts to maintain homeostasis—or by the rate of metabolism.

5. Although biological factors, such as the presence of androgens (the male sex hormone) and estrogens (the female sex hormone) prime people for sex, almost any kind of stimulus can produce sexual arousal, depending on a person's prior experience. Fantasies, thoughts, and images are also important in producing arousal.

6. Masturbation is sexual self-stimulation. The frequency of masturbation is high, particularly for males. Although attitudes toward masturbation have become more liberal, they are still somewhat negative—even thought no negative consequences have been detected.

7. Heterosexuality, or sex between a man and a woman, is the most common sexual orientation. Approval for premarital sex has risen considerably in the last few decades, as has the incidence of the behavior. The frequency of marital sex varies widely. However, younger couples tend to have sexual intercourse more frequently than older ones.

8. Homosexuals are sexually attracted to members of their own sex; bisexuals are sexually attracted to people of the same and the opposite sex. About one-quarter of males and 15 percent of females have had at least one homosexual experience, and around 5 to 10 percent of all men and women are exclusively homosexual during extended periods of their lives. Although no explanation for why people become homosexual has been confirmed, it is clear that there is no relationship between psychological adjustment and sexual preference.

9. Need for achievement refers to the stable, learned characteristic in which a person strives to attain a level of excellence. People high in need for achievement tend to seek out tasks that are of moderate difficulty, while those low in need for achievement seek out only very easy and very difficult tasks. However, inconsistent findings regarding females' need for achievement has led some researchers to suggest that women have a fear of success related to achievement motivation. Need for achievement is usually measured through the Thematic Apperception Test (TAT).

10. The need for affiliation is a concern with establishing and maintaining relationships with others, whereas the need for power is a tendency to seek impact on others.

11. One definition of emotion that seems appropriate across differing theoretical perspectives views emotions as feelings that may affect behavior and generally have both a physiological and a cognitive component. What this definition does not do is address the issue of whether there are separate systems that govern cognitive and emotional responses, and whether one has primacy over the other.

12. Among the functions of emotions are to prepare us for action, shape future behavior through learning, and help to regulate social interaction. Although the range of emotions is wide, according to one category system there are only eight primary emotions: joy, acceptance, fear, surprise, sadness, disgust, anger, and anticipation.

13. Among the general physiological responses to strong emotion are opening of the pupils, dryness of the mouth, and increases in sweating, rate of breathing, heart rate, and blood pressure. Because these physiological changes are not the full explanation of emotional experience, a number of distinct theories of emotion have been developed.

14. The James-Lange theory suggests that emotional experience is a reaction to bodily, or visceral, changes that occur as a response to an environmental event. These visceral experiences are interpreted as an emotional response. In contrast to the James-Lange theory, the Cannon-Bard theory contends that visceral movements are too slow to explain rapid shifts of emotion and the fact that visceral changes do not always produce emotion. Instead, the Cannon-Bard theory suggests that both physiological arousal *and* an emotional experience are produced simultaneously by the same nerve impulse. Therefore, the visceral experience itself does not necessarily differ among differing emotions.

15. The third explanation, the Schachter-Singer theory, rejects the view that the physiological and emotional responses are simultaneous. Instead, it suggests that emotions are determined jointly by a relatively nonspecific physiological arousal and the subsequent labeling of that arousal. This labeling process uses cues from the environment to determine how others are behaving in the same situation.

16. Emotions can be revealed through a person's facial expression. In fact, there is universality in emotional expressivity, at least for the basic emotions, across members of different cultures. In addition, there are similarities in the way members of different cultures understand the emotional expressions of others. One explanation for this similarity rests on the existence of an innate facial-affect program which activates a set of muscle movements representing the emotion being experienced.

17. The facial-feedback hypothesis suggests that facial expressions not only are a reflection of emotions but can help determine and produce emotional experience.

Key Terms and Concepts

motivation (p. 220)
motives (p. 220)
instincts (p. 222)
drive-reduction theories (p. 222)
drive (p. 222)
primary drives (p. 222)
secondary drives (p. 222)
homeostasis (p. 223)
arousal theory (p. 223)

Yerkes-Dodson law (p. 224)
incentive (p. 225)
incentive theory (p. 225)
opponent-process theory (p. 225)
intrinsic motivation (p. 226)
extrinsic motivation (p. 226)
self-actualization (p. 228)
obesity (p. 229)
hypothalamus (p. 230)

7

States of Consciousness

❖

Prologue: Donald Dorff ◆ *Looking Ahead* ◆ *Life Is but a Dream . . . : Sleep and Dreams* ◆ *Altered States of Consciousness: Hypnosis and Meditation* ◆ *The Highs and Lows of Consciousness: Drug Use* ◆ *Looking Back*

PROLOGUE: DONALD DORFF

Donald J. Dorff, whose sleeping disorder was cured.

The crowd roared as running back Donald Dorff, age 67, took the pitch from his quarterback and accelerated smoothly across the artificial turf. As Dorff braked and pivoted to cut back over tackle, a huge defensive lineman loomed in his path. One hundred twenty pounds of pluck, Dorff did not hesitate. But let the retired grocery merchandiser from Golden Valley, Minnesota, tell it:

"There was a 280-pound tackle waiting for me, so I decided to give him my shoulder. When I came to, I was on the floor in my bedroom. I had smashed into the dresser and knocked everything off it and broke the mirror and just made one heck of a mess. It was 1:30 A.M." (Long, 1987, p. 787).

Dorff, it turned out, was suffering from a rare malady found in some older men in which the mechanism that usually shuts down bodily movement during dreams does not function properly. People afflicted with the problem have been known to hit others, smash windows, punch holes in walls—all the while being fast asleep.

266

*L*OOKING AHEAD

Donald Dorff's problem had a happy ending: With the help of clonaze-pam, a drug that suppresses movement during dreams, his malady vanished, and he now sleeps through the night in welcome repose. The success of the treatment illustrates just one of the recent advances that has occurred in our understanding of sleep. In fact, our knowledge about all forms of consciousness, including sleep, has been expanding rapidly, as psychologists explore the nature of human consciousness.

Consciousness refers to a person's awareness of the sensations, thoughts, and feelings being experienced at a given moment. It is our subjective understanding of both the environment around us and our private internal world, unobservable to outsiders.

The nature of consciousness at any given moment spans several dimensions (Gazzaniga, 1988). Consciousness can range from being wide awake to being in the deepest state of sleep, with wide variation in how aware we are of outside stimuli. Furthermore, even while we are awake, consciousness can vary from an active state to a passive state (Hilgard, 1980). In more active states, we systematically carry out mental activity, thinking and considering the world around us. In passive waking states, thoughts and images come to us more spontaneously; we daydream or drift from one thought to another. Finally, consciousness can vary in terms of whether it occurs naturally, as when we drift from wakefulness into sleep, or whether it is artificially induced, as in a drug "high."

Because consciousness is so personal a phenomenon—who can say that your consciousness is the same as or, for that matter, different from anyone else's?—psychologists have sometimes been less than eager to study it. In fact, some early psychological theoreticians suggested that the study of consciousness was out of bounds for the psychologist, since it could be understood only by relying on the "unscientific" introspections of subjects about what they were experiencing at a given moment. Proponents of this view argued that the study of consciousness was better left to philosophers, who could speculate at their leisure on such knotty issues as whether consciousness is separate from the physical body, how people know they exist, how the body and mind are related to each other, and how we identify what state of consciousness we are in at a given moment in time.

Most contemporary psychologists reject the view that the study of consciousness is improper for psychology, arguing instead that there are several approaches that allow the scientific study of consciousness. For example, recent insights into the biology of the brain allow measurement of brain-wave patterns under conditions of consciousness ranging from sleep to waking to hypnotic trances. Moreover, new understandings of the effects on behavior of drugs such as marijuana and alcohol have provided insights into the way they produce their positive—and negative—

effects. Finally, psychologists have come to understand that there are actually several kinds of consciousness that may be studied separately. By concentrating on particular **altered states of consciousness**—those that differ from a normal, waking consciousness—they have been able to study the phenomenon of consciousness scientifically, even if the more difficult questions, such as whether our consciousness exists separately from our physical bodies, remain unanswered.

Although various kinds of altered states of consciousness produce widely disparate effects, all share some characteristics (Ludwig, 1969; Martindale, 1981). One is an alteration in our thinking, which may become shallow, illogical, or impaired in some way. Our sense of time may become disturbed, and our perceptions of the world and of ourselves may be changed. We may experience a loss of self-control, doing things that we would never otherwise do. Finally, we may have a sense of ineffability—the inability to understand an experience rationally or describe it in words.

This chapter considers several states of consciousness, beginning with two that we have all experienced: sleeping and dreaming. Next, we turn to states of consciousness found under conditions of hypnosis and meditation. Finally, we examine drug-induced altered states of consciousness.

After reading this chapter, you will be able to answer questions such as these:

- What are the different states of consciousness?

"If you ask me, all three of us are in different states of awareness."
Drawing by Frascino, © 1983, The New Yorker Magazine

- What happens when we sleep, and what is the meaning and function of dreams?
- How much do we daydream?
- Are hypnotized people in an altered state of consciousness, and can they be made to do things against their will?
- What are the major classifications of drugs, and what are their effects?

LIFE IS BUT A DREAM . . . : SLEEP AND DREAMS

I was sitting at my desk thinking about the movie I was going to see that evening. Suddenly I remembered that this was the day of my chemistry final! I felt awful; I hadn't studied a bit for it. In fact, I couldn't even remember where the class was held, and I had missed every lecture all semester. What could I do? I was in a panic; I knew I was going to fail and flunk out of college.

If you have ever had a dream like this one, you are not alone: It is common among people involved in academic pursuits. After you have awakened and found to your relief that the scene that moments before had seemed so real was only a dream, you may have asked yourself what such dreams mean and whether they serve any purpose—questions psychologists have themselves considered in their study of sleep and dreams. We turn now to some of the answers they have arrived at. (Before you read on, you might want to test your knowledge of sleep and dreams by answering the questions in Table 7-1.)

Awakening Our Knowledge of Sleep: The Stages of Sleep

Most of us consider sleep a time of quiet tranquillity, as we peacefully set aside the tensions of the day and spend the night in uneventful slumber. However, a closer look at sleep shows that a good deal of activity occurs throughout the night, and what at first appears to be an undifferentiated state is, in fact, quite diverse.

Most of our knowledge of what happens during sleep comes from the **electroencephalogram** or **EEG,** which, as discussed in Chapter 2, is a measurement of electrical activity within the brain. When an EEG machine is attached to the surface of a sleeping person's scalp and face, it becomes readily apparent that instead of being dormant, the brain is active throughout the night, producing electric discharges that form regular, wavelike patterns that change in height (or amplitude) and speed (or frequency) in regular sequences. Instruments that measure muscle stimulation and eye movements also reveal a good deal of physical activity.

It turns out that there are four distinct stages of sleep through which a person progresses during a night's rest. These stages come and go, cy-

TABLE 7-1 TESTING YOUR KNOWLEDGE OF SLEEP AND DREAMS

Although sleeping is something we all do for a significant part of our lives, many myths and misconceptions about the topic abound. To test your own knowledge of sleep and dreams, try answering the following questions before reading further.

1. Some people never dream. True or false? ___

2. Most dreams are caused by bodily sensations such as an upset stomach. True or false? ___

3. It has been proved that eight hours of sleep is needed to maintain mental health. True or false? ___

4. When people do not recall their dreams it is probably because they are secretly trying to forget them. True or false? ___

5. Depriving someone of sleep will invariably cause the individual to become mentally unbalanced. True or false? ___

6. If we lose some sleep, we will eventually make up all the lost sleep the next night or another night. True or false? ___

7. No one has been able to go for more than forty-eight hours without sleep. True or false? ___

8. Everyone is able to sleep and breathe at the same time. True or false? ___

9. Sleep enables the brain to rest since there is little brain activity taking place during sleep. True or false? ___

10. Drugs have been proved to provide a long-term cure for sleeping difficulties. True or false? ___

Scoring: *This is an easy set of questions to score, for every item is false. But don't lose any sleep if you missed them; they were chosen to represent the most common myths regarding sleep. (Items were drawn from a questionnaire developed by Palladino & Carducci, 1984.)*

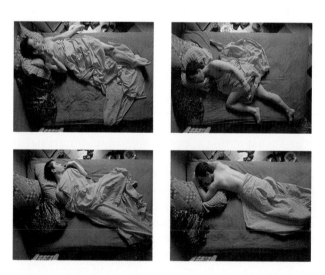

Although we generally view sleep as a period of repose and tranquillity, sleep researchers have found that a considerable amount of physical and mental activity occurs during sleep, as this series of photos taken during the course of one night suggests.

cling approximately every ninety minutes. Each of these four stages is associated with a unique pattern of brain waves, as shown in Figure 7-1. Moreover, there are specific physiological indicators of dreaming.

When people first go to sleep, they move from a waking state in which they are relaxed with their eyes closed—sometimes called stage 0 sleep—into **stage 1** sleep, which is characterized by relatively rapid, low-voltage brain waves. This is actually a stage of transition between wakefulness and sleep. During stage 1 images sometimes appear; it's as if we were viewing still photos. However, true dreaming does not occur during the initial entry into this stage.

As sleep becomes deeper, people enter **stage 2,** which is characterized by a slower, more regular wave pattern. However, there are also momentary interruptions of sharply pointed waves called, because of their configuration, "sleep spindles." It becomes increasingly difficult to awaken a

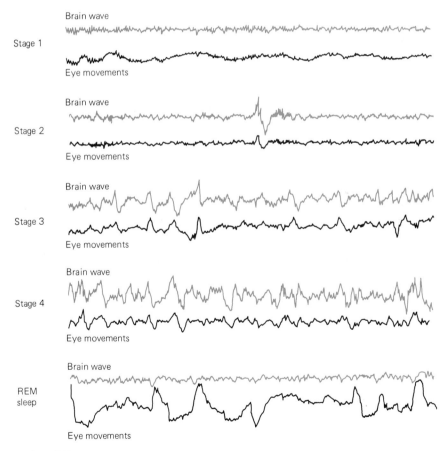

FIGURE 7-1
Brain-wave patterns (measured by an EEG apparatus) and eye movements in the different stages of sleep. (Cohen, 1979.)

person from stage 2 sleep, which accounts for about half of a college-age person's total sleep.

As people drift into **stage 3,** the next stage of sleep, the brain waves become slower, with an appearance of higher peaks and lower valleys in the wave pattern. By the time sleepers arrive at **stage 4,** the pattern is even slower and more regular, and people are least responsive to outside stimulation.

As you can see in Figure 7-2, stage 4 is most likely to occur during the early part of the night when a person has first gone to sleep. In addition to passing through regular transitions between stages of sleep, then, people tend to sleep less and less deeply over the course of the night (Dement & Wolpert, 1958).

The paradox of sleep: REM sleep. Several times a night, after sleepers cycle from higher stages back into stage 1 sleep, something curious happens: Their heart rate increases and becomes irregular, their blood pressure rises, their breathing rate increases, and males—even male infants—have erections. Most characteristic of this period is the back-and-forth movement of their eyes, as if they were watching an action-filled movie. This period of sleep is called **REM,** or **rapid eye movement** sleep. REM sleep occupies a little over 20 percent of adults' total sleeping time.

Paradoxically, while all this activity is occurring, the major muscles of the body act as if they are paralyzed—except in rare cases such as Donald Dorff's, described at the beginning of the chapter—and it is hard to awaken the sleeper. In addition, REM sleep is usually accompanied by dreams, which, whether people remember them or not, are experienced by *everyone* during some part of the night (Chase & Morales, 1990).

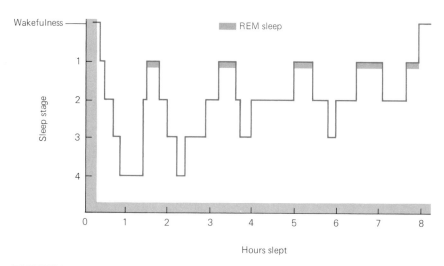

FIGURE 7-2
During the night, the typical sleeper passes through all four stages of sleep and several REM periods. (Hartmann, 1967.)

One possible but still unproven explanation for the occurrence of rapid eye movements is that the eyes follow the action that is occurring in the dream (Dement, 1979). For instance, people who have reported dreaming about watching a tennis match just before they were awakened showed regular right-left-right eye movements, as if they were observing the ball flying back and forth across the net.

There is good reason to believe that REM sleep plays an important role in everyday human functioning. People deprived of REM sleep—by being awakened every time they begin to display the physiological signs of the stage—show a **rebound effect** when allowed to rest undisturbed. With this rebound effect, REM-deprived sleepers spend significantly more time in REM sleep than they normally do. It is as if the body requires a certain amount of REM sleep in order to function properly.

Is Sleep Necessary?

Sleep, in general, seems necessary for human functioning, although surprisingly enough this fact has not been firmly established (Palca, 1989). It is reasonable to expect that the body would require a tranquil "rest and relaxation" period in order to revitalize itself. However, several arguments suggest this is not the full explanation. For instance, most people sleep between seven and eight hours each night, but there is wide variability among individuals, with some people needing as little as three hours. Sleep requirements also vary over the course of a person's lifetime; as people age, they generally need less and less sleep. If sleep played a restorative function for the body, it is hard to see why the elderly would need less sleep than those who are younger.

Furthermore, people who have participated in sleep deprivation experiments, in which they are kept awake for stretches as long as 200 hours, show no lasting effects. They do experience weariness, lack of concentration, a decline in creativity, irritability, and a tendency toward hand tremors while they are being kept awake, but after being able to sleep once again they bounce back quickly. Just having twice the amount of sleep they get in a normal night enables them to perform at predeprivation levels (Dement, 1976).

Those of us who worry that the lack of sleep due to long hours of work or study may be ruining our health should feel encouraged, then: As far as anyone can tell, we should suffer no long-term consequences of such sleep deprivation (Eckholm, 1988).

The Reality of Dreams: The Function and Meaning of Dreaming

If you have had a dream similar to the one described earlier about missing a final exam, you know how utterly convincing are the panic and fear that events in the dream can bring about. Some dreams could not seem more real.

In the case of **nightmares,** dreams are unusually frightening. Sometimes the same nightmare recurs over a period of years. Even worse are **night terrors,** dreams in which a person has a profoundly frightening dream and wakes up, in some cases screaming in horror. Often the terror of the dream is so real that people cannot get back to sleep immediately and need time to regain their emotional composure.

Nightmares are far from rare. In one study, for example, close to half of a sample of college students reported that they had experienced a nightmare within the previous two weeks. Over a one-year period, it averaged out to twenty-four times a year (Wood & Bootzin, 1990).

On the other hand, most dreams are much less dramatic, recounting such everyday events as going to the supermarket or preparing a meal. We just seem to remember the more exciting ones more readily (Webb, 1979). The most common dreams are shown in Figure 7-3.

Whether dreams have a specific function is a question that scientists have considered for many years. Sigmund Freud, for instance, used

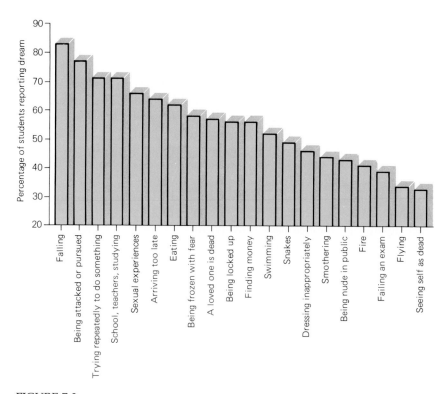

FIGURE 7-3
The twenty most common dreams reported by students. (Griffith, Miyago, & Tago, 1958.)

dreams as a guide to the unconscious (Freud, 1900). He thought that dreams represented unconscious wishes that the dreamer wanted to fulfill. However, because these wishes were threatening to the dreamer's conscious awareness, the actual wishes—called the **latent content** of the dream—were disguised. The true subject and meaning of a dream, then, may have little to do with its overt story line, called by Freud the **manifest content.**

To Freud, it was important to pierce the armor of a dream's manifest content to understand its true meaning. To do this, Freud tried to get people to discuss their dreams, associating symbols in the dreams to events in the past. He also suggested that there were certain common symbols with universal meaning that appeared in dreams. For example, to Freud, dreams in which the person was flying symbolized a wish for sexual intercourse. (See Table 7-2 for other common symbols.)

Today many psychologists reject Freud's view that dreams typically represent unconscious wishes and that particular objects and events in a dream are symbolic. Instead, the direct, overt action of a dream is considered the focal point in understanding its meaning. If we dream that we are walking down a long hallway to take an exam for which we haven't studied, for instance, it does not relate to unconscious, unacceptable wishes; rather, it simply means we are concerned about an impending test. Even more complex dreams can usually be interpreted in terms of everyday concerns.

Moreover, we now know that some dreams reflect events occurring in the dreamer's environment as he or she is sleeping. For example, sleeping subjects in one experiment were sprayed with water while they were dreaming; these unlucky volunteers reported more dreams involving water than a comparison group of subjects who were left to sleep undisturbed (Dement & Wolpert, 1958). Similarly, it is not unusual to wake up to find that the doorbell that was being rung in a dream is actually an alarm clock telling us it is time to get up.

Although the content of dreams clearly can be affected by environmental stimuli, the question of *why* we dream remains unresolved. Some

TABLE 7-2 DREAM SYMBOLISM, ACCORDING TO FREUD

Symbol	Interpretation
Climbing up a stairway, crossing a bridge, riding an elevator, flying in an airplane, walking down a long hallway, entering a room, train traveling through a tunnel	Sexual intercourse
Apples, peaches, grapefruits	Breasts
Bullets, fire, snakes, sticks, umbrellas, guns, hoses, knives	Male sex organs
Ovens, boxes, tunnels, closets, caves, bottles, ships	Female sex organs

This painting by Henry Fuseli depicts the phantoms that may inhabit our dreams. (Henry Fuseli, *The Nightmare*. Detroit Institute of Arts.)

psychologists suggest that dreaming represents an opportunity to resolve our problems and difficulties (Cartwright, 1978). By allowing our emotions to be brought to bear on personal issues in an uninhibited fashion, and by trying out different schemes for resolving our problems, we can safely "rehearse" different solutions during our dreams.

Other psychologists look at dreaming in terms of a more fundamental biological activity (Hobson & McCarley, 1977; Hartmann, 1982; Hobson, 1988). According to an influential theory, the brain produces electrical energy during REM sleep, possibly due to changes in the production of particular neurotransmitters. This electrical energy randomly stimulates different memories lodged in various portions of the brain. The brain then takes these random memories and—because we have a need to make sense of our world, even while asleep—weaves them into a logical story line, filling in the gaps to produce a rational scenario. In this view, then, dreams are closer to a self-generated game of Madlibs than to significant, meaningful psychological phenomena.

Evidence that dreaming represents a response to random brain activity comes from work with people who are injected with drugs similar to the neurotransmitter acetylcholine. Under the influence of the drug, people quickly enter REM sleep and have dreams similar in quality to those occurring in natural sleep (Schmeck, 1987).

Still another theory seeks to explain why we dream: It is possible that dreaming occurs as the by-product of a checking and consolidation process that the brain goes through during REM sleep (Evans, 1984). In a sense, this theory suggests that the dreams represent an attempt of the brain to check out its neural connections during off-peak hours, in the same way that computer operators test their machines during the late evening, when computer demands are at their lowest.

Even if dreams are a by-product of brain activity and do not (as Freud suggested) represent an active attempt to disguise unconscious wishes, this does not mean that they have no psychological significance. It is still possible that the specific content of our dreams is unique to us and represents meaningful patterns and concerns. Dreams may indeed provide clues about the things that on some level of consciousness are most important to us (Cartwright et al., 1984; Hermans, 1987).

Dreams Without Sleep: Daydreams

It is the stuff of magic: Our past mistakes can be wiped out and the future filled with noteworthy accomplishments. Fame, happiness, and wealth can be ours. In the next moment, though, the most horrible of tragedies can occur, leaving us alone, penniless, a figure of pitiful unhappiness.

The source of these scenarios is **daydreams,** fantasies that people construct while awake. Unlike dreaming that occurs while sleeping, daydreams are more under people's control, and therefore their content is often more closely related to immediate events in the environment than is the content of the dreams that occur during sleep.

Daydreams are a typical part of waking consciousness; but their extent, and the daydreamer's involvement in them, varies from person to person. For example, around 2 to 4 percent of the population spend at least half their free time fantasizing. Although most people daydream much less frequently, almost everyone fantasizes to some degree. Studies that ask people to identify what they are doing at random times during the day have shown that they are daydreaming about 10 percent of the time. As to the content of fantasies, most concern mundane, ordinary events: Paying the telephone bill, picking up the groceries, and solving a romantic problem are typical (Singer, 1975; Lynn & Rhue, 1988; Lester & Tarnacki, 1989).

People who daydream most frequently often report having had lonely childhoods and appear to have developed a pattern of fantasizing to escape a lack of stimulation. On the other hand, this pattern is not universal: Many frequent fantasizers come from rich environments and had parents who encouraged the use of imagination, sometimes to the extent of building joint fantasies about the world (Lynn & Rhue, 1985).

Although frequent daydreaming might seem to suggest psychological difficulties, there actually seems to be little relationship between psychological disturbance and daydreaming (Rhue & Lynn, 1987; Lynn & Rhue, 1988). Except in those rare cases in which a daydreamer is unable to distinguish a fantasy from reality (a mark of serious problems, as we discuss in Chapter 10), daydreaming seems to be a normal part of waking consciousness. Indeed, fantasy may contribute to the psychological well-being of some people by increasing their creativity and by permitting them to use their imagination to understand what other people are experiencing.

Slumbering Problems: Sleep Disturbances

At one time or another, almost all of us have sleeping difficulty—a condition known as **insomnia.** It may be due to a particular situation such as the death of a friend or close relative, or concern about a test score or the loss of a job. Some cases of insomnia, however, have no obvious reason or cause. Some people are simply unable to fall alseep easily, or they go to sleep readily but wake up frequently during the night. Insomnia is a problem that afflicts about a quarter of the population of the United States.

Other sleep problems are less common than insomnia. People with **sleep apnea** have difficulty breathing and sleeping simultaneously. The result is disturbed, fitful sleep, as the person is constantly reawakened when the lack of oxygen becomes sufficiently great to trigger a waking

The sleeplessness of insomnia affects almost everyone at one time or another.

response. In some cases, people with apnea wake themselves some 500 times during the course of an evening, resulting in complaints of sleepiness the next day. Sleep apnea may account for **sudden infant death syndrome,** a mysterious killer of seemingly normal infants who die while sleeping.

Narcolepsy is an uncontrollable need to sleep for short periods during the day. No matter what the activity—holding a heated conversation, exercising, or driving—the narcoleptic will suddenly drift into sleep. People with narcolepsy go directly from wakefulness to REM sleep, skipping the other stages. The causes of narcolepsy are not known, although there may be a genetic component, with narcolepsy running in some families.

We know relatively little about sleeptalking and sleepwalking, two fairly harmless sleep disturbances. Both occur during stage 4 sleep and are more frequent in children than in adults. In most cases, sleeptalkers and sleepwalkers have a vague consciousness of the world around them, and a sleepwalker may be able to walk around obstructions in a crowded room in an agile fashion. Unless a sleepwalker wanders into a dangerous environment, sleepwalking typically poses little risk. In fact, the conventional wisdom that one shouldn't awaken sleepwalkers is wrong: No harm will come from waking them, although they will probably be quite confused.

*A*SK YOURSELF

What is the definition of consciousness?

What are the four distinct stages of sleep and REM sleep?

What are the different explanations for dreams?

How can the sleep disorders of insomnia, narcolepsy, and sleep apnea be described?

Why has the psychological meaning of dreaming proven so difficult to comprehend, and how would you go about studying the meaning of dreams?

*A*LTERED STATES OF CONSCIOUSNESS: HYPNOSIS AND MEDITATION

You are feeling relaxed and drowsy. You are getting sleepier and sleepier. Your body is becoming limp. Now you are starting to become warm, at ease, more comfortable. Your eyelids are feeling heavier and heavier. Your eyes are closing; you can't keep them open any more. You are totally relaxed.

Now, as you listen to my voice, do exactly as I say. Place your hands above your head. You will find they are getting heavier and heavier—so heavy you can barely keep them up. In fact, although you are straining as hard as you can, you will be unable to hold them up any longer.

An observer watching the above scene would notice a curious phenomenon occurring: Many of the people listening to the voice would, one by one, drop their arms to their sides, as if they were holding heavy lead weights. The reason for this strange behavior is probably no surprise: The people have been hypnotized.

You Are Under My Power—Or Are You? Hypnosis

A person under **hypnosis** is in a state of heightened susceptibility to the suggestions of others. In some respects, it appears that a person in a hypnotic trance is asleep. Yet other aspects of behavior contradict this appearance, for the person is attentive to the hypnotist's suggestions and carries out suggestions that may be bizarre and silly.

At the same time, people do not lose all will of their own when hypnotized: They will not perform antisocial behaviors, and they will not carry out self-destructive acts. Moreover, people cannot be hypnotized against their will—despite the popular misconceptions.

There are wide variations in people's susceptibility to hypnosis (Sabourin et al., 1990; Piccione, Hilgard, & Zimbardo, 1989). About 5 to 10 percent of the population cannot be hypnotized at all, while some 15 percent are very easily hypnotized. Most people fall in between. Moreover, the ease with which a person is hypnotized is related to a number of other characteristics. People who are readily hypnotized are also easily absorbed while reading books or listening to music, becoming unaware of what is happening around them, and they often spend an unusual amount of time daydreaming (Hilgard, 1974; Lynn & Rhue, 1985; Lynn & Snodgrass, 1987). In sum, then, they show a high ability to concentrate and to become completely absorbed in what they are doing.

If this comic were true to life, Spiderman would have little to fear from the evil Mesmero: Despite common misconceptions to the contrary, people cannot be hypnotized against their will. (© 1981 Marvel Entertainment Group, Inc. All rights reserved. Spider-Man and the likeness thereof are trademarks of Marvel Entertainment Group, Inc. and are used with permission.)

A different state of consciousness? The issue of whether hypnosis represents a state of consciousness that is qualitatively different from normal waking consciousness has long been controversial among psychologists.

Ernest Hilgard (1975) has argued convincingly that hypnosis does represent a state of consciousness that differs significantly from other states. He contends that particular behavioral characteristics clearly differentiate hypnosis from other states, including higher suggestibility; increased ability to recall and construct images, including visual memories from early childhood; a lack of initiative; and the ability to accept uncritically suggestions that clearly contradict reality. Moreover, recent research has found changes in electrical activity in the brain that are associated with hypnosis, supporting the position that hypnotic states represent a state of consciousness different from that of normal waking (Spiegel, 1987).

Still, some theorists reject the notion that hypnosis represents an altered state of consciousness (Spanos, 1986; Spanos, James & de Groot, 1990). They argue that altered brain wave patterns are not sufficient to demonstrate that a hypnotic state is qualitatively different from normal waking consciousness, given that there are no other specific physiological changes that occur when a person is in a trance. Furthermore, some researchers have shown that people merely pretending to be hypnotized show behaviors that are nearly identical to those of truly hypnotized individuals, and that hypnotic susceptibility can be increased through training procedures (Gfeller, Lynn & Pribble, 1987; Spanos et al., 1987). There also is little support for the contention that adults can accurately recall memories of childhood events while hypnotized (Nash, 1987). Such converging evidence suggests that there is nothing qualitatively special about the hypnotic trance (Barber, 1975; Lynn, Rhue, & Weeks, 1990).

The jury remains out on whether hypnosis represents a state of consciousness that is truly unique. On the other hand, hypnosis has been applied in a number of important areas (see the Psychology and Society box), and as such represents a useful therapeutic tool.

Regulating Your Own State of Consciousness: Meditation

When traditional practitioners of the ancient eastern religion of Zen Buddhism want to achieve greater spiritual insight, they turn to a technique that has been used for centuries to alter their state of consciousness. This technique is called meditation.

Meditation is a learned technique for refocusing attention that brings about an altered state of consciousness. Although there is an exotic sound to it, some form of meditation is found within every major religion—including Christianity and Judaism. In the United States today, some of

---

PSYCHOLOGY AND SOCIETY

Using Hypnosis Outside the Laboratory

Although there is disagreement over the true nature of consciousness associated with hypnotic states, few would dispute the tremendous practical value of hypnosis in a variety of settings (Weitzenhoffer, 1989). Psychologists working in many disparate areas have found hypnosis to be a reliable, effective tool. Among the range of applications are the following:

• Medical care. Patients suffering from chronic pain may be given the suggestion, while hypnotized, that their pain is eliminated or reduced. Similarly, they may be taught to hypnotize themselves to relieve pain or to gain a sense of control over their symptoms. Hypnosis has proved to be particularly useful during childbirth and dental procedures (Erickson, Hershman, & Secter, 1990).

• Law enforcement uses. Witnesses and victims are sometimes better able to recall details of a crime when hypnotized. In one well-known case, a witness to the kidnapping of a group of California schoolchildren was placed under hypnosis and was able to recall all but one digit of the license number on the kidnapper's vehicle (*Time*, 1976). On the other hand, the evidence regarding the accuracy of recollections obtained under hypnosis is decidedly mixed. In some cases, accurate recall of specific information increases—but so does the number of errors (Dywan & Bowers, 1983). Moreover, there is an increase in a person's confidence about the recollections obtained during hypnosis, even when the memory is in error (Nogrady, McConkey & Perry, 1985). The hypnotic state may simply make people more willing to report whatever they think they remember. Because of these questions about its usefulness, the legal status of hypnosis has yet to be resolved (Council on Scientific Affairs, 1985).

• Professional sports. Athletes frequently turn to hypnosis to improve their performance. For example, championship fighter Ken Norton used hypnosis prior to a bout to prepare himself for the encounter, and baseball star Rod Carew used hypnotism to increase his concentration when batting (Udolf, 1981).

Hypnosis, then, has many potential applications. Of course, it is not invariably effective: For the significant number of people who cannot be hypnotized, it offers little help. But for people who make good hypnotic subjects, hypnosis has the potential for providing significant benefits.

---

the major proponents of meditation are followers of Maharishi Mahesh Yogi. They practice a form of meditation called *transcendental meditation,* or *TM,* although several other groups teach various forms of meditation.

The specific meditative technique used in TM involves repeating a **mantra**—a sound, word, or syllable—over and over; in other forms of meditation, the focus is on a picture, flame, or specific part of the body. Regardless of the nature of the particular initial stimulus, in most forms of meditation the key to the procedure is concentrating on it so thoroughly that the meditator becomes unaware of any outside stimulation and a different state of consciousness is reached. Following meditation, people report feeling thoroughly relaxed, having sometimes gained new insights into themselves and the problems they are facing.

Meditation has its roots in the ancient oriental religion of Zen Buddhism, but it is practiced today by many westerners in modified techniques that do not use traditional sitting postures.

Studies of the physiological changes that occur during meditation indicate that *something* different is happening in that state, but whether these changes qualify as a true change in consciousness is controversial. For example, oxygen usage decreases, heart rate and blood pressure decline, and brain-wave patterns may change (Wallace & Benson, 1972). On the other hand, similar changes occur during relaxation of any sort, so whether they indicate some special state of consciousness remains an open question (Holmes, 1985).

It *is* clear that users of meditation techniques report positive benefits, and there is even some evidence that significant long-term benefits can accumulate (Alexander et al., 1989). It is also possible to meditate without exotic trappings by using a few simple procedures developed by Herbert Benson, who has studied meditation extensively (Benson et al., 1977). The basics—which are similar in several respects to those developed as a part of Eastern religions but have no spiritual component—include sitting in a quiet room with eyes closed, breathing deeply and rhythmically, and repeating a word or sound over and over. Most people find themselves in a deeply relaxed state after just twenty minutes. Practiced twice a day, Benson's meditative techniques seem to be just as effective as more mystical methods in bringing about relaxation (Benson & Friedman, 1985).

*A*SK YOURSELF

What is the nature of hypnosis?

Does hypnosis represent a separate state of consciousness?

What is meditation?

If meditation has psychological benefits, does this suggest that we are mentally overburdened in our normal state of consciousness?

THE HIGHS AND LOWS OF CONSCIOUSNESS: DRUG USE

As the butane torch flame vaporized the cocaine in the bowl of a glass smoking pipe, Amir Vik-Kiv inhaled deeply, held the smoke in his expanded chest, then exhaled in a breathless rush. Suddenly, his eyes bulged and his hands trembled. Beads of sweat broke out on his forehead, and perspiration stains formed under his arms.

Within an hour he had "burned" about $100 worth of the drug, but what had happened in his brain just seven seconds after taking the first hit was more like an explosion. Although he had not eaten food in a day or had sex in months, he was no longer hungry for either. . . .

What would happen when the dope ran out was another story. Before long Vik-Kiv would be crawling around the kitchen floor, searching for bits of cocaine that might have spilled. When he found anything white, he would take it—and gag at the taste of what could have been anything from a burning bread crumb to a moldering roach egg. (Milloy, 1986, p. 1.)

Although few of us reach the extremes of this person—who eventually enrolled in a rehabilitation program—almost all of us are experienced drug users. From infancy on, most people take vitamins, aspirin, cold-relief medicine, and the like. These drugs have little effect on our con-

The use of cocaine, here being inhaled or "snorted," has damaged the lives of many people.

sciousness, operating primarily on our biological functions. When we speak of drugs that affect consciousness, we are referring instead to **psychoactive drugs,** drugs that influence a person's emotions, perceptions, and behavior. Even these drugs are common in most people's lives; if you have ever had a cup of coffee or sipped a beer, you have had a psychoactive drug. In fact, a large number of people have used more potent—and dangerous—psychoactive drugs than coffee and beer (see Figure 7-4).

Obviously, drugs vary in the nature of the effects they have on users. The most dangerous are those that are addictive. **Addictive drugs** produce a biological or psychological dependence in the user, and their withdrawal leads to a craving for the drug that, in some cases, may be nearly irresistible. Addictions may be biologically based, in which case the body becomes so accustomed to functioning in the presence of a drug that it cannot function in its absence. Or addictions may be psychological, in which case people believe that they need the drug in order to respond to the stresses of daily living. Although we generally associate addiction with drugs such as heroin, everyday sorts of drugs like caffeine (found in

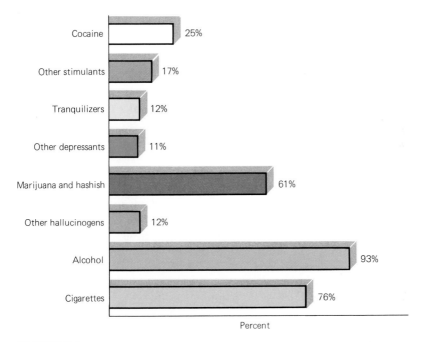

FIGURE 7-4
How many people use drugs? Results of the most recent comprehensive survey of people 18 to 25 years old, carried out by the National Institute of Drug Abuse, show the percentage of respondents who have used various substances for nonmedical purposes at least once. (National Institute of Drug Abuse, 1986.)

coffee) and nicotine (found in cigarettes) have their addictive aspects as well.

We know relatively little about the reasons underlying addiction. One of the problems in identifying the causes is that different drugs (such as alcohol and cocaine) affect the brain in very different ways—and yet may be equally addicting. Furthermore, it takes longer to become addicted to some drugs than to others, even though the ultimate consequences of addiction may be equally grave (Barnes, 1988).

Why do people take drugs in the first place? There are many reasons, ranging from the perceived pleasure of the experience itself, to the escape a drug-induced high affords from the everyday pressures of life, to an attempt to achieve a religious or spiritual state. But other factors, ones that have little to do with the nature of the experience itself, also lead people to try drugs. For instance, the models of prestigious users and the pressures of peers play a role in the decision to use drugs (Stein, Newcomb & Bentler, 1987). In some cases, the motive is simply the thrill of trying something new and perhaps illegal. Regardless of the forces that lead a person to begin to use drugs, drug addiction is among the most difficult of all behaviors to modify, even with extensive treatment (Marlatt et al., 1988).

Drug Highs: Stimulants

It's 1 A.M., and you still haven't finished reading the last chapter of the text on which you are being tested in the morning. Feeling exhausted, you turn to the one thing that may help you keep awake for the next two hours: a cup of strong, black coffee.

If you have ever found yourself in such a position, you have been relying on a major **stimulant,** caffeine, to stay awake. **Caffeine** is one of a number of stimulants that affect the central nervous system by causing a rise in heart rate, blood pressure, and muscular tension. Caffeine is not present in coffee alone; it is an important ingredient in tea, soft drinks, and chocolate as well. The major behavioral effects of caffeine are an increase in attentiveness and a decrease in reaction time. Caffeine can also bring about an improvement in mood, most likely by mimicking the effects of a natural brain chemical, adenosine.

Too much caffeine, however, can result in nervousness and insomnia. People can build up a biological dependence on the drug: If they suddenly stop drinking coffee, they may experience headaches or depression. Many people who drink large amounts of coffee on weekdays have headaches on weekends because of a sudden drop in the amount of caffeine they are consuming (Konner, 1988).

Another common stimulant is **nicotine,** found in cigarettes. The soothing effects of nicotine help explain why cigarette smoking is rewarding for smokers, many of whom continue to smoke despite clear

One of the most frequently used stimulants is nicotine, a chief ingredient of cigarettes.

evidence of its long-term health dangers. Smoking is addictive; smokers develop a dependence on nicotine, and smokers who suddenly stop develop strong cravings for the drug. According to the former U.S. Surgeon General, C. Everett Koop, who changed the designation of smoking from a "habit" to an "addiction," the use of nicotine is "driven by strong, often irresistible urges and can persist despite . . . repeated efforts to quit" (Koop, 1988).

"Speed kills": amphetamines. The phrase "speed kills" was made popular in the late 1970s when use of **amphetamines,** strong stimulants such as Dexedrine and Benzedrine (popularly known as speed), soared. In small quantities, amphetamines bring about increased confidence, a sense of energy and alertness, and a mood "high." They may also cause a loss of appetite, increased anxiety, and irritability. When taken over long periods of time, amphetamines can cause feelings of being persecuted by others, as well as a general sense of suspiciousness. If taken in too large a quantity, amphetamines cause so much stimulation of the central nervous system that convulsions and death can occur—hence the phrase "speed kills." (For a summary of the effects of amphetamines and other illegal drugs, see Table 7-3.)

Coke isn't it. Two dangerous stimulants that have grown in popularity over the last fifteen years are **cocaine** and its derivative, **crack.** Cocaine is inhaled or "snorted" through the nose, whereas crack is smoked. Both are rapidly absorbed into the bloodstream, making their effects apparent almost immediately. Although illegal and expensive, cocaine and crack use are not uncommon: There are some 3 million regular cocaine users, and about 30 percent of all college students will have tried cocaine by their senior year (Washton & Gold, 1987; NIDA, 1989).

TABLE 7-3 ILLEGAL DRUGS AND THEIR EFFECTS

Drug	Street Name	Effects	Withdrawal Symptoms	Adverse/Overdose Reactions
Stimulants				
Amphetamines		Increased confidence, mood elevation, sense of energy and alertness, decreased appetite, anxiety, irritability, insomnia, transient drowsiness, delayed orgasm	Apathy, general fatigue, prolonged sleep, depression, disorientation, suicidal thoughts, agitated motor activity, irritability, bizarre dreams	Elevated blood pressure, increase in body temperature, face-picking, suspiciousness, bizarre and repetitious behavior, vivid hallucinations, convulsions, possible death
Benzedrine	Speed			
Dexedrine	Speed			
Cocaine	Coke, blow, toot, snow, lady, crack			
Depressants				
Barbiturates		Impulsiveness, dramatic mood swings, bizarre thoughts, suicidal behavior, slurred speech, disorientation, slowed mental and physical functioning, limited attention span	Weakness, restlessness, nausea and vomiting, headaches, nightmares, irritability, depression, acute anxiety, hallucinations, seizures, possible death	Confusion, decreased response to pain, shallow respiration, dilated pupils, weak and rapid pulse, coma, possible death
Nembutal	Yellowjackets, yellows			
Seconal	Reds			
Phenobarbital				
Quaalude	Ludes, 714s			
Heroin	H, hombre, junk, smack, dope, horse, crap	Apathy, difficulty in concentration, slowed speech, decreased physical activity, drooling, itching, euphoria, nausea	Anxiety, vomiting, sneezing, diarrhea, lower back pain, watery eyes, runny nose, yawning, irritability, tremors, panic, chills and sweating, cramps	Depressed levels of consciousness, low blood pressure, rapid heart rate, shallow breathing, convulsions, coma, possible death
Morphine	Drugstore dope, cube, first line, mud			

When taken in relatively small quantities, cocaine has many of the same effects as amphetamines in general—euphoria, increased confidence, alertness, and a sense of well-being. It also allows people to work for long periods of time without feeling tired (although this can be followed by a "crash" in which the user sleeps for long periods of time).

The price paid for these effects is steep. The drug is psychologically addictive, and users may grow obsessed with obtaining it. Their lives become tied to the drug; they deteriorate mentally and physically, losing weight and growing suspicious of others. In extreme cases, cocaine can cause hallucinations; a common one is that insects are crawling over one's body (Fisher, Raskin & Uhlenhuth, 1987).

Drug Lows: Depressants

In contrast to the initial effect of stimulants, which is an increase in arousal of the central nervous system, the effect of **depressants** is to impede the nervous system by causing the neurons to fire more slowly. Small doses

TABLE 7-3 ILLEGAL DRUGS AND THEIR EFFECTS (*continued*)

Drug	Street Name	Effects	Withdrawal Symptoms	Adverse/Overdose Reactions
Hallucinogens Cannabis Marijuana Hashish Hash oil	Bhang, kif, ganja, dope, grass, pot, smoke, hemp, joint, weed, bone, Mary Jane, herb, tea	Euphoria, relaxed inhibitions, increased appetite, disoriented behavior	Hyperactivity, insomnia, decreased appetite, anxiety	Severe reactions are rare but include panic, paranoia, fatigue, bizarre and dangerous behavior, decreased production of testosterone over long term, immune-system effects
LSD	Electricity, acid, quasey, blotter acid, microdot, white lightning, purple barrels	Fascination with ordinary objects; heightened aesthetic responses to color, texture, spatial arrangements, contours, music; vision and depth distortion; hearing colors, seeing music; slowing of time; heightened sensitivity to faces and gestures; magnified feelings of love, lust, hate, joy, anger, pain, terror, despair; paranoia; panic; euphoria; bliss; impairment of short-term memory; projection of self into dreamlike images	Not reported	Nausea and chills; increased pulse, temperature, and blood pressure; trembling; slow, deep breathing; loss of appetite; insomnia; longer, more intense "trips"; bizarre, dangerous behavior possibly leading to injury or death
Phencylidine (PCP)	Angel dust, hog, rocket fuel, superweed, peace pill, elephant tranquilizer, dust, bad pizza	Increased blood pressure and heart rate, sweating, nausea, numbness, floating sensation, slowed reflexes, altered body image, altered perception of time and space, impaired immediate and recent memory, decreased concentration, paranoid thoughts and delusions	Not reported	Highly variable and possibly dose-related: disorientation, loss of recent memory, lethargy/stupor, bizarre and violent behavior, rigidity and immobility, mutism, staring, hallucinations and delusions, coma

result in at least temporary feelings of **intoxication**—drunkenness—along with a sense of euphoria and joy. When large amounts are taken, however, speech becomes slurred, muscle control becomes disjointed, causing difficulty of motion, and ultimately consciousness may be lost entirely.

The most common depressant is alcohol, although most people would probably claim that it increases their sense of sociability and well-being (Steele & Southwick, 1985; Steele & Josephs, 1990). The discrepancy between the actual and the perceived effects of alcohol lies in its initial effects: releasing tension and producing a breakdown in judgment. As the dose of alcohol increases, however, the depressive effects become clearer (Hannon et al., 1985). People may feel emotionally and physically unstable; they become incoherent and may eventually fall into a stupor and pass out (see Table 7-4).

TABLE 7-4 EFFECTS OF ALCOHOL

Distilled Spirits Consumed in 2 Hours, Ounces	Alcohol in Blood, Percent	Typical Effects, Average-size Adult
3 (2 drinks)	0.05	Judgment, thought, and restraint weakened; tension released, giving carefree sensation
4½ (3 drinks)	0.08	Tensions and inhibitions of everyday life lessened
6 (4 drinks)	0.10	Voluntary motor action affected, making hand and arm movements, walk, and speech clumsy
10 (7 drinks)	0.20	Severe impairment—staggering, loud, incoherent, emotionally unstable; 100 times greater traffic risk
14 (9 drinks)	0.30	Deeper areas of brain affected, with stimulus response and understanding confused; stuporous
18 (12 drinks)	0.40	Incapable of voluntary action, sleepy, difficult to arouse; equivalent of surgical anesthesia
22 (15 drinks)	0.50	Comatose; centers controlling breathing and heartbeat anesthetized; death

Note: A drink refers to a typical 12-ounce glass of beer, a 1.5-ounce shot of hard liquor, or a 5-ounce glass of wine.

It is only recently that scientists have begun to understand how alcohol brings about its varied effects. According to some research, alcohol affects the walls or membranes of neurons by decreasing their ability to transmit messages. When most people consume alcohol, the normal pathways of the neurons become less rigid, and messages become garbled and disoriented—resulting in the depressive effects that occur in the central nervous system.

In contrast, alcoholics—people who come to rely on alcohol and drink even though it causes serious problems—develop a tolerance for alcohol; their cell membranes remain rigid even in the presence of alcohol. When alcohol in the blood decreases, alcoholics suffer from withdrawal symptoms, since their cell membranes become unable to process messages in the absence of alcohol (U.S. Dept. of Health & Human Services, 1990; Hurley & Horowitz, 1990).

It is still unclear why certain people become alcoholic and develop a tolerance for alcohol, while others do not. Some evidence suggests a genetic cause; the chances of becoming alcoholic are considerably higher if alcoholics are present in earlier generations, implying that some people are genetically susceptible to alcoholism. On the other hand, not all alcoholics have close relatives who are alcoholics; in these cases, environmental stressors are suspected of playing a larger role (Blum et al., 1990; Hurley & Horowitz, 1990).

Whatever the specific cause of the increased tolerance to alcohol found in alcoholics, the findings pertaining to the rigidity of the cell membranes suggest some novel approaches to treating alcoholism. Because certain foods affect the density of the neuronal cell membranes, it is possible that changes in diet might help people become less susceptible to alcoholism in the same way that dietary changes are recommended to help prevent heart disease. Even more interesting is the possibility of a "sober" pill, which would prevent alcohol from affecting the cell membranes and would thereby prevent the behavioral effects of alcohol from occurring (Paul, 1986).

Barbiturates, which include such drugs as Nembutal, Seconal, and phenobarbital, are another form of depressant. Frequently prescribed by physicians to induce sleep or to reduce stress, barbiturates produce a sense of relaxation. Yet they too are psychologically and physically addictive and, when combined with alcohol, can be deadly, since such a combination relaxes the muscles of the diaphragm to such an extent that the user suffocates. The street drug known as Quaalude is closely related to the barbiturate family and has similar dangers associated with it.

Morphine and heroin. Two of the most powerful depressants, both derived from the poppy flower, are **morphine** and **heroin.** Both reduce pain and cause sleepiness. Although morphine is used medically to control severe pain, heroin is illegal in the United States. This has not prevented its widespread use.

Heroin users usually inject the drug directly into their veins with a hypodermic needle. The immediate effect has been described as a "rush" of positive feeling, similar in some respects to a sexual orgasm—and just as difficult to describe. After the rush, a heroin user experiences a sense

Heroin, which is typically injected directly into the user's vein, is a powerful drug that produces both biological and psychological addiction.

of well-being and peacefulness that lasts three to five hours. When the effects of the drug wear off, however, the user feels extreme anxiety and a desperate desire to repeat the experience. Moreover, larger amounts of heroin are needed each time to produce the same pleasurable effect. This leads to a cycle of biological and psychological addiction: The user is constantly either shooting up or attempting to obtain ever-increasing amounts of the drug. Eventually, the life of the addict becomes centered around heroin.

Because of the powerful positive feelings the drug produces, heroin addiction is particularly difficult to cure. One treatment that has shown some success is the use of methadone. **Methadone** is a chemical that satisfies a heroin user's physiological cravings for the drug without providing the "high" that accompanies heroin. When heroin users are placed on regular doses of methadone they may be able to function relatively normally. The use of methadone has one substantial drawback, however: Although it removes the psychological dependence on heroin, it replaces the biological addiction to heroin with a biological addiction to methadone. Researchers, then, are attempting to identify non-addictive chemical substitutes for heroin, as well as substitutes for other addictive drugs, that do not replace one addiction with another (Waldrop, 1989).

Flying High: Hallucinogens

What do mushrooms, jimsonweed, and morning glories have in common? Besides being fairly common plants each can be a source of a powerful **hallucinogen,** a drug that is capable of producing hallucinations, or changes in the perceptual process.

The most common hallucinogen in use today is **marijuana,** whose active ingredient—tetrahydrocannabinol (THC)—is found in a common weed, cannabis. Marijuana is typically smoked in cigarettes, although it can be cooked and eaten. At least one-third of all Americans over the age of 12 have tried it at least once, and among 18- to 25-year-olds, the figure is twice as high (National Institute of Drug Abuse, 1986). Despite its illegality, marijuana use is so prevalent that about 15 percent of those over 15 years old are likely to use it in a given week.

The effects of marijuana vary from person to person, but they typically consist of feelings of euphoria and general well-being. Sensory experiences seem more vivid and intense, and a person's sense of self-importance seems to grow. Memory may be impaired, causing the user to feel pleasantly "spaced out." On the other hand, the effects are not universally positive: Individuals who take marijuana when feeling depressed can end up even more depressed, since the drug tends to magnify both good and bad feelings.

Marijuana has the reputation of being a "safe" drug when used in moderation, and there seems to be no scientific evidence that its use is addictive or that users "graduate" to more dangerous drugs. However, the long-term effects of heavy marijuana use present some potential hazard. For instance, there is some evidence that heavy use decreases the production of the male sex hormone testosterone, potentially affecting sexual activity and sperm count (Miller, 1975). Similarly, heavy use affects the ability of the immune system to fight off germs and increases stress on the heart, although it is unclear how strong the magnitude of these effects are (Turkington, 1986). One negative consequence of smoking large quantities of marijuana is unquestionable, though: The smoke damages the lungs much the way cigarette smoke does, producing an increased likelihood of developing cancer and other lung diseases (Institute of Medicine, 1982).

In sum, the *short-term* effects of marijuana use appear to be relatively minor—if users follow obvious cautions, such as avoiding driving or using machinery. However, it is less clear whether the long-term consequences are harmful. The case regarding the use of marijuana is far from closed, and more research is necessary before the question of its safety can be settled.

The acid test: LSD and PCP. Two of the strongest hallucinogens are **lysergic acid diethylamide,** or **LSD** (known commonly as acid), and **phencyclidine,** or **PCP** (often referred to as angel dust). Both drugs seem to affect the operation of the neurotransmitter serotonin in the brain, causing an alteration in brain-cell activity and perception (Jacobs, 1987).

LSD produces vivid hallucinations. Perceptions of colors, sounds, and shapes are altered so much that even the most mundane experience— such as looking at the knots in a wooden table—can seem exciting and moving. Time perception is distorted, and objects and people may be viewed in a new way, with some users reporting that LSD increases their understanding of the world. For others, however, the experience brought on by LSD can be terrifying, particularly if users have had emotional difficulties in the past. Furthermore, people can experience flashbacks, in which they hallucinate long after the initial drug usage.

One of the most recent additions to the drug scene, PCP also causes strong hallucinations. However, the potential side effects associated with its use make the drug even more dangerous than LSD. Large doses may cause paranoid and destructive behavior, and in some cases users become violent toward themselves and others.

The Informed Consumer of Psychology: Identifying Drug and Alcohol Problems

In a society bombarded with commercials for drugs that are guaranteed to do everything from curing the common cold to giving new life to "tired blood," it is no wonder that drug-related problems present a major social issue. Yet many people with drug and alcohol problems deny they have them, and even close friends and family members may fail to realize when occasional social use of drugs or alcohol has turned into abuse.

Certain signs, however, indicate when use becomes abuse (Brody, 1982). Among them:

- Always getting high to have a good time
- Being high more often than not
- Getting high to get oneself going
- Going to work or class while high
- Missing or being unprepared for class or work because you were high
- Feeling bad later about something you said or did while high
- Driving a car while high
- Coming in conflict with the law because of drugs or alcohol
- Doing something while high that you wouldn't otherwise do
- Being high in nonsocial, solitary situations
- Being unable to stop getting high
- Feeling a need for a drink or a drug to get through the day
- Becoming physically unhealthy
- Failing at school or on the job
- Thinking about liquor or drugs all the time

Any combination of these symptoms is sufficient to alert a person to a serious drug problem. Because drug and alcohol dependence are almost impossible to cure on one's own, people who suspect that they have a problem should seek immediate attention from a psychologist, physician, or counselor.

ASK YOURSELF

What are psychoactive drugs?

What are the different types of addiction?

How can the effects of stimulants and depressants be differentiated?

What are hallucinogens?

Why is the use of psychoactive drugs and the search for altered states of consciousness found in almost every culture?

LOOKING BACK

1. Consciousness refers to a person's awareness of the sensations, thoughts, and feelings being experienced at a given moment. It can vary in terms of how aware of outside stimuli we are, from an active to passive state, and in terms of whether it is artificially induced or occurs naturally.

2. Using the electroencephalogram, or EEG, to study sleep, scientists have found that sleep proceeds through a series of stages identified by unique patterns of brain waves. In what is sometimes called stage 0, people move out of a waking state, in which they are relaxed with their eyes closed, into stage 1. Stage 1 is characterized by relatively rapid, low-voltage waves, whereas Stage 2 shows more regular, spindle patterns. In stage 3, the brain waves become slower, with higher peaks and lower valleys apparent. Finally, stage 4 sleep includes waves that are even slower and more regular.

3. REM (rapid eye movement) sleep is characterized by an increase in heart rate, a rise in blood pressure, an increase in the rate of breathing and, in males, erections. Most striking is the rapid movement of the eyes, which dart back and forth under closed eyelids. Dreams occur during this stage.

4. According to Freud, dreams have both a manifest content, their apparent story line, and a latent content, their true meaning. He suggested that the latent content provides a guide to a dreamer's unconscious, showing unfulfilled wishes or desires.

5. More recent theories view dreaming in terms of a fundamental biological activity, in which dreams are a result of random electrical energy, possibly due to changes in the production of particular neurotransmitters. This electrical energy randomly stimulates different memories, which are then woven into a coherent story line. Another theory suggests that dreaming occurs as the by-product of a checking and consolidation process that the brain goes through during REM sleep.

6. Daydreaming is a typical part of waking consciousness, although there are wide individual differences in the amount of time devoted to it.

7. Insomnia is a sleep disorder characterized by difficulty sleeping. Sleep apnea is reflected in difficulties in sleeping and breathing at the same time; people with narcolepsy have an uncontrollable urge to sleep. Sleepwalking and sleeptalking are relatively harmless.

8. Hypnosis produces a state of heightened susceptibility to the suggestions of the hypnotist. Although there are no physiological indicators that distinguish hypnosis from normal waking consciousness, significant behavioral characteristics occur, including increased concentration and suggestibility, heightened ability to recall and construct images, lack of initiative, and acceptance of suggestions that clearly contradict reality.

9. Meditation is a learned technique for refocusing attention that brings about an altered state of consciousness. In transcendental meditation, the most popular form practiced in the United States, a person repeats a mantra (a sound, word, or syllable) over and over, concentrating until he or she becomes unaware of any outside stimulation and reaches a different state of consciousness.

10. Drugs can produce an altered state of consciousness. However, they vary in whether or not they are addictive, producing a physical or psychological dependence. People take drugs for several reasons: to perceive the pleasure of the experience itself, to escape from everyday pressures, to attain religious or spiritual states, to follow the model of prestigious users or peers, or to experience the thrill of trying something new and perhaps illegal.

11. Stimulants cause arousal in the central nervous system. Two common stimulants are caffeine (found in coffee, tea, and soft drinks) and nicotine (found in cigarettes). More dangerous are amphetamines, or "speed," and cocaine. Although in small quantities they bring about increased confidence, a sense of energy and alertness, and a "high," in larger quantities they may overload the central nervous system, leading to convulsions and death.

12. Depressants decrease arousal in the central nervous system, causing the neurons to fire more slowly. They may cause intoxication along with feelings of euphoria. The most common depressant is alcohol, which initially relieves tension. Other depressants include barbiturates, morphine, and heroin. Because of their addictive qualities, morphine and heroin are particularly dangerous.

13. Alcohol is the most frequently used depressant. Alcohol affects the walls or membranes of neurons by decreasing their ability to transmit messages. However, alcoholics develop a tolerance for alcohol, and the cell membranes are unable to process messages effectively without the presence of alcohol. Both genetic causes and environmental stressors may lead to alcoholism.

14. Hallucinogens are drugs that produce hallucinations and other changes in perception. The most frequently used hallucinogen is marijuana; its use is common throughout the United States. Although occasional, short-term use of marijuana seems to be of little danger, long-term effects are less clear. Two other hallucinogens, LSD and PCP, affect the operation of neurotransmitters in the brain, causing an alteration in brain-cell activity and perception.

Key Terms and Concepts

consciousness (p. 267)
altered states of consciousness (p. 268)
electroencephalogram (EEG) (p. 269)
stage 1 sleep (p. 271)
stage 2 sleep (p. 271)
stage 3 sleep (p. 272)
stage 4 sleep (p. 272)
rapid eye movement (REM)
   sleep (p. 272)
rebound effect (p. 273)
nightmares (p. 274)
night terrors (p. 274)
latent content of dreams (p. 275)
manifest content of dreams (p. 275)
daydreams (p. 277)
insomnia (p. 278)
sleep apnea (p. 278)
sudden infant death syndrome (p. 279)
narcolepsy (p. 279)
hypnosis (p. 280)

meditation (p. 281)
mantra (p. 282)
psychoactive drugs (p. 285)
addictive drugs (p. 285)
stimulants (p. 286)
caffeine (p. 286)
nicotine (p. 286)
amphetamines (p. 287)
cocaine (p. 287)
crack (p. 287)
depressants (p. 288)
intoxication (p. 289)
barbiturates (p. 291)
morphine (p. 291)
heroin (p. 291)
methadone (p. 292)
hallucinogen (p. 292)
marijuana (p. 292)
lysergic acid diethylamide (LSD) (p. 293)
phencyclidine (PCP) (p. 293)

8

$\mathcal{D}$evelopment

❖

PROLOGUE: GERALD LEVEY AND MARK NEWMAN

Twins Jerry Levey and Mark Newman have many things in common—from their choice of occupation to their favorite brand of beer—despite the fact that they never met until the age of 31.

How many bald, 6-foot-6, 250-pound volunteer fire fighters are there in New Jersey who have droopy mustaches and aviator-style eyeglasses and wear a key ring on their belt on the right side?

The answer is: two. Gerald Levey and Mark Newman are twins, separated at birth, who did not even know each other existed until they were reunited—in a fire station—by a fellow fire fighter who knew Newman and was startled to see Levey at a fire fighters' convention.

Their lives, although separate, took remarkably similar paths. Levey went to college, studying forestry; Newman planned to study forestry in college but instead took a job trimming trees. Both had jobs in supermarkets. One has a job installing sprinkler systems; the other installed fire alarms.

Both are unmarried and find the same kind of woman attractive: "tall, slender, long hair." They share similar hobbies, enjoying hunting, fishing, going to the beach, and watching old John Wayne movies and professional wrestling. Both like Chinese food, and they drink the same brand of beer. Their mannerisms are also similar—they both throw their heads back when they laugh. And, of course, there is one more thing: They share a passion for fighting fires (Lang, 1987).

297

LOOKING AHEAD

Gerald Levey and Mark Newman have been reunited once again, as part of a large-scale, national study of twins being conducted at the Minnesota Center for Twin and Adoption Research, where researchers are finding that the strange degree of similarity between Levey and Newman is mirrored in many other sets of twins. Such coincidences are being studied not as mere curiosities, but because they provide us with important clues about one of the most fundamental questions facing psychologists: how the environment and the natural endowment with which the human being is born interact to produce a unique individual.

This question, and others, falls within the domain of developmental psychology. **Developmental psychology** is the branch of psychology that studies the patterns of growth and change occurring throughout life. In large part, developmental psychologists study the interaction between the unfolding of biologically predetermined patterns of behavior and a constantly changing, dynamic environment. They ask how our genetic background affects our behavior throughout our lives, whether our potential is limited by heredity, and how our built-in biological programming affects our day-to-day development. Similarly, they are committed to understanding the way the environment works with—or against—our genetic capabilities, how the world we live in affects our development, and how we can be encouraged to develop our full potential.

More than other psychologists, developmental psychologists consider the day-to-day patterns and changes in behavior that occur across the life span. We begin our discussion of development by examining the approaches that have been used to understand and delineate the environmental and genetic factors that direct a person's development. Then we consider the very start of development, beginning with conception and the nine months of life prior to birth.

We examine next the physical and perceptual developments that occur after birth and throughout childhood, witnessing the enormous and rapid growth that occurs during the early stages of life. We also focus on the developing child's social world and on cognitive growth, tracing changes in the way children think about the world.

Next, we discuss the major physical, emotional, and cognitive changes that occur during people's entry and passage through adulthood. We examine adolescence and continue through the later stages of life. Finally, in our discussion of old age, we examine the kinds of physical, intellectual, and social changes that occur as a consequence of the aging process.

After reading this chapter, then, you will have the answers to several fundamental questions about development:

- How do psychologists study the extent to which development is a joint function of heredity and environmental factors?
- What are the major milestones of physical, perceptual, and social growth during childhood?

- How does cognitive development proceed throughout our lives?
- What principal kinds of social and intellectual change occur in adolescence, adulthood, and old age, and what are their causes?

NATURE VERSUS NURTURE: A FUNDAMENTAL DEVELOPMENTAL QUESTION

Although the similarities displayed by twins such as Gerald Levey and Mark Newman are startling, they are no less surprising than the dissimilarities that exist among siblings who are raised in almost identical environments. Consider, for instance, the Torres family. Emmanual Torres was convicted of attempting to rape a drama student and then stabbing her to death on a New York City apartment roof; his brother, Alfredo, is a well-respected medical student. Although raised in the same house, with the same parents, the two brothers could not be more different. The differences between them were apparent from childhood; Emmanual continually misbehaved and later had difficulty holding a job, whereas Alfredo showed a fierce ambition from an early age to become a physician (Chambers, 1985).

To the developmental psychologist, one of the central challenges to understanding human development is illustrated by such contrasts, which raise a fundamental question about human development: Can we attribute behavior to causes that are **environmental**—the influence of parents, siblings, family, friends, schooling, nutrition, and all the other experiences to which a child is exposed—or to causes that are **hereditary**—those based on the genetic makeup of an individual that influence growth throughout one's life? A fundamental issue, then, is the **nature-nurture question**, where nature refers to heredity and nurture to environmental influences.

The nature-nurture issue has deep philosophical roots. English philosopher John Locke argued in the 1600s that people were born with the equivalent of a blank slate, a *tabula rasa*, on which the story of their individual experience could be written from scratch. In contrast, the French philosopher Jean Jacques Rousseau suggested a very different conception of development in the 1700s, one in which the environment was seen as corrupting and the "natural" aspects of people (namely, genetic factors) were most influential.

Although the question was first posed as the nature-*versus*-nurture question, today developmental psychologists agree that *both* nature and nurture interact to produce specific developmental patterns. The question has changed from *which* influences behavior to *how* and to what degree environment and heredity produce their effects. No one grows up without being influenced by the environment, nor does anyone develop without being affected by his or her inherited, or **genetic makeup**. However, the debate over the relative influence of the two factors remains an ongoing one, with different approaches and theories of development emphasizing the environment or heredity to a greater or lesser degree (Loehlin, 1989).

For example, some developmental theories stress the role of learning in producing changes in behavior in the developing child, relying on the basic principles of learning we discussed in Chapter 4; such theories emphasize the role of environment in accounting for development. In contrast, other approaches, grounded more closely in the biological aspects of the human being we first encountered in Chapter 2, emphasize the physiological makeup and functioning of the individual. Such theories stress the role of heredity and **maturation**—the unfolding of biologically predetermined patterns of behavior—in producing developmental change. Maturation can be seen, for instance, in the development of sex characteristics (such as breasts or body hair) that occur at the start of adolescence.

On some points, however, agreement exists among developmental psychologists of different theoretical persuasions (Plomin, 1989; 1990). It seems clear that genetic factors not only provide the potential for particular behaviors or traits to emerge, they also place limitations on the emergence of such behaviors or traits. For instance, heredity defines people's general level of intelligence, setting an upper limit which—regardless of the nature of the environment—they cannot exceed. Heredity also provides limits on physical abilities; humans simply cannot run at a speed of 60 miles an hour, nor are they going to grow as tall as ten feet, no matter what the nature of their environment.

Table 8-1 shows some of the characteristics that are most affected by heredity. As you consider the items on the list, it is important to keep in

TABLE 8-1 CHARACTERISTICS WITH STRONG GENETIC COMPONENTS

Physical Characteristics	Intellectual Characteristics	Emotional Characteristics and Disorders
Height	Memory	Shyness
Weight	Ability as measured on intelligence tests	Extraversion
Obesity		Emotionality
Tone of voice	Age of language acquisition	Neuroticism
Blood pressure	Reading disability	Schizophrenia
Tooth decay	Mental retardation	Anxiety
Athletic ability		Alcoholism
Firmness of handshake		
Age of death		
Activity level		

SOURCE Papalia & Olds, 1989; Plomin, 1989.

mind that these characteristics are not *entirely* determined by heredity—merely that the best evidence suggests that variations in these factors are due to a relatively large extent to the genetic makeup of an individual.

In most instances, environmental factors play a critical role in enabling people to reach the potential capabilities provided by their genetic background (Case, 1985; Lamb & Bornstein, 1987). Had Albert Einstein received no intellectual stimulation as a child and not been sent to school, it is unlikely that he would have reached his genetic potential. Similarly, a great athlete like baseball star Willie Mays would have been unlikely to display much physical skill had he not been raised in an environment that nurtured his native talent and gave him the opportunity to train and perfect his natural skills.

In sum, developmental psychologists take an **interactionist** position on the nature-nurture issue, suggesting that a combination of genetic predisposition and environmental influences produces development (Butterworth & Bryant, 1990). The challenge facing developmental psychologists is to identify the specific kind and relative strength of each of these influences on the individual.

The search for the influence of nature and nurture is not merely academic. Important advances in our understanding of the optimal way to treat children have come from research on heredity and the environment. For instance, the way in which we educate children, how children in institutions such as orphanages are raised, and the kinds of day-care that are considered optimal have all been influenced by our understanding of the interaction of heredity and environment.

Addressing the Nature-Nurture Question

Developmental psychologists have confronted the question of determining the relative influence of genetic and environmental factors on behavior in several different ways, although no technique is foolproof. We can, for example, experimentally control the genetic makeup of laboratory animals, carefully breeding them for specific traits. Just as the people who raise Butterball turkeys have learned to produce a breed that grows particularly quickly (so they can be brought to the marketplace less expensively), psychologists are able to breed strains of laboratory animals who share a similar genetic makeup. By observing animals with a similar genetic background in varied environments, they can then ascertain the effects of particular kinds of environmental stimulation. Ultimately, of course, we have the problem of generalizing the findings of research with animals to a human population, but the animal findings do provide fundamental information that could not be obtained ethically from human subjects.

Human twins also provide us with an important source of information about the relative effects of genetic and environmental factors (Bouchard et al., 1990). If **identical twins** (those who are genetically identical) display different patterns of development, we have to attribute such differences to variations in the environment in which they were raised. The most useful data come from identical twins (such as Gerald Levey and Mark Newman) who are adopted at birth by different sets of foster parents and raised apart from each other in different environments. Studies of nontwin siblings who are raised in different environments also shed some light on the issue. Because they share relatively similar genetic backgrounds, siblings who show similarities as adults provide strong evidence for the importance of heredity.

It is also possible to take the opposite tack. Instead of concentrating on people with similar genetic backgrounds who are raised in different environments, we may consider people raised in similar environments who have totally dissimilar genetic backgrounds. If we find, for example, that two adopted children—who have dissimilar genetic backgrounds— raised in the same family develop similarly, we have evidence for the importance of environmental influences on development. Moreover, it is possible to carry out research with animals with dissimilar genetic backgrounds; by experimentally varying the environment in which they are raised, we can determine the influence of environmental factors, independent of heredity, on development.

Studying Development: Research Methods

The specific research methods used by developmental psychologists to consider the nature-nurture issue, as well as other questions of a developmental nature, tend to fall into two categories: cross-sectional and longitudinal. In **cross-sectional research**, people of different ages are compared at the same point in time. Suppose, for instance, you were interested in the development of intellectual ability in adulthood. To carry out a cross-sectional study, you might compare a sample of 25-, 45-, and 65-year olds on an IQ test, seeing how the average scores differ.

Cross-sectional research has pitfalls, however. In our example, for instance, it is possible that any differences you found in IQ scores were due not to age differences per se but to the fact that the average educational level attained by the older subjects was lower than that of the younger sample, since far fewer people went to college forty years ago.

One way around the problem is to conduct **longitudinal research**, in which the behavior of one or more subjects is traced as the subjects age. By examining changes over several points in time, we can best understand how individual people develop.

Unfortunately, there are drawbacks to longitudinal research: It requires an enormous expenditure of time (as the researcher waits for the subjects to get older), and subjects who participate at an earlier stage may drop out, move away, or even die as the research continues. Moreover, subjects who take the same test at several points in time may become "testwise" and perform better each time they take it, just because they are becoming more familiar with the test.

To make up for the drawbacks of cross-sectional research and longitudinal research, investigators have devised an alternative method (Schaie et al., 1988). Known as cross-sequential research, it combines cross-sectional and longitudinal research by taking a number of different age groups and examining them over several points in time. For example, investigators might use a group of 3-, 5-, and 7-year-olds, examining them every six months for a period of several years. This technique allows the developmental psychologist to tease out the effects of age changes themselves from other potentially contaminating factors.

The Start of Life: Conception and Beyond

Our understanding of the biology of the start of life—when a male's sperm cell meets a female's egg cell at the moment of **conception**—makes it no less of a miracle. At that single moment, an individual's genetic endowment is established for the rest of his or her life.

When the egg becomes fertilized by the sperm, the result is a one-celled **zygote** that immediately begins to develop. The zygote contains twenty-three pairs of **chromosomes**, rod-shaped structures that contain the basic hereditary information. One member of each pair is from the mother and the other is from the father. Each chromosome contains thousands of **genes**—smaller units through which genetic information is transmitted—that, either individually or in combination, produce particular characteristics in the individual.

While some genes are responsible for the development of systems common to all members of the human species—the heart, circulatory system, brain, lungs, and so forth—others control the characteristics that make each human unique—facial configuration, height, eye color, and the like. The child's sex is also determined by a particular combination of genes. Specifically, a child inherits an X chromosome from its mother, and either an X or Y chromosome from its father. With an XX combination, it is a female; with an XY combination, it develops as a male. Recent findings suggest that male development is triggered by a single gene on the Y chromosome, and without the presence of that specific gene, the individual will develop as a female (Roberts, 1988a).

The zygote starts out as a microscopic speck, but as it divides through an intricate preprogrammed system of cell division, it grows 10,000 times larger in just four weeks, to about one-fifth of an inch long. At that point it is called an **embryo** and has developed a rudimentary heart (that beats), a brain, an intestinal tract, and a number of other organs. Although all

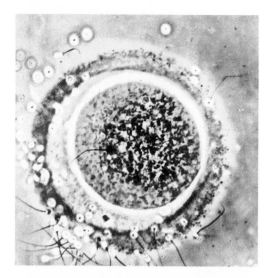

The moment—and miracle—of conception, when a male's sperm cell meets a female's egg cell.

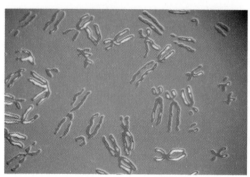

Rod-shaped chromosomes carry the basic information of heredity. Each chromosome contains thousands of genes.

these organs are at a primitive stage of development, they are clearly recognizable. Moreover, by the eighth week, the embryo is about an inch long, and arms, legs, and face can be deciphered (see Figure 8-1).

Following the eighth week, the embryo faces what is known as a **critical period**, the first of several stages in development in which specific kinds of growth must occur if the individual is to develop normally. For example, if the eyes and ears do not develop during this stage, they will never form later on, and if they form abnormally, they are permanently damaged. During critical periods, organisms are particularly sensitive to environmental influences such as the presence of certain kinds of drugs, which, as we will see later, can have a devastating effect on subsequent development (Bornstein, 1987; Bornstein & Bruner, 1989).

Beginning in the ninth week and continuing until birth, the developing individual is called a **fetus**. At the start of this period, it begins to be responsive to touch; it bends its fingers when touched on the hand. At

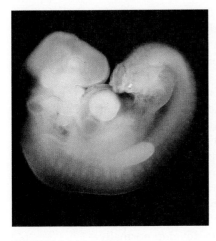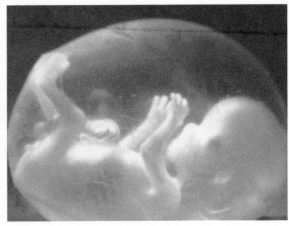

FIGURE 8-1
These remarkable photos of live fetuses display the degree of physical development at 4 and 15 weeks.

16 to 18 weeks, its movements become strong enough for the mother to sense the baby. At the same time, hair may begin to grow on the baby's head, and the facial features become similar to those the child will display at birth. The major organs begin to function, although the fetus could not be kept alive outside the mother. In addition, a lifetime's worth of brain neurons have been produced—although it is unclear whether the brain is capable of thinking in any real sense at this early stage.

By the twenty-fourth week, a fetus has many of the characteristics it will display as a newborn. In fact, when an infant is born prematurely at this age, it can open and close its eyes; suck; cry; look up, down, and around; and even grasp things placed in its hands, although it is still unable to survive for long outside the mother.

The fetus continues to develop prior to birth. It begins to grow fatty deposits under the skin and it gains weight. The fetus reaches the **age of viability**, the point at which it can survive if born prematurely, at about 28 weeks, although through advances in medical technology, this crucial age is getting earlier. At 28 weeks, the fetus weighs about three pounds and is about 16 inches long. It may be capable of learning: One study found that the infants of mothers who read a certain Dr. Seuss story aloud prior to birth preferred the sound of the Dr. Seuss story over other stories after they were born (Spence & DeCasper, 1982).

In the final weeks of pregnancy, the fetus continues to put on weight and grow, becoming increasingly fit. At the end of the normal 38 weeks of pregnancy the fetus typically weighs around $7\frac{1}{2}$ pounds and is about 20 inches in length.

Genetic influences on the fetus. The process of fetal growth that we have been discussing reflects normal development—something that happens in 95 to 98 percent of all pregnancies. Some people are less fortunate, for in the remaining 2 to 5 percent of the cases, children are delivered with major birth defects. One prime cause of such defects is genetic: The information in the chromosomes inherited from one or both of the parents causes a problem. Here are some of the most common genetic difficulties.

- *Phenylketonuria (PKU).* A child born with the inherited disease **phenylketonuria** (PKU) cannot produce an enzyme that is required for normal development. This results in accumulation of poisons that eventually cause profound mental retardation. The disease is treatable, however; if it is caught early enough—and most infants today are routinely tested for PKU—children can be placed on a special diet which allows them to develop normally.

- *Sickle-cell anemia.* About 10 percent of the American black population has the possibility of passing on **sickle-cell anemia**, a disease that gets its name from the abnormal shape of the red blood cells. Children with the disease may have poor appetites, swollen stomachs, and yellowish eyes; they rarely live beyond childhood.

- *Tay-Sachs disease.* Children born with **Tay-Sachs disease**, a problem found most often in Jews of eastern European ancestry, usually die by the age of 3 or 4 because of the body's inability to break down fat. If both parents carry the genetic defect producing the illness, their child has a 1-in-4 chance of being born with the disease (Navon & Proia, 1989).

- *Down's syndrome.* As we discuss in Chapter 9, **Down's syndrome** is a cause of mental retardation. Down's syndrome is brought about not by an inherited trait passed on by the parents, but by a malfunction whereby the zygote receives an extra chromosome at the moment of conception, causing retardation and an unusual physical appearance (which led to an earlier label for the disease: mongolism). Down's syndrome is related to the mother's and father's age; mothers over 35, in particular, stand a higher risk of having a child with the problem.

Prenatal environmental influences. Genetic factors are *not* the only causes of difficulties in fetal development; a number of environmental factors also have an effect on the course of development. The major prenatal environmental influences include:

- *The mother's nutrition and state of mind.* What a mother eats during her pregnancy can have important implications for the health of her baby. Mothers who are seriously undernourished cannot provide adequate nutrition to the growing baby, and they are likely to give birth to underweight babies or to babies that are more susceptible to disease (Wyden, 1971). Moreover, there is some evidence that the mother's emotional state affects the baby. Mothers who are anxious and tense during the end of their pregnancies are more apt to have infants who are irritable and who sleep and eat poorly (Kagan, Kearsley & Zelazo, 1978). The reason? One hypothesis is that the autonomic nervous system of the fetus becomes especially sensitive as a result of the chemical changes produced by the mother's emotional state.

- *Illness of mother.* During 1964 and 1965 an epidemic of **rubella**, or German measles, in the United States resulted in the prenatal death or malformation of close to 50,000 children. Although the disease has relatively minor effects on the mother when contracted during the early part of pregnancy, it is one of a number of illnesses that can have devastating results on the developing fetus. Other maternal diseases that may produce a permanent effect on the fetus include syphilis, diabetes, and high blood pressure.

  AIDS—acquired immune deficiency syndrome—can be passed from mother to child. Sadly, in many cases mothers may not even know they carry the disease and inadvertently transmit it to their children. According to some evidence, the AIDS virus can also be passed on through breast feeding after birth (Heyward & Curran, 1988).

- *Mother's drug intake.* Drugs taken by a pregnant woman can have a tragic effect on the unborn child. Probably the most dramatic ex-

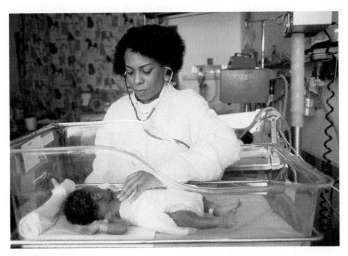

This infant, the child of a cocaine addict, was born addicted. He is undergoing treatment by Dr. Xylina Bean of King Drew Medical Center, Los Angeles, for the painful symptoms of withdrawal from the drug.

ample was the use of thalidomide, a tranquilizer that was widely prescribed during the 1960s—until it was discovered that it caused such severe birth defects as the absence of arms and legs. The hormone diethylstilbestrol (DES), prescribed until the 1950s to prevent miscarriages, is now known to have placed children of mothers who took it at risk for abnormalities of the cervix and vagina and for developing cancer of the uterus in the case of daughters, and for infertility and reproductive problems in the case of sons.

Alcohol and nicotine are also dangerous to fetal development. For example, **fetal alcohol syndrome**, an ailment resulting in mental and growth retardation, has been found in the children of mothers who consumed high levels of alcohol during pregnancy. Moreover, mothers who take physically addictive drugs run the risk of giving birth to babies similarly addicted, and their newborns suffer painful withdrawal symptoms after birth (Chavez et al., 1979; Miller, 1986).

- *Birth complications.* Although most births occur without complication, the process sometimes goes awry, resulting in injury to the infant. For example, the umbilical cord connecting the baby to the mother may become compressed, withholding oxygen from the child. If this occurs for too long, the child may suffer permanent brain damage.

Although several environmental factors have an impact upon the child prior to and during birth, it is important to keep in mind that development represents the interaction of environmental and genetic influences, and that—although we have been discussing the influences of genetics and environment separately—neither factor works alone. Moreover, while we have been flagging some of the points at which development can go awry, the vast majority of births occur without difficulty, and development follows normal patterns—which we discuss next.

ASK YOURSELF

What is the nature-nurture issue?

What is the course of prenatal development?

What are the major difficulties produced by genetic factors and environmental influences that affect prenatal development?

Why has the nature-nurture debate gone on for centuries without resolution, and why will it probably continue to interest psychologists in the future?

If you wanted to discover the extent to which some trait is inherited, how would you go about it?

HOW WE DEVELOP PHYSICALLY AND SOCIALLY

His head was molded into a long melon shape and came to a point at the back. . . . He was covered with a thick, greasy white material known as "vernix," which made him slippery to hold, and also allowed him to slip easily through the birth canal. In addition to a shock of black hair on his head, his body was covered with dark, fine hair known as "lanugo." His ears, his back, his shoulders, and even his cheeks were furry. . . . His skin was wrinkled and quite loose, ready to scale in creased places such as his feet and hands. The hair, matted with vernix, gave an odd, pasted appearance. . . . His ears were pressed to his head in unusual positions—one ear was matted firmly forward on his cheek. His nose was flattened and pushed to one side by the squeeze as he came through the pelvis (Brazelton, 1969, p. 3).

What kind of creature is this? Although the description hardly fits the Gerber baby in commercials, we are in fact talking about a normal, completely developed child just after the moment of birth. Called a **neonate**, the newborn presents itself to the world in a form that hardly meets the typical standards of beauty against which we normally measure others. Yet ask any parent: No sight is more beautiful or exciting than the first glimpse of their newborn.

The neonate's less-than-perfect appearance is brought about by a number of factors. Its travels through its mother's birth canal may have squeezed the incompletely formed bones of the skull together and squashed the nose into the head. It is covered with **vernix**, a white, greasy material which is secreted to protect its skin prior to birth, and it may have **lanugo**, a soft fuzz, over its entire body. Its eyelids may be puffy with an accumulation of fluids because of its upside-down position during birth.

All this changes during the first two weeks of life, as the neonate takes on a more familiar appearance. Even more impressive are the capabilities that the neonate begins to display from the time it is born—capabilities that grow at an astounding rate over the ensuing months and years.

The neonate is born with a number of **reflexes**—unlearned, involuntary responses that occur automatically in the presence of certain stimuli. Many of these reflexes are critical for survival and unfold naturally as a part of an infant's ongoing maturation. The **rooting reflex**, for instance, causes neonates to turn their heads toward things that touch their cheeks—such as a nipple of a mother's breast or a bottle. Similarly, a **sucking reflex** prompts the infant to suck at things that touch its lips. Among the other reflexes are a **gag reflex** (to clear its throat); the **Moro**, or **startle, reflex** (a series of movements in which the infant flings out its arms, fans it fingers, and arches its back in response to a sudden noise); and the **Babinski reflex** (the baby's toes fan out when the outer edge of the sole of its foot is stroked).

As these primitive reflexes are lost after the first few months of life, they are replaced by more complex and organized behaviors. Although at birth the neonate is capable of only jerky, limited voluntary movement,

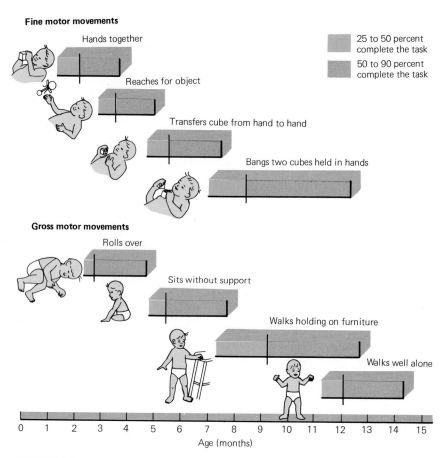

FIGURE 8-2
These landmarks of physical development illustrate the range of ages at which most infants learn various physical tasks. (Frankenburg & Dodds, 1967.)

during the first year of life the capability to move independently grows enormously. The typical baby is able to roll over by the age of 3 months; at 6 months it can sit without support; it stands alone at about $11\frac{1}{2}$ months; and by the time it is just over a year old, a baby has begun to walk. Not only does the ability to make large-scale movements improve during this time, but fine-muscle movements also become increasingly sophisticated (as illustrated in Figure 8-2).

Growth after Birth

Perhaps the most obvious sign of development is the physical growth of the child. During the first year of life, children typically triple their birth weight, and their height increases by about half. This rapid growth slows

The grasp reflex is one of the behaviors that is characteristic of newborns.

down as the child gets older—think how gigantic adults would be if that rate of growth were constant—and the average rate of growth from age 3 to the beginning of adolescence, around age 13, is a gain of about 5 pounds and 3 inches a year.

The physical changes that occur as children develop are not just a matter of increasing growth; the relationship of the size of the various body parts to one another changes dramatically as children age. For example, the head of the fetus (and the newborn) is disproportionally large. However, the head soon becomes more in proportion to the rest of the body as growth occurs mainly in the trunk and legs.

Taking in the World: Development of Perception

When proud parents pick up the neonate and peer into its eyes, is the child able to return their gaze? Although it was thought for some time that newborns could see only a hazy blur, most current findings indicate that the capabilities of neonates are much more impressive (Aslin & Smith, 1988; Haith, 1990). Their eyes have limited capacity to modify the shape of the lens, making it difficult to focus on objects that are not within a 7- to 8-inch distance from the face, yet neonates are able to follow objects moving within their field of vision (Bornstein, 1988; Bronson, 1990). They also show the rudiments of depth perception, as they react by raising their hands when an object appears to be moving rapidly toward the face.

You might think that it would be hard to figure out just how well neonates are able to see, since their lack of language ability clearly prevents them from saying what direction the E on a vision chart is facing—even if they were able to read. However, a number of ingenious methods, which rely on physiological responses and innate reflexes of the newborn, have been devised to test their perceptual skills (Haith, 1990).

One important technique relies on changes in an infant's heart rate, for heart rate is closely correlated with the baby's reaction to a stimulus that he or she is looking at—a phenomenon known as **habituation**. Habituation is a decrease in responding to repeated presentations of the same stimulus. Infants who are shown a novel stimulus will pay close attention to it, and their heart rates will show a change in speed. But if the infant is repeatedly shown the same stimulus, his or her attention to it decreases, as indicated by the return to a normal heart rate—showing that habituation has occurred.

However, when a new stimulus is subsequently presented, once again a discernible change in heart rate occurs *if* the child is able to detect that the new stimulus is different from the old one. Using this technique, then, developmental psychologists can tell when a stimulus can be detected and discriminated by a child too young to speak (Lipsitt, 1990).

Researchers have developed a number of other methods of measuring neonate and infant perception. In one technique, for instance, babies suck on a nipple attached to a computer; a change in the rate and vigor with which they suck is used to infer that they can perceive variations in stimuli (Milewski, 1976). In other studies, researchers examine babies' eye movements (Hainline & Lemerise, 1982), while still other investigators simply observe which way babies move their heads when presented with a visual stimulus (Kolata, 1987).

Using such research techniques, we now know that infants' visual perception is remarkably sophisticated from the very start of life. At birth, babies show preferences for patterns with contours and edges over less distinct patterns, indicating that they are capable of responding to the configuration of stimuli. In fact, neonates have the skill to discriminate facial expressions—and even to imitate them (Field, 1982; Phillips et al., 1990). As you can see in Figure 8-3, newborns exposed to an adult with a happy, sad, or surprised facial expression are able to produce a good imitation of the adult's expression. Even newborn children, then, have the capability of responding to the emotions and moods that their care givers' facial expressions reveal.

Other visual abilities grow rapidly after birth. By the end of their first month, babies can distinguish some colors from others, and after 4 months they can readily focus on near or far objects. By 4 or 5 months, they are able to recognize two- and three-dimensional objects, and they can make use of the gestalt patterns that we discussed in relation to adult perception in Chapter 3 (Smith, 1987). Furthermore, there are rapid improvements in perceptual abilities: Sensitivity to visual stimuli, for instance, becomes

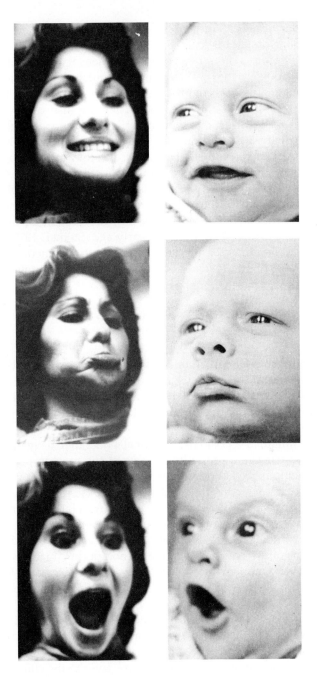

FIGURE 8-3
This newborn infant is clearly imitating the happy,
sad, and surprised expressions of the adult model in
these amazing photos.

three to four times greater at 1 year of age than it was at birth (Aslin & Smith, 1988; Norcia & Tyler, 1985).

In addition to vision, newborns' other sensory capabilities are quite impressive (Bower, 1989). They can distinguish different sounds to the point of being able to recognize their own mothers' voices at the age of three days (DeCasper & Fifer, 1980). They are also capable of making subtle linguistic distinctions that underlie the language abilities we discussed in Chapter 5: At 4 days of age babies can discriminate between such closely related sounds as *ba* and *pa,* and they are soon able to distinguish between their native tongue and foreign languages (Jusczyk & Derrah, 1987; Jusczyk, 1986). By 6 months of age, they are capable of discriminating virtually any difference in sound that is relevant to the production of language (Aslin, 1987). Moreover, they are capable of discriminating different tastes and smells at a very early age (Steiner, 1979). There even seems to be something of a built-in sweet tooth: The neonate prefers liquids that have been sweetened with sugar over unsweetened liquids.

Forming Relationships: The Growth of Social Development

As anyone who has seen an infant smiling at the sight of its mother can guess, at the same time infants are growing physically and perceptually, they are also developing socially. In fact, the nature of a child's early social development provides the foundation for social relationships that will last a lifetime.

Attachment, the positive emotional bond that develops between a child and a particular individual, is one of the most important forms of social development that occurs during infancy (Collins & Gunnar, 1990). One of the first investigators to demonstrate the importance and nature of attachment was psychologist Harry Harlow. Harlow found that infant monkeys who were given the choice of a wire "monkey" that provided food or a soft, terrycloth "monkey" that was warm but did not provide food, clearly preferred the cloth one, although they made occasional forays to the wire monkey to nurse (Harlow & Zimmerman, 1959). Clearly, the cloth monkey provided greater comfort to the infants; food alone was insufficient to create attachment (see Figure 8-4).

Building on this initial work, other researchers have suggested that attachment grows through the responsiveness of infants' care givers to the signals the babies provide, such as cries, smiles, reaching, and clinging. The greater the responsiveness of the care giver to the child's signals, the more likely it is that a secure attachment bond will be formed. Full attachment eventually develops as a result of a complex series of interactions between care giver and child (Ainsworth, 1989; Bell & Ainsworth, 1972). It is important to note that the infant plays as critical and active a role in the formation of an attachment bond as the care giver; infants who

FIGURE 8-4
Although the wire "mother" dispensed milk to the
hungry infant monkey, the soft, terry-cloth
"mother" was preferred.

respond positively to a care giver promote more positive behavior on the
part of the care giver, which in turn elicits even greater attachment from
the child.

The nature of children's attachment has far-reaching consequences on
later development. For example, one study found that boys who were
securely attached at age 1 showed fewer psychological difficulties when
they were older than did avoidant or ambivalent youngsters (Lewis et al.,
1984). Moreover, children who are securely attached to their mothers tend
to be more socially and emotionally competent than their less securely
attached peers, and they are viewed as more cooperative, capable, and
playful (Sroufe, Fox & Pancake, 1983).

The father's role. For many years, the father stood in the shadows
behind the mother—at least as far as developmental research was concerned. Because traditionally it was thought that the mother-infant bond
was the most crucial in a child's life, researchers in earlier decades focused
on the mother's relationship with her children. However, the last ten years
have seen a host of studies which focus on fathers and their interactions
with their children (Lamb, 1987).

In recent years, fathers have taken a more active role in child care.

Although by and large fathers still spend less time caring for and playing with their children than do mothers—even in households in which both parents are employed full time—fathers can produce attachment bonds as strong as those between mothers and their children. Furthermore, children can be simultaneously attached to both their parents (Lamb, 1982). Yet the nature of attachment is not always identical between mothers and fathers. For instance, infants tend to prefer to be soothed by their mothers, even though fathers are just as adept at comforting and nurturing babies.

The reason for differences in attachment between mothers and fathers may be that mothers spend a greater proportion of their time feeding and directly nurturing their children, whereas fathers spend more time, proportionally, playing with them. Moreover, the quality of fathers' play is often different from that of mothers. Fathers engage in more physical, rough-and-tumble sorts of activities, whereas mothers play more verbally oriented games and traditional physical ones such as peekaboo. Such differences in play style are very pronounced, and occur even in the small minority of families in which the mother works to support the family and the father stays at home with the children (Power & Parke, 1982; Russell & Russell, 1987).

Despite the differences between the behavior of fathers and mothers, each parent is an important attachment figure and plays a major role in the social development of a child. Furthermore, it is becoming increasingly apparent that the amount of time an adult spends with a child is less important than the quality of that time (Hetherington & Parke, 1986).

Social relationships with peers. If you have ever seen a preschooler rushing off to play with a neighborhood friend, you know the enjoyment that children derive from being with their peers. In fact, such friendships are crucial to a child's social development (Ladd, 1990). According to development psychologist Willard Hartup, experience is necessary both in "vertical" relationships (those with people of greater knowledge and social power, such as parents) *and* in "horizontal" relationships (those with people who have the same amount of knowledge and social power) in order for effective social competence to develop (Hartup, 1989).

From the age of 2 years, children become less dependent on their parents and more self-reliant, increasingly preferring to play with friends. Initially, play is relatively independent: Two-year-olds pay more attention to toys than to one another when playing. Later, however, children actively interact, modifying one another's behavior and later exchanging roles during play.

As children reach school age, their social interactions become increasingly formalized, as well as more frequent. They may engage in elaborate games, in which they pretend to be superheroes on another planet, and work out elaborate scenarios. Play also becomes more structured, involving teams and games with rigid rules (Mueller & Lucas, 1975).

It is important to realize that children's play serves other purposes than mere enjoyment. It allows them to become increasingly competent in their social interactions with others, learning to take the perspective of other people and to infer others' thoughts and feelings, even when they are not being directly expressed. Furthermore, they learn self-control: They avoid hitting an adversary who bests them, they learn to be polite, and they learn to control their emotional displays and facial expressions, smiling even when receiving a disappointing gift (Feldman & Rimé, 1991; Selman et al., 1983). Situations that provide children with opportunities for social interaction, then, may enhance their social development—a point illustrated in the Psychology and Society box, which considers the effects of child care on children.

Erikson's Theory of Psychosocial Development

In trying to trace the course of social development, some theorists have considered how society and culture present challenges that change as the individual matures. Following this path, psychoanalyst Erik Erikson developed the most comprehensive theory of social development. According to Erikson (1963), the developmental changes occurring throughout our lives can be viewed as a series of eight stages of psychosocial development. **Psychosocial development** encompasses changes in our interactions and understanding of one another as well as in our knowledge and understanding of ourselves as members of society.

Erikson suggests that passage through each of the stages necessitates resolution of a crisis or conflict. Accordingly, each of Erikson's eight stages

PSYCHOLOGY AND SOCIETY

Who Is Taking Care of the Children? Determining the Effects of Child-Care Centers

A mother and her 3-year-old son head off together at the start of the day. But they are not out for a day's excursion; instead, they head to a child-care center near the mother's office. She says goodbye to her son and leaves for work for the day, knowing that she will not see him again until she picks him up some nine hours later. It is a scene that she and her son repeat five days a week, every week of the year—except during the mother's two weeks of vacation.

One of the biggest societal changes to occur over the last two decades is the upsurge in the number of children enrolled in child-care centers. Roughly a million children, some still in their infancy, are looked after by paid child-care workers, generally in centers outside the home, from a couple of hours a day to all day long. To parents contemplating enrolling their children in such a center, certain questions are critical: What are the effects of child-care on children? How early can children start? What separates good child-care from bad? Because child-care is a necessity in many families with two working parents or in single-parent families, such questions take on particular urgency.

Fortunately, answers to these questions have begun to emerge as a result of research conducted during the last two decades, and although the long-term consequences of child-care have yet to be determined definitively, the results are encouraging: Chil-dren who attend high-quality child-care centers not only may do as well as children who stay at home with their parents but in some cases may actually do better (Bee, 1985; Scarr, 1986; Clarke-Stewart, 1989; Scarr, Phillips, & McCartney, 1990). Among the specific findings that support this suggestion are the following:

• *Social development.* Researchers have found several kinds of positive results from child-care center experiences. Children in child care have been found to be more considerate and sociable, and they interact more positively with teachers (e.g., Phillips, McCartney, & Scarr, 1987). They may also be more compliant and regulate their own behavior more effectively. Although some research suggests that children in child-care situations are more aggressive and assertive than their peers (e.g., Haskins, 1985), these outcomes may well fade as the children get older (Finkelstein, 1982).

• *Intellectual development.* For children from poor or disadvantaged homes, child care in specially enriched environments—those with many toys, books, a variety of children and high-quality care providers—often proves to be more intellectually stimulating than the children's home environment. Such child care can lead to increased intellectual achievement in terms of higher IQ scores and better language development (Lee,

is represented as a pairing of the most positive and most negative aspects of the crisis of the period. Although each crisis is never resolved entirely—life becomes increasingly complicated as we grow older—it needs to be resolved enough so that we are equipped to deal with demands that the next stage makes.

In the first stage of psychosocial development, **trust versus mistrust**

Brooks-Gunn, & Schnur, 1988). On the other hand, we don't know how long such improvements last; the intellectual benefits of early child care have yet to be demonstrated in adults who received such care as children (Holden, 1990).

It is also less than clear that child-care experiences bolster intellectual development in children who are from more affluent backgrounds. Although a few research studies do suggest that children in child-care centers score higher on tests of cognitive abilities than those who are cared for by their mothers (e.g., Clark-Stewart, 1984), most studies have been unable to demonstrate either benefits or damage resulting from participation in child care.

● *Relationship with parents.* Are children less attached to their mothers and fathers when they spend part of the day being cared for by others? This question—raised by many critics of day-care—is a difficult one to answer, and the research on the issue is contradictory. Some evidence suggests that infants who are involved in outside care more than twenty hours a week in their first year show less attachment to their mothers than do those who have not been in child-care (Belsky & Rovine, 1988). On the other hand, most other research finds little or no difference in the strength of parental attachment bonds of infants and toddlers who have been in child-care and those raised solely by their parents, regardless of how long they have been in child-care. Moreover, there is no evidence that children in child-care centers are more attached to the child-care workers than to their parents; in fact, they almost always appear to be more attached to their parents (Rutter, 1982; Ragozin, 1980). In sum, evidence is lacking that children who are in child-care are less attached to their parents than those who are not in child-care.

Overall, most research has found little difference between children who have been in child-care and those who have not—a comforting state of affairs for parents concerned about the effects of child-care on their children (Scarr, Phillips & McCartney, 1990). Furthermore, long-term follow-up research shows that first-, third-, and fifth-graders whose mothers worked performed better academically, were more socially adjusted, and were more self-reliant than children whose mothers did not work. They were also more involved in school activities and scored higher in IQ tests (Scarr, 1986).

Yet there are many unanswered questions: Is there an age before which child-care should be avoided? How do the effects of good child-care centers differ from the effects of less optimal centers? Does it matter what kind of child-care curriculum is used? What are the critical characteristics to consider when choosing a child-care center? Given the necessity of employment for a significant proportion of the parent population, these questions must be addressed. For many people, then, the significant issue is not whether to choose child-care, but how to make their child's experience as positive as possible (Clarke-Stewart, 1989; Scarr, Phillips & McCartney, 1990).

(birth to $1\frac{1}{2}$ years), infants develop feelings of trust if their physical requirements and psychological needs for attachment are consistently met and their interactions with the world are generally positive. On the other hand, inconsistent care and unpleasant interactions with others can lead to the development of mistrust and leave the infant unable to meet the challenges required in the next stage.

In the second stage, **autonomy versus shame and doubt** ($1\frac{1}{2}$ to 3 years), toddlers develop independence and autonomy if exploration and freedom are encouraged, or they experience shame, self-doubt, and un-happiness if they are overly restricted and protected. According to Erik-son, the key to the development of autonomy, rather than of shame and doubt, during this period is for the child's care givers to provide the ap-propriate amount of control. If parents provide too much control, children will be unable to assert themselves and develop their own sense of control over their environment; if parents provide too little control, children themselves become overly demanding and controlling.

The next crisis that children face is that of **initiative versus guilt** (ages 3 to 6). In this stage, the major conflict is between a child's desire to initiate activities independently and the guilt that comes from unwanted and un-expected consequences of such activities. If parents react positively to the child's attempts at independence, they help resolve the initiative-versus-guilt crisis positively.

The fourth and last stage of childhood is **industry versus inferiority** (ages 6 to 12). During this period, successful psychosocial development is characterized by increasing competency across all tasks, be they social interactions or academic skills. In contrast, difficulties in this stage lead to feelings of failure and inadequacy.

Erikson's theory suggests that psychosocial development continues throughout life, and he proposes that there are four more crises to face past childhood (which we discuss later in the chapter). Although his the-ory has been criticized on several grounds—such as the imprecision of the concepts he employs and an emphasis more on male development than female development—it remains influential and is one of the few that encompasses the entire lifespan.

ASK YOURSELF

What are the major reflexes that neonates have at birth?

What is the pattern of physical growth in childhood?

How is social development demonstrated through the growth of attachment?

According to Erikson, what are the four stages of psychosocial development during childhood?

In what ways do newborns come into the world well-equipped for the task of beginning development?

Thinking about Erikson's psychosocial stages, how would the way one stage is resolved affect the resolution of subsequent stages?

OUR MINDS: HOW WE DEVELOP COGNITIVELY

Suppose you had two drinking glasses of different shapes—one short and broad and one tall and skinny. Now imagine that you filled the short, broad one with soda about half way and then poured the liquid from that glass into the tall one. The soda appears to fill about three-quarters of the second glass. If someone asked you whether there was more soda in the second glass than there had been in the first, what would you say?

You might think that such a simple question hardly deserves an answer; of course there is no difference in the amount of soda in the two glasses.

However, most 4-year-olds would be likely to say that there is more soda in the second glass. In fact, if you then poured the soda back into the short glass, they would say there is now less soda than there was in the taller glass.

Why are young children confused by this problem? The reason is not readily apparent. Anyone who has observed preschoolers must be impressed at how far they have progressed from the early stages of development. They speak with ease, know the alphabet, count, play complex games, use a phonograph, tell stories, and communicate quite ably.

Yet, despite this outward sophistication, there are profound gaps in children's understanding of the world. Some theorists have suggested that children are incapable of understanding certain ideas about the world until they reach a particular stage of **cognitive development**—the process by which a child's understanding of the world changes as a function of age and experience. In contrast to theories of physical and social development that were discussed earlier (such as those of Erikson), theories of cognitive development seek to explain the quantitative and qualitative intellectual advances that occur during development.

Stages of Understanding: Piaget's Theory of Cognitive Development

No theory of cognitive development has had more impact than that of Swiss psychologist Jean Piaget. Piaget (1970) suggested that children proceed through a series of four separate stages in a fixed order that is universal across all children. He maintained that these stages differ not only in the *quantity* of information acquired at each, but in the *quality* of knowledge and understanding as well. Taking an interactionist point of view, he suggested that movement from one stage to the next occurred when the child reached an appropriate level of maturation *and* was exposed to relevant types of experiences. Without such experiences, children were assumed to be incapable of reaching their highest level of cognitive growth.

TABLE 8-2 A SUMMARY OF PIAGET'S STAGES

Approximate Age Range	Stage	Major Characteristics
Birth–2 years	Sensorimotor	Development of object permanence, development of motor skills, little or no capacity for symbolic representation
2–7 years	Preoperational	Development of language and symbolic thinking, egocentric thinking
7–12 years	Concrete operational	Development of conservation, mastery of concept of reversibility
12 years–adulthood	Formal operational	Development of logical and abstract thinking

Piaget's four stages are known as the sensorimotor, preoperational, concrete operational, and formal operational stages (see Table 8-2). Let's examine each of them.

Sensorimotor stage: birth to 2 years. During the initial part of the **sensorimotor stage** the child has relatively little competence in representing the environment using images, language, or other kinds of symbols. Consequently, the infant has no awareness of objects or people who are not immediately present at a given moment, lacking what Piaget calls object permanence. **Object permanence** is the awareness that objects—and people—continue to exist even if they are out of sight.

How can we know that children lack object permanence? Although we cannot ask infants, we can watch their reaction when a toy that they are playing with is hidden under a blanket. Until the age of about 9 months, children will make no attempt to locate the toy. However, soon after this age they will begin to actively search for the object when it is hidden, indicating that they have developed a mental representation of the toy. Object permanence, then, is a critical development during the sensorimotor stage.

Preoperational stage: 2 to 7 years. The most important development during the **preoperational stage** is in the use of language, described in more detail in Chapter 5. Children develop internal representational systems of the world that allow them to describe people, events, and feelings. They even use symbols in play, pretending, for example, that a book pushed across the floor is a car.

Although children's thinking is more advanced in this stage than in the earlier sensorimotor stage, it still is qualitatively inferior to that of adults. One example of this is seen in the preoperational child's **egocentric thought**, in which the world is viewed entirely from the child's own perspective. Preoperational children think that everyone shares their own perspective and knowledge. Thus, children's stories and explanations to adults can be maddeningly uninformative, as they are described without any context. For example, a preoperational child may start a story with "He wouldn't let me go," neglecting to mention who "he" is or where the storyteller wanted to go. Egocentric thinking is also seen when children at the preoperational stage play hiding games. For instance, 3-year-olds frequently hide with their faces against a wall, covering their eyes—although they are still in plain view. It seems to them that if *they* cannot see, no one else will be able to see them, since they assume that others share their view.

Another deficiency of the preoperational child is demonstrated by the **principle of conservation**, which is the knowledge that quantity is unrelated to the arrangement and physical appearance of objects. Children who have not mastered this principle do not know that the amount, volume, or length of an object does not change when its shape or configuration is changed. The question about the two glasses—one short and broad, the other tall and thin—with which we began our discussion of cognitive development illustrates this point quite clearly. Children who do not understand the principle of conservation invariably state that the amount of liquid changes as it is poured back and forth; they cannot comprehend that a transformation in appearance does not imply a transformation in amount. Instead, it seems just as reasonable to the child that there is a change in quantity as it does to the adult that there is no change.

There are a number of other ways in which the lack of understanding of the principle of conservation affects children's responses, several of which are illustrated in Figure 8-5. Research on conservation illustrates that principles which are obvious and unquestioned by adults may be completely misunderstood by children during the preoperational period,

When equal amounts of liquid are poured into containers of different sizes, adults recognize that the level of the liquid is higher in the container with the smaller diameter. A 3-year-old, however, believes that there is actually more liquid in the smaller container because it appears fuller.

and it is not until the next stage of cognitive development that children grasp the concept of conservation.

Concrete operational stage: 7 to 12 years. The beginning of the concrete operation stage is marked by mastery of the principle of conservation. However, there are still some aspects of conservation—such as conservation of weight and volume—that are not fully understood for a number of years.

During the **concrete operational stage**, children develop the ability to think in a more logical manner, and they begin to overcome some of the egocentrism characteristic of the preoperational period. One of the major principles that children learn during this stage is reversibility, the idea that some changes can be undone by reversing an earlier action. For example, children in the concrete operational stage can understand that when a ball of clay is rolled into a long sausage shape, it is possible to recreate the original ball by reversing the action. They can even conceptualize this principle in their heads, without having to see the action performed before them.

Although children make important advances in their logical capabilities during the concrete operational stage, there is still one major limitation to their thinking: They are largely bound to the concrete, physical reality of the world. For the most part, they have difficulty understanding questions of an abstract, hypothetical nature.

Formal operational stage: 12 years to adulthood. In the **formal operational stage** a new kind of thinking emerges—that which is abstract, formal, and logical. Thinking is no longer tied to events that are observed in the environment but makes use of logical techniques to resolve problems.

The emergence of formal operational thinking is illustrated by the way in which the "pendulum problem," devised by Piaget, is attacked (Piaget & Inhelder, 1958). The problem solver is asked to figure out what determines how fast a pendulum swings. Is it the length of the string, or the weight of the pendulum, or the force with which the pendulum is pushed? (For the record, the answer is the length of the string.)

Children in the concrete operational stage approach the problem haphazardly, without a logical or rational plan of action. For example, they may simultaneously change the length of the string *and* the weight on the string *and* the force with which they push the pendulum. Since they are varying all factors at once, they are unable to tell which factor is the critical one. In contrast, people in the formal operational stage approach the problem systematically. Acting as if they were scientists conducting an experiment, they examine the effects of changes in just one variable at a time. This ability to rule out competing possibilities is characteristic of formal operational thought.

Although formal operational thought emerges during the teenage years, this type of thinking is, in some cases, used only infrequently (Bur-

Type of conservation	Modality	Change in physical appearance	Average age at which invariance is grasped
Number	Number of elements in a collection 	Rearranging or dislocating elements 	6–7
Substance (mass) (continuous quantity)	Amount of a malleable substance (e.g., clay or liquid) 	Altering shape 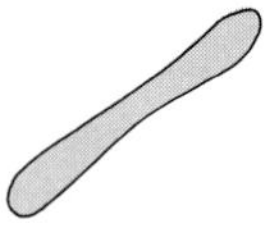	7–8
Length	Length of a line or object 	Altering shape or configuration 	7–8
Area	Amount of surface covered by a set of plane figures 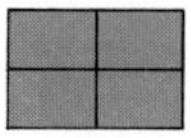	Rearranging the figures 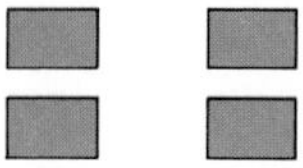	8–9
Weight	Weight of an object 	Altering shape 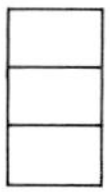	9–10
Volume	Volume of an object (in terms of water displacement) 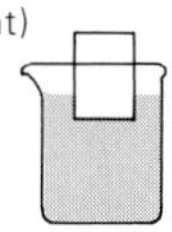	Altering shape 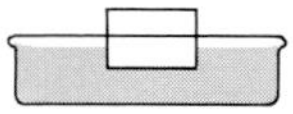	14–15

FIGURE 8-5
These tests are among those used most frequently to assess whether children have learned the principle of conservation across a variety of dimensions. (Schikendanz, Schikendanz, & Forsythe, 1982.)

bules & Linn, 1988). Moreover, it appears that many individuals never reach this stage at all; most studies show that only 40 to 60 percent of college students and adults fully reach it, with some estimates running as low as 25 percent in the general population (Keating, 1980). In addition, in certain cultures—particularly those that are less technologically so-phisticated than western societies—almost no one reaches the formal op-erational stage (Chandler, 1976; Super, 1980).

Is Piaget right?: Stages versus continuous development. No other theorist has provided us with as comprehensive a theory of cognitive development as Piaget. Still, some contemporary theorists suggest that a better description of how children develop cognitively can be provided by approaches that do not employ a series of stages (Daehler & Bukato, 1985; Bornstein & Sigman, 1986). Such researchers have found that chil-dren are not always consistent in their performance of tasks that—if Piaget's theory were accurate—ought to be performed equally well at a given stage (Tomlinson-Keasey et al., 1979). Furthermore, some devel-opmental psychologists suggest that cognitive development proceeds in a more continuous fashion than Piaget's stage theory implies; they pro-pose that cognitive developmental growth is primarily quantitative, rather than qualitative. They argue that although there are differences in when, how, and to what extent a child is capable of using given cognitive abilities—thereby reflecting quantitative changes—the underlying cogni-tive processes change relatively little with age (Gelman & Baillargeon, 1983; Sugarman, 1989).

Most developmental psychologists do agree that, although the processes that underlie changes in cognitive abilities may not be those suggested by his theory, Piaget has provided us with an accurate account of age-related changes in cognitive development. Moreover, the influence of the theory has been enormous (Ginsburg & Opper, 1988; Halford, 1989). For example, Piaget suggests that increases in cognitive performance can-not be attained unless both cognitive readiness brought about by matu-ration *and* appropriate environmental stimulation are present. This view has been influential in determining the nature and structure of educational curricula and how children are taught. Piaget's theory and methods have also been used to investigate issues surrounding animal cognition, such as whether primates show object permanence (they seem to; Dore & Dumas, 1987).

Alternatives to Piaget: Information-Processing Approaches

If cognitive development does not proceed in the stagelike fashion sug-gested by Piaget, what *does* underlie the enormous increases in children's cognitive abilities that are apparent to even the most untutored eye? To many developmental psychologists, the answer can be found in changes in **information processing,** the way in which people take in, use, and store information.

According to this approach, which reflects the cognitive aspects of behavior that we discussed in Chapter 5, quantitative changes occur in children's ability to organize and manipulate information about the world. From this perspective, children are seen as becoming increasingly adept at information processing, analogous to the way a computer program might become more sophisticated as a programmer modifies it on the basis of experience. Information-processing approaches consider the kinds of "mental programs" that children invoke when approaching problems.

Several significant changes occur in children's information processing capabilities. For one thing, speed of processing increases with age as some abilities become more automatic. The speed at which stimuli can be scanned, compared with other stimuli, and recognized increases with age. Attention span also lengthens; with increasing age, children can pay attention to stimuli longer and are less easily distracted (Manis, Keating & Morrison, 1980; Case, 1985).

Memory also improves dramatically with age. If you recall from Chapter 5, adults are able to keep seven, plus or minus two, chunks of information in short-term memory. In contrast, preschoolers can hold only two or three chunks; 5-year-olds can hold four; and 7-year-olds can hold five. The size of chunks also grows with age, as does the sophistication and organization of knowledge stored in memory (Bjorkland, 1985; Ornstein & Naus, 1988).

Finally, improvement in information processing is tied to advances in **metacognition**, an awareness and understanding of one's own cognitive processes. Metacognition involves the planning, monitoring, and revising of cognitive strategies. Younger children, who lack knowledge of their cognitive processes, are often unaware of their own incapabilities, causing them to misunderstand others and not even to recognize their errors. It is only later, when metacognitive abilities become more sophisticated, that children are able to know when they *don't* understand (Astington, Harris, & Olson, 1988; Fabricius et al., 1989; Flavell, Green, & Flavell, 1990).

The growth in metacognitive abilities is but one of the many advances we make as part of our continuing development. We have seen so far the enormous strides youngsters make as they move from relatively helpless infants to competent, able children. In the final sections of the chapter, we consider the challenges presented by adolescence and adulthood and the ways people continue to grow and change throughout their lives.

The Informed Consumer of Psychology: Maximizing Cognitive Development

Are there ways of maximizing a child's cognitive development? Although our examination of the nature-nurture issue makes clear that genetic background plays a critical role in defining the limits that we can ultimately achieve, it is also apparent that environmental factors can enhance the probability of achieving our potential. In fact, research carried out by developmental psychologists has identified several child-rearing practices that seem to be important in maximizing cognitive development (Meyerhoff & White, 1986; Gottfried, 1984; Bee, 1985; Cataldo, 1987). Among the most crucial:

- Provide children with the maximum opportunity to explore and investigate their environments. For instance, if an environment can be made safe, toddlers should not be restricted to playpens.
- Be emotionally responsive and involved with children. Parents with high-achieving children are interested in their children's lives and encourage and reinforce their efforts. They are warm and supportive, and act as children's "personal consultants."
- Use language that is highly descriptive and accurate when speaking with a child. Avoid "baby talk" and speak with children, not *at* them. Ask questions, listen to babies' responses, and provide further feedback.
- Provide *appropriate* play materials. The sheer quantity of toys and other play materials is less important than their appropriateness for the child's age and developmental level.
- Give children a chance to make mistakes. Parents of successful children tend to avoid harsh, arbitrary rules and highly restrictive control, and they do not use punishment frequently. Instead, while remaining firmly in control of their children's behavior and without being overly permissive, they are likely to guide their children with a combination of firmness and warmth, providing a rationale for the rules children must follow.
- Hold high expectations. Parents should communicate that they expect their children to do well, demonstrating to their children the importance of success and achievement.
- Don't push children too hard. Despite the rigors and demands of modern life, childhood should be a time of enjoyment and not viewed as merely a period of preparation for what comes later. Some psychologists feel that we are producing a society of "hurried children," whose lives revolve around rigid schedules and who are so pressed to succeed that their childhood is filled with stress (Elkind, 1981). Remember that—as in the rest of the life-span—it is important to step back and set priorities regarding what is and is not most important.

ASK YOURSELF

What are the major stages of cognitive development according to Piaget?

How does children's understanding of object permanence and conservation change?

What are the major distinctions between stage theories of cognitive development, such as that of Piaget, and information-processing approaches to cognitive development?

BECOMING AN ADULT: ADOLESCENCE

It is not easy to be a male adolescent in the Awa tribe: First come beatings. Seated around a fire, the boys are hit with sticks and prickly branches, not only for their own past misdeeds but in honor of tribesmen killed in warfare.

But these thrashings—which last for two or three days—are just the beginning. In the next phase of the ritual, adults jab sharpened sticks into the boys' nostrils until copious bleeding takes place. Then they force a five-foot length of vine deep into the boys' throats, until they gag and vomit. Finally, tribesmen make deep cuts in the boys' genitals, leading to severe bleeding. The boys are then released, while adult onlookers laugh, jeer, and poke at the cuts to make them bleed even more.

Although the rites that mark the coming-of-age of boys in the Awa tribe in New Guinea sound horrifying to us, they are comparable to those in other cultures, in which it may be necessary to endure public circumcision and kneeling on hot coals without displaying pain. And it is not just males who must participate in such trials: In some tribes, girls must toss wads of burning cotton from hand to hand and allow themselves to be bitten by hundreds of ants.

Although western society has no rituals as physically and psychologically taxing to represent the entry into adulthood—for which most of us will heave a sigh of relief—the period that follows childhood, adolescence, is still an important time in our lives. For most people, adolescence is marked by profound changes and, sometimes, turmoil. Considerable biological change marks the adolescent's attainment of sexual and physical maturity, rivaled by important social, emotional, and cognitive changes that occur as adolescents strive for independence and move toward adulthood.

Adolescence, which is generally thought of as a developmental stage between childhood and adulthood, represents a critical period in people's development. Given the length of education that precedes starting work in our society, the stage is a fairly lengthy one, starting just before the teenage years and ending just after them. No longer children, but considered by society to be not quite adults, adolescents face a period of rapid physical and social change that affects them for the rest of their lives.

The Changing Adolescent: Physical Development

If you think back to the start of your own adolescence, it is likely that the most dramatic changes you remember are of a physical nature. A spurt in height, the growth of breasts in girls, deepening voices in boys, the development of body hair, and intense sexual feelings are a source of curiosity, interest, and sometimes embarrassment for individuals entering adolescence.

The physical changes that occur at the start of adolescence, which are largely a result of the secretion of various hormones (see Chapter 2), affect virtually every aspect of the adolescent's life; not since infancy has development been so dramatic (see Figure 8-6). Weight and height increase rapidly; a growth spurt begins at around age $10\frac{1}{2}$ for girls and age 12 for boys, and adolescents may grow as much as 5 inches in one year.

Puberty, the period at which maturation of the sexual organs occurs, begins at about age 11 or 12 for girls and 13 or 14 for boys. However, there are wide variations, and it is not too rare for a girl to begin to menstruate—the first sign of sexual maturity in females—as early as age 10 or as late as age 16. Furthermore, the average age at which adolescents reach sexual maturity has been steadily decreasing over the last century, most likely a result of better nutrition and medical care (Dreyer, 1982). This change in the onset of puberty provides a good illustration of how changes in the environment interact with heredity to affect development.

The age at which puberty begins has important implications for the way adolescents feel about themselves—as well as how others treat them. Early-maturing boys have a distinct advantage over later-maturing boys; they do better in athletics and they are generally more popular and have higher self-concepts. The picture is less clear for girls. Although early-maturing girls are more sought after as dates and have higher self-concepts than later-maturing girls, initially their early physical maturation is less positive, since the development of such obvious characteristics as breasts sets them apart from their peers and may be a source of ridicule (Atwater, 1983).

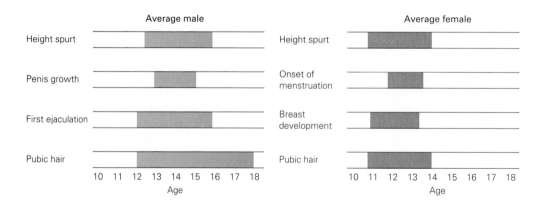

FIGURE 8-6
The range of ages during which major maturational changes occur during adolescence is shown by the colored bars. (Based on Tanner, 1978.)

Late maturers, in contrast, may suffer psychological consequences as a result of the delay. Boys who are smaller and less coordinated than their more mature peers tend to be ridiculed and seen as less attractive, and may come to view themselves in the same way. The consequences of late maturation may extend well into a male's thirties (Mussen & Jones, 1957). Similarly, late-maturing girls are at a disadvantage in junior high and high school. They hold a relatively low social status, and they may be overlooked in dating and other male-female activities (Apter et al., 1981; Clarke-Stewart & Friedman, 1987).

Clearly, the rate at which physical changes occur during adolescence can have significant effects on the way people are viewed by others and the way they view themselves. Just as important as physical changes, however, are the psychological and social changes that evolve during adolescence.

Distinguishing Right from Wrong: Moral and Cognitive Development

In Europe, a woman is near death from a special kind of cancer. The one drug that the doctors think might save her is a form of radium that a druggist in the same town has recently discovered. The drug is expensive to make, and the druggist is charging ten times the cost, or $2000, for a small dose. The sick woman's husband, Heinz, goes to everyone he knows to borrow the money, but he can get together only about $1000. He tells the druggist that his wife is dying and asks him to sell the drug cheaper or let him pay later. The druggist says, "No, I discovered the drug and I'm going to make money from it." Heinz is desperate and considers breaking into the man's store to steal the drug for his wife.

What would you tell Heinz he should do?

In the view of psychologist Lawrence Kohlberg, the advice you give Heinz is a reflection of your level of moral development. According to Kohlberg, people pass through a series of stages in the evolution of their sense of justice and in the kind of reasoning they use to make moral judgments (Kohlberg, 1984). Largely because of the various cognitive deficits that Piaget described, preadolescent children tend to think either in terms of concrete, unvarying rules ("It is always wrong to steal" or "I'll be punished if I steal") or in terms of the rules of society ("Good people don't steal" or "What if everyone stole?").

Adolescents, however, are capable of reasoning on a higher plane, typically having reached Piaget's formal operational stage of cognitive development. Because they are able to comprehend broad moral principles, they can understand that morality is not always black and white and that conflict can exist between two sets of socially accepted standards.

Kohlberg (1984) suggests that the changes occurring in moral reasoning can be understood best as a three-level sequence, which, in turn, is divided into six stages. These levels and stages are shown in Table 8-3,

TABLE 8-3 KOHLBERG'S SEQUENCE OF MORAL REASONING

Level	Stage	Sample Moral Reasoning of Subjects	
		In Favor of Stealing	*Against Stealing*
Level 1 Preconventional morality: At this level, the concrete interests of the individual are considered in terms of rewards and punishments.	*Stage 1* Obedience and punishment orientation: At this stage, people stick to rules in order to avoid punishment, and obedience occurs for its own sake.	"If you let your wife die, you will get in trouble. You'll be blamed for not spending the money to save her, and there'll be an investigation of you and the druggist for your wife's death."	"You shouldn't steal the drug because you'd be caught and sent to jail if you do. If you do get away, your conscience will bother you thinking how the police will catch up with you at any minute."
	Stage 2 Reward orientation: At this stage, rules are followed only for a person's own benefit. Obedience occurs because of rewards that are received.	"If you do happen to get caught, you could give the drug back and you wouldn't get much of a sentence. It wouldn't bother you much to serve a little jail term, if you have your wife when you get out."	"You may not get much of a jail term if you steal the drug, but your wife will probably die before you get out, so it won't do much good. If your wife dies, you shouldn't blame yourself; it isn't your fault she has cancer."
Level 2 Conventional morality: At this level, people approach moral problems as members of society. They are interested in pleasing others by acting as good members of society.	*Stage 3* "Good boy" morality: Individuals at this stage show an interest in maintaining the respect of others and doing what is expected of them.	"No one will think you're bad if you steal the drug, but your family will think you're an inhuman husband if you don't. If you let your wife die, you'll never be able to look anybody in the face again."	"It isn't just the druggist who will think you're a criminal; everyone else will too. After you steal the drug, you'll feel bad thinking how you've brought dishonor on your family and yourself; you won't be able to face anyone again."
	Stage 4 Authority and social-order-maintaining morality: People at this stage conform to society's rules and consider that "right" is what society defines as right.	"If you have any sense of honor, you won't let your wife die just because you're afraid to do the only thing that will save her. You'll always feel guilty that you caused her death if you don't do your duty to her."	"You're desperate and you may not know you're doing wrong when you steal the drug. But you'll know you did wrong after you're sent to jail. You'll always feel guilty for your dishonesty and law-breaking."
Level 3 Postconventional morality: At this level, people use moral principles which are seen as broader than those of any particular society.	*Stage 5* Morality of contract, individual rights, and democratically accepted law: People at this stage do what is right because of a sense of obligation to laws which are agreed upon within society. They perceive that laws can be modified as part of changes in an implicit social contract.	"You'll lose other people's respect, not gain it, if you don't steal. If you let your wife die, it will be out of fear, not out of reasoning. So you'll just lose self-respect and probably the respect of others too."	"You'll lose your standing and respect in the community and violate the law. You'll lose respect for yourself if you're carried away by emotion and forget the long-range point of view."
	Stage 6 Morality of individual principles and conscience: At this final stage, a person follows laws because they are based on universal ethical principles. Laws that violate the principles are disobeyed.	"If you don't steal the drug, and if you let your wife die, you'll always condemn yourself for it afterward. You won't be blamed and you'll have lived up to the outside rule of the law but you won't have lived up to your own standards of conscience."	"If you steal the drug, you won't be blamed by other people, but you'll condemn yourself because you won't have lived up to your own conscience and standards of honesty."

SOURCE: Adapted from Kohlberg, 1969.

which also includes samples of subjects' reasoning at each stage. Note that the arguments either in favor of or against stealing the drug can be categorized into the same stage of moral reasoning. It is the nature and sophistication of the argument that determine into what category it falls.

Kohlberg's category system assumes that people move through the six stages in a fixed order, and that they are not capable of reaching the highest stage until about the age of 13—primarily because of deficits in cognitive development that are not overcome until that age. However, many people never reach the highest level of moral reasoning. In fact, Kohlberg suggests that only about 25 percent of all adults rise above stage 4 of his model.

Extensive research has shown that the stages identified by Kohlberg generally provide a valid representation of moral development. Yet the research raises several methodological issues. One major problem is that Kohlberg's procedure measures moral *judgments,* not *behavior.* Although Kohlberg's theory seems to be a generally accurate account of how moral judgments develop, some research finds that such judgments are not always related to moral behavior (Snarey, 1985; Malinowski & Smith, 1985). On the other hand, other investigators suggest that a relationship between moral judgments and behavior does exist. For example, one study found that students who were most likely to commit acts of civil disobedience were those whose moral judgments were at the highest levels (Candee & Kohlberg, 1987). Still, the evidence is mixed on this question; knowing right from wrong does not mean that we will always act in accordance with our judgments (Darley & Shultz, 1990).

Moral development in women. Psychologist Carol Gilligan (1982; 1987) has pointed out an important shortcoming in Kohlberg's original research: It was first carried out using only male subjects and is thus more applicable to them than to women. Furthermore, she convincingly argues that, because of differing socialization experiences, a fundamental difference exists in the manner in which men and women view moral behavior. According to her, men view morality primarily in terms of broad principles such as justice and fairness, whereas women see it in terms of responsibility toward individuals and willingness to sacrifice to help a specific individual within the context of a particular relationship. Compassion for individuals is a more salient factor in moral behavior for women than it is for men.

Thus, because Kohlberg's model conceives of moral behavior largely in terms of principles of justice, it is inadequate in describing the moral development of females. This factor accounts for the surprising finding that women typically score at a lower level than men on tests of moral judgment using Kohlberg's stage sequence. In Gilligan's view, women's morality is centered on individual well-being rather than moral abstractions, and the highest levels of morality are represented by compassionate concern for others' welfare (Gilligan et al., 1988).

According to Gilligan's research, women's moral development proceeds in three stages. In the first stage, termed "orientation toward individual survival," a woman concentrates on what is practical and best for her. During this stage, there is a transition from selfishness to responsibility, in which the woman thinks about what would be best for others.

At the second stage of moral development, termed "goodness as self-sacrifice," a woman begins to think that she must sacrifice her own wishes to what other people want. Ultimately, though, she makes the transition from "goodness" to "truth," in which she takes into account her own needs plus those of others.

In the third stage, "morality of nonviolence," a woman comes to see that hurting anyone is immoral—including hurting herself. This realization establishes a moral equality between herself and others and represents, according to Gilligan, the most sophisticated level of moral reasoning.

As you can see, Gilligan's sequence of stages is very different from that presented by Kohlberg, and some psychologists have suggested that her rejection of Kohlberg's work is too sweeping (Colby & Damon, 1987). It is clear, though, that gender plays an important role in determining what is seen as moral, and that men and women have differing conceptions of what constitutes moral behavior (McGraw & Bloomfield, 1987).

Searching for Identity: Psychosocial Development in Adolescence

To most adolescents, answering the questions "Who am I?" and "How do I fit into the world?" is one of life's major challenges. Although these questions continue to be posed throughout a person's lifetime, they take on particular significance during the adolescent years.

Erikson's theory of psychosocial development, which we discussed earlier, places particular importance on this search for identity during the adolescent years. As noted earlier, psychosocial development encompasses how people's understanding of themselves, one another, and the world around them changes as a part of development (Erikson, 1963).

The fifth stage of Erikson's theory (summarized, with the other stages, in Table 8-4) is labeled the **identity-versus-role-confusion** period and encompasses adolescence. This stage is a time of major testing, as people try to determine what is unique and special about themselves. They attempt to discover who they are, what their skills are, and what kinds of roles they are best suited to play—in short, their **identity**. Confusion over the most appropriate role to follow in life can lead to lack of a stable identity, adoption of a socially unacceptable role such as that of a social deviant, or difficulty in maintaining close personal relationships later in life (Kahn et al., 1985).

TABLE 8-4 A SUMMARY OF ERIKSON'S STAGES

Stage	Approximate Age	Positive Outcomes	Negative Outcomes
1. Trust vs. mistrust	Birth–1½ years	Feelings of trust from environmental support	Fear and concern regarding others
2. Autonomy vs. shame and doubt	1½–3 years	Self-sufficiency if exploration is encouraged	Doubts about self, lack of independence
3. Initiative vs. guilt	3–6 years	Discovery of ways to initiate actions	Guilt from actions and thoughts
4. Industry vs. inferiority	6–12 years	Development of sense of competence	Feelings of inferiority, no sense of mastery
5. Identity vs. role confusion	Adolescence	Awareness of uniqueness of self, knowledge of role to be followed	Inability to identify appropriate roles in life
6. Intimacy vs. isolation	Early adulthood	Development of loving, sexual relationships and close friendships	Fear of relationships with others
7. Generativity vs. stagnation	Middle adulthood	Sense of contribution to continuity of life	Trivialization of one's activities
8. Ego-integrity vs. despair	Late adulthood	Sense of unity in life's accomplishments	Regret over lost opportunities of life

During the identity-versus-role-confusion period, pressures to identify what one wants to do with one's life are acutely felt. Because these pressures come at a time of major physical changes and important changes in what society expects of them, adolescents can find the period a particularly difficult one. The identity-versus-role-confusion stage has another important characteristic: a decline in reliance on adults for information, with a shift toward using the peer group as a source of social judgments. The peer group becomes increasingly important, enabling adolescents to form close, adultlike relationships and helping them clarify their personal identities (Palmonari, Pomben, & Kirchler, 1990).

During the college years, most students enter the **intimacy-versus-isolation** stage (spanning the period of early adulthood, from around age 18 to age 30), in which the focus is on developing close relationships with others. Difficulties during this stage result in feelings of loneliness and a fear of relationships with others, while successful resolution of the crises of the stage results in the possibility of forming relationships that are intimate on physical, intellectual, and emotional levels.

Erikson goes on to describe the last stages of adulthood, in which development continues. During middle adulthood, people are in the **generativity-versus-stagnation** stage. Generativity refers to a person's contribution to his or her family, community, work, and society as a whole. Success in this stage results in positive feelings about the continuity of life, while difficulties lead to feelings of triviality regarding one's activities and a sense of stagnation or of having done nothing for upcoming generations. In fact, if a person has not successfully resolved the identity crisis of adolescence, he or she may still be floundering toward identifying an appropriate career.

The last stage of psychosocial development, the **ego-integrity-versus-despair** period, comprises later adulthood and continues until death. Success in resolving the difficulties presented by this stage of life is signified by a sense of accomplishment; difficulties result in regret over what might have been achieved, but was not.

One of the most noteworthy aspects of Erikson's theory is its suggestion that development does not stop at adolescence but continues throughout adulthood. Prior to Erikson, the prevailing view was that psychosocial development was largely complete after adolescence. He helped to establish that considerable development continues throughout our lives.

Stormy Adolescence: Myth or Reality?

Does puberty invariably foreshadow a stormy, rebellious period of adolescence?

At one time most children entering adolescence were thought to enter a period fraught with stress and unhappiness, but psychologists are now finding that such a characterization is largely a myth. Most young people, it seems, pass through adolescence without appreciable turmoil in their lives (Steinberg, Belsky, & Meyer, 1991; Peterson, 1988).

This is not to say that adolescence is completely tranquil (Glyshaw, Cohen, & Towbes, 1989; Rowlison & Felner, 1988). There is clearly a rise in the amount of arguing and bickering in most families. Young teenagers, as part of their search for identity, tend to experience a tension between their attempts to become independent from their parents and their actual dependence on them. Happily, though, for the majority of families such tensions tend to stabilize during middle adolescence—around age 15 or 16—and eventually decline around age 18 (Montemayor, 1983).

One of the reasons for the increase in discord in adolescence appears to be the protracted period in which children stay at home with their parents. In prior historical periods—and in some cultures today—children leave home immediately following puberty. Today, however, sexually mature adolescents may spend as much as seven or eight years with their parents (Steinberg, 1985). In addition, adolescence brings with it a variety of stresses outside the home. Typically, adolescents change schools at least twice (from elementary to middle or junior high, then to senior high school), and friendships and peer groups are particularly volatile. Such stressors can lead to unusual tensions at home.

THE MIDDLE YEARS OF LIFE: EARLY AND MIDDLE ADULTHOOD

At some point it just dawned on me: I'm an adult now. I've got a wife, I've got children, a mortgage, I complain about my taxes—I'm not too different from my own father, in fact. Probably the biggest change in my life that made me feel like an adult was having kids. Here were other people who were dependent on me. I couldn't just say to heck with it, walk away, and go on. . . . I had responsibilities. And I couldn't think any longer, "Someday I'll do this, someday I'll do that." Someday was *here.* If I wasn't successful, if I messed up my life, there would be no second chances.

The sentiments expressed by this young adult are common during the years of life known as early and middle adulthood. During this period, people "grow up"; they are considered both legally and socially to be full-fledged adult members of society.

Psychologists generally consider early adulthood to begin at around age 20 and last until about age 40 to 45, and middle adulthood to last from about age 40 to 45 to around age 65. Despite the enormous impor-

Young adulthood often brings added responsibilities.

tance of these periods of life—in terms of both the accomplishments that occur within them and their overall length (together they span some forty years)—they have been studied less than any other stages by developmental psychologists. One reason is that the physical changes during these periods are less apparent and occur more gradually than do those at other times during the life span. In addition, the social changes are so diverse that they prevent simple categorization. Still, there has been a recent upsurge of interest in adulthood among developmental psychologists, with a special focus on the social changes that occur in terms of the family, marriage, divorce, and careers for women.

The Peak of Health: Physical Development

For most people, early adulthood marks the peak of physical health. From about 18 to 25 years of age, people's strength is greatest, their reflexes are quickest, and their chances of dying from disease are quite slim. Moreover, reproductive capabilities are at their highest level.

The changes that begin at age 25 are largely of a quantitative rather than a qualitative nature. The body begins to operate slightly less efficiently and becomes somewhat more prone to disease. Overall, however, ill health remains the exception; most people stay remarkably healthy. (Can you think of any machine other than the body that can operate without pause for so long a period?)

The major biological change that does occur pertains to reproductive capabilities during middle adulthood. On average, during their late forties or early fifties, women begin **menopause**, the point at which they stop menstruating and are no longer fertile. Because menopause is accompanied by a reduction in estrogen, a female hormone, women sometimes experience symptoms such as hot flashes, or sudden sensations of heat. Most symptoms of menopause, though, are successfully treated with artificial estrogen.

Menopause was once blamed for a host of psychological symptoms, including depression, but most research now suggests that such problems, if they do occur, are caused more by women's perceived reactions to reaching an "old" age in a society that values youth so highly than by menopause itself. Society's attitudes, then, more than the physiological changes of menopause, may produce psychological difficulties (Ballinger, 1981).

For men, the aging process during middle adulthood is somewhat more subtle, since there are no physiological signals of increasing age equivalent to the end of menstruation in women. Moreover, men remain fertile and are capable of fathering children until well into old age. However, some gradual physical declines appear: Sperm production decreases and the frequency of orgasm tends to decline. Once again, though, any psychological difficulties that do occur are usually brought about, not so much by physical deterioration, but by the inability of the aging individual to meet the exaggerated standards of youthfulness held in high regard by society.

Working at Life: Social Development

Whereas physical changes during adulthood reflect development of a quantitative nature, social developmental transitions are more profound. It is during this period that people typically launch themselves into careers, marriage, and families.

Psychologist Daniel Levinson (1986) has proposed a model of adult development based on a comprehensive study of major events in the lives of a group of forty men. Although his initial sample was small and consisted only of males, the study is important because it provided one of the first comprehensive descriptions of the stages through which people pass following adolescence. According to Levinson, six major stages occur from the entry into early adulthood through the end of middle adulthood.

After a transitional period at around age 20, the stages in early adulthood relate to leaving one's family and entering the adult world. An individual envisions what Levinson calls "The Dream"—an all-encompassing vision about what goals are desired from life, be it writing the great American novel or becoming a physician. Career choices are made, and perhaps discarded, during early adulthood, until eventually long-term decisions are reached. This leads to a period of settling down in the late thirties, during which people establish themselves in a particular set of roles and begin to evolve and work toward a vision of their own future.

Around the age of 40 or 45, people generally begin to question their lives as they enter a period called the **midlife transition**, and the idea that life is finite becomes paramount in their thinking. Rather than maintaining a future-oriented view of life, people begin to ask questions about their past accomplishments, assessing what they have done and how satisfying it has been to them (Gould, 1978). They realize that not all they had wanted to accomplish will be completed before their life ends.

In some cases, people's assessments of their lives are negative, and they may enter what has been popularly labeled a **midlife crisis**. As they face signs of physical aging, they become aware that their careers are not going to progress considerably further. Even if they have attained the heights to which they aspired—be it company president or well-respected community leader—they find that the reality of their accomplishments is not all that they had hoped it would be. As they look at their past, they may also be motivated to try to define what went wrong and how they can remedy old dissatisfactions.

In most cases, though, the passage into middle age is relatively calm, and some developmental psychologists even question whether the midlife crisis occurs in most people (Whitbourne, 1986). Most 40-year-olds view their lives and accomplishments sufficiently positively that their midlife transition proceeds relatively smoothly, and the forties and fifties are a particularly rewarding period of life. Rather than looking to the future, people at this stage concentrate on the present, and their involvement with their families, friends, and other social groups takes on new importance. A major developmental thrust of this period of life is learning to accept that the die has been cast, and that one must come to terms with one's circumstances.

Unfortunately, there is as yet no clear answer to the question of how women's social development differs from men's, since a sufficiently large body of data focusing directly on women has only begun to be accumulated. Some recent research suggests, however, that there are both similarities and differences between men and women. Levinson (in press), for example, argues that women generally go through the same stages at the same ages as men, although disparities exist in the specific details of some of the stages. For instance, important differences appear during "The Dream," the stage in which people develop a vision of what their future life will encompass. Women often have greater difficulty than men in forming a clear dream, for they may experience conflict between the goals of working and of raising a family. For men, this conflict tends to be much less important, since a man who wishes to marry and have a family usually views working as the means of taking care of his family.

One study of early adulthood suggests that there is a major period of disruption, reassessment, and reorientation around the age of 30 for women (Reinke, Holmes & Harris, 1985). Although it is not clear why this disruption occurs, the age-30 transition appears to have greater impact on women than the age-40 transition. In contrast, for men the midlife transition at age 40 is typically more powerful. Further research must be carried out, of course, before the universality of these findings can be determined.

Finally, during the last stages of middle adulthood—the fifties—people generally become more accepting of others and their lives and less concerned about issues or problems which once bothered them. Rather than being driven to achieve as they were in their thirties, they come to accept the realization that death is inevitable, and they try to understand their accomplishments in terms of the broader meaning of life (Gould, 1978). Although people may begin, for the first time, to label themselves as "old," many also develop a sense of wisdom and feel freer to enjoy life (Karp, 1989).

THE LATER YEARS: GROWING OLD

I can't quite figure out where all the time went. Seventy-six years old. It sounds ancient, even to me.

The funny part is I really don't *feel* any older. Oh, my body has its share of aches and pains, and I don't move around as fast as I used to. And I forget things. But I've been forgetting things all my life.

I guess the most surprising thing is that it doesn't bother me all that much to be old and to know that death can't be too far away. It's quite a contrast to how I felt when I was younger—I used to be so afraid of getting old and of dying. Now, though, things are different. Of course, I'm not ready to die, and I sure don't want to. But it doesn't scare me the way it once did. After all, we all die sometime, don't we?

The fact that death is indeed a universal experience has not stopped it from being a source of fear and concern to many people, just as it once was to the speaker above. And many younger people exhibit similar negative feelings toward the entire period of old age.

However, old age is rapidly being viewed in a more favorable light as **gerontologists**, specialists who study aging, have begun to debunk many misconceptions regarding old age. Focusing on the period that starts at around age 65, gerontologists have made important contributions in clarifying the capabilities of the elderly and have demonstrated that significant developmental processes continue even during old age.

The Old Body: Physical Changes in the Elderly

Napping, eating, walking, conversing. It probably doesn't surprise you that these relatively unvigorous activities represent the typical pastimes of the elderly. But what is striking about this list is that these activities are identical to the most common leisure activities reported in a survey of college students. Although the students cited more active pursuits— such as sailing and playing basketball—as their favorite activities, in actuality they engaged in such sports relatively infrequently, spending most of their free time napping, eating, walking, and conversing (Harper, 1978).

Although the leisure activities in which the elderly engage may not differ all that much from those that younger people pursue, many physical changes are, of course, brought about by the aging process. The most obvious are those of appearance—hair thinning and turning gray, skin wrinkling and folding, and sometimes a slight loss of height as the size of the disks between vertebrae in the spine decreases—but there are also more subtle changes in the body's biological functioning (Munnichs, Mussen, Obrich & Coleman, 1985).

For example, sensory acuity decreases as a result of aging; vision and hearing are less sharp, and smell and taste are not as sensitive. Reaction time slows. There are changes in physical stamina. Because oxygen intake and heart-pumping ability decline, the body is unable to replenish lost nutrients as quickly—and therefore the rebound from physical activity is slower (Shock, 1962). Of course, none of these changes begins suddenly at age 65; gradual declines in some kinds of functioning start earlier. It is in old age, however, that these changes become more apparent.

What are the reasons for these physical declines? There are two major

The physical changes that come with age can be seen in these four self-portraits by Rembrandt. (Top left, Indianapolis Museum of Art/The Clowes Fund Collection; top right, Gemaldegalerie Alte Meister/Staatliche Kunstammlungen Kassel; bottom right, National Galleries of Scotland/Duke of Sutherland; bottom left, © copyright Scala Art Resource, 1986.)

explanations: **genetic preprogramming theories** and **wear-and-tear theories** (Bergener, Ermini & Stahelin, 1985; Whitbourne, 1986). Genetic preprogramming theories suggest that there is a built-in time limit to the reproduction of human cells, and that after a certain time they are no longer able to divide (Hayflick, 1974). A variant of this idea is that some cells are genetically preprogrammed to become harmful to the body after a certain amount of time has gone by, causing the internal biology of the body to "self-destruct" (Pereira-Smith et al., 1988).

The second approach for understanding physical declines due to aging is based on the same factors that force people to buy new cars every so often: mechanical devices simply wear out. According to wear-and-tear theories, the mechanical functions of the body simply stop working efficiently. Moreover, wastes that are by-products of energy production eventually accumulate, and mistakes are made when cells reproduce. Eventually the body, in effect, wears out.

We do not know which of these theories provides a better explanation of the physical aging process; it may be that both contribute. It is important to realize, however, that physical aging is not a disease, but rather a natural biological process (Rowe & Kahn, 1987). Many physical functions do not decline with age. For example, sex remains pleasurable well into old age (although the frequency of sexual activity decreases), and some elderly people even report that the pleasure they derive from sex increases (Lobsenz, 1975).

Furthermore, neither genetic preprogramming theories nor wear-and-tear theories successfully explain a fact that is immediately apparent to anyone studying aging: Women live longer than men. Throughout the industrialized world, women outlive men by a margin of four to ten years (Holden, 1987). The female advantage begins just after conception. Although more males are conceived than females, males have a higher rate of prenatal, infant, and childhood death, and by age 30 there are equal numbers of males and females. By age 65, 84 percent of females and 70 percent of males are still alive.

Happily, though, the gender gap is not increasing—mainly because of positive changes in men's health habits, including decreased smoking and consumption of cholesterol and increased exercise. But health habits do not provide the complete explanation for the gap, and an explanation of why women live longer than men remains to be found. What is clear is that women, more often than men, must make the profound adjustments needed following the death of a spouse. Women's longer lives are something of a mixed blessing: The end of life must frequently be faced without a partner.

Thinking About—and During—Old Age: Cognitive Changes

Three women were talking about the inconveniences of growing old.

"Sometimes," one of them confessed, "when I go to my refrigerator, I can't remember if I'm putting something in or taking something out."

"Oh, that's nothing," said the second woman. "There are times when I find myself at the foot of the stairs wondering if I'm going up or if I've just come down."

"Well, my goodness!" exclaimed the third woman. "I'm certainly glad I don't have any problems like that"—and she knocked on wood. "Oh," she said, starting up out of her chair, "there's someone at the door" (Dent, 1984, p. 38).

At one time, many gerontologists would have agreed with the view—suggested by the story above—that the elderly are forgetful and confused. Today, however, most research tells us that this is far from an accurate assessment of elderly people's capabilities.

One reason for the change in view is the use of more sophisticated research techniques. For example, if we were to give a group of elderly people an IQ test, we might find that the average score was lower than for a group of younger people. We might conclude that this signifies a decline in intelligence. But if we looked a little closer at the specific test, we might find that such a conclusion was unwarranted. For instance, many IQ tests include portions based on physical performance (such as arranging a group of blocks) or on speed. In such a case, poorer performance on the IQ test may be due to increases in reaction time—a physical decline that accompanies old age—and have little or nothing to do with the intellectual capabilities of the elderly (Cornelius & Caspi, 1987; Schaie, 1988).

On the other hand, some declines in the intellectual functioning of the elderly have been found, even when using more sophisticated research methods (Cerella, 1985; Schaie & Willis, 1985; Willis, 1988). As we will discuss in Chapter 9, intelligence can be conceptualized in terms of **fluid intelligence**—the ability to deal with new problems and situations—and **crystallized intelligence**—intelligence based on the accumulation of particular kinds of knowledge and experience as well as on strategies that have been acquired through the use of fluid intelligence. Tests show clear, although not substantial, declines in fluid intelligence in old age. It is noteworthy, however, that such changes actually begin to appear in early adulthood (Baltes & Schaie, 1974; Schaie, 1985).

Crystallized intelligence, in contrast, does not decline; it actually improves with age. For example, an elderly woman asked to solve a geometry problem (which taps fluid intelligence) might have greater difficulty than she once did, but she might be better at solving verbal problems that require reasoned conclusions.

One possible reason for the developmental differences between fluid and crystallized intelligence during old age is that fluid intelligence may be more sensitive to changes in the nervous system than crystallized intelligence. Another factor may be the degree to which the two kinds of intelligence are used during a person's lifetime. Whatever the reason, people compensate for the decline. They can still learn what they want to; it just may take more time (Storandt, 1984; Horne, 1982).

Furthermore, new evidence suggests that cognitive declines might be remedied by increasing the amount of blood in the brains of the elderly. In support of this reasoning, in one experiment the drug Nimodipine—which increases blood flow—was given to a group of elderly rabbits. The rabbits that received the drug learned a classically conditioned response significantly faster than a control group of rabbits that did not receive the drug. In fact, the rabbits that received the drug learned as rapidly as a group of young rabbits (Deyo, Straube, & Disterhoft, 1989).

Are the Elderly Forgetful? Memory Changes in Old Age

One of the characteristics most frequently attributed to the elderly is for-getfulness. How accurate is this assumption?

Most evidence suggests that memory change is not inevitable in the aging process, although some elderly people show declines. Moreover, when memory deficits do exist, they most typically occur only in long-term memory; the capacity of short-term memory rarely declines, except in cases of illness (Craik, 1977).

Some cases of memory failures are due merely to changes in the lives of the elderly (Ratner, 1987). For instance, it is not surprising that a retired person, who may no longer face the same kind of consistent intellectual challenges encountered on the job, might well be less practiced in using memory or even be less motivated to remember things, leading to an apparent decline in memory. Even in cases in which long-term memory declines, the elderly person can usually profit from compensatory strate-gies. In fact, when the elderly are provided with the kind of mnemonic procedures that we discussed in Chapter 5, long-term memory not only can be prevented from deteriorating, but actually may improve (Perl-mutter & Mitchell, 1986; Brody, 1987).

In the past, elderly people with severe cases of memory decline, ac-companied by other cognitive difficulties, were viewed as suffering from senility. **Senility** is a broad, imprecise term typically applied to elderly people who experience progressive deterioration of mental abilities, including memory loss, disorientation to time and place, and general confusion.

Once thought to be an inevitable state that accompanies aging, senility is now viewed by most gerontologists as a label that has outlived its use-fulness. Rather than senility being the cause of certain symptoms, the symptoms are deemed to be caused by some other factor. In some cases there is an actual disease, such as **Alzheimer's disease**, the progressive brain disorder discussed in Chapter 5 which leads to a gradual and irre-versible decline in mental abilities. In other cases, the symptoms of senility are caused by temporary anxiety and depression, which may be success-fully treated, or may even be due to over medication. The danger is that people suffering such symptoms may be labeled senile and left untreated, thereby continuing their decline—even though treatment would have been beneficial.

Adjusting to Death

At some time in your life, you will face death—certainly your own, and probably the deaths of friends and loved ones. Although there is nothing more inevitable in life than death, it remains a frightening, emotion-laden topic. In fact, there may be nothing more stressful than the death of a loved one or the contemplation of your own imminent death, and pre-

Grand Master cyclist Fred Knoller, photographed at age 87, exemplifies the view that the elderly who age most successfully are those who maintain the activities of their earlier years.

paring for death will likely represent one of your most crucial developmental tasks.

Not too long ago, talk of death was taboo. The topic was never mentioned to dying people, and gerontologists had little to say about it. That changed, however, with the pioneering work of Elisabeth Kübler-Ross (1969), who brought the subject out into the open with her observation that those facing death move through five stages.

- Denial. In this first stage, people resist the idea that they are dying. Even if told that their chances for survival are small, they refuse to admit that they are facing death.

- Anger. After moving beyond the denial stage, dying people are angry—angry at people around them who are in good health, angry at medical professionals for being ineffective, angry at God. They ask the question "Why me?" and are unable to answer it without feeling anger.

- Bargaining. Anger leads to bargaining, in which the dying try to think of ways to postpone death. They may decide to dedicate their lives to religion if God saves them; they may say, "If only I can live to see my son married, I will accept death then." Such bargains are rarely kept, most often because the dying person's illness keeps progressing and invalidates any "agreements."

- Depression. When dying people come to feel that bargaining is of no use, they move to the next stage: depression. They realize that the die is cast, that they are losing their loved ones and their lives really are coming to an end. They are experiencing what Kübler-Ross calls "preparatory grief" for their own death.

- Acceptance. In this last stage, people are past mourning for the loss of their own lives, and they accept impending death. Usually, they are unemotional and uncommunicative; it is as if they have made peace with themselves and are expecting death without rancor.

Although not everyone experiences each of these stages in the same way, if at all, Kübler-Ross's theory remains our best description of people's reactions to their approaching death. There are, however, vast individual differences, depending on the specific cause of death as well as the person's sex, age, personality, and the type of support received from family and friends (Kastenbaum, 1975; Goleman, 1988).

*A*SK YOURSELF

What critical physical changes occur during puberty?

According to Kohlberg and Gilligan, how does moral development proceed?

Can Gilligan's and Kohlberg's theories be integrated?

Is adolescence a stormy, rebellious period for most individuals?

What are the stages of social development during adulthood?

How do genetic preprogramming theories and wear-and-tear theories explain physical declines during old age?

What changes occur in intelligence and memory in old age?

How might the aging process be affected by a society that views the elderly with greater respect and admiration than ours?

*L*OOKING BACK

1. Developmental psychology is the branch of psychology that studies growth and change throughout life. One fundamental question is how much developmental change is due to nature—heredity and genetic factors—and how much to nurture—environmental factors. Most psychologists take an interactionist position.

2. Cross-sectional research compares people of different ages with one another at the same point in time. In contrast, longitudinal research traces the behavior of one or more subjects as the subjects become older. Finally, cross-sequential research combines the two methods by taking several different age groups and examining them over several points in time.

3. At the moment of conception, a male's sperm cell and a female's egg cell unite, each contributing to the new individual's

genetic makeup. The new cell, a zygote, immediately begins to grow, becoming an embryo at four weeks. By the ninth week, the embryo is called a fetus and is responsive to touch and other stimulation. At about twenty-eight weeks it reaches the age of viability. A fetus is normally born after thirty-eight weeks of pregnancy, weighing around $7\frac{1}{2}$ pounds and measuring about 20 inches in length.

4. Genetic abnormalities produce birth defects such as phenylketonuria (PKU), sickle-cell anemia, Tay-Sachs disease, and Down's syndrome. Among the prenatal environmental influences on fetal growth are the mother's nutritional status, illnesses, drug intake, and birth complications.

5. The newborn, or neonate, has many capabilities. Among them are the rooting reflex, the Moro (startle) reflex, and the Babinski reflex. After birth, physical development is rapid; children typically triple their birth weights in a year. Perceptual abilities also increase rapidly; infants can distinguish color and depth after just one month. Infants can distinguish sounds and discriminate tastes and smells. However, the development of more sophisticated perceptual abilities depends on increased cognitive abilities.

6. Social development in infancy is marked by the phenomenon of attachment—the positive emotional bond between a child and a particular individual. As children become older, the nature of their social interactions with peers changes.

7. According to Erikson, eight stages of psychosocial development encompass people's changing interactions and understanding of themselves and others. During childhood, there are four stages.

8. Piaget's theory suggests that cognitive development proceeds through four stages in which qualitative changes occur in thinking. In the sensorimotor stage (birth to 2 years), children develop object permanence. In the preoperational stage (2 to 7 years) children display egocentric thought, and by the end of the stage they begin to understand the principle of conservation. The conservation principle is not fully grasped, however, until the concrete operational stage (7 to 12 years), in which children begin to think more logically. In the final stage, the formal operational period (12 years to adulthood), thinking becomes abstract, formal, and fully logical.

9. Some theorists suggest that the notion of developmental stages is inaccurate, saying that development is more continuous. Information-processing approaches suggest that quantitative changes occur in children's ability to organize and manipulate information about the world, such as significant increases in speed of processing, attention span, and memory. In addition, there are advances in metacognition, the awareness and understanding of one's own cognitive processes.

10. Adolescence, the developmental stage between childhood and adulthood, is marked by the onset of puberty, the point at which sexual maturity occurs. The age at which puberty begins has implications for the way people view themselves and the way they are seen by others.

11. Moral judgments during adolescence increase in sophistication, according to Kohlberg's three-stage, six-level model. Although Kohlberg's stages are an adequate description of males' moral judgments, they seem not to be as applicable in describing females' judgments. Specifically, Gilligan suggests that women view morality in terms of concern for individuals rather than in terms of broad, general principles of justice or fairness; in her view, moral development in women proceeds in three stages.

12. According to Erikson's model of psychosocial development, adolescence may be accompanied by an identity crisis, although this is by no means universal. Adolescence is followed by three stages of psychosocial development which cover the remainder of the life span.

13. Early adulthood marks the peak of physical health. Physical changes occur rela-

tively gradually in men and women during adulthood, although one major change occurs at the end of middle adulthood for women: They begin menopause, after which they are no longer fertile. For men, the aging process is more subtle, since they remain fertile.

14. Levinson's model of adult development suggests that six major stages occur, beginning with entry into early adulthood at around age 20 and ending at around age 60 or 65. Although Levinson suggests that women's lives follow the same pattern as men's, several differences have been identified for them.

15. Old age may bring marked physical declines. Although the activities of the elderly are not all that different from those of younger people, elderly people do experience reaction-time increases, as well as sensory declines and a decrease in physical stamina. These declines might be caused by genetic preprogramming or by wear and tear on the mechanical parts of the body.

16. Although intellectual declines were once thought to be an inevitable part of aging, most research suggests that this is not necessarily the case. Fluid intelligence does decline with age, and long-term memory abilities are sometimes impaired. In contrast, crystallized intelligence shows slight increases with age, and short-term memory remains at about the same levels. Senility, then, is no longer seen as a universal outcome of old age.

17. According to Kübler-Ross, dying people move through five stages as they face death: denial, anger, bargaining, depression, and acceptance.

Key Terms and Concepts

developmental psychology (p. 298)
environmental influences (p. 299)
hereditary influences (p. 299)
nature-nurture question (p. 299)
genetic makeup (p. 299)
maturation (p. 300)
interactionist (p. 301)
identical twins (p. 302)
cross-sectional research (p. 302)
longitudinal research (p. 302)
conception (p. 303)
zygote (p. 303)
chromosomes (p. 303)
genes (p. 303)
embryo (p. 303)
critical period (p. 304)
fetus (p. 304)
age of viability (p. 305)
phenylketonuria (PKU) (p. 306)
sickle-cell anemia (p. 306)
Tay-Sachs disease (p. 306)
Down's syndrome (p. 306)
rubella (p. 307)

fetal alcohol syndrome (p. 308)
neonate (p. 309)
vernix (p. 309)
lanugo (p. 309)
reflexes (p. 309)
rooting reflex (p. 309)
sucking reflex (p. 309)
gag reflex (p. 309)
Moro (startle) reflex (p. 309)
Babinski reflex (p. 309)
habituation (p. 312)
attachment (p. 314)
psychosocial development (p. 317)
trust-versus-mistrust stage (p. 318)
autonomy-versus-shame-and-doubt
    stage (p. 320)
initiative-versus-guilt stage (p. 320)
industry-versus-inferiority stage (p. 320)
cognitive development (p. 321)
sensorimotor stage (p. 322)
object permanence (p. 322)
preoperational stage (p. 322)
egocentric thought (p. 323)

9

Personality and Individual Differences

❖

PROLOGUE: FRANK COSTELLO

Frank Costello testifies before the Senate Crime Investigating Committee in 1951. Despite his criminal activities, he was also known for his charitable contributions.

His generosity was undeniable. For instance, as vice-chairman of the Salvation Army's fund-raising drive, Frank Costello helped raise $3500 at a $100-a-plate dinner he organized at the Copacabana in New York. To that sum he added $6500 of his own money, a goodly amount in 1949. He was also active in other charities and was a member of the Men's Committee of the Legal Aid Society.

Costello cut a dapper figure. His meticulous attention to his clothing was legendary among his acquaintances—a habit he insisted on even when it might have worked against him. When a lawyer suggested that wearing one of his hand-tailored suits at a trial might hurt his case with the jury, Costello refused to change to off-the-rack clothing, saying he would rather blow the case.

The fact that Frank Costello was involved in a trial at all, however, was related to another side to his personality. Along with generosity and concern over his appearance, Costello had a somewhat more unusual set of attributes: As a member of one of the

351

most prominent organized crime syndicates in the United States, he was a thief, gambler, and murder mastermind.

Costello began his life of crime at age 14, when he robbed the landlady of his parents' apartment. He quickly graduated to assault and robbery and eventually moved through the ranks of organized crime to the very top position, where he routinely arranged for the murder of those he considered his enemies (Sifakis, 1987).

*L*OOKING AHEAD

Will the real Frank Costello please stand up?

Although you probably don't know many cases as extreme as that of Costello, you may be acquainted with people who behave one way in one situation and display characteristics that are quite the opposite in another. (In fact, you might include yourself in this category.) At the same time, you probably know people whose behavior is so predictable that you can tell, almost without thinking, what they are going to do in a particular situation—people whose behavior is almost entirely consistent from one setting to the next.

To psychologists, understanding the characteristic ways in which people behave makes up the core of the branch of psychology known as **personality**. The term itself is used in two different, but related, ways: On the one hand, personality refers to the characteristics that differentiate people—those *individual differences* that make a person unique. On the other hand, personality is used as a means of explaining the stability in people's behavior that leads them to act uniformly both in different situations and over extended periods of time (Pervin, 1990).

In this chapter we consider a number of theories meant to explain personality and individual differences. We begin with the broadest and most comprehensive approach to personality: Freud's psychoanalytic theory. Next, we turn to more recent theories of personality. We consider approaches that concentrate on identifying the most fundamental personality traits that differentiate one person from another, on theories that focus on personality as a set of learned behaviors, and on approaches, known as humanistic theories, that highlight the uniquely human aspects of personality.

We then turn to a consideration of the ways in which personality is measured and how personality tests can be used. We focus on the specific aspect of human individuality that has received the greatest attention from psychologists: intelligence. We examine the differing conceptions of intelligence and the use of tests to measure it. We also consider the two groups displaying extremes of individual differences in intelligence: the mentally retarded and the gifted.

We end with a discussion of the two most controversial issues surrounding intelligence: the degree to which intelligence is influenced by heredity and the environment, and possible bias in traditional tests of intelligence toward the dominant cultural groups in society.

After reading this chapter, then, you will have the answers to questions such as these:

- How do psychologists define and use the concept of personality?
- What is the structure and development of personality according to Freud and his successors?
- What are the major aspects of trait, learning, and humanistic theories of personality?
- How can we most accurately assess personality, and what are the major types of personality measures?
- How is intelligence conceived of and defined by psychologists?
- How can the extremes of intelligence be differentiated?
- To what degree is intelligence influenced by the environment and by heredity?

*E*XPLAINING THE INNER LIFE: PSYCHOANALYTIC THEORIES OF PERSONALITY

Oscar Madison: sloppy, disheveled, unkempt. Felix Unger: neat, precise, controlled.

As anyone who has seen the play or the old television series *The Odd Couple* can attest, two people could hardly seem to possess more dissimilar personalities. Yet to one group of personality theorists, **psychoanalysts**, the two might actually be quite similar—at least in terms of the underlying part of personality that motivates their behavior. According to psychoanalysts, our behavior is triggered largely by powerful forces found in a part of personality about which we are not aware. These hidden forces, shaped to a great degree by childhood experiences, play an important role in energizing and directing our everyday behavior.

The most important of the theorists to hold such a view, and indeed one of the best-known figures in all psychology, is Sigmund Freud. An Austrian physician, Freud was the originator of **psychoanalytic theory** in the early 1900s.

What You See Is Not What You Get: Freud's Psychoanalytic Theory

The college student was intent on sounding smooth and making a good first impression with an attractive woman he spotted across a crowded room at a party. As he walked toward her, he mulled over a line he had heard in an old movie the night before: "I don't believe we've been properly introduced yet." To his horror, what came out was a bit different. After threading his way through the crowded room, he finally reached the woman and blurted out, "I don't believe we've been properly seduced yet."

Although this may seem to be merely an embarrassing slip of the tongue, according to psychoanalytic theory such a mistake is not an error at all (Motley, 1987). Rather, it is an indication of deeply felt emotions and thoughts that are harbored in the **unconscious**, a part of the personality of which a person is not aware. Many of life's experiences are painful, and the unconscious provides a "safe" haven for our recollection of such events, a place where they can remain without continually disturbing us. Similarly, the unconscious contains **instinctual drives**: infantile wishes, desires, demands, and needs that are hidden from conscious awareness because of the conflicts and pain they would cause us if they were part of our everyday lives.

To Freud, conscious experience is just the tip of the iceberg; like the unseen mass of a floating iceberg, the material found in the unconscious dwarfs the information about which we are aware. Much of people's everyday behavior is viewed as being motivated by unconscious forces about which they know little. For example, a child's concern over being unable to please his strict and demanding parents may lead him to have low self-esteem as an adult, although he may never understand why his accomplishments—which may be considerable—seem insufficient. Indeed, consciously the child may recall his childhood with great pleasure; it is his unconscious, which holds the painful memories, that provokes the low self-evaluation.

According to Freud, to fully understand personality, it is necessary to illuminate and expose what is in the unconscious. But because the unconscious disguises the meaning of material it holds, it cannot be observed directly. It is therefore necessary to interpret clues to the unconscious— slips of the tongue, fantasies, and dreams—in order to understand the unconscious processes directing behavior. A slip of the tongue, such as the one quoted earlier, might be interpreted as revealing the speaker's underlying unconscious sexual interests.

If the notion of an unconscious does not seem so farfetched to most of us, it is only because Freudian theory has had such a widespread influence, with applications ranging from literature to religion. In Freud's day, however, the idea that the unconscious could harbor painful material from which people were protecting themselves was revolutionary, and the best minds of the time summarily rejected his ideas as being without basis and even laughable. That it is now so easy to accept the existence of a portion of personality about which people are unaware—and one that is responsible for much of our behavior—is a tribute to the influence of Freud's theory.

Structuring personality: id, ego, and superego. To describe the structure of personality, Freud developed a comprehensive theory which held that personality consisted of three separate but interacting parts: the id, the ego, and the superego. Although Freud described these parts in very concrete terms, it is important to realize that they are not actual physical structures found in a certain part of the brain; instead, they represent parts of a general *model* of personality that describes the interaction of various processes and forces within one's personality that motivate behavior. Yet Freud suggested that they can be depicted diagrammatically to show how the three components of personality are related to the conscious and the unconscious (see Figure 9-1).

If personality consisted only of primitive, instinctual cravings and longings, it would have but one component: the id. The **id** is the raw, unorganized, inherited part of personality whose sole purpose is to reduce tension created by primitive drives related to hunger, sex, aggression, and irrational impulses. The id operates according to the **pleasure principle**, in which the goal is the immediate reduction of tension and the maximization of satisfaction.

Unfortunately for the id—but luckily for people and society—reality prevents the demands of the pleasure principle from being fulfilled in most cases. Instead, the world produces constraints: We cannot always eat when we are hungry, and we can discharge our sexual drives only when time, place—and partner—are willing. To account for this fact of life, Freud suggested a second part of personality, which he called the ego.

The **ego** provides a buffer between the id and the realities of the objective, outside world. In contrast to the pleasure-seeking nature of the id, the ego operates according to the **reality principle**, in which instinctual energy is restrained in order to maintain the safety of the individual and help integrate the person into society. In a sense, then, the ego is the

FIGURE 9-1
In Freud's model of personality, there are three major components: the id, the ego, and the superego. As the schematic shows, only a small portion of personality is conscious. This figure should not be thought of as an actual, physical structure, but rather as a model of the interrelationships between the parts of personality.

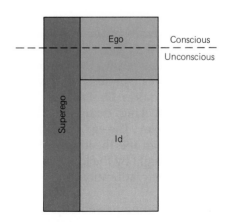

This baby may be going through what Freud described as the oral stage. An adult who has a fixation at this stage might engage in excessive eating, smoking, or chewing gum.

"executive" of personality: It makes decisions, controls actions, and allows thinking and problem solving of a higher order than the id is capable of. The ego is also the seat of higher cognitive abilities such as intelligence, thoughtfulness, reasoning, and learning.

The **superego**, the final personality structure to develop, represents the rights and wrongs of society as handed down by a person's parents, teachers, and other important figures. It becomes a part of personality when children learn right from wrong and continues to develop as people begin to incorporate into their own standards the broad moral principles of the society in which they live.

The superego actually has two parts, the **conscience** and the **ego ideal**. The conscience *prevents* us from doing morally bad things, while the ego ideal *motivates* us to do what is morally proper. The superego helps to control impulses coming from the id, making them less selfish and more virtuous.

Although on the surface the superego appears to be the opposite of the id, the two share an important feature: Both are unrealistic in that they do not consider the actualities of society. While this lack of reality within the superego pushes the person toward greater virtue, if left unchecked it would create perfectionists who were unable to make the compromises that life requires. Similarly, an unrestrained id would create a primitive, pleasure seeking, thoughtless individual, seeking to fulfill every desire without delay. The ego, then, must compromise between the demands of the superego and the id, permitting a person to obtain some of the gratification sought by the id while keeping the moralistic superego from preventing the gratification.

Developing personality: a stage approach. Freud did not stop after describing the components of adult personality; his theory also provides

TABLE 9-1 THE STAGES OF PERSONALITY DEVELOPMENT ACCORDING TO FREUD'S PSYCHOANALYTIC THEORY

Stage	Age	Major Characteristics
Oral	Birth to 12–18 months	Interest in oral gratification from sucking, eating, mouthing, biting
Anal	12–18 months to 3 years	Gratification from expelling and withholding feces; coming to terms with society's controls relating to toilet training
Phallic	3 to 5–6 years	Interest in the genitals; coming to terms with Oedipal/Electra conflict, leading to identification with same-sex parent
Latency	5–6 years to adolescence	Sexual concerns largely unimportant
Genital	Adolescence to adulthood	Reemergence of sexual interests and establishment of mature sexual relationships

a view of how personality develops throughout a series of stages during childhood.

Particularly important about the sequence, summarized in Table 9-1, is that it suggests how experiences and difficulties during a particular childhood stage may predict specific sorts of idiosyncrasies in adult personality. The theory is also unique in focusing each stage on a major biological function, which is assumed to be the focus of pleasure in a given period.

In the first period of development, called the **oral stage**, the baby's mouth is the focal point of pleasure. During the first 12 to 18 months of life, children suck, mouth, and bite anything that will fit into their mouths. To Freud, this behavior suggested that the mouth was the primary site of a kind of sexual pleasure, and if infants were either overly indulged (perhaps by being fed every time they cried) or very frustrated in their search for oral gratification, they might become fixated at this stage. Displaying **fixation** means that an adult shows personality characteristics that are related to an earlier stage of development. For example, fixation at the oral stage might produce an adult who was unusually interested in overtly oral activities—eating, talking, smoking—or who showed symbolic sorts of oral interests: being "bitingly" sarcastic or being very gullible ("swallowing" anything).

From around 12 to 18 months until 3 years of age—where the emphasis in most cultures is on toilet training—the child enters the **anal stage**. At this point, the major source of pleasure changes from the mouth to the anal region, and children derive considerable pleasure from both retention and expulsion of feces. If the external concerns of society in the form of toilet training are particularly demanding, the result may be fixation. If fixation occurs during the anal stage, Freud suggested that adults might show unusual rigidity, orderliness, punctuality—or extreme disorderliness or sloppiness, as in our earlier examples of Oscar and Felix.

At about age 3, the **phallic stage** begins, at which point there is another major shift in the primary source of pleasure for the child. This time, interest focuses on the genitals and the pleasures derived from fondling them. This is also the stage of one of the most important points of personality development, according to Freudian theory: the **Oedipal conflict**. As children focus their attention on their genitals, the differences between male and female anatomy become more salient. Furthermore, at this time Freud felt that the male begins to develop sexual interests in his mother, starts to see his father as a rival, and harbors a wish to kill his father—as Oedipus did in the ancient Greek tragedy. But because he views his father as too powerful, he develops a fear of retaliation in the form of "castration anxiety." Ultimately, this fear becomes so powerful that the child represses his desires for his mother and instead chooses to **identify** with his father, trying to be as much like him as possible.

For girls, the process—occasionally referred to as a resolution of the "Electra complex"—is a little different. Freud reasoned that girls begin to feel sexual arousal toward their fathers and—in a suggestion that was to later bring serious, and not unreasonable, accusations that he viewed women as inferior to men—that they begin to experience **penis envy**: They wish they had the anatomical part that, at least to Freud, seemed most clearly "missing" in girls. They blame their mothers for their lack of a penis, believing that their mothers are responsible for their "castration." As with males, though, they find that in order to resolve such unacceptable feelings, they must identify with the same-sex parent by behaving like her and adapting her attitudes and values. In this way, a girl's identification with her mother is completed.

At this point, the Oedipal conflict is said to be resolved, and, if things have gone smoothly, Freudian theory assumes that both males and females move on to the next stage of development. If difficulties arise during this period, however, all sorts of problems are thought to occur, including a lack of conscience and improper sex-role behavior.

Following the resolution of the Oedipal conflict, typically at around age 5 or 6, children move into the **latency period**, which lasts until puberty. During this period, not much of interest is occurring, according to Freud; sexual concerns are more or less put to rest, even in the unconscious. Then, during adolescence, sexual feelings reemerge, marking the start of the final period, the **genital stage**, which extends until death. The focus in the genital stage is on mature, adult sexuality, which Freud defined as sexual intercourse.

Dealing with the dangers from within: defense mechanisms. Freud's efforts to describe and theorize about the underlying dynamics of personality and its development were motivated by very practical problems that his patients faced in dealing with **anxiety**, an intense, negative emotional experience. According to Freud, anxiety is a danger signal to the ego. Although anxiety may arise from realistic fears—such as seeing a poisonous snake about to strike—it may also occur as **neurotic anxiety**, in which irrational impulses emanating from the id threaten to burst through and become uncontrollable. Because anxiety, naturally, is unpleasant, Freud believed that people develop a range of defense mechanisms to deal with it. **Defense mechanisms** are unconscious strategies people use to reduce anxiety by concealing the source from themselves and others (Cramer, 1987).

The primary defense mechanism is **repression**, in which unacceptable or unpleasant id impulses are pushed back into the unconscious. Repression is the most direct method of dealing with anxiety; instead of handling an anxiety-producing impulse on a conscious level, one simply ignores it. For example, a college student who feels hatred for her mother might repress these personally and socially unacceptable feelings; they remain lodged within the id, since acknowledging them would be so anxiety-provoking. This does not mean, however, that they would have no effect: True feelings might be revealed through dreams, slips of the tongue, or symbolically in some other fashion. The student might, for instance, have difficulty with authority figures such as teachers and do poorly in school. Alternatively, she might join the military, where she could give harsh orders to others and never have them questioned.

If repression is ineffective in keeping anxiety at bay, other defense mechanisms may be called upon. For example, **regression** might be used, whereby people behave as if they were at an earlier stage of development. By retreating to a younger age—for instance by complaining and throwing tantrums—they might succeed in having fewer demands put upon them.

Anyone who has ever been angered by a professor and then returned to the dorm and yelled at his or her roommate knows what displacement is all about. In **displacement**, the expression of an unwanted feeling or thought is redirected from a more threatening, powerful person to a weaker one. A classic case is yelling at one's secretary after being criticized by the boss.

Rationalization, another defense mechanism, occurs when we distort reality by justifying what happens to us: We develop explanations that allow us to protect our self-esteem. If you've ever heard someone say that he didn't mind being stood up for a date because he really had a lot of work to do that evening, you have probably seen rationalization at work.

In **denial**, a person simply refuses to accept or acknowledge an anxiety-producing piece of information. For example, when told that his wife has died in an automobile crash, a husband may at first deny the tragedy, saying that there must be some mistake, and only gradually come

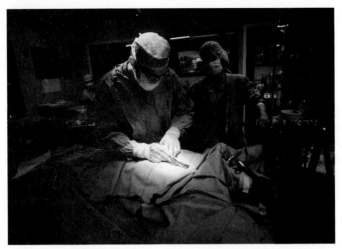

One of the healthier defense mechanisms is sublimation, in which people channel their unwanted impulses into socially approved behavior. For example, Freud might suggest that a surgeon's choice of profession is influenced by unconscious aggressive tendencies.

to conscious acceptance that she actually has been killed. In extreme cases, denial may linger; the husband may continue to expect that his wife will return home.

Projection is a means of protecting oneself by attributing unwanted impulses and feelings to someone else. For example, a man who feels sexually inadequate may complain to his wife that *she* is sexually inept.

Finally, one defense mechanism that Freud considered to be particularly healthy and socially acceptable is **sublimation**. In sublimation, people divert unwanted impulses into socially approved thoughts, feelings, or behaviors. For example, a person with strong feelings of aggression may become a butcher—and hack away at meat instead of people. Sublimation allows the butcher the opportunity not only to release psychic tension but to do so in a way that is socially acceptable.

All of us employ defense mechanisms to some degree, according to Freudian theory. Yet some people use them so much that a large amount of psychic energy must be constantly directed toward hiding and rechanneling unacceptable impulses, making everyday living difficult. In this case, the result is a neurosis, a term referring to mental disorders produced by anxiety that we will discuss in the chapter on abnormal behavior.

Evaluating Freudian theory. More than almost any other psychological theory we have discussed, Freud's personality theory presents an elaborate and complicated set of propositions—some of which are so removed from everyday explanations of behavior that they may appear difficult to accept. But laypeople are not the only ones to be concerned about the validity of Freud's theory; personality psychologists, too, have been quick to criticize its inadequacies.

Among the most compelling of these criticisms is the lack of scientific data to support the theory. Although there are a wealth of individual assessments of particular people that *seem* to support the theory, we lack definitive evidence showing that the personality is structured and operates along the lines Freud laid out—due, in part, to the fact that Freud's conception of personality is built on unobservable abstractions. Moreover, while we can readily employ Freudian theory in after-the-fact explanations, it is extremely difficult to predict how certain developmental difficulties will be displayed in the adult. For instance, if a person is fixated at the anal stage, he might, according to Freud, be unusually messy—or he might be unusually neat. Freud's theory offers no guidance for predicting which manifestations of the difficulty will occur. It produces good history, then, but not such good science. Finally, Freud made his observations—albeit insightful ones—and derived his theory from a limited population: primarily upper-class Austrian women living in the strict, puritanical era of the early 1900s. How far one can generalize beyond this population is a matter of considerable question.

Despite these criticisms, which cannot be dismissed, Freud's theory has had an enormous impact on the field of psychology—and indeed on all of western thinking. The ideas of the unconscious, anxiety, defense mechanisms, and the childhood causes of adult psychological difficulties have permeated people's views of the world and their understanding of the causes of their own behavior and that of others (Moore & Fine, 1990).

Furthermore, Freud's emphasis on the unconscious has been partially supported by some of the current research findings of cognitive psychologists. This work has revealed that mental processes about which people are unaware have an important impact on thinking and actions. In addition, new experimental techniques have been developed that allow the unconscious to be studied in a more scientifically sophisticated manner, overcoming the reliance of traditional Freudian approaches on single-subject case studies and unconfirmable theoretical interpretations of dreams and slips of the tongue for support (Kihlstrom, 1987; Kline, 1987; Western, 1990).

The importance of psychoanalytic theory is underscored by the fact that it spawned a significant—and enduring—method of treating psychological disturbances, as we will discuss further in Chapter 11. For a variety of reasons, then, Freud's psychoanalytic theory remains a significant contribution to our understanding of personality.

Revising Freud: The Neo-Freudian Psychoanalysts

One particularly important outgrowth of Freud's theorizing was the work done by a series of successors who were trained in traditional Freudian theory but who later strayed from some of its major points. These theorists are known as **neo-Freudian psychoanalysts**.

The neo-Freudians placed greater emphasis than did Freud on the functions of the ego, suggesting that it had more control than the id over day-to-day activities. They also paid greater attention to social factors and the effects of society and culture on personality development. Carl Jung (pronounced "yoong"), for example, who initially adhered closely to Freud's thinking, later rejected the notion of the primary importance of unconscious sexual urges—a key notion of Freudian theory—and instead looked at the primitive urges of the unconscious more positively. He suggested that people had a **collective unconscious**, a set of influences we inherit from our own particular ancestors, the whole human race, and even animal ancestors from the distant past. This collective unconscious is shared by everyone and is displayed by behavior that is common across diverse cultures—such as love of mother, belief in a supreme being, and even behavior as specific as fear of snakes.

Jung went on to propose that the collective unconscious contained **archetypes**, universal symbolic representations of a particular person, object, or experience. For instance, a mother archetype, which contains both our own experiences with our mother and reflections of our ancestors' relationships with mother figures, is suggested by the prevalence of moth-

To Jung, Superman and his enemy General Zod would represent broad archetypes of good and evil. (*Superman II*, A Warner Bros. Release/© DC Comics Inc./Film Stills Archive, The Museum of Modern Art, New York)

ers in art, religion, literature, and mythology. (Think of the Virgin Mary, Earth Mother, wicked stepmothers of fairy tales, Mother's Day, and so forth!) A more sinister archetype is the shadow, which Jung said contained the more depraved attributes from our prehuman predecessors. The shadow archetype forms the basis for representations of sin and the devil which are found throughout religious history.

To Jung, archetypes play an important role in determining our day-to-day reactions, attitudes, and values. For instance, Jung might explain the popularity of a movie such as *Batman* as being due to its use of broad archetypes of good (Batman), evil (the Joker), and innocence (Vicki Vail).

Alfred Adler, another important neo-Freudian psychoanalyst, considered Freudian theory's emphasis on sexual needs as misplaced. Instead, Adler proposed that the primary human motivation was a striving for superiority, not in terms of superiority over others, but as a quest to achieve self-improvement and perfection. Adler used the term **inferiority complex** to describe situations in which adults have not been able to overcome the feelings of inferiority that they developed as children, when they were small and limited in their knowledge about the world. Early social relationships with parents have an important effect on how well children are able to outgrow feelings of personal inferiority and instead orient themselves toward attaining more socially useful goals such as improving society.

Other neo-Freudians, such as Erik Erikson (whose theory we discussed in Chapter 8) and Karen Horney (1937), also focused less than Freud on inborn sexual and aggressive motivation and more on the social and cultural factors behind personality. Horney, for example, suggested that personality developed in terms of social relationships and depended particularly on the relationship between parents and child and how well the child's needs were met. She rejected Freud's suggestion that women had penis envy, asserting that what women coveted most in men was not their anatomy but the independence, success, and freedom that women were often denied. Horney was one of the first feminist psychologists.

*A*SK YOURSELF

What are the three components of personality according to Freud's psychoanalytic theory?

In Freud's view, how does personality develop?

What are the major defense mechanisms?

How have neo-Freudian psychoanalysts modified psychoanalytic theory?

Can you identify any of Freud's defense mechanisms that you have employed in the past week?

*I*N SEARCH OF PERSONALITY: TRAIT, LEARNING, AND HUMANISTIC APPROACHES

"Tell me about Roger, Sue," said Wendy.

"Oh, he's just terrific. He's the friendliest guy I know—goes out of his way to be nice to everyone. He hardly ever gets mad. He's just so even-tempered, no matter what's happening. And he's really smart, too. About the only thing I don't like is that he's always in such a hurry to get things done; he seems to have boundless energy, much more than I have."

"He sounds great to me, especially in comparison to Richard," replied Wendy. "He is so self-centered and arrogant it drives me crazy. I sometimes wonder why I ever started going out with him."

Friendly. Even-tempered. Smart. Energetic. Self-centered. Arrogant.

If we were to analyze the conversation printed above, the first thing we would notice is that it is made up of a series of trait characterizations of the two people being discussed. In fact, most of our understanding of the reasons behind others' behavior is based on the premise that people possess certain traits that are assumed to be consistent across different situations. A number of formal theories of personality employ variants of this approach. We turn now to a discussion of these and other personality theories, all of which provide alternatives to the psychoanalytic emphasis on unconscious processes in determining behavior.

Labeling Personality: Trait Theories

If someone were to ask you to characterize another person, it is probable that—like the two people in the conversation just presented—you would come up with a list of that individual's personal qualities, as you see them. But how would you know which of these qualities were most important in determining the person's behavior?

Personality psychologists have asked similar questions themselves. In order to answer them, they have developed a sophisticated model of personality known as **trait theory. Traits** are enduring dimensions of personality characteristics along which people differ from one another.

Trait theorists do not assume that some people have a trait and others do not; rather, they propose that all people have certain traits, but that the degree to which the trait applies to a specific person varies and can be quantified. For instance, you might be relatively friendly, whereas I might be relatively unfriendly. But we both have a "friendliness" trait, although you would be quantified with a higher score and I with a lower one. The major challenge for trait theorists taking this approach has been to identify the specific primary traits necessary to describe personality—and, as we shall see, different theorists have come up with surprisingly different sets (Buss, 1989).

Getting down to basics: Allport's trait theory. When personality psychologist Gordon Allport carefully leafed through an unabridged dictionary, he came up with some 18,000 separate terms that could be used to describe personality. Although he was able to pare down the list to a mere 4500 descriptors after eliminating synonyms, he obviously was still left with a problem crucial to all trait theories: Which of these were the most crucial?

Allport answered this question by suggesting that there were three basic categories of traits: cardinal, central, and secondary (Allport, 1961, 1966). A **cardinal trait** is a single characteristic that directs most of a person's activities. For example, a totally selfless woman might direct all her energy toward humanitarian activities; another person might be driven by all-consuming power needs.

Most people, however, do not develop all-encompassing cardinal traits; instead, they possess a handful of central traits that make up the core of personality. **Central traits**, such as honesty and sociability, are the major characteristics of the individual; they usually number from five to ten in any one person. Finally, **secondary traits** are characteristics that affect behavior in fewer situations and are less influential than central or cardinal traits. For instance, a preference for ice cream or a dislike of modern art would be considered a secondary trait.

Factoring out personality: The theories of Cattell and Eysenck. More recent attempts at discovering primary traits have centered on a statistical technique known as factor analysis. **Factor analysis** is a method of summarizing the relationships among a large number of variables into fewer, more general patterns. For example, a personality researcher might administer a questionnaire to many subjects, asking them to describe themselves along an extensive list of traits. By statistically combining responses and computing which traits are associated with one another in the same person, a researcher can identify the most fundamental patterns or combinations of traits—called factors—that underlie subjects' responses.

Using factor analysis, personality psychologist Raymond Cattell (1965) suggested that the characteristics that can be observed in a given situation represent 46 **surface traits**, or clusters of related behaviors. For example, you might encounter a friendly, gregarious librarian who goes out of his way to be helpful to you, and from your interactions with him decide that he possesses the trait of sociability—in Cattell's terms, a surface trait.

However, such surface traits are based on people's perceptions and representations of personality; they do not necessarily provide the best description of the underlying personality dimensions that are at the root of all behavior. Carrying out further factor analysis, Cattell found that sixteen **source traits** represented the basic dimensions of personality. Us-

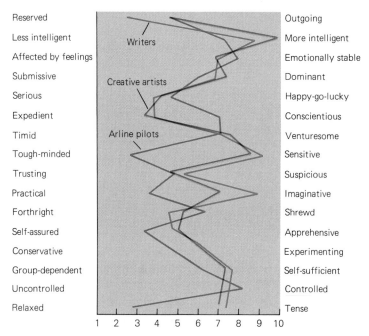

Reserved		Outgoing
Less intelligent	Writers	More intelligent
Affected by feelings		Emotionally stable
Submissive	Creative artists	Dominant
Serious		Happy-go-lucky
Expedient		Conscientious
Timid	Arline pilots	Venturesome
Tough-minded		Sensitive
Trusting		Suspicious
Practical		Imaginative
Forthright		Shrewd
Self-assured		Apprehensive
Conservative		Experimenting
Group-dependent		Self-sufficient
Uncontrolled		Controlled
Relaxed		Tense

1 2 3 4 5 6 7 8 9 10

FIGURE 9-2
Personality profiles for source traits developed by Cattell for three groups of subjects: airline pilots, creative artists, and writers. The average score for the general population is between 4.5 and 6.5 on each scale. (Adapted from Cattell, Ebver, & Tatsuoka, 1970. Copyright © 1970 by the Institute for Personality and Ability Testing. Reproduced by permission.)

ing these source traits, he developed the Sixteen Personality Factor Questionnaire, or 16 PF, a measure that provides scores for each of the source traits. Figure 9-2 shows the pattern of average scores on each of the source traits for three different groups of subjects—airplane pilots, creative artists, and writers.

Another trait theorist, psychologist Hans Eysenck (Eysenck & Eysenck, 1975, 1985), also used factor analysis to identify patterns within traits, but he came to a very different conclusion about the nature of personality. He found that personality could best be described in terms of just two major dimensions: **introversion-extroversion** and **neuroticism-stability**. On the one extreme of the introversion-extroversion dimension are people who are quiet, careful, thoughtful, and restrained (the introverts), and on the other are those who are outgoing, sociable, and active (the extroverts). Independent of that, people can be rated as neurotic (moody, touchy, sensitive) versus stable (calm, reliable, even-tempered). By evaluating people along these two dimensions, Eysenck has been able to make accurate predictions of behavior in a number of situations (see Figure 9-3).

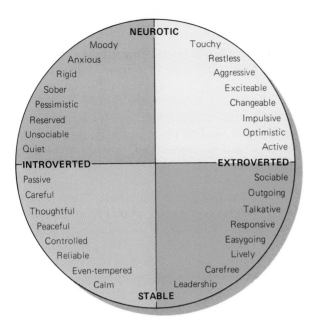

FIGURE 9-3
According to Eysenck, personality can be viewed as
lying along two major dimensions: introversion-
extroversion and neuroticism-stability. Other personality characteristics can be ordered along the circular figure depicted here. (Eysenck, 1973.)

Still other theorists, also using factor analysis, have produced trait
models that encompass anywhere from three to seven primary dimensions. For example, one study determined that five major factors produce
the optimal description of personality: sociability, activity, impulsivity,
socialization (autonomy versus conformity), and emotionality (Zuckerman, Kuhlman & Camac, 1988). However, the specific number and kinds
of traits remain a source of heated debate among trait theorists.

**Which theorist's traits are the right ones? Evaluating trait theories
of personality.** Trait theories have several virtues. They provide a clear,
straightforward explanation of people's behavioral consistencies. Furthermore, traits allow us to readily compare one person with another.
Because of these advantages, trait conceptions of personality have had an
important practical influence on the development of several personality
measures that we discuss later in the chapter.

On the other hand, trait theories have several drawbacks. For example, we have seen that trait theories describing personality come to quite
different conclusions about which traits are the most fundamental and
descriptive. The difficulty in determining which of the theories is most

accurate has led many psychologists to question the validity of trait conceptions of personality in general.

Actually, there is an even more fundamental difficulty with trait approaches. Even if we are able to identify a set of primary traits, we are left with little more than a label or description of personality—rather than an explanation of behavior. If we say that someone donates money to charity because he or she has the trait of generosity, we still do not know *why* the person became generous in the first place, or the reasons for displaying generosity in a given situation. Traits, then, provide nothing in the way of explanations of behavior; they are merely descriptive labels.

Is personality a myth?: Personality versus situational factors. Perhaps the biggest problem with trait conceptions is one that is fundamental to the entire area of personality: Is behavior really as consistent over different situations as trait conceptions would imply? How, for instance, would a trait theorist explain Frank Costello's behavior described at the beginning of this chapter? Trying to answer this question has provided personality theory with one of its most vexing and controversial problems.

When personality psychologist Walter Mischel began to review the literature on the strength of the relationship between people's personality traits and their behavior in the late 1960s, he found a curious situation: Broad personality traits could be used to explain only a minor, insignificant portion of behavior. Instead, it seemed to Mischel that most behavior could be explained primarily by the nature of the situation in which the people found themselves—not by their personalities (Mischel, 1968).

Mischel's views fanned the flames of a raging controversy that continues to be one of the major issues dividing personality theorists: the degree to which people's behavior is caused by personality versus situational factors. On one side of the controversy are traditional personality theorists who argue that traits, if measured appropriately, provide a valid explanation of behavior across diverse situations. For instance, Seymour Epstein argued that it is necessary to consider behavior over repeated settings and times to get a true picture of the degree of consistency displayed. When this was done—a group of subjects were repeatedly assessed over a period of months—there were strong indications of consistency, contrary to Mischel's suggestions (Epstein & O'Brien, 1985; Epstein, 1990).

In response, Mischel has argued that even though his critics may have demonstrated consistency over time, they have not shown consistency over situations. For instance, an office supervisor may be verbally aggressive toward her staff day in and day out, thereby showing consistency over time, but may not be verbally aggressive toward her boss—demonstrating *in*consistency over situations. It is this inconsistency across situations that makes personality-trait approaches suspect to Mischel (Mischel & Peake, 1982, 1983; Mischel, 1990).

Although the controversy shows little indication of abating, several important facts have emerged as a result of it (Kenrick & Funder, 1988). Trait ratings are most accurate when they are done by raters who are thoroughly familiar with the person being rated, when multiple ratings and multiple raters are used, and when the observed behavior is directly relevant to the trait in question. On the other hand, lower accuracy is apt to be obtained in situations in which only one sample of behavior is observed or in which powerful forces are pushing an individual toward certain behavior. Thus, when a sergeant orders a private to peel potatoes, the subsequent behavior could hardly be viewed as an indication of a trait relating to the private's culinary interest.

The controversy has also led personality theorists to focus more directly on the nature of person-situation interactions—how the specific characteristics of a situation will influence the behavior of an individual with a specific type of personality (Magnusson & Endler, 1977). By considering such person-situation interactions, personality psychologists are developing a more accurate portrait of the role of personality in the particular situations and environments that are part of people's everyday lives (Kenrick & Funder, 1988). Still, the final chapter in the controversy over the consistency of behavior across situations has yet to be written.

Explaining the Outer Life, Disregarding the Inner Life: Learning Theories of Personality

Whereas psychoanalytic and trait theories concentrate on the inner person—the stormy fury of an unobservable but powerful id or a hypothetical but critical set of traits—learning theories of personality focus on the outer person. In fact, to a strict learning theorist, personality is simply the sum of learned responses to the external environment. Internal events such as thoughts, feelings, and motivations are ignored; though their existence is not denied, learning theorists say that personality is best understood by looking at features of a person's environment.

According to the most influential of the learning theorists, B. F. Skinner (whom we mentioned first in discussing operant conditioning in Chapter 4), personality is a collection of learned behavior patterns (Skinner, 1975). Similarities in responses across different situations are caused by similar patterns of reinforcement that have been received in such situations in the past. If I am sociable both at parties and at meetings, it is because I have been reinforced previously for displaying social behaviors—not because I am fulfilling some unconscious wish based on experiences during my childhood or because I have an internal trait of sociability.

Strict learning theorists, such as Skinner was, are less interested in the consistencies in behavior across situations, however, than in ways of modifying behavior. In fact, their view is that humans are infinitely changeable; if one is able to control and modify the patterns of reinforcers in a situation, behavior that other theorists would view as stable and unyielding can be changed and ultimately improved. Learning theorists are optimistic in their attitudes about the potential for resolving personal and societal problems through treatment strategies based on learning theory—methods we will discuss further in Chapter 10.

Where Freud meets Skinner: Dollard and Miller's stimulus-response theory. Not all learning theories of personality take such a strict view in rejecting the importance of what is "inside" the person by focusing solely on the "outside." John Dollard and Neal Miller (1950) are two theorists who tried to meld psychoanalytic notions with traditional stimulus-response learning theory in an ambitious and influential explanation of personality.

Dollard and Miller translated Freud's notion of the pleasure principle—trying to maximize one's pleasure and minimize one's pain—into terms more suitable for learning theory by suggesting that both biological *and* learned drives energize an organism. If the consequence of a particular behavior is a reduction in drive, the drive reduction is viewed as reinforcing. This in turn increases the probability of the behavior occurring again in the future.

According to Dollard and Miller, the Freudian notion of repression, in which anxiety-producing thoughts are pushed into the unconscious through innate processes, can be looked at instead as an example of "learned not-thinking." Suppose the thought of sexual intercourse makes you anxious. Freud might propose that you deal with the anxiety by avoiding conscious thought about intercourse and instead relegating the idea to your unconscious—that is, by repressing the thought, where repression is an unlearned phenomenon. In contrast, Dollard and Miller might suggest that "not thinking" about the topic will become reinforcing to you because you find that doing so leads to a reduction in the unpleasant state of anxiety that thinking about the topic evokes. "Not thinking," then, will become an increasingly likely behavior.

Where the inner person meets the outer one: Social learning theories of personality. Unlike other learning theories of personality, **social learning theory** emphasizes the influence of a person's thoughts, feelings, expectations, and values in determining personality. According to Albert Bandura, the main proponent of this point of view, people are able to foresee the possible outcomes of certain behaviors in a given setting without actually having to carry them out. This takes place mainly through the mechanism of **observational learning**—viewing the actions of others and observing the consequences (Bandura, 1977).

For instance, as we first discussed in Chapter 4, children who view a model behaving in, say, an aggressive manner tend to copy the behavior if the consequences of the model's behavior are seen to be positive. If, on the other hand, the model's aggressive behavior has resulted in no consequences or negative consequences, children are considerably less likely to act aggressively. According to social learning theory, personality thus is developed by repeated observation of others' behavior.

More than other learning theories, social learning theory considers how we can modify our own personalities through the exercise of self-reinforcement. We are constantly judging our own behavior on the basis of our internal expectations and standards and then providing ourselves with cognitive rewards or punishments. For instance, a person who cheats on her income tax may mentally punish herself, feeling guilty and displeased with herself. If, just before mailing her tax return, she corrects her "mistake," the positive feelings she will experience will be rewarding and will serve to reinforce her view of herself as a law-abiding citizen.

Social learning theories are also distinct in the emphasis they place on the reciprocity between individuals and their environment. Not only is the environment assumed to affect personality, but people's behavior and personalities are assumed to "feed back" and modify the environment—which in turn affects behavior (Bandura, 1981).

Evaluating learning theories of personality. By ignoring the internal processes that are uniquely human, traditional learning theorists such as Skinner have been accused of oversimplifying personality so much that the concept becomes meaningless. In fact, reducing behavior to a series of stimuli and responses, and excluding thoughts and feelings from the realm of personality, leaves behaviorists practicing an unrealistic and inadequate form of science, at least in the eyes of their critics.

Of course, some of these criticisms are blunted by social learning theory, which explicitly considers the role of cognitive processes in personality. Still, all learning theories share a highly **deterministic** view of human behavior, a view maintaining that behavior is shaped primarily by forces outside the control of the individual. In the eyes of some critics, determinism disregards the ability of people to pilot their own course through life.

On the other hand, learning approaches have had a major impact in a variety of ways. For one thing, they have helped make the study of personality an objective, scientific venture by focusing on observable features of people and the environments in which they live. Beyond this, learning theories have produced important, successful means of treating personality disorders. The degree of success these treatments have enjoyed provides confidence that learning theory approaches have merit.

Understanding the Self: Humanistic Theories of Personality

Where, in all these theories of personality, is an explanation for the saintliness of a Mother Teresa, the creativity of a Michelangelo, the brilliance and perseverance of an Einstein? An understanding of such unique in-

Mother Teresa's selflessness can be explained by humanistic theories of personality.

dividuals—as well as more ordinary sorts of people who share some of the same attributes—comes from humanistic theory.

According to humanistic theorists, the theories of personality that we have discussed share a fundamental error in their views of human nature. Instead of seeing people as controlled by unconscious, unseen forces (as does psychoanalytic theory), a set of stable traits (trait theory), or situational reinforcements (learning theory), **humanistic theory** emphasizes people's basic goodness and their tendency to grow to higher levels of functioning. It is this conscious, self-motivated ability to change and improve, along with people's unique creative impulses, that make up the core of personality.

The major representative of the humanistic point of view is Carl Rogers (1971). Rogers suggests that people have a need for positive regard that reflects a universal requirement to be loved and respected. Because others provide this positive regard, we grow dependent on them. We begin to see and judge ourselves through the eyes of other people, relying on their values.

According to Rogers, one outgrowth of placing import on the values of others is that there is often some degree of mismatch between a person's experiences and his or her **self-concept**, or self-impression. If the discrepancy is minor, so are the consequences. But if it is great, it will lead to psychological disturbances in daily functioning, such as the experience of frequent anxiety.

Rogers suggests that one way of overcoming the discrepancy between experience and self-concept is through the receipt of unconditional positive regard from others—a friend, a spouse, or a therapist. As we will discuss further in Chapter 11, **unconditional positive regard** consists of supportive behavior on the part of an observer, no matter what a person says or does. This support, says Rogers, allows people the opportunity to evolve and grow both cognitively and emotionally as they are able to develop more realistic self-concepts.

To Rogers and other humanistic personality theorists (such as Abraham Maslow, whose theory of motivation we discussed in Chapter 6), an ultimate goal of personality growth is **self-actualization**. Self-actualization is a state of self-fulfillment in which people realize their highest potential: This, Rogers would argue, occurs when their experience with the world and their self-concept are closely matched. People who are self-actualized accept themselves as they are in reality, which enables them to achieve happiness and fulfillment.

Evaluating humanistic theories. Although humanistic theories suggest the value of providing unconditional positive regard toward people, unconditional positive regard toward humanistic theories has been less forthcoming from many personality theorists. The criticisms have centered on the difficulty of verifying the basic assumptions of the theory, as well as on the question of whether unconditional positive regard does, in fact, lead to greater personality adjustment.

Humanistic approaches have also been criticized for making the assumption that people are basically "good"—a notion which is unverifiable and, equally important, one in which nonscientific values are used to build supposedly scientific theories. Still, humanistic theories have been important in highlighting the uniqueness of human beings and in guiding the development of a significant form of therapy designed to alleviate psychological difficulties.

Answering the Enduring Question: Which Theory Is Right?

By now, you have come across the question of which theory is right a number of times in connection with psychology. The response, once again, is the same: This is not the most appropriate question to be asking. Each theory looks at somewhat different aspects of personality and holds different premises, and in many cases personality is most reasonably viewed from a number of perspectives simultaneously. Of course, the potential exists that someday there will be a unified theory of personality, but the field has not yet reached that point, and the likelihood of its happening in the near future is slim.

In the meantime, it is possible to highlight and compare the major differences between each of the theories. Listed below are the most important dimensions along which the theories differ:

- The unconscious versus the conscious. Psychoanalytic theory emphasizes the importance of the unconscious; humanistic theory stresses the conscious; and trait and learning theories largely disregard both.
- Nature (genetic factors) versus nurture (environmental factors). Psychoanalytic theory stresses genetic factors; learning theory focuses on the environment; trait theory varies; and humanistic theory stresses the interaction between both in the development of personality.
- Freedom versus determinism. Humanistic theories stress the freedom of individuals to make choices in their lives; other theories stress determinism, the view that behavior is directed and caused by factors outside people's willful control. Determinism is particularly evident in psychoanalytic and learning theories, as well as in most trait theories; in such approaches, people's behavior is assumed to be brought about by factors largely outside their control.
- Stability versus modifiability of personality characteristics. Psychoanalytic and trait theories emphasize the stability of characteristics across a person's life; learning and humanistic theories stress that personality remains flexible and resilient throughout the life span.
- Nomothetic versus idiographic approaches. **Nomothetic** approaches to personality accentuate the broad uniformities across behavior, whereas **idiographic** approaches to personality emphasize what makes one person unique—different from all others. Although each of the theories contains nomothetic and idiographic aspects, psychoanalytic theory, which posits broad developmental stages, and trait theory, which searches for universal characteristics, are more closely allied to nomothetic approaches than the others. Learning theory and humanistic theory are more idiographic, stressing the consequences of a person's particular background and environment on personality.

*A*SK YOURSELF

What do trait theories attempt to do?

What are the principal traits according to Allport, Cattell, and Eysenck?

How do learning theories explain personality?

In what way do humanistic theories view personality?

What are the major dimensions along which personality theories differ?

Think about a trait you use to describe yourself. How consistently does it show itself, and in what situations might you act differently or even in opposition to the trait?

Do different theories of personality really contradict one another, or is it possible that the various theorists are often just using different levels of analysis or focusing on different aspects of human behavior?

DETERMINING WHAT MAKES YOU SPECIAL: ASSESSING PERSONALITY

You have a need for other people to like and admire you.

You have a tendency to be critical of yourself.

You have a great deal of unused potential that you have not turned to your advantage.

Although you have some personality weaknesses, you are generally able to compensate for them.

Your adjustment to the opposite sex has presented problems to you.

More disciplined and self-controlled outside, you tend to be worrisome and insecure inside.

At times you have serious doubts as to whether you have made the right decision or done the right thing.

You prefer a certain amount of change and variety and become dissatisfied when hemmed in by restrictions and limitations.

You do not accept others' statements without satisfactory proof.

You have found it unwise to be too frank in revealing yourself to others.

If you think these statements provide a surprisingly accurate account of your personality, you are not alone: Most college students think that the statements are tailored just to them. In fact, though, the descriptions are intentionally designed to be so vague as to be applicable to just about anyone (Forer, 1949; Russo, 1981).

The ease with which we can agree with such imprecise statements underscores the difficulty in coming up with accurate and meaningful assessments of people's personalities (Johnson, Cain, Falke, Hayman & Perillo, 1985). Just as trait theorists were faced with the problem of determining the most critical and important traits, psychologists interested in assessing personality must be able to define the most meaningful measures of discriminating between one person's personality and another's. To do this, they use **psychological tests**, standard measures devised to assess behavior objectively. Such tests are used by psychologists to help people make decisions about their lives and understand more about themselves; they are also employed by researchers interested in the causes and consequences of personality.

The Keys to Personality Assessment: Reliability and Validity

When we use a ruler, we expect to find that it measures an inch in the same way as the last time we used it. When we weigh ourselves on the bathroom scale, we hope that the variations we see on the scale are due to changes in our weight and are not errors on the part of the scale (unless the change in weight is in an unwanted direction!).

In the same way, we hope that psychological tests have **reliability**— that they measure what they are trying to measure consistently. We need to be sure that each time we administer the test, a person taking the test will get the same results—assuming that nothing about the person has changed relevant to what is being measured.

Suppose, for instance, that when you first took the College Board exams you scored a 300 on the verbal section of the test. Then, when taking the test again a few months later, you scored a 700. Upon receiving your new score, you might well stop celebrating for a moment to question whether the test is reliable, since it is unlikely that your abilities could have changed enough to raise your score by 400 points.

But suppose your score changed hardly at all, and both times you received a score of about 300. Though you couldn't complain about a lack of reliability, if you knew your verbal skills were above average you might be concerned that the test did not adequately measure what it was supposed to measure. The question has now become one of validity rather than of reliability. A test has **validity** when it actually measures what it is supposed to measure.

Knowing that a test is reliable is no guarantee that it is also valid. For instance, we could devise a very reliable means for measuring the circumference of the skull, if we decided that skull size is related to trustworthiness. But there is certainly no guarantee that the test is valid, since one can assume with little danger of being contradicted that skull size has nothing to do with trustworthiness. In this case, then, we have reliability without validity.

On the other hand, if a test is unreliable, it cannot be valid. Assuming that all other factors—a person's motivation, knowledge of the material, health, and so forth—are similar, if someone scores high the first time she takes a specific test and low the second time, the test cannot be measuring what it is supposed to measure, and is therefore both unreliable and not valid.

Test validity and reliability are prerequisites for accurate personality assessment—as well as for any other measurement task carried out by psychologists. Thus the intelligence tests that we discuss later in this chapter, clinical psychologists' assessments of psychological disorders that we will consider in Chapters 10 and 11, and social psychologists' measures of attitudes must meet the tests of validity and reliability in order for the results to be meaningful. We turn now to some of the specific sorts of measures used by psychologists in their study of personality.

Asking a Little to Learn Much: Self-Report Measures of Personality

If someone wanted to assess your personality, one useful method would be to carry out an extensive interview with you in order to determine the most important events of your childhood, your social relationships, and your successes and failures. Obviously, though, such a technique would be extraordinarily costly in terms of time and effort.

It is also unnecessary. Just as physicians do not need to drain your entire blood supply in order to test it, psychologists can utilize **self-report measures** that ask people about a relatively small sample of their behavior. This sampling of self-reports is then used to infer the presence of particular personality characteristics.

One of the best examples of a self-report measure, and the most frequently used personality test, is the **Minnesota Multiphasic Personality Inventory-2 (MMPI-2)**, developed by a group of researchers in the 1940s and recently revised (Hathaway & McKinley, 1989). Although the original purpose of the measure was to differentiate people with specific sorts of psychological difficulties from those without disturbances, it has been found to predict a variety of other behaviors. For instance, MMPI scores have been shown to be good predictors of whether college students will marry within ten years and whether they will get an advanced degree (Dworkin & Widom, 1977). Police departments use the test to measure whether police officers are prone to use their weapons. The Soviets even administer a modified form of the MMPI to their cosmonauts and Olympic athletes (Holden, 1986).

The test itself consists of a series of 567 items to which a person responds "true," "false," or "cannot say." The questions cover a variety of issues, ranging from mood ("I feel useless at times") to opinions ("people should try to understand their dreams") to physical and psychological health ("I am bothered by an upset stomach several times a week" and "I have strange and peculiar thoughts"). There are no right or wrong answers, of course. Instead, interpretation of the results rests on the pattern of responses. The test yields scores on ten separate scales (see Figure 9-4) plus three scales meant to measure the validity of the respondent's answers. For example, there is a "lie scale" that indicates (from items such

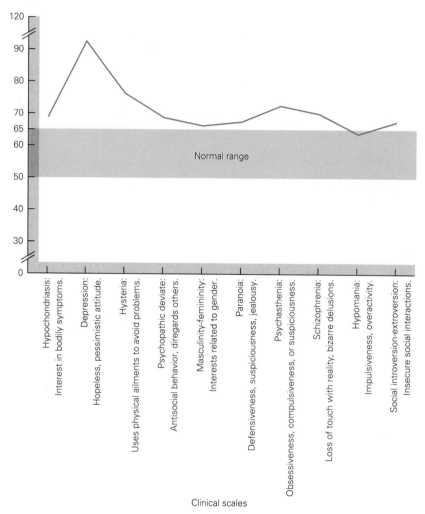

FIGURE 9-4
A sample profile on the MMPI-2 of a person who has been diagnosed as suffering from severe depression.

as "I can't remember ever having a bad night's sleep") when people are falsifying their responses in order to present themselves more favorably.

How did the authors of the MMPI know what specific patterns of responses indicate? The procedure they used is typical of personality test construction—a process known as test standardization. To devise the test, groups of psychiatric patients with a specific diagnosis, such as depression or schizophrenia, were asked to complete a large number of items. The test authors then determined which items best differentiated members of these groups from a comparison group of normal subjects, and these specific items were included in the final version of the test. By systematically carrying out this procedure on groups with different diagnoses, the test authors were able to devise a number of subscales which identified different forms of abnormal behavior.

As with any test standardization procedure, it was necessary for the MMPI authors to establish **norms**, standards of test performance. To develop a norm, test designers calculate the average score, and also establish the amount and nature of scores that differ from the norm. Test takers are then able to consider the meaning of their raw scores relative to the scores of others who have taken the test, giving them a qualitative sense of their performance.

When the MMPI is used for the purposes for which it was devised— identification of personality disorders—it has proved to do a reasonably good job (Graham, 1990). However, like other personality tests, it presents the opportunity for abuse. For instance, employers who use it as a screening tool for job applicants may interpret the results improperly, relying too heavily on the results of individual scales instead of taking into account the overall patterns of results, which require skilled interpretation. Other tests, such as the California Psychological Inventory and the Edwards Personal Preference Schedule are more appropriately used for screening job applicants, as well as for providing people with information about their personalities to help them make informed career choices and to identify their strengths and weaknesses (see the Psychology and Society box).

Looking Into the Unconscious: Projective Methods

If you were shown the kind of inkblot presented in Figure 9-5 and asked what it represented to you, you might not think that your impressions would mean very much. But to a psychoanalytic theoretician, your responses to such an ambiguous figure would provide valuable clues to the state of your unconscious, and ultimately to your general personality characteristics (Lerner, 1990).

The inkblot in the figure is representative of **projective personality tests**, in which a person is shown an ambiguous stimulus and asked to describe it or tell a story about it. The responses are then considered to be "projections" of what the person is like.

The best-known projective test is the **Rorschach test**. Devised by Swiss psychiatrist Hermann Rorschach (1924), the test consists of showing a series of symmetrical stimuli, similar to the one in Figure 9-5, to people who are then asked what the figures represent to them. Their responses are recorded, and through a complex set of clinical judgments on the part of the examiner, people are classified into different personality types. For instance, respondents who see a bear in one inkblot are thought to have a strong degree of emotional control, according to the rules developed by Rorschach.

PSYCHOLOGY AND SOCIETY

Can You Pass the Job Personality Test?

Wanted: *People with "kinetic energy," "emotional maturity" and the ability to "deal with large numbers of people in a fairly chaotic situation."*

This job description may seem as if it specifies qualities required for a co-host of *Wheel of Fortune*. In actuality, American MultiCinema (AMC), one of the major movie theater chains in America, was searching for candidates who possessed such skills to manage its theaters (Dentzer, 1986). To find them, AMC developed a battery of personality measures for aspiring job applicants to complete. In developing its tests, AMC joined scores of companies, ranging from General Motors to J. C. Penney, which employ personality tests to help determine who gets hired and, once on the job, who gets promoted or even who gets fired.

Companies in the United States now spend about $50 million a year on testing procedures, and the amount is rising annually (Tuller, 1985). One reason for the growth of such tests is computerization. Before the advent of inexpensive microcomputers, many companies had to send test responses to a central scoring facility, waiting as long as two weeks for results. Today, however, scores can be determined immediately through computerized scoring procedures, aiding in timely decision making.

An even more important factor in the growth of testing has been the development of more sophisticated, valid, and bias-free tests (Fuchsberg, 1990). For instance, a group of power companies devised a series of tests for a number of job categories. The companies now have specific tests to measure decision-making capability for systems operators, mechanical aptitude for maintenance workers, and language skills

for clerical positions. The power companies have estimated that they are saving at least $20 million per year because of the improvement in employee selection procedures (Tuller, 1985).

The use of personality tests for employee selection is not without its potential dangers, however. For one thing, although personality tests may be good at predicting the abilities of large numbers of people, any one individual—particularly someone who has difficulties performing well on standardized tests—may not receive an adequate assessment of his or her abilities. Furthermore, no single test, by itself, gives a complete picture of the range of skills, traits, and abilities a person may have (Angleitner & Wiggins, 1986). Finally, it is difficult to construct a test that is both reliable and valid, and tests designed by nonexperts may be worse than no test at all.

A more controversial use of employment assessment has come in the form of "integrity tests." These tests are designed to predict the honesty of employees, weeding out those who are likely to steal goods or cheat their employer in some manner. The controversy arises not only because the validity of the tests has yet to be established, but also because between 40 and 60 percent of people who are identified by such tests as likely to be dishonest are, in fact, honest employees (Office of Technology Assessment, 1990). Consequently, substantial numbers of honest workers may be unable to get jobs because of the tests' deficiencies.

Despite their potential shortcomings, the use of personality tests is on the rise in employment settings (Sweetland & Keyser, 1988). Given their increasing use, you should not be surprised if the first thing you are given when you apply for a new job is not a traditional job interview, but a personality test.

FIGURE 9-5
This inkblot is similar to the type used in the Rorschach personality test. What do *you* see in it?

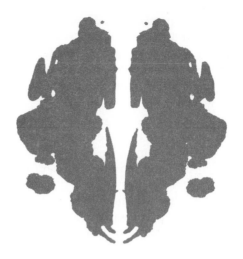

The **Thematic Apperception Test (TAT)** is another well-known projective test. As noted when we discussed achievement motivation in Chapter 6, the TAT consists of a series of pictures about which a person is asked to write a story. The stories are then used to draw inferences about the writer's personality characteristics.

By definition, tests with stimuli as ambiguous as the Rorschach and TAT require particular skill and care in their interpretation. In fact, they are often criticized as requiring too much inference on the part of the examiner. However, they are widely used, particularly in clinical settings, and their proponents suggest that their reliability and validity are high.

The Informed Consumer of Psychology: Assessing Personality Assessments

It is not unusual today to be required to take a personality test before being offered a job. Likewise, there are many organizations which—for a hefty fee—will give you a battery of personality tests that purport to steer you toward a career for which your personality is particularly suited.

Before you rely on the results of such testing too heavily—as a potential employee, employer, or consumer of testing services—you should keep the following points in mind:

- Understand what the test purports to measure. Standard personality measures are accompanied by information that discusses how the test was developed, to whom it is most applicable, and how the results should be interpreted. If possible, you should read the accompanying literature; it will help you understand the meaning of any results.

- Remember that decisions should not be based solely on the results of any one test. Test results should be interpreted in the context of other information—academic records, social interests, and home and community activities. Without these data, individual scores are relatively uninformative at best and may even be harmful.

- Tests are not infallible. The results may be in error; the test may be unreliable or invalid; you may have had a "bad day" when you took the test; the person scoring and interpreting the test may have made a mistake. You should not place undue stock in the results of the single administration of any test.

In sum, it is important to keep in mind the complexity of human behavior—particularly your own. No one test can provide an understanding of the intricacies of someone's personality without considering a good deal more information than can be provided in a single testing session.

*A*SK YOURSELF

What makes a psychological test reliable and valid?

How do self-reports measure personality?

What are projective personality tests?

How is behavioral assessment used to measure personality?

*I*NTELLIGENCE

It is typical for members of the Trukese tribe, a small Micronesian society, to sail a hundred miles in open ocean waters. Although their destination may be just a small dot of land less than a mile across, the Trukese are able to sail unerringly toward it—without the aid of compass, chronometer, sextant, or any of the other sailing tools that are at the heart of modern western navigation. They are able to sail accurately even when prevailing winds do not allow a direct approach to the island and they must take a zigzag course (Gladwin, 1964).

How are the Trukese able to navigate so effectively? If you ask them, they could not explain it. They might tell you that they use a process that takes into account the rising and setting of the stars and the appearance, sound, and feeling of the waves against the side of the boat. But at any given moment as they are sailing along, they could not identify their position or say why they are doing what they are doing. Nor could they explain the navigational theory underlying their sailing technique.

Some might say the inability of the Trukese to explain how their sailing technique works is a sign of primitive and even unintelligent behavior. In fact, if we made Trukese sailors take a standardized western test of

The flawless Trukese navigational techniques, although primitive by western standards, are indicative of intelligence that is not easily measured on traditional intelligence tests.

navigational knowledge and theory, or for that matter a traditional test of intelligence, they might very well do poorly on it. Yet, as a practical matter, it is hard to accuse the Trukese of being unintelligent: Despite their inability to explain how they do so, they are able to navigate successfully through the open ocean waters.

The way in which the Trukese navigate points out the difficulty in coming to grips with what is meant by intelligence. To a westerner, traveling in a straight line along the most direct and quickest route using a sextant and other navigational tools would likely represent the most "intelligent" kind of behavior; a zigzag course, based on the "feel" of the waves, would not seem very reasonable. To the Trukese, however, who are used to their own system of navigation, the use of complicated navigational tools might well seem so overly complex and unnecessary that they might think of western navigators as lacking in intelligence.

It is clear that the term "intelligence" can take on many different meanings. If, for instance, you lived in a remote African village, the way you differentiate between more intelligent and less intelligent people might be unlike the way someone living in the middle of New York City would distinguish individual differences. To the African, high intelligence might be represented by extraordinary hunting or other survival skills; to the New Yorker, it might be exemplified by dealing effectively with a mass-transit system, by achieving success as a member of a high-salaried, prestigious profession, or by getting good grades at a rigorous private school.

In fact, each of these conceptions of intelligence is reasonable, for each represents an instance in which more intelligent people are better able to use the resources of their environment than are less intelligent people, a distinction that we would assume to be basic to any definition of intelligence. Yet it is also clear that these conceptions represent very different views of intelligence.

That two such different sets of behavior can exemplify the same psychological concept has proved to be a problem to psychologists. They have long grappled with the issue of devising a general definition of intelligence that would remain independent of a person's specific culture and other environmental factors. Interestingly, untrained laypersons have fairly clear conceptions of intelligence (Sternberg, 1985b). For example, in one survey that asked a group of people to define what they meant by intelligence, three major components of intelligence emerged (Sternberg, Conway, Ketron & Bernstein, 1981). First, there was problem-solving ability: People who reason logically and identify more solutions to problems were seen as intelligent. Second, verbal abilities were thought to exemplify intelligence. Finally, intelligence was assumed to be indicated by social competence: the ability to show interest in others and interact effectively with them.

The definition of intelligence that psychologists employ is more focused, although it contains many of the same elements contained in the layperson's conception. To psychologists, **intelligence** is the capacity to understand the world, think with rationality, and use resources effectively when faced with challenges (Wechsler, 1975).

Unfortunately, neither the layperson's nor the psychologist's conception of intelligence is much help when it comes to distinguishing, with any degree of precision, more intelligent people from less intelligent ones. To overcome this problem, psychologists interested in intelligence have focused much of their attention on the development of batteries of tests, known, quite appropriately, as **intelligence tests**, and have relied on such tests to identify a person's level of intelligence. These tests have proved to be of great benefit in identifying students in need of special attention in school, in diagnosing cognitive difficulties, and in helping people make optimal educational and vocational choices. At the same time, their use has proved quite controversial.

Separating the Intelligent from the Unintelligent: Measuring Intelligence

The first intelligence tests followed a simple premise: If performance on certain tasks or test items improved with age, then performance could be used to distinguish more intelligent people from less intelligent ones within a particular age group. Using this principle, Alfred Binet, a French psychologist, devised the first formal intelligence test, which was de-

The French psychologist Alfred Binet developed the first intelligence test.

signed to identify the "dullest" students in the Paris school system in order to provide them with remedial aid.

Binet began by presenting tasks to same-age students who had been labeled "bright" or "dull" by their teachers. If a task could be completed by the bright students but not by the dull ones, he retained the task as a proper test item; otherwise it was discarded. In the end he came up with a test that distinguished between the bright and dull groups, and—with further work—one that distinguished among children in different age groups (Binet & Simon, 1916).

On the basis of the Binet test, children were assigned a score that corresponded to their **mental age**, the average age of children taking the test who achieved the same score. For example, if a 10-year-old boy received a score of 45 on the test and this was the average score received by 8-year-olds, his mental age would be considered to be 8 years. Similarly, a 14-year-old girl who scored an 88 on the test—matching the mean score for 16-year-olds—would be assigned a mental age of 16 years.

Although assigning a mental age to students provided an indication of whether they were performing at the same level as their peers, it did not allow for adequate comparisons among people of different physical, or **chronological ages**. By using mental age alone, for instance, we would assume that an 18-year-old responding at a 16-year-old's level would be as bright as a 5-year-old answering at a 3-year-old's level, when actually the 5-year-old would be displaying a much greater *relative* degree of slowness.

To resolve this concern, psychologists developed the **intelligence quotient**, or **IQ score**, a measure of intelligence that takes into account an individual's mental *and* chronological ages. To calculate an IQ score, the following formula is used, in which MA stands for mental age and CA for chronological age: ＇

$$\text{IQ score} = \frac{\text{MA}}{\text{CA}} \times 100$$

Using this formula, we can return to the earlier example of an 18-year-old performing at a mental age of 16 and calculate an IQ score of (16 ÷ 18) × 100 = 88.9. In contrast, the 5-year-old performing at a mental age of 3 comes out with a considerably lower IQ score: (3 ÷ 5) × 100 = 60.

As a bit of trial and error with the formula will show you, anyone who has a mental age equal to his or her chronological age will have an IQ equal to 100. Moreover, people with a mental age that is greater than their chronological age will have IQs that exceed 100.

Although the basic principles behind the calculation of an IQ score still hold, IQ scores are figured in a somewhat different manner today and are known as **deviation IQ scores**. First, the average test score for everyone of the same age who takes the test is determined, and this average score is assigned an IQ of 100. Then, with the aid of mathematically sophisticated techniques, IQ values are assigned to other test scores for the age group on the basis of how much the test score deviates from the average for that group.

As you can see in Figure 9-6, approximately two-thirds of all individuals fall within 15 IQ points of the average score of 100. As scores increase or fall beyond that range, the percentage of people in a category falls considerably.

Measuring IQ: Stanford-Binet, Wechsler, et al.

Just what is an IQ test like? It is probable that sometime during your academic career you have taken one; almost all of us are given IQ tests at one time or another.

The original test is still with us, although it has been revised many times and in its modern incarnation bears little resemblance to the original version. Now called the **Stanford-Binet test**, it was last revised in 1985 (Hagen, Sattler & Thorndike, 1985; Thorndike, Hagan & Sattler, 1986). The test consists of a series of items which vary in nature according to the age of the person being tested. For example, young children are asked to copy figures or answer questions about everyday activities. Older people are asked to solve analogies, explain proverbs, and describe similarities that underlie sets of words.

The test is administered orally. An examiner begins by finding a mental age level at which the person is able to answer all questions correctly and then moves on to successively difficult problems. When a mental age

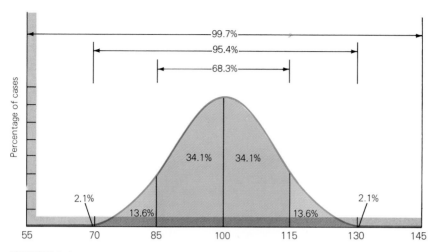

FIGURE 9-6
The average and most frequent IQ score is 100, and approximately 68 percent of all people are within a 30-point range centered on 100. Some 95 percent of the population have scores that are within 30 points above or below 100, and 99.7 percent have scores that are between 55 and 145.

level is reached at which no items can be answered, the test is over. By examining the pattern of correct and incorrect responses, the examiner is able to compute an IQ score for the person being tested.

The other IQ test frequently used in America was devised by psychologist David Wechsler and is known as the **Wechsler Adult Intelligence Scale—Revised**, or, more commonly, the **WAIS-R**. There is also a children's version, the **Wechsler Intelligence Scale for Children—Revised**, or **WISC-R**. Both the WAIS-R and the WISC-R have two major parts: a verbal scale and a performance—or nonverbal—scale. As you can see from the sample questions in Figure 9-7, the two scales include questions of very different types. Whereas verbal tasks consist of more traditional kinds of problems, including vocabulary definition and comprehension of various concepts, the nonverbal part consists of assembling small objects and arranging pictures in a logical order. Although an individual's scores on the verbal and performance sections of the test are generally close to each other, the scores of a person with a language deficiency or from a background of severe environmental deprivation may show a relatively large discrepancy. By providing separate scores, the WAIS-R and WISC-R give a more precise picture of a person's specific abilities.

Because the Stanford-Binet, WAIS-R, and WISC-R all require individualized administration, it is relatively difficult and time-consuming to administer and score them on a wide-scale basis. Consequently, there are now a number of IQ tests that allow for group administration (Anastasi, 1988). Rather than having one examiner ask one person at a time to re-

Verbal scale

Information
Where does milk come from?
Who invented the telephone?

Comprehension
Why do we put food in the refrigerator?
What should you do if you see a person leave his or her groceries on a bus?

Arithmetic
Stacey had two crayons and the teacher gave her two more. How many did
she have all together?
How long will it take a train traveling at 80 miles an hour to reach the
station 320 miles away?

Similarities
In what way are cows and horses alike?
In what way are rivers and roads the same?

Digit span
Repeat the following numbers: 5, 8, 2
Repeat the following numbers in reverse order: 3, 2, 9, 7, 4, 1, 4.

Vocabulary
What is a candle?
What does administer mean?

Performance scale

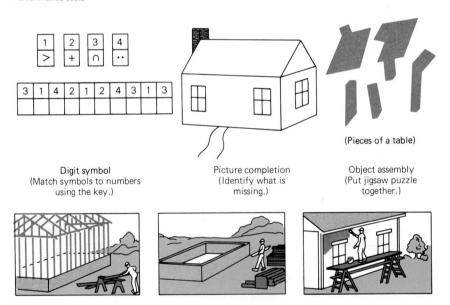

Digit symbol
(Match symbols to numbers
using the key.)

Picture completion
(Identify what is
missing.)

Object assembly
(Put jigsaw puzzle
together.)

Picture arrangement
(Arrange pictures to tell a logical story.)

FIGURE 9-7
Typical kinds of items found on the verbal and performance scales of the
Wechsler Intelligence Scale for Children (WISC-R).

spond to individual items, group IQ tests are strictly paper-and-pencil
measures, in which those taking the tests read the questions and provide
their answers in writing. The primary advantage of group tests is their
ease of administration.

There are, however, sacrifices made in group testing which, in some cases, may outweigh the benefits. For instance, group tests generally sample a narrower range of behaviors than tests administered individually. Furthermore, people may be more motivated to perform at their highest ability level when working on a one-to-one basis with a test administrator. Finally, in some cases, it is simply impossible to employ group tests, particularly with young children or people with unusually low IQs.

Achievement and aptitude tests. IQ tests are not the only kind of tests that you have taken during the course of your schooling. Two other kinds of tests related to intelligence but designed to measure somewhat different phenomena are achievement tests and aptitude tests. An **achievement test** is a test meant to ascertain the level of knowledge in a given subject area; rather than measuring general ability as an intelligence test does, an achievement test concentrates on the specifics of what a person has learned.

An **aptitude test** is designed to predict a person's ability in a particular area or line of work. You may have already taken the most famous aptitude test of them all: the Scholastic Aptitude Test, or SAT. The SAT is meant to predict how well people will do in college and has proved over the years to correlate very strongly with college grades.

Although in theory the distinction between intelligence, aptitude, and achievement tests can be precisely drawn, as a practical matter there is a good deal of overlap between them. For example, the SAT has been roundly criticized for being less of a predictive aptitude test than one that actually measures achievement. It is difficult, then, to devise tests that predict future performance but do not rely on past achievement.

IQ Tests Don't Tell All: Alternative Formulations of Intelligence

Although Binet's procedure for measuring intelligence, exemplified by the modern Stanford-Binet and WAIS-R intelligence tests, remains one of the most frequently employed, some theorists argue that it lacks an underlying conception of what intelligence is. To Binet and his followers, intelligence was generally conceived of as what his test measured. That was, and remains, an eminently practical approach, but it depends not on an understanding of the nature of intelligence but primarily on comparing one person's performance with that of others. For that reason, the intelligence test of Binet and his successors does little to increase our understanding of what intelligence is all about; it merely measures behavior that is assumed to exemplify intelligence.

This does not mean, however, that researchers and theoreticians have ignored the question of what intelligence really is. One important issue is whether intelligence is a single, unitary factor, or whether it is made up of particular subcomponents (Weinberg, 1989; Lohman, 1989). The earliest psychologists interested in intelligence made the assumption that there was a general factor for mental ability, called **g**, or the **g-factor** (Spearman, 1927). This factor was thought to underlie performance on every aspect of intelligence, and it was the g factor that was presumably being measured on tests of intelligence.

Contemporary theoreticians have suggested that there are really two different kinds of intelligence, as we first saw in Chapter 8: fluid intelligence and crystallized intelligence (Cattell, 1967, 1987). **Fluid intelligence** is the ability to deal with new problems and encounters. If you were asked to group a series of letters according to some criterion or to remember a set of numbers, you would be using fluid intelligence. **Crystallized intelligence** is the store of information, skills, and strategies that people have acquired through their use of fluid intelligence. You would likely rely on crystallized intelligence, for instance, if you were asked to solve a puzzle or deduce the solution to a mystery, drawing upon your past unique experience. The differences between fluid and crystallized intelligence become particularly evident in the elderly, who—as we noted in Chapter 8—show declines in fluid, but not crystallized, intelligence.

Other theoreticians divide intelligence into even more detailed subdivisions. For instance J. P. Guilford (1968, 1982) suggested that an even finer-grained analysis of intelligence was in order. In his **structure-of-intellect model**, Guilford provided the most detailed representation of human intelligence to date. On the basis of observations of people's performance on a wide variety of tasks, he proposed that there are 150 separate mental abilities underlying intelligence. These abilities could be sorted along three major dimensions: the content of a task (made up of five subdivisions), the requirements—called "operations"—involved in carrying out the task (made up of five subdivisions), and the product of the task (made up of six subdivisions).

Although such minute distinctions between different components of intelligence present difficulties in terms of reliable measurement, Guilford's model, as well as those of other theorists who propose that intelligence is multifaceted, has led to a number of advances in our understanding of the nature of intelligence. For example, one outgrowth of the models is the development of test items in which more than one answer can be correct, providing the opportunity for the demonstration of creative thinking. According to these approaches, then, different kinds of intelligence may produce contradictory—but equally valid—responses to the same question.

Is Information Processing Intelligence? Contemporary Approaches

The most recent contributions to understanding intelligence employ an information-processing approach, which assumes that the way people store material in memory and use the material to solve intellectual tasks provides the most accurate conception of intelligence. Rather than focusing on the structure of intelligence in the form of its subcomponents, cognitive approaches have examined the *processes* underlying intelligent behavior (Lohman, 1989).

By breaking tasks and problems into their component parts and identifying the nature and speed of problem-solving processes, researchers have noted distinct differences between those who score high on traditional IQ tests and those who score lower. Take, for example, a college student who is asked to solve the following analogy problem (Sternberg, 1982):

lawyer is to *client* as *doctor* is to:

(a) *patient* or **(b)** *medicine*

A student presented with this analogy tends to move through a series of stages in attempting to reach a solution (see Figure 9-8). First she will *encode* the initial information, which means providing each item with identifying cues that help retrieve relevant information buried in long-term memory. For instance, she may think of lawyer in terms of law school, the Supreme Court, L.A. Law, and a courtroom. Each of the other terms will be similarly encoded. Next, she will *infer* any possible relationship between lawyer and client. She may infer that the relevant relationship is that a client employs a lawyer, or alternatively, that a lawyer gives services to a client.

Once she has inferred the relationship, she must *map* the higher-order relationship between the first half of the analogy and the second half—both deal with people who provide professional services for a fee. The crucial stage that follows is one of *application*, in which she tries out each answer option with the relationship she has inferred. She will presumably decide that a doctor provides professional services to a patient, not to medicine. Finally, the last component of solving the problem is responding.

By breaking problems into component parts in this manner, it is possible to identify systematic differences in both quantitative and qualitative aspects of problem solving, and to demonstrate that people with higher intelligence levels differ not only in the number of correct solutions they come up with, but in their method of solving problems. For instance, high scorers are apt to spend more time on the initial encoding stages of a problem, identifying the parts of the problem and retrieving relevant information from long-term memory. This initial emphasis on recalling relevant information pays off in the end; those who spend relatively less time on the initial stages tend to be less able to find a solution. People's use of such information-processing abilities, therefore, may underlie the differences in intelligence.

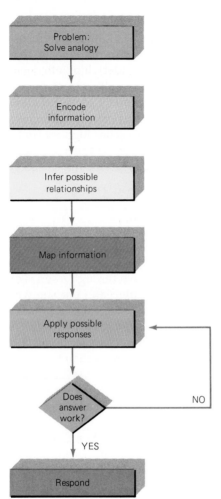

FIGURE 9-8
Information-processing stages in solving analogies. (Sternberg, 1982.)

Applying this cognitive approach to intelligence, psychologist Robert Sternberg (1985*b*) developed what he calls a triarchic theory of intelligence. The **triarchic theory of intelligence** suggests that there are three major aspects to intelligence: componential, experiential, and contextual. The componential aspect focuses on the mental components involved in analyzing information to solve problems, particularly those processes operating when a person displays intelligent behavior. In contrast, the experiential aspect focuses on how a person's prior experiences are related to intelligence and how those experiences are brought to bear on problem-solving situations. Finally, the contextual aspect of intelligence takes into account the success people experience in facing the demands of their everyday environment.

Recent approaches to intelligence have focused most heavily on Sternberg's third aspect of intelligence (Sternberg & Detterman, 1986). Several new theories emphasize **practical intelligence**—intelligence related to overall success in living, rather than to intellectual and academic performance (e.g., Epstein & Meier, 1989). These theories are designed to overcome one of the most glaring limitations of measures of intelligence based on traditional formulations of intelligence: Although literally hundreds of studies have shown that students with high IQs tend to get high grades and those with low IQs tend to be less successful in school, the fact remains that IQ does not relate to *career* success. Although only at the early stages of development, tests of practical intelligence may prove to have important applications in such fields as business.

ABOVE AND BELOW THE NORM: VARIATIONS IN INTELLECTUAL ABILITY

Bill never liked school all that much. For the first few years he managed to get by, although his parents had to push hard to get him to do a minimally acceptable level of first- and second-grade work. He always seemed slower at learning things that the other kids had no trouble with, and—while he wasn't exactly a poorly behaved child—his attention span was short and he had trouble following what was going on in class. He also seemed tired much of the time, but a physical examination ruled out any medical problems. His teachers began to suspect he was simply lazy and unmotivated, though he did, on occasion, show great interest in lessons that involved working with his hands. Finally, out of desperation, his teachers and parents arranged for him to be evaluated by a psychologist. To their surprise, they found out he had an IQ of 63—so far below average that his fell into the range of IQ scores classified as mentally retarded.

Bill is one of more than 6.5 million people in the United States who have been identified as having intelligence far enough below average to regard it as a serious deficit. Both those people with low IQs, known as the mentally retarded, and those with unusually high IQs, referred to as the intellectually gifted, make up classes of individuals who require special attention to reach their full potential.

Falling Below the Norm: Mental Retardation

Although sometimes thought of as a rare phenomenon, mental retardation occurs in 1 to 3 percent of the population. There is wide variation among those labeled as mentally retarded—in large part because of the inclusiveness of the definition developed by the American Association on Mental Deficiency. The association suggests that **mental retardation** exists when there is "significantly subaverage general intellectual functioning existing concurrently with deficits in adaptive behavior and manifested during the developmental period" (Grossman, 1983). What this means is that people classified as mentally retarded can range from individuals whose performance differs little in a qualitative sense from those with higher IQs, to those who virtually cannot be trained and who must receive institutional treatment throughout their lives (Reynolds & Mann, 1987).

Most mentally retarded people have relatively minor deficits and are classified as **mildly retarded**. These individuals have IQ scores ranging from 55 to 69, and they constitute some 90 percent of all retarded individuals. Although their development is typically slower than that of their peers, they can function quite independently by adulthood and are able to hold jobs and have families of their own.

At greater levels of retardation—**moderate retardation** (IQs of 40 to 54), **severe retardation** (IQs of 25 to 39), and **profound retardation** (IQs below 25)—the difficulties are more pronounced. With the moderately retarded, deficits are obvious early, with language and motor skills lagging behind those of peers. Although these people can hold simple jobs, they need to have a moderate degree of supervision throughout their lives. The severely and profoundly retarded are generally unable to function independently. Often they have no language ability, poor motor control, and even an inability to be toilet-trained. These people are typically institutionalized for their entire lives.

What are the causes of mental retardation? In nearly one-third of the cases there is a known biological cause, the most common being Down syndrome. **Down syndrome**, which was once referred to as mongolism because the facial configuration of those with the disorder had an oriental appearance, is caused by the presence of an extra chromosome. Birth complications, such as a temporary lack of oxygen, may also cause retardation.

The majority of cases of mental retardation are classified as familial retardation. In **familial retardation** there is no known biological defect but a history of retardation within the person's family. Whether that history is caused by environmental factors—such as extreme, continuous

Mentally retarded people can lead productive lives as adults; pictured here is the first retarded person to be hired as a page in the U.S. Senate.

poverty leading to malnutrition—or by some underlying genetic factor inherited from one's parents is usually impossible to determine for certain. What is characteristic of familial retardation is the presence of more than one retarded person in the immediate family.

Regardless of the cause of mental retardation, important advances in the care and treatment of the mentally retarded have been made in the last fifteen years (Turkington, 1987; Garber, 1988; Landesman & Ramey, 1989). Much of this change was instigated by the Education for All Handicapped Children Act of 1975 (Public Law 94-142). In this federal law, Congress ruled that the mentally retarded are entitled to a full education and that they must be educated in the **least-restrictive environment**. The law increased the educational opportunities for the retarded, facilitating their integration into regular classrooms as much as possible—a process known as **mainstreaming**.

The philosophy behind mainstreaming suggests that the interaction of retarded and nonretarded students in regular classrooms will improve the educational opportunities for the mentally retarded, increase their social acceptance, and facilitate their integration into society as a whole. The philosophy was once to segregate the retarded into special-education classes where they could learn at their own pace along with other handicapped students. Mainstreaming attempts to prevent the isolation inherent in special-education classes and to reduce the social stigma of retardation by allowing the handicapped to interact with their age peers as much as possible (Mastropieri & Scruggs, 1987).

In mainstreaming, the mentally retarded are educated and trained in the least restrictive environment, often being integrated into regular classrooms.

Of course, there are still special-education classes; some retarded individuals function at too low a level to benefit from placement in regular classrooms. Moreover, retarded children mainstreamed into regular classes typically attend special classes for at least part of the day. Still, mainstreaming holds the promise of increasing the integration of the mentally retarded into society and allowing them to make their own contributions to the world at large.

The Other End of the Spectrum: The Intellectually Gifted

While the uniqueness of the mentally retarded is readily apparent, members of another group differ equally from the norm. Instead of having low intelligence, the **intellectually gifted** have higher-than-average intelligence.

Comprising 2 to 4 percent of the population, the intellectually gifted have IQ scores greater than 130. The stereotype associated with the gifted suggests that they are awkward, shy, social misfits unable to get along well with peers, but most research suggests just the opposite: The intellectually gifted are outgoing, well-adjusted, popular people who are able to do most things better than the average person (Stanley, 1980; Horowitz & O'Brien, 1987).

For example, in a long-term study by Lewis Terman that started in the early 1920s and is still going on, 1500 children who had IQ scores above 140 were followed and examined periodically through the next 60 years (Sears, 1977; Terman & Oden, 1947). From the very start, members of this group were physically, academically, and socially more able than their nongifted peers. They were generally healthier, taller, heavier, and stronger than average. Not surprisingly, they did better in school as well. They also showed better social adjustment than average. And all these advantages paid off in terms of career success: As a group, the gifted received more awards and distinctions and higher incomes and made more contributions in art and literature. For example, by the time the members of the group were 40 years old they had written over 90 books, 375 plays and short stories, and 2000 articles and had registered more than 200 patents. Perhaps most important, they reported greater satisfaction in life than the nongifted.

On the other hand, the picture of these intellectually gifted people was not unvaryingly positive. Not every member of the group Terman studied was successful, and in fact there were some notable failures. Moreover, other research suggests that high intelligence is not a homogeneous quality; a person with a high overall IQ is not necessarily gifted in every academic subject but may excel in just one or two (Stanley, 1980; Sternberg & Davidson, 1986). A high IQ, then, does not guarantee success in everything.

INDIVIDUAL DIFFERENCES IN INTELLIGENCE: HEREDITY, ENVIRONMENT—OR BOTH?

Kwang is often washed with a pleck tied to a _____.

(*a*) rundel   (*c*) pove

(*b*) flink   (*d*) quirj

If you found this kind of item on an intelligence test, you would probably complain that the test was totally absurd and had nothing to do with your intelligence or anyone else's. How could anyone be expected to respond to items presented in a language that was completely unfamiliar?

But suppose you found the following item, which at first glance might look equally foreign:

Which word is most out of place here?

(*a*) splib   (*d*) spook

(*b*) blood   (*e*) black

(*c*) gray

Just as absurd, you say? On the contrary, there is considerably more reason to use this second item on an intelligence test than the first example, which was made up of nonsense syllables. Although this second item may appear meaningless to the white population of the United States, to urban blacks the question might be a reasonable test of their knowledge.

The item is drawn from a test created by sociologist Adrian Dove, who tried to illustrate a problem that has plagued the developers of IQ tests from the beginning. By using terminology that would be familiar to urban blacks with inner-city backgrounds, but typically unfamiliar to whites (and to blacks raised within the dominant white culture), he dramatized the fact that cultural experience could play a critical role in determining intelligence test scores.

The importance of devising fair intelligence tests that measure knowledge unrelated to cultural and family background and experience would be minor if it were not for one important and persistent finding: Members of certain racial and cultural groups consistently score lower than members of other groups (MacKenzie, 1984). For example, as a group, blacks tend to average 15 IQ points lower than whites. Does this reflect a true difference in intelligence, or are the questions biased in the kinds of knowledge they test? Clearly, if whites perform better because of their greater familiarity with the kind of information that is being tested, their higher IQ scores are not necessarily an indication that they are more intelligent than members of other groups.

In fact, there is good reason to believe that some standardized IQ tests contain elements that discriminate against minority-group members whose experiences differ from those of the white majority. Consider the question "What would you do if another child grabbed your hat and ran with it?" Most white middle-class children answer that they would tell an adult, and this response is scored as "correct." On the other hand, a reasonable response might be to chase the person and fight to get the hat back, the answer that is chosen by many urban black children—but one that is scored as incorrect (Albee, 1978; Miller-Jones, 1989).

The possibility of bias and discrimination against minority-group members in traditional IQ tests has led some jurisdictions to ban their use. For example, the state of California does not permit public schools to give black students IQ tests to decide whether they should be placed in special-education classes—regardless of the students' academic background or socioeconomic status, or even following parental request—unless express permission is obtained from the courts (Baker, 1987). (Ironically, because the ban pertains only to black students, and not to whites, Hispanics, and other racial and ethnic groups, some people have argued that the ban itself is discriminatory.)

The Basic Controversy: Heredity versus Environment

In an attempt to produce what has come to be called a **culture-fair IQ test**, one that does not discriminate against members of any minority cultural group, psychologists have tried to devise test items which assess experiences common to all cultures or which emphasize questions that do not require language usage. However, test makers have found this difficult to do, and some culture-fair tests have produced even larger discrepancies between majority and minority groups than traditional tests which rely more heavily on verbal skills (Anastasi, 1988).

The efforts of psychologists to produce culture-fair measures of intelligence relate to a lingering controversy over differences in intelligence between members of minority and majority groups. In attempting to identify whether there are differences between such groups, psychologists have been faced with the broader issue of determining the relative contribution to intelligence of genetic factors (heredity) and experience (environment).

Arthur Jensen, an educational psychologist, fueled the fires of the debate with a 1969 article. He argued that an analysis of IQ differences between whites and blacks demonstrated that, although environmental factors played a role, there were also basic genetic differences between the two races. Jensen based his argument on a number of findings. For instance, on average, whites score 15 points higher than blacks on traditional IQ tests even when socioeconomic class is taken into account. According to Jensen, middle- and upper-class blacks score lower than middle- and upper-class whites, just as lower-class blacks score lower on average than do lower-class whites. Intelligence differences between blacks and whites, Jensen concluded, could not be attributed to environmental differences alone.

Moreover, intelligence in general shows a high degree of **heritability**, a measure of the degree to which a characteristic is related to genetic, inherited factors (Bouchard et al., 1990). As can be seen in Figure 9-9, the closer the genetic link between two people, the greater the correspondence of IQ scores. Using data such as these, Jensen argued that fully 75 to 80 percent of the variability in IQ scores could be attributed solely to genetic factors. If we rule out environmental causes of differences between races in IQ scores, then, we are left with the conclusion—claimed by Jensen—that these differences in IQs are caused by genetically-based differences in intelligence.

The psychology community reacted quickly to Jensen's contentions

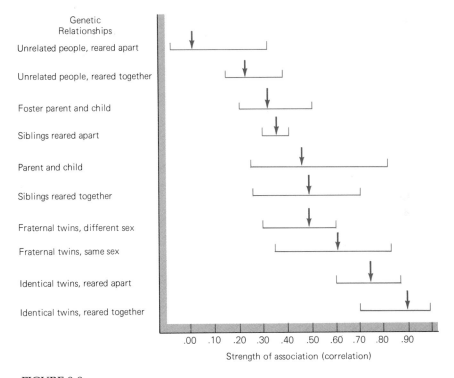

FIGURE 9-9
Summary findings on IQ and closeness of genetic relationship. The length of the line indicates the range of correlations found in different studies, and the arrows show the average correlation. Note, for example, that the average correlation for unrelated people reared apart is quite low, while the correlation for identical twins, reared together, is substantially higher. The more similar the genetic and environmental background of two people, the greater the correlation. (Jencks et al., 1972; Kamin, 1979; Walker & Emory, 1985; Scarr & Carter-Saltzmann, 1985.)

and convincingly refuted many of his claims. For one thing, even when socioeconomic conditions are supposedly held constant, there remain wide variations among individual households, and no one can convincingly assert that living conditions of blacks and whites are identical even when their socioeconomic status is similar. Second, as we discussed earlier, there is reason to believe that traditional IQ tests may discriminate against lower-class urban blacks, asking for information on experiences to which they are unlikely to have been exposed.

Moreover, there is direct evidence that blacks who are raised in enriched environments do not tend, as a group, to have lower IQ scores than whites in similar environments. For example, a study by Sandra Scarr and Richard Weinberg examined black children who were adopted at an early age by white middle-class families of above-average intelligence (Scarr & Weinberg, 1976). The IQ scores of the children averaged 106—about 15 points above the average IQ scores of unadopted black children reared in their own homes, and above the average in scores of the general population. In addition, the younger a child was when adopted, the higher his or her IQ score tended to be. The evidence that genetic factors play the major role in determining racial differences in IQ, then, is not compelling—although the question still evokes controversy (MacKenzie, 1984).

Ultimately, it is crucial to remember that IQ scores and intelligence have greatest relevance in terms of individuals, not groups, and that by far the greatest discrepancies in IQ occur not among mean *group* IQ scores but among the IQ scores of *individuals.* There are blacks who score high on IQ tests and whites who score low, just as there are whites who score high and blacks who score low. For the concept of intelligence to aid in the betterment of society, we must examine how *individuals* perform, not the groups to which they belong, as well as the degree to which intelligence can be improved in a given person (Angoff, 1988).

Other issues make the heredity-versus-environment debate somewhat irrelevant to practical concerns. For example, as we discussed earlier, there are many kinds of intelligence, and traditional IQ scores do not tap many of them. Indeed, some psychologists argue that IQ scores are only weakly linked to intelligence (Flynn, 1987). Furthermore, IQ scores are often inadequate predictors of ultimate work and academic success; and actual school achievement differences between whites and blacks appear to be narrowing (Jones, 1984). In sum, questions concerning differences in white and black intelligence levels may prove to be less pertinent than those relating to understanding individual differences in IQ, without regard to race.

Neither Heredity nor Environment: Putting the Question in Perspective

There is no absolute resolution to the question of the degree to which intelligence is influenced by heredity and by environment. The reason is that we are dealing with an issue for which true experiments to un-equivocally determine causality cannot be devised. (A moment's thought about how we might experimentally assign infants to enriched or de-prived environments will reveal the impossibility of devising ethically reasonable experiments!)

The more critical question to ask, then, is not so much whether it is primarily heredity or environment that underlies intelligence but whether there is anything we can do to maximize the intellectual development of each individual (Scarr & Carter-Saltzman, 1982; Angoff, 1988). We then will be able to make changes in the environment—which may take the form of more enriched homes and schools—that can lead each person to reach his or her highest potential.

ASK YOURSELF

How is intelligence defined and measured?

What are the major formulations of intelligence?

How are mental retardation and intellectual giftedness concep-tualized?

What are the controversies regarding the existence of racial dif-ferences in intelligence and the degree to which intelligence is influenced by heredity and by the environment?

Why does intelligence have so many different definitions?

Why is it so difficult to determine whether group differences in IQ scores are due to heredity or environment?

LOOKING BACK

1. Personality is thought of in two different, but related, ways: First, it refers to the characteristics that differentiate one per-son from another. Second, it provides a means of explaining the stability in peo-ple's behavior that leads them to act uni-formly both in different situations and over extended periods of time.

2. According to psychoanalysts, much of be-havior is caused by parts of personality which are found in the unconscious, and of which we are unaware. Freud's theory suggests that personality is composed of the id, the ego, and the superego.

3. Freud's psychoanalytic theory suggests that personality develops through a series of stages, each of which is associated with a major biological function: the oral stage, anal stage, phallic stage, the Oedipal con-flict, latency period, and the genital stage, a period of mature sexuality.

4. Defense mechanisms, used for dealing with anxiety relating to impulses from the id, provide people with unconscious strategies to reduce anxiety. The most common defense mechanisms are repres-sion, regression, displacement, ration-alization, denial, projection, and sub-limation.

5. Freud's psychoanalytic theory has pro-voked a number of criticisms. Still, the theory remains a pivotal one. For in-stance, the neo-Freudian psychoanalytic theorists built on Freud's work, although

they placed greater emphasis on the role of the ego and paid greater attention to social factors in determining behavior.

6. Trait theories have tried to identify the most basic and relatively enduring dimensions along which people differ from one another—dimensions known as traits. For example, Allport suggested that there were three kinds of traits. Later theorists employed a statistical technique called factor analysis to identify the most crucial traits. Using this method, Cattell identified sixteen basic traits, while Eysenck found two major dimensions.

7. Learning theories of personality concentrate on observable behavior. In fact, to the strict learning theorist, personality is the sum of learned responses to the external environment. In contrast, Dollard and Miller's stimulus-response theory combines psychoanalytic concepts with learning approaches, and social learning theory concentrates on the role of thoughts, feelings, expectations, and values in determining personality. Social learning theory pays particular attention to observational learning.

8. Humanistic theory emphasizes the basic goodness of people and their tendency to grow into higher levels of functioning. It considers as the core of personality a person's unique creative impulses and his or her ability to change and improve. Rogers' concept of the need for positive regard suggests that a universal requirement to be loved and respected underlies personality.

9. The major personality theories differ along a number of important dimensions, including the role of the unconscious versus the conscious, nature versus nurture, freedom versus determinism, stability versus modifiability of personality characteristics, and nomothetic versus idiographic approaches.

10. Psychological tests are standard assessment tools that objectively measure behavior. They must be reliable, measuring what they are trying to measure consistently, and valid, measuring what they are supposed to measure.

11. Self-report measures ask people about a sample range of their behaviors. These reports are used to infer the presence of particular personality characteristics. The most commonly used self-report measure is the Minnesota Multiphasic Personality Inventory-2 (MMPI-2).

12. Projective personality tests present an ambiguous stimulus; the observer's responses are then used to infer information about the observer. The two most frequently used projective tests are the Rorschach and the Thematic Apperception Test (TAT).

13. Because intelligence can take many forms, defining it presents a challenge to psychologists. One commonly accepted view is that intelligence is the capacity to understand the world, think rationally, and use resources effectively when faced with challenges.

14. Intelligence tests are used to measure intelligence. They provide a mental age which, when divided by a person's chronological age and then multiplied by 100, gives an IQ, or intelligence quotient, score. Specific tests of intelligence include the Stanford-Binet test, the Wechsler Adult Intelligence Scale—Revised (WAIS-R), and the Wechsler Intelligence Scale for Children—Revised (WISC-R). In addition to intelligence tests, other standardized tests take the form of achievement tests and aptitude tests.

15. Although intelligence tests are able to identify individual differences in intelligence, they do not provide us with an understanding of the underlying nature of intelligence. One of the major issues here is whether there is a single, unitary factor underlying intelligence or whether intelligence is made up of particular subcomponents.

16. The earliest psychologists interested in intelligence made the assumption that there was a general factor for mental ability called g. However, later psychologists disputed the view that intelligence was unidimensional.

17. Some researchers suggest that there are two kinds of intelligence: fluid intelli-

gence and crystallized intelligence. Guilford's structure-of-intellect model theorizes that there are 150 separate mental abilities.

18. Information-processing approaches suggest that intelligence should be conceptualized as the way in which people represent and use material cognitively. Rather than focusing on the structure of intelligence, they examine the processes underlying intelligent behavior. One example of an information-processing approach is Sternberg's triarchic theory of intelligence, which suggests three major aspects to intelligence: componential, experiential, and contextual.

19. At the two extremes of intelligence are the mentally retarded and the intellectually gifted. About one-third of the cases of retardation have a known biological cause, with Down's syndrome being the most common. Most cases, however, are classified as ones of familial retardation, in which there is no known biological cause.

20. There have been a number of recent advances in the treatment of both the mentally retarded and the intellectually gifted, particularly after federal law mandated that the mentally retarded be educated in the least-restrictive environment.

21. Traditional intelligence tests have frequently been criticized for being biased in favor of the white middle-class population majority. That controversy has led to attempts to devise culture-fair tests, IQ measures which avoid questions that depend on a particular cultural background.

22. Two major controversies have grown out of research on intelligence: whether there are racial differences in intelligence and the degree to which intelligence is influenced by heredity and by the environment. Because individual IQ scores vary far more than group IQ scores, it is most critical to ask what we can do to maximize the intellectual development of each individual.

Key Terms and Concepts

personality (p. 352)
psychoanalyst (p. 353)
psychoanalytic theory (p. 353)
unconscious (p. 354)
instinctual drives (p. 354)
id (p. 355)
ego (p. 355)
superego (p. 355)
pleasure principle (p. 355)
reality principle (p. 355)
conscience (p. 356)
ego ideal (p. 356)
oral stage (p. 357)
fixation (p. 357)
anal stage (p. 357)
phallic stage (p. 358)
Oedipal conflict (p. 358)
identification (p. 358)
penis envy (p. 358)
latency period (p. 358)
genital stage (p. 358)

anxiety (p. 359)
neurotic anxiety (p. 359)
defense mechanisms (p. 359)
repression (p. 359)
regression (p. 359)
displacement (p. 359)
rationalization (p. 359)
denial (p. 359)
projection (p. 360)
sublimation (p. 360)
neo-Freudian psychoanalyst (p. 362)
collective unconscious (p. 362)
archetypes (p. 362)
inferiority complex (p. 363)
trait theory (p. 364)
traits (p. 364)
cardinal trait (p. 365)
central trait (p. 365)
secondary trait (p. 365)
factor analysis (p. 365)
surface trait (p. 365)

source trait (p. 365)
introversion-extroversion (p. 366)
neuroticism-stability (p. 366)
social learning theory (p. 370)
observational learning (p. 370)
determinism (p. 371)
humanistic theory (of personality) (p. 372)
self-concept (p. 372)
unconditional positive regard (p. 373)
self-actualization (p. 373)
nomothetic approaches to personality
    (p. 374)
idiographic approaches to personality
    (p. 374)
psychological tests (p. 375)
reliability (p. 376)
validity (p. 376)
self-report measures (p. 377)
Minnesota Multiphasic Personality
    Inventory-2 (MMPI-2) (p. 377)
norms (for tests) (p. 379)
projective personality test (p. 379)
Rorschach test (p. 379)
Thematic Apperception Test (TAT) (p. 381)
intelligence (p. 384)
intelligence test (p. 384)
mental age (p. 385)
chronological age (p. 385)

intelligence quotient (IQ) score (p. 385)
deviation IQ score (p. 386)
Stanford-Binet test (p. 386)
Wechsler Adult Intelligence Scale—Revised
    (WAIS-R) (p. 387)
Wechsler Intelligence Scale for Children—
    Revised (WISC-R) (p. 387)
achievement test (p. 389)
aptitude test (p. 389)
g or g-factor (p. 390)
fluid intelligence (p. 390)
crystallized intelligence (p. 390)
structure-of-intellect model (p. 390)
triarchic theory of intelligence (p. 392)
practical intelligence (p. 393)
mental retardation (p. 393)
mild retardation (p. 394)
moderate retardation (p. 394)
severe retardation (p. 394)
profound retardation (p. 394)
Down syndrome (p. 394)
familial retardation (p. 394)
least-restrictive environment (p. 395)
mainstreaming (p. 395)
intellectually gifted (p. 396)
culture-fair IQ test (p. 398)
heritability (p. 399)

10

Abnormal Behavior

❖

Prologue: Joyce Brown ♦ *Looking Ahead* ♦ *Normal versus Abnormal: Making the Distinction* ♦ *From Superstition to Science: Models of Abnormality* ♦ *The ABCs of DSM-III-R: Classifying Types of Abnormal Behavior* ♦ *The Major Disorders* ♦ *Looking Back*

PROLOGUE: JOYCE BROWN

After being released from the hospital through the intervention of a civil-rights organization, Joyce Brown worked for a short time as an office volunteer.

There was nothing out of place in the scene of the secretary expertly fielding calls to the office. Well-dressed, intelligent, and attractive, Joyce Brown, 40 years old, looked as if she had spent years polishing her secretarial skills. Yet just a few months earlier, Brown had spent her days and nights on a New York City sidewalk over a hot-air vent in front of a restaurant. She hurled insults and obscenities at passers-by and used the street as her bathroom.

Her background gave no clue to the unusual transformation that she had undergone during the course of her life. Brown grew up in Elizabeth, New Jersey, where, after graduating from high school, she held a series of jobs at Bell Laboratories and at the local Human Rights Commission. At some point, though, she became dependent on heroin and later cocaine. Her mental health deteriorated, and she was eventually hospitalized. After her release, she fought with her family and moved to New York, where she eventually found her way to the heating grate that was her "home" for about a year.

She gained notoriety when she became the first person chosen by New York City mental health professionals to be hospitalized under a program in which severely mentally ill street people were forcibly removed from the streets and treated. Yet once she was hospitalized, Brown, with the help of lawyers from the American Civil Liberties

Union, eloquently argued that she had a constitutional right to be free—and a judge accepted her arguments. After twelve weeks of hospitalization and refusal to accept treatment, she was allowed to leave the hospital, and she quickly gained celebrity status.

Brown dined in the best restaurants and shopped at Bloomingdale's and Lord & Taylor; people stopped her and asked for her autograph. She was interviewed on national television and received a number of movie and book offers.

However, there remained suggestions that all was not well with her. Her former roommate at a residence for homeless women reported that, although basically considerate and nonargumentative, Brown talked to herself. Others overheard her mumbling racial slurs. And a few weeks after lecturing at Harvard Law School on the plight of the homeless, she was back on the street, begging for money and shouting obscenities.

Brown had explanations for these apparent setbacks. When asked why she panhandled, she said she did so only because she had run out of money—not because she was mentally disordered. She admitted using obscenities, but only as a reaction to being harassed by people who passed by her on the street (Barbanel, 1988).

To Brown, her behavior was no more abnormal than anyone else's.

LOOKING AHEAD

Many of us would disagree with Joyce Brown's own assessment of her behavior as "quite normal." Yet her case presents a series of perplexing questions. Why did she live in the streets, hurling obscenities? Why did she spurn housing in shelters provided for the homeless and instead choose to live over a hot-air vent? Was she correct in claiming her behavior was normal? What factors in her background led to her behavior? Could she have been spared a life in the streets through early treatment? How do we distinguish normal from abnormal behavior, and how can Brown's behavior be categorized and classified and the specific nature of her problem pinpointed?

Although these questions cannot be answered definitively, especially with a case as complex as Brown's, we can start to address some of the issues raised by her atypical behavior in this and the following chapter. We begin by discussing the distinction between normal and abnormal behavior, considering the subtle distinctions that must be made. We examine the various approaches that have been used to explain abnormal behavior, ranging from explanations based on superstition to those based on contemporary, scientific approaches, and apply these approaches to the case of Joyce Brown, showing how the various explanations complement one another.

The heart of the chapter consists of a description of the various types of abnormal behaviors. Using a classification system employed by mental health practitioners, we examine the most significant kinds of disorders. The chapter also includes a discussion of the problems and dangers of self-diagnosis, and the signals people might see in themselves that could lead them to consider seeking help from a mental health professional.

In sum, after reading this chapter, you will have the answers to several fundamental questions about mental health:

- How can we distinguish normal from abnormal behavior?
- What are the major models of abnormal behavior used by mental health professionals?
- How can we apply these approaches to specific cases, such as that of Joyce Brown?
- What is the classification system used to categorize abnormal behavior, and what are the major mental health disorders?
- What are the major indicators that signal a need for the help of a mental health practitioner?

NORMAL VERSUS ABNORMAL: MAKING THE DISTINCTION

Universally that person's acumen is esteemed very little perceptive concerning whatsoever matters are being held as most profitable by mortals with sapience endowed to be studied who is ignorant of that which the most in doctrine erudite and certainly by reason of that in them high mind's ornament deserving of veneration constantly maintain when by general consent they affirm that other circumstances being equal by no exterior splendour is the prosperity of a nation more efficaciously asserted than by the measure of how far forward may have progressed the tribute of its solicitude for that proliferent continuance which of evils the original if it be absent when fortunately present constitutes the certain sign of omnipollent nature's incorrupted benefaction.

It would be easy to conclude that these words were the musings of a madman; the passage does not seem, at least at first consideration, to make any sense at all. But literary scholars would disagree; in actuality this passage is from James Joyce's classic *Ulysses*, which has been hailed as one of the major works of twentieth-century literature (Joyce, 1934, p. 377).

As this example illustrates, making a cursory examination of a person's writing is insufficient to determine the degree to which he or she is "normal." But even when we consider more extensive samples of someone's behavior, we find that there may be only a fine line between behavior that is considered normal and that which is considered abnormal.

Approaches to Abnormality

The difficulty in distinguishing normal from abnormal behavior has led to a diversity of approaches for devising a precise, scientific definition of "abnormal behavior." Over the years, in fact, the definitions of what constitutes normal and abnormal behavior have taken a number of twists. We examine next the four major approaches most commonly employed.

Different equals abnormal: Deviation from the average. Perhaps the most obvious approach defines abnormality as deviation from the average—a statistical definition. In order to determine abnormality, we simply observe what behaviors are rare or infrequent in a given society or culture and label these deviations from the norm as abnormal (Ullman & Krasner, 1975).

Although such a definition may be appropriate in some instances, its drawback is that some behaviors that are statistically rare clearly do not lend themselves to classification as abnormal. If most people prefer to have orange juice with breakfast, but you prefer apple juice, this hardly makes your behavior abnormal. Similarly, such a conception of abnormality would unreasonably necessitate labeling a person who has an unusually high IQ as abnormal, because it is statistically rare to have a high IQ. A definition of abnormality that rests on deviation from the average, then, is insufficient.

Aiming for perfection: Deviation from the ideal. An alternative approach to defining abnormality is one that takes into account not what most people do (the average), but the standard toward which most people are striving—the ideal. Under this sort of definition, behavior is considered abnormal if it deviates a sufficient degree from some kind of ideal or standard. Unfortunately, the definition suffers from even more difficulties than the deviation-from-the-average definition, since society has so few standards about which people agree. Moreover, the standards that do arise tend to change over time, leaving the deviation-from-the-ideal approach inadequate.

Normal feels right: Abnormality as a sense of subjective discomfort. Given the drawbacks of both the deviation-from-the-average and deviation-from-the-ideal definitions of normality, we must turn to more subjective approaches. In fact, one of the most useful definitions of abnormal behavior is one that concentrates on the psychological consequences of the behavior for the individual. In this approach, behavior is considered abnormal if it produces a sense of distress, anxiety, or guilt in an individual—or if it is harmful to others in some way.

Of course, even a definition that rests on subjective discomfort has its

Although membership in a cult such as the Hare Krishna is statistically rare, it would be inaccurate to classify all Hare Krishnas as abnormal.

drawbacks, for in some particularly severe forms of mental disturbance people report feeling euphoric and on top of the world—yet to others, their behavior is bizarre. In this case, then, there is a subjective state of well-being, yet the behavior is clearly within the realm of what most people would consider abnormal—suggesting that a definition of abnormality that does not consider people's ability to function effectively is inadequate. Thus psychologists have developed one final approach to distinguishing normal and abnormal behavior.

Getting along in the world: Abnormality as the inability to function effectively. Most people are able to feed themselves, hold a job, get along with others, and in general live as productive members of society. Yet there are those who are unable to adjust to the demands of society or function effectively.

According to this last view of abnormality, people who are unable to function effectively and adapt to the demands of society are considered abnormal. For example, an unemployed, homeless woman living on the street—such as Joyce Brown—might be considered unable to function effectively; therefore her behavior would be considered abnormal, even if she had made the choice to live in this particular fashion. It is her inability to adapt to the requirements of society that makes her "abnormal," according to this approach.

Drawing the Line on Abnormality: The Continuum of Abnormal and Normal Behavior

None of the four definitions alone is sufficiently broad to cover all instances of abnormal behavior, and the division between normal and abnormal behavior often remains indistinct, sometimes even to trained professionals. Probably the best way to deal with this imprecision is to consider abnormal and normal behavior not as absolute states but rather as marking the opposite ends of a *continuum* (or scale) of behavior, with completely normal functioning at one end and totally abnormal behavior at the other. Obviously, behavior will usually fall somewhere between these two extremes.

Because the difference between normal and abnormal behavior is indistinct, the issue of when society should intervene and require treatment of people displaying abnormal behavior is also ambiguous. For example, did Joyce Brown, whose behavior was clearly out of the ordinary but who presented little danger to others, warrant the intervention of New York City officials who demanded that she receive treatment?

There is no clear-cut answer to the question, both in Brown's case and in those of many others. However, lawyers and forensic psychologists— psychologists who specialize in the law—have attempted to define the circumstances under which legal intervention in cases of abnormal behavior is appropriate. In most states, a person must meet four criteria prior to intervention (Schwitzgebel & Schwitzgebel, 1980): The person must be (1) dangerous to himself or herself; (2) incapable of providing for basic physical needs; (3) unable to make reasonable decisions about whether treatment is required; and (4) in need of treatment or care. Of course, these four criteria still do not clearly answer the question of when treatment should be provided to an individual since the criteria are fraught with ambiguity. The determination, then, of when society should intervene in the presence of abnormal behavior is clearly a difficult one to make.

The Mental State of the Union: The Prevalence of Mental Disorders

Given the difficulties in satisfactorily defining abnormality, it should come as no surprise that determining the number of people showing signs of abnormal behavior is no simple task. But a survey conducted by the U.S. government in the mid-1980s does provide a sense of how many Americans show signs of mental disorder (Reiger et al., 1984, 1988).

The survey, conducted in five communities and including about 18,000 Americans, found that close to 20 percent of the adults queried had a mental disorder, and that the rates were about equal for men and women. In individual interviews that lasted two hours, each subject answered 200 questions about particular kinds of problems, such as feeling panicky when leaving the house and losing interest in normally pleasant activities. By using standard categories of mental disturbance that we will explore later in the chapter, the researchers were able to produce a statistical profile of the "mental state of the union."

Projecting the results to the nation as a whole indicates that over 29 million Americans have one or more mental disorders or have suffered from one within the past six months. For example, 13 million have difficulties related to anxiety, 10 million abuse alcohol or some other drug, and some 11 million have irrational fears. (Because subjects could report more than one problem, there is overlap in these statistics.) Surprisingly, just one in five of those with a problem seeks help. These results suggest that abnormal behavior is far from rare.

ASK YOURSELF

What are the major approaches to defining what is abnormal behavior?

Why is it reasonable to view abnormal and normal behavior as marking the two ends of a continuum?

How prevalent are mental disorders in the United States?

FROM SUPERSTITION TO SCIENCE: MODELS OF ABNORMALITY

The disease occurred at the height of the summer heat. People, asleep or awake, would suddenly jump up, feeling an acute pain like the sting of a bee. Some saw the spider, others did not, but they knew that it must be the tarantula. They ran out of the house into the street, to the marketplace, dancing in great excitement. Soon they were joined by others who like them had been bitten, or by people who had been stung in previous years. . . .

Thus groups of patients would gather, dancing wildly in the queerest attire. . . . Others would tear their clothes and show their nakedness, losing all sense of modesty. . . . Some called for swords and acted like fencers, others for whips and beat each other. . . . Some of them had still stranger fancies, liked to be tossed in the air, dug holes in the ground, and rolled themselves into the dirt like swine. They all drank wine plentifully and sang and talked like drunken people . . . (Sigerist, 1943, pp. 103, 106–107).

This description of a peculiar form of abnormal behavior that occurred during the thirteenth century—behavior attributed, at the time, to the bite of an imagined tarantula spider—indicates that mental disturbance and theories about its causes are nothing new. Yet our understand-

ing of the causes of such behavior has become considerably more sophisticated.

For much of the past, abnormal behavior was linked to superstition
and witchcraft; people displaying abnormal behavior were accused of
being possessed by the devil or some sort of demonic god (Howells &
Osborn, 1984). Authorities felt justified in "treating" abnormal behavior
by attempting to drive out the source of the problem. This typically involved whipping, immersion in hot water, starvation, or other forms of
torture in which the cure was often worse than the affliction.

Contemporary approaches to abnormal behavior take a more enlight-
ened view, and five major models of abnormal behavior predominate: the
medical model, the psychoanalytic model, the behavioral model, the humanistic model, and the sociocultural model. These models suggest not
only different causes of abnormal behavior but—as we shall see in the
next chapter—different treatment approaches as well.

Abnormal Behavior as a Biological Disease: The Medical Model

When a person displays the symptoms of tuberculosis, we generally find
the tuberculin germ in his or her body tissue. In the same way, the **medical
model of abnormality** suggests that when an individual displays the
symptoms of abnormal behavior, the root cause will be found in an examination of some physical aspect of the individual, such as a hormonal
imbalance, a chemical deficiency, or an injury to part of the body. Indeed,
when we speak of mental "illness," the "symptoms" of abnormal behavior, and mental "hospitals," we are using terminology related to the medical model.

As we will discuss later, because many sorts of abnormal behaviors
have been linked to physiological causes, the medical model would seem
to be a reasonable approach. In fact, the medical model does represent a
major advance over explanations of abnormal behavior based on superstitions. Yet serious criticisms have been leveled against it. For one thing,
there are many instances in which no physiological cause has been identified for abnormal behavior, thus negating the basic assumption of the
medical model. Other criticisms have equally important, though less obvious, implications. For instance, some critics have argued that the use of
the term "illness" implies that there is something "wrong" with a person,
something that is in need of a cure (Szasz, 1982; 1987). Using such terms
suggests that people displaying abnormal behavior hold little control over
their actions and have no responsibility for them—and that any "cure" is
entirely in the hands of someone else (who, given the assumptions of the
medical model, would presumably be a physician).

Conflicting Causes of Abnormal Behavior: The Psychoanalytic Model

On the surface, Joyce Brown's background shows little difference from that of anyone else. Yet could certain aspects of her past, of which she was unaware, have brought about her unusual behavior? Such a possibility is suggested by the psychoanalytic model of abnormal behavior.

Whereas the medical model suggests that physiological causes are at the root of abnormal behavior, the **psychoanalytic model of abnormality** holds that abnormal behavior stems from childhood conflicts over opposing wishes regarding sex and aggression. As we discussed in Chapter 9, Freud believed that children pass through a series of stages in which sexual and aggressive impulses take different forms that require resolution. If the conflicts of childhood are not successfully dealt with, they remain unresolved in the unconscious and eventually bring about abnormal behavior during adulthood.

In order to understand the roots of a person's disordered behavior, the psychoanalytic model scrutinizes his or her early life history. For example, if we knew more details of Joyce Brown's childhood, we might discover experiences that produced unresolved insecurities and conflicts in adulthood. Of course, it would be difficult to prove a direct link between her childhood experiences and later abnormal behavior—pointing to one of the major objections that critics have raised regarding psychoanalytic theorizing. Because there is no conclusive way of linking people's childhood experiences with the abnormal behaviors they display as adults, we can never be sure that the mechanisms suggested by psychoanalytic theory are accurate. Moreover, psychoanalytic theory, like the medical model, paints a picture of people as having little control over their behavior and of behavior as being guided by unconscious impulses, implying that the treatment of abnormal behavior is dependent on others.

On the other hand, the contributions of psychoanalytic theory have been great (Moore & Fine, 1990). More than any other approach to abnormal behavior, it highlights the fact that people can have a rich, involved inner life and that prior experiences can have a profound effect on current psychological functioning.

When Behavior Itself Is the Problem: The Behavioral Model

The medical model and the psychoanalytic model display a common approach to behavior disorders: They both look at abnormal behaviors as *symptoms* of some underlying problem. In contrast, the **behavioral model of abnormality** looks at the behavior itself as the problem. According to theorists using this approach, one need not look beyond a person's display

Until the twentieth century, abnormal behavior was blamed on "evil spirits." As a result, its treatment involved (a) religious ceremonies or (b) bizarre paraphernalia designed to drive out the demons.

of abnormal behavior or past the environment to be able to understand and ultimately change that behavior.

Using the principles of learning we discussed in Chapter 4, behavioral theorists can thus explain why people behave abnormally—or normally. Both normal and abnormal behaviors are seen as responses to a set of stimuli, responses that have been learned through past experience and are guided in the present by the stimuli that one finds in one's environment. Indeed, in its most extreme form, the behavioral model rejects the notion that it is important to understand what a person is thinking. What is critical is analyzing how an abnormal behavior has been learned and observing the circumstances in which it is displayed in order to explain why such behavior is occurring. For example, a behavioral approach would explain an individual's inability to get work done on time as being due to a lack of skill in time management. This could be remedied by teaching the individual techniques for working more efficiently. Other approaches, in contrast, would try to determine the underlying causes of the person's inability to manage time.

The emphasis on overt observable behavior represents both the greatest strength and the greatest weakness of the behavioral approach to abnormal behavior. Because of its emphasis on the present, the behavioral approach is the most precise and objective in examining manifestations of abnormal behavior. Rather than hypothesizing elaborate, underlying, unobservable mechanisms to explain abnormal behavior, behavioral theorists concentrate on immediate behavior. They have developed many techniques (presented in the next chapter) to modify such behavior successfully.

On the other hand, the behavioral approach has received its share of criticism. For example, behavioral theories, like medical and psycho-analytic explanations, tend to view people's behavior as being caused by factors largely outside of their own control, although for different reasons. Moreover, according to critics, one cannot overlook the very real fact that people have complex unobservable thoughts that influence their behavior. This latter criticism has led some behavioral theorists to modify their position and consider approaches in which a change in cognitions—people's thoughts and beliefs—is the goal of treatment, rather than a direct change in overt behavior. For example, they may teach a student who, on taking every exam, thinks, "This exam is crucial to my future," to modify her thoughts to make them more realistic (and less threatening and less potentially debilitating): "My entire future is not dependent on this one exam." The basic principles of learning theory are still used; what is different is the target of behavior change. Although not all behavioral theorists subscribe to these views, the behavioral model has been broadened by the addition of such cognitive approaches.

Putting the Person in Control: The Humanistic Model

You might wonder if there is any model of abnormal behavior that considers a person to be in complete control of her or his behavior, and in fact this is a reasonable question in light of the three models we have discussed. In each of these models the individual is seen, to a greater or lesser degree, as something of a pawn, beset by physiological difficulties, unconscious conflicts, or environmental stimuli that direct and motivate behavior.

Psychologists who subscribe to the humanistic approach, in contrast, emphasize the control and responsibility that people have for their own behavior—even when such behavior is abnormal. The **humanistic model of abnormality** concentrates on what is uniquely human, viewing people as basically rational, oriented toward a social world, and motivated to get along with others (Rogers, 1980).

Although diverse in many ways, humanistic approaches to abnormal behavior focus on the relationship of the individual to the world, on the ways people view themselves in relation to others and see their place in the world in a philosophical sense. People have an awareness of life and of themselves that leads them to search for meaning and self-worth. So-called abnormal behavior is basically a sign of a person's inability to fulfill his or her human needs and capabilities. Moreover, humanistic approaches take a much less judgmental view of atypical behavior than other models. Rather than assuming that a "cure" is required, the humanistic model suggests that individuals can, by and large, set their own limits of what is acceptable behavior. As long as they are not hurting others and do not feel personal distress, people should be free to choose the behaviors they engage in. It is only if *they* feel that their behavior needs some correction that they ought to consider taking responsibility for modifying it, and the way to bring about such modification is by exploring ways to reach higher levels of self-fulfillment.

Humanistic models consider abnormal behavior, then, in a less negative light than the models we discussed earlier. Rather than assuming there is something wrong with an individual, humanistic theorists view abnormal behavior as an understandable reaction to circumstances arising in the person's daily life. Moreover, the humanistic model suggests that people have a relatively high degree of control over their lives and can make informed and rational choices to overcome their difficulties.

The humanistic model is not without its detractors. For instance, it has been criticized for its reliance on unscientific, unverifiable information, as well as for its vague, almost philosophical formulation related to such concepts as "human striving" and "fulfillment of human needs." Despite these criticisms, the humanistic model offers a view of abnormal behavior that stresses the unique aspects of being human and provides a number of important suggestions for helping those with psychological problems.

Society as the Cause of Abnormal Behavior: The Sociocultural Model

Sociocultural approaches to abnormal behavior make the assumption that people's behavior—both normal and abnormal—is shaped by the kind of family group, society, and culture in which they live. We all are part of a social network of family, friends, acquaintances, and even strangers, and the kinds of relationships that evolve with others may support abnormal behaviors and even cause them to occur. According to the **sociocultural model of abnormality**, then, the kinds of stresses and conflicts people experience—not in terms of unconscious processes, but as part of their daily interactions with those around them—can promote and maintain abnormal behavior.

In fact, some proponents of this view take the extreme position that there really is no such thing as abnormal behavior. Although people who violate social rules may be labeled by society as showing abnormal behavior, in reality there is nothing wrong with such individuals. Rather, there is something wrong with a society that is unwilling to tolerate deviant behavior.

To support the position that sociocultural factors shape abnormal behavior, theorists say statistics show that certain kinds of abnormal behavior are far more prevalent among certain social classes than others, and poor economic times tend to be linked to general declines in psychological functioning. For instance, diagnoses of schizophrenia tend to be higher among members of lower socioeconomic classes than among members of more affluent groups (Hollingshead & Redlich, 1958). The reason may relate to the way abnormal behavior is interpreted by diagnosticians, who tend to be psychiatrists and psychologists from upper socioeconomic classes. Alternatively, it may be that stresses on members of lower socio-economic classes are greater than those on people in higher classes. What-ever the reason, there is frequently a link between sociocultural factors and abnormal behavior, suggesting the possibility of a cause-and-effect sequence (Lindsey & Paul, 1989).

As with the other theories, the sociocultural model does not have unequivocal support. Alternative explanations abound for the association between abnormal behavior and social factors. For example, people of lower classes may be less likely than those of higher classes to seek help until their symptoms become relatively severe and warrant a more serious diagnosis (Gove, 1982). Moreover, sociocultural explanations provide relatively little in the way of direct guidance for the treatment of individ-uals showing mental disturbance, since the focus is on broader societal factors.

Applying the Models: The Case of Joyce Brown

We began this chapter by discussing Joyce Brown's case. Perhaps you are wondering which of these models brings us closer to understanding the reasons for her behavior. Indeed, you may be looking for the answer to a more encompassing question: Which of these approaches provides the best model for explaining abnormal behavior in general?

The most appropriate answer to both questions is, in fact, that *all* of them can be reasonably and profitably used. As in other branches of their field, psychologists have found that there is more than one workable ap-proach to the problems of abnormal behavior; as we shall see, effective and worthwhile approaches to resolving psychological problems have been made using each of the different models. Indeed, it is possible to address various parts of a given problem simultaneously using each model.

Consider Joyce Brown. We might first use the medical model to ex-amine whether Brown had any physical problems—such as continued dependence on heroin or cocaine, a brain tumor, a chemical imbalance in the brain, or some type of disease—that could possibly account for her unusual behavior.

A psychoanalytic theorist would take a very different approach, seek-ing out information about Brown's past, concentrating on her childhood and probing her memories to determine the nature of conflicts residing in her unconscious. A behavioral theorist would take still another ap-proach, concentrating on the nature of the rewards and punishments that Brown received for behaving in the way she did, as well as the stimuli in the environment that maintained or reinforced her behavior. For instance, Brown's street life certainly made her a center of attention in the neighborhood in which she lived. Finally, humanistic and sociocultural approaches would concentrate on Brown's view of herself, in relation to other people and to the world in general.

Humanistic theories might suggest that, by living on the streets and refusing to stay in the mental hospital, Brown had made a series of choices—although unconventional ones—about the way she wanted to lead her life. Sociocultural approaches, in contrast, would focus on the ways society contributed to Brown's problems, looking at how her relationships with others, possible economic difficulties, family structure, and cultural background influenced her behavior. Taking an extreme view, a sociocultural theorist might suggest that living over a hot-air grate was a legitimate alternative lifestyle and that society should not intervene in Brown's preferences. In fact, this argument was raised by her public defense lawyers, who argued that she had a constitutional right to choose whether she wanted treatment and that legally she could not be held against her will in a mental hospital. (For consideration of another legal issue associated with abnormal behavior, see the Psychology and Society box.)

As you can see, finding support for one or another of these approaches does not automatically make the others wrong; each focuses on somewhat different aspects of Brown's behavior and life. Of course, if her background were analyzed in depth, one approach ultimately might provide a better explanation than any other. But because the theories consider abnormal behavior at different levels, and because people's lives are made up of so many facets, a single approach may be insufficient to provide a full explanation for a person's abnormal behavior.

Do You Feel Abnormal?

As we conclude this introduction to abnormal behavior and begin to consider its specific classifications and treatment, it is important to note a phenomenon that has long been known to medical students, and one that you, too, may find yourself susceptible to—a phenomenon called **medical student's disease**. Although in the present case it might be more aptly labeled "psychology student's disease," the basic symptoms are the same: deciding that you suffer from the same sorts of problems you are studying.

Most often, of course, your concerns will be unwarranted. As we have discussed, the differences between normal and abnormal behavior are often so fuzzy that it is easy to jump to the conclusion that one has the same symptoms that are involved in serious forms of mental disturbance.

Before coming to such a conclusion, though, it is important to keep in mind that from time to time we all experience a wide range of emotions and subjective experiences, and it is not unusual to feel deeply unhappy,

PSYCHOLOGY AND SOCIETY

When Law and Psychology Mix: The Insanity Defense

When 26-year-old John Hinckley pulled the trigger and shot Ronald Reagan early in Reagan's first term, he did more than almost kill the former president. Ultimately, he set into motion a series of events that came close to dealing a lethal blow to the legal plea of insanity. For when Hinckley was found not guilty by reason of insanity, the public outrage at the verdict was so intense that Congress soon considered legislation to change the way in which that defense could be used.

Whether or not he had shot Reagan was never an issue, of course, during Hinckley's trial. Millions of people had witnessed the shooting on videotapes that were played repeatedly on television following the incident. What was at issue was Hinckley's state of mind: Was he legally insane at the time of the shooting?

According to law in twenty-two states, insanity—which is a legal, not a psychological term—means that defendants at the time they commit a criminal act cannot understand the difference between right and wrong. In twenty-six other states, however, a somewhat different definition is used; defendants are considered insane if they are substantially confused or unable to control themselves. And two other states—Idaho and Montana—do not accept insanity pleas at all.

As a defendant in a federal crime, Hinckley had to prove that he was incapable of knowing that his actions were wrong when he shot President Reagan. To prove this, the defense called expert witness after expert witness to the stand to portray Hinckley as a man overcome by schizophrenia, as well as an assortment of other severe mental problems. On the other hand, expert witnesses for the prosecution contended that Hinckley had made a conscious and rational decision to shoot Reagan, and that although he was self-centered and manipulative, he suffered from only minor mental health problems. To the jury, the task of determining which side was right seemed impossible; one juror, Maryland Copelin, said afterward, "If the expert psychiatrists could not decide whether the man was sane, then how are we supposed to decide?" (Time, July 5, 1982, p. 25).

In the end, the jury decided that Hinckley had been legally insane. The verdict produced rage and indignation, with a clear majority of people polled in an ABC news survey maintaining that the verdict was unjust. Some individuals called for drastic modification of the plea. For example, the Denver Post editorialized, "It's the system which found him innocent that's insane." Others called for complete abolition of the insanity plea. Their outrage increased a few years later, when Hinckley received several weekend passes from the mental hospital in which he had been confined after the jury decision.

Nonetheless, most people, while acknowledging the drawbacks to a plea about which even experts could not agree, believed that it was unreasonable to abolish the plea completely. Surely there was something wrong with Hinckley, whether or not he met the legal criteria for insanity, and abolishing the plea might prove to be like throwing out the baby with the bath water. Hopefully, as our understanding of abnormal behavior advances, it will be possible to provide more conclusive answers about the nature of a person's state of mind. Until that happens, however, we are going to have to grapple with the issues raised by Hinckley's trial (Rogers, 1987).

to fantasize about bizarre situations, or to feel anxiety about life's circumstances. It is the persistence, depth, and consistency of such behavior that sets normal reactions apart from abnormal ones. If you have not previously had serious doubts about the normality of your behavior, it is unlikely that reading about others' abnormality should prompt you to reevaluate your earlier conclusion.

ASK YOURSELF

Historically, how was abnormal behavior viewed?

What are the five major models of abnormality?

How can we most reasonably answer the question, "Which model provides the most complete explanation of abnormal behavior?"

How might the frequency of various disorders change across history?

THE ABCs OF DSM-III-R: CLASSIFYING TYPES OF ABNORMAL BEHAVIOR

Crazy. Nutty as a fruitcake. Loony. Insane. Neurotic. Strange. Demented. Odd. Possessed.

Society has long placed labels on people displaying abnormal behavior. Unfortunately, most of the time these labels have been pejorative, and they have been used without giving much thought to what they signify.

Providing appropriate and specific names and classifications for abnormal behavior has presented a major challenge to psychologists. It is not too hard to understand why, given the difficulties we discussed earlier in simply distinguishing normal from abnormal behavior. Yet classification systems are necessary in order to be able to describe and ultimately understand abnormal behavior.

Over the years many different classification systems have been used, varying in terms of their utility and how universally they have been accepted by mental health workers. Today, however, one standard system—devised by the American Psychiatric Association—has emerged and is employed by most professionals to classify abnormal behavior. The classification system is known as **DSM-III-R**—the *Diagnostic and Statistical Manual of Mental Disorders*, **Third Edition—Revised**.

Published in 1987, DSM-III-R presents comprehensive and relatively precise definitions for more than 230 separate diagnostic categories. By following the criteria presented in the system, diagnosticians can provide a clear description of the specific problem an individual is experiencing. (Table 10-1 provides a brief outline of the major diagnostic categories.)

TABLE 10-1 MAJOR DSM-III-R DIAGNOSTIC CATEGORIES

The following list of disorders represents the major categories from DSM-III-R, presented in the order in which they are discussed in the text. This is only a partial list of the 230 disorders found in DSM-III-R.

Anxiety disorders (problems in which anxiety impedes daily functioning)
   Subcategories: generalized anxiety disorder, panic disorder, phobic disorder, obsessive-compulsive disorder, posttraumatic stress disorder

Somatoform disorders (psychological difficulties displayed through physical problems)
   Subcategories: hypochondriasis, conversion disorder

Dissociative disorders (the splitting apart of crucial parts of personality that are usually integrated)
   Subcategories: multiple personality, psychogenic amnesia, psychogenic fugue

Mood disorders (emotions of depression or euphoria that are so strong they intrude on everyday living)
   Subcategories: major depression, bipolar disorder

Schizophrenia (declines in functioning, thought, and language disturbances, perception disorders, emotional disturbance, and withdrawal from others)
   Subcategories: disorganized, paranoid, catatonic, undifferentiated, residual

Personality disorders (problems that create little personal distress but that lead to an inability to function as a normal member of society)
   Subcategories: antisocial (sociopathic) personality disorder, narcissistic personality disorder

Sexual disorders (problems related to sexual arousal from unusual objects or problems related to sexual functioning)
   Subcategories: paraphilias, sexual dysfunction

Psychoactive substance-use disorders (problems related to drug dependence and abuse)
   Subcategories: alcohol, cocaine, hallucinogens, marijuana

Organic mental disorders (problems produced by physical deterioration of the brain)
   Subcategories: Alzheimer's disease, delirium, dementia

DSM-III-R evaluates a person's behavior according to five dimensions, or axes. The first three axes assess the person's present condition according to the particular maladaptive behaviors being exhibited; the nature of any long-standing personality problems in adults or any specific developmental problems in children and adolescents that may be relevant to treatment; and any physical disorders or illnesses that may also be present. The fourth and fifth axes take into account a broader consideration of the person, focusing on the severity of stressors present and the general level of functioning over the past year in social relationships, work, and the use of leisure time.

One particularly noteworthy feature of DSM-III-R is that it is meant to be primarily descriptive and devoid of suggestions as to the underlying causes of an individual's behavior and problems (Klerman, 1984). Hence, the term "neurotic"—a label that is commonly used by people in their everyday descriptions of abnormal behavior—is not listed as a DSM-III-R category. The reason is that "neurotic" derives directly from Freud's theory of personality (discussed in Chapter 9). Because the term refers to problems with a specific cause and theoretical approach, neurosis is no longer listed as a category.

DSM-III-R has the advantage, then, of providing a descriptive system that does not specify the cause or reason behind the problem. Instead, it paints a picture of the behavior that is being manifested. Why should this be important? For one thing, it allows communication between mental health professionals of diverse backgrounds and approaches and does not immediately suggest that there is only one appropriate treatment. Another important point is that precise classification enables researchers to go forward and to explore the causes of a problem. If the manifestations of an abnormal behavior cannot be reliably described, researchers will be hard-pressed to find ways of investigating the difficulties. Finally, DSM-III-R provides a kind of conceptual shorthand through which professionals can describe the behaviors that tend to occur simultaneously in an individual.

It is also important to note that the DSM is designed to be revised periodically. Reflecting the fact that changes in society affect what behaviors are viewed as abnormal, DSM-IV is scheduled to be completed in the near future.

Of course, DSM-III-R has its drawbacks, as does any classification system (Vaillant, 1984). Perhaps the strongest criticism is its possible overreliance on a medical model. Because it was drawn up by psychiatrists—who are physicians—it was criticized as viewing abnormal behaviors primarily in terms of symptoms of some underlying physiological disorder. Moreover, some critics suggest that DSM-III-R pigeonholes people into inflexible categories, and that it would be more reasonable to use systems that classify people along some sort of continuum or scale.

Other concerns with DSM-III-R are more subtle but equally important. For instance, Szasz (1961) argues that labeling an individual as a deviant provides a lifetime stigma that is dehumanizing. Moreover, there is a tendency for a diagnosis itself to be mistaken for an explanation of a problem. Saying, for instance, that a woman with schizophrenia hears voices may make it seem as though schizophrenia is an *explanation* for her behavior—when in fact schizophrenia is simply a label that gives no clue as to *why* the woman hears voices (Rosenhan, 1975). Furthermore, after an initial diagnosis is made, other diagnostic possibilities may be overlooked by mental health professionals, who concentrate on the initial diagnostic category.

Despite these drawbacks, DSM-III-R remains the major categorization system in use today. It has increased both the reliability and validity of diagnostic categorization; it also provides a logical way to organize our examination of the major types of mental disturbance, to which we turn next.

In our discussion of the major disorders, we will consider the disorders that are most common, serious, or debilitating. We begin with disorders in which anxiety plays a predominate role, those in which psychological difficulties take on a physical form, and disorders in which the parts of personality are no longer integrated. Although these disorders are discussed in a dispassionate manner, it is important to keep in mind that each represents a very human set of difficulties that influence and in some cases play havoc with people's lives.

*T*HE MAJOR DISORDERS

I remember walking up the street, the moon was shining and suddenly everything around me seemed unfamiliar, as it would be in a dream. I felt panic rising inside me, but managed to push it away and carry on. I walked a quarter of a mile or so, with the panic getting worse every minute. . . . By now, I was sweating, yet trembling; my heart was pounding and my legs felt like jelly. . . . Terrified, I stood not knowing what to do. The only bit of sanity left in me told me to get home. Somehow this I did very slowly, holding onto the fence in the road. I cannot remember the actual journey back, until I was going into the house, then I broke down and cried helplessly (Melville, 1977, pp. 1, 14).

Anxiety Without Reason: Anxiety Disorders

All of us, at one time or another, experience **anxiety**, a feeling of apprehension or tension, in reaction to stressful situations. There is nothing "wrong" with such anxiety; everyone feels it to some degree, and usually it is a reaction to stress that helps, rather than hinders, our daily functioning. Without anxiety, for instance, most of us would not be terribly motivated to study hard, to undergo physical exams, or to spend long hours at our jobs.

But some people—such as the person who wrote the passage above— experience anxiety in situations in which there is no external reason or cause. When anxiety occurs without external justification and begins to impede people's daily functioning, it is considered a psychological problem known as an **anxiety disorder**. There are four main types of anxiety disorders: generalized anxiety disorder, panic disorder, phobic disorder, and obsessive-compulsive disorder.

Generalized anxiety disorder. As the name implies, **generalized anxiety disorder** refers to a disorder in which an individual experiences long-term, consistent anxiety without knowing why. Such people feel afraid of *something,* but are unable to articulate what it is. Because of their anxiety they are unable to function normally. They cannot concentrate and cannot set their fears aside, and their lives become centered around their anxiety. Such anxiety may eventually result in the development of physiological problems. Because of heightened muscle tension and arousal, individuals with generalized anxiety disorder may begin to experience headaches, dizziness, heart palpitations, or insomnia.

Panic disorder. In another type of anxiety disorder, **panic disorder**, there are instances of **panic attacks** that last from a few seconds to as much as several hours. During an attack, such as the one described at the start of this section of the chapter, the anxiety that a person has been chronically experiencing suddenly rises to a peak, and the individual feels a sense of impending, unavoidable doom. Although symptoms differ from person to person, they may include heart palpitations, shortness of breath, unusual amounts of sweating, faintness and dizziness, an urge to urinate, gastric sensations and—in extreme cases—a sense of imminent death. After an attack such as this, it is no wonder that people tend to feel exhausted (Barlow, 1988).

Phobic disorder. What do Bob Newhart, Wayne Gretzky, Maureen Stapleton, Aretha Franklin, and Isaac Asimov have in common? All have a fear of flying that is severe enough to disrupt their lives (Zeman, 1989).

Such fears as fear of flying represent a class of psychological disorder known as phobias. **Phobias** are intense, irrational fears of specific objects or situations. For example, claustrophobia is a fear of enclosed places, acrophobia a fear of high places, and xenophobia a fear of strangers. Although the objective danger posed by an anxiety-producing stimulus (which can be just about anything, as you can see from the list in Table 10-2) is typically small or nonexistent, to the individual suffering from the

To Virginia Artus or anyone else suffering from acrophobia (the fear of heights), climbing or descending even a short flight of stairs may present major difficulties.

TABLE 10-2 GIVING FEAR A PROPER NAME

Phobia	Stimulus	Phobia	Stimulus
Acrophobia	Heights	Herpetophobia	Reptiles
Aerophobia	Flying	Hydrophobia	Water
Agoraphobia	Open spaces	Mikrophobia	Germs
Ailurophobia	Cats	Murophobia	Mice
Amaxophobia	Vehicles, driving	Mysophobia	Dirt or germs
Anthophobia	Flowers	Numerophobia	Numbers
Anthrophobia	People	Nyctophobia	Darkness
Aquaphobia	Water	Ochlophobia	Crowds
Arachniphobia	Spiders	Ophidiophobia	Snakes
Astraphobia	Lightning	Ornithophobia	Birds
Brontophobia	Thunder	Phonophobia	Speaking out loud
Claustrophobia	Closed spaces	Pyrophobia	Fire
Cynophobia	Dogs	Thanatophobia	Death
Dementophobia	Insanity	Trichophobia	Hair
Gephyrophobia	Bridges	Xenophobia	Strangers

phobia it represents great danger, and a full-blown panic attack may follow exposure to the stimulus. Phobic disorders differ from generalized anxiety disorders and panic disorders in that there is a specific, identifiable stimulus that sets off the anxiety reaction.

Phobias may have only a minor impact on people's lives if the people who suffer from them can avoid the things they fear. Unless one is a professional fire fighter or tightrope walker, for example, a fear of heights may have little impact on one's daily life. On the other hand, a fear of strangers presents a more debilitating problem. In one extreme case, a Washington housewife left her home just three times in thirty years—once to visit her family, once for an operation, and once to purchase ice cream for a dying companion (Adler, 1984; Baker, 1989).

Obsessive-compulsive disorder. In **obsessive-compulsive disorder**, people are plagued by unwanted thoughts, called obsessions, or feel that they must carry out some actions, termed compulsions, against their will.

An **obsession** is a thought or idea that keeps recurring in one's mind. For example, a student may not be able to stop feeling that he has neglected to put his name on a test and may think about it constantly for the two weeks it takes to get the paper back; a man may go on vacation and wonder the whole time whether he locked his house; a woman may hear the same tune running through her head over and over again. In each case, the thought or idea is unwanted and difficult to put out of mind. Of course, many of us suffer from mild obsessions from time to time, but usually such thoughts persist for a short period only. For people with serious obsessions, however, the thoughts persist for days or months and may consist of bizarre, troubling images. In one classic case of an obsession, the patient

> complained of having "terrible thoughts." When she thought of her boyfriend she wished he were dead; when her mother went down the stairs, she "wished she'd fall and break her neck"; when her sister spoke of going to the beach with her infant daughter, the patient "hoped that they would both drown." These thoughts "make me hysterical. I love them; why should I wish such terrible things to happen? It drives me wild, makes me feel I'm crazy and don't belong to society" (Kraines, 1948, p. 199).

As part of an obsessive-compulsive disorder, people may also experience **compulsions**, urges to repeatedly carry out some act that seems strange and unreasonable, even to them. Whatever the compulsive behavior, people experience extreme anxiety if they cannot carry it out, even if it is something they want to stop. The acts involved may be relatively trivial, such as repeatedly checking the stove to make sure all the burners are turned off, or more unusual, such as a continuous need to wash oneself (Rachman & Hodgson, 1980). For example, consider this case report of a 27-year-old woman with a cleaning ritual:

> Bess would first remove all of her clothing in a preestablished sequence. She would lay out each article of clothing at specific spots on her bed, and examine each one for any indications of "contamination." She would then thoroughly scrub her body, starting at her feet and working meticulously up to the top of her head, using certain washcloths for certain areas of her body. Any articles of clothing that appeared to have been "contaminated" were thrown into the laundry. Clean clothing was put in the spots that were vacant. She would then dress herself in the opposite order from which she took the clothes off. If there were any deviations from this order, or if Bess began to wonder if she had missed some contamination, she would go through the entire sequence again. It was not rare for her to do this four or five times in a row on certain evenings (Meyer & Osborne, 1982, p. 156).

Unfortunately for people experiencing an obsessive-compulsive disorder, there is no reduction of anxiety from carrying out a compulsive ritual. They tend to lead lives filled with unrelenting tension.

When the Psychological Leads to the Physical: Somatoform Disorders

Most of us know people who cannot wait to regale us with their latest physical problems; even an innocent "How are you?" brings a long list of complaints in response. People who consistently report physical problems, have a preoccupation with their health, and have unrealistic fears of disease may be experiencing a problem known as **hypochondriasis**. In hypochondriasis there is a constant fear of illness, and physical sensations are misinterpreted as signs of disease. It is not that the "symptoms" are faked; hypochondriacs actually experience the aches and pains that most of us feel as we go through an active existence (Costa & McCrae, 1985). It is the misinterpretation of these sensations as symptoms of some dread disease—often in the face of unarguable medical evidence to the contrary—that characterizes hypochondriasis.

Hypochondriasis is just one example of a class of disorders known as **somatoform disorders**—psychological difficulties that take on a physical (somatic) form of one sort or another. Even though an individual reports physical symptoms, there is no underlying physical problem, or, if a physical problem does exist, the person's reaction greatly exaggerates what would be expected from the medical problem alone. Only when a physical examination rules out actual physiological difficulties can a diagnosis of somatoform disorder be made.

In addition to hypochondriasis, the other major somatoform disorder is **conversion disorder**. In contrast to hypochondriasis, in which there is no actual physical problem, conversion disorders involve an actual physical disturbance such as the inability to use a sensory organ or the complete or partial inability to move an arm or leg. The *cause* of such a physical disturbance is purely psychological; there is no biological reason for the problem. Some of Freud's classic cases involved conversion disorders. For instance, one patient of Freud's was suddenly unable to use her arm, without any apparent physiological cause; later, just as abruptly, she regained its use.

Conversion disorders are often characterized by their rapid onset. People wake up one morning blind or deaf, or they experience numbness that is restricted to a certain part of the body. A person's hand, for example, might become entirely numb, while an area above the wrist—controlled by the same nerves—remains inexplicably sensitive to touch. Such a condition is referred to as "glove anesthesia," because the area that is numb is the part of the hand covered by a glove, and not a region related to pathways of the nervous system (see Figure 10-1).

Interestingly, one of the characteristics of conversion disorders is a surprising lack of concern over the symptoms that one would expect to be highly anxiety-producing. For instance, a person in good health who wakes up blind might react in a bland, matter-of-fact way. Considering how most people would feel if it happened to them, this reaction hardly seems appropriate.

Most conversion disorders occur when an individual is under emotional stress that can be reduced by a physical symptom. The physical condition allows the person to escape or reduce the source of stress. An emotional problem is turned, then, into a physical ailment that acts to relieve the source of the original emotional problem.

In one large-scale example of conversion disorder, Mucha and Reinhardt (1970) found that some 16 percent of the student aviators at the U.S. Naval Aerospace Medical Institute suffered symptoms for which there

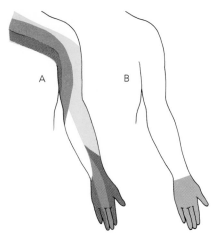

FIGURE 10-1
A person who suffered from actual nerve damage in the arm would show numbness in the entire area shown in (*a*). However, a person with "glove anesthesia" would experience numbness in just the area that would be covered by a glove (*b*), which is a region of the body that is unrelated to the pathways of the nervous system. Therefore, the phenomenon can only be attributed to psychological causes.

was no underlying physical problem. The difficulties most frequently included blurred vision, double vision, and the development of blind spots and focusing trouble. Investigation revealed that the students found outright quitting an unacceptable response to the stress they were experiencing and instead developed physical responses that allowed them to avoid the demands of the program. Their stress was thus relieved through a face-saving physical problem.

One Becomes Two (or More): Dissociative Disorders

The most dramatic and celebrated cases of psychological dysfunctioning—although they are actually quite rare—have been **dissociative disorders**. The movie *The Three Faces of Eve*, the book *Sybil* (about a girl with sixteen personalities), and cases of people found wandering the

Although in reality quite rare, the disorder of multiple personality has been featured in many novels and films. For instance, movie buffs will recall *Sybil*, the story of a girl who, as her psychiatrist eventually discovered, had no fewer than sixteen separate personalities.

streets with no notion of who they are or where they came from exemplify dissociative disorders. The key factor in such problems is the splitting apart (or dissociation) of critical parts of personality that are normally integrated and work together. This lack of integration acts to allow certain parts of a personality to avoid stress—since another part can be made to face it. By dissociating themselves from key parts of their personality, individuals with the disorder can eliminate anxiety.

There are three major types of dissociative disorders: multiple personality, psychogenic amnesia, and psychogenic fugue. A person with a multiple personality displays characteristics of two or more distinct personalities. Each personality has a unique set of likes and dislikes and its own reactions to situations. In fact, some people with multiple personalities carry several pairs of glasses because their vision changes with each personality. Moreover, each individual personality can be well adjusted, when considered on its own (Braun, 1985; Ross, 1989).

The problem, of course, is that there is only one body available to the various personalities, forcing the personalities to take turns. Because there can be strong variations in personalities, the person's behavior—considered as a whole—can appear very inconsistent. For instance, in the famous case portrayed in *The Three Faces of Eve,* the meek, bland Eve White provided a stunning contrast to the dominant and carefree Eve Black.

Psychogenic amnesia, another dissociative disorder, is a failure or inability to remember past experiences. Psychogenic amnesia is unlike simple amnesia, which, as we discussed in Chapter 5, involves an actual loss of information from memory, typically due to a physiological cause. In contrast, in cases of psychogenic amnesia, the "forgotten" material is still present in memory—it simply cannot be recalled.

In the most severe forms, individuals cannot recall their names, are unable to recognize parents and other relatives, and do not know their addresses. In other respects, though, they may appear quite normal: Apart from an inability to remember certain facts about themselves, they may be able to recall skills and abilities that they developed earlier. For instance, even though a chef may not remember where he grew up and received training, he may still be able to prepare gourmet meals.

In some cases of psychogenic amnesia, the memory loss is quite profound. For example, a woman—dubbed Jane Doe by her rescuers—was found by a Florida park ranger in the early 1980s. Incoherent, thin, and only partially clothed, Doe was unable to recall her name, her past, and even how to read and write. On the basis of her accent, authorities thought the woman was from Illinois, and interviews conducted under drugs revealed that she had had a Catholic education. However, the childhood memories she revealed were so universal that her background could not be further pinpointed. In a desperate attempt to rediscover her identity, she appeared on the television show *Good Morning America,* and ultimately a couple from Roselle, Illinois, whose daughter had moved to Florida, stepped forward, saying that they were her parents. However, Jane Doe never regained her memory (Carson, Butcher & Coleman, 1988).

This woman, identified only as "Jane Doe" by the hospital where she was treated, was a victim of psychogenic amnesia.

A more unusual form of amnesia is a condition known as **psychogenic fugue**. In this state, people take an impulsive, sudden trip, often assuming a new identity. After a period of time—days, months, or sometimes even years—they suddenly realize that they are in a strange place and completely forget the time that they have spent wandering. Their last memories are those just before they entered the fugue state.

What the dissociative disorders have in common is that they allow people to escape from some anxiety-producing situation. Either the person produces a new personality to deal with stress, or the situation that caused the stress is forgotten or left behind as the individual journeys to some new—and perhaps less anxiety-ridden—situation.

ASK YOURSELF

What is the major classification system used to describe psychological disorders?

What are the major characteristics of anxiety disorders?

How can somatoform disorders be described?

When do dissociative disorders occur?

What are the advantages and disadvantages of a classification system such as DSM-III-R, and what are the limitations of consolidating people together into categories?

The Feeling Is Wrong: Mood Disorders

I do not care for anything. I do not care to ride, for the exercise is too violent. I do not care to walk, for walking is too strenuous. I do not care to lie down, for I should either have to remain lying, and I do not care to do that, or I should have to get up again, and I do not care to do that either. . . . I do not care at all.

Have you ever taken a test for which you had studied for days and days, felt afterward that you had done well, but later found that you had received a very low grade? Although the reactions you experienced were probably not as strong as those felt by the Danish philosopher Søren Kierkegaard, who wrote the passage above, it is likely that you experienced a feeling of depression, an emotional reaction of sadness and melancholy. More than likely, however, you soon returned to a more pleasant frame of mind.

We all experience mood swings. Sometimes we are happy, perhaps even euphoric; at other times we feel upset, saddened, or depressed. Such changes in mood are a normal part of everyday life. In some people, however, moods are so pronounced and so long-lasting that they interfere with the ability to function effectively. In extreme cases a mood may become life-threatening, and in others it may cause the person to lose touch with reality. Situations such as these represent **mood disorders**, disturbances in emotional feelings strong enough to intrude on everyday living.

Feeling down: Major depression. Moses. Rousseau. Dostoevsky. Queen Victoria. Lincoln. Tchaikovsky. Freud.

The common link among these people? Each suffered from periodic attacks of **major depression**, one of the most common forms of mood disorders. In fact, the percentage of people who are likely to experience major depression during their lifetime is 8 to 12 percent for men and 20 to 26 percent for women (Boyd & Weissman, 1981). Depression is the most frequent problem diagnosed in outpatient clinics, affecting about one-third of the patients (Woodruff, Clayton & Guze, 1975; Winokur, 1983). Furthermore, the rate of depression is increasing, with people experiencing much more depression than they did two generations ago. Even children can display depression; for instance, a sample of 3000 third-, fourth-, and fifth-graders found that around 5 percent were depressed (Lefkowitz & Tesiny, 1985; Seligman, 1988).

When psychologists speak of major depression they do not mean the sadness that comes from experiencing one of life's disappointments. Some

While temporary depression is a normal response to one of life's disappointments, in some cases depression is so severe and lingering that it represents a major psychological disorder.

depression is normal following the break-up of a long-term relationship, the death of a loved one, or the loss of a job. It is even normal for less serious problems: doing badly in school or not getting into the college of one's choice. In fact, many college students experience some form of "normal" depression during their years in school (Blatt, D'Afflitti, & Quinlan, 1976).

Individuals who suffer from major depression experience similar sorts of feelings, but the severity tends to be considerably greater. They may feel useless, worthless, and lonely and may despair over the future—feelings that may continue for months and years. They may have uncontrollable crying jags and disrupted sleep. The depth of such behavior and the length of time it lasts are the hallmarks of major depression.

Ups and downs: Mania and bipolar disorders. While some people are sinking into the depths of depression, others are emotionally soaring high, experiencing what is called mania. **Mania** refers to an extended state of intense euphoria and elation. People experiencing mania feel intense happiness, power, invulnerability, and energy. They may become involved in wild schemes, believing that they will succeed at anything they attempt. There are many cases on record of people squandering all their money while in a state of mania; consider, for example, the following description of an individual who experienced a manic episode:

> Mr. O'Reilly took a leave of absence from his civil service job. He purchased a large number of cuckoo clocks and then an expensive car, which he planned to use as a mobile showroom for his wares, anticipating that he would make a great deal of money. He proceeded to "tear around town" buying and selling clocks and other merchandise, and when he was not out, he was continuously on the phone making "deals." He rarely slept and, uncharacteristically, spent every evening in neighborhood bars drinking heavily and, according to him, "wheeling and dealing." . . . He was $3000 in debt and had driven his family to exhaustion with his excessive activity and talkativeness. He said, however, that he felt "on top of the world" (Spitzer, Skodol, Gibbon & Williams, 1983, p. 115).

Mania is often found paired with bouts of depression. This alternation of mania and depression is called **bipolar disorder** (or, as it used to be known, manic-depressive disorder). The swings between highs and lows may occur as frequently as a few days apart or they may alternate over a period of years. In addition, the periods of depression tend to be longer in most individuals than the periods of mania, although this pattern is reversed in some.

Interestingly, it has been suggested that some of society's most creative individuals may suffer from a mild form of bipolar disorder. The imagination, drive, excitement, and energy that they display during manic stages allows them to make unusually creative contributions. On the other hand, most people who display mania go beyond the bounds of what

Historical and biographical information has enabled experts to diagnose these three Romantic composers as sufferers of bipolar disorder: Robert Schumann, Hector Berlioz, and Gustav Mahler.

would generally be considered normal, and their behavior clearly causes self-harm (Fieve, 1975; Georgotas & Cancro, 1988).

Causes of mood disorders. Because they represent a major mental health problem, mood disorders—in particular, depression—have received a good deal of study, and a number of approaches have been used to explain their occurrence. Psychoanalytic approaches, for example, see depression as the result of anger at oneself. In this view, people feel responsible for the bad things that happen to them and direct their anger inward. On the other hand, there is convincing evidence that heredity plays a role in depression, since major depression seems to run in certain families (Rosenthal, 1970; Wender et al., 1986; Egeland et al., 1987).

Furthermore, some researchers have found a chemical imbalance in the brains of some depressed patients: Certain abnormalities have been identified in the neurotransmitters involved in the communication between nerve cells (Wender & Klein, 1981). Other research has identified a genetic defect that provides evidence that bipolar disorder is linked to inherited factors (Egeland et al., 1987). This chemical and genetic evidence suggests that people's moods may be determined in part by biological factors rather than the psychological factors suggested by psychoanalytic approaches (McNeal & Cimbolic, 1986).

There are still other explanations for mood disorders. For instance, Seligman (1975) suggests that depression is a response to learned helplessness, a state in which a person perceives and eventually learns that there is no way to escape from or cope with stress and simply gives up fighting it—a proposition that has received a good deal of research support (Robins, 1988).

One of the most puzzling questions about depression is why there has been an increase in its incidence over past generations. Martin Seligman (1988) suggests that the increase is due to a change in societal values, in which individuals now feel an increased commitment to themselves and a lowered commitment to the traditional institutions of religion, family, the nation, and the community. In the past, such institutions helped people from feeling despair at times of personal failure. Without these institutions to lean on in time of stress, people sink into depression more readily than in earlier years.

Societal factors also may provide the elusive answer to another difficult question facing researchers: Why is the incidence of depression almost two times higher for women than for men? One possibility is that the stress experienced by women may be greater than men at certain points in women's lives—such as cases in which a woman must simultaneously earn a living and be primary caretaker for her children (McGrath, 1988). But biological factors may also explain some women's depression. For example, 25 to 50 percent of women who take oral contraceptives report symptoms of depression, and depression that occurs following the birth of a child is linked to hormonal changes (Strickland, 1988).

It is clear, though, that researchers have discovered no definitive solutions to the puzzle of depression, and there are many alternative explanations (e.g., Hyland, 1987; Pyszczynski, Holt & Greenberg, 1987; Dykman & Abramson, 1990). Most likely, mood disorders are caused by a complex interaction of several factors.

When Reality Is Lost: Schizophrenia

> For many years she has heard voices, which insult her and cast suspicion on her chastity. They mention a number of names she knows, and tell her she will be stripped and abused. The voices are very distinct, and, in her opinion, they must be carried by a telescope or a machine from her home. Her thoughts are dictated to her; she is obliged to think them, and hears them repeated after her. She is interrupted in her work, and has all kinds of uncomfortable sensations in her body, to which something is "done." In particular, her "mother parts" are turned inside out, and people send a pain through her back, lay ice water on her heart, squeeze her neck, injure her spine, and violate her (Kraepelin, 1904).

The label given to the most severe forms of mental disturbance, such as that described in the famous case study above, is **schizophrenia**. Schizophrenics make up by far the largest percentage of those hospitalized for mental disorders and in most respects are the least likely to recover from their difficulties.

Schizophrenia refers to a class of disorders in which severe distortion of reality occurs. Thinking, perception, and emotion may deteriorate; there may be a withdrawal from social interaction; and there may be displays of bizarre behavior. Although several types of schizophrenia (see Table 10-3) have been observed, the distinctions between them are not always clear-cut (e.g., Zigler & Glick, 1988). Moreover, the symptoms displayed by a schizophrenic person may vary considerably over time, and people with schizophrenia show significant differences in the pattern of symptoms even when they are labeled with the same diagnostic category. Nonetheless, a number of characteristics reliably distinguish schizophrenia. They include:

- Decline from a previous level of functioning. An individual can no longer carry out activities he or she was once able to do.
- Disturbances of thought and language. Schizophrenics use logic and language in a peculiar way; their thinking does not make sense and they do not follow conventional linguistic rules. Consider, for example, the following response to the question "Why do you think people believe in God?"

Uh, let's, I don't know why, let's see, balloon travel. He holds it up for you, the balloon. He don't let you fall out, your little legs sticking down through the clouds. He's down to the smokestack, looking through the smoke trying to get the balloon gassed up you know. Way they're flying on top that way, legs sticking out. I don't know, looking down on the ground, heck, that'd make you so dizzy you just stay and sleep you know, hold down and sleep there. I used to be sleep outdoors, you know, sleep outdoors instead of going home (Chapman & Chapman, 1973, p. 3).

TABLE 10-3 THE MAJOR TYPES OF SCHIZOPHRENIA

Type	Symptoms
Disorganized (hebephrenic) schizophrenia	Inappropriate laughter and giggling, silliness, incoherent speech, infantile behavior, strange and sometimes obscene behavior
Paranoid schizophrenia	Delusions and hallucinations of persecution or of greatness, loss of judgment, erratic and unpredictable behavior
Catatonic schizophrenia	Major disturbances in movement; in some phases, loss of all motion, with patient frozen into a single position, remaining that way for hours and sometimes even days; in other phases, hyperactivity and wild, sometimes violent, movement
Undifferentiated schizophrenia	Variable mixture of major symptoms of schizophrenia; classification used for patients who cannot be typed into any of the more specific categories
Residual schizophrenia	Minor signs of schizophrenia following a more serious episode

 As this selection illustrates, although the basic grammatical structure may be intact, the substance of schizophrenics' thinking is often illogical, garbled, and lacking in meaningful content (see Figure 10-2).

- Delusions. People with schizophrenia often have **delusions**, firmly held, unshakable beliefs with no basis in reality. Among the most frequent ones are the beliefs that they are being controlled by someone else, that they are being persecuted by others, and that their thoughts are being broadcast so that others are able to know what they are thinking.

- Perceptual disorders. Schizophrenics do not perceive the world as most other people do. They may see, hear, or smell things differ-

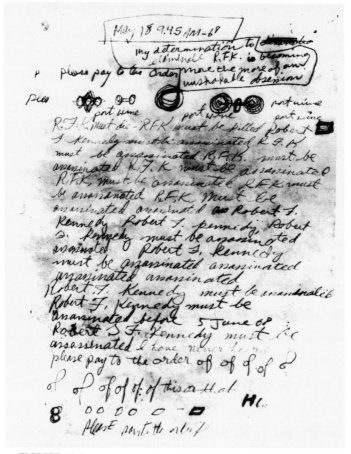

FIGURE 10-2
This excerpt from the diary of Sirhan Sirhan, the killer of Robert F. Kennedy, shows the disturbances of thought and language characteristic of schizophrenia.

ently from others and do not even have a sense of their bodies in the way that others do. Some reports suggest that schizophrenics have difficulty determining where their own bodies stop and the rest of the world begins (Ritzler & Rosenbaum, 1974). They may also have **hallucinations**, the experience of perceiving things that do not actually exist.

- Emotional disturbances. People with schizophrenia sometimes show a bland lack of emotion in which even the most dramatic events produce little or no emotional response. Conversely, they may display emotion that is inappropriate to a situation. For example, a schizophrenic might laugh uproariously at a funeral or may react with anger when being helped by someone.

- Withdrawal. Schizophrenics tend to have little interest in others. They tend not to socialize or hold real conversations with others, although they may talk *at* another person. In the most extreme cases they do not even acknowledge the presence of other people, appearing to be in their own isolated world.

The symptoms of schizophrenia follow two primary courses. In **process schizophrenia**, the symptoms develop relatively early in life, slowly and subtly. There may be a gradual withdrawal from the world, excessive daydreaming, a blunting of emotion, until eventually the disorder reaches the point where others cannot overlook it. In other cases—known as **reactive schizophrenia**—the onset of symptoms is sudden and conspicuous. The treatment outlook for reactive schizophrenia is relatively favorable; process schizophrenia has proved to be much more difficult to treat.

A relatively recent addition to the classifications used in schizophrenia distinguishes positive-symptom from negative-symptom schizophrenia (Opler et al., 1984; Andreasen, 1985; Kay & Murrill, 1990). Negative-symptom schizophrenia means an absence or loss of normal functioning, such as social withdrawal or blunted emotions. In contrast, positive-symptom schizophrenia is indicated by the presence of disordered behavior such as hallucinations, delusions, and extremes of emotionality. The distinction, although controversial, is becoming increasingly important because it suggests that two different underlying processes may explain the roots of schizophrenia—which remains one of the greatest mysteries facing psychologists who deal with abnormal behavior.

Solving the puzzle: The causes of schizophrenia. Although it is clear that schizophrenic behavior departs radically from normal behavior, its causes are less apparent. It does appear, however, that schizophrenia has genetic, brain-structural, biochemical, and environmental components at its roots (Mirsky & Duncan, 1986; Watt, 1985).

Genetic components. Because schizophrenia is more common in some families than in others, genetic factors seem to be involved in producing at least a susceptibility to or readiness for developing schizophrenia (Faraone & Tsuang, 1985; Holzman & Matthysse, 1990). For example, researchers have found evidence of a link between schizophrenia and an abnormally functioning gene (Gurling et al., 1988). In addition, some studies show that people who have been classified as suffering from schizophrenia have about a 25 percent chance of having children with severe psychological problems. Furthermore, if one of a pair of identical twins has schizophrenia, the other has as much as a 42 percent chance of developing it (Gottesman & Schields, 1972; Kringlen, 1978). However, if genetics alone were entirely accountable, the chance of the other identical twin having schizophrenia would be 100 percent, since identical twins share the same genetic makeup. The development of schizophrenia, then, is due to more than just genetic factors.

Structural abnormalities in the brain. One explanation of schizophrenia suggests that abnormalities in the structure of the brain produce symptoms of the disturbance. For instance, comparisons of the brains of long-term schizophrenics and nonschizophrenics after they have died show differences in the organization of cells. In one study, for example, the nerve cells of nonschizophrenics were found to be arranged in orderly rows, whereas the cells of those with schizophrenia were in disarray (Scheibel, 1984; Altshuler et al., 1987).

Furthermore, one recent study examined brain scans of twins, one of whom was diagnosed as schizophrenic and the other of whom was not. Results of the study showed that most of those diagnosed as schizophrenic had a smaller hippocampus and enlarged lateral ventricles in comparison to their normal twin (Suddath et al., 1990).

Although we cannot rule out the hypothesis that structural problems in the brains of people with schizophrenia are a consequence of schizophrenia—rather than its cause—the findings of current research do suggest that schizophrenic symptoms may be produced at least in part by irregularities in the structure of the brain. Such abnormalities may occur during an early period of fetal development.

Biochemical components. One of the most intriguing hypotheses to explain schizophrenia is that there is some sort of biochemical imbalance in the brains of people with the disorder (Asnis & Ryan, 1983; Noll & Davis, 1983; Johnson, 1989). One form of this theory suggests that schizophrenia occurs when a person's body in a condition of stress produces chemicals that cause hallucinations or disorganized thought—similar to the effects of a drug such as LSD—in a sort of self-induced chemical overdose (Carson, 1983).

On the other hand, alternative theories resting on the notion of a biochemical imbalance are also plausible. For instance, the **dopamine hypothesis** suggests that schizophrenia occurs when there is excess activity in those areas of the brain that use the chemical dopamine to transmit impulses across nerve cells (Wong et al., 1988; Snyder, 1978). This hypothesis came to light after the discovery that drugs that block dopamine action in brain pathways can be highly effective in reducing the symptoms of schizophrenia.

Unfortunately, the dopamine hypothesis does not provide the whole story. Drugs that block dopamine action produce a biological reaction in just a few hours after they're taken—yet the symptoms of schizophrenia don't subside for weeks. If the hypothesis were entirely correct, we would expect an immediate improvement in schizophrenic symptoms. Moreover, these drugs are effective in reducing symptoms not only in schizophrenics but also in those suffering from very different sorts of psychological problems such as mania and depression (Carson, 1983). Nevertheless, the dopamine hypothesis provides a starting point in understanding biochemical factors in schizophrenia.

Environmental components. Given that genetic, brain-structural, and biochemical factors do not provide a full explanation for schizophrenia, we need to consider past and current experiences found in the environments of people who develop the disturbance (Keith & Matthews, 1983). Psychoanalytic approaches suggest that schizophrenia is a form of regression to earlier experiences and stages of life. Freud said, for instance, that people with schizophrenia lack strong enough egos to cope with their unacceptable impulses. They regress to the oral stage—a time in which the id and ego are not yet separated. Therefore, individuals suffering from schizophrenia essentially lack an ego and act out impulses without concern for reality.

Although this is theoretically reasonable, there is little evidence to support psychoanalytic explanations. More compelling are theories that look toward the family and other major figures in the lives of people with schizophrenia. One influential theory, known as the **double-bind hypothesis**, states that individuals with schizophrenia may have received simultaneous messages from their mothers that contradicted one another (Bateson, 1960). Consider, for example, how you would react if someone told you to "come here," and then, as you approached, waved you away. According to the hypothesis, this is essentially what happens in some families: The mother is warm and loving on a verbal level but anxious and rejecting on an emotional and nonverbal level. The results are so devastating to the child that eventually he or she develops schizophrenia.

Although the details of the double-bind hypothesis have not received much support, there is firm evidence that families with members who have schizophrenia often have abnormal communication patterns (Wynne, Singer, Bartko & Toohey, 1975). These families may differ in a number of other dimensions as well, including socioeconomic status, anxiety level, and general degree of stress present (Lidz, 1973; Lidz & Fleck, 1985).

Theorists taking a behavioral perspective believe these differences support a **learned-inattention theory** of schizophrenia (Ullmann & Krasner, 1975). According to the learned-inattention view, schizophrenia is a learned behavior consisting of a set of inappropriate responses to social stimuli. Instead of responding to others, people with schizophrenia have learned to ignore appropriate stimuli and pay attention instead to stimuli that are not related to normal social interaction. Because this results in bizarre behavior, others respond to them in a negative way, leading to social rejection and unpleasant interactions and ultimately to an even less appropriate response by the individual in the future. Eventually, the individual begins to "tune out" appropriate stimuli and develops schizophrenic characteristics.

The causes of schizophrenia—not one, but many?   As we have seen, there is research supporting genetic, brain-structural, biochemical, and environmental causes of schizophrenia. It is likely, then, that not just one but several causes jointly explain the onset of the problem. The predominant approach used today, the **predisposition model**, considers a number of factors simultaneously (Zubin & Spring, 1977). This model suggests that individuals may inherit a predisposition or an inborn sensitivity to schizophrenia which makes them particularly vulnerable to stressful factors in the environment. The stressors may vary—a poor family environment, social rejection, or dysfunctional communication patterns—but if they are sufficiently strong and are coupled with a genetic predisposition, the result will be the onset of schizophrenia (see Figure 10-3). Similarly, if the genetic predisposition is strong enough, schizophrenia may occur even when the environmental stressors are relatively weak.

In sum, schizophrenia may be produced by several different combinations of biological predisposition and environmental stress. It is increasingly clear, then, that schizophrenia is not produced by any single factor but is an amalgamation of interrelated problems.

Lacking Distress: Personality Disorders

I had always wanted lots of things; as a child I can remember wanting a bullet that a friend of mine had brought in to show the class. I took it and put it into my school bag and when my friend noticed it was missing, I was the one who stayed after school with him and searched the room, and I was the one who sat with him and bitched about the other kids and how one of them took his bullet. I even went home with him to help him break the news to his uncle, who had brought it home from the war for him.

But that was petty compared with the stuff I did later. I wanted a Ph.D. very badly, but I didn't want to work very hard—just enough to get by. I

FIGURE 10-3
According to the predisposition model of schizophrenia, schizophrenic behavior occurs when environmental stressors are particularly high, even if the predisposition is relatively low (person A). Similarly, schizophrenic behavior can occur if the predisposition is relatively high, even if stressors are relatively low (person B). On the other hand, even though the stress level is high, person X will not display schizophrenic behavior, because the predisposition is sufficiently low. Similarly, person Y will behave normally, despite the strong predisposition, because the stress is low. (Adapted from Zubin & Spring, 1977.)

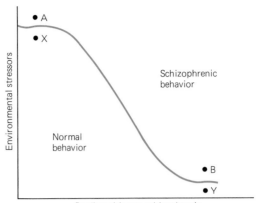

never did the experiments I reported; hell, I was smart enough to make up the results. I knew enough about statistics to make anything look plausible. I got my master's degree without even spending one hour in a laboratory. I mean, the professors believed anything. I'd stay out all night drinking and being with my friends, and the next day I'd get in just before them and tell 'em I'd been in the lab all night. They'd actually feel sorry for me. I did my doctoral research the same way, except it got published and there was some excitement about my findings. The research helped me get my first college teaching job.

Before you think that all college professors have backgrounds like this one, it should be stated that this person represents a clear example of someone with a **personality disorder**. Personality disorders are different from the other problems that we have discussed in this chapter, because there is often little sense of personal distress associated with the psychological maladjustment of those affected. In fact, people with personality disorders frequently lead seemingly normal lives—until one looks just below the surface. There one finds a set of inflexible, maladaptive personality traits that do not permit the individual to function appropriately as a member of society.

The best-known type of personality disorder is the **antisocial** or **sociopathic personality disorder**. Individuals with this disorder tend to display no regard for the moral and ethical rules of society or for the rights of others. Although they appear intelligent and are usually likeable at first, they can be seen as manipulative and deceptive upon closer examination. Moreover, they tend to share certain other characteristics (Coleman, Butcher & Carson, 1988):

- A lack of conscience, guilt, or anxiety over transgressions. When those with an antisocial personality behave in a way that injures someone else, they understand intellectually that they have caused the harm but feel no remorse.
- Impulsive behavior and an inability to withstand frustration. Antisocial personalities are unable to withstand frustration without reacting in some way—which may include violating the rights of others, if doing so allows them to remove the frustration.
- Manipulation of others. Antisocial personalities frequently have very good interpersonal skills: They are charming, engaging, and able to convince others to do what they want. In fact, some of the best con men have antisocial personalities and are able to get people to hand over their life savings without a second thought. The misery that follows in the wake of such activities is not cause for concern to the antisocial personality.

What causes such an unusual constellation of problems? A variety of factors have been suggested, ranging from a biological inability to experience emotions to problems in family relationships (e.g., Newman & Kosson, 1986). For example, in many cases of antisocial behavior the individual has come from a home in which a parent has died or left, or one in which there is a lack of affection, a lack of consistency in discipline, or outright rejection. Other explanations concentrate on sociocultural factors, since an unusually high proportion of antisocial personalities come from lower socioeconomic groups. Some researchers have suggested that the breakdown of societal rules, norms, and regulations that may be found in severely deprived economic environments may encourage the development of antisocial personalities (Melges & Bowlby, 1969). Still, no one has been able to pinpoint the specific causes of antisocial personalities, and it is likely that some combination of factors is responsible.

Another example of a personality disturbance is the **narcissistic personality disorder**, which is characterized by an exaggerated sense of self-importance. Those with the disorder expect special treatment from others, while at the same time they disregard others' feelings. In some ways, in fact, the main attribute of the narcissistic personality is an inability to experience empathy for other people.

There are several other categories of personality disorder, ranging in severity from individuals who may simply be regarded by others as eccentric, obnoxious, or difficult, to people who act in a manner that is criminal and dangerous to others. Although they are not out of touch with reality in the way that schizophrenics are, people with personality disorders lead lives on the fringes of society.

Beyond the major disorders. The various forms of abnormal behavior described in DSM-III-R cover much wider ground than we have been able to discuss in this chapter. Some are relevant to topics covered in earlier parts of the book, such as **sexual disorders**, in which one's sexual activity is unsatisfactory, and **psychoactive substance-use disorder**, in which problems arise from the abuse of drugs. Another important class of disorders that we have previously touched on is **organic mental disorders,** problems that have a purely biological basis. Other disorders are so rare that they have not been mentioned at all; and each of the disorders that we have discussed can be divided into several subcategories.

In some ways, then, our discussion of psychological disturbances has only skimmed the surface. The challenge facing psychologists interested in abnormal behavior is to improve their understanding of the nature and causes of these psychological disorders in order to improve the lives of those who suffer from them, as well as to prevent their occurrence in the first place—issues we discuss in the next chapter.

The Informed Consumer of Psychology: Deciding When You Need Help

After you consider the range and variety of psychological disturbances that can afflict people, it would not be surprising if you felt that you were suffering from one (or more) of the problems we have discussed. This is a perfectly natural reaction, for, as we mentioned earlier, people often conclude that they have the same problems they are studying—the classic medical student's disease. Because this is such a common phenomenon, it is important that you be well aware of the pitfalls of self-diagnosis.

One of the truisms of the legal profession is that lawyers who defend themselves have fools for clients. Similarly we might say that people who try to categorize their own mental disorders are making a foolish mistake. With categories that are subjective under the best of circumstances, and with problems that can be elusive and fleeting even to well-trained, experienced mental health professionals, it is unreasonable to expect that after reading a chapter in an introductory psychology book anyone could make a valid diagnosis.

On the other hand, there are guidelines you can use to determine when some kind of professional help is warranted. The following signals suggest the possible necessity of outside intervention:

- Long-term feelings of psychological distress that interfere with your sense of well-being, competence, and ability to function effectively in daily activities
- Occasions in which you experience overwhelmingly high stress, accompanied by feelings of inability to cope with the situation
- Prolonged depression or feelings of hopelessness, particularly when they do not have any clear cause (such as the death of someone close)

- Withdrawal from other people
- A chronic physical problem for which no physical cause can be determined
- A fear or phobia that prevents you from engaging in normal everyday activities
- Feelings that other people are out to get you or are talking about and plotting against you
- The inability to interact effectively with others, preventing the development of friendships and loving relationships

The above criteria can serve as a rough set of guidelines for determining when the normal problems of everyday living are beyond the point that you are capable of dealing with them yourself. In such situations, the least reasonable approach would be to pore over the psychological disorders we have discussed in an attempt to pigeonhole yourself into a specific category. A more reasonable strategy is to consider seeking professional help—something we discuss in the next chapter.

ASK YOURSELF

What are mood disorders?

What is the disorder that is most commonly diagnosed for those hospitalized for mental disturbance?

How do people with personality disorders differ from those with other kinds of abnormal behavior?

How would you refute the argument that because people with personality disorders experience little or no personal distress, they do not really require treatment?

LOOKING BACK

1. The most satisfactory definition of abnormal behavior is one based on the psychological consequences of the behavior, which is thought of as abnormal if it produces a sense of distress, anxiety, or guilt, or if it is harmful to others. Another useful definition considers people who cannot adapt to society and who are unable to function effectively to be abnormal.

2. No single definition is totally adequate; therefore it is reasonable to consider abnormal and normal behavior as marking two ends of a continuum, or scale.

3. The medical model of abnormal behavior views abnormality as a symptom of an underlying disease that requires a cure. Psychoanalytic models suggest that abnormal behavior is caused by conflicts in the unconscious stemming from past experience. In order to resolve psychological problems, people need to resolve the unconscious conflicts.

4. In contrast, behavioral approaches view abnormal behavior not as a symptom of some underlying problem, but as the problem itself. To resolve the problem, one must change the behavior. Although traditional behavioral models ignore a person's "inner life" and focus instead on overt behavior, some behavioral theorists suggest it is appropriate to take a cognitive approach in which the modification of cognitions (thoughts and beliefs) is carried out.

5. Humanistic approaches view people as rational and motivated to get along with others; abnormal behavior is seen as a difficulty in fulfilling one's needs. People are considered to be in control of their lives and able to resolve their own problems.

6. Sociocultural approaches view abnormal behavior in terms of difficulties arising from family and other social relationships. The sociocultural model concentrates on such factors as socioeconomic status and the social rules society creates to define normal and abnormal behavior.

7. Students of psychology are susceptible to the same sort of "disease" that afflicts medical students: the perception that they suffer from the problems about which they are studying. Unless their psychological difficulties are persistent, have depth, and are consistent, however, it is unlikely that their concerns are valid.

8. The system for classifying abnormal behaviors that is used most widely today is DSM-III-R—*Diagnostic and Statistical Manual of Mental Disorders*, Third Edition—Revised.

9. Anxiety disorders are present when a person experiences so much anxiety that it impedes daily functioning. Specific types of anxiety disorders include generalized anxiety disorder, panic disorder, phobic disorder, and obsessive-compulsive disorder.

10. Somatoform disorders refer to psychological difficulties that are displayed through physical problems. An example is hypochondriasis and conversion disorder.

11. Dissociative disorders are marked by the splitting apart, or dissociation, of crucial parts of personality that are usually integrated. The three major kinds of dissociative disorders are multiple personality, psychogenic amnesia, and psychogenic fugue.

12. Mood disorders are characterized by emotions of depression or euphoria so strong that they intrude on everyday living. In major depression, people experience sorrow so deep that they may become suicidal. In bipolar disorder, stages of mania, in which there is an extended sense of elation and powerfulness, alternate with depression.

13. Schizophrenia is one of the most severe forms of mental illness. The manifestations of schizophrenia include declines in functioning, thought and language disturbances, perceptual disorders, emotional disturbance, and withdrawal from others. There is strong evidence linking schizophrenia to genetic, biochemical, brain structural, and environmental factors.

14. People with personality disorders experience little or no personal distress, but they do suffer from an inability to function as normal members of society. The best-known type of personality disorder is the antisocial or sociopathic personality disorder. The narcissistic personality is characterized by an exaggerated sense of importance.

15. There are many other categories of disorders, including sexual disorders, psychoactive substance-use disorders, and organic mental disorders.

16. A number of signals indicate a need for professional help. These include long-term feelings of psychological distress, feelings of inability to cope with stress, withdrawal from others, prolonged feelings of hopelessness, chronic physical problems with no apparent causes, phobias and compulsions, paranoia, and an inability to interact with others.

Key Terms and Concepts

medical model of abnormality (p. 412)
psychoanalytic model of abnormality
    (p. 413)
behavioral model of abnormality (p. 413)
humanistic model of abnormality (p. 415)
sociocultural model of abnormality (p. 416)
medical student's disease (p. 418)
(DSM-III-R) *Diagnostic and Statistical Manual
    of Mental Disorders,* Third Edition—
    Revised) (p. 420)
anxiety (p. 423)
anxiety disorder (p. 423)
generalized anxiety disorder (p. 423)
panic disorder (p. 424)
panic attack (p. 424)
phobic disorder (p. 424)
phobia (p. 424)
obsessive-compulsive disorder (p. 425)
obsession (p. 425)
compulsion (p. 426)
hypochondriasis (p. 426)
somatoform disorder (p. 427)
conversion disorder (p. 427)
dissociative disorder (p. 428)
multiple personality (p. 429)

psychogenic amnesia (p. 429)
psychogenic fugue (p. 430)
mood disorder (p. 431)
major depression (p. 431)
mania (p. 432)
bipolar disorder (p. 432)
schizophrenia (p. 434)
delusions (p. 436)
hallucinations (p. 437)
process schizophrenia (p. 437)
reactive schizophrenia (p. 437)
dopamine hypothesis (p. 439)
double-bind hypothesis (p. 439)
learned-inattention theory of schizophrenia
    (p. 440)
predisposition model of schizophrenia
    (p. 440)
personality disorder (p. 441)
antisocial (sociopathic) personality disorder
    (p. 441)
narcissistic personality disorder (p. 442)
sexual disorders (p. 443)
psychoactive substance-use disorder (p. 443)
organic mental disorders (p. 443)

11

Treatment of Abnormal Behavior

❖

Prologue: Joanna ◆ *Looking Ahead* ◆ *Psychotherapy: Psychological Approaches to Treatment*
◆ *The Medical Model at Work: Biological Treatment Approaches* ◆ *Looking Back*

PROLOGUE: JOANNA

Though many psychotherapy sessions may look alike, the content of what is said is likely to vary greatly according to the training of the therapist and the needs of the client.

JOANNA: I just feel nervous a lot of the time.

THERAPIST: What is the feeling like?

JOANNA: I don't know. It's hard to describe. . . . I just feel nervous.

THERAPIST: [*I think I'm going to have some difficulty in getting her to elaborate on her problems. Maybe I'll hold off on trying to push for specifics for a little bit, and instead try to get her to feel more comfortable about describing and elaborating on her feelings, and just talking in general.*] So you know what the feeling is like, but it's kind of difficult to describe it in words.

JOANNA: Yes, it is. You know, it's just a feeling of uneasiness and apprehension. Like when you know something bad may happen, or at least you're afraid that it might.

THERAPIST: So emotionally, and perhaps physically, there's a fear that something might happen, although you may not be certain exactly what.

JOANNA: Yes.

447

THERAPIST: When you're feeling that way, what do you experience physically?

JOANNA: Well, my heart starts pounding and I feel myself tense up all over. It's not always that bad; sometimes it's only mild.

THERAPIST: [*I can make a smooth transition at this point and try to find out the situations in which the intensity of her anxiety varies.*] In other words, depending upon the circumstances, you may feel more or less anxious.

JOANNA: Yes.

THERAPIST: Tell me something about the situations that make you *most* anxious.

JOANNA: Well, it's usually when I deal with other people.

THERAPIST: I would find it particularly helpful to hear about some typical situations that may upset you.

JOANNA: It's hard to come up with something specific.

THERAPIST: [*I'm having doubts as to how hard to press her for details. If she has too much difficulty in coming up with specifics, the whole process of questioning might just make our relationship too aversive. I sense by the expression on her face that she may be somewhat uneasy about her inability to give me the information I want. I should probably attend to that before moving on.*] I can understand how it may be hard to come up with specific examples right on the spot. That's not at all uncommon. Let me see if I can help to make it a little easier for you. Let's take the past week or so. Think of what went on either at work or at home, or when you were out socially, that might have upset you.

JOANNA: OK. Something just occurred to me. We went out to a party last weekend, and as we were driving to the place where the party was being held, I felt myself starting to panic.

THERAPIST: Can you tell me more about that situation?

JOANNA: Well, the party was at ... (Goldfried & Davison, 1976, pp. 40–42).

LOOKING AHEAD

This actual transcript of an initial therapy session represents the view that most people have of what treatment for psychological disorders is all about. Popularized by the media, the notion that treatment always involves a therapist asking a series of probing questions and a client searching for answers to a difficult problem has come to represent society's general view of the nature of therapy.

In fact—although many kinds of therapy do encompass the situation described in the transcript—treatment approaches are much broader than this example of an initial interview with a person experiencing anxiety might suggest. Therapists today use over 250 different kinds of treatment, ranging from informal one-session discussions to long-term treatments involving powerful drugs. However, no matter what type of therapy is employed, all have a common goal: the relief of psychological disorder, ultimately enabling individuals to achieve richer, more meaningful, and more fulfilling lives.

This chapter explores a number of important issues related to abnormal behavior: How do we treat individuals with psychological disorders? Who is the most appropriate person to provide treatment? What is the future like for people with severe disturbances? What is the most reasonable therapeutic approach to use? Is one form of therapy better than others? Does any therapy *really* work? How does a person choose the "right" kind of therapy and therapist?

Most of the chapter focuses on the various approaches used by providers of treatment for psychological disturbances—approaches which, despite their diversity, boil down to two main categories: psychologically based and biologically based therapy. Psychologically based therapy, or **psychotherapy,** is the process in which a patient (often referred to as the client) and a professional attempt to remedy psychological difficulties. In psychotherapy, the emphasis is on change as a result of discussions and interactions between therapist and client. In contrast, biologically based therapy uses drugs and other medical procedures to improve psychological functioning.

As we discuss the various approaches to therapy, it is important to keep in mind that, although the distinctions may seem clear-cut, there is a good deal of overlap in the classifications and procedures employed, and even in the training and titles of various kinds of therapists (see Table 11-1). In fact, many therapists today use a variety of methods with a given person, in what is referred to as an **eclectic approach to therapy**. Assuming that abnormal behavior is often the product of both psychological and biological processes, eclectic therapists may draw from several perspectives simultaneously, merging them into a "package" of treatment procedures that address both psychological and biological aspects of a person's problems (Karasu, 1989).

After reading this chapter, then, you will be able to answer the following questions:

- What are the differences between psychologically and biologically based treatment approaches?
- What are the basic kinds of psychotherapies, and how do we evaluate them?

TABLE 11-1 GETTING HELP FROM THE RIGHT PERSON

Clinical psychologist	Ph.D. who specializes in assessment and treatment of psychological difficulties
Counseling psychologist	Psychologist with Ph.D. or master's who usually treats day-to-day adjustment problems in a counseling setting, such as a university mental health clinic
Psychiatrist	M.D., with postgraduate training in abnormal behavior, who can prescribe medication as part of treatment
Psychoanalyst	Either an M.D. or a psychologist who specializes in psychoanalysis, a treatment technique first developed by Freud
Psychiatric social worker	Professional with a master's degree and specialized training in treating people in home and community settings

Each of these trained professionals could be expected to give helpful advice and direction, although the nature of the problem a person is experiencing may make one or the other more appropriate. For example, a person who is suffering from severe disturbance and has lost touch with reality will typically require some sort of biologically based drug therapy. In that case, a psychiatrist—who is a physician—would clearly be the professional of choice. On the other hand, those suffering from milder disorders, such as difficulty in adjusting to the death of a family member, have a broader choice that might include any of the professionals listed above. The decision can be made easier because mental health facilities in communities, colleges, and health organizations often provide guidance, during an initial consultation, in selecting an appropriate therapist.

- How are drug, electroconvulsive, and psychosurgical techniques used today in the treatment of mental disorders?
- What is the best kind of therapy and therapist for a given situation?

PSYCHOTHERAPY: PSYCHOLOGICAL APPROACHES TO TREATMENT

Although diverse in many respects, all psychological approaches see treatment as a way of solving psychological problems by modifying people's behavior and helping them gain a better understanding of themselves and their past, present, and future. We will consider three major kinds of psychotherapies: psychodynamic, behavioral, and humanistic, all of which are based on the different models of abnormal behavior we discussed in Chapter 10.

Piercing the Unconscious: Psychodynamic Treatment

Psychodynamic therapy is based on the premise, first suggested by Freud, that the primary source of abnormal behavior is unresolved past conflicts and anxiety over the possibility that unacceptable unconscious impulses will enter the conscious part of a person's mind. To guard against this undesirable possibility, individuals employ **defense mechanisms**—psychological strategies that protect them from these unconscious impulses (see Chapter 9). Even though repression, the most common defense mechanism (in which threatening conflicts and impulses are pushed back into the unconscious), typically occurs, our unacceptable conflicts and impulses can never be completely buried. Therefore, some of the anxiety associated with them can produce abnormal behavior in the form of what Freud called **neurotic symptoms**.

How does one rid oneself of the anxiety caused by the repression of unconscious, unwanted impulses and drives? To Freud, the answer was to confront the conflicts and impulses by bringing them out of the unconscious part of the mind and into the conscious part. Freud assumed that, by this technique, anxiety over the past would be reduced and the patient could participate in his or her daily life more effectively.

The challenge facing a psychodynamic therapist, then, is how to facilitate patients' attempts to explore and understand their unconscious. The technique that has evolved has a number of components, but basically it consists of leading patients to consider and discuss their past experiences from the time of their first memories, in explicit detail. Through this process, it is assumed that patients will eventually stumble upon long-hidden crises, traumas, and conflicts that are producing anxiety in their adult lives. They will then be able to "work through"—understand and rectify—these difficulties.

Freud's therapy: Psychoanalysis. Classic Freudian psychodynamic therapy—called **psychoanalysis**—tends to be a lengthy and expensive affair. Patients typically meet with their therapists an hour a day, four to six days a week, for several years. In their sessions, they often use a technique developed by Freud called **free association**. Patients are told to say whatever comes to mind, regardless of its apparent irrelevance or senselessness. In fact, they are urged *not* to try to make sense of things or impose logic upon what they are saying, since it is assumed that the ramblings evoked during free association actually represent important clues to the unconscious, which has its own logic. It is the analyst's job to recognize and label the connections between what is being said and the patient's unconscious (Cooper, Kernberg & Person, 1990).

Another important tool of the therapist is **dream interpretation**. As we discussed in Chapter 9, this is an examination of the patients' dreams to find clues to the unconscious conflicts and problems being experienced. According to Freud, dreams provide a closer look at the unconscious be-

"And then I say to myself, 'If I really wanted to talk to her, why do I keep forgetting to dial 1 first?'"

Drawing by Modell, © 1981 The New Yorker Magazine, Inc.

cause people's defenses tend to be lowered when they are asleep. But even in dreaming there is a censoring of thoughts; events and people in dreams are usually represented by symbols. Because of this, one must move beyond the surface description of the dream—the **manifest content**—and

Psychodynamic therapy attempts to uncover long-suppressed conflicts through an exploration of past experiences and relationships. Some therapists encourage their clients to use physical symbols and exercises to represent persons, places, or situations.

consider its underlying meaning—the **latent content**—which reveals the true message of the dream.

The processes of free association and dream interpretation do not always move easily forward. The same unconscious forces that initially produced repression may work to keep past difficulties out of the conscious, producing resistance. **Resistance** is an inability or unwillingness to discuss or reveal particular memories, thoughts, or motivations. Resistance can be expressed in a number of ways. For instance, patients may be discussing a childhood memory and suddenly forget what they were saying, or they may completely change the subject. It is the therapist's job to pick up instances of resistance and to interpret their meaning, as well as to ensure that patients return to the subject—which is likely to hold difficult or painful memories for them.

Because of the close, almost intimate interaction between patient and psychoanalyst, the relationship between the two often becomes emotionally charged and takes on a complexity unlike most others (Luborsky, Barber & Crits-Cristoph, 1990). In fact, patients may come to see the analyst as symbolic of significant others in their past, perhaps a parent or a lover, and apply some of their feelings for that person to the analyst—a phenomenon known as **transference**.

Transference can be used by a therapist to help the patient recreate past relationships that were psychologically difficult. For instance, if a patient undergoing transference views his therapist as symbolic of his father—with whom he had a difficult relationship—the patient and therapist may "redo" an earlier interaction, this time including more positive aspects. Through this process, conflicts regarding the real father may be resolved.

Contemporary alternatives to psychoanalysis: Is Freud dead? If time is money, patients in psychoanalysis need a lot of both. As you can imagine, few people have the time, money, or patience that participating in years of traditional psychoanalysis requires. Moreover, there is no conclusive evidence that psychoanalysis, as originally conceived by Freud, works better than other, more contemporary versions of psychodynamic therapy. Today, for instance, psychodynamic therapy tends to be shorter, usually lasting no longer than three months or twenty sessions. The therapist takes a more active role than Freud would have liked, controlling the course of therapy and prodding and advising the patient with considerable directness. Finally, there is less emphasis on a patient's past history and childhood. Instead, a more here-and-now approach is used, in which the therapist concentrates on an individual's current relationships and level of functioning (Strupp, 1981; Garfield, 1989; Goldfried, Greenberg, & Marmar, 1990).

Even with its current modifications, psychodynamic therapy has its critics. It is still relatively time-consuming and expensive, especially in comparison with other forms of psychotherapy that we will discuss later.

Moreover, only certain kinds of patients tend to be well suited for this method: those who suffer from anxiety disorders and those who are highly articulate—characteristics enshrined in a (facetious) acronym, YAVIS, for the perfect patient: young, attractive, verbal, intelligent, and successful (Schofield, 1964).

Ultimately, the most important concern about psychodynamic treatment is whether it actually works, and here we find no pat answer. Psychodynamic treatment techniques have been controversial since Freud introduced them. Part of the problem is the difficulty in establishing whether or not patients have improved following psychodynamic therapy. One must depend on reports from the therapist or the patients themselves, reports that are obviously open to bias and subjective interpretation (Luborsky & Spence, 1978; Peterfreund, 1984).

Critics have questioned the entire theoretical basis of psychodynamic theory, maintaining that there is no proof that such constructs as the unconscious exist. Despite the considerable criticism, though, the psychodynamic treatment approach has remained a viable technique, not only providing effective treatment in many cases of psychological disturbances but permitting the potential development of an unusual degree of insight into and understanding of people's lives.

Learning the Good and Unlearning the Bad: Behavioral Approaches to Treatment

Perhaps, as a child, you would be rewarded by your parents with an ice cream cone if you were especially good . . . or sent to your room if you misbehaved. As we saw in Chapter 4, the principles behind such a child-rearing strategy are quite valid: Good behavior is maintained by rewards, and unwanted behavior can be eliminated by punishment.

These principles represent the basic underpinnings of behavioral treatment approaches. Building upon the fundamental processes of learning—classical and operant conditioning—**behavioral treatment approaches** make a fundamental assumption: both abnormal and normal behavior is *learned* (Kazdin, 1989). People who display abnormal behavior have either failed to learn the skills needed to cope with the problems of everyday living or they have acquired faulty skills and patterns that are being maintained through some form of reinforcement. To modify abnormal behavior, then, people must learn new behavior to replace the faulty skills they have developed and unlearn their maladaptive behavior patterns.

To behavioral psychologists, it is not necessary to delve into people's pasts or dig into their psyches; rather than viewing abnormal behavior as a symptom of some underlying problem, they consider the abnormal behavior itself as the problem in need of modification. Changing people's behavior to allow them to function more effectively solves the problem—

with no need for concern about the underlying cause. In this view, then, if you can change abnormal behavior, you've cured it.

Learning to hate what you love and love what you hate: Classical conditioning approaches. Suppose you bite into your favorite candy bar and find that it is infested with ants and that you've swallowed a bunch of them. You immediately become sick to your stomach and throw up. Your long-term reaction? You never eat that kind of candy bar again; in fact, it may be months before you eat any type of candy.

This simple example hints at how classical conditioning might be used to modify behavior. You might remember from our discussion in Chapter 4 that, when a stimulus that naturally evokes a negative response (such as an unpleasant taste or a puff of air in the face) is paired with a previously neutral stimulus (such as the sound of a bell), a state of affairs is produced in which the neutral stimulus can bring about a similar negative reaction by itself. Using this procedure, first developed by Ivan Pavlov, we may create unpleasant reactions to stimuli that previously were enjoyed—possibly to excess—by an individual. The technique, known as **aversive conditioning**, has been used in cases of alcoholism, drug abuse, and smoking.

The basic procedure in aversive conditioning is relatively straightforward. For example, a person with a drinking problem might be given an alcoholic drink along with a drug that causes severe nausea and vomiting. After these two are paired a few times, the alcohol alone becomes asso-

One treatment for people who want to stop smoking involves aversive conditioning, in which smoking and cues relating to smoking are repeatedly paired with unpleasant stimuli.

ciated with the vomiting and loses its appeal. In fact, what typically happens is that just the sight or smell of alcohol triggers the aversive reaction.

Although aversion therapy works reasonably well to inhibit substance-abuse problems such as alcoholism and certain kinds of sexual deviation, its long-term effectiveness is questionable. Moreover, there are important ethical drawbacks to aversion techniques employing such potent stimuli as electric shock—used only in the most extreme cases (for example, self-mutilation)—instead of drugs that merely induce gastric discomfort (Russo, Carr & Lovaas, 1980; Sulzer-Azaroff & Mayer, 1991). It is clear, though, that aversion therapy is an important procedure for eliminating maladaptive responses for some period of time—which provides, even if only temporarily, the opportunity to encourage more adaptive behavior patterns.

The most successful treatment based on classical conditioning is known as systematic desensitization. In **systematic desensitization**, a stimulus that evokes pleasant feelings is repeatedly paired with a stimulus that evokes anxiety in the hope that the positive feelings will eventually become associated with the anxiety-producing stimulus, thereby alleviating the anxiety (Rachman & Hodgson, 1980; Wolpe, 1969).

Suppose, for instance, you were afraid of flying. In fact, the very thought of being in an airplane made you begin to sweat and shake, and you'd never even been able to get yourself near enough to an airport to know how you'd react if you actually had to fly somewhere. Using systematic desensitization to treat your problem, you would first be trained in muscle-relaxation techniques by a behavior therapist (see Table 11-2), learning to relax your body fully—a highly pleasant state, as you might imagine. The next step would involve the construction of a **hierarchy of**

TABLE 11-2 LEARNING TO RELAX

To get a sense of how behavior therapists train people to relax, try this procedure developed by Herbert Benson (1975).

1. Sit quietly in a comfortable position.
2. Close your eyes.
3. Deeply relax all your muscles, beginning at your feet and progressing to your face—keep them relaxed.
4. Breathe through your nose. Become aware of your breathing. As you breathe out, say the word "one" silently to yourself. For example, breathe in ... out, "one"; in ... out, "one"; and so on. Breathe easily and naturally.
5. Continue for ten to twenty minutes. You may open your eyes to check the time, but do not use an alarm. When you finish, sit quietly for several minutes, at first with your eyes closed and later with your eyes open. Do not stand up for a few minutes.
6. Do not worry about whether you are successful in achieving a deep level of relaxation. Maintain a passive attitude and permit relaxation to occur at its own pace. When distracting thoughts occur, try to ignore them by not dwelling upon them, and return to repeating "one."

With practice, the response should come with little effort. Practice the techniques once or twice daily, but not within two hours after any meal, since the digestive processes seem to interfere with the elicitation of the relaxation response (Benson, 1975, pp. 114–115).

fears—a list, in order of increasing severity, of the things that are associated with your fears. For instance, your hierarchy might resemble the following:

- Watching a plane fly overhead
- Going to an airport
- Buying a ticket
- Stepping into the plane
- Seeing the plane door close
- Having the plane taxi down the runway
- Taking off
- Being in the air

Once this hierarchy had been developed and you had learned relaxation techniques, the two sets of responses would be associated with each other. To do this, your therapist might ask you to put yourself into a relaxed state and then to imagine yourself in the first situation identified in your hierarchy. After you were able to consider that first step while remaining relaxed, you would move on to the next situation, eventually moving up the hierarchy in gradual stages until you could imagine yourself being in the air without experiencing anxiety. In some cases, all this would take place in a psychologist's office, while in others people are actually placed in the fear-evoking situation. Thus, it would not be surprising if you were brought, finally, to an airplane to use your relaxation techniques.

Systematic desensitization has proved to be an effective treatment for a number of problems, including phobias, anxiety disorders, and even impotence and fear of sexual contact (Kazdin, 1989; Westover & Lanyon, 1990). As you see, we *can* learn to enjoy the things we once feared.

Following the "fearless peer": Observational learning and modeling. If we had to be hit by a car in order to learn the importance of looking both ways before we crossed the street, the world would likely be suffering from a serious underpopulation problem. Fortunately, this is not necessary, for we learn a significant amount through **observational learning,** by **modeling** the behavior of other people.

Behavior therapists have used modeling to systematically teach people new skills and ways of handling their fears and anxieties. For example, some people have never learned fundamental social skills such as maintaining eye contact with those they are speaking to. A therapist can model the appropriate behavior and thereby teach it to someone deficient in such skills (Sarason, 1976). Children with dog phobias have also been able to lose their fears by watching another child—called the "Fearless Peer"—

repeatedly walk up to a dog, touch it, pet it, and finally play with it (Bandura, Grusec & Menlove, 1967). Modeling, then, can play an effective role in resolving some kinds of behavior difficulties, especially if the model is rewarded for his or her behavior.

Reward the good, extinguish the bad: Operant conditioning approaches. Consider the A we get for a good paper . . . the raise for fine on-the-job performance . . . the gratitude for helping an elderly person cross the street. Such rewards for our behavior produce a greater likelihood that we will repeat that behavior in the future. Similarly, behavioral approaches using operant conditioning techniques (which demonstrate the effects of rewards and punishments on future behavior) are based on the notion that we should reward people for carrying out desirable behavior, and extinguish behavior—either through ignoring or punishing it—that we wish to eliminate.

Probably the best example of the systematic application of operant conditioning principles is the **token system**, whereby a person is rewarded with a token such as a poker chip or some kind of play money for desired behavior. The behavior may range from such simple things as keeping one's room neat to personal grooming to interacting with other people. The tokens that are earned for such behavior can then be exchanged for some desired object or activity, such as snacks, new clothes, or in extreme cases, being able to sleep in one's own bed (as opposed to on the floor).

Although it is most frequently employed in institutional settings for individuals with relatively serious problems, the system is not unlike what parents do when they give children money for being well behaved—money that they can later exchange for something they want. In fact, **contingency contracting**, a variant of the more extensive token system, has proved quite effective in producing behavior modification. In contingency contracting, a written agreement is drawn up between a therapist and patient (or teacher and student or parent and child). The contract states a series of behavioral goals that the patient hopes to attain. It also specifies the consequences for the patient if the goals are reached—usually some explicit reward such as money or additional privileges. Contracts frequently state negative consequences if the goals are not met.

For instance, suppose a person is having difficulty quitting smoking. He and his therapist might devise a contract in which he would pledge that for every day he went without a cigarette he would receive a reward. On the other hand, the contract could include punishments for failure. If the patient smoked on a given day, the therapist might send a check—written out in advance by the patient and given to the therapist to hold—to a cause the patient had no interest in supporting (for instance, the National Rifle Association if the patient is a staunch advocate of gun control).

Albert Ellis is the founder and Executive Director of the Institute for Rational-Emotive Therapy.

Where thinking better leads to feeling better: Cognitive-behavioral approaches and rational-emotive therapy. Consider the following assumptions:

- It is necessary to be loved or approved by virtually every significant other person for everything we do.
- We should be thoroughly competent, adequate, and successful in all possible respects if we are to consider ourselves worthwhile.
- It is horrible when things don't turn out the way we want them to.

Although each of these statements verges on the absurd, psychologist Albert Ellis suggests that many people lead unhappy and sometimes even psychologically disordered lives because they harbor these very kinds of irrational, unrealistic ideas about themselves and the world (Ellis, 1962, 1975; Ellis et al., 1989). In developing a treatment approach based on this premise—called **rational-emotive therapy**—he has suggested that the goal of therapy should be to restructure a person's belief system into a more realistic, rational, and logical set of views of the world.

In order to make their clients adopt more effective thinking, rational-emotive therapists take an active, directive role during therapy, openly challenging patterns of thought that appear to be dysfunctional. For example, a therapist might bluntly dispute the logic employed by a person in treatment by saying, "Why does the fact that your girlfriend left you mean that *you* are a bad person?" or "How does failing an exam indicate that you have *no* good qualities?" By pointing out the problems in clients' logic, therapists employing this form of treatment believe that people can come to adopt a more realistic view of themselves and their circumstances (Ellis & Dryden, 1987; Bernard & Di Giuseppe, 1989).

Rational-emotive techniques exemplify an approach known as **cognitive-behavioral therapy** (Beck, 1985; Hollon & Garber, 1990). Rather than relying exclusively on overt behaviors as indicators of psychological disorder, cognitive-behavioral therapists attempt to change faulty cognitions that people hold about the world and themselves. Cognitive-behavioral therapists, then, bring an eclectic point of view to behavioral therapy, combining ideas derived from cognitive psychology with a behavioral approach (Freeman et al., 1989).

The crucial question: How does behavior therapy stack up? Behavior therapy is quite good for certain kinds of problems. Depending on the specific problem being addressed, the success rate can range from 50 percent to as high as 90 percent. For instance, behavior therapy works well for phobias and compulsions, for establishing control over impulses, and for learning complex social skills to replace maladaptive behavior. More than any of the other therapeutic techniques, it has produced methods that can be employed by nonprofessionals to change their own behavior (see the Psychology and Society box). Moreover, it tends to be economical in terms of time, since it is directed toward the solution of carefully defined problems (Marks, 1982; Wilson et al., 1987; Bellack, Hersen, & Kazdin, 1990).

*A*SK YOURSELF

What is the distinction between psychologically based therapy and biologically based therapy?

What is psychodynamic therapy and how does it approach the treatment of psychological difficulties?

How do behavioral approaches to therapy view abnormal behavior?

What are the major approaches used by behavioral therapists?

According to psychodynamic psychotherapists, what is the value of insight?

Why might other kinds of theorists suggest that gaining mere insight into one's problems may be insufficient for solving them?

Helping People Help Themselves: Humanistic Approaches to Therapy

As you know from your own experience, it is impossible to master the material covered in a course without some hard work, no matter how good the teacher and the textbook are. It is *you* who must take the time

When Being Your Own Therapist Works: Self-Management through Behavior Modification

A fellow student, whom you don't know all that well, asks to borrow your class notes. This is the fourth time this semester he has asked you, and you feel that it is grossly unfair. But, feeling that he might become angry at you if you refuse his request, you quietly hand over your notebook.

This is not the first time you've felt that others take advantage of you, and you begin to wonder if you have a serious problem with lack of assertiveness. In fact, you begin to feel so bad about your inability to be assertive that you think about entering therapy. One day, though, a friend mentions that she was able to become more assertive entirely on her own, without professional assistance, through a technique known as behavioral self-management—and she assures you that you can do the same thing yourself.

Although the dangers of self-diagnosis and treatment have been emphasized a number of times—and caution should indeed always be used—there is one treatment approach that specifically allows people suffering from minor problems to "cure" themselves: behavioral self-management. In **behavioral self-management** people are taught to identify their problems and design their own ways of resolving them by using behavioral techniques.

Using techniques derived from behavioral treatment approaches, self-management has been shown to be effective in many cases for a variety of problems, including alcoholism, drug dependence, high blood pressure, stress control, poor study habits, and insomnia. Although many different strategies have been employed, they basically consist of altering the cues that promote an undesirable behavior, directly modifying a response that should be changed, and/or providing reinforcement or punishment for desirable or undesirable behavior.

The problems associated with self-asser-tion provide an excellent illustration of a problem that is responsive to self-management techniques. In a typical procedure, people are first asked to identify the cues and circumstances associated with a lack of assertiveness. For a student named Jim, such cues included being unable to refuse when asked for a favor and being unable to talk to strangers at a party.

To remedy his lack of assertiveness, the general strategy employed was to find some way to modify his reaction to cues that had become associated with unassertiveness. To do this, a number of goals and "rules" were set up about when, where, and how Jim should be assertive. For example, he set a goal of initiating conversations with at least two strangers at any party he went to. To accomplish this, he made a list of ways to initiate conversations, such as asking a question or making a comment on the situation, complimenting a person, and asking for help, advice, information, or an opinion.

Jim also used role playing to learn strategies for dealing with situations in which he was asked a favor. For example, he practiced scenarios in his mind—and sometimes out loud with a close friend—in which, when asked a favor, he requested time to think it over, asked for more information before agreeing or disagreeing, or simply said no to the person asking the favor.

Jim also developed a system of self-reinforcement, in which he would reward himself after acting assertively by treating himself to a movie. Moreover, he used self-punishment; when he hadn't acted assertively, he forced himself to send a check for $5 to a political party whose views he completely opposed.

By using such self-management procedures, Jim was able to become more assertive. Behavioral self-management techniques provide a means by which people can, in a sense, be their own therapists.

to study, to memorize the vocabulary, to learn the concepts. Nobody else can do it for you. If you choose to put in the effort, you'll succeed; if you don't, you'll fail. The responsibility is primarily yours.

Humanistic therapy draws upon this philosophical point of view of self-responsibility in developing treatment techniques. Although many different types of therapy fit into this category, the ideas that underlie them are the same: We have control of our own behavior; we can make choices about the kinds of lives we want to live, and it is up to us to solve the difficulties that we encounter in our daily lives. Instead of being the directive figures they are in some psychodynamic and behavioral approaches, humanistic therapists view themselves as guides or facilitators, leading people to realizations about themselves and to ways of changing in order to come closer to the ideal they hold for themselves. In this view, abnormal behavior is one result of people's inability to find meaning in life, of feeling lonely and unconnected with others, and of believing that they are pawns in a world that acts upon them without their being able to respond adequately.

Client, heal thyself: Client-centered therapy. Consider the following dialogue between a therapist and a client named Alice who is seeking treatment:

Humanistic therapy aims to help clients make better use of their own abilities.

"Of course you have strengths, dear. It's just that you don't communicate them."

Drawing by Lorenz, © 1977 The New Yorker Magazine, Inc.

ALICE: I was thinking about this business of standards. I somehow developed a sort of a knack, I guess, of—well—habit—of trying to make people feel at ease around me, or to make things go along smoothly. . . .

COUNSELOR: In other words, what you did was always in the direction of trying to keep things smooth and to make other people feel better and to smooth the situation.

ALICE: Yes. I think that's what it was. Now the reason why I did it probably was—I mean, not that I was a good little Samaritan going around making other people happy, but that was probably the role that felt easiest for me to play. I'd been doing it around home so much. I just didn't stand up for my own convictions, until I don't know whether I have any convictions to stand up for.

COUNSELOR: You feel that for a long time you've been playing the role of kind of smoothing out the frictions or differences or what not. . . .

ALICE: M-hm.

COUNSELOR: Rather than having any opinion or reaction of your own in the situation. Is that it?

ALICE: That's it. Or that I haven't been really honest being myself, or actually knowing what my real self is, and that I've been just playing a sort of false role . . . (Rogers, 1951, pp. 151–153).

If you carefully consider the responses of the counselor, you will see that they are not interpretations or answers to questions that the client has raised. Instead, they tend to clarify or reflect back in some way what the client has said. This therapeutic technique is known as **nondirective counseling**, and it is at the heart of client-centered therapy. First practiced by Carl Rogers (1951, 1980), **client-centered therapy** is the best-known and most frequently used type of humanistic therapy.

The goal of client-centered therapy is to enable people to better reach the potential for self-actualization that is assumed to be characteristic of everyone. By providing a warm and accepting environment, therapists hope to motivate clients to air their problems and feelings, which, in turn, will enable people to make realistic and constructive choices and decisions about the things that bother them in their current lives. Instead of directing the choices clients make, then, the therapist provides what Rogers calls **unconditional positive regard**—expressing acceptance and understanding, regardless of the feelings and attitudes the client expresses—thereby creating an atmosphere in which clients are able to come to decisions that can improve their lives. It does not mean that the therapist must approve of everything the client says or does; rather, it means that the therapist must convey that the client's thoughts and behaviors are seen as genuine reflections of what the client is experiencing (Lietaer, 1984).

It is relatively rare for client-centered therapy to be used today in its purest form. Contemporary approaches are apt to be somewhat more directive, nudging clients toward insights rather than merely reflecting back their statements. However, clients' insights are still seen as central to the therapeutic process.

Freeing the fear of freedom: Existential therapy. What is the meaning of life? We have all probably pondered this thought at one time or another, but for some people it is a central issue in their daily existence. For those individuals who experience psychological problems as a result of difficulty in finding a satisfactory answer, existential therapy is one particularly appropriate place to turn, because this question is central to existential therapeutic techniques.

In contrast to other humanistic approaches that view humans' unique freedom and potential as a positive force, **existential therapy** is based on the premise that the inability to deal with such freedom can produce anguish, fear, and concern (May, 1969). In existential therapy, the goal is to allow individuals to come to grips with the freedom they have, to begin to understand how they fit in with the rest of the world, and to devise a system of values that permits them to give meaning to their lives. Existential therapists try to make their patients aware of the importance of free choice and the fact that they have the ultimate responsibility for making their own choices about their lives.

The specific processes used in existential therapy are more varied than in client-centered approaches. The therapist is considerably more directive in existential therapy, probing and challenging the client's views of the world. In addition, therapists will try to establish a deep and binding relationship with their clients, attempting to be as open with them about their own feelings and points of view as possible. Their objective is to allow clients to see that they share in the difficulties and experiences that arise in trying to deal with the freedom that is part of being human.

Making people whole in a fragmented world: Gestalt therapy. Have you ever thought back to some childhood incident in which you were treated unfairly and again felt the rage that you had experienced at that time? To therapists working in a gestalt perspective, the healthiest thing for you to do psychologically might be to act out that rage—by hitting a pillow, kicking a chair, or yelling in frustration. In fact, this sort of activity represents an important part of what goes on in gestalt therapy sessions, in which the client is encouraged to act out past conflicts and difficulties.

The rationale for this approach to treatment is that it is necessary for people to integrate their thoughts, feelings, and behaviors into a gestalt, the German term for "whole" (as we discussed in reference to perception in Chapter 3). According to Fritz Perls (1967, 1970), who developed **gestalt therapy**, the way to do this is for people to examine their earlier experience and complete any "unfinished business" from their past that still affects

In gestalt therapy, people closely examine, and sometimes try to recreate, experiences from their childhood.

and colors present-day relationships. Specifically, Perls assumed that people should reenact the specific conflicts that they experienced earlier. For instance, a client might first play the part of his angry father, and then play himself when his father yelled at him, in order to experience the different parts of a conflict. By increasing their perspectives on a situation, clients are better able to understand their problems and to experience life in a more unified, honest, and complete way.

Can you become more human in the consulting room?: Humanistic approaches in perspective. You may be bothered by the lack of specificity of the humanistic treatments, and this is a problem that has also troubled its critics. Humanistic approaches are, in fact, not very precise and are probably the least scientifically and theoretically developed type of treatment. Moreover, this form of treatment is best suited for the same type of highly verbal client who profits most from psychoanalytic treatment.

On the other hand, the emphasis of humanistic approaches on what is uniquely human and their acknowledgment that the freedom we possess can lead to psychological difficulties work to provide an unusually supportive environment for therapy. In turn, this atmosphere can aid in finding solutions to difficult psychological problems.

Group Therapy

Although most treatment takes place with a single individual and therapist, some forms of therapy involve groups of people seeking treatment.

In **group therapy**, several unrelated people meet with a therapist to discuss some aspect of their psychological functioning.

People typically discuss their problems with the group, which is often centered around a particular difficulty, such as alcoholism or a lack of social skills. The other members of the group provide emotional support, as well as dispensing advice on ways in which they have coped effectively with similar problems (Lewis, 1987; Drum, 1990).

Groups vary a great deal not only in the particular model that is employed (there are psychoanalytic groups, humanistic groups, and groups corresponding to the other therapeutic approaches) but also in the degree of guidance the therapist provides. In some groups, the therapist is quite directive; in others, the members of the group set their own agenda and determine how the group will proceed.

Because several people are treated simultaneously in group therapy, it is a much more economical means of treatment than individual psychotherapy. On the other hand, critics argue that group settings do not afford the individual attention inherent in one-to-one therapy, and especially shy and withdrawn individuals may not receive the necessary attention in a group.

Family therapy. One specialized form of group therapy is family therapy. As the name implies, **family therapy** involves two or more members of the same family, one (or more) of whose problems led to treatment. But rather than focusing simply on members of the family who present the initial problem, family therapists consider the family as a whole unit, to which each member contributes. By meeting with the entire family simultaneously, family therapists attempt to obtain a sense of how the family members interact with one another (Barnes, 1990).

Family therapists view the family as a "system," and they assume that the separate individuals in the family cannot improve without understanding the conflicts that are to be found in the interactions of the family members. Thus each member is expected to contribute to the resolution of individual problems.

Many family therapists assume that family members fall into rigid roles or set patterns of behavior, with one person acting as the scapegoat, another as a bully, and so forth. In their view, family disturbances are perpetuated by the system of roles. One goal of this type of therapy, then, is to get the family to adopt new, more constructive patterns of roles (Minuchin, 1974).

Comparing Psychotherapeutic Approaches

We have seen that there are a variety of forms of psychotherapy. In order to compare them, we can classify them along several dimensions. Among the most important are (Carson, Butcher & Coleman, 1988):

- Directive versus nondirective. In some forms of therapy, the therapist takes considerably more responsibility for the person being treated than in others. In directive therapy, the therapist takes an active role, whereas in nondirective therapy, the therapist acts more as a facilitator, helping clients clarify their own feelings. Among the most directive are the behavioral approaches. In contrast, psychodynamic and humanistic approaches are considerably less directive.

- Inner control of behavior versus environmental control of behavior. In the psychodynamic and humanistic approaches, behavior is seen as largely under the control of the individual. In contrast, behavioral approaches to therapy view behavior primarily as the result of environmental factors. Cognitive-behavioral approaches take an intermediate view, seeing behavior determined not only by environmental factors but by internal cognitions as well.

- Long-term versus short-term therapy. Therapeutic approaches vary widely in terms of the typical length of treatment. Traditional psychoanalysis is the longest lasting, potentially stretching on for years. Today, however, most therapy is considerably shorter and may take as few as two or three sessions, depending on the nature of the problem being addressed.

- Historical focus versus here-and-now focus. Some kinds of therapy pay primary attention to events from the past that are assumed to be affecting current behavior. Psychodynamic approaches fall into such a category. In contrast, behavioral approaches stress the present, minimizing the consequences of early experiences. Other approaches fall in between.

- Cognitive change versus behavior change. Some kinds of therapy, particularly psychodynamic and cognitive-behavioral approaches, emphasize changes in attitudes, perceptions, feelings, and cognitions about the world and assume that a change in those characteristics will produce more adaptive behavior. In contrast, behavioral approaches emphasize the change of behavior itself.

It is important to remember, although they are presented in an either/or fashion, that each of these dimensions of therapy marks the end point of a continuum. Most therapeutic approaches will not fall squarely on one or the other end of the continuum but rather will lie somewhere in between.

Evaluating Psychotherapy

Your best friend at school, Maria, comes to you because she just hasn't been feeling right about things lately. She's upset because she and her boyfriend aren't getting along, but her difficulties go beyond that. She can't concentrate on her studies, has a lot of trouble getting to sleep, and— this is what really bothers her—she's begun to think that people are ganging up on her, talking about her behind her back. It just seems that no one really cares about or understands her or makes any effort to see why she's become so miserable.

Maria is aware that she ought to get *some* kind of help, but she is not sure where to turn. She is fairly skeptical of psychologists and psychiatrists, thinking that a lot of what they say is just mumbo-jumbo, but she's willing to put her doubts aside and try anything to feel better. She also knows there are many different types of therapy, and she doesn't have a clue as to which would be best for her. She turns to you for advice, since she knows you are taking a psychology course. She asks, "Which kind of therapy works best?"

Such a question requires a complex response, for there is no easy answer. In fact, identifying which form of treatment is most appropriate is a controversial, and still unresolved, task for psychologists specializing in abnormal behavior. For example, even before considering whether any one form of therapy works better than another, we need to determine whether therapy in *any* form is effective in alleviating psychological disturbances.

The answer to even this question has proven to be controversial for the last four decades. For example, in 1952, psychologist Hans Eysenck published an influential article that challenged the view that psychotherapy was an effective strategy for resolving psychological difficulties. After reviewing published literature on the subject, he claimed that people who received psychodynamic treatment and related therapies were no better off at the end of treatment than those who were placed on a waiting list for treatment—but never received it. According to his analysis, about two-thirds of the people who reported suffering from "neurotic" symptoms believed that those symptoms had disappeared after two years, regardless of whether or not they had been in therapy. Eysenck concluded that people suffering from neurotic symptoms would go into **spontaneous remission,** recovery without treatment, if they were simply left alone— certainly a cheaper and simpler process.

As you can imagine, Eysenck's review was controversial from the start, and its conclusions were quickly challenged. Critics pointed to the inadequacy of the data he reviewed, suggesting that he was basing his conclusions on studies that contained a number of flaws.

Many potential sources of error exist in studies of the effectiveness of psychotherapy. Most often, the data are based on therapist and patient self-reports, which may be biased and unreliable. All the parties involved are motivated to see themselves as successful, so all may report an improvement in psychological functioning when none really exists. Only when independent judges are used to determine how much progress a person has made can we be assured that the self-report is accurate. Even the use of judges has its drawbacks, however, since no well-agreed-upon set of criteria exists to determine what constitutes good and bad mental health. For all these reasons, then, critics of Eysenck's review rejected his findings.

Nonetheless, Eysenck's early review did serve to stimulate a continuing stream of better-controlled, carefully crafted studies on the effectiveness of psychotherapy, and today we can say, with confidence, that psychotherapy *is* effective. For instance, several recent comprehensive reviews indicate that therapy brings about greater improvement than does no treatment at all—although it still represents surprisingly controversial issue (Luborsky, Singer & Luborsky, 1975; Smith, Glass & Miller, 1980; Garfeld, 1983; Landman & Dawes, 1984; Bowers & Clum, 1988). Furthermore, the rate of spontaneous remission is fairly low; in most cases the symptoms of abnormal behavior do not go away by themselves if left untreated (Bergin & Lambert, 1978).

Which kind of therapy works best? Although most psychologists feel confident that psychotherapeutic treatment *in general* is more effective than no treatment at all, the question of whether any specific form of treatment is superior to any others has yet to be answered definitively (Bowers & Clum, 1988; Orwin & Condray, 1984). In part, this is due to methodological issues. For instance, it is difficult to equate the "cures" that various forms of treatment produce, because qualitatively they may be very different. Is the reduction of depression-related anxiety obtained from psychodynamic treatment equivalent to the reduction of phobia-related anxiety brought about by behavior therapy? In both cases the problems are alleviated—but, if we were keeping a tally of cures versus noncures for the two forms of treatment, would they each receive one point? You can see the difficulties involved in comparing types of treatment (Garfield, 1990; Marmar, 1990).

The problems, however, are not insurmountable. One solution has been to compare the "cure" rate for a particular form of treatment with the "cure" rate for a group of untreated controls. Next, we could do the same thing with another type of treatment and compare this cure rate with its own untreated control. Finally, we could see which of the two forms of therapy produced a higher cure rate. For instance, we could take a sample of people who, because of the nature of their problems, would be "eligible" for psychodynamic treatment, treat half of them, and compare their results to the untreated half. By following the same procedure with a group of people "eligible" for another form of treatment, we could infer which kind of treatment was most successful.

Using this kind of procedure, Smith, Glass & Miller (1980) came to the conclusions displayed in Figure 11.1. As you can see, although there is some variation among the success rates of the various treatment forms, most are fairly close to one another, ranging from about 70 to 85 percent greater success for treated than for untreated individuals. There is a slight tendency for behavioral approaches and cognitive-behavioral approaches

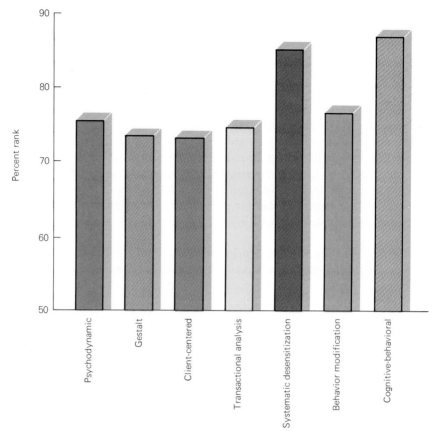

FIGURE 11-1

Estimates of the effectiveness of different types of treatment, in comparison to control groups of untreated people. The percentile score shows how much more effective a particular type of treatment is for the average patient than is no treatment. For example, people given psychodynamic treatment score, on average, more positively on outcome measures than about 75 percent of untreated people. (Adapted from Smith, Glass, & Miller, 1980).

to be a bit more successful, although this may be due to differences in the severity of cases treated (Orwin & Condray, 1984). In sum, research generally finds only minor differences among the success rates for various types of therapy (Berman, Miller & Massman, 1985).

This finding does not mean that every problem will be resolved equally well by different sorts of therapy. Recall the way that therapy-comparison studies are typically carried out: They initially consider only problems appropriate for a given treatment approach, and then compare treated versus untreated people within that specific approach to see which group of people does better. Such studies say little about whether specific sorts of problems are better treated by one approach or another (Garfield,

1983). Furthermore, in some cases—perhaps as many as 10 percent—psychotherapy actually *hurts* participants: They would have been better off if they had not undertaken it (Lambert, Shapiro & Bergin, 1986; Luborsky, 1988).

It is clear, then, that particular kinds of therapies are more appropriate for some problems than for others—a point made when we considered each of the specific treatment approaches earlier (Klerman, 1983). For example, if someone is suffering from the kind of general unhappiness and anxiety described by Maria in the earlier scenario, psychodynamic or humanistic approaches, which emphasize gaining insight into one's problems, would probably be most appropriate. On the other hand, if Maria's problems had been focused more on a particular set of circumstances that brought about her anxiety—such as a phobia or a lack of good study skills that was preventing her from doing well in school—then a behavioral approach might be more reasonable.

Similarly, it might be more appropriate for therapists with certain personal characteristics to work with particular people, and certain kinds of people may be more appropriately treated by one approach than another. For example, a behavioral approach may be more suitable for people who have difficulty expressing themselves verbally or who lack the patience or ability to engage in sustained introspection, qualities that are necessary for a psychodynamic approach.

Finally, there are an increasing number of eclectic approaches to therapy, in which a therapist uses techniques taken from a variety of approaches to treat a person's problems. By using eclectic procedures, the therapist is able to choose the appropriate mix in accordance with the specific needs of the individual (APA, 1989; Patterson, 1989).

The question of which therapy works best, then, cannot be answered without reference to the specific type of psychological problem that is being treated. The accuracy of the match between individual problems and therapeutic methods best determines the likelihood of success. Overall, though, it is clear that psychotherapy, in general, provides an effective means for solving psychological difficulties.

Given the general agreement that psychotherapy is effective, some recent research efforts have been devoted to answering the question of whether the judgments of clinical psychologists relating to the diagnosis and treatment of abnormal behavior are best made on the basis of "clinical" versus "actuarial" methods (Dawes, Faust, & Meehl, 1989). In "clinical" methods—the traditional judgment technique—decisions are made on the basis of knowledge, prior experience, and information available in the psychologist's head.

In contrast, "actuarial" judgments are based on a formal statistical rule or formula in which specific information is combined in a predetermined way. The particular rule or formula that is employed is developed on the basis of the prior collection of data relevant to the decision. For example, a psychologist using an actuarial judgment process might administer a series of standardized tests and, using a rule based on earlier research, combine the test results and define anyone who scored above a certain level on each of the tests as being severely depressed. Such a procedure would contrast with the more traditional "clinical" approach, in which the psychologist would make more intuitive judgments, based on his or her previous experience and understanding of how test scores fit together (Garb, 1989).

Because the actuarial method challenges more traditional clinical practices, its use has been controversial. While some clinical psychologists argue that it provides a more objective, scientific means of making diagnoses and treatment judgments, critics respond that subjective appraisal is a critical component of treatment for psychological disorders and that applying statistics about groups to individuals ignores the individuality of particular cases. Furthermore, critics suggest that the use of actuarial methods dehumanizes patients.

It is far too early to tell if actuarial methods will come to replace clinical techniques, and clinical judgment approaches remain the choice of most psychologists. Still, if actuarial approaches become more sophisticated and are developed to cover a wide domain of psychological disorders, their use is likely to increase (Dawes, Faust, & Meehl, 1989).

ASK YOURSELF

How do humanistic approaches view therapy and the role of the therapist?

What are the major types of humanistic therapies?

What are the major dimensions along which therapies can be evaluated?

Why is psychotherapy, regardless of the type, usually better than no therapy at all?

What do all therapies have in common that might make them helpful to people suffering psychological problems?

THE MEDICAL MODEL AT WORK: BIOLOGICAL TREATMENT APPROACHES

If you get a kidney infection, you're given some penicillin and, with luck, about a week later your kidney is as good as new. If your appendix becomes inflamed, a surgeon removes it and your body functions normally once more. Could an analogous approach, focusing on the body's physiology, be taken with psychological disturbances?

According to biological approaches to treatment, the answer is affirmative. In fact, biologically based treatments are used routinely for certain kinds of problems. The basic model suggests that, rather than focusing on a patient's psychological conflicts, past traumas, or environmental factors that may support abnormal behavior, it is more appropriate in certain cases to treat brain chemistry and other neurological factors directly. This can be done through the use of drugs, electric shock, or surgery.

Medicine for Mental Disturbances: Drug Therapy

Are we close to the day when we will take a pill each morning to maintain good psychological health, in the same way that we now take a vitamin pill to help us stay physically healthy? Although that day has not yet arrived, there are quite a few forms of **drug therapy** that successfully alleviate symptoms of a number of psychological disturbances.

Antipsychotic drugs. Probably no greater change has occurred in mental hospitals than the successful introduction in the mid-1950s of **antipsychotic drugs**—drugs used to alleviate psychotic symptoms such as agitation and overactivity. Previously, mental hospitals typically fulfilled all the stereotypes of the insane asylum—with screaming, moaning, clawing patients displaying the most bizarre behaviors. Suddenly, in just a matter of months, the hospital wards became considerably calmer environments in which professionals could do more than just try to get the patients through the day without serious harm to themselves or others.

This dramatic change was brought about by the introduction of a drug from the phenothiazine family called **chlorpromazine**. This drug, and oth-

Antipsychotic drugs have alleviated the symptoms of several different types of serious mental disturbances.

ers of similar type, rapidly became the most popular—and successful—treatment for schizophrenia. Today drug therapy is the preferred treatment for most cases of severely abnormal behavior, used for almost 90 percent of all hospitalized patients (Carson, 1983; Poling, Gadow, & Cleary, 1990; Spiegel, 1989).

How do antipsychotic drugs work? They seem to function by blocking the production of dopamine at the sites where nerve impulses travel across nerve receptors, a process we discussed in Chapter 10. Unfortunately, they do not produce a "cure" in the same way that, say, penicillin cures an infection—because as soon as the drug is withdrawn, the original symptoms tend to reappear. Moreover, such drugs can have long-term side effects, such as dryness of the mouth and throat, dizziness, and even the development of tremors and loss of muscle control that may continue even after drug treatments are stopped (Kane, 1983).

Perhaps even more devastating than these physical side effects are the numbing effects of antipsychotic drugs on the emotional responses of patients. For example, Mark Vonnegut (son of author Kurt Vonnegut) describes his reactions to the use of the antipsychotic drug Thorazine while he was institutionalized for schizophrenia:

> What the drug is supposed to do is keep away hallucinations. What I think it does is just fog up your mind so badly you don't notice the hallucinations or much else.... On Thorazine everything's a bore. Not a bore, exactly. Boredom implies impatience. You can read comic books ... you can tolerate talking to jerks forever.... The weather is dull, the flowers are dull, nothing's very impressive (Vonnegut, 1975, pp. 196–197).

Antidepressant drugs. As you might guess from the name, **antidepressant drugs** are a class of medications used in cases of severe depression to improve the moods of patients. They were discovered quite by accident: It was found that patients suffering from tuberculosis who were given the drug iproniazid suddenly became happier and more optimistic. When the same drug was tested on people suffering from depression, a similar result occurred, and drugs became an accepted form of treatment for depression (McNeal & Cimbolic, 1986).

Most antidepressant drugs work by allowing an increase in the concentration of certain neurotransmitters in the brain (see Chapter 2). For example, tricyclic drugs modify the amount of norepinephrine and serotonin within the brain; others, such as bupropion, operate by affecting the neurotransmitter dopamine (Schmeck, 1988). Although antidepressant drugs may produce side effects such as drowsiness and faintness, the overall success rate is quite good (Prien, 1983; Siris & Rifkin, 1983). In fact, unlike antipsychotic drugs, antidepressants can produce lasting, long-term recoveries from depression; in many cases, even after the drugs are no longer being taken, the depression does not return.

Lithium, a form of simple mineral salts, is another drug that has been used very successfully in cases of bipolar disorders. Although no one knows definitely why it works (it has no known physiological function), it is very effective in reducing manic episodes, ending manic behavior some 70 percent of the time. On the other hand, its effectiveness in resolving depression is not as impressive. It works only in certain cases, and, like other antidepressants, it can produce a number of side effects (Coopen, Metcalfe & Wood, 1982).

Lithium has a quality that sets it apart from other drug treatments: It represents, more than any other drug, a *preventive* treatment. People who have been subject to manic-depressive episodes in the past often can, after returning to a normal state, take a daily dose of lithium that prevents a recurrence of their symptoms. Lithium, then, presents one thought-provoking vision of the future, suggested by medical-model aproaches to abnormal behavior: a future in which people take drugs regularly to make them psychologically healthier. The reality, though, is that for better or for worse, such a future is far away.

The minor tranquilizers: Antianxiety drugs. Valium, Miltown, Librium—perhaps you are familiar with these drug names, which are among the most common of all the drugs physicians prescribe. A cure for infection? Relief of the common cold? On the contrary, these drugs have nothing to do with physical symptoms. Instead, they are members of a class of drugs known as **antianxiety drugs** (sometimes known as minor tranquilizers) which are prescribed—often by family physicians—to alleviate the stress and anxiety experienced by patients during particularly difficult periods of their lives. In fact, more than half of all Americans have a family member who has taken such a drug at one time or another.

As the name implies, antianxiety drugs reduce the level of anxiety experienced, essentially by reducing excitability and in part by increasing drowsiness. They are used not only to reduce general tension in people who are experiencing temporary difficulties but also to aid in the treatment of more serious anxiety disorders.

Although the popularity of antianxiety drugs suggests that they are relatively risk-free, in fact they can produce a number of potentially serious side effects. For instance, they can cause fatigue, and long-term use can lead to dependence. Moreover, taken in combination with alcohol, some antianxiety drugs can become lethal. But a more important question concerns their use to suppress anxiety. Since almost every theoretical approach to psychological disturbance views continuing anxiety as a symptom of some sort of problem, drugs that mask anxiety may be hiding difficulties that might be more appropriately faced and solved—rather than simply being glossed over.

Electroconvulsive Therapy (ECT)

If you thought that people who have epilepsy—a disorder characterized by seizures and convulsions—were immune to schizophrenia, what might you conclude? A number of psychiatrists in the 1930s, who mistakenly believed that a relationship did exist, concluded that if some way could be found to actually induce convulsions in patients with schizophrenia, they might be cured. To this end, two Italian physicians, Cerletti and Bini (Bini, 1938) tried to induce convulsions by administering shocks to the heads of patients suffering from schizophrenia—and reported some success in alleviating its symptoms.

The use of **electroconvulsive therapy (ECT)** has continued to the present, although the way in which it is administered has been improved. An electric current of 70 to 150 volts is passed through the head of a patient for about a second and a half, causing the patient to lose consciousness and often experience a seizure. Usually the patient is sedated and receives muscle relaxants prior to administration of the current, helping to prevent violent contractions. The typical patient receives about ten such treatments in the course of a month (Breggin, 1979; Weiner, 1982).

As you might expect, ECT is a controversial technique. Apart from the obvious distastefulness of a treatment that evokes images of capital punishment, there are frequent side effects. For instance, following treatment, patients often experience disorientation, confusion, and sometimes memory loss that may remain for months. Moreover, many patients fear ECT, even though they are anesthetized during the actual treatment and

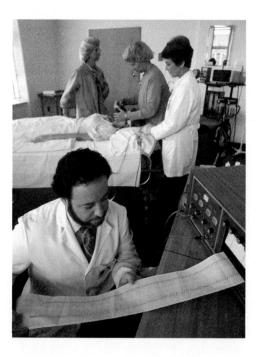

Dr. Richard B. Weiner of Duke University Medical Center reads a patient's EEG as technicians administer electroconvulsive therapy. ECT is used in the treatment of severe depression.

thus experience no pain. Finally, we still do not know how or why ECT works, and although it has never been proved, there is the reasonable fear that the treatment may produce permanent neurological damage to the brain (Fisher, 1985).

Given the drawbacks to ECT, why is it used at all? The basic reason is that in many cases it still seems to be an effective treatment for severe cases of depression (Sackheim, 1985). Indeed, although it is less popular today than it once was, some surveys suggest that the use of ECT rose in the 1980s (Harvard Medical School, 1987). Still, ECT tends to be used only in cases when other treatments have proved ineffective.

Psychosurgery

If ECT strikes you as a questionable procedure, the use of **psychosurgery**—brain surgery in which the object is to alleviate symptoms of mental disorder—will likely appear even more so. A technique that has largely disappeared, psychosurgery was first introduced as a treatment of "last resort" in the 1930s. The procedure—specifically, a **prefrontal lobotomy**—consists of surgically destroying or removing certain parts of a patient's frontal lobes, which control emotionality. The rationale for this procedure was that destroying the connections between various parts of the brain would make patients less subject to emotional impulses, and their general behavior would improve.

In fact, psychosurgery often did improve a patient's behavior—but not without drastic side effects. For along with remission of symptoms of mental disorder, patients sometimes suffered personality changes, becoming bland, colorless, and unemotional. In other cases, patients became aggressive and unable to control their impulses; in the worst cases, the patients died from treatment.

Despite these problems—and the obvious ethical questions regarding the appropriateness of forever altering someone's personality—psychosurgery was used in thousands of cases in the 1930s and 1940s. In fact, the treatment became so routine that in some places fifty patients a day received psychosurgery (Freeman, 1959).

With the advent of effective drug treatments, psychosurgery became practically obsolete. It is still used, in modified form, in very rare cases when all other procedures have failed and the patient's behavior presents a high risk to self and others or when there is severe, uncontrollable pain in terminal cases. When psychosurgery is used today, more precise techniques are employed, and only extremely small areas of brain tissue are destroyed. Still, even in these cases, important ethical issues are raised, and psychosurgery remains a highly controversial treatment (Valenstein, 1980).

Can Abnormal Behavior Be Cured?
Biological Treatment in Perspective

In some respects, there has been no greater revolution in the field of mental health than that represented by the biological approaches to treatment. Mental hospitals have been able to concentrate more on actually helping patients and less on custodial functions as previously violent, uncontrollable patients have been calmed by the use of drugs. Similarly, patients whose lives have been disrupted by depression or manic-depressive episodes have been able to function normally, and other forms of drug therapy in particular have shown remarkable results (Poling, Gadow, & Cleary, 1990).

On the other hand, biological therapies can be criticized. For one thing, in many cases they merely provide relief of the *symptoms* of mental disorder; as soon as the drugs are withdrawn, the symptoms return. Although it is considered a major step in the right direction, biological treatment does not solve the underlying problem that may continue to haunt a patient even while he or she is undergoing treatment. Moreover, biological therapies can have numerous side effects, ranging from physical reactions to the development of *new* symptoms of abnormal behavior (Elkin, 1986). For these reasons, then, biologically based treatment approaches do not represent a cure-all for psychological disorders.

Are biologically based treatment approaches more effective than psychotherapy? Although the definitive answer to this question has yet to be found, research is beginning to address the issue. For example, one major longitudinal study is examining the question of which type of therapy is best for the treatment of depression.

In the initial results of the study, conducted under the auspices of the National Institute of Mental Health, a team of researchers has found that two forms of psychotherapy appear to be as effective as a standard drug regimen in treating depression (Elkin et al., 1989). Both cognitive behavior therapy and a type of treatment labeled "interpersonal" psychotherapy—which focuses on patients' interpersonal problems and social functioning—have been shown to be at least as effective as drug therapy in reducing the symptoms of depression and improving patients' functioning. Furthermore, members of a control group who received no therapy showed significantly less improvement than patients who received some form of therapy, irrespective of its type.

On the other hand, not all the patients in the study responded similarly to the treatments. For example, when just the most severely depressed patients were considered, the drug treatment proved more effective than either of the two psychotherapies.

It is important to realize that the initial results of this study aren't definitive. The research is ongoing; follow-up research at six-month intervals may eventually determine which of the different kinds of therapy provides the most lasting improvement. In the meantime, the question of whether psychologically based or biologically based therapy is most effective remains unanswered. In fact, it is likely that no simple answer to the question will be found. The success of treatment lies in a complex interaction involving the causes and nature of the disorder and the characteristics of the patient.

Focus on Prevention: Community Psychology

All the treatments that we have reviewed in this chapter have a common element: They are "restorative" treatments, aimed at alleviating psychological difficulties that already exist. However, a new movement, dubbed **community psychology**, is geared toward a different aim: to prevent or minimize psychological disorders.

Community psychology came of age in the 1960s, when plans were developed for a nationwide network of community mental-health centers. These centers were meant to provide low-cost mental-health services, including short-term therapy and community educational programs. Moreover, over the last thirty years, the population of mental hospitals plunged, as drug treatments made physical restraint of patients unnecessary. The influx of former mental patients into the community, known as **deinstitutionalization**, further spurred the community psychology movement, which was concerned with ensuring not only that the deinstitutionalized received proper treatment but that their civil rights were maintained (Melton & Garrison, 1987).

Although the original goals of the field of community psychology have not yet been met—the incidence of mental disorders has shown no decline, for instance, and many people who need treatment do not get it (Shapiro et al., 1984)—the movement has yielded several encouraging byproducts. One of these is the installation of telephone "hot lines" in cities throughout the United States. People undergoing acute stress can call a telephone number at any time of day or night and talk to a trained, sympathetic listener who can give immediate—although quite limited—treatment.

The college crisis center is another innovation to grow out of the community psychology movement. Modeled after suicide prevention hotline centers (places for potential suicide victims to call and speak to someone about their difficulties), campus crisis centers provide callers with the opportunity to discuss life crises with a sympathetic listener, who is most often a student volunteer.

Although not professionals, the volunteers receive careful training in telephone counseling. They role-play particular problems and are told how to respond to the difficulties they may confront with callers. The volunteers also hold group meetings to discuss the kinds of problems they are encountering and to share experiences about the kinds of strategies that are most effective.

Because they are not professionals, the staff members of college crisis centers do not, of course, offer long-term therapy to those who contact them. But they are able to provide callers with a supportive, constructive response—often when it is most needed. They are also able to refer callers to appropriate agencies on and off campus to get the long-term help they need.

The Informed Consumer of Psychology: Choosing the Right Therapist

Suppose your friend Maria, who sought your advice on the most effective kind of therapy, decides on the general nature of the treatment that she wants and begins therapy. How does she know that she has chosen the right therapist?

Once again, there is no simple answer (Talley, Strupp, & Morey, 1990). There are, however, a number of factors that informed consumers of psychological services can and should take into consideration to determine whether they have made the right choice.

- The relationship between client and therapist should be a comfortable one; the client should not be afraid or in awe of the therapist but should trust the therapist and feel free to discuss the most personal issues without fearing a negative reaction.
- The therapist should have appropriate training and credentials for the type of therapy that he or she is conducting and should be licensed by appropriate state and local agencies. Far from being a breach of etiquette to ask a therapist on an initial visit about the kind of training that he or she received, it behooves a wise consumer of psychological services to make such an inquiry.
- Clients should feel that they are making progress toward resolving their psychological difficulties after therapy has begun, despite occasional setbacks (Goleman, 1988). Although there is no set timetable, the most obvious changes resulting from therapy tend to occur relatively early in the course of treatment (Howard & Zola, 1988). (Later, however, change may take longer, as more deep-seated problems are attacked.) If a client has no sense of improvement after repeated visits, this issue should be frankly discussed, with an eye toward the possibility of making a change. Most therapy today is of fairly brief duration, especially that involving college students—who average just five therapy sessions (Nowicki & Duke, 1978).
- Clients should be aware that they will have to put in a great deal of effort in therapy. Although ours is a culture that promises quick cures for any problem—as anyone who has perused the self-help

shelves of bookstores knows—in reality solving difficult problems is far from easy (Rosen, 1987). People must be committed to making therapy work and should know that it is they, and not the therapist, who must do most of the work to resolve their problems. The potential is there for the effort to pay off handsomely—as people experience more positive, fulfilling, and meaningful lives.

ASK YOURSELF

What are the major kinds of drug therapies?

How is electroconvulsive therapy (ECT) used to treat abnormal behavior?

What is the major goal of community psychology?

What does the effectiveness of drug therapy tell us about the nature of mental illness?

If drug therapy and some forms of psychotherapy are equally effective in treating depression, are there reasons to prefer one over the other?

LOOKING BACK

1. Psychologically based therapy, known as psychotherapy, and biologically based therapy share the goal of resolving psychological problems by modifying people's thoughts, feelings, expectations, evaluations, and ultimately their behavior.

2. Psychoanalytic treatment is based on Freud's psychodynamic theory. It seeks to bring unresolved past conflicts and unacceptable impulses from the unconscious into the conscious, where the problems may be dealt with more effectively.

3. Behavioral approaches to treatment view abnormal behavior itself as the problem, rather than viewing the behavior as a symptom of some underlying cause. In order to bring about a "cure," this view suggests that the outward behavior must be changed. Aversive conditioning, systematic desensitization, and observational learning are major behavioral treatments. Rational-emotive therapy is an example of a class of behavioral treatments known as cognitive-behavioral therapy.

4. Humanistic therapy is based on the premise that people have control of their behavior, that they can make choices about their lives, and that it is up to them to solve their own problems. Humanistic therapists take a nondirective approach, acting more as guides who facilitate a client's search for answers. Examples of humanistic therapy are client-centered therapy and gestalt therapy.

5. Most research suggests that, in general, therapy is more effective than no therapy, although how much more effective is not known. The answer to the more difficult question of which therapy works best is even less clear, in part because the therapies are so qualitatively different and in part because the definition of "cure" is so vague.

6. Biological treatment approaches suggest that therapy ought to focus on the physiological causes of abnormal behavior, rather than considering psychological factors. Drug therapy, the best example of

biological treatments, has been effective in bringing about dramatic reductions in the appearance of severe signs of mental disturbance.

7. Antipsychotic drugs such as chlorpromazine are very effective in reducing psychotic symptoms, although they can produce serious side effects. Antidepressant drugs reduce depression. The antianxiety drugs, or minor tranquilizers, are among the most frequently prescribed medications of any sort; they act to reduce the experience of anxiety.

8. Electroconvulsive therapy (ECT) consists of passing an electric current of 70 to 150 volts through the head of a patient, who loses consciousness and has a strong seizure. This procedure is an effective treatment for severe cases of schizophrenia and depression. Another biological treatment is psychosurgery, although it is rarely used today.

9. Community psychology aims to prevent or minimize psychological disorders. The movement was spurred in part by deinstitutionalization, in which previously hospitalized mental patients were released into the community.

Key Terms and Concepts

psychotherapy (p. 449)
eclectic approach to therapy (p. 449)
psychodynamic therapy (p. 451)
defense mechanisms (p. 451)
neurotic symptoms (p. 451)
psychoanalysis (p. 451)
free association (p. 451)
dream interpretation (p. 451)
manifest content (p. 452)
latent content (p. 453)
resistance (p. 453)
transference (p. 453)
behavioral treatment approaches (p. 454)
aversive conditioning (p. 455)
systematic desensitization (p. 456)
hierarchy of fears (p. 456)
observational learning (p. 457)
modeling (p. 457)
token system (p. 458)
contingency contracting (p. 458)
rational-emotive therapy (p. 459)
cognitive-behavioral therapy (p. 460)

behavioral self-management (p. 461)
humanistic therapy (p. 462)
nondirective counseling (p. 463)
client-centered therapy (p. 463)
unconditional positive regard (p. 463)
existential therapy (p. 464)
gestalt therapy (p. 464)
group therapy (p. 466)
family therapy (p. 466)
spontaneous remission (p. 468)
drug therapy (p. 473)
antipsychotic drugs (p. 473)
chlorpromazine (p. 473)
antidepressant drugs (p. 474)
lithium (p. 474)
antianxiety drugs (p. 475)
electroconvulsive therapy (ECT) (p. 476)
psychosurgery (p. 477)
prefrontal lobotomy (p. 477)
community psychology (p. 479)
deinstitutionalization (p. 479)

12

Social Psychology

❖

PROLOGUE: ROBERT CHAMBERS

Robert Chambers was sentenced to five to fifteen years in prison for murdering Jennifer Levin.

No one disputed the basic facts. At 4:30 on an August morning, 19-year-old Robert Chambers left a bar on New York City's Upper East Side with Jennifer Levin, 18, and walked into Central Park. A few hours later, Chambers strangled Levin with his bare hands.

At issue is exactly why Levin was killed by Chambers, a handsome six-footer who had dropped out of college. According to his version, Chambers unintentionally killed her during a wild, rough sexual encounter. In this scenario, Levin grabbed Chambers so hard during sex that he was momentarily blinded with pain and flipped Levin over, crushing her throat. In support of this explanation, medical personnel testified at Chambers's trial that it could take only five

483

seconds for someone to die if choked in the particular way that Chambers described the incident. According to Chambers, then, it was Levin's fault that she died.

To friends and family of Levin, however, Chambers's explanation was grotesquely hollow. They pointed out that the grisly injuries she sustained during her last moments suggested a prolonged struggle. Furthermore, the suggestion that it was her own fault that she died was seen by many legal experts as an example of a blame-the-victim argument, a classic legal tactic. Lawyers using this explanation for a defendant's actions try to paint a picture in which it is the victim's behavior that is the cause of the crime, not the defendant's. By employing a blame-the-victim strategy, lawyers portray victims as responsible for, and even deserving of, whatever harm comes their way.

Although we'll probably never know what really happened that night in Central Park, we can be sure about what happened to Chambers: While the jury in his trial was deliberating, he struck a deal with the prosecution and agreed to plead guilty to a first-degree manslaughter charge without waiting for the jury's decision. He is currently serving a five- to fifteen-year sentence in prison.

LOOKING AHEAD

The pivotal questions faced by the jurors in the trial were these: Why did Chambers kill Levin, and, more specifically, how could the reasons behind his behavior be determined?

In fact, these sorts of questions are ones frequently posed by all of us, who continually face the problem in our everyday lives of understanding other people and the causes of their behavior. To one branch of psychology—social psychology—these issues are central. **Social psychology** is the study of how people's thoughts, feelings, and actions are affected by others. Social psychologists consider the nature and causes of individual behavior in social situations.

The broad scope of social psychology is conveyed by the kinds of questions social psychologists ask, such as: How can we convince people to change their attitudes or to adopt new ideas and values? In what ways do we come to understand what others are like? How are we influenced by what others do and think? Why do people display such violence, aggression, and cruelty toward others that people throughout the world live in fear of annihilation? And why, at other times, do people place their own lives at risk to help others?

In this chapter, we explore social psychological approaches to several of these issues. Not only do we examine those processes that underlie social behavior; we also discuss solutions and approaches to a variety of problems and issues that all of us face—ranging from achieving a better understanding of persuasive tactics to forming more accurate impressions of others.

We begin with a look at attitudes, our evaluations of people and other stimuli. Next, we discuss the ways people form judgments about others and the causes of their behavior. We examine the way we glean the meaning of others' behavior and the kinds of biases that affect our understanding of others. Finally, we discuss **social influence**, the area of social psychology that considers situations in which the actions of an individual or group affect the behavior of others. We explore how others' words and actions affect our everyday activities, including circumstances in which we are submissive—or resistant—to authority.

In sum, after reading this chapter you'll have the answers to these questions:

- What are attitudes and how are they formed, maintained, and changed?
- How do we form impressions of what others are like and the causes of their behavior?
- What are the biases that color the way we view others' behavior?
- How can our judgments about others be made more accurate?
- What are the major sources of social influence and the tactics used to bring them about?

*A*TTITUDES, BEHAVIOR, AND PERSUASION

"You can't beat the feeling."

"It's a good time for the great taste of . . ."

"You've come a long way baby."

"Who can ask for anything more?"

You've heard it all before, and you know you'll hear it over and over again. We are constantly bombarded with advertisements designed to persuade us to purchase specific products. In fact, these attempts illustrate basic principles that have been articulated by social psychologists who study **attitudes,** learned predispositions to respond in a favorable or unfavorable manner to a particular person or object (Fishbein & Ajzen, 1975; Ajzen, 1988).

Attitudes, of course, are not restricted to consumer products; they also relate to specific individuals, as well as to more abstract issues. For example, when you think of the various people in your life, you no doubt hold vastly differing attitudes toward them, depending on the nature of your interactions with them. These attitudes may range from highly positive, as in the case of a lover, to extremely negative, as with a despised rival. Attitudes are also likely to vary in importance (Pratkanis, Breckler, & Greenwald, 1989). Whereas our attitudes toward friends, family, and peers are generally central to our interactions in the social world, our attitudes toward, say, television newscasters may be relatively insignificant.

Social psychologists generally consider attitudes to follow the **ABC model,** suggesting that an attitude has three components: affect, behavior, and cognition. The **affect component** encompasses our positive or negative emotions about something—how we feel about it. The **behavior component** consists of a predisposition or intention to act in a particular manner that is relevant to our attitude. Finally, the **cognition component** refers to the beliefs and thoughts we hold about the object of our attitude. For example, someone's attitude toward Bruce Springsteen may consist of a positive emotion (the affect component), an intention to buy his latest recording (the behavior component), and the belief that he is a good singer (the cognition component).

Every attitude can be viewed as having these three interrelated components. However, most social psychologists assume that the parts vary in terms of which element predominates and in the nature of their relationship. In fact, some recent formulations argue against the notion of a three-part model, suggesting, for example, that attitudes are composed primarily of an evaluative element (Tesser & Shaffer, 1990). Regardless of the number of components attitudes are ultimately proven to have, though, it is clear that several general principles govern their formation, maintenance, and change—principles that we discuss next.

Forming and Maintaining Attitudes

Although people do not enter the world holding well-defined attitudes toward any particular person or object, anyone who has seen an infant smile at her parents knows that at least certain attitudes develop quickly. Interestingly, some of the same principles governing how attitudes in the youngest of children are acquired and develop continue to operate throughout life.

Classical conditioning and attitudes. One of the basic processes that underlies attitude formation and development relates to learning principles (McGuire, 1985). Research has shown that the same classical conditioning processes that made Pavlov's dogs salivate at the sound of a bell (see Chapter 4) can explain how attitudes are acquired. In one experiment, for example, subjects were exposed to paired auditory and visual stimuli in which the names of particular countries were paired with words that had positive connotations (such as "gift" and "happy"), neutral connotations, or negative connotations. When the name of a country toward

Advertising is often designed to appeal to the emotions of the buying public. This engaging photo has been used to sell dozens of products and services including picture frames, wine, real estate, employment counseling, and garden hoses.

which the experimenter wanted the subjects to form a positive attitude was flashed on a screen, the experimenter said a word with a positive connotation.

After repeated trials in which each country's name appeared eighteen times, subjects' attitudes toward each of the nationalities were assessed. In general, the results showed that subjects held more positive attitudes toward the nationalities associated with positive words and more negative attitudes toward nationalities that had been associated with negative words. In technical terms, the nationalities became conditioned stimuli, evoking conditioned responses in the form of new attitudes (Staats, 1967; Staats & Staats, 1958).

Advertisers are well aware of results such as these, and often try to link a product they want consumers to buy with a positive feeling or event (Alsop, 1988). For instance, many advertisements feature young, attractive, healthy men and women using a product—even if it is one as uninteresting as toothpaste. The idea behind such advertisements is to create a classically conditioned response to the product, so that just seeing a tube of Crest toothpaste evokes a positive feeling.

Praise for the "right" attitude: Reinforcement approaches to attitude acquisition. Another basic learning process, operant conditioning, underlies attitude acquisition. Attitudes that are reinforced, either verbally or nonverbally, tend to be maintained, whereas a person who states an attitude that elicits ridicule from others may modify or abandon the attitude. But it is not only direct reinforcement or punishment that can influence attitudes. **Vicarious learning,** in which a person learns something through the observation of others, also accounts for attitude development—particularly when the individual has no direct experience with the object about which the attitude is held. It is through vicarious learning processes that children pick up the prejudices of their parents. For example, even if they have never met a blind person, children whose parents say that "blind people are incompetent" may adopt such attitudes themselves.

We also learn attitudes vicariously through television, films, and other media. For instance, movies that glorify violence reinforce positive attitudes regarding aggression (as we discuss more in Chapter 13), and portrayals of women as subservient to men shape and bolster sexist attitudes (Tuchman, 1978).

Persuasion: Changing Attitudes

What is it about Bill Cosby that leads people to buy Jell-O? How does Michael Jackson get people to drink Pepsi?

According to professionals working in the field of advertising, each of these is a carefully selected match between the product and the individual chosen to represent it. It is not just a matter of finding a well-known celebrity; the person must also be believable, trustworthy, and representative of the qualities that advertisers want their particular product to project (Alwitt, Barnet & Mitchell, 1985; Kanner, 1989).

The work of advertisers draws heavily upon findings from social psychology regarding persuasion. This research has identified a number of factors (see Figure 12-1) that promote effective persuasion—many of which you will recognize if you consider for a moment some of the advertisements with which you are most familiar.

- Message source. The individual who delivers a persuasive message has a major impact on the effectiveness of that message (Wu & Shaffer, 1987). Communicators who are both physically and socially attractive seem to produce greater attitude change (Chaiken, 1979). Moreover, the expertise and trustworthiness of a communicator are related to the impact of a message—except in situations in which

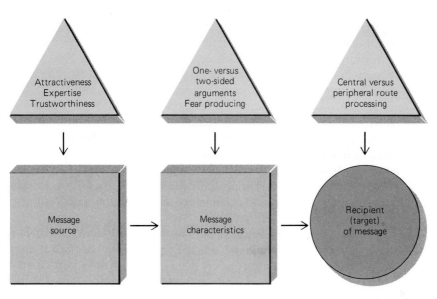

FIGURE 12-1
In this model of the critical factors affecting persuasion, the message source and message characteristics are shown to influence the recipient or target of a persuasive message.

the communicator is believed to have an ulterior motive. If a prestigious communicator seems to be benefiting from persuading others, the message may be discounted (Hovland, Janis & Kelly, 1953; Eagly, Wood, & Chaiken, 1978). For example, a prestigious scientist who argues in favor of opening a nuclear power plant would generally be a particularly influential source, unless it is revealed that the scientist owns stock in the power plant and stands to benefit financially from its opening.

- Characteristics of the message. As you might expect, it is not just *who* delivers a message but *what* the message is like that affects attitude and behavior change. One-sided arguments—in which only the communicator's side is presented—are probably best if the communicator is initially viewed favorably by the audience. But if the audience receives a message presenting an unpopular viewpoint, two-sided messages—which include both the communicator's position and the one he or she is arguing against—are more effective, probably because they are seen as more precise and thoughtful (Karlins & Abelson, 1979). In addition, fear-producing messages ("If you don't use our dental floss, your teeth are sure to fall out") are effective only if they include precise recommendations for actions to avoid danger. Otherwise, messages that arouse fear tend to evoke people's defense mechanisms and may be ignored (Leventhal, 1970).

- Characteristics of the recipient or target. Once a message has been communicated, the characteristics of the audience of the message determine whether it will be accepted. For example, we might expect that recipients' intelligence would be related to their persuasibility—and it is, although the relationship is complex. High intelligence both aids and hinders persuasion. Because higher intelligence enables people to understand a message better and later recall it more easily, persuasion is more likely. On the other hand, greater intelligence is associated with more confidence in one's own opinions, and therefore messages of opposing viewpoints are more likely to be rejected. Therefore, in many cases, these two factors cancel each other out, and intelligence is unrelated to persuasibility (McGuire, 1968).

Some gender differences in persuasibility also seem to exist. For instance, social psychologist Alice Eagly (1989) has found that women are somewhat more easily persuaded than men, particularly when they have less knowledge of the message topic. However, the magnitude of the differences between men and women are not large.

One factor that is important in determining whether a message is accepted is the nature of information processing carried out by the recipient. There are two routes to persuasion: central and peripheral (Petty & Cacioppo, 1981; Cialdini, 1984; Eagly, 1983). **Central route processing** occurs when the recipient thoughtfully considers the issues and arguments involved in persuasion. In contrast, **peripheral route processing** occurs when the recipient uses more easily understood information that requires less thought, such as the nature of the source or other information less central to the issues involved in the message itself (Mackie, 1987; Petty & Cacioppo, 1986).

In general, central route processing results in the most lasting attitude change. However, if central route processing cannot be employed (for instance, if the target is inattentive, bored, or distracted), then the nature of the message becomes less important, and peripheral factors more critical (Petty & Cacioppo, 1984). Advertising that uses celebrities to sell a product, then, tends to produce change through the peripheral route. In fact, it is possible that well-reasoned, carefully crafted messages will be *less* effective when delivered by a celebrity than by an anonymous source—if the target pays greater attention to the celebrity (leading to peripheral route processing) than to the message (which would have led to central route processing). On the other hand, since recipients of advertising messages are often in a fairly inattentive state, the use of celebrities is probably an excellent strategy. Advertisers are correct, then, in their assumption that well-known individuals can have a significant persuasive impact.

The Link Between Attitudes and Behavior: Striving for Consistency

Not surprisingly, attitudes influence behavior. If you like hamburgers (the affect component), are predisposed to eat at McDonald's or Burger King (the behavior component), and believe hamburgers are healthy for you (the cognitive component), it is hardly surprising that you will eat hamburgers frequently. The strength of the link between particular attitudes and behavior varies, of course, but generally people strive for consistency between their attitudes and their behavior. Furthermore, people tend to be fairly consistent in the different attitudes they hold: You would probably not hold the attitude that eating meat is immoral and still have a positive attitude toward hamburgers.

Interestingly, the consistency that leads attitudes to influence behavior sometimes works the other way around, for in some cases it is our behavior that shapes our attitudes. Consider, for instance, the following incident:

> You've just spent what you feel is the most boring hour of your life, turning pegs for a psychology experiment. Just as you're finally finished and about to leave, the experimenter asks you to do him a favor. He tells you that he needs a confederate to tell subsequent subjects about the task. All you have to do is tell them how interesting it was. For this, you'll be paid $1.

If you agree to such a request, you may be setting yourself up for a state of psychological tension that is known as **cognitive dissonance.** According to a major social psychologist, Leon Festinger (1957), cognitive dissonance occurs when a person holds two attitudes or thoughts (referred to as **cognitions**) that contradict each other. For example, a smoker who knows that smoking leads to lung cancer holds contradictory cognitions: (1) I smoke; and (2) smoking leads to lung cancer. The theory predicts that these two thoughts will lead to a state of cognitive dissonance. More important, it predicts that the individual will be motivated to reduce such dissonance by one of the following methods: (1) modifying one or both of the cognitions; (2) changing the perceived importance of one cognition; (3) adding cognitions; or (4) denying that the two cognitions are related to each other. Hence the smoker might decide that he really doesn't smoke all that much (modifying the cognition), that the evidence linking smoking to cancer is weak (changing the importance of a cognition), that the amount of exercise he gets compensates for the smoking (adding cognitions), or that there is no evidence linking smoking and cancer (denial). Whatever technique is used, the result is a reduction in dissonance (see Figure 12-2).

If we consider the situation in which a subject in an experiment is paid just $1 to tell someone else that a boring task was interesting, as in the situation described above, we have set up classic dissonance-produc-

"Nothing there appeals to me."

Drawing by B. Tobey, © 1978 The New Yorker Magazine, Inc.

As this cartoon aptly illustrates, cognitive dissonance arising from the two contradictory cognitions of "I want a good meal" and "I can't afford a good meal" may be reduced by deciding that one really doesn't want a good meal after all.

ing circumstances. A subject in such a situation is left with two contradictory thoughts: (1) I believe the task is boring; but (2) I said it was interesting with only little justification (one dollar's worth).

According to the theory, dissonance should be aroused. But how can such dissonance be reduced? One can't very well deny having said that the task was interesting without making a fairly strong break with reality. But, relatively speaking, it is easy to change one's attitude toward the task—and thus the theory predicts that dissonance will be reduced as the subjects change their attitudes to be more positive.

This prediction was confirmed in a classic experiment (Festinger & Carlsmith, 1959). The experiment followed essentially the same procedure outlined earlier, in which a subject was offered $1 to describe a boring task as interesting. In addition, as a control, a condition was included in which subjects were offered $20 to say that the task was interesting. The reasoning behind this condition was that $20 was so much money that subjects in this condition had a good reason to be telling something that was incorrect; dissonance would *not* be aroused, and *less* attitude change would be expected. The results supported this notion: Subjects changed

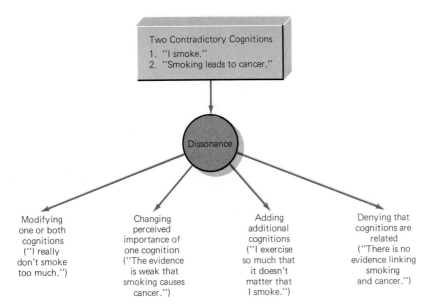

FIGURE 12-2
The presence of two contradictory cognitions ("I smoke" and "Smoking leads to cancer") produces dissonance, which may be reduced through several methods.

their attitudes more (becoming more positive toward the peg-turning task) when they were paid $1 than subjects who were paid $20.

We now know that dissonance explains a number of everyday occurrences involving attitudes and behavior. For example, consider what happens when you decide to make a major purchase, such as a new car. First you will probably get as much information as possible about a range of models by talking to people and reading about different cars. But after you make your decision, what happens? Most people experience some degree of dissonance because the car they've chosen has some undesirable characteristics, whereas those models that were rejected have some positive features. What typically happens to reduce such dissonance is that people's attitudes toward the rejected models become *more* negative, while their attitudes toward the chosen model become *more* positive (Converse & Cooper, 1979). Moreover, a **selective exposure** phenomenon occurs: In order to minimize dissonance, people selectively expose themselves to information that supports their own choice and attempt to avoid information that is contrary to their choice (Sears, 1968; Sweeney & Gruber, 1984).

Since its development in the late 1950s, dissonance theory has generated a tremendous amount of research, most of which has supported the theory (Aronson, 1990). Research continues today, with investigators expanding our understanding of the specific factors that underlie the state of dissonance (e.g., Croyle & Cooper, 1983; Scher & Cooper, 1989). However the theory has not been without its critics. Some psychologists have criticized the methodology used in dissonance experiments, while others have suggested alternative theoretical explanations.

One of the most plausible alternatives was suggested by Darryl Bem (1967, 1972) in his **self-perception theory.** Bem put forth the idea that people form attitudes by observing their own behavior, employing the same principles that they use when they observe others' behavior to draw conclusions about others' attitudes. In other words, people are sometimes unclear about the reasons for which they have just demonstrated a certain behavior. In those instances, they will look at their behavior and try to figure out just why they did what they did.

For example, if I were the subject who received $1 for saying that a task I hated was actually very interesting, I might look at what I said and try to figure out why I said it. The most likely explanation is "Well, if I agreed to say I liked the task for a paltry $1, then I probably didn't dislike it all that much. In fact, I probably liked it." Therefore, when asked by the experimenter to indicate my attitude, I might respond with a relatively positive attitude toward the task. Of course, this is the same result that dissonance theory would predict—more positive attitude change in the lower-incentive condition ($1) than in the higher-incentive condition ($20)—but the underlying reason is different. Whereas the dissonance explanation suggests that attitude change is due to the presence (in the $1 condition) of the unpleasant state of dissonance that a subject tries to overcome, the self-perception theory suggests it is due to an active search for an understanding of one's behavior.

Although we cannot be sure whether dissonance or self-perception theory provides the more accurate description of how people react to inconsistencies between their attitudes and their behavior, it is clear most of us try to make sense of our own attitudes and behavior and maintain consistency between them. When we behave in a way that is inconsistent with our attitudes, we tend to change our attitudes to make them fit better with our behavior.

ASK YOURSELF

What are the three components of attitudes?

How are attitudes acquired via classical and operant conditioning?

When does cognitive dissonance occur?

If you wanted to convince a reluctant friend to vote for your favorite candidate, how might you engage in effective persuasion?

How can you use knowledge of attitude change research to guard against the abundant persuasive messages presented to you by advertisers?

UNDERSTANDING OTHERS: SOCIAL COGNITION

Regardless of whether they agreed with his policies and ideology, in spite of how they felt he garbled the facts at news conferences, and irrespective of the trouble his subordinates found themselves in, most Americans genuinely *liked* President Ronald Reagan. Reagan's unfavorable experiences never seemed to adhere to him, and he was dubbed the "Teflon president" by the press. Perceived as a "nice guy," he remained one of the most popular presidents of the century throughout the course of his presidency.

Phenomena such as these illustrate the power of our impressions and suggest the importance of determining how people develop an understanding of others. In fact, one of the dominant areas of study in social psychology during the last few years has focused on learning how people come to understand what others are like and to explain the reasons underlying others' behavior (Ross & Fletcher, 1985; Jones, 1990).

Understanding What Others Are Like

Consider for a moment the enormous amount of information about other people to which we are exposed. How are we able to decide what is important and what is not and to make judgments about the characteristics of others? Social psychologists interested in this question study **social cognition**—the processes that underlie our understanding of the social world. They have learned that individuals have highly developed **schemas,** sets of cognitions about people and social experiences. These schemas organize information stored in memory, represent in our minds the way the social world operates, and give us a framework to categorize and interpret information relating to social stimuli (Fiske & Taylor, 1991).

We typically hold schemas for particular types of people in our environments. Our schema for "teacher," for instance, generally consists of a number of characteristics: knowledge of the subject matter he or she is teaching, a desire to impart that knowledge, and an awareness of the student's need to understand what is being said. Or we may hold a schema for "mother" that includes the characteristics of warmth, nurturance, and caring. Regardless of their accuracy—and, as we shall see, very often their inaccuracies—schemas are important because they organize the way in which we recall, recognize, and categorize information about others. Moreover, they allow us to make predictions of what others are like on the basis of relatively little information, since we tend to fit people into schemas even when there is not much concrete evidence to go on (Smith, 1984; Snyder & Cantor, 1979).

Impression formation. How do we decide that Gail is a flirt, or Andy is a jerk, or Jon is a really nice guy? The earliest work on social cognition was designed to examine **impression formation,** the process by which an individual organizes information about another individual to form an overall impression of that person. In one classic study, for instance, students were told that they were about to hear a guest lecturer (Kelley, 1950). One group of students was told that the lecturer was "a rather warm person, industrious, critical, practical, and determined," while a second group was told that he was "a rather cold person, industrious, critical, practical, and determined."

The simple substitution of "cold" for "warm" was responsible for drastic differences in the way the students in each group perceived the lecturer, even though he gave the same talk in the same style in each condition. Students who had been told he was "warm" rated him considerably more positively than students who had been told he was "cold."

The findings from this experiment led to a good deal of research on impression formation that focused on the way people pay particular attention to certain unusually important traits—known as **central traits**—to help them form an overall impression of others. According to this work, the presence of a central trait alters the meaning of other traits (Asch, 1946; Widmeyer & Loy, 1988). Hence the description of the lecturer as "industrious" presumably meant something different according to whether it was associated with the central trait "warm" or "cold."

Other work on impression formation has used information-processing approaches (see Chapter 5) to develop mathematically oriented models of how individual personality traits are combined to create an overall impression (Anderson, 1974; Casselden & Hampson, 1990). Generally, the results of this research suggest that, in forming an overall judgment of a person, we use a psychological "average" of the individual traits we see, in a manner that is analogous to finding a mathematical average of several numbers (Kaplan, 1975).

Of course, as we gain more experience with people and see them exhibiting behavior in a variety of situations, our impressions of them become more complex (Gilbert, Pelham & Krull, 1987; Anderson & Cole, 1990). But, because there usually are gaps in our knowledge of others, we still tend to fit them into personality schemas that represent particular "types" of people. For instance, we might hold a "gregarious person" schema, made up of the traits of friendliness, aggressiveness, and openness. The presence of just one or two of these traits might be sufficient to make us assign a person to a particular schema.

Unfortunately, the schemas that we employ are susceptible to a variety of factors that affect the accuracy of our judgments (Kenny & Albright, 1987; Gordon & Wyer, 1987; DePaulo et al., 1987). For example, our mood affects how we perceive others. People who are happy form more favorable impressions and make more positive judgments than people who are sad (Forgas & Bower, 1987).

Even when schemas are not entirely accurate, they serve an important function. They allow us to develop expectations about how others will behave, permitting us to plan our interactions with others more easily, and serving to simplify a complex social world.

The Negative Side of Social Cognition: Stereotypes

What do we think of when someone is described as, "elderly" or "black" or a "woman driver"? If we're honest, most of us would have to admit we readily form some sort of immediate impression of what that individual is like. This fact illustrates an important point: Although schemas can be helpful in organizing the social world, they also have a negative side— particularly when they promote an oversimplified understanding of other people (Zarate & Smith, 1990). **Stereotypes,** beliefs and expectations about members of groups held simply on the basis of their membership in those groups, represent one particularly damaging instance of this approach to impression formation.

Some of the most prevalent stereotypes have to do with racial and ethnic categorizations. Over the years, various groups have been called, for example, "lazy" or "shrewd" or "cruel" with varying degrees of regularity by nongroup members (Katz & Brayly, 1933; Weber & Crocker, 1983). But stereotypes are by no means confined to racial and ethnic groups. Sex and age stereotyping are all too common as well. There is even a general stereotype relating to *any* group, known as the **ingroup–outgroup bias** (Crocker & Luhtanen, 1990; Perdue, Dovidio, Gurtman, & Tyler, 1990). We tend to hold less favorable opinions about members of groups of which we are not a part **(outgroups)** and more favorable opinions about members of groups to which we belong **(ingroups).**

Although there is little evidence to support the accuracy of most stereotypes, they can have harmful consequences. When negative stereotypes are acted on, they result in **discrimination**—negative behavior toward members of a particular group. Discrimination can produce exclusion from jobs, neighborhoods, or educational opportunities, and may result in members of particular groups receiving lower salaries and benefits.

Stereotypes not only produce overt discrimination; they can actually *cause* members of stereotyped groups to behave in ways that reflect the stereotype through a phenomenon known as a **self-fulfilling prophecy** (Archibald, 1974). Self-fulfilling prophecies are expectations about the occurrence of a future event or behavior that act to increase the likelihood that the event or behavior *will* occur. For example, if people think that members of a particular group are lazy, they may treat them in a way that actually brings about their laziness (Skrypnek & Snyder, 1982). Similarly, people holding a stereotype may be "primed" to interpret the behavior of the stereotyped group as representative of the stereotype, even when the behavior depicts something entirely different (Slusher & Anderson, 1987).

ASK YOURSELF

What are schemas?

How do we form impressions of others?

What are stereotypes?

How do we manage to process and make sense of the almost overwhelming number of social stimuli that we receive?

How do the basic processes of impression formation and social cognition lead to destructive stereotypes?

UNDERSTANDING THE CAUSES OF BEHAVIOR: ATTRIBUTION PROCESSES

When Barbara Washington, a new employee at the Staditron Computer Company, completed a major staffing project two weeks early, her boss, Marian Gonzales, was delighted. At the next staff meeting, she announced how pleased she was with Barbara and explained that *this* was an example of the kind of performance she was looking for in her staff. The other staff members looked on resentfully, trying to figure out why Barbara had worked night and day to finish the project not just on time, but two weeks early. She must be an awfully compulsive person, they decided.

Most of us have, at one time or another, puzzled over the reasons behind someone's behavior. Perhaps it was in a situation similar to the one above, or it may have been under more formal circumstances, such as the task faced by the jurors in the Robert Chambers trial described at the beginning of the chapter. In contrast to work on social cognition, which describes how people develop an overall impression about others' personality traits, **attribution theory** seeks to explain how we decide, on the basis of samples of an individual's behavior, what the specific causes of the person's behavior are (Harvey & Weary, 1985; Weiner, 1985; Graham & Folkes, 1990).

When trying to understand the causes underlying a given behavior, individuals typically try first to determine whether the cause is situational or dispositional (Heider, 1958). **Situational causes** are those brought about by something in the environment. For instance, someone who knocks over a quart of milk and then cleans it up is probably doing so not because he or she is a terribly neat person, but because the *situation* is one that requires it. In contrast, a person who spends hours shining the kitchen floor is probably doing so because he or she *is* a neat person—hence, the behavior has a **dispositional cause,** prompted by the person's disposition (his or her internal traits or personality characteristics).

In our example involving Barbara, her fellow employees, in trying to attribute her behavior to either the situation or her disposition, assumed that her disposition was the cause. But from a logical standpoint, it is equally plausible that there was something about the situation that caused the behavior. If asked, Barbara might attribute her accomplishment to situational factors, explaining that she had so much other work to do that she just had to get the project out of the way, or that the project was not all that difficult and that it was easy to complete ahead of schedule. To her, then, the reason for her behavior might not be dispositional at all; it could be situational.

How do we determine whether Barbara's behavior is motivated by situational or dispositional factors? Harold Kelley (1967) suggested that people use three types of information to answer this question. First, there is **consensus information**—the degree to which other people behave similarly in the same situation. For instance, if most people would have completed the project two weeks early, Barbara's behavior would be high in consensus, but if most people would have procrastinated, her behavior would be low in consensus. Second, there is **consistency information**—the degree to which an individual would behave similarly in a similar situation. If Barbara always gets her work in early on the job, no matter what the project, she is high in consistency. Finally, there is **distinctiveness information,** the extent to which the behavior occurs across other situations. If Barbara gets her work done early only on her job but procrastinates everywhere else, her behavior is high in distinctiveness.

By simultaneously considering all three kinds of information, people are able to make an attribution that is based primarily on dispositional factors or on situational factors. As shown in Figure 12-3, information that is high in consensus, high in consistency, and high in distinctiveness leads to attributions that are situational: In our example, Barbara's behavior would be attributed to the demands of the job. But with situations in which consensus and distinctiveness are low and consistency is high, people tend to make dispositional attributions, assuming the behavior is related to one's personality.

To Err Is Human: Biases in Attribution

If we always processed information in the rational manner that Kelley's model suggests, the world might run a lot more smoothly. Unfortunately, although Kelley's attribution formulation generally makes accurate predictions—at least for cases in which people have concrete, firsthand

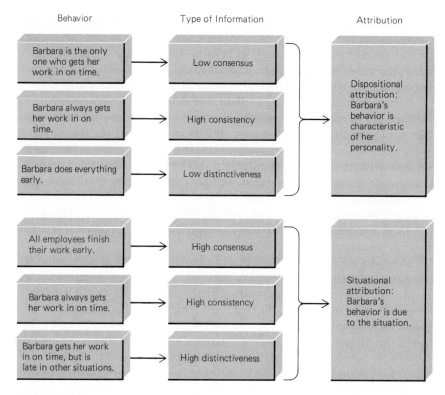

Behavior   Type of Information   Attribution

Barbara is the only one who gets her work in on time. → Low consensus

Barbara always gets her work in on time. → High consistency

Barbara does everything early. → Low distinctiveness

Dispositional attribution: Barbara's behavior is characteristic of her personality.

All employees finish their work early. → High consensus

Barbara always gets her work in on time. → High consistency

Barbara gets her work in on time, but is late in other situations. → High distinctiveness

Situational attribution: Barbara's behavior is due to the situation.

FIGURE 12-3

An illustration of Kelley's model of attribution. Learning that Barbara's behavior represents low consensus, high consistency, and low distinctiveness leads to a dispositional attribution. In contrast, determining that Barbara's behavior represents high consensus, high consistency, and high distinctiveness leads to a situational attribution.

knowledge of consensus, consistency, and distinctiveness (Wells & Harvey, 1978)—people do not always process information about others in as logical a fashion as the theory seems to suggest (Funder, 1987; Cheng & Novick, 1990). In fact, research shows that there tend to be consistent biases in the way attributions are made. Among the most typical:

- *The fundamental attribution bias.* One of the most common biases in people's attributions is the tendency to attribute others' behavior to dispositional causes—but one's own behavior to situational causes. Known as the **fundamental attribution bias,** this tendency is quite prevalent (Watson, 1982). For example, an analysis of letters and advice in newspaper columns such as "Dear Abby" and "Ann Landers" showed that writers tended to attribute their own problems to situational factors, while they described the problems of others as due to dispositional causes (Schoeneman & Rubanowitz, 1985).

In our own example, we saw how Barbara attributed her behavior to constraints of the environment (situational factors), while Barbara's colleagues thought her behavior was due to her personality characteristics (dispositional factors).

Why should the fundamental attribution bias be so common? One reason has to do with the nature of information that is available to the people making an attribution. When we view the behavior of another person in a particular setting, the information that is most conspicuous is the person's behavior itself. Because the individual's environment is relatively stable and invariant, the person is the center of our attention. But when we consider our own behavior, changes in the environment are going to be more obvious, and we are more likely to make attributions based on situational factors.

One consequence of the fundamental attribution bias is that we may excuse our own failures by attributing them to extenuating circumstances ("I couldn't finish my paper because the library didn't have the book I needed"), but when others have a problem we blame their personality flaws ("He's just too lazy to finish his paper on time"; Snyder & Higgins, 1988).

- *The halo effect.* Harry is intelligent, kind, and loving. Is he also conscientious?

If you were to hazard a guess, your most likely response would be "yes." Your guess reflects the **halo effect,** a phenomenon in which an initial understanding that a person has positive traits is used to infer other uniformly positive characteristics (Cooper, 1981). The opposite would also hold true: Learning that Harry was unsociable and argumentative would probably lead you to assume he was lazy as well.

The reason for the halo effect is that we hold **implicit personality theories,** theories reflecting our notions of what traits are found together in individuals. These theories are based on a combination of experience and logic. Our perception of the world may be flawed, however, because application of our theory can be singularly inappropriate for a given individual, or it may simply be wrong. Most people have neither uniformly positive nor uniformly negative traits but instead possess a combination of the two.

- *The Pollyanna effect.* In some respects, people have a blind optimism that is not too different from that of Pollyanna, the heroine of Eleanor Porter's 1913 novel who could see no evil in the world. Because we are typically motivated to view the world as a pleasant, enjoyable place, our perceptions of others are colored in a positive direction (Sears, 1982). This **Pollyanna effect** produces a tendency to rate others in a generally positive manner.

There are several examples of the Pollyanna effect. For instance, the public's evaluation of the U.S. president and other public figures historically is generally positive. Similarly, ratings of other people made by subjects in experiments normally fall in the positive range—even when the people have just met. Humorist Will Rogers may have been reflecting a widespread feeling when he claimed, "I never met a man I didn't like."

- *Assumed-similarity bias.* How similar to you—in terms of attitudes, opinions, and likes and dislikes—are your friends and acquaintances? Most people feel that their friends and acquaintances are fairly similar to themselves. But this feeling goes beyond just people we know; there is a general tendency—known as the **assumed-similarity bias**—to think of people as being similar to oneself, even when meeting them for the first time (Ross, Greene & House, 1977; Hoch, 1987; Marks & Miller, 1987).

  If other people are, in fact, different from oneself, the assumed-similarity bias reduces the accuracy of the judgments being made. Moreover, it suggests an interesting possibility: It may be that a judgment about another individual better defines the judge's characteristics than those of the person being rated. In some cases, then, the portrait we draw of another person—particularly one about whom we have little information—may in reality be a sketch of the way we view ourselves.

Understanding Our Own Behavior: Self-Perception Theory

The fundamental attribution bias illustrates an important point about attributional processes: People not only make attributions about others; they can sometimes act as observers of their *own* behavior and make attributions on the basis of what they see themselves doing. As we discussed earlier in the chapter in reference to attitudes, Bem's theory of self-perception suggests that people monitor their own behavior and make judgments about themselves on the basis of what they see themselves doing (Bem, 1967). The theory suggests, then, that when situational cues are weak or past experience does not provide relevant information, people will look to their own behavior to make attributions about themselves.

How does the theory work? Suppose you are asked to handle advertising for a play being produced by the campus drama club during the next term. You are pleased to be asked but not too sure you can spare the time, so you tell the person making the request you will get back to her with your decision in a few days. As the days drag on, though, you never seem to have the time to call her back, and you just can't make up your mind. After a few weeks have gone by, you begin to wonder why you can't reach a decision. As you ponder the question, you conclude that your reluctance indicates that you are unenthusiastic and really don't want the job.

Your decision to decline the request is based on self-perception. Using your own behavior as an indication of your underlying motivation, you determine that the hesitancy you observe in yourself is based on a lack of desire to take on the job. Here you are acting much like an outside observer, making an inference on the basis of your behavior. In sum, self-perception theory suggests that we derive knowledge about ourselves by examining our own actions.

Another facet of self-perception is illustrated by research showing that people habitually use a particular style in explaining events in their lives. For example, some of us tend to be more optimistic in explaining bad events in our lives, whereas others tend to be more pessimistic. Pessimists typically see unfavorable events, such as failing a test, as being due to a personal deficit that will plague them for the rest of their lives. Optimists, in contrast, may view the failure as a temporary setback, one that can be remedied by making changes in their lives.

The kinds of explanations we employ have important consequences on many areas of our lives. For example, people who employ more optimistic explanations enjoy better health, have greater job success, and actually seem to live longer than those who are more pessimistic (Scheier, 1986; Peterson, Seligman & Vaillant, 1988). The explanation for these consequences may be that people who characteristically use pessimistic explanations may act more passively in the face of adversity. When they are ill, for example, they may not seek medical advice or may not follow it once they receive it. In contrast, optimists may feel more strongly that their own actions can in fact have an impact upon their future health and consequently may be more receptive to and compliant with medical advice. (For another application of self-perception theory, see the Psychology and Society box.)

ASK YOURSELF

How does attribution theory seek to explain the processes that underlie the causes of others' behavior?

What are the major biases in attribution?

How does self-perception theory explain the way in which we monitor our own behavior?

If an acquaintance walks by you in the hallway without saying hello, you might think, "What an unfriendly and inconsiderate nerd." According to the fundamental attribution bias, how might your acquaintance interpret the same event?

PSYCHOLOGY AND SOCIETY

Improving Your Grades
by Improving Your Attributions

If you are like most people, when you first began college, you were concerned about whether you'd be able to make the grade. Could you do well enough to meet the competition of your classmates? Would you be able to meet the standards set by your professors? Would you, in short, be smart enough to do well?

For some first-year students, these concerns become so great that they produce anxiety that interferes with work. Any difficulties that such students experience early in their college careers are viewed as confirmations that they are ill-equipped to do college-level work. This attribution leads to further disruption of their studying and ultimately to even poorer performance (Peterson & Barrett, 1987).

In actuality, statistics show that *most* students' performance improves over the course of their college careers, so it is not unusual to expect that first-year performance will be less than optimal. This finding led social psychologists Timothy Wilson and Patricia Linville (1982, 1985) to devise a program to change the way first-year college students who were concerned about their grades attributed the causes of their academic performance.

Wilson and Linville hypothesized that academic performance would improve by exposing students to information that showed that poor first-year performance was likely caused by temporary factors that were susceptible to change, rather than by permanent, unchangeable conditions. To test this reasoning, Wilson and Linville carried out a series of simple experiments. In them, university freshmen who had expressed concern about their first-year grades viewed videotapes of interviews with juniors and seniors who stated that their grades had improved since they had started college. In addition, the freshmen were given statistical information indicating that grades typically improve among college students in general.

The program showed clear success. In contrast to a control group for students who received no treatment, students who viewed the videotapes and were exposed to the information showed an improvement in their grades in the semester following the study, and also had a lower dropout rate.

In sum, exposure to a one-time program designed to change attributions was sufficient to produce better performance. These results are promising, as are those for similar programs (Försterling, 1985), for other everyday problems may be solved simply by changing people's attributions regarding the causes of their behavior (Baumgardner, Heppner & Arkin, 1986).

SOCIAL INFLUENCE

You have just transferred to a new college and are attending your first class. When the professor enters, you find that your fellow classmates all rise, bow down, and then face the back of the room. You have no understanding of this behavior. Is it more likely that you will (1) jump up to join the rest of the class or (2) remain seated?

Based on what research has told us about social influence, the answer to such a question would almost always be (1). As you undoubtedly know from your own experience, pressures to conform can be painfully strong, and they can bring about changes in behavior that, when considered in perspective, would never have otherwise occurred.

Doing What Others Do: Conformity

Conformity is a change in behavior or attitudes brought about by a desire to follow the beliefs or standards of other people. The classic demonstration of pressure to conform comes from a series of studies carried out in the 1950s by Solomon Asch (Asch, 1951). In the experiments, subjects thought they were participating in a test of perceptual skills with a group of six other subjects. The subjects were shown one card with three lines of varying length and a second card which had a fourth line that matched one of the first three (see Figure 12-4). The task was seemingly straightforward: The subjects had to announce aloud which of the first three lines was identical in length to a "standard" line. Because there was always an obvious answer, the task seemed easy to the participants.

Indeed, since the subjects all agreed on the first few trials, the procedure was quite a simple one. But then something odd began to happen. From the perspective of the subject in the group who got to answer last, all of the first six subjects' answers seemed to be wrong—in fact, unanimously wrong. And this continued: Over and over again, the first six subjects provided answers that contradicted what the last subject felt was the correct one. The dilemma that this situation posed for the last subject was whether to follow his or her own perceptions or to follow the group and repeat the answer that everyone else was giving.

As you might have guessed, the situation in the experiment was more contrived that it first appeared. The first six subjects were actually confederates of the experimenter and had been instructed to give unani-

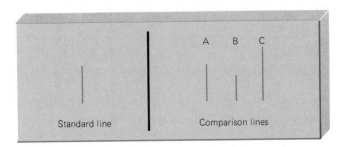

FIGURE 12-4
Subjects in Asch's conformity experiment were first shown a "standard" line and then asked to identify which of the three comparison lines was identical in length. As this example illustrates, there was always an obvious answer.

mously erroneous answers in many of the trials. And the study had nothing to do with perceptual skills. Instead, the issue under investigation was that of conformity.

What Asch found was that in about one-third of the trials, subjects conformed to the unanimous but erroneous group answer. About 75 percent of all subjects conformed at least once. However, there were strong individual differences: Some subjects conformed nearly all the time, whereas others never did so.

Since Asch's pioneering work, literally hundreds of studies have examined the factors affecting conformity, and we now know a great deal about the phenomenon (Moscovici, 1985; Tanford & Penrod, 1984). Among the most important variables producing conformity are the following:

- The nature of the group. The more attractive the group, the greater its ability to produce conformity. The lower the **status**—the social rank held within a group—of a person and the greater the similarity of the individual to the group, the greater is the power of the group over the individual's behavior.

- The nature of the individual's response. Conformity is considerably higher when people must make a response publicly than when they can respond privately, as our founding fathers noted when they authorized secret ballots in voting.

- The kind of task. People working on tasks and questions that are ambiguous (having no clear answer) are more susceptible to social pressure. Giving an opinion, such as on what type of clothing is fashionable, is more likely to produce conformity than answering a question of fact. Moreover, tasks at which an individual is less competent relative to the group create conditions in which conformity is more likely.

- Unanimity of the group. Conformity pressures are most pronounced in groups that are unanimous in their support of a position. But what of the case in which people with dissenting views have an ally in the group—known as a **social supporter**—who agrees with them? Having just one person present who shares the unpopular point of view is sufficient to reduce conformity pressures (Allen, 1975).

Gender differences in conformity. One of the most inconsistent findings to emerge from the work on conformity relates to gender differences. For many years, the prevailing wisdom was that women were more easily influenced than men (Allen, 1965)—a view that held until the late 1970s. At that time, however, research conducted by social psychologist Alice Eagly (1978) suggested that the difference was more apparent than real. For example, it seemed that the tasks employed in conformity experiments often were more familiar to men than to women, leading females to conform because of differences in their perceived lack of expertise (Eagly, 1983; Eagly & Carli, 1981).

More recent reviews of the literature, however, seem to support the earlier point of view: women do seem to conform more to others than do men, relatively independent of the topic at hand (Eagly, 1989). Thus, the best summation of the research on conformity to date is an old one: women are more susceptible to social influence than men. Still, the topsy-turvy nature of the interpretation of the conformity research suggests that we have not heard the last word on this issue.

Doing What Others Tell Us to Do: Compliance

When we discuss conformity, we are usually talking about a phenomenon in which the social pressure is not in the form of a direct order. But in some situations social pressure is much more obvious, and there is direct, explicit pressure to endorse a certain point of view or to behave in a particular way. Social psychologists call the type of behavior that occurs in response to direct social pressure **compliance**.

When a small request leads to a larger one: The foot in the door. A salesperson comes to your door and asks you to accept a small sample. You agree, thinking you have nothing to lose. A little while later comes a larger request, which, because you have already agreed to the first one, you have a harder time turning down.

The salesperson in this case is employing a tried-and-true strategy that social psychologists call the foot-in-the-door technique. According to the **foot-in-the-door technique**, you first ask that a person agree to a small request and later ask the person to comply with a more important one. It turns out that compliance with the ultimate request increases significantly when the person first agrees to the smaller favor.

The foot-in-the-door phenomenon was first demonstrated in a study in which a number of experimenters went door to door asking residents to sign a petition in favor of safe driving (Freedman & Fraser, 1966). Almost everyone complied with this small, benign request. However, a few weeks later, different experimenters contacted the residents again and asked for a much larger request: that they erect a huge sign reading "Drive Carefully" on their front lawns. The results were clear: 55 percent of those who had signed the petition agreed to the request, whereas only 17 percent of people in a control group who had not been asked to sign the petition agreed.

Subsequent research has confirmed the effectiveness of the foot-in-the-door technique (Beaman et al., 1983). Why does it work? One reason is that involvement with the small request leads to an interest in an issue, and taking an action—any action—makes the individual more committed to the issue, thereby increasing the likelihood of future compliance. Another explanation revolves around people's self-perceptions. By complying with the initial request, individuals may come to see themselves as the kind of person who provides help when asked. Then, when confronted with the larger request, they agree in order to maintain the kind of consistency in attitudes and behavior that we discussed earlier. Although we don't know which of these two explanations is more accurate, it is clear that the foot-in-the-door strategy is an effective one.

Where a large request leads to a smaller one: The door-in-the-face. A fund raiser comes to your door and asks for a $500 contribution. You laughingly refuse, telling her that the amount is way out of your league. She then asks for a $10 contribution. What do you do? If you are like most people, you'll probably be a lot more compliant than if she hadn't asked for the huge contribution first. The reason lies in the **door-in-the-face technique**, in which a large request, refusal of which is expected, is followed by a smaller one. Clearly a totally opposite strategy to the foot-in-the-door approach, the door-in-the-face technique has also proved to be effective.

One example of its success was shown in a field experiment in which college students were stopped on the street and asked to agree to a substantial favor—acting as unpaid counselors for juvenile delinquents two hours a week for two years (Cialdini et al., 1975). Not surprisingly, no one agreed to such an outrageous request. But when they were later asked the considerably smaller favor of taking a group of delinquents on a two-hour trip to the zoo, half the people complied. In comparison, only 17 percent of a control group of subjects who had not first received the larger request agreed.

The use of this technique is widespread in everyday life. For instance, children who ask their parents for an increase in their allowance would be well advised to ask for a very large increase and later settle for less. Similarly, television writers sometimes sprinkle their scripts with obscenities that they know will be cut out by network censors, hoping to keep other key phrases intact (Cialdini, 1988).

Why is the door-in-the-face procedure effective? Two explanations have been suggested (Baron & Byrne, 1987). One possibility rests on reciprocal concessions between the person making the request and the individual being asked. In **reciprocal concessions**, requesters are seen to make a compromise (reducing their initial request), thereby inviting a compromise on the part of those who initially refused the request. The result is that people are more willing to comply with the smaller request.

Another explanation rests in our desire to present ourselves well to others. When we first refuse, we feel we have acted reasonably, but a second refusal can make us feel that we are coming across as unreasonable. We comply, then, to enhance the way we present ourselves to others.

Obedience to Authority

Both the foot-in-the-door and the door-in-the-face techniques provide a means by which people are gently led toward agreement with another person's request. In some cases, however, requests are couched in terms of **obedience**, a change in behavior that is due to the commands of others. Although obedience is considerably less common than conformity and compliance, it does occur in several specific kinds of relationships. For example, we may show obedience to our boss, teacher, or parent, merely because of the power they hold to reward or punish us.

To consider the phenomenon of obedience, think, for a moment, about how you might respond if a stranger said to you:

> I've devised a new way of improving memory. All I need is for you to teach people a list of words and then give them a test. The test procedure requires only that you give learners a shock each time they make a mistake on the test. To administer the shocks you will use a "shock generator" that gives shocks ranging from 30 to 450 volts. You can see that the switches are labeled from "slight shock" through "danger: severe shock" at the top level, where there are three red X's. But don't worry; although the shocks may be painful, they will cause no permanent damage.

Presented with this situation, you would likely think that neither you, nor anyone else, would go along with the stranger's unusual request. Clearly, it lies outside the bounds of what we consider good sense.

Or does it? Suppose the stranger asking for your help were a psychologist conducting an experiment. Or suppose it were your teacher, your employer, or your military commander—all people in authority with some seemingly legitimate reason for their request.

If you still think it unlikely that you would comply, you might reconsider. For the situation represented above describes a now-classic experiment conducted by social psychologist Stanley Milgram in the 1960s (Milgram, 1974). In the study, subjects were placed in a situation in which they were told by an experimenter to give increasingly strong shocks to another person as part of a study on learning (see Figure 12-5). In reality, the experiment had nothing to do with learning; the real issue under consideration was the degree to which subjects would comply with the experimenter's requests. In fact, the person supposedly receiving the shocks was actually a confederate who never really received any punishment.

Most people who hear a description of the experiment feel that it is unlikely that *any* subject would give the maximum level of shock—or, for that matter, any shock at all. Even a group of psychiatrists who had the situation described to them predicted that fewer than 2 percent of the subjects would comply completely and administer the strongest shocks. However, the actual results contradicted both experts' and nonexperts' predictions: Almost two-thirds of the subjects eventually used the highest setting on the shock generator to "electrocute" the learner.

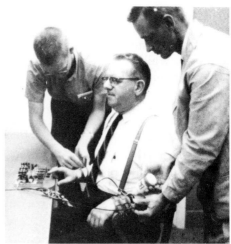

FIGURE 12-5
This impressive-looking "shock generator" was used to lead participants to believe they were administering electric shocks to another person, who was connected to the generator by electrodes that were attached to the skin. (Copyright © 1965 by Stanley Milgram. From the film *Obedience*, distributed by the New York University Film Library and Pennsylvania State University, PCR.)

Why did so many individuals comply fully with the experimenter's demands? Extensive interviews carried out with subjects following the experiment showed that they were obedient primarily because they believed that the experimenter would be responsible for any potential ill effects that befell the learner. The experiment's orders were accepted, then, because the subjects thought that they personally could not be held accountable for their actions—they could always blame the experimenter.

Although the Milgram experiment has been criticized for creating an extremely trying set of circumstances for the subjects—thereby raising serious ethical questions—and on methodological grounds (Miller, 1986; Orne & Holland, 1968), it remains one of the strongest laboratory demonstrations of compliance. We need only consider actual instances of compliance to authority to witness some frightening real-life parallels. A major defense of Nazi officers after World War II, for instance, was that they were "only following orders." Milgram's results force each of us to consider how able we would be to withstand the intense power of authority.

The Informed Consumer of Psychology: Strategies for Maintaining Your Own Point of View

We have seen how susceptible people are to the influence of others, whether it be relatively indirect, as with subtle conformity pressure, or direct, as with a straightforward order. How can one remain independent in the face of these sorts of pressures? Social psychological theory and research have suggested a number of techniques for helping one to remain faithful to one's own point of view:

- Inoculation. To avoid smallpox, people receive a shot containing a small dose of smallpox germs. This injection produces antibodies in the body that can repel a major invasion of smallpox germs, should the individual be exposed to the disease in the future. Similarly, one procedure for helping people remain independent of future attempts at persuasion is for them to expose themselves to a sample of counterarguments to which they might be subjected in the future. In an example of this technique, William McGuire (1964) showed that subjects could be made more resistant to persuasion if they were first exposed to a sample of opposing arguments along with information that refuted those arguments. Exposure to the opposing arguments—**inoculation**, as he called it—led to less subsequent change in beliefs than exposing subjects to information that bolstered their own initial views.

- Forewarning. Telling people that a persuasive message is coming and what that message involves, a strategy called **forewarning**, is sometimes sufficient to reduce social influence, even if counterarguments are not provided. This is particularly true if the issues are important and the target of influence has a large amount of information available (Cacioppo & Petty, 1979; Petty & Cacioppo, 1977). Simply knowing that a persuasive message is likely to be received without knowing the specific content of the upcoming message can reduce subsequent attitude change. The reason? When people are aware that they are going to receive information counter to their attitudes, they tend to develop their own arguments in support of their original attitudes. Forewarned is thus forearmed.

- Consistency. One technique that is not only effective in reducing persuasibility but that can actually change the attitude of the persuader is **consistency**. Under certain conditions, particularly in group settings where a majority is attempting to influence a minority, the unyielding persistence of the minority in its point of view can actually bring about a change in the majority's attitudes (Moscovici & Mugny, 1983; Tanford & Penrod, 1984). Apparently, the unyielding repetition of one's own point of view can cause others to rethink their position and, ultimately, to be persuaded by the minority's opinion.

   On the other hand, some evidence suggests that a somewhat different approach is more appropriate. Social psychologist Edwin Hollander (1980) has addressed situations in which a minority is attempting to remain independent of a majority position. He suggests a strategy in which individuals conform initially to the views of the source of influence. After doing so, which establishes them as competent and reasonable group members, they can behave more independently and espouse views that are contrary to the majority's views. According to Hollander's theory, instead of remaining consistently firm in a deviant position, as Moscovici's consistency approach suggests, people should first conform—but after establishing their "credentials," they should then press their minority views.

Experimental evidence supports both approaches (Maass & Clark, 1984). Such research makes it clear that social influence is not a one-way street; when we are the targets of social influence, we have a fighting chance to remain independent.

ASK YOURSELF

What is the distinction between conformity, compliance, and obedience?

What are the primary techniques for remaining independent from group pressure?

Would you have conformed in Asch's study or obeyed in Milgram's experiment? How do you imagine their subjects would have answered the same question before they participated?

LOOKING BACK

1. In this chapter, we discussed social psychology, the study of the way people's thoughts, feelings, and actions are affected by others, and the nature and causes of individual behavior in social situations.

2. Attitudes, a central area of study in social psychology, are learned predispositions to respond in a favorable or unfavorable manner to a particular object. The ABC model of attitudes suggests that they have three components: the affect component, the behavior component, and the cognition component. We acquire attitudes through classical conditioning and operant conditioning.

3. A number of theories suggest that people try to maintain consistency between attitudes. Cognitive dissonance occurs when two cognitions—attitudes or thoughts—contradict each other and are held simultaneously by an individual. To resolve the contradiction, the person may modify the cognition, change its importance, or deny it, thereby bringing about a reduction in dissonance. However, alternative explanations based on self-perception theory have been proposed to explain dissonance phenomena.

4. Impressions of others are formed through social cognition—the study of the processes that underlie our understanding of the social world. People develop schemas, which organize information about people and social experiences in memory. Such schemas represent our social life and allow us to interpret and categorize information about others.

5. One of the ways in which people form impressions of others is through the use of central traits, personality characteristics that are given unusually heavy weight when an impression is formed. Information-processing approaches have

found that we tend to average sets of traits to form an overall impression.

6. Stereotypes are beliefs and expectations about members of groups held on the basis of membership in those groups. Although they most frequently are used for racial and ethnic groups, stereotypes are also found in categorizations of sex- and age-group membership.

7. Attribution theory tries to explain how we understand the causes of behavior, particularly with respect to situational or dispositional factors. To determine causes, people use consensus, consistency, and distinctiveness information.

8. Even though logical processes are involved, attribution is still prone to error, as the fundamental attribution bias and the prevalence of stereotyping demonstrate. Other biases include the halo effect, the Pollyanna effect, and the assumed-similarity bias.

9. Self-perception theory suggests that attribution processes similar to those we use with others may be used to understand the causes of our own behavior.

10. Conformity refers to changes in behavior or attitudes that occur as the result of a desire to follow the beliefs or standards of others. Among the factors affecting conformity are the nature of the group, the nature of the response required, the kind of task, and the unanimity of the group.

11. Compliance is behavior that occurs as a result of direct social pressure. Two means of eliciting compliance are the foot-in-the-door and the door-in-the-face techniques.

12. In contrast to compliance, obedience is a change in behavior that results from the commands of others. Among the ways to remain independent of group pressure are inoculation, forewarning, and consistency.

Key Terms and Concepts

13

Interacting with Others in a Complex World

❖

Prologue: Cathy Collins ◆ Looking Ahead ◆ Liking and Loving: Interpersonal Attraction and the Development of Relationships ◆ Hurting and Helping Others: Aggression and Prosocial Behavior ◆ Stress and Coping ◆ Looking Back

PROLOGUE: CATHY COLLINS

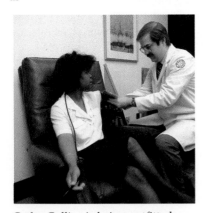

Cathy Collins is being outfitted with the apparatus that measures how much stress she experiences during a normal workday.

It is now 10:26 A.M. Cathy Collins of Teaneck, New Jersey, administrative aide in a metropolitan hospital, has already been up for five hours, having left breakfast for her children and taken two buses to reach her tiny, windowless office.

She is standing with a phone cradled on her shoulder, contending with:

- A patient sitting at her desk, waiting to ask her some questions
- A secretary with a question about another patient's chart
- Two calls on hold, and her intercom buzzing
- A desk piled with forms, which she attempts to fill out between calls
- A stack of paperwork 3 inches high in her "in" box
- A boss who has just walked out of his office and asked for something to be copied

514

At this moment, a mechanism strapped to Cathy's waist and arm measures her blood pressure and heartbeat, finding that they are elevated 25 and 15 percent, respectively, over earlier readings. As it happened, it was not the biggest increase of the day for Collins (Tierney, 1988).

LOOKING AHEAD

Because Cathy Collins was participating in a hospital study of stress in the workplace, we know for certain about her hidden physiological reactions to the events of the moment. And although no measurements were taken of her emotional reactions, few of us would have difficulty in guessing what she would report experiencing during this same period: stress.

Cathy Collins's life is hardly unique. The complexities of the contemporary world make it a stressful and complex place, and the impact of everyday events can be at times overwhelming. Even our relationships with others can be complex and confusing.

In this chapter, we consider several aspects of the complexity of modern-day society that relate to human behavior. We begin by considering our social relationships with others. We consider what social psychologists have learned about the ways people are attracted to one another, form relationships, and fall in love.

We then look at the factors that underlie some of the most negative and positive social behaviors that we find in today's world: aggression and helping. We consider whether aggression is inevitable and if helpfulness is as much a part of the human condition as aggressive behavior. Finally, we consider the causes and consequences of stress, examining ways of coping with it.

In sum, after reading this chapter, you will be able to answer questions such as these:

- Why are we attracted to certain people?
- What factors underlie aggression?
- Under what conditions do people act in a prosocial manner?
- What is stress, how does it affect us, and how can we best cope with it?

LIKING AND LOVING: INTERPERSONAL ATTRACTION AND THE DEVELOPMENT OF RELATIONSHIPS

When nineteenth-century poet Elizabeth Barrett Browning wrote "How do I love thee? Let me count the ways," she was expressing feelings about a topic that is central to most people's lives—and one that has developed into a major subject of investigation by social psychologists: loving and liking. Known more formally as the study of **interpersonal attraction** or **close relationships**, this topic encompasses the factors that lead to positive feelings for others.

How Do I Like Thee? Let Me Count the Ways

By far the greatest amount of research has focused on liking, probably because it has always proved easier for investigators conducting short-term experiments to produce states of liking in strangers who have just met than to promote and observe loving relationships over long periods of time. Hence traditional studies have given us a good deal of knowledge about the factors that initially attract two people to each other (Berscheid, 1985; Duck, 1990). Among the most important factors considered by social psychologists are the following:

- Proximity. If you live in a dormitory or an apartment, consider the friends you made when you first moved in. Chances are you became friendliest with those who lived closest to you. In fact, this is one of the best-established findings in the interpersonal attraction literature; **proximity** leads to liking (Festinger, Schachter & Back, 1950; Nahemon & Lawton, 1975).

The proximity of neighbors is one factor that leads us to like them. We tend to be attracted to those who are geographically close to us.

- Mere exposure. Repeated exposure to a person is often sufficient to produce attraction. Interestingly, repeated exposure to *any* stimulus—be it a person, picture, record, or what have you—most frequently makes us like the stimulus more (Zajonc, 1968; Bornstein, 1989). Becoming familiar with a stimulus can evoke positive feelings; these positive feelings stemming from familiarity are then transferred to the stimulus itself. There are exceptions, though: In cases in which the initial interactions are strongly negative, repeated exposure is unlikely to cause us to like another person more; instead, we may end up disliking such an individual more the more we are exposed to him or her.

- Similarity. We tend to like those who are similar to us; discovering that others are similar in terms of attitudes, values, or traits promotes liking for them (Byrne, 1969; Hill & Stull, 1981). Moreover, the more similar others are, the more we like them. One reason behind the relationship between similarity and interpersonal attraction is that we assume that people with similar attitudes will evaluate us positively (Condon & Crano, 1988). Because there is a strong **reciprocity-of-liking effect** (a tendency to like those who like us), knowing that someone evaluates us positively will promote attraction to that person. In addition, we assume that when we like someone else, that person likes us in return (Metee & Aronson, 1974; Tagiuri, 1958).

- Need complementarity. There are exceptions to the general case that similarity and attraction are found together. People don't always seek out others like themselves: Some people seem to be attracted to others who are unlike them. One reason for this may be that we are attracted to those people who fulfill the greatest number of needs for us. Thus a dominant person may seek out someone who is submissive; at the same time, the submissive individual may be seeking someone who is dominant. Although their dissimilarity often makes others expect them to be incompatible, by forming a relationship they are able to fulfill each other's complementary needs.

    The hypothesis that people are attracted to others who fulfill their needs—dubbed the **need-complementarity hypothesis**—was first proposed in the late 1950s in a classic study which found that a sample of married couples appeared to have complementary needs (Winch, 1958). However, there has been little evidence since that time to support the hypothesis, with most studies finding that attraction is related more to similarity in needs than to complementarity (e.g., Meyer & Pepper, 1977). In general, then, similarity—be it in attitudes, values, or personality traits—remains one of the best predictors of whether two people will be attracted to each other.

- Physical attractiveness. For most people, the equation *beautiful* =

good is a very real one. As a result, people who are physically attractive are more popular than those who are physically unattractive, if all other factors are equal. This finding, which contradicts the values that most people would profess, is apparent even in childhood—with nursery-school-age children rating popularity on the basis of attractiveness—and continues into adulthood (Dion & Berscheid, 1974; Langlois, Roggman, & Rieser-Danner, 1990). Indeed, physical attractiveness may be the single most important element promoting initial liking in college dating situations, although its influence decreases when people get to know each other better (Berscheid & Walster, 1974; Hatfield & Sprecher, 1986).

Physical attractiveness is a drawback in some cases, however. Although good looks lead to more positive impressions of men in job-related situations, beauty can work against women in managerial positions. The reason is a common (although totally unfounded) stereotype that successful, attractive women attain their position as a result of looks rather than ability (Heilman & Stopek, 1985). In general, though, physical attractiveness is an asset in social situations. It is a powerful factor in determining to whom people are attracted and the kind of social life they will have (Reis et al., 1982; Hatfield & Sprecher, 1986).

The factors that we have discussed are not, of course, the only constituents of liking. For example, survey research has sought to identify the factors critical in friendships. In one questionnaire answered by some 40,000 respondents, the qualities that were most valued in a friend were identified as the ability to keep confidences, loyalty, and warmth and affection, followed closely by supportiveness, frankness, and a sense of humor (Parlee, 1979). The results are summarized in Figure 13-1.

How Do I Love Thee? Let Me Count the Ways

Whereas our knowledge of what makes people like one another is extensive, our understanding of love is a more limited and relatively recent phenomenon. For some time, many social psychologists believed that love represented a phenomenon too difficult to observe and study in a controlled, scientific way. However, love is such a central issue in most people's lives that, in time, social psychologists could not resist its allure and became infatuated with the topic (Sternberg & Grajek, 1984; Hendrick & Hendrick, 1989).

As a first step, researchers tried to identify the distinguishing characteristics between mere liking and full-blown love (Sternberg, 1987). Using this approach, they discovered that love is not simply liking of a greater quantity, but a qualitatively different psychological state (Walster & Walster, 1978). For instance, at least in its early stages, love includes relatively intense physiological arousal, an all-encompassing interest in

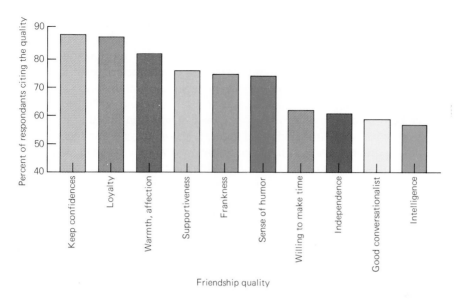

FIGURE 13-1
These are the key qualities looked for in a friend, according to some 40,000
respondents to a questionnaire. (Parke, 1979.)

another individual, fantasizing about the other, and relatively rapid
swings of emotion. Similarly, Davis (1985) suggests that love has elements
of fascination, exclusiveness, sexual desire, and intense caring that liking
lacks.

Social psychologist Zick Rubin (1970, 1973) has tried to differentiate
between love and liking using a paper-and-pencil scale. As can be seen
from the sample items in Table 13-1, each question refers to the person to
whom the individual is attracted. Researchers have found that couples
scoring high on the love scale differ considerably from those with low
scores. They gaze at each other more, and their relationships are more

TABLE 13-1 LOVING AND LIKING

Sample love items:
    I feel that I can confide in _____ about virtually everything.
    I would do almost anything for _____.
    I feel responsible for _____'s well-being.

Sample liking items:
    I think that _____ is unusually well adjusted.
    I think that _____ is one of those people who quickly wins
      respect.
    _____ is one of the most likable people I know.

SOURCE: Rubin, 1973

likely to be intact six months later than are the relationships of those who score low on the scale.

Other experiments have found evidence suggesting that the heightened physiological arousal hypothesized to be characteristic of loving is indeed present when a person reports being in love. Interestingly, though, it may not be just arousal of a sexual nature. Berscheid & Walster (1974) have theorized that when we are exposed to *any* stimulus that increases physiological arousal—such as danger, fear, or anger—our feelings for another person present at the time of the arousal may be labeled as love, if there are situational cues that suggest that "love" is an appropriate label for the feelings being experienced. In sum, we perceive we are in love when instances of general physiological arousal are coupled with the thought that the cause of the arousal is most likely love.

This theory explains why a person who keeps being rejected or hurt by another can still feel "in love" with that person. If the rejection leads to physiological arousal, but the arousal still happens to be attributed to love—and not to rejection—then a person will still feel "in love."

Other researchers have theorized that there are actually several kinds of love (Hendrick, Hendrick & Adler, 1988; Hendrick & Hendrick, 1989). Some distinguish between two main types of love: passionate love and companionate love. **Passionate (or romantic) love** represents a state of intense absorption in someone. It includes intense physiological arousal, psychological interest, and caring for the needs of another. In contrast, **companionate love** is the strong affection that we have for those with whom our lives are deeply involved. The love we feel for our parents, other family members, and even some close friends falls into the category of companionate love.

According to psychologist Robert Sternberg (1986), an even finer differentiation between types of love is in order. He proposes that love is made up of three components: an intimacy component, encompassing feelings of closeness and connectedness; a passion component, made up of the motivational drives relating to sex, physical closeness, and romance; and a decision/commitment component, encompassing the cognition that one loves someone (in the short term) and longer-term feelings of commitment to maintain love. As can be seen in Table 13-2, particular combinations of the three components produce eight kinds of love.

The Rise and Fall of Liking and Loving: Understanding the Course of Relationships

With one out of two marriages ending in divorce and broken love affairs a common phenomenon, it is not surprising that social psychologists have begun to turn their attention increasingly toward understanding how relationships develop, are maintained—and, in some cases, dissolve (Duck, 1990; Hendrick, 1989; Clark & Reis, 1988; Berscheid, Snyder & Omoto, 1989).

TABLE 13-2 THE KINDS OF LOVE

	Component*		
	Intimacy	Passion	Decision/Commitment
Nonlove	−	−	−
Liking	+	−	−
Infatuated love	−	+	−
Empty love	−	−	+
Romantic love	+	+	−
Companionate love	+	−	+
Fatuous love	−	+	+
Consummate love	+	+	+

*+ = component present; − = component absent.
SOURCE: Sternberg, 1986, Table 2.

The behavior of couples in developing relationships changes in fairly predictable patterns (Berscheid, 1985). The most frequent pattern follows this course:

- People interact more often, for longer periods of time, and in a widening array of settings.
- They seek each other's company.
- They increasingly "open up" to each other, disclosing secrets and sharing physical intimacies. They are more willing to share both positive and negative feelings and are increasingly willing to provide praise and criticism.
- They begin to understand each other's point of view and way of looking at the world.
- Their goals and behavior form greater synchrony, and they begin to share greater similarity in attitudes and values.
- Their investment in the relationship—in terms of time, energy, and commitment—increases.
- They begin to feel that their psychological well-being is tied to the well-being of the relationship. The relationship comes to be seen as unique and irreplaceable.
- They start behaving as a couple, rather than as two separate individuals.

Although these transitions in relationships are typical, it is difficult to predict the exact point at which each will occur. One important reason is that at the same time the relationship is evolving, the two individuals may be going through personal growth and change themselves.

Once a relationship has evolved, how can we distinguish successful ones from those that will ultimately fail? Some answers come from a study by Jeanette and Robert Lauer (1985), who surveyed couples who reported being happily married for 15 years or more. When asked to indicate what it was that had made their marriages last, both the husbands and the wives gave remarkably similar responses. As you can see in Table 13-3, the most frequently named reason was perceiving one's spouse as one's best friend and liking him or her "as a person." There was also a strong belief in marriage as a commitment and a desire to make the relationship work, as well as agreement about aims and goals. On the other hand, there was not blind commitment to the other person: People acknowledged their partner's flaws, but they tended to overlook them. As one husband said, "She isn't perfect. But I don't worry about her weak points, which are very few. Her strong points overcome them too much" (Lauer & Lauer, 1985).

TABLE 13-3 MOST-OFTEN-CITED REASONS* FOR SUCCESS IN MARRIAGE

Cited by Husbands	Cited by Wives
My spouse is my best friend.	My spouse is my best friend.
I like my spouse as a person.	I like my spouse as a person.
Marriage is a long-term commitment.	Marriage is a long-term commitment.
Marriage is sacred.	Marriage is sacred.
We agree on aims and goals.	We agree on aims and goals.
My spouse has grown more interesting.	My spouse has grown more interesting.
I want the relationship to succeed.	I want the relationship to succeed.
An enduring marriage is important to social stability.	We laugh together.
We laugh together.	We agree on a philosophy of life.
I am proud of my spouse's achievements.	We agree on how and how often to show affection.
We agree on a philosophy of life.	An enduring marriage is important to social stability.
We agree about our sex life.	We have a stimulating exchange of ideas.
We agree on how and how often to show affection.	We discuss things calmly.
I confide in my spouse.	We agree about our sex life.
We share outside hobbies and interests.	I am proud of my spouse's achievements.

*In order of frequency.
SOURCE: Lauer & Lauer, 1985.

Another factor affecting the long-term success of loving relationships concerns the rate at which the various components of love develop. According to Sternberg's theory of love, the three individual components of love—intimacy, passion, and decision/commitment—vary in their influence over time and follow distinct courses, as illustrated in Figure 13-2. In strong loving relationships, the level of commitment peaks and then remains stable, while intimacy continues to grow over the course of a relationship. Passion, on the other hand, shows a marked decline over time, reaching a plateau fairly early in a relationship. Still, it remains an important component of loving relationships.

The decline of a relationship. What is it that causes some relationships to flounder? Social psychologist George Levinger (1983) has speculated on the reasons behind the deterioration of relationships. One important factor appears to be a change in judgments about the meaning of a partner's behavior. Behavior that was once viewed as "charming forgetfulness" becomes seen as "boorish indifference," and the partner becomes less valued. In addition, communications may be disrupted; rather than listening to what the other person is saying, each partner becomes bent on justifying himself or herself, and communication deteriorates. Eventually, a partner may begin to invite and agree with criticism of the other partner from people outside the relationship and look to others for the fulfillment of basic needs that were previously met by the partner.

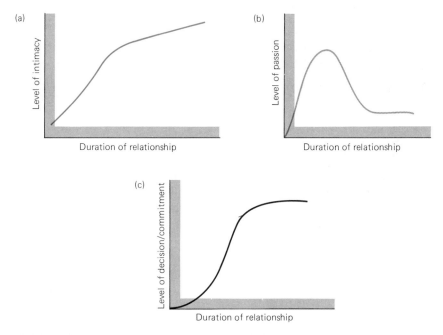

FIGURE 13-2
The changing ingredients of love. The three components of love vary in strength over the course of a relationship. (Sternberg, 1986.)

"When I fell in love with you, suddenly your eyes didn't seem close together. Now they seem close together again."

Drawing by Wm. Hamilton, © 1976 The New Yorker Magazine, Inc.

When relationships begin to deteriorate, flaws that were previously viewed as charming come to be perceived in a more negative light.

Just as developing relationships tend to follow a common pattern, relationships that are on the decline conform to a pattern of stages (Duck, 1982). The first phase occurs when a person decides that he or she can no longer tolerate being in a relationship. During this stage, called the **interpsychic phase**, there is a focus on the other person's behavior and an evaluation of the extent to which this behavior provides a basis for terminating the relationship.

In the **dyadic phase**, a person decides to confront the partner and determines whether to attempt to repair, redefine, or terminate the relationship. For example, a redefinition might encompass a qualitative change in the level of the relationship. ("We can still be friends" might replace "I'll love you forever.")

If the decision is made to terminate the relationship, the person then enters the **social phase**, in which there is public acknowledgment that the relationship is being dissolved and an accounting is made to others regarding the events that led to the termination of the relationship. The last stage is the **grave-dressing phase**, in which the major activity is to physically and psychologically end the relationship. One of the major concerns of this period is to rethink the entire relationship, making what happened seem reasonable and in keeping with one's self-perceptions.

ASK YOURSELF

What are the most important elements that produce liking?

How can love and liking be differentiated?

What are the factors that relate to the maintenance and decline of relationships?

Are the TV and movie versions of romantic love consistent with the factors actually related to successful, long-term relationships?

Does the research described in this chapter adequately capture your experience of being in love?

HURTING AND HELPING OTHERS: AGGRESSION AND PROSOCIAL BEHAVIOR

A 22-year-old woman who stopped in a bar for a drink late one evening was sexually assaulted and repeatedly raped on a pool table by a group of four men. Despite her desperate pleas to at least nine bystanders, no one came to her aid. In fact, instead of helping her, the other people in the bar simply stood by, and some even cheered.

◆ ◆ ◆

When he saw a man slumped in the seat of a burning car, Darrell Van Etten rushed to save him, "just as any other . . . human being would have done." Aware that the car could blow up at any second, Van Etten struggled to remove the unconscious man from the flaming vehicle. His efforts came just in time: When he was eight feet away from the car, it exploded.

In these two incidents, we see the worst and the best of humanity. In the first—a true sequence of events dramatized in the film *The Accused*—we see violence unrestrained by bystanders. In the second, we get a considerably more positive view of the world, in a deed that won a Carnegie award for heroism.

Psychologists have long pondered the issues of what motivates helping behavior and its counterpart, aggression. Much of the work was inspired by an incident—described in Chapter 1—that occurred some twenty years ago when a young woman named Kitty Genovese was heard screaming, "Oh, my God, he stabbed me," and "Please help me," by no fewer than thirty-eight of her neighbors. Not one witness came forward to help, and it was not until thirty minutes had gone by that even one person bothered to call the police. Genovese subsequently died in an alleyway before the police arrived—the victim of a vicious attack by a mugger.

If events such as these foster only a negative, pessimistic interpretation of human capacities, other, equally dramatic incidents promote a more optimistic view of humankind. In addition to dramatic incidents of heroism such as those performed by Darrell Van Etten, ponder the cases of people like Raoul Wallenberg, who risked death to help Jews escape from the Nazis in German-occupied countries during World War II. Or consider the simple kindnesses of life: lending a valued recording, stopping to help a child who has fallen off her bicycle, or merely sharing a candy bar with a friend. Such instances of helping are no less characteristic of human behavior than the more distasteful examples. In this part of the chapter we explore the work that social psychologists have done in an effort to explain instances of both aggressive and helping behavior.

Hurting Others: Aggression

We need look no further than our daily paper or the nightly news to be bombarded with examples of aggression, both on a societal level (war, invasion, assassination) and on an individual level (crime, child abuse, and the many petty cruelties that humans are capable of inflicting on one another). Is such aggression an inevitable part of the human condition, or is aggression primarily a function of particular circumstances that might be alleviated by changing the conditions that cause it?

Social psychologists investigating this issue have begun by attempting to define the term "aggression" (Krebs & Miller, 1985). This is not as simple as it may at first appear, since many examples of inflicted pain or injury may or may not qualify as aggression, depending upon one's definition. Although it is clear, for instance, that a rapist is acting aggressively toward his victim, it is less certain that a physician carrying out an emergency medical procedure without an anesthetic, thereby causing incredible pain to the patient, should be considered aggressive.

Most social psychologists define aggression in terms of the intent and purpose behind the behavior: **Aggression** is intentional injury of or harm to another person (Berkowitz, 1974). Under this definition, it is clear that the rapist in our example is acting aggressively, whereas the physician causing pain during a medical procedure is not.

Aggression as a release: Instinct approaches. If you have ever punched an adversary in the nose, you may have experienced a certain satisfaction, despite your better judgment. Instinct theories, noting the prevalence of aggression not only in humans but in animals as well, propose that aggression is primarily the outcome of innate—or inborn—urges.

The major proponent of the instinct approach is Konrad Lorenz, an ethologist (a scientist who studies animal behavior) who suggested that humans, along with members of other species, have a fighting instinct, which in earlier times ensured protection of food supplies and weeded out the weaker of the species (Lorenz, 1966, 1974). The controversial notion arising from Lorenz's instinct approach is the idea that aggressive energy is constantly being built up within an individual until it is finally discharged in a process called **catharsis**. The longer the energy is built up, says Lorenz, the greater will be the magnitude of the aggression displayed when it is discharged.

Probably the most controversial idea to come out of instinct theories of aggression is Lorenz's proposal that society ought to provide acceptable means of catharsis through, for instance, participation in sports and games, in order to prevent its discharge in less socially desirable ways. However, although the notion makes logical sense, there is no possible way to devise an adequate experiment to test it. In fact, relatively little support exists for instinct theories in general because of the difficulty in finding evidence for any kind of pent-up reservoir of aggression (Berkowitz, 1974; Geen & Donnerstein, 1983). Most social psychologists suggest that we should look to other approaches to explain aggression.

Aggression as a reaction to frustration: Frustration-aggression approaches. Have you ever worked painstakingly on a model or puzzle, only to have someone clumsily knock it over and ruin it just as you were about to complete it? The feelings you experienced toward the person who destroyed your work probably placed you on the verge of real aggression, and you no doubt seethed inside.

Frustration-aggression theory tries to explain aggression in terms of events such as the one described above. When first put forward, the theory said flatly that frustration *always* led to aggression of some sort, and that aggression was *always* the result of some frustration, where **frustration** is defined as the thwarting or blocking of some ongoing, goal-directed behavior (Dollard, Doob, Miller, Mowrer & Sears, 1939). More recent formulations, however, have modified the original one, suggesting instead that frustration produces anger, leading to a *readiness* to act aggressively. Whether or not actual aggression occurs depends on the presence of **aggressive cues**, stimuli that have been associated in the past with actual aggression or violence and that will trigger aggression again (Carlson, Marcus-Newhall, & Miller, 1990). In addition, frustration is assumed to produce aggression only to the extent that the frustration produces negative feelings (Berkowitz, 1989, 1990).

What kinds of stimuli act as aggressive cues? They can range from the most overt, such as the presence of weapons, to the most subtle, such as the mere mention of the name of an individual who has behaved violently in the past. For example, in one experiment angered subjects behaved significantly more aggressively when in the presence of a rifle and revolver than in a comparable situation in which the guns were not present (Berkowitz & LePage, 1967; daGloria et al., 1989). Similarly, frustrated subjects in an experiment who had viewed a violent movie were more aggressive to a confederate with the same name as the star of the movie than to a confederate with a different name (Berkowitz & Geen, 1966). It appears, then, that frustration does lead to aggression, at least when aggressive cues are present.

Learning to hurt others: Observational learning approaches. Do we learn to be aggressive? The observational learning (sometimes called "social learning") approach to aggression says we do. Taking an almost opposite view from the instinct theories, which focus on the innate aspects of aggression, observational learning theory (which we discussed first in Chapter 4) emphasizes how social and environmental conditions can teach individuals to be aggressive. Aggression is seen not as inevitable, but rather as a learned response that can be understood in terms of rewards and punishments (Bandura, 1973; Zillman, 1978).

Suppose, for instance, that a girl hits her younger brother when he damages one of her new toys. Whereas instinct theory would suggest that the aggression had been pent up and was now being discharged, and frustration-aggression theory would examine the girl's frustration at no longer being able to use her new toy, observational learning theory would look for a previous reinforcement that the girl had received for being aggressive. Perhaps she had learned that aggression resulted in her getting attention from her parents, or perhaps in the past her brother had apologized after being hit. In either case, observational learning theory views the aggression as a result of past rewards the girl had obtained for such behavior.

Observational learning theory pays particular attention not only to direct rewards and punishments that individuals themselves receive, but to the rewards and punishments that models—individuals who provide a guide to appropriate behavior—receive for their aggressive behavior.

After observing an adult model behaving aggressively, angered children carried out behaviors remarkably similar to those they had seen earlier.

According to observational learning theory, people observe the behavior of models and the subsequent consequences of the behavior. If the consequences are positive, the behavior is likely to be imitated when the observer finds himself or herself in a similar situation.

This basic formulation of observational learning theory has received wide support. For example, nursery-school-age children who have watched an adult behave aggressively display the same behavior themselves if they have been previously angered (Bandura, Ross & Ross, 1963). It turns out, though, that exposure to models typically leads to spontaneous aggression only if the observer has been angered, insulted, or frustrated after exposure (Bandura, 1973). This finding has important implications for understanding the effects of aggression observed in the media.

Does it hurt to watch TV? Media aggression. The average American child between the ages of 5 and 15 is exposed to no fewer than 13,000 violent deaths on television; the number of fights and aggressive sequences that children view is still higher. Even Saturday mornings, once filled with relatively peaceful fare, now include cartoons sporting titles such as "Teenage Mutant Ninja Turtles" and "Robo Cop," which include long sequences of aggressive action (Gerbner et al., 1978; Berkowitz, 1984; Freedman, 1984).

Does observation of this kind of violent television fare, as well as observation of aggression in other forms of media, suggest that our world is destined to become even more violent than it already is? Because observational learning research on modeling shows that people frequently learn and imitate the aggression that they observe, this question is one of the most important being addressed by social psychologists.

Most research suggests that there is a significant association between watching violent television programs and displaying aggressive behavior (Eron, 1982; Huesmann & Eron, 1986). For example, one experiment showed that subjects who watched a lot of television as third-graders became more aggressive adults than those who didn't watch so much TV (Eron, Huesmann, Lefkowitz & Walden, 1972). Of course, these results cannot prove that viewing television was the *cause* of the adult aggression; some additional factor, such as socioeconomic status, may have led both to higher levels of television viewing and to increased aggression.

Still, most experts agree that watching media violence can lead to a greater readiness to act aggressively, if not invariably to acting overtly with direct aggression, and to desensitization to the suffering of victims of violence (Linz, Donnerstein, & Penrod, 1988). Several reasons, beyond mere modeling, help explain why the observation of media violence may produce aggression. For one thing, watching violence seems to lower inhibitions against the performance of aggression—watching television portrayals of violence makes aggression seem a legitimate response to particular situations. Furthermore, viewing violence may make our understanding of the meaning of others' behavior shift: We may be predisposed to view even nonaggressive acts of others as aggressive after watching media aggression, and subsequently may act upon these new interpretations by responding aggressively. Finally, a continual diet of aggression may leave us desensitized to violence, and what previously would have repelled us now produces little emotional response. The pain and suffering brought about by aggression may be lost, and we may find it easier to act aggressively ourselves (Geen & Donnerstein, 1983). For more on the connection between media violence and aggression, see the Psychology and Society box.

PSYCHOLOGY AND SOCIETY

The Link between Aggressive Pornography and Violence toward Women

Does viewing pornography lead to violence toward women? This question is a complex one, but recent evidence suggests that there may, in fact, be a link between certain kinds of erotic material and aggression.

In an experiment examining this issue, angered male subjects who viewed an erotic movie that contained violence toward a woman showed significantly more subsequent aggression toward a female than if they viewed an erotic movie that contained no violence (Donnerstein & Berkowitz, 1981). Other experiments have found that long-term exposure to violent and sexually degrading depictions of women lead to emotional and physiological desensitization. In one study, for example, subjects who saw a series of R-rated violent "slasher" movies later showed less anxiety and depression when exposed to violence against women, and they were less sympathetic toward rape victims than subjects who saw nonviolent films (Linz, Donnerstein, & Penrod, 1988; Linz, Donnerstein, & Adams, 1989).

Overall, research in this area suggests that the viewing of pornography that contains violence toward women leads to emotional and physiological desensitization regarding aggression directed at women and an increased likelihood of aggression toward women (Donnerstein, Linz, & Penrod, 1987). What appears to be particularly crit-

ical is whether the pornography contains violence toward women; aggressive content in erotic materials clearly raises the level of aggression subsequently displayed by those exposed to it.

On the other hand, in some cases even standard X-rated movies showing sex between consenting adults may be sufficient to produce unwanted effects. For instance, in one study a group of subjects were shown a series of six 8-minute films during six weekly sessions (Zillman & Bryant, 1984). Some subjects saw films that were entirely sexual in content; others saw half sexual and half nonsexual films; and a third group saw only nonsexual films. At the end of the six weeks, subjects completed a questionnaire that described a rapist who had been convicted, and they were asked to recommend a sentence. The greater the exposure to the films with sexual content, the lower the recommended sentence. Exposure to even nonviolent pornography, then, can result in a decrease in the perceived repugnance of the crime of rape.

Whether these findings mean that pornography should be banned is a debatable question—such a move would certainly infringe on first-amendment rights to free speech—but they do alert us to the danger of exposure to pornography depicting aggression against women.

Reducing and preventing aggression. Billy, a seventh-grader, gets into fights almost weekly on the school playground. His teacher thinks he ought to get involved in football in order to, as she says, "get rid of his aggression." His father thinks Billy is frustrated over his inability to read very well. His mother thinks they ought to withhold Billy's allowance until he has gone without a fight for two weeks. The school counselor suggests still another approach: Every week that Billy displays no aggression, he should receive a $5 reward.

Who is right? Looking back at the different explanations of aggression, we find that each of these approaches may have some merit. Instinct theories of aggression suggest that aggression builds up until it is discharged; this hypothesis—known as the catharsis hypothesis, and expressed by the teacher's point of view that Billy should play football—suggests that by behaving aggressively in socially acceptable ways people can relieve aggressiveness that would otherwise be expressed in less desirable ways. Unfortunately, the scientific evidence in support of the theory is quite inconsistent (Ebbesen, Duncan & Konečni, 1975), and the only circumstance in which catharsis is seemingly effective is when a person's aggression is directed toward an individual who caused that person to be angry (Doob & Wood, 1972). Moreover, as we discussed earlier, exposure to aggression in media forms can actually lead to an increase in aggression. In sum, instinct approaches have not garnered much scientific support.

More promising approaches to reducing aggression are provided by frustration-aggression and observational learning theories. As suggested by the father's point that Billy's inability to read leads to frustration, removing frustration is effective in reducing aggression. However, the difficulty with such a technique is that life is full of all sorts of frustrations, and removing them all is an impossibility. One cannot create an environment completely free of frustration, and techniques for reducing aggression that are based on frustration-aggression theory may not be practical.

To date, the most promising approach to reducing aggression comes from learning theory, which deals with the modification of the rewards and punishments that follow aggression. The mother's suggestion to withhold Billy's allowance is an example of the most frequently used technique to control aggression and is built on observational-learning-theory approaches: the use of punishment following aggressive behavior. Interestingly, though, the use of punishment turns out to be a relatively ineffective technique for reducing aggression. One reason is that the people who do the punishing, especially when they use physical punishment, can actually serve as aggressive models themselves and thereby increase the likelihood of future aggression. Moreover, research shows that in most cases the effects of punishment tend to be relatively transitory (Sulzer-Azaroff & Mayer, 1991).

There is clear evidence, however, in support of the school counselor's strategy of reinforcing Billy's nonaggressive behavior, for research demonstrates that providing rewards for nonaggressive behavior can lead to a reduction in aggression. In fact, even exposure to nonaggressive models leads to reduced aggression, at least in laboratory studies (Baron & Kepner, 1970).

Helping Others: The Brighter Side of Human Nature

Turning away from aggression, we move now to the opposite—and brighter—side of the coin of human nature: helping behavior. Helping behavior, or **prosocial behavior** as it is more formally known, has been investigated under many different approaches, but the question that has been looked at most closely relates to bystander intervention in emergency situations. What are the factors that lead someone to give help to a person who is in need?

As we noted in Chapter 1, one critical factor relates to the number of others present. When more than one person bears witness to an emergency situation, there can be a sense of diffusion of responsibility among bystanders. **Diffusion of responsibility** is the tendency for people to feel that responsibility for acting is shared, or diffused, among those present. The more people present in an emergency, then, the less personally responsible each individual feels—and therefore the less help is provided (Latané & Nida, 1981).

Although the majority of research on helping behavior supports the diffusion-of-responsibility formulation, other factors clearly are involved in helping behavior. According to a model developed by Latané and Darley (1970), the process of helping involves four basic steps (see Figure 13-3).

- Noticing a person, event, or situation that may require help.
- Interpreting the event as one that requires help. Even if an event is noticed, it may be sufficiently ambiguous to be interpreted as a non-emergency situation (Shotland, 1985). It is here that the presence of others first affects helping behavior: The presence of inactive others may indicate to the observer that a situation does not require help—a judgment not necessarily made if the observer is alone.
- Assuming responsibility for taking action. It is at this point that diffusion of responsibility is likely to occur if others are present. Moreover, a bystander's particular expertise is apt to play a role in whether helping occurs. For instance, if people with training in medical aid or lifesaving techniques are present, untrained bystanders are less apt to intervene because they feel they have less expertise. This point was well illustrated in a study by Jane and Irving Piliavin (1972), who conducted a field experiment in which an individual seemed to collapse in a subway car with blood trickling out of the corner of his mouth. The results of the experiment showed

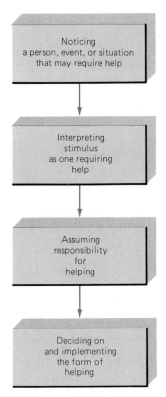

FIGURE 13-3
The basic steps of helping. (Based on Latané &
Darley, 1970.)

that bystanders were less likely to help when a person (actually a confederate) appearing to be an intern was present than when the "intern" was not present.

- Deciding on and implementing the form of assistance. After an individual assumes responsibility for helping, the decision must be made as to how assistance will be provided. Helping can range from very indirect forms of intervention, such as calling the police, to more direct forms, such as giving first aid or taking the victim to a hospital. Most social psychologists use a **rewards-costs approach** for helping to predict the nature of assistance that a bystander will choose to provide. The general notion is that the rewards of helping, as perceived by the bystander, must outweigh the costs if helping is to occur (Lynch & Cohen, 1978), and most research tends to support this notion.

After the nature of assistance is determined, there is still one step remaining: the actual implementation of the assistance. A rewards-costs analysis suggests that the least costly form of implementation is the most likely to be used. However, this is not the whole story: In some cases, people behave altruistically (Dovidio, Allen & Schroeder, 1990; Batson,

The model provided by this person helping an elderly woman is likely to encourage passers-by to act more compassionately.

1990). **Altruism** is helping behavior that is beneficial to others but clearly requires self-sacrifice. For example, an instance in which a person runs into a burning house to rescue a stranger's child might be considered altruistic, particularly when compared with the alternative of simply calling the fire department.

Some research suggests that individuals who intervene in emergency situations tend to have certain personality characteristics that differentiate them from nonhelpers. For example, Shotland (1984) suggests that helpers tend to be more self-assured. Other research has found that individuals who are characteristically high in **empathy**—a personality trait in which an individual observing another person experiences the emotions of that person—are more likely to respond to others' needs (Eisenberg-Berg, 1978; Cialdini et al., 1987). Still, most social psychologists agree that there is no single set of attributes that differentiate helpers from nonhelpers; situational factors play the predominant role in determining whether an individual intervenes in a situation requiring aid (e.g., Carlson, Charlin & Miller, 1988).

*A*SK YOURSELF

What is the most widely used definition of aggression?

How do different theories explain aggression?

What are the four steps in helping in an emergency?

If you were calling for help in an emergency, would you probably
be better off if there were several potential helpers or just one
within earshot?

STRESS AND COPING

For better or worse, most of us need little introduction to the phenomenon
of **stress**, formally defined as the response to events that threaten or challenge a person. Whether it be a paper or exam deadline, a family problem,
or even a cumulative series of small events such as those faced by Cathy
Collins on the job, life is full of circumstances—known as **stressors**—that
produce threats to our well-being. Even pleasant events—such as planning a party or beginning a sought-after job—can produce stress, although negative events result in greater detrimental consequences than
positive ones (Sarason, 1976; Brown & McGill, 1989).

All of us face stress in our lives; in fact, some psychologists believe
that daily life involves a series of repeated sequences of perceiving a
threat, considering ways of coping with it, and ultimately adapting to the
threat, with greater or lesser success (Gatchel & Baum, 1983). Although
adaptation is often minor and occurs without our being aware of it, in
those cases in which the stress is more severe or longer lasting, adaptation
requires major effort and may produce physiological and psychological
responses that result in health problems.

The High Cost of Stress

Stress can take its toll in many ways, producing physiological and psychological consequences. Often the most immediate reaction to stress is a
physiological one, for exposure to stress induces a rise in certain hormones
secreted by the adrenal glands, an increase in heart rate and blood pressure, and changes in how well the skin conducts electrical impulses (Mason, 1975; Selye, 1976). On a short-term basis, these responses may be
adaptive because they produce an "emergency reaction"—the response
of the sympathetic nervous system discussed in Chapter 2—and may allow more effective coping with the stressful situation.

However, continued exposure to stress results in a decline in the
body's overall level of biological functioning because of the continued
secretion of the stress-related hormones. Over time, in fact, stressful reactions can promote actual deterioration of body tissues such as the blood
vessels and the heart. Ultimately, we become more susceptible to disease
as our ability to fight off germs is lowered (Kiecolt-Glaser & Glaser, 1986;
Schneiderman, 1983).

In addition to major health difficulties, many of the minor aches and
pains that we experience may be caused or worsened by stress. These

TABLE 13-4 PREDICTING THE ILLNESS OF THE FUTURE
FROM THE STRESS OF THE PAST

Is there a stress-related illness in your future? Survey research has shown that the number of stressors in a person's life is associated with the experience of a major illness (Rahe & Arthur, 1978).

To find out the degree of stress in your life, take the stressor value given beside each event you have experienced and multiply it by the number of occurrences over the past year (up to a maximum of four), then add up these scores.

50 Entered college

77 Married

38 Had trouble with your boss

43 Held a job while attending school

87 Experienced the death of a spouse

34 Had a major change of sleeping habits

77 Experienced the death of a close family member

30 Had a major change in eating habits

41 Changed your choice of major field of study

45 Revised personal habits

68 Experienced the death of a close friend

22 Were found guilty of minor violations of the law

40 Had an outstanding personal achievement

68 Experienced pregnancy or fathered a pregnancy

56 Experienced a major change in the health or behavior of a family member

58 Had sexual difficulties

42 Had trouble with in-laws

26 Had a major change in the number of family get-togethers

53 Had a major change in financial status

50 Gained a new family member

42 Changed residence or living conditions

50 Had a major conflict or change in values

36 Had a major change in church activities

58 Experienced a marital reconciliation with your mate

62 Were fired from work

76 Were divorced

50 Changed to a different line of work

50 Had a major change in the number of arguments with your spouse

47 Had a major change in responsibilities at work

---

include headaches, backaches, skin rashes, indigestion, fatigue, and constipation (Brown, 1984). Moreover, a whole class of medical problems, known as **psychosomatic disorders**, often result from stress. These medical problems are caused by an interaction of psychological, emotional, and physical difficulties. Among the most common psychosomatic disorders are ulcers, asthma, high blood pressure, and eczema. In fact, the likelihood of onset of any major illness seems to be related to the number of stressful events a person experiences (see Table 13-4).

On a psychological level, high levels of stress prevent people from coping with life adequately. Their view of the environment can become clouded (a minor criticism made by a professor is blown out of proportion), and—at the greatest levels of stress—emotional responses may be so severe that people are unable to act at all. Moreover, people become less able to deal with new stressors. The ability to contend with future stress, then, declines as a result of past stress (Eckenrode, 1984).

TABLE 13-4 *(Continued)*

41 Had your spouse begin or cease work outside the home

42 Had a major change in working hours or conditions

74 Experienced a marital separation from mate

37 Had a major change in type and/or amount of recreation

52 Had a major change in use of drugs

52 Took on a mortgage or loan of more than $10,000

65 Had a major personal injury or illness

46 Experienced a major change in use of alcohol

43 Had a major change in social activities

38 Had a major change in amount of participation in school activities

49 Had a major change in amount of independence and responsibility

33 Took a trip or vacation

54 Became engaged to be married

50 Changed to a new school

41 Changed dating habits

44 Had trouble with school administration

60 Ended a marital engagement or a steady relationship

57 Had a major change in self-concept or self-awareness

Scoring If your total score is above 1435, you are in a high-stress category, which, according to Marx, Garrity & Bowers (1975), puts you at risk for experiencing a stress-related illness in the future. On the other hand, you should not assume that a high score destines you to a future illness. Because the research on stress and illness is correlational, major stressful events cannot be viewed as necessarily causing illness (Dohrenwend, Dohrenwend, Dodson & Shrout, 1984; Lakey & Heller, 1985). Moreover, some research suggests that future illness is better predicted by the daily, ongoing hassles of life, rather than by the major events depicted in the questionnaire (Lazarus, DeLoungis, Folkman & Gruen, 1985). Still, a high level of stressful events in one's life is a concern, and it is not unreasonable to take measures to reduce stress (Marx, Garrity & Bowers, 1975, p. 97; Maddi, Bartone & Puccetti, 1987).

Characterizing Stress: The General Adaptation Syndrome Model

The effects of stress are best illustrated by a model developed by Hans Selye, a major stress theorist (Selye, 1976). This model, the **general adaptation syndrome (GAS)**, suggests that the same set of physiological reactions to stress occurs regardless of the particular cause of stress. As shown in Figure 13-4, the model has three phases. The first stage, the **alarm and mobilization stage**, occurs when people become aware of the presence of a stressor. Suppose, for instance, you learned at the end of the first term of college that you were on academic probation because of your low grades. You likely would respond first with alarm, feeling concerned and upset. Subsequently, though, you would probably begin to mobilize your efforts, making plans and promises to yourself to study harder for the rest of the school year.

Stressor	Alarm and mobilization	Resistance	Exhaustion
	Meeting and resisting stressor.	Coping with stress and resistance to stressor.	Negative consequences of stress (such as illness) occur when coping is inadequate.

FIGURE 13-4
The general adaptation syndrome suggests that there are three major stages in people's response to stress. (Selye, 1976.)

In the next stage of the model, the **resistance stage**, you would prepare yourself to fight the stressor. During resistance, a person uses various means to cope with the stressor—sometimes successfully—but at a cost of some degree of physical or psychological general well-being. For instance, your resistance might take the form of devoting long hours to studying. You may ultimately be successful in raising your grades, but it may be at the expense of a loss of sleep and hours of worry.

If resistance is not adequate, the last stage of the model, exhaustion, is reached. During the **exhaustion stage**, a person's ability to adapt to the stressor declines to the point where negative consequences of stress appear: physical illness, psychological symptoms in the form of an inability to concentrate, heightened irritability, or, in severe instances, disorientation and a loss of touch with reality. If you become overwhelmed by pressure to perform well in your courses, for example, you may become sick or find it impossible to study altogether.

The GAS has had a substantial impact on our understanding of stress. For instance, by suggesting that the exhaustion of resources in the third stage of the model produces physiological damage, it has provided a specific model to explain how stress can lead to illness. Furthermore, the model offers a general explanation for stress that cuts across humans and animals.

On the other hand, some of the specifics of the GAS model have been questioned. Among the most important criticisms is that certain stressors seem to produce distinct physiological reactions, such as the secretion of specific hormones (Mason, 1974). Furthermore, the model's reliance on physiological factors leaves little room for attention to psychological factors, particularly in terms of the way in which stressors are appraised differently by different people (Mikhail, 1981). Still, the model provides a substantial foundation for our understanding of stress.

My Stress Is Your Pleasure: The Nature of Stressors

The general adaptation syndrome model is useful in explaining how people respond to stress, but it is not specific about what constitutes a stressor for a given person. Although it is clear that certain kinds of events—such as the death of a loved one or participation in combat during a war—are almost universally stressful, other situations may or may not be stressful to a particular person (Fleming, Baum & Singer, 1984; Lazarus & Cohen, 1977). Consider, for instance, automobile racing. Some of us would find driving cars at breakneck speeds to be a very stressful event, and the activity would be likely to produce reactions similar to those of other stressful occurrences. However, there are those for whom car racing is a challenging and fun-filled activity; instead of experiencing stress, they look forward to driving around a track at 200 miles per hour. Whether or not car racing is stressful depends in part, then, on individual perceptions of the activity.

For people to consider an event to be stressful, they must perceive it as threatening and must lack the resources to deal with it effectively (Folkman et al., 1986). Consequently, the same event may at times be stressful and at other times evoke no stress at all. For instance, a young man might experience stress when he is turned down for a date—if he attributes the refusal to his unattractiveness or unworthiness. But if he attributes it to some factor unrelated to his self-esteem, such as a previous commitment of the woman he asked, the experience of being refused might create no stress at all.

A number of factors also influence the severity of stress. For example, stress is greater when the importance and number of goals that are threatened are high, when the threat is immediate, or when the anticipation of the threatening event extends over a long period (Paterson & Neufeld, 1987).

Categorizing stressors. What kinds of events tend to be seen as stressful? There are three general classes of events: cataclysmic stressors, personal stressors, and background stressors (Gatchel & Baum, 1983; Lazarus & Cohen, 1977). **Cataclysmic events** are strong stressors that occur suddenly and affect many people simultaneously. Natural disasters, such as tornadoes and plane crashes, are examples of cataclysmic events that can affect hundreds or thousands of people simultaneously. Curiously, however, cataclysmic events may sometimes be less stressful in the long run than events that are initially less intense. One reason is that such events have a clear resolution: once they are over and done with, people can look forward to the future knowing that the worst is behind them. Moreover, the stress induced by cataclysmic events is shared by others who have also experienced the disaster (Cummings, 1987). This permits people to provide one another with social support and a firsthand understanding of the difficulties the others are going through.

On the other hand, some victims of major catastrophes can experience a **posttraumatic stress syndrome**, in which the original events and the feelings associated with them are reexperienced in vivid flashbacks or dreams. Fifteen percent of the veterans of the Vietnam War suffer from posttraumatic stress syndrome, which leads to sleep difficulties, problems in relating to others, and—in some cases—alcohol and drug abuse (Roberts, 1988b). The fact that the suicide rate for Vietnam veterans is 86 percent higher than for the general population indicates the difficulties faced by veterans of this war (Roberts, 1988b; Oei, Lim & Hennessy, 1990).

Personal stressors include major life events such as the death of a parent or spouse, the loss of one's job, a major personal failure, and diagnosis of a life-threatening illness. Typically, personal stressors produce an immediate major reaction that soon tapers off. For example, stress arising from the death of a loved one tends to be greatest just after the time of death, but people begin to feel less stressed and are better able to cope with the loss after the passage of time.

In some cases, though, the effects of stress are lingering. Victims of rape sometimes suffer lasting consequences long after the event, facing major difficulties in adjustment. Similarly, the malfunction of the Three Mile Island nuclear plant in Pennsylvania in 1979, which exposed people to the stressor of a potential nuclear meltdown, produced emotional, behavioral, and physiological consequences that lasted more than a year and a half (Baum, Gatchel & Schaeffer, 1983).

Standing in a long line at a bank and getting stuck in a traffic jam are examples of **background stressors** or, more informally, "daily hassles" (Lazarus & Cohen, 1977). These stressors represent the minor irritations of life that we all face time and time again: delays, noisy cars and trucks, broken appliances, other people's irritating behavior, and so on. Background stressors also consist of long-term, chronic problems such as dissatisfaction with school or job, unhappy relationships, or living in crowded quarters without privacy.

By themselves, daily hassles do not require much coping or even response on the part of the individual, although they certainly do produce unpleasant emotions and moods (Bolger et al., 1989; Clark & Watson, 1988). Yet daily hassles add up—and ultimately they may produce as great a toll as a single, more stressful incident. In fact, there is an association between the number of daily hassles that people face and the number of psychological symptoms they report. Even health problems (such as flu, sore throat, headaches, and backaches) have been linked to daily hassles (DeLongis, Folkman & Lazarus, 1988; Jones, Brantley & Gilchrist, 1988; Jung & Khalsa, 1989).

Although the nature of daily hassles differs from day to day and from person to person, background stressors do have certain characteristics in common. One critical factor is related to the degree of control people have over aversive, unpleasant stimuli in the environment (Folkman, 1984; Rodin, 1986). When people feel that they can control a situation and determine its outcome, stress reactions are reduced considerably. For instance, people exposed to high levels of noise suffer fewer adverse effects if they know they are able to control the noise than those exposed to the same amount of noise who are unable to control its intensity and duration (Glass & Singer, 1972).

The flip side of hassles are **uplifts**, those minor positive events that make one feel good—even if only temporarily. As indicated in Table 13-5,

TABLE 13-5 THE TEN MOST FREQUENTLY REPORTED HASSLES AND UPLIFTS

Below are the items that a group of people identified as the hassles and uplifts they experienced most frequently over a nine-month period. The "percentage of times checked" figures represent the mean number of times an item was checked each month, averaged over the nine monthly administrations.

Items	Percentage of Times Checked
Hassles	
1. Concerns about weight	52.4
2. Health of a family member	48.1
3. Rising price of common goods	43.7
4. Home maintenance	42.8
5. Too many things to do	38.6
6. Misplacing or losing things	38.1
7. Yard work or major outside home maintenance	38.1
8. Property investment or taxes	37.6
9. Fears of crime	37.1
10. Physical appearance	35.9
Uplifts	
1. Relating well with spouse or lover	76.3
2. Relating well with friends	74.4
3. Completing a task	73.3
4. Feeling healthy	72.7
5. Getting enough sleep	69.7
6. Eating out	68.4
7. Meeting your responsibilities	68.1
8. Visiting, phoning, or writing someone	67.7
9. Spending time with family	66.7
10. Home (inside) pleasing to you	65.5

SOURCE: Kanner, A. D., Coyne, J. C., Schaefer, C., & Lazarus, R. S. (1981). "Comparison of two modes of stress measurement: Daily hassles and uplifts versus major life events." *Journal of Behavioral Medicine*, 4:14, Table 3. Used with permission.

uplifts range from relating well to a companion to finding one's surroundings pleasing. What is especially intriguing about these uplifts is that they are associated with people's psychological health in just the opposite way that hassles are: The greater the number of uplifts experienced, the fewer the psychological symptoms people later report.

Coping with Stress

Stress is a normal part of living. As Hans Selye has noted, to avoid stress totally, a person would likely have to cease living. Yet, as we have seen, too much stress can take its toll on both physical and psychological health. How do people deal with stress? Is there a way to reduce its negative effects?

The efforts to control, reduce, or learn to tolerate the threats that lead to stress are known as **coping**. We habitually use certain coping responses to help ourselves deal with stress. Most of the time, we're not aware of these responses—just as we may be unaware of the minor stressors of life until they build up to sufficiently aversive levels.

One means of dealing with stress that occurs on an unconscious level is the use of **defense mechanisms**. As we discussed in Chapter 9, defense mechanisms are reactions that maintain a person's sense of control and self-worth by distorting or denying the actual nature of the situation. For example, one study showed that California students who live close to a geological fault in dormitories which are rated as being unlikely to withstand an earthquake were significantly more likely to deny the seriousness of the situation and to doubt experts' predictions of an impending earthquake than those who lived in safer structures (Lehman & Taylor, 1988).

Another defense mechanism sometimes used to cope with stress is emotional insulation, in which a person stops experiencing any emotions at all, thereby remaining unaffected and unmoved by both positive and negative experiences. The problem with defense mechanisms, of course, is that they do not deal with reality but merely hide the problem.

A sense of control over one's daily activities is vital to mental health, for the elderly as well as for younger people. This gentleman spends part of his week volunteering in a local school.

People use other, more direct and potentially more positive means for coping with stress, as shown in several studies (Aldwin & Revenson, 1987; Compas, 1987; Miller, Brody & Summerton, 1988). For example, in one experiment 100 men and women were asked to record how they coped with a number of different stressors in their lives over a seven-month period. The results showed that people used two major sorts of techniques for dealing with stress: the conscious regulation of emotions, called **emotion-focused coping**, and the management of the stressful problem or stimulus, called **problem-focused coping**. Examples of emotion-focused coping included such strategies as "accepted sympathy and understanding from someone" and "tried to look on the bright side," whereas examples of problem-focused strategies included "got the person responsible to change his or her mind" and "made a plan of action and followed it." In over 98 percent of the stressful incidents reported, *both* emotion-focused and problem-focused strategies were employed. However, more emotion-focused strategies were used in circumstances perceived as being unchangeable, and more problem-focused approaches were used in situations seen as relatively modifiable (Folkman and Lazarus, 1980).

The Informed Consumer of Psychology: Coping Strategies That Work

How does one cope most effectively with stress? Researchers working in the area have made a number of recommendations for dealing with the problem. There is no universal solution for coping with stress, of course, since effective coping depends on the nature of the stressor and the degree to which control is possible. Still, some general guidelines can be followed (Folkman, 1984; Holahan & Moos, 1987, 1990; Everly, 1989).

- *Turning threat into challenge.* When a stressful situation might be controllable, the best coping approach is to treat the situation as a challenge, focusing on ways to control it. For instance, if you are stressed by poor academic performance, one reasonable approach is to analyze your performance and develop strategies for more effective studying.

- *Making a threatening situation less threatening.* When a stressful situation seems to be uncontrollable, a different approach must be taken. It is possible to change one's appraisal of the situation, to view it in a different light, and to modify one's attitudes toward it (Abella & Heslin, 1989; Smith & Ellsworth, 1987). The old truism "Look for the silver lining in every cloud" seems to be supported by research findings that show that people who discover something good in negative situations show less distress and better coping ability than those who do not look for the positive side of things (Silver & Wortman, 1980).

- *Changing one's goals.* When a person is faced with an uncontrollable situation, another reasonable strategy is to adopt new goals that are practical in view of the particular situation. For example, a dancer who has been in an automobile accident and has lost full use of her legs may no longer aspire to a career in dance—but might modify her goals and try to become a dance instructor. Similarly, an executive who has lost his job may change his goal of becoming wealthy to that of obtaining a more modest, but secure, source of income.

- *Taking physical action.* Another approach to coping with stress is to bring about changes in one's physiological reactions to it. For example, biofeedback, discussed in Chapter 2, can alter basic physiological processes, allowing people to reduce blood pressure, heart rate, and other consequences of heightened stress. In addition, exercise can be effective in reducing stress. Finally, sometimes a change in diet is helpful in coping with stress. For instance, people who drink large quantities of caffeine are susceptible to feeling jittery and anxious; simply decreasing the amount they consume may be sufficient to reduce the experience of stress. Similarly, being overweight may itself be a stressor, and losing excess weight may be an effective measure for reducing stress—unless dieting is so tension-filled that it becomes stressful.

- *Preparing for stress before it happens.* A final strategy for coping with stress is **inoculation**: preparing for stress *before* it is encountered. First developed as a means of preventing postsurgical emotional problems among hospital patients, inoculation methods prepare

"Stress inoculation" is the technique of preparing oneself for a stressful event before it happens, as this patient about to undergo a spinal tap operation is doing.

people for stressful experiences—of either a physical or an emotional nature—by explaining, in as much detail as possible, the difficult events they are likely to encounter. As part of the process, people are asked to imagine how they will feel about the circumstances and to consider various ways of dealing with their reactions—all before the experience has actually occurred. Probably the most crucial element, however, is providing individuals with clear, objective strategies for handling the situation, rather than simply telling them what to expect (Janis, 1984).

When carried out properly, inoculation works. Coping is greater for people who have received inoculation treatments prior to facing a stressful event than for those who have not (MacDonald & Kuiper, 1983; Anderson, 1987).

*A*SK YOURSELF

What is stress?

What are the three stages of Selye's general adaptation model?

What are the three general categories of stressors?

Describe the major ways of coping.

You have three exams next week, you are behind in all your readings, and your car just broke down. In dealing with the stress, how would you employ problem-based coping and how would you use emotion-based coping?

*L*OOKING BACK

1. The study of interpersonal attraction, or close relationships, considers liking and loving. Among the primary determinants of liking are proximity, mere exposure, similarity, and physical attractiveness.

2. Love is distinguished from liking by the presence of intense physiological arousal, an all-encompassing interest in another, fantasies about the other, rapid swings of emotion, fascination, sexual desire, exclusiveness, and strong feelings of caring. According to one approach, love can be distinguished into two types: passionate and romantic. Sternberg's theory further subdivides love into eight kinds.

3. Recent work has examined the development, maintenance, and deterioration of relationships. Partners in lasting marriages tend to be remarkably similar in their perceptions of what makes their marriage endure.

4. Aggression is intentional injury of or harm to another person. Instinct approaches suggest that humans have an innate drive to behave aggressively and that if aggression is not released in socially desirable ways, it will be discharged in some other form—a point for which there is relatively little research support. Frustration-aggression theory suggests that frustration produces a readiness to be aggressive—if aggressive cues are present. Finally, observational learning theory hypothesizes that aggression is learned through reinforce-

ment—particularly reinforcement that is given to models. Each of these approaches suggests means of reducing aggressive behavior.

5. Helping behavior in emergencies is determined in part by the phenomenon of diffusion of responsibility, which results in a lower likelihood of helping when more people are present. Deciding to help is the outcome of a four-stage process consisting of noticing a possible need for help, interpreting the situation as requiring aid, assuming responsibility for taking action, and deciding on and implementing a form of assistance.

6. Stress is a response to threatening or challenging environmental conditions. People's lives are filled with stressors—the circumstances that produce stress—of both a positive and negative nature.

7. Stress produces immediate physiological reactions. In the short term, these reactions are adaptive, but in the long term they may have negative consequences. These reactions may be explained in part by Selye's general adaptation syndrome (GAS), which suggests that there are three stages to stress responses: alarm and mobilization, resistance, and exhaustion.

8. Although the stimuli that produce stress are not universal, there are three general classes that tend to provoke stress: cataclysmic events, personal stressors, and background stressors or daily hassles.

9. Stress can be reduced by developing a sense of control over one's circumstances. Coping with stress can take a number of forms, including the unconscious use of defense mechanisms and the use of emotion-focused or problem-focused coping strategies.

Key Terms and Concepts

Glossary

❖

ABC model The model suggesting that an attitude has three components: affect, behavior, and cognition (ch. 12, p. 486)

absolute refractory period The period following the triggering of a neuron in which the neuron recovers and prepares for another impulse (ch. 2, p. 45)

absolute threshold The smallest amount of physical intensity by which a stimulus can be detected (ch. 3, p. 81)

accommodation The ability of the lens to vary its shape in order to focus incoming images on the retina (ch. 3, p. 89)

acetylcholine A common neurotransmitter that produces contractions of skeletal muscles (ch. 2, p. 49)

achievement test A test intended to determine a person's level of knowledge in a given subject (ch. 9, p. 389)

acquired immune deficiency syndrome (AIDS) A fatal, sexually transmitted disease that is caused by a virus that destroys the body's immune system and has no known cure (ch. 6, p. 239)

action potential An electric nerve impulse that travels through a neuron when it is set off by a "trigger," changing the cell's charge from negative to positive (ch. 2, p. 45)

acupuncture A Chinese technique of relieving pain through the placement of needles in specific areas of the body (ch. 3, p. 107)

adaptation An adjustment in sensory capacity following prolonged exposure to stimuli (ch. 3, p. 84)

addictive drugs Drugs that produce a physical or physiological dependence in the user (ch. 7, p. 285)

adolescence The developmental stage between childhood and adulthood during which many physical, cognitive, and social changes take place (ch. 8, p. 329)

affect component That part of an attitude encompassing how one feels about the object of one's attitude (ch. 12, p. 486)

afterimage The image appearing when one moves one's eyes from a particular image to a blank area (ch. 3, p. 95)

age of viability The point at which a fetus can survive if born prematurely (ch. 8, p. 365)

aggression Intentional injury of or harm to another person (ch. 13, p. 526)

aggressive cues Stimuli that have been associated with aggression in the past (ch. 13, p. 527)

alarm and mobilization stage In Selye's general adaptation syndrome, a person's initial awareness of the presence of a stressor (ch. 13, p. 537)

algorithm A set of rules that, if followed, guarantee a problem's solution, though the reason they work may not be understood (ch. 5, p. 201)

all-or-none law The principle governing the state of neurons, which are either on (firing) or off (resting) (ch. 2, p. 45)

altered states of consciousness Experiences of sensation or thought that differ from one's normal experience (ch. 7, p. 268)

altruism Helping behavior that is beneficial to others while requiring sacrifice on the part of the helper (ch. 13, p. 539)

Alzheimer's disease An illness associated with aging that includes severe memory loss, physical deterioration, and loss of language abilities (ch. 2, p. 50, ch. 5, p. 195, ch. 8, p. 345)

amnesia Memory loss unaccompanied by other mental difficulties (ch. 5, p. 195)

amphetamines Strong stimulants that cause a temporary feeling of confidence and alertness but may increase anxiety and appetite loss and, taken over a period of time, suspiciousness and feelings of persecution (ch. 7, p. 287)

anal stage According to Freud, a stage, from 12–18 months to 3 years of age, in which a child's pleasure is centered on the anus (ch. 9, p. 357)

anorexia nervosa An eating disorder usually striking young women with symptoms including self-starvation or near self-starvation in an attempt to avoid obesity (ch. 6, p. 234)

anterograde amnesia Memory loss of events following an injury (ch. 5, p. 195)

antianxiety drugs Drugs that alleviate stress and anxiety (ch. 11, p. 475)

antidepressant drugs Medication that improves a patient's mood and feeling of well-being (ch. 11, p. 474)

antipsychotic drugs Drugs that temporarily alleviate psychotic symptoms such as agitation and overactivity (ch. 11, p. 473)

antisocial (sociopathic) personality disorder A disorder in which individuals display no regard for moral and ethical rules or for the rights of others (ch. 10, p. 441)

anvil A tiny bone in the middle ear that transfers vibrations to the stirrup (ch. 3, p. 98)

anxiety A feeling of apprehension or tension (ch. 9, p. 359, ch. 10, p. 423)

anxiety disorder The occurrence of anxiety without obvious external cause, intruding on daily functioning (ch. 10, p. 423)

aphasia A disorder resulting in problems with verbal expression due to brain injury (ch. 2, p. 68)

apraxia The inability to perform activities in a logical way (ch. 2, p. 68)

aptitude test A test designed to predict ability in a particular line of work (ch. 9, p. 389)

archetypes According to Jung, universal, symbolic representations of a particular person, object, or experience (ch. 9, p. 362)

archival research The examination of written records for the purpose of understanding behavior (ch. 1, p. 23)

arousal theory The belief that we try to maintain certain levels of stimulation and activity, increasing or reducing them as necessary (ch. 6, p. 223)

arrangement problems Problems whose solution requires the rearrangement of a group of elements in order to satisfy a certain criterion (ch. 5, p. 198)

association area One of the major areas of the brain, the site of the higher mental processes such as thought, language, memory, and speech (ch. 2, p. 68)

assumed-similarity bias The tendency to think of people as being similar to oneself (ch. 12, p. 502)

attachment The positive emotional bond that develops between parents and their children (ch. 8, p. 314)

attitudes Learned predispositions to respond in a favorable or unfavorable manner to a particular object (ch. 12, p. 486)

attribution theory The theory that seeks to explain how we decide, on the basis of samples of an individual's behavior, what the specific causes of that behavior are (ch. 12, p. 498)

auditory canal A tubelike passage in the ear through which sound moves to the eardrum (ch. 3, p. 98)

autonomic division The part of the nervous system that controls involuntary movement (the actions of the heart, glands, lungs, and other organs) (ch. 2, p. 54)

autonomy-versus-shame-and-doubt stage The period during which, according to Erikson, toddlers (ages 18 months to 3 years) develop independence and autonomy if exploration and freedom are encouraged, or shame and self-doubt if they are restricted and overprotected (ch. 8, p. 328)

availability heuristic A rule for judging the probability that an event will occur by the ease with which it can be recalled from memory (ch. 5, p. 201)

aversive conditioning A technique used to help people break unwanted habits by associating the habits with very unpleasant stimuli (ch. 11, p. 455)

aversive stimulus Unpleasant or painful stimulus (ch. 4, p. 146)

axon A long, slim, tubelike extension from the end of a neuron that carries messages (ch. 2, p. 43)

babble Speechlike but meaningless sounds (ch. 5, p. 212)

Babinski reflex The reflex action in which an infant fans out its toes in response to a stroke on the outside of its foot (ch. 8, p. 309)

background stressors Daily hassles, such as being stuck in traffic, that cause minor irritations but no long-term ill effects, unless they continue or are compounded by other stressful events (ch. 13, p. 540)

barbiturates Depressants used to induce sleep and reduce stress, the abuse of which, especially when combined with alcohol, can be deadly (ch. 7, p. 291)

basilar membrane A structure dividing the cochlea into an upper and a lower chamber (ch. 3, p. 99)

behavioral model The psychological model that suggests that observable behavior should be the focus of study (ch. 1, p. 16)

behavioral model of abnormality The model that suggests that abnormal behavior itself is the problem to be treated, rather than viewing behavior as a symptom of some underlying medical or psychological problem (ch. 10, p. 413)

behavioral self-management A procedure in which people learn to identify and resolve their problems using techniques based on learning theory (ch. 11, p. 461)

behavioral treatment approaches Approaches to abnormal behavior that assume that both normal and abnormal behaviors are learned and that treatment consists of learning new behavior or unlearning maladaptive behavior (ch. 11, p. 454)

behavior component A predisposition to act in a way that is relevant to one's attitude (ch. 12, p. 486)

behavior modification A formalized technique for promoting the frequency of desirable behaviors and decreasing the incidence of unwanted ones (ch. 4, p. 168)

binocular disparity The difference between the images that reach the retina of each eye; this disparity allows the brain to estimate distance (ch. 3, p. 115)

biofeedback A technique for learning to control internal physiological processes through conscious thought (ch. 2, p. 73)

biological constraints Built-in limitations in an organism's ability to learn particular behaviors (ch. 4, p. 161)

biological model The psychological model that views behavior in terms of biological functioning (ch. 1, p. 14)

biopsychologists Psychologists who study the ways biological structures and body functions affect behavior (ch. 2, p. 40)

biopsychology The branch of psychology that studies the biological basis of behavior (ch. 1, p. 6)

bipolar cells Nerve cells leading to the brain that are triggered by nerve cells in the eye (ch. 3, p. 91)

bipolar disorder A disorder in which a person alternates between euphoric feelings of mania and bouts of depression (ch. 10, p. 432)

bisexuality A sexual attraction to members of both sexes (ch. 6, p. 243)

bottom-up processing Recognition and processing of individual components of a stimulus (ch. 3, p. 118)

brain scan A method of "photographing" the brain without opening the skull (ch. 2, p. 56)

Broca's aphasia A syndrome in which speech production is disturbed (ch. 2, p. 68)

bulimia An eating disorder characterized by a vast intake of food that may be followed by self-induced vomiting (ch. 6, p. 239)

caffeine A stimulant found most abundantly in coffee, soda, and chocolate (ch. 7, p. 286)

Cannon-Bard theory of emotion The belief that both physiological and emotional arousal are produced simultaneously by the same nerve impulse (ch. 6, p. 255)

cardinal trait A single personality trait that directs most of a person's activities (e.g., greed, lust, kindness) (ch. 9, p. 365)

case study An in-depth interview of an individual in order to better understand that individual and to make inferences about people in general (ch. 1, p. 23)

cataclysmic events Strong stressors that occur suddenly, affecting many people at once (e.g., natural disasters) (ch. 13, p. 539)

catharsis The notion that aggression is built up and must be discharged through violent acts (ch. 13, p. 527)

central core The "old brain," which controls such basic functions as eating and sleeping and is common to all vertebrates (ch. 2, p. 58)

central nervous system (CNS) The system that includes the brain and the spinal cord (ch. 2, p. 52)

central route processing Message interpretation characterized by thoughtful consideration of the issues and arguments used to persuade (ch. 12, p. 490)

central traits A set of major characteristics that make up the core of a person's personality, used for forming impressions of others (ch. 9, p. 365, ch. 12, p. 497)

cerebellum The part of the brain that controls bodily balance (ch. 2, p. 60)

cerebral cortex The "new brain," responsible for the most sophisticated information processing in the brain; contains the lobes (ch. 2, p. 63)

channels Paths along which verbal and non-verbal behavioral messages are communicated (e.g., facial expressions, eye contact, body movements) (ch. 6, p. 259)

chlorpromazine An antipsychotic drug that is used in the treatment of schizophrenia (ch. 11, p. 473)

chromosomes Rod-shaped structures that contain basic hereditary information (ch. 8, p. 303)

chronological age A person's physical age (ch. 9, p. 385)

chunk A meaningful grouping of stimuli that can be stored as a unit in short-term memory (ch. 5, p. 179)

classical conditioning A kind of learning in which a previously neutral stimulus comes to elicit a response through its association with a stimulus that naturally brings about the response (ch. 4, p. 136)

client-centered therapy Therapy in which the therapist reflects back the patient's statements in a way that causes the patient to find his or her own solutions (ch. 11, p. 467)

clinical psychology The branch of psychology that studies diagnosis and treatment of abnormal behavior (ch. 1, p. 8)

closure The tendency to group according to enclosed or complete figures rather than open or incomplete ones (ch. 3, p. 110)

cocaine A stimulant that initially creates feelings of confidence, alertness, and well-being, but eventually causes mental and physical deterioration (ch. 7, p. 287)

cochlea A coiled tube filled with fluid that receives sound via the oval window or through bone conduction (ch. 3, p. 99)

cognition The higher mental processes through which we understand the world, process information, make judgments and decisions, and communicate knowledge to others (ch. 5, p. 174, ch. 12, p. 491)

cognition component (of attitude) The belief and thoughts held about the object of one's attitude (ch. 12, p. 486)

cognitive-behavioral therapy A process by which people's faulty cognitions about themselves and the world are changed to more accurate ones (ch. 11, p. 460)

cognitive complexity The use of and preference for elaborate, intricate, and complex stimuli and thinking patterns (ch. 5, p. 209)

cognitive development The process by which a child's understanding of the world changes as a function of age and experience (ch. 8, p. 321)

cognitive dissonance The conflict that arises when a person holds contrasting cognitions (ch. 12, p. 491)

cognitive learning theory The study of the thought processes that underlie learning (ch. 4, p. 162)

cognitive map A mental "picture" of locations and directions (ch. 4, p. 163)

cognitive model The psychological model that focuses on how people know, understand, and think about the world (ch. 1, p. 16)

cognitive psychology The branch of psychology that considers higher mental processes including thinking, language, memory, problem solving, knowing, reasoning, judging, and decision making (ch. 1, p. 7, ch. 5, p. 174)

collective unconscious A concept developed by Jung proposing that we inherit certain personality characteristics from our ancestors and the human race as a whole (ch. 9, p. 362)

community psychology A branch of psychology aimed at preventing and treating psychological disorders in the community (ch. 11, p. 479)

companionate love The strong affection felt for those with whom our lives are deeply involved (ch. 13, p. 520)

compliance Behavior that occurs in response to direct social pressure (ch. 12, p. 507)

compulsion An urge to repeatedly carry out an act that even the sufferer realizes is unreasonable (ch. 10, p. 426)

computerized axial tomography (CAT) scan A scanning procedure that shows the structures within the brain (ch. 2, p. 56)

conception Process by which an egg cell is fertilized by a sperm cell (ch. 8, p. 303)

concrete operational stage According to Piaget, the period from 7 to 12 years of age that is characterized by logical thought and a loss of egocentrism (ch. 8, p. 324)

conditioned response (CR) A response that, after conditioning, follows a previously neutral stimulus (e.g., salivation at the sound of a tuning fork) (ch. 4, p. 136)

conditioned stimulus (CS) A once-neutral stimulus that has been paired with an unconditioned stimulus to bring about a response formerly caused only by the unconditioned stimulus (ch. 4, p. 136)

cones Cone-shaped, light-sensitive receptor cells in the retina that are responsible for sharp focus and color perception, particularly in bright light (ch. 3, p. 89)

confederate A participant in an experiment who has been instructed to behave in ways that will affect the responses of other subjects (ch. 1, p. 31)

confirmation bias A bias in problem solving favoring an initial hypothesis and disregarding contradictory information suggesting alternative solution (ch. 5, p. 208)

conformity A change in behavior or attitudes brought about by a desire to follow the beliefs or standards of other people (ch. 12, p. 506)

conscience The part of the superego that prevents us from doing what is morally wrong (ch. 9, p. 356)

consciousness A person's awareness of the sensations, thoughts, and feelings that he or she is experiencing at a given moment (ch. 7, p. 267)

consensus information The degree to which people behave similarly in the same situation (ch. 12, p. 499)

consistency The persistence of those holding an unpopular view, eventually bringing about a change in the attitude of the majority (ch. 12, p. 511)

consistency information The degree to which an individual behaves similarly in similar situations (ch. 12, p. 499)

constructive processes Processes in which memories are influenced by the interpretation and meaning we give to events (ch. 5, p. 190)

contingency contracting Acting upon a written contract between a therapist and a patient (or parent and child, etc.) that sets behavioral goals, with rewards for achievement (ch. 11, p. 458)

continuous reinforcement The reinforcing of a behavior every time it occurs (ch. 4, p. 150)

control group The experimental group receiving no treatment (ch. 1, p. 26)

convergent thinking A type of thinking which produces responses based on knowledge and logic (ch. 5, p. 209)

conversion disorder Psychological disturbances characterized by actual physical disturbances, such as the inability to speak or move one's arms (ch. 10, p. 467)

coping The efforts to control, reduce, or learn to tolerate the threats that lead to stress (ch. 13, p. 442)

cornea A transparent, protective window into the eyeball (ch. 3, p. 87)

correlational research Research to determine whether there is a relationship between certain behaviors and responses (ch. 1, p. 25)

counseling psychology The branch of psychology that focuses on educational, social, and career adjustment issues (ch. 1, p. 8)

creativity The combining of responses or ideas in novel ways (ch. 5, p. 208)

critical period The first of several stages of development in which specific kinds of growth must occur to enable further crucial development (ch. 8, p. 304)

cross-sectional research A research method in which people of different ages are compared at the same point in time (ch. 8, p. 302)

cross-sequential research A research method which combines cross-sectional and longitudinal research (ch. 8, p. 302)

crystallized intelligence Intelligence based on the store of specific information, skills, and strategies that people have acquired through experience (ch. 8, p. 390, ch. 9, p. 344)

culture-fair IQ test A test that does not discriminate against members of any minority culture group (ch. 9, p. 398)

cumulative recorder A device that automatically records and graphs the pattern of responses made in reaction to a particular reinforcement schedule (ch. 4, p. 151)

dark adaptation A heightened sensitivity to light resulting from being in low-level light (ch. 3, p. 94)

daydreams Fantasies people construct while awake (ch. 7, p. 277)

decay The loss of information through non-use (ch. 5, p. 192)

decibel A measure of sound loudness or intensity (ch. 3, p. 100)

defense mechanisms Psychological strategies that protect people from unconscious impulses (ch. 9, p. 359, ch. 11, p. 451, ch. 13, p. 542)

deinstitutionalization The transfer of former mental patients from institutions into the community (ch. 11, p. 479)

delusions Firmly held beliefs with no basis in reality (ch. 10, p. 436)

dendrites Fibers at one end of a neuron that receive messages from other neurons (ch. 2, p. 43)

denial A refusal to accept or acknowledge anxiety-producing information (ch. 9, p. 359)

dependent variable The variable that is measured and is expected to change as a result of experimenter manipulation of the independent variable (ch. 1, p. 26)

depressants Drugs that slow down the nervous system (ch. 7, p. 288)

depth perception The ability to view the world in three dimensions and to perceive distance (ch. 3, p. 115)

determinism The view suggesting that people's behavior is shaped primarily by factors outside their control (ch. 9, p. 371)

developmental psychology The branch of psychology that studies people's growth and change over the life span (ch. 1, p. 8, ch. 8, p. 298)

deviation IQ score A calculation of an IQ score that allows one person's performance to be measured in relation to others' (ch. 9, p. 386)

Diagnostic and Statistical Manual of Mental Disorders, Third Edition—**Revised (DSM-III-R)** A manual that presents comprehensive definitions of more than 230 separate diagnostic categories for identifying problems and behaviors (ch. 10, p. 420)

dichotic listening A procedure in which an individual wears earphones through which different messages are sent to each ear at the same time (ch. 3, p. 119)

difference threshold The smallest detectable difference between two stimuli (ch. 3, p. 83)

diffusion of responsibility The tendency for people to feel that responsibility for helping is shared among those present (ch. 13, p. 532)

discrimination Negative behavior toward members of a particular group (ch. 12, p. 497)

discriminative stimulus A stimulus to which an organism learns to respond as part of stimulus control training (ch. 4, p. 154)

displacement The expression of an unwanted feeling or thought, directed toward a weaker person instead of a more powerful one (ch. 9, p. 359)

dispositional causes of behavior Causes of behavior that are based on internal traits or personality factors (ch. 12, p. 499)

dissociative disorder The splitting apart of critical personality facets, allowing stress avoidance by escape (ch. 10, p. 428)

distinctiveness information The extent to which a given behavior occurs across different situations (ch. 12, p. 499)

divergent thinking The ability to generate unusual, but appropriate, responses to problems or questions (ch. 5, p. 209)

door-in-the-face technique A strategy in which a large request, refusal of which is expected, is followed by a smaller request (ch. 12, p. 508)

dopamine (DA) A common neurotransmitter that inhibits certain neurons and excites others (ch. 2, p. 50)

dopamine hypothesis A theory that suggests that schizophrenia occurs when there is excess activity in those areas of the brain using dopamine to transmit nerve impulses (ch. 10, p. 439)

double-bind hypothesis A theory that suggests that people suffering from schizophrenia may have received simultaneous contradictory messages from their mothers and never learned what behavior was appropriate (ch. 10, p. 439)

double-blind procedure The technique by which both the experimenter and the subject are kept from knowing which subjects received a drug, making any observed behavior variations more reliable (ch. 1, p. 13)

Down syndrome A disorder caused by the presence of an extra chromosome, resulting in mental retardation (ch. 8, p. 306, ch. 9, p. 394)

dream interpretation An examination of a patient's dreams to find clues to the unconscious conflicts and problems being experienced (ch. 11, p. 451)

drive A motivational tension or arousal that energizes behavior in order to fulfill a need (ch. 6, p. 222)

drive-reduction theory The theory which claims that drives are produced to obtain our basic biological requirements (ch. 6, p. 222)

drug therapy Control of psychological problems through drugs (ch. 11, p. 473)

dyadic phase The second phase in the decline of a relationship, in which a person confronts a partner and determines whether to attempt to repair, redefine, or terminate the relationship (ch. 13, p. 524)

eardrum The part of the ear that vibrates when sound waves hit it (ch. 3, p. 98)

echoic memory The storage of information obtained from the sense of hearing (ch. 5, p. 176)

eclectic approach to therapy An approach to therapy that uses a variety of treatment methods rather than just one (ch. 11, p. 449)

ecological theory A theory suggesting that the relationship between objects in a scene gives clues about the objects' sizes (ch. 3, p. 114)

educational psychology The branch of psychology that considers how the educational process affects students (ch. 1, p. 8)

ego The part of personality that provides a buffer between the id and the outside world according to Freud (ch. 9, p. 355)

egocentric thought Viewing the world entirely from one's own perspective (ch. 8, p. 323)

ego-ideal The part of the superego that motivates us to do what is morally proper (ch. 9, p. 356)

ego-integrity-versus-despair stage According to Erikson, a period from late adulthood until death during which we review life's accomplishments and failures (ch. 8, p. 336)

elaborative rehearsal Organizing information into a logical framework to assist in recalling it (ch. 5, p. 181)

electroconvulsive therapy (ECT) Treatment involving the administration of an electric current to a patient's head to treat depression (ch. 11, p. 416)

electroencephalogram (EEG) A measure of the brain's electrical activity (ch. 2, p. 56, ch. 7, p. 269)

embryo A developed zygote that has a heart, a brain, and other organs (ch. 8, p. 303)

emotion-focused coping The conscious regulation of emotion as a means of dealing with stress (ch. 13, p. 543)

emotions Feelings (such as happiness and sorrow) that generally have both physiological and cognitive elements and that influence behavior (ch. 6, p. 250)

empathy One person's experiencing of another's emotions, leading to an increased likelihood of responding to the other's needs (ch. 13, p. 534)

encoding The process by which information is initially recorded in a form usable to memory (ch. 5, p. 175)

endocrine system A chemical communication network that sends messages throughout the nervous system and secretes hormones that affect body growth and functioning (ch. 2, p. 60)

endorphins Chemicals produced by the body that interact with an opiate receptor to reduce pain (ch. 2, p. 51)

episodic memories Stored information relating to personal experiences (ch. 5, p. 182)

excitatory message A chemical secretion that "tells" a receiving neuron to fire (ch. 2, p. 98)

exhaustion stage The third stage of Selye's general adaptation syndrome: failure to adapt to a stressor, leading to physical, psychological, and emotional problems (ch. 13, p. 538)

existential therapy A humanistic approach that addresses the meaning of life, allowing a client to devise a system of values that gives purpose to his or her life (ch. 11, p. 464)

experiment A study carried out to investigate the relationship between two or more factors in order to establish causality (ch. 1, p. 225)

experimental bias Factors that could lead an experimenter to an erroneous conclusion about the effect of the independent variable on the dependent variable (ch. 1, p. 29)

experimental manipulation The intentional alteration of factors in an experiment to affect responses or behaviors (ch. 1, p. 25)

experimental psychology The branch of psychology that studies the processes of sensing, perceiving, learning, and thinking about the world (ch. 1, p. 8)

experimenter expectations An experimenter's unintentional message to a subject about results expected from the experiment (ch. 1, p. 30)

extinction The weakening and eventual disappearance of a learned response (ch. 4, p. 139)

extrinsic motivation Motivation in which people participate in an activity for a tangible reward (ch. 6, p. 226)

facial-affect program The activation of a set of nerve impulses that make the face display the appropriate expression (ch. 6, p. 261)

facial-feedback hypothesis The notion that facial expressions are involved in determining the experience of emotions and in labeling them (ch. 6, p. 261)

factor analysis A statistical technique for combining traits into broader, more general patterns of consistency (ch. 9, p. 365)

familial retardation Mental retardation in which there is a history of retardation in a family but no evidence of biological causes (ch. 9, p. 394)

family therapy An approach that focuses on the family as a whole unit to which each member contributes (ch. 11, p. 486)

fear of success A fear that being successful will have a negative influence on the way one is perceived (ch. 6, p. 297)

feature detection The activation of neurons in the cortex by visual stimuli of specific shapes or patterns (ch. 3, p. 93)

fetal alcohol syndrome An ailment producing mental and physical retardation in a baby as a result of the mother's high alcohol intake while pregnant (ch. 8, p. 308)

fetus A developing child, from nine weeks after conception until birth (ch. 8, p. 304)

figure/ground Figure refers to the object being perceived, whereas ground refers to the background of or spaces within the object (ch. 3, p. 111)

fixation Behavior reflecting an earlier stage of development (ch. 9, p. 357)

fixed-interval schedule A schedule whereby a reinforcer is given at established time intervals (ch. 4, p. 152)

fixed-ratio schedule A schedule whereby reinforcement is given only after a certain number of responses are made (ch. 4, p. 152)

flashbulb memories Memories of a specific event that are so clear that they seem like "snapshots" of the event (ch. 5, p. 188)

fluid intelligence The ability to deal with new problems and situations (ch. 8, p. 344, ch. 9, p. 390)

foot-in-the-door technique A technique in which compliance with an important request is more likely following compliance with a smaller, previous request (ch. 12, p. 507)

forewarning A procedure in which a subject is told in advance that a persuasive message is forthcoming, sometimes reducing the effects of social influence (ch. 12, p. 511)

formal operational stage According to Piaget, the period from age 12 to adulthood that is characterized by abstract thought (ch. 8, p. 329)

fovea A very sensitive region of the retina that aids in focusing (ch. 3, p. 89)

free association A Freudian therapeutic technique in which a patient says everything that comes to mind to give the therapist a clue to the workings of the patient's unconscious (ch. 11, p. 451)

free will The human ability to make decisions about one's own life (ch. 1, p. 17)

frequency The number of wave crests occurring each second in any particular sound (ch. 3, p. 100)

frequency theory of hearing The theory that suggests that the entire basilar membrane acts like a microphone, vibrating in response to sound (ch. 3, p. 102)

frontal lobes The brain structure located at the front center of the cortex containing major motor and speech and reasoning centers (ch. 2, p. 64)

frustration A state produced by the thwarting or blocking of some ongoing, goal-directed behavior (ch. 13, p. 527)

functional fixedness The tendency to think of an object in terms of its most typical use (ch. 5, p. 205)

functionalism An early approach to psychology that considered the role of mental activity in adapting to one's environment (ch. 1, p. 13)

fundamental attribution bias A tendency to attribute others' behavior to dispositional causes but to attribute one's own behavior to situational causes (ch. 12, p. 500)

gag reflex An infant's reflex to clear its throat (ch. 8, p. 309)

ganglion cells Nerve cells that collect and summarize information from rods and carry it to the brain (ch. 3, p. 91)

gate-control theory of pain The theory that suggests that particular nerve receptors lead to specific areas of the brain related to pain; when these receptors are activated by an injury or bodily malfunction, a "gate" to the brain is opened and pain is sensed (ch. 3, p. 107)

general adaptation syndrome (GAS) A theory developed by Selye that suggests that a person's response to stress consists of three stages: alarm and mobilization, resistance, and exhaustion (ch. 13, p. 537)

generalized anxiety disorder The experience of long-term anxiety with no explanation (ch. 10, p. 423)

generativity-versus-stagnation stage According to Erikson, a period in middle adulthood during which we take stock of our contributions to family and society (ch. 8, p. 336)

genes The parts of a chromosome through which genetic information is transmitted (ch. 8, p. 303)

genetic makeup Pertaining to the biological factors that transmit hereditary information (ch. 8, p. 299)

genetic preprogramming theories of aging Theories that suggest a built-in time limit to the reproduction of human cells (ch. 8, p. 342)

genital stage According to Freud, a period from puberty until death, marked by mature sexual behavior (i.e., sexual intercourse) (ch. 9, p. 358)

gerontologists Specialists who study aging (ch. 8, p. 341)

gestalt laws of organization A series of principles that describe how we organize pieces of information into meaningful wholes; they include closure, proximity, similarity, and simplicity (ch. 3, p. 110)

gestalt psychology An approach to psychology that focuses on the organization of perception and thinking in a "whole" sense, rather than on the individual elements of perception (ch. 1, p. 113)

gestalts Patterns studied by the gestalt psychologists (ch. 3, p. 110)

gestalt therapy An approach that attempts to integrate thoughts, feelings, and behavior into a whole (ch. 11, p. 464)

glaucoma A dysfunction of the eye in which fluid pressure builds up and causes a decline in visual acuity (ch. 3, p. 92)

g or g-factor A single general factor accounting for mental ability (ch. 9, p. 390)

grammar The framework of rules that determine how our thoughts can be expressed (ch. 5, p. 211)

grave-dressing phase The fourth and final stage in the decline of a relationship in which the relationship is physically and psychologically ended (ch. 13, p. 524)

group therapy Therapy in which people discuss problems with a group (ch. 11, p. 466)

habituation A decrease in responding to repeated presentations of the same stimulus (ch. 8, p. 312)

hair cells Tiny cells covering the basilar membrane that, when bent by vibrations entering the cochlea, transmit neural messages to the brain (ch. 3, p. 99)

hallucinations Perceptions of things that do not actually exist (ch. 10, p. 437)

hallucinogen A drug that is capable of producing changes in perception, or hallucinations (ch. 7, p. 292)

halo effect A phenomenon in which an initial understanding that a person has positive traits is used to infer other uniformly positive characteristics (ch. 12, p. 501)

hammer A tiny bone in the middle ear that transfers vibrations to the anvil (ch. 3, p. 98)

health psychology The branch of psychology that explores the relationship of physical and psychological factors (ch. 1, p. 8)

hemispheres Symmetrical left and right halves of the brain (ch. 2, p. 70)

hereditary influences Influences on behavior that are transmitted biologically from patients to a child (ch. 8, p. 299)

heritability A measure of the degree to which a characteristic is related to genetic, inherited factors, as opposed to environmental factors (ch. 9, p. 399)

heroin A powerful depressant, usually injected, that gives an initial rush of good feeling but leads eventually to anxiety and depression; extremely addictive (ch. 7, p. 291)

heterosexuality Sexual behavior between a man and a woman (ch. 6, p. 240)

heuristic A rule of thumb that may bring about a solution to a problem but is not guaranteed to do so (ch. 5, p. 201)

hierarchy of fears A list, in order of increasing severity, of the things that are associated with one's fears (ch. 11, p. 456)

higher-order conditioning A form of conditioning that occurs when an already-conditioned stimulus is paired with a neutral stimulus until the neutral stimulus evokes the same response as the conditioned stimulus (ch. 4, p. 192)

homeostasis The process by which an organism tries to maintain an internal biological balance or steady state (ch. 2, p. 60, ch. 6, p. 223)

homosexuality A sexual attraction to a member of one's own sex (ch. 6, p. 243)

hormones Chemicals that circulate throughout the blood and affect the functioning and growth of parts of the body (ch. 2, p. 61)

humanistic model The psychological model that suggests that people are in control of their lives (ch. 1, p. 17)

humanistic model of abnormality The model that suggests that people are basically rational, and that abnormal behavior results from an inability to fulfill human needs and capabilities (ch. 10, p. 414)

humanistic theory (of personality) The theory emphasizing people's basic goodness and their natural tendency to rise to higher levels of functioning (ch. 9, p. 372)

humanistic therapy Therapy in which the underlying assumption is that people have control of their behavior, can make choices about their lives, and are essentially responsible for solving their own problems (ch. 11, p. 462)

hypnosis A state of heightened susceptibility to the suggestions of others (ch. 7, p. 280)

hypochondriasis A constant fear of illness and misinterpretation of normal aches and pains (ch. 10, p. 426)

hypothalamus Located below the thalamus of the brain, its major function is to maintain homeostasis (ch. 2, p. 60, ch. 6, p. 230)

hypothesis A prediction that can be tested experimentally (ch. 1, p. 22)

iconic memory The storage of visual information (ch. 5, p. 176)

id The raw, unorganized, inherited part of personality whose purpose is to reduce tension created by biological drives and irrational impulses (ch. 9, p. 355)

identical twins Twins with identical genetic makeup (ch. 8, p. 302)

identification A child's attempt to be similar to his or her same-sex parent (ch. 9, p. 358)

identity The distinguishing character of the individual: who each of us is, what our roles are, and what we are capable of (ch. 8, p. 334)

identity-versus-role-confusion stage According to Erikson, a time in adolescence of testing to determine one's own unique qualities (ch. 8, p. 334)

idiographic approaches to personality A study of personality emphasizing what makes one person different from others and unique (ch. 9, p. 374)

imaginal code Memory storage based on visual images (ch. 5, p. 183)

implicit personality theory Theory reflecting our notions of what traits are found together in individuals (ch. 12, p. 501)

impression formation The process by which an individual organizes information about another individual to form an overall impression of that person (ch. 12, p. 496)

incentive An external stimulus anticipated as a reward which directs and energizes behavior (ch. 6, p. 225)

incentive theory The theory explaining motivation in terms of external stimuli (ch. 6, p. 225)

independent variable The variable that is manipulated in an experiment (ch. 1, p. 26)

inducing structure problems Problems whose solution requires the identification of existing relationships among elements presented so as to construct a new relationship among them (ch. 5, p. 198)

industrial-organizational psychology The branch of psychology that studies the psychology of the workplace, considering productivity, job satisfaction, and related issues (ch. 1, p. 9)

industry-versus-inferiority stage According to Erikson, the period during which children aged 6 to 12 years may develop positive social interactions with others or may feel inadequate and become less sociable (ch. 8, p. 320)

inferiority complex A phenomenon whereby adults have continuing feelings of weakness and insecurity (ch. 9, p. 363)

information processing The way in which

people take in, use, and store information (ch. 8, p. 326)

informed consent A document signed by subjects prior to an experiment in which the study and conditions and risks of participation are explained (ch. 1, p. 33)

ingroup Group to which an individual belongs (ch. 12, p. 497)

ingroup-outgroup bias The tendency to hold less favorable opinions about groups to which we do not belong (outgroups), while holding more favorable opinions about groups to which we do belong (ingroups) (ch. 12, p. 497)

inhibitory message A chemical secretion that prevents a receiving neuron from firing (ch. 2, p. 48)

initiative-versus-guilt stage According to Erikson, the period during which children aged 3 to 6 years experience conflict between independence of action and the sometimes negative results of that action (ch. 8, p. 320)

inner ear The interior structure that changes sound vibrations into a form that can be transmitted to the brain (ch. 3, p. 98)

inoculation Exposure to arguments opposing one's beliefs, making the subject more resistant to later attempts to change those beliefs (ch. 12, p. 511)

inoculation (for stress) Preparation for stress before it is encountered (ch. 13, p. 544)

insight Sudden awareness of the relationships among various elements that had previously appeared to be independent of one another (ch. 5, p. 202)

insomnia An inability to get to sleep or stay asleep (ch. 7, p. 278)

instinct An inborn pattern of behavior that is biologically determined (ch. 6, p. 222)

instinctual drives Infantile wishes, desires, demands, and needs hidden from conscious awareness (ch. 9, p. 354)

intellectually gifted Individuals characterized by higher-than-average intelligence, with IQ scores above 130 (ch. 9, p. 396)

intelligence The capacity to understand the world, think rationally, and use resources effectively when faced with challenges (ch. 9, p. 384)

intelligence quotient (IQ) score A measure of intelligence that takes into account an individual's mental and chronological ages (ch. 9, p. 385)

intelligence tests A battery of measures to determine a person's level of intelligence (ch. 9, p. 384)

intensity A feature of wave patterns that allows us to distinguish between loud and soft sounds (ch. 3, p. 100)

interactionist One believing that a combination of genetic predisposition and environmental influences determines the course of development (ch. 8, p. 301)

interference The phenomenon by which recall is hindered because of other information in memory (ch. 5, p. 193)

interneurons Neurons that transmit information between sensory and motor neurons (ch. 2, p. 52)

interpersonal attraction Positive feelings for others (ch. 13, p. 516)

interpsychic phase The first phase in the decline of a relationship, characterized by a focus on the other person's behavior and an evaluation of the extent to which this behavior provides reason for terminating the relationship (ch. 13, p. 524)

intimacy-versus-isolation stage According to Erikson, a period during early adulthood during which close relationships develop (ch. 8, p. 335)

intoxication A state of drunkenness (ch. 7, p. 289)

intrinsic motivation Motivation by which people participate in an activity for their own enjoyment, not for the reward it will get them (ch. 6, p. 226)

introspection A method in which subjects are asked to describe in detail their thoughts and feelings (ch. 1, p. 12)

introversion-extroversion According to Eysenck, a dimension of personality traits encompassing the shyest to the most sociable people (ch. 9, p. 366)

iris The colored part of the eye (ch. 3, p. 87)

James-Lange theory of emotion The belief that emotional experience is a reaction to bodily events occurring as a result of an external situation ("I feel sad because I am crying") (ch. 6, p. 254)

just noticeable difference (See difference threshold) (ch. 3, p. 83)

Korsakoff's syndrome A disease among long-term alcoholics involving memory impairment (ch. 5, p. 195)

language The systematic arrangement of symbols to convey meaning (ch. 5, p. 211)

language-acquisition device A neural system of the brain hypothesized to permit understanding of language (ch. 5, p. 214)

lanugo A soft fuzz covering the body of a newborn (ch. 8, p. 309)

latency period According to Freud, the period, between the phallic stage and puberty, during which children's sexual concerns are temporarily put aside (ch. 9, p. 358)

latent content of dreams The "true" message hidden within a dream (ch. 7, p. 275, ch. 11, p. 453)

latent learning Learning in which a new behavior is acquired but not readily demonstrated until reinforcement is provided (ch. 4, p. 162)

lateral hypothalamus The part of the brain which, when damaged, results in an organism's starving to death (ch. 6, p. 230)

lateralization The dominance of one hemisphere of the brain in specific functions (ch. 2, p. 70)

law of effect Thorndike's theory that responses that satisfy are more likely to be repeated, and those that don't satisfy will be discontinued (ch. 4, p. 144)

learned helplessness An organism's learned belief that it has no control over the environment (ch. 4, p. 166)

learned-inattention theory (of schizophrenia) A theory that suggests that schizophrenia is a learned behavior consisting of a set of inappropriate responses to social stimuli (ch. 10, p. 440)

learning A relatively permanent change in behavior brought about by experience (ch. 4, p. 133)

least-restrictive environment The official phrase from PL94-142 that guarantees the right of full education for retarded people in an environment that is most similar to the educational environment of typical children (ch. 9, p. 395)

lens The part of the eye located behind the pupil that bends rays of light to focus them on the retina (ch. 3, p. 89)

levels-of-processing theory The theory which suggests that the way information is initially perceived and learned determines recall (ch. 5, p. 184)

light The stimulus that produces vision (ch. 3, p. 86)

light adaptation The eye's temporary insensitivity to light dimmer than that to which it has become accustomed (ch. 3, p. 93)

limbic system The part of the brain located outside the "new brain" that controls eating and reproduction (ch. 2, p. 62)

linear perspective The phenomenon by which distant objects appear to be closer together than nearer objects (ch. 3, p. 116)

linguistic code Memory storage relying on language (ch. 5, p. 183)

linguistic-relativity hypothesis The theory claiming that language shapes and may even determine the way people perceive and understand the world (ch. 5, p. 215)

lithium A drug used in the treatment of bipolar disorders (ch. 11, p. 474)

longitudinal research A research method which investigates behavior as subjects age (ch. 8, p. 302)

long-term memory The storage of information on a relatively permanent basis, although retrieval may be difficult (ch. 5, p. 176)

lysergic acid diethylamide (LSD) One of the most powerful hallucinogens, affecting the operation of neurotransmitters in the brain and causing brain cell activity to be altered (ch. 7, p. 293)

magnitude The strength of a stimulus (ch. 3, p. 80)

mainstreaming The integration of retarded people into regular classroom situations (ch. 9, p. 395)

major depression A severe form of depression that interferes with concentration, decision making, and sociability (ch. 10, p. 431)

mania An extended state of intense euphoria and elation (ch. 10, p. 432)

manifest content of dreams According to Freud, the surface description of dreams (ch. 7, p. 275, ch. 11, p. 452)

mantra A sound, word, or syllable repeated over and over to take one into a meditative state (ch. 7, p. 282)

marijuana A common hallucinogen, usually smoked (ch. 7, p. 292)

masturbation Sexual self-stimulation (ch. 6, p. 240)

maturation The unfolding of biologically predetermined patterns of behavior due to aging (ch. 4, p. 134, ch. 8, p. 300)

means-ends analysis Repeated testing to determine and reduce the distance between real and desired outcomes in problem solving (ch. 5, p. 201)

medical model of abnormality The model that suggests that when an individual displays symptoms of abnormal behavior, the cause is physiological (ch. 10, p. 412)

medical student's disease The feeling that symptoms and illnesses about which one studies are characteristic of oneself (ch. 10, p. 418)

meditation A learned technique for refocusing attention that brings about an altered state of consciousness (ch. 7, p. 281)

medulla The part of the central core of the brain that controls functions such as breathing and heartbeat (ch. 2, p. 58)

memory The capacity to record, retain, and retrieve information (ch. 5, p. 175)

memory trace A physical change in the brain corresponding to the memory of material (ch. 5, p. 192)

menopause The point at which women stop menstruating, generally at around age 45 (ch. 8, p. 338)

mental age The typical intelligence level found for people at a given chronological age (ch. 9, p. 385)

mental retardation A significantly subaverage level of intellectual functioning accompanying deficits in adaptive behavior (ch. 9, p. 393)

mental set The tendency for old patterns of problem solving to persist (ch. 5, p. 205)

metabolism Rate at which energy is produced and expended by the body (ch. 6, p. 239)

metacognition An awareness and understanding of one's own cognitive processes (ch. 8, p. 327)

methadone A chemical used to detoxify heroin addicts (ch. 7, p. 292)

middle ear A tiny chamber containing three bones—the hammer, the anvil, and the stirrup—which transmit vibrations to the oval window (ch. 3, p. 98)

midlife crisis The negative feelings that accompany the realization that we have not accomplished in life what we had hoped to (ch. 8, p. 339)

midlife transition Beginning around the age of 40, a period during which we come to the realization that life is finite (ch. 8, p. 339)

mild retardation Mental retardation charac-

terized by an IQ between 55 and 69 and the ability to function independently (ch. 9, p. 394)

Minnesota Multiphasic Personality Inventory (MMPI) A test used to identify people with psychological difficulties (ch. 9, p. 377)

mnemonics Formal techniques for organizing material to increase the likelihood of its being remembered (ch. 5, p. 181)

model A person serving as an example to an observer; if a model's behavior is rewarded, the observer may imitate that behavior (ch. 1, p. 11, ch. 4, p. 165)

modeling Imitating the behavior of others (models) (ch. 11, p. 457)

moderate retardation Mental retardation characterized by an IQ between 40 and 54 (ch. 9, p. 394)

monocular cues Signals that allow us to perceive distance and depth with just one eye (ch. 3, p. 116)

mood disorder Disturbance severe enough to interfere with normal living (ch. 10, p. 431)

Moro (startle) reflex The reflex action in which an infant, in response to a sudden noise, flings it arms, arches its back, and spreads its fingers (ch. 8, p. 309)

morphine Derived from the poppy flower, a powerful depressant that reduces pain and induces sleep (ch. 7, p. 291)

motion parallax The movement of the image of objects on the retina as the head moves, providing a monocular cue to distance (ch. 3, p. 116)

motivation The factors that direct and energize behavior (ch. 6, p. 220)

motives Desired goals that prompt behavior (ch. 6, p. 220)

motor area One of the major areas of the brain, responsible for voluntary movement of particular parts of the body (ch. 2, p. 66)

motor code Memory storage based on physical activities (ch. 5, p. 183)

motor (efferent) neurons Neurons that transmit information from nervous system to muscles and glands (ch. 2, p. 52)

Müller-Lyer illusion An illusion in which two lines of the same length appear to be of different lengths because of the direction of the arrows at the ends of each line; the line with arrows pointing out appears shorter than the line with arrows pointing in (ch. 3, p. 129)

multiple personality A disorder in which a person displays characteristics of two or more distinct personalities (ch. 10, p. 429)

myelin sheath An axon's protective coating, made of fat and protein (ch. 2, p. 44)

narcissistic personality disorder A personality disorder characterized by an exaggerated sense of self and an inability to experience empathy for others (ch. 10, p. 442)

narcolepsy An uncontrollable need to sleep for short periods during the day (ch. 7, p. 479)

naturalistic observation Observation without interference, in which the researcher records information about a naturally occurring situation in a way that does not influence the situation (ch. 1, p. 23)

nature-nurture question The issue of the degree to which environment and heredity influence behavior (ch. 8, p. 299)

need-complementarity hypothesis The hypothesis that people are attracted to others who fulfill their needs (ch. 13, p. 517)

need for achievement A stable, learned characteristic in which satisfaction comes from striving for and achieving a level of excellence (ch. 6, p. 245)

need for affiliation A need to establish and maintain relationships with other people (ch. 6, p. 298)

need for power A tendency to want to make an impression or have an impact on others in order to be seen as a powerful individual (ch. 6, p. 248)

negative reinforcer A stimulus whose removal is reinforcing, leading to a greater probability that the response bringing about this removal will occur again (ch. 4, p. 146)

neo-Freudian psychoanalysts Theorists who place greater emphasis than did Freud on the functions of the ego and its influence on our daily activities (ch. 9, p. 362)

neonate A newborn child (ch. 8, p. 309)

nervous system The brain and its pathways extending throughout the body (ch. 2, p. 40)

neurons The basic elements of the nervous system that carry messages (ch. 2, p. 92)

neuroscientists Individuals from diverse fields who study the nervous system (ch. 2, p. 40)

neurotic anxiety Anxiety caused when irrational impulses from the id threaten to become uncontrollable (ch. 9, p. 359)

neuroticism-stability Eysenck's personality spectrum encompassing people from the moodiest to the most even-tempered (ch. 9, p. 366)

neurotic symptoms According to Freud, abnormal behavior brought about by anxiety associated with unwanted conflicts and impulses (ch. 11, p. 451)

neurotransmitter A chemical, secreted when a nerve impulse comes to the end of an axon, that carries messages between neurons (ch. 2, p. 47)

neutral stimulus A stimulus that, before conditioning, has no effect on the desired response (ch. 4, p. 136)

nicotine A stimulant present in cigarettes (ch. 7, p. 286)

nightmares Unusually frightening dreams (ch. 7, p. 274)

night terrors Profoundly frightening nightmares which wake the dreamer (ch. 7, p. 274)

noise Background stimulation that interferes with the perception of other stimuli (ch. 3, p. 81)

nomothetic approaches to personality A study of personality accentuating the broad uniformities across behavior (ch. 9, p. 374)

nondirective counseling A therapeutic technique in which the therapist creates a warm, supportive environment to allow the client to better understand and work out his or her problems (ch. 11, p. 463)

norms (for tests) Standards of test performance (ch. 9, p. 379)

nuclear magnetic resonance (NMR) scan A scan produced by a magnetic field which shows brain structure in great detail (ch. 2, p. 56)

obedience A change in behavior due to the commands of others (ch. 12, p. 509)

obesity The state of being more than 20 percent above the average weight for a person of a particular height (ch. 6, p. 229)

object permanence The awareness that objects do not cease to exist if they are out of sight (ch. 8, p. 326)

observational learning Learning through observation of others (models) (ch. 4, p. 165, ch. 9, p. 370, ch. 11, p. 457)

obsession A thought or idea that keeps re-curring (ch. 10, p. 425)

obsessive-compulsive disorder A disorder characterized by obsessions or compul-sions (ch. 10, p. 425)

occipital lobes The structures of the brain lying behind the temporal lobes (ch. 2, p. 64)

Oedipal conflict A child's sexual interests in his or her opposite-sex parent, typically re-solved through identification with the same-sex parent (ch. 9, p. 358)

olfactory cells The receptor cells of the nose (ch. 3, p. 105)

operant The learning process involving one's operation of the environment (see operant conditioning) (ch. 4, p. 143)

operant conditioning Learning that occurs as a result of certain positive or negative con-sequences; the organism operates on its environment in order to produce a result (ch. 4, p. 193)

operationalization The process of translating a hypothesis into experimental procedures (ch. 1, p. 22)

opiate receptor A neuron that acts to reduce the experience of pain (ch. 2, p. 51)

opponent-process theory The theory that suggests that increases in arousal produce a calming reaction in the nervous system, and vice versa (ch. 6, p. 225)

opponent-process theory of color vision The theory that suggests that members of pairs of different receptor cells are linked to-gether to work in opposition to each other (ch. 3, p. 95)

optic chiasma A point between and behind the eyes at which nerve impulses from the optic nerves are reversed and "righted' in the brain (ch. 3, p. 91)

optic nerve A bundle of ganglion axons in the back of the eyeball that carry visual infor-mation to the brain (ch. 3, p. 91)

oral stage According to Freud, a stage from birth to 12–18 months, in which an infant's center of pleasure is the mouth (ch. 9, p. 357)

organic mental disorders Problems having a purely biological basis (ch. 10, p. 443)

otoliths Crystals in the semicircular canals that sense body acceleration (ch. 3, p. 102)

outer ear The visible part of the ear that acts as a sound collector (ch. 3, p. 98)

outgroups Groups to which an individual does not belong (ch. 12, p. 497)

oval window A thin membrane between the middle ear and the inner ear that transmits vibrations while increasing their strength (ch. 3, p. 98)

ovaries The female reproductive organs (ch. 6, p. 236)

overregularization Applying rules of speech in instances in which they are inappro-priate (ch. 5, p. 213)

ovulation The monthly release of an egg from an ovary (ch. 6, p. 236)

panic attack Sudden anxiety characterized by heart palpitations, shortness of breath, sweating, faintness, and great fear (ch. 10, p. 424)

panic disorder Anxiety that manifests itself in the form of panic attacks (ch. 10, p. 424)

paraplegia The inability, as a result of injury to the spinal cord, to move any muscles in the lower half of the body (ch. 2, p. 53)

parasympathetic division The part of the autonomic division of the peripheral nervous system that calms the body, bringing functions back to normal after an emergency has passed (ch. 2, p. 54)

parietal lobes The brain structure to the rear of the frontal lobes; the center for bodily sensations (ch. 2, p. 64)

partial reinforcement The reinforcing of a be-havior some, but not all of the time (ch. 4, p. 150)

passionate (or romantic) love A state of in-tense absorption in someone that is char-acterized by physiological arousal, psy-chological interest, and caring for another's needs (ch. 13, p. 520)

penis envy According to Freud, a girl's wish, developing around age 3, that she had a penis (ch. 9, p. 358)

perception The sorting out, interpretation, analysis, and integration of stimuli from our sensory organs (ch. 3, p. 78)

perceptual constancy The phenomenon by which physical objects are perceived as unvarying despite changes in their ap-pearance or the surrounding environment (ch. 3, p. 112)

peripheral nervous system All parts of the nervous system except the brain and the spinal cord (includes somatic and auto-nomic divisions) (ch. 2, p. 53)

peripheral route processing Message inter-pretation characterized by consideration of the source and related general information rather than of the message itself (ch. 12, p. 490)

peripheral vision The ability to see objects behind the eye's main center of focus (ch. 3, p. 89)

personality The sum total of characteristics that differentiate people, or the stability in a person's behavior across different situations (ch. 9, p. 352)

personality disorder A mental disorder characterized by a set of inflexible, maladaptive personality traits that keep a person from functioning properly in society (ch. 10, p. 441)

personality psychology The branch of psychology that studies consistency and change in people's behavior and the characteristics that differentiate people (ch. 1, p. 7)

personal stressors Major life events, such as the death of a family member, that have immediate negative consequences which generally fade with time (ch. 13, p. 540)

phallic stage According to Freud, a period beginning around age 3 during which a child's interest focuses on the genitals (ch. 9, p. 358)

phencyclidine (PCP) A powerful hallucinogen that alters brain-cell activity (ch. 7, p. 293)

phenylketonuria (PKU) The inability to produce an enzyme that resists certain poisons, causing profound mental retardation (ch. 8, p. 306)

pheromones Chemicals that produce a reaction in other members of a species (ch. 3, p. 104)

phobia Intense, irrational fear of specific objects or situations (ch. 10, p. 424)

phobic disorder Disorders characterized by unrealistic fears (phobias) that may keep people from carrying out routine daily behaviors (ch. 10, p. 424)

phonemes The smallest units of sound used to form words (ch. 5, p. 211)

phonology The study of the sounds we make when we speak and of how we use those sounds to produce meaning by forming them into words (ch. 5, p. 211)

pitch The "highs" and "lows" in sound (ch. 3, p. 100)

pituitary gland The "master gland," the major component of the endocrine system, which secretes hormones that control growth (ch. 2, p. 61)

placebo A biologically ineffective pill used in an experiment to keep subjects, and sometimes experimenters, from knowing whether or not the subjects have received a behavior-altering drug (ch. 1, p. 30)

place theory of hearing The theory that states that different frequencies are responded to by different areas of the basilar membrane (ch. 3, p. 101)

pleasure principle The principle by which the id operates, in which the person seeks the immediate reduction of tension and the maximization of satisfaction (ch. 9, p. 355)

Poggendorf illusion An illusion involving a line that passes diagonally through two parallel lines (ch. 3, p. 129)

Pollyanna effect The tendency to rate others in a generally positive manner (ch. 12, p. 501)

pons The part of the brain that joins the halves of the cerebellum, transmitting motor information to coordinate muscles and integrate movement between the right and left sides of the body (ch. 2, p. 58)

positive reinforcer A stimulus added to the environment that brings about an increase in the response that preceded it (ch. 4, p. 146)

positron emission tomography (PET) scan A scan technique which indicates how the brain is functioning at a given moment (ch. 2, p. 58)

posttraumatic stress syndrome A phenomenon in which victims of major catastrophes reexperience the original stress event and associated feelings in flashbacks or dreams (ch. 13, p. 540)

practical intelligence A person's style of thought and approach to problem solving, which may differ from traditional measures of intelligence (ch. 9, p. 392)

predisposition model (of schizophrenia) A model that suggests that individuals may inherit a predisposition toward schizophrenia that makes them particularly vulnerable to stressful factors in the environment (ch. 10, p. 440)

prefrontal lobotomy The surgical destruction of certain areas of a patient's frontal lobes to improve the control of emotionality (ch. 11, p. 477)

preoperational stage According to Piaget, the period from 2 to 7 years of age that is characterized by language development (ch. 8, p. 322)

primary drives Biological needs such as hunger, thirst, fatigue, and sex (ch. 6, p. 222)

primary reinforcer A reward that satisfies a biological need (e.g., hunger or thirst) and works naturally (ch. 4, p. 145)

principle of conservation The knowledge that quantity is unrelated to the arrangement and physical appearance of objects (ch. 8, p. 323)

proactive interference The phenomenon by which information stored in memory interferes with recall material learned later (ch. 5, p. 193)

problem-focused coping The management of a stressful stimulus as a way of dealing with stress (ch. 13, p. 543)

process schizophrenia One course of schizophrenia in which symptoms begin early in life and develop slowly and subtly (ch. 10, p. 437)

profound retardation Mental retardation characterized by an IQ below 25 and an inability to function independently (ch. 9, p. 394)

programmed instruction Development of learning by building gradually on basic knowledge, with review and reinforcement when appropriate (ch. 4, p. 159)

projection A defense mechanism in which people attribute their own inadequacies or faults to someone else (ch. 9, p. 360)

projective personality test An ambiguous stimulus presented to a person for the purpose of determining personality characteristics (ch. 9, p. 379)

prosocial behavior Helping behavior (ch. 13, p. 532)

proximity The tendency to group together those elements that are close together (ch. 3, p. 110, ch. 13, p. 516)

psychoactive drugs Drugs that influence a person's emotions, perceptions, and behavior (ch. 7, p. 285)

psychoactive substance-use disorder Disordered behavior involving drug abuse (ch. 10, p. 443)

psychoanalysis Psychodynamic therapy that involves frequent sessions and often lasts for many years (ch. 11, p. 451)

psychoanalyst Physician or psychologist who specializes in psychoanalysis (ch. 9, p. 353)

psychoanalytic model of abnormality The model that suggests that abnormality stems from childhood conflicts over opposing wishes (ch. 10, p. 412)

psychoanalytic theory Freud's theory that unconscious forces act as determinants of personality (ch. 9, p. 353)

psychodynamic model The psychological model based on the belief that behavior is brought about by unconscious inner forces over which an individual has little control (ch. 1, p. 15)

psychodynamic therapy Therapy based on the notion that the basic sources of abnormal behavior are unresolved past conflicts and anxiety (ch. 11, p. 451)

psychogenic amnesia A failure to remember past experience (ch. 10, p. 429)

psychogenic fugue An amnesiac condition in which a person takes sudden, impulsive trips, sometimes assuming a new identity (ch. 10, p. 403)

psychological tests Standard measures devised to objectively assess behavior (ch. 9, p. 375)

psychology The scientific study of behavior and mental processes (ch. 1, p. 2)

psychophysics The study of the relationship between the physical nature of stimuli and a person's sensory responses to them (ch. 3, p. 81)

psychosocial development Development of individuals' interactions and understanding of each other and of their knowledge and understanding of themselves as members of society (ch. 8, p. 317)

psychosomatic disorders Medical problems caused by an interaction of psychological, emotional, and physical difficulties (ch. 13, p. 536)

psychosurgery Brain surgery, once used to alleviate symptoms of mental disorder but rarely used today (ch. 11, p. 477)

psychotherapy The process in which a patient (client) and a professional attempt to remedy the client's psychological difficulties (ch. 11, p. 451)

puberty The period during which maturation of the sexual organs occurs (ch. 8, p. 330)

punishment An unpleasant or painful stimulus that is added to the environment after a certain behavior occurs, decreasing the likelihood that the behavior will occur again (ch. 4, p. 146)

pupil A dark hole in the center of the eye's iris which changes size as the amount of incoming light changes (ch. 3, p. 87)

random assignment to condition The assignment of subjects to given conditions on a chance basis alone (ch. 1, p. 27)

rapid eye movement (REM) sleep Sleep occupying around 20 percent of an adult's sleeping time, characterized by increased heart rate, blood pressure, and breathing rate; erections; eye movements; and the experience of dreaming (ch. 7, p. 272)

rational-emotive therapy Psychotherapy based on Ellis's suggestion that the goal of therapy should be to restructure one's beliefs into a more realistic, rational, and logical system (ch. 11, p. 454)

rationalization A defense mechanism whereby people justify a negative situation in a way that protects their self-esteem (ch. 9, p. 359)

reactive schizophrenia One course of schizophrenia in which the onset of symptoms is sudden and conspicuous (ch. 10, p. 437)

reality principle The principle by which the ego operates, in which instinctual energy is restrained in order to maintain an individual's safety and integration into society (ch. 9, p. 355)

rebound effect An increase in REM sleep after one has been deprived of it (ch. 7, p. 273)

recall drawing from memory a specific piece of information for a specific purpose (ch. 5, p. 186)

reciprocal concessions A phenomenon in which requesters are perceived as compromising their initial request, thereby inviting a compromise from the individual being asked to comply (ch. 12, p. 508)

reciprocity-of-liking effect The tendency to like those who like us (ch. 13, p. 517)

recognition Acknowledging prior exposure to a given stimulus, rather than recalling the information from memory (ch. 5, p. 186)

reflexes Unlearned, involuntary responses to certain stimuli (ch. 2, p. 52, ch. 8, p. 309)

regression Behavior reminiscent of an earlier stage of development, carried out in order to have fewer demands put upon oneself (ch. 9, p. 359)

rehearsal The transfer of material from short- to long-term memory via repetition (ch. 5, p. 180)

reinforcer Any stimulus that increases the probability that a preceding behavior will be repeated (ch. 4, p. 145)

relative refractory period The period during which a neuron, not yet having returned to its resting state, requires more than the normal stimulus to be set off (ch. 2, p. 45)

relative size The phenomenon by which, if two objects are the same size, the one that makes a smaller image on the retina is perceived to be farther away (ch. 3, p. 116)

reliability Consistency in the measurements made by a test (ch. 9, p. 376)

replication The repetition of an experiment in order to verify the results of the original experiment (ch. 1, p. 32)

representativeness heuristic A rule in which people and things are judged by the degree to which they represent a certain category (ch. 5, p. 201)

repression The primary defense mechanism, in which unacceptable or unpleasant id impulses are pushed back into the unconscious (ch. 9, p. 359)

research Systematic inquiry aimed at discovering knowledge (ch. 1, p. 22)

resistance An inability or unwillingness to discuss or reveal particular memories, thoughts, or motivations (ch. 11, p. 453)

resistance stage The second stage of Selye's general adaptation syndrome: coping with the stressor (ch. 13, p. 538)

resting state The nonfiring state of a neuron when the charge equals about -70 millivolts (ch. 2, p. 45)

reticular formation A group of nerve cells in the brain that arouses the body to prepare it for appropriate action and screens out background stimuli (ch. 2, p. 60)

retina The part of the eye that converts the electromagnetic energy of light into useful information for the brain (ch. 3, p. 89)

retrieval The process by which material in memory storage is located, brought into awareness, and used (ch. 5, p. 175)

retrieval cue A stimulus such as a word, smell, or sound that allows one to more easily recall information located in long-term memory (ch. 5, p. 186)

retroactive interference The phenomenon by which new information interferes with the recall of information learned earlier (ch. 5, p. 193)

retrograde amnesia Memory loss of occurrences prior to some event (ch. 5, p. 195)

reuptake The reabsorption of neurotransmitters by a terminal button (ch. 2, p. 49)

rewards-costs approach The notion that, in a

situation requiring help, a bystander's perceived rewards must outweigh the costs if helping is to occur (ch. 13, p. 533)

rhodopsin A complex reddish-purple substance that changes when energized by light, causing a chemical reaction (ch. 3, p. 91)

rods Long, cylindrical, light-sensitive receptors in the retina that perform well in poor light but are largely insensitive to color and small details (ch. 3, p. 89)

rooting reflex A neonate's tendency to turn its head toward things that touch its cheek (ch. 8, p. 309)

Rorschach test A test consisting of inkblots of indefinite shapes, the interpretation of which is used to assess personality characteristics (ch. 9, p. 379)

rubella German measles; when contracted by pregnant women, it can cause severe birth defects (ch. 8, p. 307)

Schachter-Singer theory of emotion The belief that emotions are determined jointly by a nonspecific kind of physiological arousal and its interpretation, based on environmental cues (ch. 6, p. 256)

schedules of reinforcement The frequency and timing of reinforcement following desired behavior (ch. 4, p. 150)

schemas Sets of cognitions about people and social experiences (ch. 5, p. 190, ch. 12, p. 495)

schizophrenia A class of disorders characterized by a severe distortion of reality, resulting in antisocial behavior, silly or obscene behavior, hallucinations, and disturbances in movement (ch. 10, p. 434)

school psychology Branch of psychology that considers the academic and emotional problems of elementary and secondary school students (ch. 1, p. 8)

secondary drives Drives in which no biological need is fulfilled (e.g., need for achievement) (ch. 6, p. 222)

secondary reinforcer A stimulus that becomes reinforcing by its association with a primary reinforcer (e.g., money, which allows us to obtain food, a primary reinforcer) (ch. 4, p. 146)

secondary traits Less important personality traits (e.g., preferences for certain clothes or movies) that do not affect behavior as much as central and cardinal traits do (ch. 9, p. 305)

selective exposure An attempt to minimize dissonance by exposing oneself only to information that supports one's choice (ch. 12, p. 493)

self-actualization In Maslow's theory, a state of self-fulfillment in which people realize their highest potential (ch. 6, p. 228, ch. 9, p. 373)

self-concept The impression one holds of oneself (ch. 9, p. 373)

self-fulfilling prophecy An expectation about the occurrence of an event or behavior that increases the likelihood that the event or behavior will happen (ch. 12, p. 497)

self-perception theory Bem's theory that people form attitudes by observing their own behavior and applying the same principles to themselves as they do to others (ch. 12, p. 494)

self-report measures A method of gathering data about people by asking them questions about a sample of their behavior (ch. 9, p. 377)

semantic memories Stored, organized facts about the world (e.g., mathematical and historical data) (ch. 5, p. 182)

semantics The rules governing the meaning of words and sentences (ch. 5, p. 212)

semicircular canals Part of the inner ear containing fluid that moves when the body moves to control balance (ch. 3, p. 102)

senility A broad, imprecise term used in reference to elderly people who experience progressive deterioration of mental abilities, including memory loss, confusion of time and place, and general disorientation (ch. 8, p. 345)

sensation The process by which an organism responds to a stimulus (ch. 3, p. 78)

sensorimotor stage According to Piaget, the stage from birth to 2 years during which a child has little competence in representing the environment using images, language, or other symbols (ch. 8, p. 322)

sensory area The site in the brain of the tissue that corresponds to each of the senses, the degree of sensitivity relating to amount of tissue (ch. 2, p. 66)

sensory memory The initial, short-lived storage of information recorded as a meaningless stimulus (ch. 5, p. 176)

sensory (afferent) neurons Neurons that transmit information from the body to the nervous system (ch. 2, p. 52)

serial reproduction The passage of interpretive information from person to person, often resulting in inaccuracy through personal bias and misinterpretation (ch. 5, p. 190)

severe retardation Mental retardation characterized by an IQ between 25 and 39 and difficulty in functioning independently (ch. 9, p. 394)

sexual disorders A form of abnormal behavior in which one's sexual activity is unsatisfactory (ch. 10, p. 493)

shadowing A technique used during dichotic listening in which a subject is asked to repeat one of the messages aloud as it comes into one ear (ch. 3, p. 120)

shaping The process of teaching a complex behavior by rewarding closer and closer approximations of the desired behavior (ch. 4, p. 158)

short-term memory The storage of information for fifteen to twenty-five seconds (ch. 5, p. 176)

sickle-cell anemia A disease of the blood that affects about 10 percent of America's black population (ch. 8, p. 306)

signal detection theory The theory that addresses the questions of whether a person can detect a stimulus and whether a stimulus is actually present at all (ch. 3, p. 82)

similarity The tendency to group together those elements that are similar in appearance (ch. 3, p. 111)

simplicity The tendency to perceive a pattern in the most basic, straightforward, organized manner possible—the overriding gestalt principle (ch. 3, p. 111)

situational causes of behavior Causes of behavior that are based on environmental factors (ch. 12, p. 498)

skin senses The senses that include touch, pressure, temperature, and pain (ch. 3, p. 106)

sleep apnea A sleep disorder characterized by difficulty in breathing and sleeping simultaneously (ch. 7, p. 278)

social cognition The processes that underlie our understanding of the social world (ch. 12, p. 495)

social influence The area of social psychology concerned with situations in which the actions of an individual or group affect the behavior of others (ch. 12, p. 485)

social learning theory The theory that suggests that personality develops through observational learning (ch. 9, p. 370)

social phase The third phase in the decline of a relationship in which there is public acknowledgment that the relationship is being dissolved, and others are given an account of events that led to the relationship's termination (ch. 13, p. 524)

social psychology The branch of psychology that studies how people's thoughts, feelings, and actions are affected by others (ch. 1, p. 9, ch. 12, p. 484)

social supporter A person who shares an unpopular opinion or attitude of another group member, thereby encouraging nonconformity (ch. 12, p. 506)

sociocultural model of abnormality The model that suggests that people's behavior, both normal and abnormal, is shaped by family, society, and cultural influences (ch. 10, p. 416)

somatic division The part of the nervous system that controls voluntary movements of the skeletal muscles (ch. 2, p. 53)

somatoform disorder Psychological difficulties that take on a physical (somatic) form (ch. 10, p. 427)

somatosensory area The area within the cortex corresponding to the sense of touch (ch. 2, p. 66)

sound The movement of air molecules brought about by the vibration of an object (ch. 3, p. 98)

source traits The sixteen basic dimensions of personality that Cattell identified as the root of all behavior (ch. 9, p. 365)

spinal cord A bundle of nerves running along the spine, carrying messages between the brain and the body (ch. 2, p. 52)

spontaneous recovery The reappearance of a previously extinguished response after a period of time during which the conditioned stimulus has been absent (ch. 4, p. 140)

spontaneous remission Recovery without treatment (ch. 11, p. 468)

stage 1 sleep The state of transition between wakefulness and sleep (ch. 7, p. 271)

stage 2 sleep A sleep deeper than that of stage 1, characterized by sleep spindles (ch. 7, p. 271)

stage 3 sleep Sleep characterized by slow brain waves, with greater peaks and valleys in the wave pattern (ch. 7, p. 271)

stage 4 sleep The deepest stage of sleep, during which we are least responsive to outside stimulation (ch. 7, p. 272)

Stanford-Binet test A test of intelligence that includes a series of items varying in nature according to the age of the person being tested (ch. 9, p. 386)

status The evaluation by others of the roles we play in society (ch. 12, p. 506)

stereotype A kind of schema in which beliefs and expectations about members of a group are held simply on the basis of their membership in that group (ch. 12, p. 497)

stimulants Drugs that affect the central nervous system, causing increased heart rate, blood pressure, and muscle tension (ch. 7, p. 286)

stimulus A source of physical energy that activates a sense organ (ch. 3, p. 80)

stimulus control training Training in which an organism is reinforced in the presence of a certain specific stimulus, but not in its absence (ch. 4, p. 154)

stimulus discrimination The process by which an organism learns to differentiate among stimuli, restricting its response to one in particular (ch. 4, p. 141)

stimulus generalization Response to a stimulus similar to but different from a conditioned stimulus; the more similar the two stimuli, the more likely generalization is to occur (ch. 4, p. 140)

stirrup A tiny bone in the middle of the ear that transfers vibrations to the oval window (ch. 3, p. 98)

storage The location in the memory system in which material is saved (ch. 5, p. 175)

stress The response to events that are threatening or challenging (ch. 13, p. 535)

stressors Circumstances that produce threats to our well-being (ch. 13, p. 535)

Stroop task An exercise requiring the division of our attention between two competing stimuli—the meaning of words and the colors in which they are written (ch. 3, p. 120)

structuralism An early approach to psychology which focused on the fundamental elements underlying thoughts and ideas (ch. 1, p. 21)

structure-of-intellect model A model of intelligence based on performance along three different dimensions: task content, task requirements, and product (ch. 9, p. 390)

subject A participant in research (ch. 1, p. 26)

subject expectations A subject's interpretation of what behaviors or responses are expected in an experiment (ch. 1, p. 30)

sublimation A defense mechanism, considered healthy by Freud, in which a person diverts unwanted impulses into socially acceptable thoughts, feelings, or behaviors (ch. 9, p. 320)

sucking reflex A reflex that prompts an infant to suck at things that touch its lips (ch. 8, p. 309)

sudden infant death syndrome A disorder in which seemingly healthy infants die in their sleep (ch. 7, p. 279)

superego The part of personality that represents the morality of society as presented by parents, teachers, and others (ch. 9, p. 356)

superstitious behavior The mistaken belief that particular ideas, objects, or behavior will cause certain events to occur, learning based on the coincidental association between the idea, object, or behavior and subsequent reinforcement (ch. 4, p. 155)

surface traits According to Cattell, clusters of a person's related behavior that can be observed in a given situation (ch. 9, p. 365)

survey research Sampling a group of people by assessing their behavior, thoughts, or attitudes, then generalizing the findings to a larger population (ch. 1, p. 24)

sympathetic division The part of the autonomic division of the peripheral nervous system that prepares the body to respond in stressful emergency situations (ch. 2, p. 54)

synapse The gap between neurons through which chemical messages are communicated (ch. 2, p. 47)

syntax The rules that indicate how words are joined to form sentences (ch. 5, p. 211)

systematic desensitization A procedure in which a stimulus that evokes pleasant feelings is repeatedly paired with a stimulus that evokes anxiety in the hope that the anxiety will be alleviated (ch. 4, p. 139, ch. 11, p. 456)

taste buds The location of the receptor cells of the tongue (ch. 3, p. 105)

Tay-Sachs disease A genetic defect preventing the body from breaking down fat and typically causing death by the age of 3 or 4 (ch. 8, p. 306)

telegraphic speech Sentences containing

only the most essential words (ch. 5, p. 213)

temporal lobes The portion of the brain located beneath the frontal and parietal lobes (ch. 2, p. 64)

terminal buttons Small branches at the end of an axon that relay messages to other cells (ch. 2, p. 44)

testes The male reproductive organs responsible for secreting androgens (ch. 6, p. 236)

thalamus The part of the brain's central core that transmits messages from the sense organs to the cerebral cortex and from the cerebral cortex to the cerebellum and medulla (ch. 2, p. 60)

Thematic Apperception Test (TAT) A test consisting of a series of ambiguous pictures about which a person is asked to write a story, which is then taken to be a reflection of the writer's personality (ch. 6, p. 296, ch. 9, p. 381)

theories Broad explanations and predictions concerning phenomena of interest (ch. 1, p. 21)

tip-of-the-tongue phenomenon The inability to recall information that one realizes one knows (ch. 5, p. 185)

token system A procedure whereby a person is rewarded for performing certain desired behaviors (ch. 11, p. 458)

top-down processing Perception guided by knowledge, experience, expectations, and motivations (ch. 3, p. 118)

traits Enduring dimensions of personality characteristics differentiating people from one another (ch. 9, p. 364)

trait theory A model that seeks to identify the basic traits necessary to describe personality (ch. 9, p. 364)

transcutaneous electrical nerve stimulation (TENS) A method of providing relief from pain by passing a low-voltage electric current through parts of the body (ch. 3, p. 108)

transference A patient's transferal of certain strong feelings for others to the analyst (ch. 11, p. 453)

transformation problems Problems to be solved using a series of methods to change an initial state into a goal state (ch. 5, p. 198)

treatment The manipulation implemented by the experimenter to influence results in a segment of the experimental population (ch. 1, p. 26)

treatment group The experimental group re-

ceiving the treatment, or manipulation (ch. 1, p. 26)

triarchic theory of intelligence A theory suggesting three major aspects of intelligence: componential, experiential, and contextual (ch. 9, p. 392)

trichromatic theory of color vision The theory that suggests that the retina has three kinds of cones, each responding to a specific range of wavelengths, perception of color being influenced by the relative strength with which each is activated (ch. 3, p. 94)

trust-versus-mistrust stage According to Erikson, the first stage of psychosocial development, occurring from birth to 18 months of age, during which time infants develop feelings of trust or lack of trust (ch. 8, p. 318)

tunnel vision An advanced stage of glaucoma in which vision is reduced to the narrow circle directly in front of the eye (ch. 3, p. 93)

unconditional positive regard Supportive behavior from another individual, regardless of one's words or actions (ch. 9, p. 373, ch. 11, p. 463)

unconditioned response (UCR) A response that is natural and needs no training (e.g., salivation at the smell of food) (ch. 4, p. 136)

unconditioned stimulus (UCS) A stimulus that brings about a response without having been learned (ch. 4, p. 136)

unconscious A part of the personality of which a person is unaware and which is a potential determinant of behavior (ch. 9, p. 354)

unconscious inference theory A theory stating that unconscious inferences about an object's location are made on the basis of prior experience with the object's size (ch. 3, p. 114)

universal grammar An underlying structure shared by all languages, the basis of Chomsky's theory that certain language characteristics are based in the brain's structure and are, therefore, common to all people (ch. 5, p. 219)

uplifts Minor positive events that make one feel good (ch. 13, p. 541)

validity The ability of a test to measure what it is supposed to measure (ch. 9, p. 376)

variable A behavior or event that can be changed (ch. 1, p. 25)

variable-interval schedule A schedule whereby reinforcement is given at various times, usually causing a behavior to be maintained more consistently (ch. 4, p. 153)

variable-ratio schedule A schedule whereby reinforcement occurs after a varying number of responses rather than after a fixed number (ch. 4, p. 152)

ventromedial hypothalamus The part of the brain which, when injured, results in extreme overeating (ch. 6, p. 230)

vernix A white lubricant that covers a fetus, protecting it during birth (ch. 8, p. 309)

vicarious learning Learning by observing others (ch. 12, p. 488)

visceral experience The "gut" reaction experienced internally, triggering an emotion (see James-Lange theory of emotion) (ch. 6, p. 254)

visual illusion A physical stimulus that consistently produces errors in perception (often called an optical illusion) (ch. 3, p. 122)

visual spectrum The range of wavelengths to which humans are sensitive (ch. 3, p. 87)

von Restorff effect The phenomenon by which distinctive stimuli are recalled more readily than less distinctive ones (ch. 5, p. 189)

wear-and-tear theories of aging Theories that suggest that the body's mechanical functions cease efficient activity and, in effect, wear out (ch. 8, p. 343)

Weber's law The principle that states that the just noticeable difference is a constant proportion of the magnitude of an initial stimulus (ch. 3, p. 84)

Wechsler Adult Intelligence Scale—Revised (WAIS-R) A test of intelligence consisting of verbal and nonverbal performance sections, providing a relatively precise picture of a person's specific abilities (ch. 9, p. 387)

Wechsler Intelligence Scale for Children—Revised (WISC-R) An intelligence test for children; see Wechsler Adult Intelligence Scale—Revised (ch. 9, p. 387)

weight set point The particular level of weight the body strives to maintain (ch. 6, p. 231)

Wernicke's aphasia A syndrome involving problems with understanding language, resulting in fluent but nonsensical speech (ch. 2, p. 69)

Yerkes-Dodson law The theory that a particular level of motivational arousal produces optimal performance of a task (ch. 6, p. 224)

zygote The one-celled product of fertilization (ch. 8, p. 303)

References

❖

Abella, R., & Heslin, R. (1989). Appraisal processes, coping and the regulation of stress-related emotions in a college examination. *Basic and Applied Social Psychology*, *10*, 311–328.

Abrahamson, L. Y., Garber, J., & Seligman, M. E. P. (1980). Learned helplessness in humans: An attributional analysis. In J. Garber and M. E. P. Seligman (Eds.), *Human helplessness: Theory and applications.* New York: Academic Press.

Adelmann, P. K., & Zajonc, R. B. (1989). Facial efference and the experience of emotion. *Annual Review of Psychology*, *40*, 249–280.

Adler, J. (1984, April 23). The fight to conquer fear. *Newsweek*, pp. 66–72.

Adler, J. (1985, March 25). A teen-pregnancy epidemic. *Newsweek*, p. 90.

Adler, J. (1985, September 23). The AIDS conflict. *Newsweek*, pp. 18–24.

Ainsworth, M. D. S. (1989). Attachments beyond infancy. *American Psychologist*, *44*, 709–716.

Ajzen, I. (1988). *Attitudes, personality, and behavior.* Stratford, England: Open University Press.

Akmajian, A., Demers, R. A., & Harnish, R. M. (1984). *Linguistics.* Cambridge, MA: MIT Press.

Albee, G. W. (1978, February 12). I.Q. tests on trial. *New York Times*, p. E-13.

Aldwin, C. M., & Revenson, T. A. (1987). Does coping help? A reexamination of the relation between coping and mental health. *Journal of Personality and Social Psychology*, *53*, 337–348.

Alexander, C. N., Langer, E. J., Newman, R. I., Chandler, H. M., & Davies, J. L. (1989). Transcendental meditation, mindfulness, and longevity: An experimental study with the elderly. *Journal of Personality and Social Psychology*, *57*, 950–964.

Allen, M. (1988, January 25). When jurors are ordered to ignore testimony, they ignore the order. *Wall Street Journal*, p. 33.

Allen, V. L. (1965). Situational factors in conformity. In L. Berkowitz (Ed.), *Advances in experimental social psychology*, Vol. 1. New York: Academic Press.

Allen, V. L. (1975). Social support for nonconformity. In L. Berkowitz (Ed.), *Advances in experimental and social psychology* (Vol. 8). New York: Academic Press.

Allport, G. W., & Postman, L. J. (1958). The basic psychology of rumor. In E. D. Maccoby, T. M. Newcomb, & E. L. Hartley (Eds.), *Readings in social psychology* (3rd ed.). New York: Holt, Rinehart and Winston.

Alsop, R. (1988, May 13). Advertisers put consumers on the couch. *Wall Street Journal*, p. 21.

Altman, I. (1987). Community psychology twenty years later: Still another crisis in psychology? *American Journal of Community Psychology*, *15*, 613–627.

Altshuler, L. L., Conrad, A., Kovelman, J. A., & Scheibel, A. (1987). Hippocampal pyramidal cell orientation in schizophrenia. *Archives of General Psychiatry*, *44*, 1094–1096.

Alwitt, L., & Mitchell, A. A. (1985). *Psychological processes and advertising effects: Theory, research, and applications.* Hillsdale, NJ: Erlbaum.

American Psychological Association. (1980). *Careers in psychology.* Washington, DC: American Psychological Association.

American Psychological Association (1988). *Behavioral research with animals.* Washington, DC: American Psychological Association.

American Psychological Association. (1990). *Ethical standards of psychologists.* Washington, DC: American Psychological Association.

Amsel, A. (1988). *Behaviorism, neobehaviorism, and cognitivism in learning theory.* Hillsdale, NJ: Erlbaum.

Anastasi, A. (1988). *Psychological testing* (6th ed.). New York: Macmillan.

Andersen, S. M., & Cole, S. W. (1990). "Do I know you?": The role of significant others in general social perception. *Journal of Personality and Social Psychology, 59,* 384–399.

Anderson, E. (1987). Preoperative preparation for cardiac surgery facilitates recovery, reduces psychological distress, and reduces the incidence of acute postoperative hypertension. *Journal of Consulting and Clinical Psychology, 55,* 513–520.

Anderson, J. R., & Bower, G. H. (1972). Recognition and retrieval processes in free recall. *Psychological Review, 79,* 97–123.

Anderson, N. H. (1974). Cognitive algebra integration theory applied to social attribution. In L. Berkowitz (Ed.), *Advances in experimental social psychology* (Vol. 7, pp. 1–101). New York: Academic Press.

Andreasen, N. C. (1985). Positive vs. negative schizophrenia: A critical evaluation. *Schizophrenia, 11,* 380–389.

Angleitner, A., & Wiggins, J. S. (Eds.) (1986). *Personality assessment via questionnaires: Current issues in theory and measurement.* Berlin: Springer-Verlag.

Angoff, W. H. (1988). The nature-nurture debate, aptitudes, and group differences. *American Psychologist, 43,* 713–720.

Annett, M. (1985). *Left, right, hand, and brain: The right shift theory.* Hillsdale, NJ: Erlbaum.

Appleyard, D. (1976). *Planning a pluralistic city.* Cambridge, MA: MIT Press.

Apter, A., Galatzer, A., Beth-Halachmi, N., & Laron, Z. (1981). Self-image in adolescents with delayed puberty and growth retardation. *Journal of Youth and Adolescence, 10,* 501–505.

Arafat, I., & Cotton, W. L. (1974). Masturbation practices of males and females. *Journal of Sex Research, 10,* 293–307.

Archibald, W. P. (1974). Alternative explanations for the self-fulfilling prophecy. *Psychological Bulletin, 81,* 74–84.

Arena, J. M. (1984, April). A look at the opposite sex. *Newsweek on Campus,* p. 21.

Aronoff, J., Barclay, A. M., & Stevenson, L. A. (1988). The recognition of threatening facial stimuli. *Journal of Personality and Social Psychology, 54,* 647–655.

Aronson, E. (1988). *The Social Animal* (3rd ed.). San Francisco: Freeman.

Aronson, E. (1990, April). Dissonance theory. Presidential address at the meeting of the Western Psychological Society. Los Angeles, CA.

Asch, S. E. (1946). Forming impressions of personality. *Journal of Abnormal and Social Psychology, 41,* 258–290.

Asch, S. E. (1951). Effects of group pressure upon the modification and distortion of judgments. In H. Guetzkow (Ed.), *Groups, leadership, and men.* Pittsburgh: Carnegie Press.

Aslin, R. N. (1987). Visual and auditory development in infancy. In J. Osofsky (Ed.), *Handbook of infant development* (2nd ed.). New York: Wiley.

Aslin, R. N., & Smith, L. B. (1988). Perceptual development. *Annual Review of Psychology, 39,* 435–473.

Asnis, G., & Ryan, N. D. (1983). The psychoneuroendocrinology of schizophrenia. In A. Rifkin (Ed.), *Schizophrenia and effective disorders: Biology and drug treatment* (pp. 205–236). Boston: John Wright.

Astington, J. W., Harris, P. L., & Olson, D. R. (1988). Developing theories of mind. Cambridge, England: Cambridge University Press.

Atkinson, J. W., & Feather, N. T. (1966). *Theory of achievement motivation.* New York: Krieger.

Atkinson, J. W., & Raynor, J. O. (Eds.) (1974). *Motivation and achievement.* Washington, DC: Winston.

Atkinson, R. C., & Shiffrin, R. M. (1968). Human memory: A proposed system and its control processes. In K. W. Spence and J. T. Spence (Eds.), *The psychology of learning and motivation: Advances in research and theory* (Vol. 2, pp. 80–195). New York: Academic Press.

Atwater, E. (1983). *Adolescence.* Englewood Cliffs, NJ: Prentice-Hall.

Azrin, N. H., & Holt, N. C. (1966). Punishment. In W. A. Honig (Ed.), *Operant behavior: Areas of research and application* (pp. 380–447). New York: Appleton.

Bach-Y-Rita, P. (1982). Sensory substitution in rehabilitation. In L. Illis, M. Sedwick, & H. Granville (Eds.), *Rehabilitation of the neurological patient* (pp. 361–382). Oxford, England: Blackwell Press.

Backer, T. E., Batchelor, W. F., Jones, J. M., & Mays, V. M. (1988). Introduction to the special issue: Psychology and AIDS. *American Psychologist, 43,* 835–836.

Baddeley, A. (1982). *Your memory: A user's guide.* New York: Macmillan.

Baddeley, A., & Wilson, B. (1985). Phonological coding and short-term memory in patients without speech. *Journal of Memory and Language, 24,* 490–502.

Bahill, T. A., & Laritz, T. (1984). Why can't batters keep their eyes on the ball? *American Scientist, 72,* 249–253.

Baker, J. N. (1987, July 27). Battling the IQ-test ban. *Newsweek,* p. 53.

Baker, R. (Ed.) (1989). *Panic disorder: Theory, research and therapy.* New York: Wiley.

Ballinger, C. B. (1981). The menopause and its syndromes. In J. G. Howells (Ed.), *Modern perspectives in the psychiatry of middle age* (pp. 279–303). New York: Brunner/Mazel.

Baltes, P. B., & Schaie, K. W. (1974, March). The myth of the twilight years. *Psychology Today,* pp. 35–38ff.

Bandura, A. (1973). *Aggression: A social learning analysis.* Englewood Cliffs, NJ: Prentice-Hall.

Bandura, A. (1977). *Social learning theory.* Englewood Cliffs, NJ: Prentice-Hall.

Bandura, A. (1981). In search of pure unidirectional determinants. *Behavior Therapy, 12,* 30–40.

Bandura, A., Grusec, J. E., & Menlove, F. L. (1967). Vicarious extinction of avoidance behavior. *Journal of Personality and Social Psychology, 5,* 16–23.

Bandura, A., Ross, D., & Ross, S. (1963). Imitation of film-mediated aggressive models. *Journal of Abnormal and Social Psychology, 66,* 3–11. (a)

Bandura, A., Ross, D., & Ross, S. (1963). Vicarious reinforcement and imitative learning. *Journal of Abnormal and Social Psychology, 67,* 601–607. (b)

Barbanel, J. (1988, February 15). Joyce Brown's ascent from anonymity. *New York Times,* pp. B-1, B-4.

Barber, T. X. (1975). Responding to "hypnotic" suggestions: An introspective report. *American Journal of Clinical Hypnosis, 18,* 6–22.

Barker, L. M., Best, M. E., & Domjan, M. (Eds.) (1977). *Learning mechanisms in food selection.* Waco, TX: Baylor University Press.

Barlow, D. H. (1988). *Anxiety and its disorders: The nature and treatment of anxiety and panic.* New York: Guilford.

Barnes, D. M. (1988). The biological tangle of drug addiction. *Science, 24,* 415–417.

Barnes, G. G. (1990). Making family therapy work: Research findings and family therapy practice. *Journal of Family Therapy, 12,* 17–30.

Baron, J. B., & Sternberg, R. J. (1986). *Teaching thinking skills.* New York: Freeman.

Baron, R. A., & Byrne, D. (1987). *Social psychology: Understanding human interaction* (5th ed.). Boston: Allyn & Bacon.

Baron, R. A., & Kepner, C. R. (1970). Model's behavior and attraction toward the model as determinants of adult aggressive behavior. *Journal of Personality and Social Psychology, 14,* 335–344.

Barron, F. (1969). *Creative person and creative process.* New York: Holt.

Barron, F., & Harrington, D. M. (1981). Creativity, intelligence, and personality. *Annual Review of Psychology, 32,* 439–476.

Bartlett, F. (1932). *Remembering: A study in experimental and social psychology.* Cambridge, England: Cambridge University Press.

Bartoshuk, L. M. (1971). The chemical senses: I. Taste. In J. N. Kling & L. A. Riggs (Eds.), *Experimental psychology* (3rd ed.). New York: Holt, Rinehart and Winston.

Bateson, G. (1960). Minimal requirements for a theory of schizophrenia. *Archives of General Psychiatry, 2,* 477–491.

Batson, C. D. (1990). How social an animal? The human capacity for caring. *American Psychologists, 45,* 336–346.

Baum, A., Gatchel, R. J., & Schaeffer, M. A. (1983). Emotional, behavioral, and physiological effects of chronic stress at Three Mile Island. *Journal of Consulting and Clinical Psychology, 51,* 565–572.

Bauman, L. J., & Siegel, K. (1987). Misperception among gay men of the risk for AIDS associated with their sexual behavior. *Journal of Applied Social Psychology, 17,* 329–350.

Baumgardner, A. H., Heppner, P. P., & Arkin, R. M. (1986). Role of causal attribution in personal problem solving. *Journal of Personality and Social Psychology, 50,* 636–643.

Beaman, A. L., Cole, C. M., Preston, M., Klentz, B., & Steblay, N. M. (1983). Fifteen years of foot-in-the-door research: A meta-analysis. *Personality and Social Psychology Bulletin, 9*, 181–196.

Beaton, A. (1986). *Left side, right side: A review of laterality research*. New Haven: Yale University Press.

Beck, A. T. (1985). Cognitive therapy of depression: New perspectives. In P. J. Clayton & J. E. Barret (Eds.), *Treatment of depression: Old controversies and new approaches* (pp. 265–290). New York: Raven Press.

Beck, J., Hope, B., & Rosenfeld, A. (Eds.) (1983). *Human and machine vision*. New York: Academic Press.

Bee, H. L. (1985). *The developing child* (4th ed.). New York: Harper & Row.

Bell, A., & Weinberg, M. S. (1978). *Homosexuality: A study of diversities among men and women*. New York: Simon & Schuster.

Bell, S. M., & Ainsworth, M. D. S. (1972). Infant crying and maternal responsiveness. *Child Development, 43*, pp. 1171–1190.

Bellack, A. S., Hersen, M., & Kazdin, A. E. (Eds.) (1990). *International handbook of behavior modification and therapy*. New York: Plenum.

Belsky, J., & Rovine, M. (1988). Nonmaternal care in the first year of life and infant-parent attachment security. *Child Development, 59*, 157–167.

Bem, D. J. (1967). Self-perception: An alternative interpretation of cognitive dissonance phenomena. *Psychological Review, 74*, 183–200.

Bem, D. (1972). Self-perception theory. In L. Berkowitz (Ed.), *Advances in experimental social psychology* (Vol. 6, pp. 1–62). New York: Academic Press.

Benjamin, L. T., Jr. (1988). A history of teaching machines. *American Psychologist, 43*, 703–712.

Bennett, W., & Gurin, J. (1982). *The dieter's dilemma: Eating less and weighing more*. New York: Basic Books.

Benson, H. (1975). *The relaxation response*. New York: Morrow.

Benson, H., & Friedman, R. (1985). A rebuttal to the conclusions of Davis S. Holme's article, "Meditation and somatic arousal reduction." *American Psychologist*, 725–726.

Benson, H., Kotch, J. B., Crassweller, K. D., & Greenwood, M. (1977). Historical and clinical considerations of the relaxation response. *American Scientist, 65*, 441–445.

Bergener, M., Ermini, M., & Stahelin, H. B. (Eds.). (1985, February). *Thresholds in aging*. The 1984 Sandoz Lectures in Gerontology (Basel, Switzerland).

Berger, J. (1988, March 16). Teachers of the gifted fight accusations of elitism. *New York Times*, p. 36.

Bergin, A. E., & Lambert, M. J. (1978). The evaluation of therapeutic outcomes. *Handbook of psychotherapy and behavior change: An empirical analysis* (2nd ed.). New York: Wiley.

Berkowitz, L. (1974). Some determinants of impulsive aggression: The role of mediated associations with reinforcements for aggression. *Psychological Review, 81*, 165–176.

Berkowitz, L. (1984). Aversive conditioning as stimuli to aggression. In R. J. Blanchard & C. Blanchard (Eds.), *Advances in the study of aggression* (Vol. 1). New York: Academic Press.

Berkowitz, L. (1989). Frustration-aggression hypothesis: Examination and reformulation. *Psychological Bulletin, 106*, 59–73.

Berkowitz, L. (1990). On the formation and regulation of anger and aggression: A cognitive-neoassociationistic analysis. *American Psychologist, 45*, 494–503.

Berkowitz, L., & Geen, R. G. (1966). Film violence and the cue properties of available targets. *Journal of Personality and Social Psychology, 3*, 525–530.

Berkowitz, L., & LePage, A. (1967). Weapons as aggression-eliciting stimuli. *Journal of Personality and Social Psychology, 7*, 202–207.

Berlyne, D. (1967). Arousal and reinforcement. In D. Levine (Ed.), *Nebraska symposium on motivation*. Lincoln: University of Nebraska Press.

Berman, J. S., Miller, R. C., & Massman, P. J. (1985). Cognitive therapy versus systematic desensitization: Is one treatment superior? *Psychological Bulletin, 97*, 451–461.

Bernard, M. E., & DiGiuseppe, R. (Eds.) (1989). *Inside rational-emotive therapy: A critical appraisal of the theory and therapy of Albert Ellis*. San Diego, CA: Academic Press.

Berscheid, E. (1985). Interpersonal attraction. In G. Lindzey & E. Aronson (Eds.), *Handbook of social psychology* (3rd ed.). New York: Random House.

Berscheid, E., Snyder, M., & Omoto, A. M. (1989). The relationship closeness inventory: Assessing the closeness of interpersonal relationships. *Journal of Personality and Social Psychology, 57,* 792–807.

Berscheid, E., & Walster, E. (1974). Physical attractiveness. In L. Berkowitz (Ed.), *Advances in experimental social psychology* (Vol. 7, pp. 157–215). New York: Academic Press.

Best, C. T. (Ed.) (1985). *Hemispheric function and collaboration in the child.* New York: Academic Press.

Bieber, I., et al. (1962). *Homosexuality: A psychoanalytic study.* New York: Basic Books.

Binet, A., & Simon, T. (1916). *The development of intelligence in children* (The Binet-Simon Scale). Baltimore, MD: Williams & Wilkins.

Bini, L. (1938). Experimental research on epileptic attacks induced by the electric current. *American Journal of Psychiatry,* Supplement 94, 172–183.

Birch, H. G. (1945). The role of motivation factors in insightful problem solving. *Journal of Comparative Psychology, 38,* 295–317.

Bishop, J. E. (1988, March 2). Memory on trial: Witnesses of crimes are being challenged as frequently fallible. *Wall Street Journal,* pp. 1, 18.

Bjorklund, D. F. (1985). The role of conceptual knowledge in the development of organization in children's memory. In C. J. Brainerd & M. Pressley (Eds.), *Basic process in memory development.* New York: Springer-Verlag.

Bjorklund, D. F. (1989). *Children's thinking: Developmental function and individual differences.* Pacific Groves, CA: Brooks/Cole.

Blakeslee, S. (1984, August 14). Scientists find key biological causes of alcoholism. *New York Times,* p. C-1.

Blank, J. P. (1983, October). "I can see feeling good." *Readers Digest, 123,* 98–104.

Blatt, S. J., D'Afflitti, J. P., & Quinlan, D. M. (1976). Experiences of depression in normal young adults. *Journal of Abnormal Psychology, 85,* 383–389.

Blumstein, P. W., & Schwartz, P. (1983). *American couples.* New York: Morrow.

Blusztajn, J. K., & Wurtman, R. J. (1983). Choline and cholinergic neurons. *Science, 221,* 614–620.

Boakes, R. A., Popplewell, D. A., & Burton, M. J. (Eds.) (1987). *Eating habits: Food, physiology, and learned behaviour.* New York: Wiley.

Bolger, N., DeLongis, A., Kessler, R. C., & Schilling, E. A. (1989). Effects of daily stress on negative mood. *Journal of Personality and Social Psychology, 57,* 808–818.

Bolles, R. C., & Fanselow, M. S. (1982). Endorphins and behavior. *Annual Review of Psychology, 33,* 87–101.

Borland, J. H. (1989). *Planning and implementing programs for the gifted.* New York: Teachers College Press.

Bornstein, M. H. (1984). Perceptual development. In M. H. Bornstein & M. E. Lamb (Eds.), *Developmental psychology: An advanced textbook.* Hillsdale, NJ: Erlbaum.

Bornstein, M. H. (1987). *Sensitive periods in development: Interdisciplinary perspectives.* Hillsdale, NJ: Erlbaum.

Bornstein, M. H. (1989). Sensitive periods in development: Structural characteristics and causal interpretations. Psychological Bulletin, *105,* 179–197.

Bornstein, M. H., & Bruner, J. S. (Eds.) (1989). *Interaction in human development.* Hillsdale, NJ: Erlbaum.

Bornstein, M. H., & Sigman, M. D. (1986). Continuity in mental development from infancy. *Child Development, 57,* 251–274.

Bornstein, R. F. (1989). Exposure and affect: Overview and meta-analysis of research, 1968–1987. *Psychological Bulletin, 106,* 265–289.

Botstein, D. (1986, April 11). The molecular biology of color vision. *Science, 232,* 142–143.

Bouchard, T. J., Jr., Lykken, D. T., McGue, M., Segal, N. L., & Tellegen, A. (1990, October 12). *Science, 250,* 223–228.

Bourne, L. E., Dominowski, R. L., Loftus, E. F., & Healy, A. F. (1986). *Cognitive processes* (2nd ed.). Englewood Cliffs, NJ: Prentice-Hall.

Bower, T. G. (1989). The perceptual world of the newborn child. In A. M. Slater & J. Gavin Bremner (Eds.), *Infant development.* Hillsdale, NJ: Erlbaum.

Bowers, T. G., & Clum, G. A. (1988). Relative contribution of specific and nonspecific treatment effects: Meta-analysis of placebo-controlled behavior therapy research. *Psychological Bulletin, 103,* 315–323.

Boyd, J. H., & Weissman, M. M. (1981). Epidemiology of affective disorders: A re-examination and future directions. *Archives of General Psychiatry, 38,* pp. 1039–1045.

Boynton, R. M. (1988). Color vision. *Annual Review of Psychology, 39,* 69–100.

Braun, B. (1985, May 21). Interview by D. Goleman: New focus on multiple personality. *New York Times,* p. C-1.

Brazelton, T. B. (1969). *Infants and mothers: Differences in development.* New York: Dell.

Breggin, P. R. (1979). *Electroshock: Its brain-disabling effects.* New York: Springer-Verlag.

Brehm, J. W., & Self, E. A. (1989). The intensity of motivation. *Annual Review of Psychology, 40,* 109–131.

Breland, K., & Breland, M. (1961). Misbehavior of organisms. *American Psychologist, 16,* 681–684.

Brewer, W. F., & Dupree, D. A. (1983). Use of plan schemata in the recall and recognition of goal-directed actions. *Journal of Experimental Psychology: Learning, Memory, and Cognition, 9,* 117–129.

Brody, J. (1982). *New York Times guide to personal health.* New York: Times Books.

Brody, J. E. (1987, May 5). Talking to the baby: Some expert advice. *New York Times,* p. C-11. (a)

Brody, J. E. (1987, March 24). Research lifts blame from many of the obese. *New York Times,* pp. C-1, C-6. (b)

Bronson, G. W. (1990). Changes in infants' visual scanning across the 2- to 14-week period. *Journal of Experimental Child Psychology, 49,* 101–125.

Brown, B. (1984). *Between health and illness.* Boston: Houghton Mifflin.

Brown, J. D., & McGill, K. L. (1989). The cost of good fortune: When positive life events produce negative health consequences. *Journal of Personality and Social Psychology, 57,* 1103–1110.

Brown, P. K., & Wald, G. (1964). Visual pigments in single rod and cones of the human retina. *Science, 144,* pp. 45–52.

Brown, R. (1958). How shall a thing be called? *Psychological Review, 65,* 14–21.

Brown, R. (1986). *Social psychology.* New York: Macmillan.

Brown, R., & Kulik, J. (1977). Flashbulb memories. *Cognition, 5,* 73–99.

Bruce, V., & Green, P. R. (1990). *Visual perception: Physiology, psychology and ecology.* (2nd ed.) Hillsdale, NJ: Erlbaum.

Brumberg, J. J. (1988). *Fasting girls: The emergence of anorexia nervosa as a modern disease.* Cambridge, MA: Harvard University Press.

Buckhout, R. (1975). Eyewitness testimony. *Scientific American,* pp. 23–31.

Budiansky, S. (1987, June 29). Taking the pain out of pain. *U.S. News and World Report,* pp. 50–57.

Burbules, N. C., & Linn, M. C. (1988). Response to contradiction: Scientific reasoning during adolescence. *Journal of Educational Psychology, 80,* 67–75.

Burnham, D. K. (1983). Apparent relative size in the judgment of apparent distance. *Perception, 12,* 683–700.

Burns, H. L., Parlett, J. W., & Luckhardt-Redfield, C. (1990). *Intelligent tutoring systems: Evolutions in design.* Hillsdale, NJ: Erlbaum.

Buss, A. H. (1989). Personality as traits. *American Psychologist, 44,* 1378–1388.

Butcher, J. N. (1990). *The MMPI-2 in psychological treatment.* New York: Oxford University Press.

Butler, R. A. (1954). Incentive conditions which influence visual exploration. *Journal of Experimental Psychology, 48,* 19–23.

Butterworth, G., & Bryant, P. (Eds.) (1990). *Causes of development: Interdisciplinary perspectives.* Hillsdale, NJ: Erlbaum.

Byrne, D. (1969). Attitudes and attraction. In L. Berkowitz (Ed.), *Advances in experimental social psychology* (Vol. 4, pp. 35–89). New York: Academic Press.

Cacioppo, J. T., & Petty, R. E. (1979). Attitudes and cognitive response: An electrophysiological approach. *Journal of Personality and Social Psychology, 37,* 2181–2199.

Cairns, H. S., & Cairns, C. E. (1976). *Psycholinguistics: A cognitive view of language.* New York: Holt, Rinehart and Winston.

Candee, D., & Kohlberg, L. (1987). Moral judgment and moral action: A reanalysis of Haan, Smith, and Block's (1968) free-speech data. *Journal of Personality and Social Psychology, 52,* 554–564.

Cannon, W. B. (1929). Organization for physiological homeostatics. *Physiological Review, 9,* 280–289.

Carlson, M., Charlin, V., & Miller, N. (1988). Positive mood and helping behavior: A test of six hypotheses. *Journal of Personality and Social Psychology, 55,* 211–229.

Carlson, M., Marcus-Newall, A., & Miller, N. (1990). Effects of situational aggression cues: A quantitative review. *Journal of Personality and Social Psychology, 58,* 622–633.

Caroll, J. B. (1982). The measurement of intelligence. In R. J. Sternberg (Ed.), *The handbook of human intelligence* (pp. 29–120). Cambridge, MA: Cambridge University Press.

Carson, R. C. (1983). The schizophrenias. In H. E. Adams & P. B. Sutker (Eds.), *Handbook of clinical behavior therapy.* New York: Plenum Press.

Carson, R. C., Butcher, J. N., & Coleman, J. C. (1988). *Abnormal psychology and modern life* (8th ed.). Glenview, IL: Scott, Foresman.

Cartwright, R. D. (1978). *A primer on sleep and dreaming.* Reading, MA: Addison-Wesley.

Cartwright, R. D., Lloyd, S., Knight, S., & Trenholme, I. (1984). Broken dreams: A study of the effects of divorce and depression on dream content. *Psychiatry, 47,* 251–259.

Case, R. (1985). *Intellectual development: Birth to adulthood.* New York: Academic Press.

Casey, K. L., & Morrow, T. J. (1983). Ventral posterior thalamic neurons differentially responsive to noxious stimulation of the awake monkey. *Science, 223,* 675–677.

Casselden, P. A., & Hampson, S. E. (1990). Forming impressions from incongruent traits. *Journal of Personality and Social Psychology, 59,* 353–362.

Catalano, E. M., & Johnson, K. (Eds.) (1987). *A patient's guide to the management of chronic pain.* Oakland, CA: New Harbinger.

Cataldo, C. Z. (1987). *Parent education for early childhood.* New York: Columbia University Press.

Cattell, R. B. (1965). *The scientific analysis of personality.* Baltimore: Penguin.

Cattell, R. B. (1967). *The scientific analysis of personality.* Baltimore: Penguin.

Cattell, R. B. (1987). *Intelligence: Its structure, growth, and action.* Amsterdam: North-Holland.

Ceci, S. J., Peters, D., & Plotkin, J. (1985). Human subjects review: Personal values and the regulation of social science research. *American Psychologist, 40,* 994–1002.

Cerella, J. (1985). Information-processing rates in the elderly. *Psychological Bulletin, 98,* 67–83.

Chaiken, S. (1979). Communicator physical attractiveness and persuasion. *Journal of Personality and Social Psychology, 37,* 1387–1397.

Chambers, M. (1985, June 29). Torres is guilty in the slaying of actress. *New York Times,* p. 29.

Chandler, M. J. (1976). Social cognition and life-span approaches to the study of child development. In H. W. Reese & L. P. Lipsitt (Eds.), *Advances in child development and behavior* (Vol. 11), New York: Academic Press.

Chapman, L. J., & Chapman, J. P. (1973). *Disordered thought in schizophrenia.* New York: Appleton-Century Crofts.

Charlier, M. (1988, February 24). Fasting plans are fast becoming a popular way to combat obesity. *Wall Street Journal,* p. 28.

Chase, M. H., & Morales, F. R. (1990). The atonia and myoclonia of active (REM) sleep. *Annual Review of Psychology, 41,* 557–584.

Chavez, C. J., Ostrea, E. M., Stryker, J. C., & Smialek, Z. (1979). Sudden infant death syndrome among infants of drug-dependent mothers. *Journal of Pediatrics, 95,* 407–409.

Cheng, P. W., & Novick, L. R. (1990). A probabilistic contrast model of causal induction. *Journal of Personality and Social Psychology, 58,* 545–567.

Cherry, E. C. (1953). Some experiments on the recognition of speech with one and two ears. *Journal of the Acoustical Society of America, 25,* 975–979.

Chomsky, N. (1968). *Language and mind.* New York: Harcourt Brace Jovanovich.

Chomsky, N. (1969). *The acquisition of syntax in children from five to ten.* Cambridge, MA: MIT Press.

Chomsky, N. (1978). On the biological basis of language capacities. In G. A. Miller & E. Lennenberg (Eds.), *Psychology and biology of language and thought* (pp. 199–220). New York: Academic Press.

Christensen, L. (1988). Deception in psychological research: When is its use justified? *Personality and Social Psychology Bulletin, 14,* 664–675.

Chwalisz, K., Diener, E., & Gallagher, D. (1988). Autonomic arousal feedback and emotional experience: Evidence from the spinal-cord injured. *Journal of Personality and Social Psychology, 54,* 820–828.

Cialdini, R. B. (1984). *Social influence.* New York: William Morrow.

Cialdini, R. B. (1988). *Influence: Science and practice* (2nd ed.). Glenview, IL: Scott, Foresman.

Cialdini, R. B., Schaller, M., Houlihan, D., Arps, K., Fultz, J., & Beaman, A. L. (1987). Empathy-based helping: Is it selflessly or selfishly motivated? *Journal of Personality and Social Psychology, 52,* 749–758.

Cialdini, R. B., Vincent, J. E., Lewis, S. K., Catalan, J., Wheeler, D., & Darby, B. L. (1975). Reciprocal concessions procedure for inducing compliance: The door-in-the-face technique. *Journal of Personality and Social Psychology, 31,* 206–215.

Clark, L. A., & Watson, D. (1988). Mood and the mundane: Relations between daily life events and self-reported mood. *Journal of Personality and Social Psychology, 54,* 296–308.

Clark, M. (1987, November 9). Sweet music for the deaf. *Newsweek,* 73.

Clark, M. S., & Reis, H. T. (1988). Interpersonal processes in close relationships. *Annual Review of Psychology, 39,* 609–672.

Clarke-Stewart, A. (1984). Day care: A new context for research and development. In M. Perlmutter (Ed.), *The Minnesota Symposia on Child Psychology: Vol. 27. Parent-child interaction and parent-child relations in child development.* Hillsdale, NJ: Erlbaum.

Clarke-Stewart, A., & Friedman, S. (1987). *Child development: Infancy through adolescence.* New York: Wiley.

Clarke-Stewart, K. A. (1989). Infant day care: Maligned or malignant? *American Psychologist, 44,* 266–273.

Cohen, D. B. (1979). *Sleep and dreaming: Origins, nature, and functioning.* New York: Pergamon.

Cohen, T. E., & Lasley, D. J. (1986). Visual sensitivity. In Rosenweig & Porter (Eds.), *Annual Review of Psychology, 37.* Palo Alto, CA: Annual Reviews.

Colby, A., & Damon, W. (1987). Listening to a different voice: A review of Gilligan's *In a different voice.* In M. R. Walsh (Ed.), *The Psychology of Women.* New Haven, CT: Yale University Press.

Coleman, J. C., Butcher, J. N., & Carson, R. C. (1984). *Abnormal psychology and modern life.* Glenview, IL: Scott, Foresman.

Collins, W. A., & Gunnar, M. (1990). Social and personality development. *Annual Review of Psychology, 41,* 387–416.

Commons, M. L., Nevin, J. A., & Davison, M. C. (Eds.) (19XX). *Signal detection: Mechanism, models and applications.* Hillsdale, NJ: Erlbaum.

Compas, B. E. (1987). Coping with stress during childhood and adolescence. *Psychological Bulletin, 101,* 393–403.

Condon, J. W., & Crano, W. D. (1988). Inferred evaluation and the relation between attitude similarity and interpersonal attraction. *Journal of Personality and Social Psychology, 54,* 789–797.

Converse, J., Jr., & Cooper, J. (1979). The importance of decisions and free-choice attitude change: A curvilinear finding. *Journal of Experimental Social Psychology, 15,* 48–61.

Cooper, A. M., Kernberg, O. F., & Person, E. S. (1990). New Haven, CT: Yale University Press.

Cooper, J. D., Heron, T. E., & Heward, W. L. (1987). *Applied behavior analysis.* Columbus, OH: Merrill.

Cooper, W. H. (1981). Ubiquitous halo. *Psychological Bulletin, 90,* 218–244.

Coppen, A., Metcalfe, M., & Wood, K. (1982). Lithium. In E. S. Paykel (Ed.), *Handbook of affective disorders.* New York: Guilford Press.

Corballis, M. C., & Beale, I. L. (1983). *The ambivalent mind: The neuro-psychology of left and right.* Chicago: Nelson-Hall.

Coren, S., & Aks, D. J. (1990). Moon illusion in pictures: A multimechanism approach. *Journal of Experimental Psychology, 16,* 365–380.

Coren, S., & Ward, L. M. (1989). *Sensation and perception.* (3rd ed.). San Diego: Harcourt Brace Jovanovich.

Cornelius, S. W., & Caspi, A. (1987). Everyday problem solving in adulthood and old age. *Psychology and Aging, 2,* 144–153.

Costa, P. T., Jr., & McCrae, R. R. (1985). Hypochondriasis, neuroticism, and aging. *American Psychologist, 40,* 19–28.

Council of Scientific Affairs (1985, April 5). Scientific status of refreshing recollection by the use of hypnosis. *Journal of the American Medical Association, 253*(13).

Covington, M. V., & Omelich, C. L. (1987). "I knew it cold before the exam": A test of the anxiety-blockage hypothesis. *Journal of Educational Psychology, 79,* 393–400.

Craik, F. I. M. (1977). Age differences in human memory. In J. E. Birren & K. W. Schaie (Eds.). *Handbook of the psychology of aging.* New York: Van Nostrand Reinhold.

Craik, F. I., & Lockhart, R. S. (1972). Levels of processing: A framework for memory research. *Journal of Verbal Behavior, 11,* 671–684.

Cramer, P. (1987). The development of defense mechanisms. *Journal of Personality, 55,* 597–614.

Crandall, C. S. (1988). Social contagion of binge eating. *Journal of Personality and Social Psychology, 55,* 588–598.

Crapo, L. (1985). Hormones: Messengers of life.

Crocetti, G. (1983). *GRE: Graduate record examination general aptitude test.* New York: Arco.

Crocker, J., & Luhtanen, R. (1990). Collective self-esteem and ingroup bias. *Journal of Personality and Social Psychology, 58,* 60–67.

Crowley, G. (1990, June 25). AIDS: The next ten years. *Newsweek,* 20–27.

Croyle, R. T., & Cooper, J. (1983). Dissonance arousal: Physiological evidence. *Journal of Personality and Social Psychology, 45,* 782–791.

Cummings, J. (1987, October 6). An earthquake aftershock: Calls to mental health triple. *New York Times,* p. A-1.

Cusack, O. (1984, April). Pigeon posses. *Omni,* p. 34.

Cutler, B. L., & Penrod, S. D. (1988). Improving the reliability of eyewitness identification: Lineup construction and presentation. *Journal of Applied Psychology, 73,* 281–290.

Daehler, M., & Bukato, D. (1985). *Cognitive development.* New York: Random House.

daGloria, J., Duda, D., Pahlavan, F., & Bonnet, P. (1989). ''Weapons effect'' revisited: Motor effects of the reception of aversive stimulation and exposure to pictures of firearms. *Aggressive Behavior, 15,* 265–272.

Darley, J. M., & Shultz, T. R. (1990). Moral judgments: Their content and acquisition. *Annual Review of Psychology, 41,* 525–556.

Darwin, C. J., Turvey, M. T., & Crowder, R. G. (1972). An auditory analogue of the Sperling partial-report procedure: Evidence for brief auditory storage. *Cognitive Psychology, 3,* 255–267.

Davis, R. (1986). Assessing the eating disorders. *The Clinical Psychologist, 39,* 33–36.

Dawes, R. M., Faust, D., & Meehl, P. E. (1989, March 31). Clinical versus actuarial judgment. *Science, 243,* 1668–1674.

DeCasper, A. J., & Fifer, W. D. (1980). Of human bonding: Newborns prefer their mothers' voices. *Science, 208,* 1174–1176.

DeCharms, R., & Moeller, G. H. (1962). Values expressed in American children's readers, 1800–1950. *Journal of Abnormal and Social Psychology, 64,* 136–142.

Deci, E. L., & Ryan, R. M. (1985). *Intrinsic motivation and self-determination in human behavior.* New York: Plenum Press.

deGroot, A. D. (1966). Perception and memory versus thought: Some old ideas and recent findings. In B. Kleinmuntz (Ed.), *Problem solving: Research, method, and theory.* New York: Wiley.

DeLeon, P. H. (1988). Public policy and public service: Our professional duty. *American Psychologist, 43,* 309–315.

DeLongis, A., Folkman, S., & Lazarus, R. S. (1988). The impact of daily stress on health and mood: Psychological social resources as mediators. *Journal of Personality and Social Psychology, 54,* 486–495.

deLuce, J., & Wilder, H. T. (1983). *Language in primates: Perspectives and implications.* New York: Springer-Verlag.

Dement, W. C. (1976). *Some must watch while some must sleep.* New York: Norton.

Dement, W. C. (1979). Two kinds of sleep. In D. Goleman & R. J. Davidson (Eds.), *Consciousness: Brain, states of awareness, and mysticism* (pp. 72–75). New York: Harper & Row.

Dement, W. C., & Wolpert, E. A. (1958). The relation of eye movements, body mobility, and external stimuli to dream content. *Journal of Experimental Psychology, 55,* 543–553.

Dent, J. (1984, March). *Readers Digest, 124,* 38.

Dentzer, S. (1986, May 5). Can you pass the job test? *Newsweek,* pp. 46–53.

DePaulo, B. M., Kenny, D. A., Hoover, C. W., Webb, W., & Oliver, P. V. (1987). Accuracy of person perception: Do people know what kinds of impressions they convey? *Journal of Personality and Social Psychology, 52,* 303–315.

Deregowski, J. B. (1973). Illusion and culture. In R. L. Gregory & G. H. Combrich (Eds.), *Illusion in nature and art* (pp. 161–192). New York: Scribner.

Deyo, R. A., Straube, K. T., & Disterhoft,

J. F. (1989, February 10). Nimodipine facilitates associative learning in aging rabbits. *Science, 243,* 809–811.

Dion, K. K., & Berscheid, E. (1974). Physical attractiveness and peer perception among children. *Sociometry, 37,* 1–12.

Dohrenwend, B. S., Dohrenwend, B. P., Dodson, M., & Shrout, P. E. (1984). Symptoms, hassles, social supports, and life events: The problem of confounded measures. *Journal of Abnormal Psychology, 93,* 222–230.

Dolce, J. J., & Raczynski, J. M. (1985). Neuromuscular activity and electromyography in painful backs: Psychological and biomechanical models in assessment and treatment. *Psychological Bulletin, 97,* 502–520.

Dollard, J., Doob, L., Miller, N., Mower, O. H., & Sears, R. R. (1939). *Frustration and aggression.* New Haven, CT: Yale University Press.

Dollard, J., & Miller, N. E. (1950). *Personality and psychotherapy: An analysis in terms of learning, thinking and culture.* New York: McGraw-Hill.

Donnerstein, E., & Berkowitz, L. (1981). Victim reactions in aggressive erotic films as a factor in violence against women. *Journal of Personality and Social Psychology, 41,* 710–724.

Donnerstein, E., Linz, D., & Penrod, S. (1987). *The question of pornography: Research findings and policy implications.* New York: Free Press.

Doob, A. N., & Wood, L. (1972). Catharsis and aggression: The effects of annoyance and retaliation on aggressive behavior. *Journal of Personality and Social Psychology, 22,* 156–162.

Dore, F. Y., & Dumas, C. (1987). Psychology of animal cognition: Piagetian studies. *Psychological Bulletin, 102,* 219–233.

Doty, R. L. (1986). Development and age-related changes in human olfactory function. In W. Breipohl & R. Apfelbach (Eds.), *Ontogeny of olfaction in vertebrates.* Berlin: Springer-Verlag.

Dovidio, J. F., Allen, J. L., & Schroeder, D. A. (1990). Specificity of empathy-induced helping: Evidence for altruistic motivation. *Journal of Personality and Social Psychology, 59,* 249–260.

Dreyer, P. H. (1982). Sexuality during adolescence. In B. B. Wolman (Ed.), *Handbook of developmental psychology.* Englewood Cliffs, NJ: Prentice-Hall.

Drum, D. J. (1990). Group therapy review. *The Counseling Psychologist, 18,* 131–140.

Duck, S. W. (Ed.) (1982). *Personal relationships: Vol. 4. Dissolving personal relationships.* New York: Academic Press.

Duck, S. W. (Ed.) (1990). *Personal relationships and social support.* Newbury Park, CA: Sage.

Duke, M., & Nowicki, S., Jr. (1979). *Abnormal psychology: Perspectives on being different.* Monterey, CA: Brooks/Cole.

Duncker, K. (1945). On problem solving. *Psychological Monographs, 58,* (5, whole no. 270).

Dutton, D. G., & Aron, A. P. (1974). Some evidence for heightened sexual attraction under conditions of high anxiety. *Journal of Personality and Social Psychology, 30,* 510–517.

Dworkin, R. H., & Widom, C. S. (1977). Undergraduate MMPI profiles and the longitudinal prediction of adult social outcome. *Journal of Consulting and Clinical Psychology, 45,* 620–625.

Dykman, B. M., & Abramson, L. Y. (1990). Contributions of basic research to the cognitive theories of depression. *Personality and Social Psychology Bulletin, 16,* 42–57.

Dywan, J., & Bowers, K. (1983). The use of hypnosis to enhance recall. *Science, 222,* 184–185.

Eagly, A. (1987). *Sex differences in social behavior: A social-role interpretation.* Hillsdale, NJ: Erlbaum.

Eagly, A. (1989, May). Meta-analysis of sex differences. Annual conference on adversity. University of Massachusetts, Amherst, Massachusetts.

Eagly, A. H. (1978). Sex differences in influenceability. *Psychological Bulletin, 85,* 86–116.

Eagly, A. H. (1983). Gender and social influence: A social psychological analysis. *American Psychologist, 38,* 971–981.

Eagly, A. H., & Carlie, L. L. (1981). Sex of researchers and sex-typed communications as determinants of sex differences in influenceability: A meta-analysis of social influence studies. *Psychological Bulletin, 90,* 1–20.

Eagly, A. H., Wood, W., & Chaiken, S. (1978). Causal inferences about communicators and their effect on opinion change. *Journal of Personality and Social Psychology, 36,* 424–435.

Ebbesen, E. B., Duncan, B., & Konečni, V. J. (1975). Effects of content of verbal aggression on future verbal aggression: A field experiment. *Journal of Experimental Social Psychology, 11,* 192–204.

Ebbinghaus, H. (1885/1913). *Memory: A contribution to experimental psychology.* (H. A. Roger & C. E. Bussenius, Trans.) New York: Columbia University Press.

Eberts, R., & MacMillan, A. C. (1985). Misperception of small cars. In R. Eberts & C. Eberts (Eds.), *Trends in ergonomics/human factors, III.* Amsterdam: Elsevier.

Eckenrode, J. (1984). Impact of chronic and acute stressors on daily reports of mood. *Journal of Personality and Social Psychology, 46,* 907–918.

Eckholm, E. (1988, April 17). Exploring the forces of sleep. *New York Times Magazine,* pp. 26–34.

Egan, D. E., & Schwartz, B. J. (1979). Chunking in recall of symbolic drawings. *Memory and Cognition, 7,* 149–158.

Egeland, J. A., Gerhard, D. S., Pauls, D. L., Sussex, J. N., Kidd, K. K., Allen, C. R., Hostetter, A. M., & Housman, D. E. (1987). Bipolar effective disorders linked to DNA markers on chromosome 11. *Nature, 325,* 783–787.

Eisenberg, N., & Miller, P. A. (1987). The relation of empathy to prosocial and related behaviors. *Psychological Bulletin, 101,* 91–119.

Eisenberg-Berg, N., & Mussen, P. (1978). Empathy and moral development in adolescence. *Developmental Psychology, 14,* 185–186.

Ekman, P. (1972). Universals and cultural differences in facial expressions of emotion. In J. Cole (Ed.), *Darwin and facial expression: A century of research in review* (pp. 169–222). New York: Academic Press.

Ekman, P., Friesen, W. V., & Ellsworth, P. (1982). *Emotion in the human face.* Elmsford, NY: Pergamon Press.

Ekman, P., Friesen, W. V., O'Sullivan, M., Chan, A., Diacoyanni-Tarlatzis, I., Heider, K., Krause, R., LeCompte, W. A., Pitcairn, T., Ricci-Bitti, P. E., Scherer, K., Tomita, M., & Tzavaras, A. (1987). Universals and cultural differences in the judgments of facial expressions of emo-

tion. *Journal of Personality and Social Psychology, 53,* 712–717.

Ekman, P., Levenson, R. W., & Friesen, W. V. (1983, September 16). Autonomic nervous system activity distinguishes among emotions. *Science, 223,* 1208–1210.

Elkin, I. (1986, May). *NIMH treatment of depression: Collaborative research program.* Paper presented at the annual meeting of the American Psychiatric Association (Washington, DC).

Elkin, I., et al. (1989). National Institute of Mental Health treatment of depression collaborative research program: General effectiveness of treatments. *Archives of General Psychiatry, 46,* 971–982.

Elkind, D. (1981). *The hurried child.* Reading, MA: Addison-Wesley.

Ellis, A. (1962). *Reason and emotion in psychotherapy.* New York: Lyle Stuart.

Ellis, A. (1975). Creative job and happiness: The humanistic way. *The Humanist, 35* (1), 11–13.

Ellis, A., & Dryden, W. (1987). *The practice of rational-emotive therapy (RET).* New York: Springer.

Ellis, A., Sichel, J. L., Yeager, R. J., DiMattia, D. J., & DiGiuseppe, R. (1989). *Rational-emotive couples therapy.* New York: Pergamon.

Engen, T. (1982). *Perception of odors.* New York: Academic Press.

Engen, T. (1987, September–October). Remembering odors and their names. *American Scientist, 75,* 497–503.

Epstein, R. (1987). The spontaneous interconnection of four repertoires of behavior in a pigeon. *Journal of Comparative Psychology, 101,* 197–201.

Epstein, R., Kirshnit, C. E., Lanza, R. P., & Rubin, L. C. (1984). Insight in the pigeon: Antecedents and determinants of intelligent performance. *Nature, 308,* 61–62.

Epstein, S. (1990). Cognitive-experiential self-theory. In L. A. Pervin (Ed.), *Handbook of personality theory and research.* New York: Guilford.

Epstein, S., & Meier, P. (1989). Constructive thinking: A broad coping variable with specific components. *Journal of Personality and Social Psychology, 57,* 332–350.

Epstein, S., & O'Brien, E. J. (1985). The person-situation debate in historical and current perspective. *Psychological Bulletin, 98,* 513–537.

Erikson, E. H. (1963). *Childhood and society* (2nd ed.). New York: Norton.

Erickson, M. H., Hershman, S., & Secter, I. I. (1990). *The practical application of medical and dental hypnosis.* New York: Brunner/Mazel.

Eron, L. D. (1982). Parent-child interaction, television violence, and aggression of children. *American Psychologist, 37,* 197–211.

Eron, L. D., & Huesmann, L. R. (1985). The control of aggressive behavior by changes in attitude, values, and the conditions of learning. In R. J. Blanchard and C. Blanchard (Eds.), *Advances in the study of aggression.* New York: Academic Press.

Eron, L. D., Huesmann, L. R., Lefkowitz, M. M., & Walden, L. O. (1972). Does television cause aggression? *American Psychologist, 27,* 253–263.

Evans, C. (1984). *Landscapes of the night: How and why we dream.* New York: Viking Press.

Everly, Jr., G. S. (1989). *A clinical guide to the treatment of the human stress response.* New York: Plenum.

Eysenck, H. J. (1973). *Eysenck on extraversion.* New York: Wiley.

Eysenck, H. J., & Eysenck, M. W. (1985). *Personality and individual differences: A natural science approach.* New York: Plenum.

Eysenck, H. J., & Eysenck, S. B. G. (1975). *Manual of the Eysenck personality questionnaire.* San Diego, CA: Educational and Industrial Testing Service.

Fabricius, W. V., Schwanenflugel, P. J., Kyllonen, P. C., Barclay, C. R., & Denton, S. M. (1989). Developing theories of the mind: Children's and adults' concepts of mental activities. *Child Development, 60,* 1278–1290.

Fanelli, R. J., Burright, R. G., & Donovick, P. J. (1983). A multivariate approach to the analysis of genetic and septal lesion effects on maze performance in mice. *Behavioral Neuroscience, 97,* 354–369.

Farone, S. V., & Tsuang, M. T. (1985) Quantitative models of the genetic transmission of schizophrenia. *Psychological Bulletin, 98,* 41–66.

Fay, R. E., Turner, C. F., Klassen, A. D., & Gagnon, J. H. (1989). Prevalence and patterns of same-gender sexual contact among men. *Science, 243,* 338–348.

Feldman, R. S., & Rimé, B. (Eds.) (1991). *Fundamentals of nonverbal behavior.* Cambridge, England: Cambridge University Press.

Feldman, R. S., & Schwartzberg, S. (1990). *Critical thinking: A psychology student's guide to evaluating research and theory.* New York: McGraw-Hill.

Festinger, L. (1957). *A theory of cognitive dissonance.* Stanford, CA: Stanford University Press.

Festinger, L., & Carlsmith, J. M. (1959). Cognitive consequences of forced compliance. *Journal of Abnormal and Social Psychology, 58,* 203–210.

Festinger, L., Schachter, S., & Back, K. W. (1950). *Social pressure in informal groups.* New York: Harper.

Feynman, R. P. (1988, February). An outsider's view of the *Challenger* inquiry. *Physics Today,* pp. 26–37.

Fichter, M. M. (Ed.) (1990). *Bulimia nervosa: Basic research, diagnosis and therapy.* New York: Wiley.

Field, T. (1982). Individual differences in the expressivity of neonates and young infants. In R. S. Feldman (Ed.), *Development of nonverbal behavior in children.* New York: Springer-Verlag.

Fieve, R. R. (1975). *Moodswing.* New York: Morrow.

Fineberg, H. V. (1988, October). The social dimensions of AIDS. *Scientific American, 259,* 128–134.

Fink, A., & Kosecoff, J. (1985). *How to conduct surveys: A step-by-step guide.* Beverly Hills, CA: Sage.

Finkelstein, N. (1982). Aggression: Is it stimulated by day care? *Young Children, 37,* 3–9.

Fischoff, B. (1977). Perceived informativeness of facts. *Journal of Experimental Psychology: Human Perception and Performance, 3,* 349–358.

Fishbein, M., & Ajzen, I. (1975). *Belief, attitude, intention, and behavior: An introduction to theory and research.* Reading, MA: Addison-Wesley.

Fisher, K. (1985, March). ECT: New studies on how, why, who. *APA Monitor,* pp. 18–19.

Fisher, S., Raskin, A., & Uhlenhuth, E. H. (Eds.) (1987). *Cocaine: Classical and biobehavioral aspects.* New York: Oxford University Press.

Fiske, S. T., & Taylor, S. E. (1991). *Social cognition* (2nd ed.). Reading, MA: Addison-Wesley.

Flavell, J. H., Green, F. L., & Flavell, E. R. (1990). Developmental changes in young children's knowledge about the mind. *Cognitive Development, 5,* 1–28.

Fleming, R., Baum, A., & Singer, J. E. (1984). Toward an integrative approach to the study of stress. *Journal of Personality and Social Psychology, 46,* 939–949.

Flor, H., & Turk, D. C. (1989). Psychophysiology of chronic pain: Do chronic pain patients exhibit symptom-specific psychophysiological responses? *Psychological Bulletin, 105,* 215–259.

Flynn, J. R. (1987). Massive IQ gains in 14 nations: What IQ tests really measure. *Psychological Bulletin, 101,* 171–191.

Foa, E. B., & Kozak, M. S. (1986). Emotional processing of fear: Exposure to corrective information. *Psychological Bulletin, 99,* 20–35.

Folkman, S. (1984). Personal control and stress and coping processes: A theoretical analysis. *Journal of Personality and Social Psychology, 46,* 839–852.

Folkman, S., & Lazarus, R. S. (1980). An analysis of coping in a middle-aged community sample. *Journal of Health and Social Behavior, 21,* 219–239.

Folkman, S., Lazarus, R. S., Dunkel-Schetter, C., DeLongis, A., & Green, R. J. (1986). Dynamics of a stressful encounter: Cognitive appraisal, coping, and encounter outcome. *Journal of Personality and Social Psychology, 50,* 992–1003.

Fordyce, W. E. (1988). Pain and suffering: A reappraisal. *American Psychologist, 43,* 276–283.

Forer, B. (1949). The fallacy of personal validation: A classroom demonstration of gullibility. *Journal of Abnormal and Social Psychology, 44,* 118–123.

Forgas, J. P., & Bower, G. H. (1987). Mood effects on person-perception judgments. *Journal of Personality and Social Psychology, 53,* 53–60.

Försterling, F. (1985). Attributional retraining: A review. *Psychological Bulletin, 98,* 495–512.

Frankenburg, W. K., & Dodds, J. B. (1967). The Denver developmental screening test. *Journal of Pediatrics, 71,* 181–191.

Freedman, J. L. (1984). Effects of television violence on aggressiveness. *Psychological Bulletin, 96,* 227–246.

Freedman, J. L., & Fraser, S. C. (1966). Compliance without pressure: The foot-in-the-door technique. *Journal of Personality and Social Psychology, 4,* 195–202.

Freeman, A., Simon, K. M., Beutler, L. E., & Arkowitz, H. (Eds.) (1989). *Comprehensive handbook of cognitive therapy.* New York: Plenum.

Freeman, W. (1959). Psychosurgery. In *American handbook of psychiatry* (Vol. 2, pp. 1521–1540). New York: Basic Books.

Freud, S. (1900). *The interpretation of dreams.* New York: Basic Books.

Freud, S. (1922/1959). *Group psychology and the analysis of the ego.* London: Hogarth.

Frijda, N. H. (1987). Emotion, cognitive structure, and action tendency. *Cognition and Emotion, 1,* 115–143.

Frijda, N. H. (1988). The laws of emotion. *American Psychologist, 43,* 349–358.

Frijda, N. H., Kuipers, P., & terSchure, E. (1989). Relations among emotion, appraisal, and emotional action readiness. *Journal of Personality and Social Psychology, 57,* 212–228.

Fuchsberg, G. (1990, June 15). Pencil's sharp? E.T.S. to offer employee tests. *Wall Street Journal,* B1, B6.

Funder, D. C. F. (1987). Errors and mistakes: Evaluating the accuracy of social judgment. *Psychological Bulletin, 101,* 75–90.

Galanter, E. (1962). Contemporary psychophysics. In R. Brown, E. Galanter, E. Hess, & G. Maroler (Eds.), *New directions in psychology* (pp. 87–157). New York: Holt.

Gallup, G. G., Jr., & Suarez, S. D. (1985). Alternatives to the use of animals in psychological research. *American Psychologist, 40,* 1104–1111.

Gama, E. M. P. (1985). Achievement motivation of women: Effects of achievement and affiliation arousal. *Psychology of Women, 9,* 89–103.

Garb, H. N. (1989). Clinical judgment, clinical training, and professional experience. *Psychological Bulletin, 105,* 387–396.

Garber, H. L. (1988). *The Milwaukee Project: Preventing mental retardation in children at risk.* Washington, DC: American Association on Mental Retardation.

Gardner, H. (1975). *The shattered mind: The person after brain damage.* New York: Knopf.

Gardner, H. (1983). *Frames of mind: The theory of multiple intelligences.* New York: Basic Books.

Garfield, S. L. (1983). Psychotherapy: Efficacy, generality, and specificity. In J. B. N. Williams & R. L. Spitzer (Eds.), *Psycho-*

therapy research: Where are we and where should we go? (pp. 295–305). New York: Guilford Press.

Garfield, S. L. (1989). *The practice of brief psychotherapy.* New York: Pergamon.

Garfield, S. L. (1990). Issues and methods in psychotherapy process research. *Journal of Consulting and Clinical Psychology, 58,* 273–280.

Garling, T. (1989). The role of cognitive maps in spatial decisions. *Journal of Environmental Psychology, 9,* 269–278.

Gartell, N. N. (1982). Hormones and homosexuality. In W. Paul et al. (Eds.), *Homosexuality: Social, psychological, and biological issues.* Beverly Hills, CA: Sage.

Gatchel, R. J., & Baum, A. (1983). *An introduction to health psychology.* Reading, MA: Addison-Wesley.

Gawin, F. H., & Ellinwood, E. H. (1988). Cocaine and other stimulants: Actions, abuse, and treatment. *New England Journal of Medicine, 18,* 1173.

Gazzaniga, M. S. (1983). Right-hemisphere language following brain bisection: A twenty-year perspective. *American Psychologist, 38,* 525–537.

Gazzaniga, M. S. (1985, November). The social brain. *Psychology Today,* pp. 29–38.

Gazzaniga, M. S. (1988). Mind matters: How mind and brain interact to create our conscious lives. Boston: Houghton Mifflin.

Gazzaniga, M. S. (1989, September 1). Organization of the human brain. *Science, 245,* 947–952.

Geen, R. G. (1984). Human motivation: New perspectives on old problems. In A. M. Rogers & C. J. Scheirer (Eds.), *The G. Stanley Hall Lecture Series* (Vol. 4). Washington, DC: American Psychological Association.

Geen, R. G., & Donnerstein, E. (1983). *Aggression: Theoretical and empirical reviews.* New York: Academic Press.

Gelman, R., & Baillargeon, R. (1983). A review of some Piagetian concepts. In J. H. Flavell & E. M. Markman (Eds.), *Handbook of child psychology: Vol. 3, Cognitive development* (4th ed.). New York: Wiley.

Georgotas, A., & Cancro, R. (Eds.) (1988). *Depression and mania.* New York: Elsevier.

Gerbner, G., Gross, L., Jackson-Beeck, M., Jeffries-Fox, S., & Signorielli, N. (1978). Cultural indicators: Violence profile No. 9. *Journal of Communication, 28,* 176–207.

Gerrard, M. (1988). Sex, sex guilt, and contraceptive use revisited: The 1980s. *Journal of Personality and Social Psychology, 57,* 973–980.

Gescheider, G. A. (1985). *Psychophysics: Method, theory, and application.* Hillsdale, NJ: Erlbaum.

Geschwind, N., & Galuburda, A. M. (1985). Cerebral lateralization. Biological mechanisms, associations, and pathology: I. A hypothesis and a program for research. *Archives of Neurology, 17,* 128–457.

Gfeller, J. D., Lynn, S. J., & Pribble, W. E. (1987). Enhancing hypnotic susceptibility: Interpersonal and rapport factors. *Journal of Personality and Social Psychology, 52,* 586–595.

Gibbons, A. (1990, July 13). New maps of the human brain. *Science, 249,* 122–123.

Gibson, E. J. (1988). Explanatory behavior in the development of perceiving, acting, and the acquiring of knowledge. *Annual Review of Psychology, 39,* 1–41.

Gibson, J. J. (1979). *The ecological approach to visual perception.* Boston: Houghton Mifflin.

Gilbert, A. N., & Wysocki, C. J. (1987, October). The smell survey results. *National Geographic, 172,* 514–525.

Gilbert, D. T., Pelham, B. W., & Krull, D. S. (1987). On cognitive busyness: When person perceivers meet persons perceived. *Journal of Personality and Social Psychology, 54,* 733–740.

Gill, T. J., III, Smith, G. J., Wissler, R. W., & Kunz, H. W. (1989, July 21). The rat as an experimental animal. *Science, 245,* 269–276.

Gilligan, C. (1982). *In a different voice.* Cambridge, MA: Harvard University Press.

Gilligan, C. (1987). In a different voice: Women's conception of self and of morality. In M. R. Walsh (Ed.), *The psychology of women.* New Haven, CT: Yale University Press.

Gilligan, C., Ward, J. V., & Taylor, J. M. (Eds.) (1988). *Mapping the moral domain: A contribution of women's thinking to psychological theory and education.* Cambridge, MA: Harvard University Press.

Ginsburg, H. P., & Opper, S. (1988). *Piaget's theory of intellectual development* (3rd ed.). Englewood Cliffs, NJ: Prentice-Hall.

Gladue, B. (1984). Hormone markers for homosexuality. *Science, 225,* 198.

Gladwin, T. (1964). Culture and logical process. In N. Goodenough (Ed.), *Explorations in cultural anthropology: Essays in honor of George Peter Murdoch*. New York: McGraw-Hill.

Glaser, R. (1990). The reemergence of learning theory within instructional research. *American Psychologist, 45*, 29–39.

Glass, A., & Holyoak, K. J. (1985). *Cognition* (2nd ed.). Reading, MA: Addison-Wesley.

Glass, D. C., & Singer, J. E. (1972). *Urban stress*. New York: Academic Press.

Glyshaw, K., Cohen, L. H., & Towbes, L. C. (1989). Coping strategies and psychological distress: Prospective analyses of early and middle adolescents. *American Journal of Community Psychology, 17*, 607–624.

Gold, P. W., Gwirtsman, H., Avgerinos, P. C., Nieman, L. K., Gallucci, W. T., Kaye, W., Jimerson, D., Ebert, M., Rittmaster, R., Loriaux, L., & Chrousos, G. P. (1986). Abnormal hypothalmic-pituitary-adrenal function in anorexia nervosa. *New England Journal of Medicine, 314*, 1335–1342.

Goldfried, M., & Davison, G. (1976). *Clinical behavior therapy*. New York: Holt, Rinehart and Winston.

Goldfried, M. R., Greenberg, L., & Marmar, C. (1990). Individual psychotherapy: Process and outcome. *Annual Review of Psychology, 41*, 659–688.

Goleman, D. (1988, March 29). Study of normal mourning process illuminates grief gone awry. *New York Times*, pp. C-1, C-6. (c)

Goodall, J. (1987, November–December). A plea for chimpanzees. *American Scientist, 75*, 574–577.

Gordon, S. E., & Wyer, R. S., Jr. (1987). Person memory: Category-set-size effects on the recall of a person's behaviors. *Journal of Personality and Social Psychology, 53*, 648–662.

Gottesman, I. I., & Shields, J. (1972). *Schizophrenia and genetics*. New York: Academic Press.

Gottfried, A. W. (Ed.) (1984). *Home environment and early cognitive development*. New York: Academic Press.

Gould, R. L. (1978). *Transformations*. New York: Simon and Schuster.

Gove, W. R. (1982). Labeling theory's explanation of mental illness: An update of recent evidence. *Deviant Behavior, 3*, 307–327.

Graham, J. R. (1990). *MMPI-2: Assessing personality and psychopathology*. New York: Oxford University Press.

Graham, S., & Folkes, V. S. (Eds.) (1990). *Attribution theory: Applications to achievement, mental health, and interpersonal conflict*. Hillsdale, NJ: Erlbaum.

Green, R. (1978). Sexual identity of 37 children raised by homosexual or transsexual parents. *American Journal of Psychiatry, 135*, 687–692.

Greeno, J. G. (1978). Nature of problem-solving abilities. In W. K. Estes (Ed.), *Handbook of learning and cognitive processes*. Hillsdale, NJ: Erlbaum.

Gregory, R. L. (1978). *The psychology of seeing* (3rd ed.). New York: McGraw-Hill.

Greig, G. L. (1990). On the shape of energy-detection ROC curves. *Perception & Psychophysics, 48*, 77–81.

Greist-Bousquet, S., & Schiffman, H. R. (1986). The basis of the Poggendorff effect: An additional clue for Day and Kasperczyk. *Perception and Psychophysics, 39*, 447–448.

Griffith, R. M., Miyago, O., & Tago, A. (1958). The universality of typical dreams: Japanese vs. Americans. *American Anthropologist, 60*, 1173–1179.

Groner, R., Groner, M., & Bischof, W. F. (Eds.) (1983). *Methods of heuristics*. Hillsdale, NJ: Erlbaum.

Grossman, H. J. (Ed.) (1983). *Classification in mental retardation*. Washington, DC: American Associations on Mental Deficiency.

Guilford, J. P. (1968). The structure of intelligence. In D. K. White (Ed.), *Handbook of measurement and assessment in behavioral sciences*. Reading, MA: Addison-Wesley.

Guilford, J. P. (1982). Cognitive psychology's ambiguities: Some remedies. *Psychological Review, 89*, 48–59.

Gur, R. C., Gur, R. E., Obrist, W. D., Hungerbuhler, J. P., Younkin, D., Rosen, A. D., Skilnick, B. E., & Reivich, M. (1982). Sex and handedness differences in cerebral blood flow during rest and cognitive activity. *Science, 217*, 659–661.

Haber, R. N. (1983). Stimulus information processing mechanisms in visual space perception. In J. Beck, B. Hope, & A. Rosenfeld (Eds.), *Human and machine vision*. New York: Academic Press.

Hagen, E., Sattler, J. M., & Thorndike, R. L.

(1985). *Stanford-Binet test.* Chicago: Riverside.

Hahn, W. K. (1987). Cerebral lateralization of function: From infancy through childhood. *Psychological Bulletin, 10,* 376–392.

Hainline, L., & Lemerise, E. (1982). Infants' scanning of geometric forms varying in size. *Journal of Experimental Child Psychology, 33,* 235–256.

Haith, M. M. (1990). Progress in the understanding of sensory and perceptual processes in early infancy. *Merrill-Palmer Quarterly, 36,* 1–26.

Halford, G. S. (1989). Reflections on 25 years of Piagetian cognitive developmental psychology, 1963–1988. *Human Development, 32,* 325–387.

Hannon, R., Butler, C. P., Day, C. L., Khan, S. A., Quitoriano, L. A., Butler, A. M., & Meredith, L. A. (1985). Alcohol use and cognitive functioning in men and women college students. In M. Galanter (Ed.), *Recent developments in alcoholism* (Vol. 3, pp. 241–252). New York: Plenum Press.

Harlow, H. F., Harlow, M. K., & Meyer, D. R. (1950). Learning motivated by a manipulation drive. *Journal of Experimental Psychology, 40,* 228–234.

Harlow, H. F., & Zimmerman, R. R. (1959). Affectional responses in the infant monkey. *Science, 130,* 421–432.

Harlow, J. M. (1869). Recovery from the passage of an iron bar through the head. *Massachusetts Medical Society Publication, 2,* 329–347.

Harper, T. (1978, November 15). It's not true about people 65 or over. *Green Bay (Wis.) Press-Gazette,* D–1.

Harte, R. A., Travers, J. A., & Savich, P. (1948). Voluntary caloric intake of the growing rat. *Journal of Nutrition, 36,* 667–679.

Hartmann, E. (1967). *The biology of dreaming.* Springfield, IL: Thomas.

Hartmann, E. (1982). From the biology of dreaming to the biology of the mind. *Psychoanalytic Study of the Child, 37,* 303–335.

Hartup, W. W. (1989). Social relationships and their developmental significance. *American Psychologist, 44,* 120–126.

Harvard Medical School (1987, December). *Mental health letter,* p. 4.

Harvey, J. G., & Weary, G. (Eds.) (1985). *Attribution: Basic issues and applications.* Orlando, FL: Academic Press.

Haskins, R. (1985). Public school aggression among children with varying day care experience. *Child Development, 56,* 689–703.

Hassett, J., & Dukes, S. (1986, September). The new employee trainer: A floppy disk. *Psychology Today, 20,* 30–34.

Hastie, R., Penrod, S., & Pennington, N. (1983). *Inside the jury.* Cambridge, MA: Harvard University Press.

Hatfield, E., & Sprecher, S. (1986). *Mirror, mirror: The importance of looks in everyday life.* Albany: State University of New York Press.

Hathaway, B. (1984, July). Running to ruin. *Psychology Today,* pp. 14–15.

Hathaway, S. R., & McKinley, J. C. (1989). *MMPI-2: Minnesota Multiphasic Personality Inventory-2.* Minneapolis: University of Minnesota Press.

Hayes, J. R. (1966). Memory, goals, and problem solving. In B. Kleinmuntz (Ed.), *Problem solving: Research, method, and theory.* New York: Wiley.

Hayes, J. R. (1989). *The complete problem solver* (2nd ed.). Hillsdale, NJ: Erlbaum.

Hayflick, L. (1974). The strategy of senescence. *Journal of Gerontology, 14,* 37–45.

Haymes, M., Green, L., & Quinto, R. (1984). Maslow's hierarchy, moral development, and prosocial behavioral skills within a child psychiatric population. *Motivation and Emotion, 8,* 23–31.

Hearst, N., & Hulley, S. B. (1988, April 22–29). Preventing the heterosexual spread of AIDS: Are we giving our patients the best advice? *Journal of the American Medical Association, 259,* 2428–2432.

Hebb, D. O. (1955). Drive and the CNS. *Psychological Review, 62,* 243–254.

Heckhausen, H., Schmalt, H. D., & Schneider, K. (1985). *Achievement motivation in perspective.* (M. Woodruff & R. Wicklund, Trans.) Orlando, FL: Academic Press.

Heider, F. (1958). *The psychology of interpersonal relations.* New York: Wiley.

Heilman, M. E., & Stopeck, M. H. (1985). Attractiveness and corporate success: Different causal attributions for men and women. *Journal of Applied Psychology, 70,* 379–388.

Hellerstein, D. (1988, May 22). Plotting a theory of the brain. *New York Times Magazine,* pp. 17–19, 27–28, 55–64.

Hellige, J. B. (1990). Hemispheric asymmetry. *Annual Review of Psychology, 41,* 55–80.

Hendrick, C. (Ed.) (1989). *Close relationships.* Newbury Park, CA: Sage.

Hendrick, C., & Hendrick, S. (1989). Research on love: Does it measure up? *Journal of Personality and Social Psychology, 56,* 784–794.

Hendrick, S., Hendrick, C., & Adler, N. L. (1988). Romantic relationships: Love, satisfaction, and staying together. *Journal of Personality and Social Psychology, 54,* 980–988.

Herman, C. P., & Polivy, J. (1975). Anxiety, restraint, and eating behavior. *Journal of Abnormal Psychology, 84,* 666–672.

Hermans, H. J. M. (1987). The dream in the process of valuation: A method of interpretation. *Journal of Personality and Social Psychology, 53,* 163–175.

Hershenson, M. (1989). *The moon illusion.* Hillsdale, NJ: Erlbaum.

Hetherington, E. M., & Parke, R. D. (1986). *Child psychology: A contemporary viewpoint* (3rd ed.). New York: McGraw-Hill.

Heyward, W. L., & Curran, J. W. (1988, October). The epidemiology of AIDS in the U.S. *Scientific American, 72–81.*

Higbee, K. L., & Kunihira, S. (1985). Cross-cultural applications of Yodni mnemonics in education. *Educational Psychologist, 20,* 57–64.

Hilgard, E. R. (1974). Imaginative involvement: Some characteristics of the highly hypnotizable and the nonhypnotizable. *International Journal of Clinical and Experimental Hypnosis, 22,* 138–156.

Hilgard, E. R. (1975). Hypnosis. *Annual Review of Psychology, 26,* 19–44.

Hilgard, E. R. (1980). Consciousness in contemporary psychology. *Annual Review of Psychology, 31,* 1–26.

Hill, C. T., & Stull, D. E. (1981). Sex differences in effects of social and value similarity in same-sex friendship. *Journal of Personality and Social Psychology, 41,* 488–502.

Hiroto, D. S., & Seligman, M. E. P. (1975). Generality of learned helplessness in man. *Journal of Personality and Social Psychology, 31,* 311–327.

Hobson, J. A. (1988). *The dreaming brain.* New York: Basic Books.

Hobson, J. A., & McCarley, R. W. (1977). The brain as a dream state generator: An activation-synthesis hypothesis of the dream process. *American Journal of Psychiatry, 134,* 1335–1348.

Hoch, S. J. (1987). Perceived consensus and predictive accuracy: The pros and cons of projection. *Journal of Personality and Social Psychology, 53,* 221–234.

Hochberg, J. E. (1978). *Perception.* Englewood Cliffs, NJ: Prentice-Hall.

Hoffman, C., Lau, I., & Johnson, D. R. (1986). The linguistic relativity of person cognition: An English–Chinese comparison. *Journal of Personality and Social Psychology, 51,* 1097–1105.

Holahan, C. J., & Moos, R. H. (1990). Life stressors, resistance factors, and improved psychological functioning: An extension of the stress resistance paradigm. *Journal of Personality and Social Psychology, 58,* 909–917.

Holden, C. (1986, September 19). Researchers grapple with problems of updating classic psychological test. *Science, 233,* 1249–1251. (c)

Holden, C. (1987, October 9). Why do women live longer than men? *Science, 238,* 158–160. (b)

Holden, C. (1988, January 29). Animal stealer convicted. *Science, 239,* 458.

Holden, C. (1990, March 23). Head Start enters adulthood. *Science, 247,* 1400–1402.

Hollander, E. P. (1980). Leadership and social exchange processes. In K. J. Gargon, M. Greenberg & R. Willis (Eds.), *Social exchange: Advances in theory and research.* New York: Plenum Press.

Hollingshead, A. B., & Redich, F. C. (1958). *Social class and mental illness.* New York: Wiley.

Hollon, S. D., & Garber, J. (1990). Cognitive therapy for depression: A social cognitive perspective. *Personality and Social Psychology Bulletin, 16,* 58–73.

Holmes, D. S. (1985). To meditate or rest?: The answer is rest. *American Psychologist, 40,* 728–731.

Holzman, P. S., & Matthysse, S. (1990). The genetics of schizophrenia: A review. *Psychological Science, 1,* 279–286.

Hoon, P. W., Bruce, K., & Kinchloe, B. (1982). Does the menstrual cycle play a role in sexual arousal? *Psychophysiology, 19,* 21–26.

Horn, M. C., & Bachrach, C. A. (1985). *1982 National Survey of Family Growth.* Washington, DC: National Center for Health Statistics.

Horne, J. L. (1982). The theory of fluid and crystallized intelligence in relation to concepts of cognitive psychology and aging in adulthood. In F. I. M. Craik & S. Trehub (Eds.), *Aging and cognitive processes*. New York: Plenum.

Horner, M. (1972). Toward an understanding of achievement-related conflicts in women. *Journal of Social Issues, 28*, 157–175.

Horney, K. (1937). *Neurotic personality of our times*. New York: Norton.

Horowitz, F. D., & O'Brien, M. (Eds.) (1987). *The gifted and talented: Developmental perspectives*. Washington, DC: American Psychological Association.

Houston, L. N. (1981). Romanticism and eroticism among black and white college students. *Adolescence, 16*, 263–272.

Hovland, C., Janis, I., & Kelly, H. H. (1953). *Communication and persuasion*. New Haven, CT: Yale University Press.

Howard, A., Pion, G. M., Gottfredson, G. D., Flattau, P. E., Oskamp, S., Pfafflin, S. M., Bray, D. W., & Burstein, A. D. (1986). The changing face of American psychology: A report from the committee on employment and human resources. *American Psychologist, 41*, 1311–1327.

Howard, K. I., & Zola, M. A. (1988). Paper presented at the annual meeting of the Society for Psychotherapy Research.

Howells, J. G., & Osborn, M. L. (1984). *A reference companion to the history of abnormal psychology*. Westport, CT: Greenwood Press.

Hoyenga, K., & Hoyenga, K. (1984). *Motivation*. Monterey, CA: Brooks-Cole.

Hsu, L. K. G. (1990). *Eating disorders*. New York: Guilford.

Hubel, D. H., & Wiesel, T. N. (1979). Brain mechanisms of vision. *Scientific American, 241*, 150–162.

Huesmann, L. R., & Eron, L. D. (Eds.) (1986). *Television and the aggressive child: A cross-national comparison*. Hillsdale, NJ: Erlbaum.

Huesmann, L. R., Eron, L. D., Klein, R., Brice, P., & Fischer, P. (1983). Mitigating the imitation of aggressive behaviors by changing children's attitudes about media violence. *Journal of Personality and Social Psychology, 5*, 899–910.

Hull, C. L. (1943). *Principles of behavior*. New York: Appleton-Century-Crofts.

Hunt, M. (1974). *Sexual behaviors in the 1970s*. New York: Dell.

Hurley, J., & Horowitz, J. (1990). *Alcohol and health*. New York: Hemisphere.

Hurst, R. (1984). *Pilot error*. London: Granada.

Hutchison, J. B. (Ed.) (1978). *Biological determinants of sexual behavior*. New York: Wiley.

Hyland, M. E. (1987). Control theory interpretation of psychological mechanisms of depression: Comparison and integration of several theories. *Psychological Bulletin, 102*, 109–121.

Ingelfinger, F. J. (1944). The late effects of total and subtotal gastrectomy. *New England Journal of Medicine, 231*, 321–377.

Institute of Medicine. (1982). *Marijuana and health*. Washington, DC: National Academy Press.

Izard, C. (1988, August). The structure and function of human emotions. Paper presented at the annual meeting of the American Psychological Association.

Izard, C. E. (1977). *Human emotions*. New York: Plenum.

Izard, C. E. (1990). Facial expressions and the regulation of emotions. *Journal of Personality and Social Psychology, 54*, 487–498.

Izard, C. E., Kagan, J., & Zajonc, R. B. (1989). *Emotions, cognition, and behavior*. Cambridge, England: Cambridge University Press.

Jackson, J. M., Buglione, S. A., & Glenwick, D. S. (1988). Major league baseball performance as a function of being traded: A drive theory analysis. *Personality and Social Psychology Bulletin, 14*, 46–56.

Jacobs, B. L. (1987, July–August). How hallucinogenic drugs work. *American Scientist, 75*, 386–392.

James, W. (1890). *The principles of psychology*. New York: Holt.

Janis, I. (1984). Improving adherence to medical recommendations: Descriptive hypothesis derived from recent research in social psychology. In A. Baum, J. E. Singer, & S. E. Taylor (Eds.), *Handbook of medical psychology* (Vol. 4). Hillsdale, NJ: Erlbaum.

Jaroff, L. (1987, July 13). Steps toward a brave new world. *Time*, pp. 56–57.

Jencks, C., et al. (1972). *Inequality*. New York: Basic Books.

Jenkins, S. R. (1987). Need for achievement and women's careers over 14 years: Evidence for occupational structure effects. *Journal of Personality and Social Psychology, 53*, 922–932.

Johnson, D. L. (1989). Schizophrenia as a

brain disease: Implications for psychologists and families. *American Psychologist, 44*, 553–555.

Johnson, D. M., Parrott, G. R., & Stratton, R. P. (1968). Production and judgment of solutions to five problems. *Journal of Educational Psychology Monograph Supplement, 59* (6, pt. 2).

Johnson, J. T., Cain, L. M., Falke, T. L., Hayman, J., & Perillo, E. (1985). The "Barnum Effect" revisited: Cognitive and motivational factors in the acceptance of personality descriptions. *Journal of Personality and Social Psychology, 49*, 1378–1391.

Johnson, T. E. (1986, March 17). Kids and cocaine. *Newsweek*, pp. 58–65.

Jones, E. E. (1990). *Interpersonal perception.* New York: W. H. Freeman.

Jones, G. N., Brantley, P. J., & Gilchrist, J. C. (1988, August). The relation between daily stress and health. Paper presented at the annual meeting of the American Psychological Association (Atlanta).

Jones, L. V. (1984). White-black achievement differences: The narrowing gap. *American Psychologist, 39*, 1207–1213.

Josephs, R. A., & Steele, C. M. (1990). The two faces of alcohol myopia: Attentional mediation of psychological stress. *Journal of Abnormal Psychology, 99*, 115–126.

Jung, J., & Khalsa, H. K. (1989). The relationship of daily hassles, social support, and coping to depression in black and white students. *Journal of General Psychology, 116*, 407–418.

Jusczyk, P. W. (1986). Toward a model of the development of speech perception. In J. S. Perkell & D. H. Klatt (Eds.), *Invariance and variability in speech processes.* Hillsdale, NJ: Erlbaum.

Jusczyk, P. W., & Derrah, C. (1987). Representation of speech sounds by young infants. *Developmental Psychology, 23*, 648–654.

Justice, T. C., & Looney, T. A. (1989). Another look at "superstitions" in pigeons. *Bulletin of the Psychonomic Society, 28*, 64–66.

Kagan, J., Kearsley, R. B., & Zelazo, P. R. (1978). *Infancy: Its place in human development.* Cambridge, MA: Harvard University Press.

Kahn, S., Zimmerman, G., Csikszentmihalyi, M., & Getzels, J. W. (1985). Relations between identity in young adulthood and intimacy at midlife. *Journal of Personality and Social Psychology, 49*, 1316–1322.

Kahneman, D., & Tversky, A. (1972). Subjective probability: A judgment of representativeness. *Cognitive Psychology, 3*, 430–454.

Kahneman, D., & Tversky, A. (1973). On the psychology of prediction. *Psychology Review, 80*, 237–251.

Kane, J. M. (1983). Hypotheses regarding the mechanism of action of antidepressant drugs: Neurotransmitters in affective disorders. In A. Rifkin (Ed.), *Schizophrenia and affective disorders: Biology and drug treatment* (pp. 19–34). Boston: John Wright.

Kanner, A. D., Coyne, J. C., Schaefer, C., & Lazarus, R. (1981). Comparison of two modes of stress measurement: Daily hassles and uplifts versus major life events. *Journal of Behavioral Medicine, 4*, 14.

Kaplan, M. F. (1975). Information integration in social judgment: Interaction of judge and informational components. In M. Kaplan & S. Schwartz (Eds.), *Human development and decision processes.* New York: Academic Press.

Karasu, T. B. (1982). Psychotherapy and psychopharmacology: Toward an integrative model. *American Journal of Psychiatry, 139*, 1102–1113.

Karasu, T. B. (Ed.) (1989). *Treatments of psychiatric disorders: A task force report of the American Psychiatric Association.* Washington, DC: American Psychiatric Association.

Karlins, M., & Abelson, H. I. (1979). *How opinions and attitudes are changed.* New York: Springer-Verlag.

Karp, D. A. (1988). A decade of remembrances: Changing age consciousness between fifty and sixty years old. *The Gerontologist, 28*, 727–738.

Kasa, P. (1986). The cholinergic systems in brain and spinal cord. *Progress in Neurobiology, 26*, 211–272.

Kassin, S. M. (1985). Eyewitness identification: Retrospective self-awareness and the accuracy-confidence correlation. *Journal of Personality and Social Psychology, 41*, 878–893.

Kastenbaum, R. (1975). Is death a life crisis? On the confrontation with death in theory and practice. In N. Datan & L. H. Ginsberg (Eds.), *Life-span developmental psychology: Normative life crisis.* New York: Academic Press.

Katz, D., & Braly, K. W. (1933). Racial stereotypes of 100 college students. *Journal of Abnormal and Social Psychology, 4,* 280–290.

Kay, S. F., & Merrill, L. M. (1990). Predicting outcome of schizophrenia: Significance of symptom profiles and outcome dimensions. *Comprehensive Psychiatry, 31,* 91–102.

Kazdin, A. E. (1989). *Behavior modification in applied settings* (4th ed.). Pacific Grove, CA: Brooks/Cole.

Kazdin, A. E., & Wilson, G. T. (1978). *Evaluation of behavior therapy: Issues, evidence, and research strategies.* Cambridge, MA: Ballinger.

Keating, D. (1980). Thinking processes in adolescence. In J. Adelson (Ed.), *Handbook of Adolescent Psychology.* New York: Wiley.

Keating, D. P., & Clark, L. V. (1980). Development of physical and social reasoning in adolescence. *Developmental Psychology, 16,* 23–30.

Keerdoja, E. (1985, July 8). Scaling the walls of silence. *Newsweek,* p. 66.

Keesey, R. E., & Powley, T. L. (1986). The regulation of body weight. *Annual Review of Psychology,* p. 37.

Keith, S. J., & Matthews, S. M. (1983). Schizophrenia: A review of psychosocial treatment strategies. In J. W. W. Williams & R. L. Spitzer (Eds.), *Psychotherapy research: Where are we and where should we go?* (pp. 70–88). New York: Guilford Press.

Keith-Spiegel, P., & Koocher, G. P. (1985). *Ethics in psychology.* San Francisco: Random House-Knopf.

Kelley, H. (1950). The warm-cold variable in first impressions of persons. *Journal of Personality and Social Psychology, 18,* 431–439.

Kelley, H. H. (1967). Attribution theory in social psychology. In D. Levine (Ed.), *Nebraska Symposium on Motivation.* Lincoln: University of Nebraska Press.

Kemper, T. D. (Ed.) (1990). *Research agendas in the sociology of emotions.* Albany, NY: State University of New York Press.

Kendrick, D. T., & Funder, D. C. (1988). Profiting from controversy: Lessons from the person-situation debate. *American Psychologist, 43,* 23–34.

Kenny, D. A., & Albright, L. (1987). Accuracy in interpersonal perception: A social relations analysis. *Psychological Bulletin, 102,* 390–402.

Kertesz, A. E. (1983). Cyclofusion and stereopsis. *Perception and Psychophysics, 33,* 99–101.

Kiecolt-Glaser, J. K., & Glaser, R. (1986). Behavioral influences on immune function: Evidence for the interplay between stress and health. In T. Field, P. McCabe, & N. Schneiderman (Eds.), *Stress and coping* (Vol. 2). Hillsdale, NJ: Erlbaum.

Kienker, P. K., Sejnowski, T. J., Hinton, G. E., & Schumacher, L. E. (1986). Separating figure from ground with a parallel network. *Perception, 15,* 197–216.

Kihlstrom, J. F. (1987, September 18). The cognitive unconscious. *Science, 237,* 1445–1452.

King, G. R., & Logue, A. W. (1990). Humans' sensitivity to variation in reinforcer amount: Effects of the method of reinforcer delivery. *Journal of the Experimental Analysis of Behavior, 53,* 33–46.

Kinsey, A. C., Pomeroy, W. B., & Martin, C. E. (1948). *Sexual behavior in the human male.* Philadelphia: Saunders.

Klassen, A. D., Williams, C. J., Levitt, E. E., & O'Gorman, H. J. (Eds.) (1989). *Sex and morality in the U.S.* Middletown, CT: Wesleyan University Press.

Klein, S. B., & Mowrer, R. R. (1989). *Contemporary learning theories* (Vol. I: Pavlovian conditioning and the status of tradition.). Hillsdale, NJ: Erlbaum. (a)

Klein, S. B., & Mowrer, R. R. (1989). *Contemporary learning theories* (Vol. II: Instrumental conditioning theory and the impact of biological constraints on learning.). Hillsdale, NJ: Erlbaum. (b)

Klerman, G. L. (1983). Evaluating the efficacy of psychotherapy. In P. J. Clayton & J. E. Barret (Eds.), *Treatment of depression: Old controversies and new approaches* (pp. 291–298). New York: Raven Press.

Klerman, G. L. (1984). The advantages of DSM-III. *American Journal of Psychiatry, 141,* 539–542.

Kline, P. (1987). The experimental study of the psychoanalytic unconscious. *Personality and Social Psychology Bulletin, 13,* 363–378.

Knittle, J. L. (1975). Early influences on development of adipose tissue. In G. A. Bray (Ed.), *Obesity in perspective.* Washington, DC: U.S. Government Printing Office.

Kohlberg, L. (1969). Stage and sequence: The cognitive-developmental approach to socialization. In D. Goslin (Ed.), *Handbook of socialization theory and research.* Chicago: Rand McNally.

Kohlberg, L. (1984). *The psychology of moral*

development: Essays on moral development (Vol. 2). San Francisco: Harper & Row.

Köhler, W. (1927). The mentality of apes. London: Routledge & Kegan Paul.

Kohn, A. (1988, April). What they say. Psychology Today, pp. 36–41.

Kohn, A. (1990). You know what they say. New York: HarperCollins.

Kohn, V. (1987, February). The body prison: A bulimic's compulsion to eat more, eat less, add muscle, get thinner. Life, p. 44.

Kolata, G. (1987, August 14). What babies know, and noises parents make. Science, 237, 726. (b)

Kolata, G. (1988, February 25). New obesity studies indicate metabolism is often to blame. New York Times, pp. A-1, B-5.

Konner, M. (1988, January 17). Caffeine high. New York Times Magazine, pp. 47–48.

Koop, C. E. (1988). The health consequences of smoking. Washington, DC: U.S. Government Printing Office.

Kosslyn, S. M. (1988). Aspects of a cognitive neuroscience of mental imagery. Science, 240, 1621–1626.

Koveces, Z. (1987). The container metaphor of emotion. Paper presented at the University of Massachusetts, Amherst.

Kraepelin, E. (1904/1968). Lectures on clinical psychiatry. New York: Hafner.

Kraft, C. L., & Elworth, C. L. (1969). Measurement of aircrew performance: The flight deck workload and its relation to pilot performance (NTIS70-19779/A; 699934-DTIC).

Kraines, S. H. (1948). The therapy of the neuroses and psychoses (3rd ed.). Philadelphia: Lea and Febiger.

Kravitz, E. A. (1988). Hormonal control of behavior: Amines and the biasing of behavioral output in lobsters. Science, 241, 1775–1782.

Krebs, D. L., & Miller, D. T. (1985). Altruism and aggression. In G. Lindzey & E. Aronson (Eds.), Handbook of social psychology (3rd ed.). New York: Random House.

Kreuger, L. E. (1989). The world of touch. Hillsdale, NJ: Erlbaum.

Kringlen, E. (1978). Adult offspring of two psychotic parents, with special reference to schizophrenia. In L. C. Wynne, R. L. Cromwell, & S. Matthysee (Eds.), The nature of schizophrenia: New epidemiological-clinical twin study. Oslo: Univesitsforlaget.

Kübler-Ross, E. (1969). On death and dying. New York: Macmillan.

Kucharski, D., & Hall, W. G. (1987). New routes to early memories. Science, 238, 786–788.

Ladd, G. W. (1990). Having friends, keeping friends, making friends, and being liked by peers in the classroom: Predictors of children's early school adjustment? Child Development, 61, 1081–1100.

Lakey, B., & Heller, K. (1985). Response biases and the relation between negative life events and psychological symptoms. Journal of Personality and Social Psychology, 49, 1662–1668.

Lamb, M. (1982). The bonding phenomenon: Misinterpretations and their implications. Journal of Pediatrics, 101, 555–557.

Lamb, M., & Bornstein, M. H. (1987). The father's role. Hillsdale, N.J.: Erlbaum.

Lamb, M. E. (1982). Paternal influences on early socio-emotional development. Journal of Child Psychology and Psychiatry and Allied Disciplines, 23, 185–190.

Lamb, M. E. (Ed.) (1987). The father's role. Hillsdale, NJ: Erlbaum.

Lambert, M. J., Shapiro, D. A., & Bergin, A. E. (1986). The effectiveness of psychotherapy. In S. L. Garfield & A. E. Bergin (Eds.), Handbook of psychotherapy and behavior change (3rd ed.). New York: Wiley.

Landesman, S., & Ramey, C. (1989). Developmental psychology and mental retardation: Integrating scientific principles with treatment practices. American Psychologist, 44, 409–415.

Landman, J., & Dawes, R. M. (1984). Reply to Orwin and Cordray. American Psychologist, 39, 72–73.

Landwehr, (1990). Ecological perception research, visual communication and aesthetics. New York: Springer-Verlag.

Lang, J. S. (1987, April 13). Happiness is a reunited set of twins. U.S. News and World Report, pp. 63–66.

Langer, E., & Janis, I. (1979). The psychology of control. Beverly Hills, CA: Sage.

Langer, E., Janis, I. L., & Wolfer, J. A. (1975). Reduction of psychological stress in surgical patients. Journal of Experimental Social Psychology, 11, 155–165.

Langlois, J. H., Roggman, L. A., Rieser-Danner, L. A. (1990). Infants' differential social responses to attractive and unattractive faces: Developmental Psychology, 26, 153–159.

Latané, B., & Darley, J. M. (1970). The unresponsive bystander: Why doesn't he help? New York: Appleton-Century-Crofts.

Latané, B., & Nida, S. (1981). Ten years of research on group size and helping. Psychological Bulletin, 89, 308–324.

Lauer, J., & Lauer, R. (1985, June). Marriages made to last. Psychology Today, pp. 22–26.

Lazarus, R. S. (1984). On the primacy of cognition. American Psychologist, 39, 124–129.

Lazarus, R. S., & Cohen, J. B. (1977). Environmental stress. In I. Altman & J. F. Wohlwill (Eds.), Human behavior and the environment: Current theory and research (Vol. 2). New York: Plenum Press.

Lazarus, R. S., DeLongis, A., Folkman, S., & Gruen, R. (1985). Stress and adaptational outcomes: The problem of confounded measures. American Psychologist, 40, 770–779.

Lechtenberg, R. (1982). The psychiatrist's guide to diseases of the nervous system. New York: Wiley.

Lee, V. E., Brooks-Gunn, J., & Schnur, E. (1988). Does Head Start work? A one-year follow-up comparison of disadvantaged children attending Head Start, no preschool, and other preschool programs. Developmental Psychology, 24, 210–222.

Lefkowitz, M. M., & Tesiny, E. P. (1985). Depression in children: Prevalence and correlates. Journal of Consulting and Clinical Psychology, 53, 647–656.

Lehman, D. R., & Taylor, S. E. (1988). Date with an earthquake: Coping with a probable, unpredictable disaster. Personality and Social Psychology Bulletin, 13, 546–555.

Lepper, M. R. (1985). Intrinsic motivation and instruction: Conflicting views on the role of motivation processes in computer-based education. Educational Psychologist, 20, 217–230. (a)

Lepper, M. R. (1985). Microcomputers in education: Motivational and social issues. American Psychologist, 40, 1–18. (b)

Lerner, P. M. (1990) Rorschach assessment of primitive defenses: A review. Journal of Personality Assessment, 54, 30–46.

Lester, D., & Tarnacki, P. A. (1989). Frequencies of dreams and day-dreams and locus of control. Perceptual and Motor Skills, 69, 954–955.

Leventhal, H. (1970). Findings and theory in the study of fear communications. In L. Berkowitz (Ed.), Advances in experimental social psychology (Vol. 5). New York: Academic Press.

Leventhal, H., & Tomarken, A. J. (1986). Emotion: Today's problems. Annual Review of Psychology, 37, 565–610.

Levinger, G. (1983). Development and change. In H. H. Kelley et al., Close relationships. San Francisco: Freeman.

Levinson, D. J. (1986). A conception of adult development. American Psychologist, 41, 3–13.

Levy, W. B., Anderson, J. A., & Lehmkuhle, S. (1984). Synaptic modification, neuron selectivity, and nervous system organization. Hillsdale, NJ: Erlbaum.

Lewin, R. (1987, July 17). Dramatic results with brain grafts. Science, 237, 245–247.

Lewin, R. (1988, April 22). Cloud over Parkinson's therapy. Science, 240, 390–392.

Lewis, P. (1987). Therapeutic change in groups: An interactional perspective. Small Group Behavior, 18, 548–556.

Lewis, M., Feiring, C., McGuffog, C., & Jaskir, J. (1984). Predicting psychopathology in six-year-olds from early social relations. Child Development, 55, 123–136.

Lidz, T. (1973). The origin and treatment of schizophrenic disorders. New York: Basic Books.

Lidz, T., & Fleck, S. (1985). Schizophrenia and the family (2nd ed.). New York: International Universities Press.

Lietaer, G. (1984). Unconditional positive regard: A controversial basic attitude in client-centered therapy. In R. F. Levant & L. M. Shlien (Eds.), Client-centered therapy and the person-centered approach. New York: Praeger.

Lindsay, P. H., & Norman, D. A. (1977). Human information processing (2nd ed.). New York: Academic Press.

Lindsey, K. P., & Paul, G. L. (1989). Involuntary commitments to public mental institutions: Issues involving the overrepresentation of blacks and assessment of relevant functioning. Psychological Bulletin, 106, 171–183.

Lindvall, O., Brundin, P., Widner, H., Rehncrona, S., Gusavii, B., Frackowiak, R., Leenders, K. L., Sawle, G., Rothwell, J. C., Marsden, C. D., & Bjorklund, A. (1990, February 2). Grafts of fetal dopamine neurons survive and improve motor function in Parkinson's Disease. Science, 247, 574–577.

Linz, D., Donnerstein, E., & Adams, S. M. (1989). Physiological desensitization and judgments about female victims of violence. Human Communication Research, 15.

Linz, D. G., Donnerstein, E., & Penrod, S. (1988). Effects of long-term exposure to violent and sexually degrading depictions of women. *Journal of Personality and Social Psychology, 55,* 758–768.

Lipsitt, L. P. (1990). Learning and memory in infants. *Merrill-Palmer Quarterly, 36,* 53–66.

Lobsenz, M. M. (1975). *Sex after sixty-five.* Public Affairs Pamphlet #519, New York Public Affairs Committee.

Loehlin, J. C. (1989). Partitioning environmental and genetic contributions to behavioral development. *American Psychologist, 44,* 1285–1292.

Loftus, E. F., & Palmer, J. C. (1974). Reconstruction of automobile destruction: An example of the interface between language and memory. *Journal of Verbal Learning and Verbal Behavior, 13,* 585–589.

Lohman, D. F. (1989). Human intelligence: An introduction to advances in theory and research. *Review of Educational Research, 59,* 333–373.

Long, A. (1987, December). What is this thing called sleep? *National Geographic, 172,* 786–821.

Long, G. M., & Beaton, R. J. (1982). The case for peripheral persistence: Effects of target and background luminance on a partial-report task. *Journal of Experimental Psychology: Human Perception and Performance, 8,* 383–391.

Long, P. (1986, January). Medical mesmerism. *Psychology Today.*

Lorenz, K. (1966). *On aggression.* New York: Harcourt Brace Jovanovich.

Lorenz, K. (1974). *Civilized man's eight deadly sins.* New York: Harcourt Brace Jovanovich.

Lovaas, O. I., & Koegel, R. (1973). Behavior therapy with autistic children. In C. Thoreson (Ed.), *Behavior Modification and Education.* Chicago: University of Chicago Press.

Luborsky, L. (1988). *Who will benefit from psychotherapy?* New York: Basic Books.

Luborsky, L., Barber, J. P., & Crits-Christoph, P. (1990). Theory-based research for understanding the process of dynamic psychotherapy. *Journal of Consulting and Clinical Psychology, 58,* 281–287.

Luborsky, L., Singer, B., & Luborsky, L. (1975). Comparative studies of psychotherapies: Is it true that everyone has won and all must have prizes? *Archives of General Psychiatry, 32,* 995–1008.

Luborsky, L., & Spence, D. P. (1978). Quantitative research on psychoanalytic therapy. In S. L. Garfield & A. E. Bergin (Eds.), *Handbook of psychotherapy and behavior change: An empirical analysis* (2nd ed.). New York: Wiley.

Luchins, A. S. (1946). Classroom experiments on mental set. *American Journal of Psychology, 59,* 295–298.

Ludwig, A. M. (1969). Altered states of consciousness. In C. T. Tart (Ed.), *Altered states of consciousness.* New York: Wiley.

Luria, A. R. (1968). *The mind of a mnemonist.* New York: Basic Books.

Lynch, J. G., Jr., & Cohen, J. L. (1978). The use of subjective expected utility theory as an aid to understanding variables that influence helping behavior. *Journal of Personality and Social Psychology, 36,* 1138–1151.

Lynn, S. J., & Rhue, J. (1985, September). Daydream believers. *Psychology Today, 14–15.*

Lynn, S. J., & Rhue, J. W. (1988). Fantasy-proneness: Hypnosis, developmental antecedents, and psychopathology. *American Psychologist, 43,* 35–44.

Lynn, S. J., Rhue, J. W., & Weekes, J. R. (1990). Hypnotic involuntariness: A social cognitive analysis. *Psychological Review, 97,* 169–184.

Lynn, S. J., & Snodgrass, M. (1987). Goal-directed fantasy, hypnotic susceptibility, and expectancies. *Journal of Personality and Social Psychology, 53,* 933–938.

Maass, A., & Clark, R. D., III (1984). Hidden impact of minorities: Fifteen years of minority influence research. *Psychological Bulletin, 95,* 428–450.

McCanne, T. R., & Anderson, J. A. (1987). Emotional responding following experimental manipulation of facial electromyographic activity. *Journal of Personality and Social Psychology, 52,* 759–768.

McCauley, C., & Swann, C. P. (1978). Male-female differences in sexual fantasy. *Journal of Research in Personality, 12,* 76–86.

McClelland, D. C. (1985). How motives, skills, and values determine what people do. *American Psychologist, 40,* 812–825. (a)

McClelland, D. C. (1985). *Human motivation.* Glenview, IL: Scott, Foresman. (b)

McClelland, D. C., Atkinson, J. W., Clark, R. A., & Lowell, E. L. (1953). *The achievement motive.* New York: Appleton-Century-Crofts.

McCloskey, M., Wible, C. G., & Cohen, N. J. (1988). Is there a special flashbulb-memory mechanism? *Journal of Experimental Psychology: General, 117,* 171–181.

McConnell, J. V. (1985). On Gazzaniga and right hemisphere language. *American Psychologist, 40,* 1273.

MacDonald, M. R., & Kuiper, N. A. (1983). Cognitive-behavioral preparations for surgery: Some theoretical and methodological concerns. *Clinical Psychology Review, 3,* 27–39.

McDougall, W. (1908). *Introduction to social psychology.* London: Methuen.

MacFadyen, J. T. (1987, November). Educated monkeys help the disabled help themselves. *Smithsonian,* pp. 125–133.

McGrath, E. (1988, August). A different kind of treatment: Medicine, education and research. Paper presented at the annual meeting of the American Psychological Association (Atlanta).

McGraw, K. M., & Bloomfield, J. (1987). Social influence on group moral decisions: The interactive effects of moral reasoning and sex-role orientation. *Journal of Personality and Social Psychology, 53,* 1080–1087.

McGuire, W. J. (1964). Inducing resistance to persuasion. In L. Berkowitz (Ed.), *Advances in experimental social psychology* (Vol. 1). New York: Academic Press.

McGuire, W. J. (1968). Personality and susceptibility to social influence. In E. F. Borgatta & W. W. Lambert (Eds.), *Handbook of personality theory and research.* Chicago: Rand McNally.

McGuire, W. J. (1985). Attitudes and attitude change. In G. Lindzey & E. Aronson (Eds.), *Handbook of social psychology* (Vol. 2, 3rd ed.). New York: Random House.

Mackenzie, B. (1984). Explaining race differences in IQ: The logic, the methodology, and the evidence. *American Psychologist, 39,* 1214–1233.

Mackie, D. M. (1987). Systematic and nonsystematic processing of majority and minority persuasive communications. *Journal of Personality and Social Psychology, 53,* 41–52.

McKusick, L., Horstman, W., & Coates, T. J. (1985). AIDS and sexual behavior reported by gay men in San Francisco. *American Journal of Public Health, 75,* 493–496.

McNeal, E. T., & Cimbolic, P. (1986). Antidepressants and biochemical theories of depression. *Psychological Bulletin, 99,* 361–374.

Maddi, S. R., Bartone, P. T., & Puccetti, M. C. (1987). Stressful events are indeed a factor in physical illness: Reply to Schroeder and Costa (1984). *Journal of Personality and Social Psychology, 52,* 833–843.

Maeroff, G. I. (1977, August 21). The unfavored gifted few. *New York Times Magazine.*

Magnusson, D., & Endler, N. S. (1977). Interactional psychology: Present status and future prospects. In D. Magnusson & N. S. Endler (Eds.), *Personality at the crossroads: Current issues in interactional psychology.* Hillsdale, NJ: Erlbaum.

Malin, J. T. (1979). Information-processing load in problem solving by network search. *Journal of Experimental Psychology: Human Perception and Performance, 5,* 379–390.

Malinowski, C. I., & Smith, C. P. (1985). Moral reasoning and moral conduct: An investigation prompted by Kohlberg's theory. *Journal of Personality and Social Issues, 49,* 1016–1027.

Mandl, H., & Lesgold, A. (1988). *Learning issues for intelligent tutoring systems.* New York: Springer-Verlag.

Manis, F., Keating, D. P., & Morrison, F. J. (1980). Developmental differences in the allocation of processing capacity. *Journal of Experimental Child Psychology, 29,* 156–159.

Marks, G., & Miller, N. (1987). Ten years of research on the false-consensus effect: An empirical and theoretical review. *Psychological Bulletin, 102,* 72–90.

Marks, I. M. (1982). Toward an empirical clinical science: Behavioral psychotherapy in the 1980s. *Behavioral Therapies, 13,* 63–81.

Marlatt, G. A., Baer, J. S., Donovan, D. M., & Kivlahan, D. R. (1988). Addictive behaviors: Etiology and treatment. *Annual Review of Psychology, 39,* 223–252.

Marmar, C. R. (1990). Psychotherapy process research: Progress, dilemmas, and future directions. *Journal of Consulting and Clinical Psychology, 58,* 265–272.

Marshall, G., & Zimbardo, P. (1979). The affective consequences of "inadequately explained" physiological arousal. *Journal of Personality and Social Psychology, 37,* 970–988.

Martindale, C. (1981). *Cognition and consciousness*. Homewood, IL: Dorsey Press.

Marx, M. B., Garrity, T. F., & Bowers, F. R. (1975). The influence of recent life experience on the health of college freshmen. *Journal of Psychosomatic Research, 19,* 87–98.

Marx, M. H., & Hillix, W. A. (1987). *Systems and theories in psychology* (4th ed.). New York: McGraw-Hill.

Maslow, A. H. (1970). *Motivation and personality*. New York: Harper & Row.

Maslow, A. H. (1987). *Motivation and personality* (3rd ed.). New York: Harper & Row.

Mason, J. W. (1974). Specificity in the organization of neuroendocrine response profiles. In P. Seeman and G. M. Brown (Eds.), *Frontiers in neurology and neuroscience research*. First International Symposium of the Neuroscience Institute. Toronto: University of Toronto Press.

Mason, J. W. (1975). A historical view of the stress field. *Journal of Human Stress, 1,* 6–12, 22–37.

Masters, W. H., & Johnson, V. E. (1979). *Homosexuality in perspective*. Boston: Little, Brown.

Masters, W. H., Johnson, V. E., & Kolodny, R. C. (1988). *CRISIS: Heterosexual behavior in the age of AIDS*. New York: Grove Press.

Mastropierei, M. A., & Scruggs, T. (1987). *Effective instruction for special education*. Boston: College-Hill Press/Little, Brown.

Matrazzo, J. D. (1987). There is only one psychology, no specialties, but many applications. *American Psychologist, 42,* 893–903.

Matsuda, L., Lolait, S., Brownstein, M., Young, A., & Bonner, T. (1990, August 9). *Nature*

Matsumoto, D. (1987). The role of facial response in the experience of emotion: More methodological problems and a meta-analysis. *Journal of Personality and Social Psychology, 52,* 769–774.

Mawhinney, V. T., Boston, D. E., Loaws, O. R., Blumenfeld, G. T., & Hopkins, B. L. (1971). A comparison of students' studying behavior produced by daily, weekly, and three-week testing schedules. *Journal of Applied Behavior Analysis, 4,* 257–264.

May, R. (1969). *Love and will*. New York: Norton.

Mayer, R. E. (1982). Different problem-solving strategies for algebra word and equation problems. *Journal of Experimental Psychology: Learning, Memory, and Cognition, 8,* 448–462.

Melges, F. T., & Bowlby, J. (1969). Types of hopelessness in psychopathological process. *Archives of General Psychiatry, 70,* 690–699.

Melton, G. B., & Garrison, E. G. (1987). Fear, prejudice, and neglect: Discrimination against mentally disabled persons. *American Psychologist, 42,* 1007–1026.

Melville, J. (1977). *Phobias and obsessions*. New York: Coward, McCann.

Melzack, R., & Wall, P. D. (1965). Pain mechanisms: A new theory. *Science, 150,* pp. 971–979.

Merzenich, M. M., & Kass, J. H. (1980). Principles of organization of sensory-perceptual systems in mammals. In J. M. Sprague & A. N. Epstein (Eds.), *Progress in psychology and physiological psychology* (Vol. 9). New York: Academic Press.

Metcalfe, J. (1986). Premonitions of insight predict impending error. *Journal of Experimental Psychology: Learning, Memory, and Cognition, 12,* 623–634.

Metee, D. R., & Aronson, E. (1974). Affective reactions to appraisal from others. In T. L. Huston (Ed.), *Foundations of interpersonal attraction* (pp. 235–283). New York: Academic Press.

Meyer, J. P., & Pepper, S. (1977). Need compatibility and marital adjustment in young married couples. *Journal of Personality and Social Psychology, 35,* 331–342.

Meyer, R. G., & Osborne, Y. V. H. (1987). *Case studies in abnormal behavior* (2nd ed.). Boston: Allyn & Bacon.

Meyerhoff, M. K., & White, B. L. (1986, September). Making the grade as parents. *Psychology Today,* pp. 38–45.

Mikhail, A. (1981). Stress: A psychophysiological conception. *Journal of Human Stress, 7,* 9–15.

Milewski, A. E. (1976). Infants' discrimination of internal and external pattern elements. *Journal of Experimental Child Psychology, 22,* 229–246.

Milgram, S. (1974). *Obedience to authority*. New York: Harper & Row.

Miller, A. G. (1986). *The obedience experiments: A case study of controversy in social science*. New York: Praeger.

Miller, G. A. (1956). The magical number seven, plus or minus two: Some limits on our capacity for processing information. *Psychology Review, 63*, 81–97.

Miller, L. L. (Ed.) (1975). *Marijuana: Current research.* New York: Academic Press.

Miller, M. W. (1986, September 19). Effects of alcohol on the generation and migration of cerebral cortical neurons. *Science, 213,* 1308–1310.

Miller, N. E. (1985). The value of behavioral research on animals. *American Psychologist, 40*, 423–440 (b).

Miller, S. M., Brody, D. S., & Summerton, J. (1988). Styles of coping with threat: Implications for health. *Journal of Personality and Social Psychology, 54,* 142–148.

Miller-Jones, D. (1989). Culture and testing. *American Psychologist, 44,* 360–366.

Milloy, C. (1986, June 22). Crack user's highs, lows. *Washington Post*, p. A-1.

Milner, B. (1966). Amnesia following operation on temporal lobes. In C. W. M. Whitty & P. Zangwill (Eds.), *Amnesia.* London: Butterworth.

Mineka, S., & Hendersen, R. W. (1985). Controllability and predictability in acquired motivation. *Annual Review of Psychology, 36,* 495–529.

Minuchin, S. (1974). *Families and family therapy.* Cambridge, MA: Harvard University Press.

Mirsky, A. F., & Duncan, C. C. (1986). Etiology and expression of schizophrenia: Neurological and psychosocial factors. *Annual Review of Psychology, 37.*

Mischel, W. (1968). *Personality and assessment.* New York: Wiley.

Mischel, W. (1990). Personality dispositions revisited and revised: A view after three decades. In L. A. Pervin (Ed.), *Handbook of personality theory and research.* New York: Guilford.

Mischel, W., & Peake, P. K. (1982). Analyzing the construction of consistency in personality. *Nebraska Symposium on Motivation,* 233–262 (a).

Mischel, W., & Peake, P. K. (1982). Beyond deja vu in the search for cross-situational consistency. *Psychological Review, 89,* 730–755 (b).

Mischel, W., & Peake, P. K. (1983). Some facets of consistency: Replies to Epstein, Funder, and Bem. *Psychological Review, 90,* 394–402.

Molotsky, I. (1984, November 30). Implant to aid the totally deaf is approved. *New York Times*, pp. A-1, B-10.

Money, J. (1987). Sin, sickness, or status? Homosexuality, gender identity, and psychoneuroendocrinology. *American Psychologist, 42,* 384–399.

Monmaney, T. (1987, December 7). Keeping it in the family. *Newsweek,* p. 81.

Montemayor, P. (1983). Parents and adolescents in conflict: All families some of the time and some families most of the time. *Journal of Early Adolescence, 3,* 83–103.

Moore, B. E., & Fine, B. D. (1990). *Psychoanalytic terms and concepts.* New Haven, CT: Yale University Press.

Moore, B. S., & Isen, A. M. (Eds.) (1990). *Affect and social behavior.* Cambridge, England: Cambridge University Press.

Moscovici, S. (1985). Social influence and conformity. In G. Lindzey & E. Aronson (Eds.), *Handbook of social psychology* (3rd ed.). New York: Random House.

Moscovici, S., & Mugny, G. (1983). Minority influence. In P. B. Paulus (Ed.), *Basic group processes.* New York: Springer-Verlag.

Motley, M. T. (1987, February). What I meant to say. *Psychology Today,* pp. 25–28.

Mucha, T. F., & Reinhardt, R. F. (1970). Conversion reactions in student aviators. *American Journal of Psychiatry, 127,* 493–497.

Mueller, E., & Lucas, T. (1975). A developmental analysis of peer interaction among toddlers. In M. Lewis & L. A. Rosenblum (Eds.), *Friendship and peer relations.* New York: Wiley-Interscience.

Mumford, M. D., & Gustafson, S. B. (1988). Creativity syndrome: Integration, application, and innovation. *Psychological Bulletin, 103,* 27–43.

Munnichs, U., Mussen, P., Olbrich, E., & Coleman, P. (Eds.) (1985). *Life-span and change in a gerontological perspective.* New York: Academic Press.

Mussen, P. H., & Jones, M. C. (1957). Self-conceptions, motivations, and interpersonal attitudes of late- and early-maturing boys. *Child Development, 28,* 243–256.

Nahemon, L., & Lawton, M. P. (1975). Similarity and propinquity in friendship formation. *Journal of Personality and Social Psychology, 32,* 205–213.

Namir, S., Wolcott, D. L., Fawzy, F. I., & Alumbaugh, M. J. (1987). Coping with AIDS: Psychological and health implications. *Journal of Applied Social Psychology, 17,* 309–328.

Nash, M. (1987). What, if anything, is regressed about hypnotic age regression? A review of the empirical literature. *Psychological Bulletin, 102,* 42–52.

Nathans, J., Davenport, C. M., Maumenee, I. H., Lewis, R. A., Hejtmancik, J. F., Litt, M., Lovrien, E., Weleber, R., Bachynski, B., Zwas, F., Klingaman, R., & Fishman, G. (1989, August 25). Molecular genetics of human blue cone monochromacy. *Science, 245,* 831–838.

Nathans, J., Piantanidu, T. P., Eddy, R. L., Shows, T. B., & Hogness, D. S. (1986, April 11). Molecular genetics of inherited variation in human color vision. *Science, 232,* pp. 203–210.

National Institute of Drug Abuse. (1986). *Annual survey of drug use.* Washington, D.C.: U.S. Government Printing Office.

Navon, R., & Proia, R. L. (1989, March 17). The mutations in Ashkenazi Jews with adult G(M2) Gangliosidosis, the adult form of Tay-Sachs Disease. *Science, 243,* 1471–1474.

Newman, J. P., & Kosson, D. S. (1986). Passive avoidance learning in psychopathic and nonpsychopathic offenders. *Journal of Abnormal Psychology, 95,* 252–256.

Nisbett, R. E. (1968). Taste, deprivation, and weight determinants of eating behavior. *Journal of Personality and Social Psychology, 10,* 107–116.

Nisbett, R. E. (1972). Hunger, obesity and the ventromedial hypothalamus. *Psychological Review, 79,* 433–453.

Nogrady, H., McConkey, K. M., & Perry, C. (1985). Enhancing visual memory: Trying hypnosis, trying imagination, and trying again. *Journal of Abnormal Psychology, 94,* 105–204.

Noll, K. M., & Davis, J. M. (1983). Biological theories in schizophrenia. In A. Rifkin (Ed.), *Schizophrenia and affective disorders: Biology and drug treatment* (pp. 139–204). Boston: John Wright.

Norcia, A. M., & Tyler, C. W. (1985). Spatial frequency sweep VEP: Visual acuity during the first year of life. *Vision Research, 25,* 1399–1408.

Novak, M. A., & Suomi, S. J. (1988). Psychological well-being of primates in captivity. *American Psychologist, 43,* 765–773.

Nowicki, S., & Duke, M. (1978). An examination of counseling variables within a social learning framework. *Journal of Counseling Psychology, 25,* 1–7.

O'Brien, C. P., et al. (1988). Pharmacological and behavioral treatments of cocaine dependence: Controlled studies. *Journal of Clinical Psychiatry, 49,* 17.

Oei, T. P. S., Lim, B., & Hennessy, B. (1990). Psychological dysfunction in battle: Combat stress reactions and posttraumatic stress disorder. *Clinical Psychology Review, 10,* 355–388.

Office of Technology Assessment (1990). *Integrity tests.* Washington, DC: Office of Technology Assessment.

O'Keeffe, M. K., Nesselhof-Kendall, S., & Baum, A. (1990). Behavior and prevention of AIDS: Bases of research and intervention. *Personality and Social Psychology Bulletin, 16,* 166–180.

Olds, J., & Milner, P. (1954). Positive reinforcement produced by electrical stimulation of septal area and other regions of rat brain. *Journal of Comparative and Physiological Psychology, 47,* 411–427.

Opler, L. A., Kay, S. R., Rosado, V., & Lindenmayer, J. P. (1984). Positive and negative syndromes in chronic schizophrenic inpatients. *Journal of Nervous and Mental Disease, 172,* 317–325.

Orne, M. T., & Holland, C. C. (1968). On the ecological validity of laboratory deceptions. *International Journal of Psychiatry, 6,* 282–293.

Ornstein, P. A., & Naus, M. J. (1988). Effects of the knowledge base on children's memory strategies. In H. W. Reese (Ed.), *Advances in Child Development and Behavior* (Vol. 19). New York: Academic Press.

Ornstein, R. E. (1977). *The psychology of consciousness* (2nd ed.). New York: Harcourt Brace Jovanovich.

Orwin, R. G., & Condray, D. S. (1984). Smith and Glass' psychotherapy conclusions need further probing: On Landman and Dawes' re-analysis. *American Psychologist, 39,* 71–72.

Osherson, D. N. (Ed.) (1990). *An invitation to cognitive science.* Cambridge, MA: Bradford.

Oskamp, S. (1988). Nontraditional employment opportunities for applied psychologists. *American Psychologist, 43,* 484–485.

Palca, J. (1989, 28 July). Sleep researchers awake to possibilities. *Science, 245,* 351–352.

Palmonari, A., Pombeni, M. L., & Kirchler, E. (1990). Adolescents and their peer groups. *Social Behaviour, 5,* 33–34.

Papalia, D., & Olds, S. (1989). *Human development* (4th ed.). New York: McGraw-Hill.

Parlee, M. B. (1979, October). The friendship bond. *Psychology Today, 13,* pp. 43–45.

Paterson, R. J., & Neufeld, R. W. J. (1987). Clear danger: Situational determinants of the appraisal of threat. *Psychological Bulletin, 101,* 404–416.

Patterson, C. H. (1989). Foundations for a systematic eclectic psychotherapy. *Psychotherapy, 26,* 427–435.

Paul, S. (1986, December 5). A selective imidazobenzodiazepine antagonist of ethanol in the rat. *Science, 234,* 1245.

Pavlov, I. P. (1927). *Conditioned reflexes.* London: Oxford University Press.

Payne, D. G. (1986). Hyperamnesia for pictures and words: Testing the recall level hypothesis. *Journal of Experimental Psychology: Learning, Memory, and Cognition, 12,* 16–29.

Pennebaker, N. N., Burnam, M. A., Schaeffer, N. A., & Harper, D. C. (1977). Lack of control as a determinant of perceived physical symptoms. *Journal of Personality and Social Psychology, 35,* 167–174.

Perdue, C. W., Dovidio, J. F., Gurtman, M. B., & Tyler, R. B. (1990). Us and them: Social categorization and the process of intergroup bias. *Journal of Personality and Social Psychology, 59,* 475–486.

Pereira-Smith, O., Smith, J., et al. (1988, August). Paper presented at the annual meeting of the International Genetics Congress (Toronto).

Perkins, D. N. (1983). Why the human perceiver is a bad machine. In J. Beck, B. Hope & A. Rosenfeld (Eds.), *Human and machine vision.* New York: Academic Press.

Perlmutter, M., & Mitchell, D. B. (1986). The appearance and disappearance of age differences in adult memory. In I. M. Craik & S. Trehub (Eds.), *Aging and cognitive processes.* New York: Plenum Press.

Perls, F. S. (1967). Group vs. individual therapy. *ETC: A review of general semantics, 34,* 306–312.

Perls, F. S. (1970). *Gestalt therapy now: Therapy, techniques, applications.* Palo Alto, CA: Science and Behavior Books.

Pervin, L. A. (Ed.) (1990). *Handbook of personality theory and research.* New York: Guilford.

Peterson, A. C. (1988, September). Those gangly years. *Psychology Today,* pp. 28–34.

Peterson, C., & Barrett, L. C. (1987). Explanatory style and academic performance among university freshmen. *Journal of Personality and Social Psychology, 53,* 603–607.

Peterson, C., & Raps, C. S. (1984). Helplessness and hospitalization: More remarks. *Journal of Personality and Social Psychology, 46,* 82–83.

Peterson, C., Seligman, M. E. P., & Vaillant, G. E. (1988). Pessimistic explanatory style is a risk factor for physical illness: A thirty-five-year longitudinal study. *Journal of Personality and Social Psychology, 55,* 23–27.

Peterson, L. R., & Peterson, M. J. (1959). Short-term retention of individual items. *Journal of Experimental Psychology, 58,* 193–198.

Petty, R. E., & Cacioppo, J. T. (1977). Cognitive responding and resistance to persuasion. *Journal of Personality and Social Psychology, 35,* 645–655.

Petty, R. E., & Cacioppo, J. T. (1981). *Attitudes and persuasion: Classic and contemporary approaches.* Dubuque, IA: Brown.

Petty, R. E., & Cacioppo, J. T. (1984). The effects of involvement on responses to argument quantity and quality: Central and peripheral routes to persuasion. *Journal of Personality and Social Psychology, 46,* 69–81.

Petty, R. E., & Cacioppo, J. T. (1986). The elaboration likelihood model of persuasion. In L. Berkowitz (Ed.), *Advances in experimental social psychology* (Vol. 10). New York: Academic Press.

Phillips, D., McCartney, K., & Scarr, S. (1987). Child-care quality and children's social development. *Developmental Psychology, 23,* 537–543.

Phillips, R. D., Wagner, S. H., Fells, C. A., & Lynch, M. (1990). *Infant behavior and development, 13,* 71–84.

Piaget, J. (1970). Piaget's theory. In P. H. Mussen (Ed.), *Carmichael's manual of child psychology* (Vol. I, 3rd ed.). New York: John Wiley.

Piaget, J., & Inhelder, B. (1958). *The growth of logical thinking from childhood to adolescence.* Translated by A. Parsons & S. Seagrin. New York: Basic Books.

Piccione, C., Hilgard, E. R., & Zimbardo, P. G. (1989). On the degree of stability of measured hypnotizability over a 25-year period. *Journal of Personality and Social Psychology, 56,* 289–295.

Piliavin, J. A., & Piliavin, I. M. (1972). Effect of blood on reactions to a victim. *Journal of Personality and Social Psychology, 23,* 353–362.

Pi-Sunyer, F. X. (1987). Exercise effects on caloric intake. In R. Wurtman (Ed.), *Obesity.* New York: New York Academy of Science.

Plomin, R. (1989). Environment and genes: Determinants of behavior. *American Psychologist, 44,* 105–111.

Plomin, R. (1989, April 13). The role of inheritance in behavior. *Science, 248,* 183–188.

Poling, A., Gadow, K. D., & Cleary, J. (1990). *Drug therapy for behavior disorders: An introduction.* New York: Pergamon.

Polivy, J., & Herman, L. P. (1985). Dieting and binging: A causal analysis. *American Psychologist, 40,* 193–201.

Pollack, A. (1987, September 15). More human than ever, computer is learning to learn. *New York Times,* pp. C-1, C-6.

Porter, R. H., Cernich, J. M., & McLaughlin, F. J. (1983). Maternal recognition of neonates through olfactory cues. *Physiology and Behavior, 30,* 151–154.

Posner, M. I., & Presti, D. E. (1987). Selective attention and cognitive control. *Trends in Neurosciences, 10,* 13–17.

Power, T. G., & Parke, R. D. (1982). Play as a context for early learning: Lab and home analyses. In L. M. Laosa & I. E. Sigal (Eds.), *The family as a learning environment.* New York: Plenum.

Pribram, K. H. (1984). Emotion: A neurobehavioral analysis. In K. R. Scherer & P. Ekman (Eds.), *Approaches to emotion.* Hillsdale, NJ: Erlbaum.

Prien, R. F. (1983). Lithium and the long-term maintenance treatment of tricyclic antidepressant drugs and therapeutic response. In P. J. Clayton & J. E. Barret (Eds.), *Treatment of depression: Old controversies and new approaches* (pp. 105–114). New York: Raven Press.

Pyszczynski, T., Holt, K., & Greenberg, J. (1987). Depression, self-focused attention, and expectancies for positive and negative future life events for self and others. *Journal of Personality and Social Psychology, 52,* 994–1001.

Rachlin, H. (1990, August). *Context in classical and instrumental conditioning.* G. Stanley Hall Lecture presented at the annual meeting of the American Psychological Association, Boston.

Rachman, S., & Hodgson, R. (1980). *Obsessions and compulsions.* Englewood Cliffs, NJ: Prentice-Hall.

Ragozin, A. S. (1980). Attachment behavior of day care children: Naturalistic and laboratory observations. *Child Development, 51,* 409–415.

Rahe, R. H., & Arthur, R. J. (1978). Life change and illness studies: Past history and future directions. *Human Stress, 4,* 3–15.

Raphael, B. (1976). *The thinking computer.* San Francisco: Freeman.

Rasmussen, J. (1981). Models of mental strategies in process control. In J. Rasmussen & W. Rouse (Eds.), *Human detection and diagnosis of system failures.* New York: Plenum Press.

Reed, C. F. (1984). Terrestrial passage theory of the moon illusion. *Journal of Experimental Psychology: General, 113,* 489–500.

Reed, S. K. (1988). *Cognition: Theories and applications* (2nd ed.). Monterey, CA: Brooks/Cole.

Reich, P. A. (1986). *Language development.* Englewood Cliffs, NJ: Prentice-Hall.

Reiger, D. A., Boyd, J. H., Burke, J. D., Jr., Rae, D. S., Myers, J. K., Kramer, M., Robins, L. N., George, L. K., Karno, M., & Locke, B. Z. (1988). One-month prevalence of mental disorders in the United States. *Archives of General Psychiatry, 45,* 977–986.

Reiger, D. A., Myers, J. K., Kramer, M., Robins, L. N., Blazer, D. G., Hough, R. L., Eaton, W. W., & Lock, B. Z. (1984). The NIMH epidemiological catchment area program. *Archives of General Psychiatry, 41,* 934–941.

Reinke, B. J., Holmes, D. S., & Harris, R. L. (1985). The timing of psychosocial changes in women's lives: The years 25 to 45. *Journal of Personality and Social Psychology, 48,* 1353–1364.

Reis, H. T., Wheeler, L., Spiegel, N., Kerris, M. H., Nezlek, J., & Perri, M. (1982). Physical attractiveness in social interaction: II. Why does appearance affect social experience? *Journal of Personality and Social Psychology, 43,* 979–996.

Reis, S. M. (1989). Reflections on policy affecting the education of gifted and talented students. *American Psychologist, 44,* 399–408.

Reisenzein, R. (1983). The Schachter theory of emotion: Two decades later. *Psychological Bulletin, 94*, 239–264.

Reiss, B. F. (1980). Psychological tests in homosexuality. In J. Marmor (Ed.), *Homosexual behavior* (pp. 296–311). New York: Basic Books.

Reitman, J. S. (1965). *Cognition and thought.* New York: Wiley.

Rescorla, R. A. (1988). Pavlovian conditioning: It's not what you think it is. *American Psychologist, 43*, 151–160.

Reuman, D. A., Alwin, D. F., & Veroff, J. (1984). Assessing the validity of the achievement motive in the presence of random measurement error. *Journal of Personality and Social Psychology, 47*, 1347–1362.

Reynolds, C., & Mann, L. (Eds.) (1987). *Encyclopedia of special education.* New York: Wiley.

Reynolds, R. I., & Takooshian, H. (1988, January). Where were you August 8, 1985? *Bulletin of the Psychonomic Society, 26*, 23–25.

Rhue, J. W., & Lynn, S. J. (1987). Fantasy-proneness and psychopathology. *Journal of Personality and Social Psychology, 53*, 327–336.

Rice, A. (1984, May). Imagination to go. *Psychology Today*, pp. 48–52.

Rice, B. (1981, December). Call-in therapy: Reach out and shrink someone. *Psychology Today*, pp. 39–47, 87.

Rice, M. L. (1989). Children's language acquisition. *American Psychologist, 44*, 149–156.

Richards, R., Kinney, D. K., Benet, M., & Merzel, A. P. C. (1988). Assessing everyday creativity: Characteristics of the lifetime creativity scales and validation with three large samples. *Journal of Personality and Social Psychology, 54*, 476–485.

Rinn, W. E. (1984). The neuropsychology of facial expression: A review of neurological and psychological mechanisms for producing facial expressions. *Psychological Bulletin, 95*, 52–77.

Ritzler, B., & Rosenbaum, G. (1974). Proprioception in schizophrenics and normals: Effects of stimulus intensity and interstimulus interval. *Journal of Abnormal Psychology, 83*, 106–111.

Roberts, A. H. (1985). Biofeedback: Research, training, and clinical roles. *American Psychologist, 40*, 938–941.

Roberts, L. (1988, January 1). Zeroing in on the sex switch. *Science, 239*, 21–23. (a)

Roberts, L. (1988, July 8). Vietnam's psychological toll. *Science, 241*, 159–161. (b)

Robins, C. J. (1988). Attributions and depression: Why is the literature so inconsistent? *Journal of Personality and Social Psychology, 54*, 880–889.

Rock, I. (1983). *The logic of perception.* Cambridge, MA: MIT Press.

Rodin, J. (1981). Current status of the internal-external hypothesis of obesity: What went wrong? *American Psychologist, 34*, 361–372.

Rodin, J. (1985). Insulin levels, hunger, and food intake: An example of feedback loops in body-weight regulation. *Health Psychology, 4*, 1–18.

Rodin, J. (1986, September 19). Aging and health: Effects of the sense of control. *Science, 233*, 1271–1276.

Rogers, C. R. (1951). *Client-centered therapy.* Boston: Houghton-Mifflin.

Rogers, C. R. (1971). A theory of personality. In S. Maddi (Ed.), *Perspectives on personality.* Boston: Little, Brown.

Rogers, C. R. (1980). *A way of being.* Boston: Houghton Mifflin.

Rogers, M. (1988, February 15). The return of 3-D movies—on TV. *Newsweek*, pp. 60–62. (a)

Rogers, M. (1988, October 3). Here comes hypermedia. *Newsweek*, pp. 44–45. (b)

Rogers, R. (1987). APA's position on the insanity defense. *American Psychologist, 42*, 840–848.

Rohter, L. (1987, July 21). Inside the operating room: A day of bold brain surgery. *New York Times*, pp. C-17, C-20.

Rorschach, H. (1924). *Psychodiagnosis: A diagnostic test based on perception.* New York: Grune and Stratton.

Rosen, G. M. (1987). Self-help treatment books and the commercialization of psychotherapy. *American Psychologist, 42*, 46–51.

Rosenberg, M. B., Friedmann, T., Robertson, R. C., Tuszynski, M., Wolff, J. A., Breakefield, X. O., & Gage, F. H. (1988). Grafting genetically modified cells to the damaged brain: Restorative effects of NGF expression. *Science, 242*, 1575–1578.

Rosenhan, D. L. (1975). The contextual nature of psychiatric diagnosis. *Journal of Abnormal Psychology, 84*, 462–474.

Rosenthal, D. (1970). *Genetic theory and abnormal behavior.* New York: McGraw-Hill.

Ross, C. A. (1989). *Multiple personality disorder: Diagnosis, clinical features and treatment.* New York: Wiley.

Ross, L., Greene, D., & House, P. (1977). The false consensus effect: An egocentric bias in social perception and attribution processes. *Journal of Experimental Social Psychology, 13,* 279–301.

Ross, M., & Fletcher, G. J. O. (1985). Attribution and social perception. In G. Lindzy & E. Aronson (Eds.), *Handbook of social psychology* (3rd ed.). New York: Random House.

Rouse, W. B., & Morris, N. M. (1986). On looking into the black box: Prospects and limits in the search for mental models. *Psychological Bulletin, 100,* 349–363.

Routtenberg, A., & Lindy, J. (1965). Effects of the availability of rewarding septal and hypothalmic stimulation on bar pressing for food under conditions of deprivation. *Journal of Comparative and Physiological Psychology, 60,* 158–161.

Rowe, J. W., & Kahn, R. L. (1987, July 10). Human aging: Usual and successful. *Science, 237,* 143–149.

Rowlison, R. T., & Felner, R. D. (1988). Major life events, hassles, and adaptation in adolescence: Confounding in the conceptualization and measurement of life stress and adjustment revisited. *Journal of Personality and Social Psychology, 55,* 432–444.

Royer, J. M., & Feldman, R. S. (1984). *Educational psychology: Applications and theory.* New York: Knopf.

Rozin, P. (1977). The significance of learning mechanisms in food selection: Some biology, psychology and sociology of science. In L. M. Barker, M. R. Best, & M. Donijan (Eds.), *Learning mechanisms in food selection.* Waco, TX: Baylor University Press.

Rubenstein, C. (1982, July). Psychology's fruit flies. *Psychology Today,* pp. 83–84.

Rubin, D. C. (1985, September). The subtle deceiver: Recalling our past. *Psychology Today, 19,* pp. 39–46.

Rubin, Z. (1970). Measurement of romantic love. *Journal of Personality and Social Psychology, 16,* 265–273.

Rubin, Z. (1973). *Liking and loving.* New York: Holt, Rinehart and Winston.

Russell, G., & Russell, A. (1987). Mother-child and father-child relationships in middle childhood. *Child Development, 58,* 1573–1585.

Russo, D. C., Carr, E. G., & Lovaas, O. I. (1980). Self-injury in pediatric populations. *Comprehensive handbook of behavioral medicine* (Vol. 3: Extended applications and issues). Holliswood, NY: Spectrum.

Russo, N. (1981). In L. T. Benjamin, Jr., & K. D. Lowman (Eds.), *Activities handbook for the teaching of psychology.* Washington, DC: American Psychological Association.

Rutter, M. (1982). Social-emotional consequences of day-care for preschool children. In E. F. Zigler & E. W. Gordon (Eds.), *Day-care: Scientific and social policy issues.* Boston: Auburn House.

Sabourin, M. E., Cutcomb, S. D., Crawford, H. J., & Pribram, K. (1990). EEG correlates of hypnotic susceptibility and hypnotic trance: Spectral analysis and coherence. *International Journal of Psychophysiology, 10,* 125–142.

Sackheim, H. A. (1985, June). The case for E.C.T. *Psychology Today,* pp. 36–40.

Sanders, M. S., & McCormick, E. J. (1987). *Human factors in engineering and design* (6th ed.). New York: McGraw-Hill.

Sarason, I. G. (1976). A modeling and informational approach to delinquency. In E. Ribes-Inesta & A. Bandura (Eds.), *Analysis of delinquency and aggression.* Hillsdale, NJ: Erlbaum.

Sarason, I. G., Johnson, J. H., & Siegel, J. M. (1978). Assessing the impact of life changes: Development of the Life Experiences Survey. *Journal of Consulting and Clinical Psychology, 46,* 932–946.

Scarr, S. (1986, August). Child-care decisions and working mothers' dilemmas. Address given at the annual meeting of the American Psychological Association (Washington, DC).

Scarr, S., & Carter-Saltzman, L. (1982). Genetics and intelligence. In R. J. Sternberg (Ed.), *Handbook of human intelligence* (pp. 792–896). Cambridge: Cambridge University Press.

Scarr, S., Phillips, D., & McCartney, K. (1990). Facts, fantasies and the future of child care in the United States. *Psychological Science, 1,* 26–35.

Scarr, S., & Weinberg, R. A. (1976). I.Q. test performance of black children adopted by white families. *American Psychologist, 3,* 726–739.

Schachter, S. (1959). *The psychology of affiliation.* Stanford, CA: Stanford University Press.

Schachter, S. (1971). Some extraordinary facts about obese humans and rats. *American Psychologist, 26,* 129–144.

Schachter, S., Goldman, R., & Gordon, A. (1968). Effects of fear, food deprivation, and obesity on eating. *Journal of Personality and Social Psychology, 10,* 91–97.

Schachter, S., & Singer, J. E. (1962). Cognitive, social, and physiological determinants of emotional state. *Psychological Review, 69,* 379–399.

Schaie, K. W. (1985). *Longitudinal studies of psychological development.* New York: Guilford Press.

Schaie, K. W. (1988). Ageism in psychological research. *American Psychologist, 43,* 179–183.

Schaie, K. W., Campbell, R. T., Meredith, W., & Rawlings, S. C. (Eds.) (1988). *Methodological issues in aging research.* New York: Springer-Verlag.

Schaie, K. W., & Willis, S. L. (1985, August). *Differential ability decline and its remediation in late adulthood.* Paper presented at annual meeting of the American Psychological Association (Los Angeles).

Scharf, B., & Buus, S. (1986). Audition. In K. R. Boff, L. Kaufman, & J. P. Thomas (Eds.), *Handbook of perception and human performance* (Vol. 1). New York: Wiley.

Scheibel, A. (1984). Personal communication.

Scheier, M. F. (1986). Coping with stress: Divergent strategies of optimists and pessimists. *Journal of Personality and Social Psychology, 51,* 1257–1264.

Scher, S. J., & Cooper, J. (1989). Motivational basis of dissonance: The singular role of behavioral consequences. *Journal of Personality and Social Psychology, 56,* 899–906.

Scherer, K. R. (1984). Les émotions: Fonctions et composantes. [Emotions: Functions and components.] *Cahiers de psychologie cognitive, 4,* 9–39.

Scherer, K. R., & Ekman, P. (Eds.) (1984). *Approaches to emotion.* Hillsdale, NJ: Erlbaum.

Schickedanz, J. A., Schickedanz, D. I., & Forsyth, P. D. (1982). *Toward understanding children.* Boston: Little, Brown.

Schiffman, H. R. (1982). *Sensation and perception: An integrated approach* (2nd ed.). New York: Wiley.

Schlundt, D. G., & Johnson, W. G. (1990). *Eating disorders: Assessment and treatment.* Boston: Allyn & Bacon.

Schmeck, H. M., Jr. (1984, March 6). Explosion of data on brain cell reveals its great complexity. *New York Times,* pp. C-1–C-2.

Schmeck, H. M., Jr. (1987, December 29). New light on the chemistry of dreams. *New York Times,* pp. C-1, C-2.

Schmeck, H. M., Jr. (1988, February 16). Depression: Studies bring new drugs and insights. *New York Times,* pp. C-1, C-10.

Schneiderman, N. (1983). Animal behavior models of coronary heart disease. In D. S. Krantz, A. Baum, & J. E. Singer (Eds.), *Handbook of psychology and health* (Vol. 3). Hillsdale, NJ: Erlbaum.

Schoeneman, T. J., & Rubanowitz, D. E. (1985). Attributions in the advice columns: Actors and observers, causes and reasons. *Journal of Personality and Social Psychology, 11,* 315–325.

Schofield, W. (1964). *Psychotherapy: The purchase of friendship.* Englewood Cliffs, NJ: Prentice-Hall.

Schwartz, G. E., Davidson, R., & Maer, F. (1975). Right hemisphere lateralization for emotion in the human brain: Interactions with cognition. *Science, 286*–288.

Schwartz, S. H., & Inbar-Saban, N. (1988). Value self-confrontation as a method to aid in weight loss. *Journal of Personality and Social Psychology, 54,* 396–404.

Schwitzgabel, R. L., & Schwitzgabel, R. K. (1980). *Law and psychological practice.* New York: Wiley.

Sears, D. D. (1968). The paradox of de facto selective exposure without preferences for supportive information. In R. P. Abelson (Ed.), *Theories of cognitive consistency.* Chicago: Rand McNally.

Sears, D. O. (1982). The person-positivity bias. *Journal of Personality and Social Psychology, 44,* 233–250.

Sears, D. O. (1986). College sophomores in the laboratory: Influences of a narrow data base on social psychology's view of human nature. *Journal of Personality and Social Psychology, 51,* 515–530.

Sears, R. R. (1977). Sources of life satisfaction of the Terman gifted men. *American Psychologist, 32,* 119–128.

Segall, M. H., Campbell, D. T., & Herskovits, M. J. (1966). *The influence of culture on visual perception.* New York: Bobbs-Merrill.

Seligman, M. E. P. (1975). *Helplessness: On*

depression, development, and death. San Francisco: Freeman.

Seligman, M. E. P. (1988, October). Baby boomer blues. *Psychology Today,* p. 54.

Selman, R. L., Schorin, M. Z., Stone, C. R., & Phelps, E. (1983). A naturalistic study of children's social understanding. *Developmental Psychology, 19,* 82–102.

Selye, H. (1976). *The stress of life.* New York: McGraw-Hill.

Shapiro, S., Skinner, E. A., Kessler, L. G., VonKorff, M., German, P. S., Shapiro, D. H., & Walsh, R. N. (Eds.) (1984). *Meditation: Classical and contemporary perspectives.* New York: Aldine.

Shapley, R. (1990). Visual sensitivity and parallel retinocortical channels. *Annual Review of Psychology, 41,* 635–658.

Shepherd, G. M. (Ed.) (1990). *The synaptic organization of the brain* (3rd ed.). New York: Oxford University Press.

Shock, N. W. (1962, January). The physiology of aging. *Scientific American,* 100–110.

Shotland, R. L. (1984, March). Paper presented at the Catherine Genovese Memorial Conference on Bad Samaritanism, Fordham University.

Shotland, R. L. (1985, June). When bystanders just stand by. *Psychology Today, 19,* pp. 50–55.

Sifakis, C. (1987). *The mafia encyclopedia.* New York: Facts on File.

Sigerist, H. E. (1943). *Civilization and disease.* Ithaca, NY: Cornell University Press.

Silver, R. L., & Wordman, C. B. (1980). Coping with undesirable life events. In J. Barber & M. E. P. Seligman (Eds.), *Human helplessness: Theory and application.* New York: Academic Press.

Simmons, J. V., Jr. (1984). U.S. Patent Office Document #4,261,284 (1981). Washington, D.C.: U.S. Government Printing Office.

Singer, J. L. (1975). *The inner world of daydreaming.* New York: Harper & Row.

Siris, S. G., & Rifkin, A. (1983). Side effects of drugs used in the treatment of affective disorders. In A. Rifkin (Ed.), *Schizophrenia and affective disorders: Biology and drug treatment* (pp. 117–138). Boston: John Wright.

Skinner, B. F. (1957). *Verbal behavior.* New York: Appleton-Century-Crofts.

Skinner, B. F. (1975). The steep and thorny road to a science of behavior. *American Psychologist, 30,* 42–49.

Skrypnek, B. J., & Snyder, M. (1982). On the self-perpetuating nature of stereotypes about women and men. *Journal of Experimental Social Psychology, 18,* 277–291.

Slusher, M. P., & Anderson, C. A. (1987). When reality monitoring fails: The role of imagination in stereotype maintenance. *Journal of Personality and Social Psychology, 52,* 653–662.

Smith, C. A., & Ellsworth, P. C. (1987). Patterns of appraisal and emotion related to taking an exam. *Journal of Personality and Social Psychology, 52,* 475–488.

Smith, E. R. (1984). Attributions and other inferences: Processing information about the self versus others. *Journal of Experimental Social Psychology, 20,* 97–115.

Smith, L. (1987). From global similarities to kinds of similarities: The construction of dimensions in development. In S. Voniadou & A. Ortony (Eds.), *Similarity and analogy.* Cambridge, England: Cambridge University Press.

Smith, M. B. (1990). Psychology in the public interest: What have we done? What can we do? *American Psychologist, 45,* 530–536.

Smith, M. L., Glass, G. V., & Miller, T. J. (1980). *The benefits of psychotherapy.* Baltimore: John Hopkins.

Snarey, J. R. (1985). Cross-cultural universality of social-moral development: A critical review of Kohlbergian research. *Psychological Bulletin, 97,* 202–232.

Snyder, C. R., & Higgins, R. L. (1988). Excuses: Their effective role in the negotiation of reality. *Psychological Bulletin, 104,* 23–35.

Snyder, M., & Cantor, N. (1979). Testing hypotheses about other people: The use of historical knowledge. *Journal of Experimental Social Psychology, 15,* 330–343.

Snyder, S. H. (1978). Dopamine and schizophrenia. In L. C. Wynne, R. L. Cromwell, & S. Matthysse (Eds.), *The nature of schizophrenia: New approaches to research and treatment* (pp. 87–94). New York: Wiley.

Snyder, S. H. (1980). *Biological aspects of mental disorder.* New York: Oxford University Press.

Snyder, S. H. (1987, April 30). Parkinson's disease: A cure using brain transplants? *Nature, 326,* 824–825.

Solomon, R. L., & Corbit, J. D. (1974). An opponent-process theory of motivation: I. Temporal dynamics of affect. *Psychological Review, 81,* 119–145.

Spanos, N. P. (1986). Hypnotic behavior: A social psychological interpretation of amnesia, analgesia, and "trance logic." *Behavioral and Brain Science, 9,* 449–467.

Spanos, N. P., Cross, W. P., Menary, E. P., Brett, P. J., & deGroic, M. (1987). Attitudinal and imaginal ability predictors of social cognitive skill-training enhancements in hypnotic susceptibility. *Personality and Social Psychology Bulletin, 13,* 379–398.

Spanos, N. P., James, B., & deGroot, H. P. (1990). Detection of simulated hypnotic amnesia. *Journal of Abnormal Psychology, 99,* 179–182.

Spear, N. E., Miller, J. S., & Jagielo, J. A. (1990). Animal memory and learning. *Annual Review of Psychology, 41,* 169–211.

Spearman, C. (1927). *The abilities of man.* London: Macmillan.

Spence, J. T. (1985, August). *Achievement American style: The rewards and costs of individualism.* Presidential address. 93rd Annual Convention of the American Psychological Association (Los Angeles).

Spence, J. T. (1987). Centrifugal versus centripetal tendencies in psychology: Will the center hold? *American Psychologist, 42,* 1052–1054.

Spence, M. J., & DeCasper, A. J. (1982, March). Human fetuses perceive maternal speech. Paper presented at the meeting of the International Conference on Infant Studies (Austin, Texas).

Sperling, G. (1960). The information available in brief visual presentation. *Psych Monographs, 74* (whole no. 498).

Spiegel, H. (1987). The answer is: Psychotherapy plus. Special Issue: Is hypnotherapy a placebo? *British Journal of Experimental and Clinical Hypnosis, 4,* 163–164.

Spiegel, R. (1989). *Psychopharmacology: An introduction* (2nd ed.). New York: Wiley.

Spitzer, R. L., Skodol, A. E., Gibbon, M., & Williams, J. B. W. (1983). *Psychopathology: A case book.* New York: McGraw-Hill.

Springer, S. P., & Deutsch, G. (1989). *Left brain, right brain* (3rd ed.) New York: Freeman.

Sroufe, L. A., Fox, N. E., & Pancake, V. R. (1983). Attachment and dependency in a developmental perspective. *Child Development, 54,* 1615–1627.

Staats, A. W. (1967). Outline of an integrated learning theory of attitude formation and function. In M. Fishbein (Ed.), *Attitude theory and measurement.* New York: Wiley.

Staats, A. W., & Staats, C. K. (1958). Attitudes

established by classical conditioning. *Journal of Abnormal and Social Psychology, 57,* 37–40.

Stanley, J. C. (1980). On educating the gifted. *Educational Researcher, 9,* 8–12.

Stapp, J., Tucker, A. M., & VandenBos, G. R. (1985). Census of psychology personnel. *American Psychologist, 40,* 1317–1351.

Stava, L. J., & Jaffa, M. (1988). Some operationalizations of the neodissociation concept and their relationship to hypnotic susceptibility. *Journal of Personality and Social Psychology, 54,* 989–996.

Steele, C. M., & Southwick, L. (1985). Alcohol and social behavior I: The psychology of drunken excess. *Journal of Personality and Social Psychology, 48,* 18–34.

Stein, J. A., Newcomb, M. D., & Bentler, P. M. (1987). An 8-year study of multiple influences on drug use and drug-use consequences. *Journal of Personality and Social Psychology, 53,* 1094–1105.

Steinberg, L. (1987, September). Bound to bicker. *Psychology Today,* pp. 36–39.

Steinberg, L., Belsky, J., & Meyer, R. B. (1991). *Infancy, childhood, & adolescence.* New York: McGraw-Hill.

Steiner, J. E. (1979). Human facial expressions in response to taste and smell stimulation. In H. Reese & L. P. Lipsitt (Eds.), *Advances in child development and behavior* (Vol. 13). New York: Academic Press.

Sternbach, R. A. (Ed.) (1987). *The psychology of pain.* New York: Raven Press.

Sternberg, R. J. (1982). Reasoning, problem solving, and intelligence. In R. J. Sternberg (Ed.), *Handbook of human intelligence* (pp. 225–307). Cambridge, MA: Cambridge University Press.

Sternberg, R. J. (1985). Implicit theories of intelligence, creativity, and wisdom. *Journal of Personality and Social Psychology, 49,* 607–627. (a)

Sternberg, R. J. (1985). *Beyond IQ: A triarchic theory of human intelligence.* New York: Cambridge University Press. (b)

Sternberg, R. J. (1986). Triangular theory of love. *Psychological Review, 93,* 119–135.

Sternberg, R. J. (1987). Liking versus loving: A comparative evaluation of theories. *Psychological Bulletin, 102,* 331–345.

Sternberg, R. J., Conway, B. E., Ketron, J. L., & Bernstein, M. (1981). Peoples' conceptions of intelligence. *Journal of Personality and Social Psychology, 41,* 37–55.

Sternberg, R. J., & Davidson, J. E. (Eds.)

(1986). *Conceptions of giftedness.* New York: Cambridge University Press.

Sternberg, R. J., & Detterman, D. (1986). *What is intelligence?* Norwood, NJ: Ablex.

Sternberg, R. J., & Grajek, S. (1984). The nature of love. *Journal of Personality and Social Psychology, 47,* 312–329.

Storandt, M., et al. (1984). Psychometric differentiation of mild senile dementia of the Alzheimer type. *Archives of Neurology, 41,* 497–499.

Streufert, S. (1984, October). The stress of excellence. *Across the Board,* 9–16.

Stricker, E. M., & Zigmond, M. J. (1976). Recovery of function after damage to catecholamine-containing neurons: A neurochemical model for hypothalmic syndrome. In J. M. Sprague & A. N. Epstein (Eds.), *Progress in psychobiology and physiological psychology* (Vol. 6). New York: Academic Press.

Strickland, B. (1988, August). Winning the battle against depression: Strategies for women. Paper presented at the annual meeting of the American Psychological Association (Atlanta).

Stroop, J. R. (1935). Studies of interference in serial verbal reactions. *Journal of Experimental Psychology, 18,* 643–662.

Strupp, H. H. (1981). Toward a refinement of time-limited dynamic psychotherapy. *Forms of brief therapy.* New York: Guilford Press.

Suddath, R. L., Christison, G. W., Torrey, E. F., Casanova, M. F., & Weinberger, D. R. (1990, March 22). Anatomical abnormalities in the brains of monozygotic twins discordant for schizophrenia. *New England Journal of Medicine, 322,* 789–794.

Sue, D. (1979). Erotic fantasies of college students during coitus. *Journal of Sex Research, 15,* 299–305.

Sugarman, S. (1989). *Piaget's construction of the child's reality.* Cambridge, England: Cambridge University Press.

Sulzer-Azaroff, B., & Mayer, G. R. (1986). *Achieving educational excellence with behavioral strategies.* New York: Holt, Rinehart and Winston.

Super, C. M. (1980). Cognitive development: Looking across at growing up. In C. M. Super & S. Harakness (Eds.), *New directions for child development: Anthropological perspectives on child development* (pp. 59–69). San Francisco: Jossey-Bass.

Sweeney, P. D., & Gruber, L. L. (1984). Selective exposure: Voter information preferences and the Watergate affair. *Journal of Personality and Social Psychology, 46,* 1208–1221.

Sweetland, R. C., & Keyser, D. J. (1988). *Tests: A comprehensive reference for assessments in psychology, education, and business.* Kansas City: Test Corporation of America.

Szasz, T. (1961). *The myth of mental illness.* New York: Harper & Row.

Szasz, T. (1982). The psychiatric will: A new mechanism for protecting persons against "psychosis" and psychiatry. *American Psychologist, 37,* 762–770.

Szasz, T. (1987). *Insanity and its consequences.* New York: Wiley.

Tagiuri, R. (1958). Social preference and its perception. In R. Tagiuri & L. Petrullo (Eds.), *Person, perception, and interpersonal behavior* (pp. 316–336). Stanford, CA: Stanford University Press.

Talley, P. F., Strupp, H. H., & Morey, L. C. (1990). Matchmaking in psychotherapy: Patient-therapist dimensions and their impact on outcome. *Journal of Consulting and Clinical Psychology, 58,* 182–188.

Tamura, T., Nakatani, K., & Yau, K. -W. (1989, August 18). Light adaptation in cat retinal rods. *Science, 245,* 755–758.

Tanford, S., & Penrod, S. (1984). Social influence model: A formal integration of research on majority and minority influence processes. *Psychological Bulletin, 95,* 189–225.

Terman, L. M., & Oden, M. H. (1947). *Genetic studies of genius, IV: The gifted child grows up.* Stanford, CA: Stanford University Press.

Tesser, A., & Shaffer, D. (1990). Attitudes and attitude change. *Annual Review of Psychology, 41,* 479–524.

Thatcher, R. W., Walker, R. A., & Giudice, S. (1987, May 29). Human cerebral hemispheres develop at different rates and ages. *Science, 236,* 1110–1114.

Thorndike, E. L. (1932). *The fundamentals of learning.* New York: Teachers College.

Thorndike, R. L., Hagan, E., & Sattler, J. (1986). *Stanford-Binet* (4th ed.). Chicago: Riverside.

Thurstone, L. L. (1928). Attitudes can be measured. *American Journal of Sociology, 33,* 529–554.

Tierney, J. (1988, May 15). Wired for stress. *New York Times Magazine,* pp. 49–85.

Time. (1976, September). Svengali squad: L.A. police. *Time*, p. 76.

Tolman, E. C., & Honzik, C. H. (1930). Introduction and removal of reward and maze performance in rats. *University of California Publications in Psychology, 4,* 257–275.

Tomlinson-Keasey, C., Eisert, D. C., Kahle, L. R., Hardy-Brown, K., & Keasey, B. (1979). The structure of concrete operations. *Child Development,* 1153–1163.

Treisman, A., & Gormican, S. (1988). Feature analysis in early vision: Evidence from search asymmetries. *Psychological Review, 95,* 15–48.

Treisman, M. (1960). Motion sickness: An evolutionary hypothesis. *Science,* pp. 493–495.

Tross, S., & Hirsch, D. A. (1988). Psychological distress and neuropsychological complications of HIV infection and AIDS. *American Psychologist, 43,* 924–934.

Tuchman, G. (1978). The symbolic annihilation of women by the mass media. In G. Tuchman, A. K. Daniels, & J. Benet (Eds.), *Hearth and home: Images of women in the mass media.* New York: Oxford University Press.

Tuller, D. (1985, February 24). What's new in employment testing? *New York Times,* p. 17.

Tulving, E. (1983). *Elements of episodic memory.* New York: Oxford University Press.

Tulving, E., & Psotka, J. (1971). Retroactive inhibition in free recall: Inaccessibility of information available in the memory store. *Journal of Experimental Psychology, 87,* 1–8.

Tulving, E., & Schachter, D. L. (1990, January 19). Priming and human memory systems. *Science, 247,* 301–306.

Tulving, E., & Thompson, D. M. (1973). Encoding specificity and retrieval processes in episodic memory. *Psychological Review, 80,* 352–373.

Turkington, C. (1985, September). Computer unlocks secrets in folds, functions of brain. *APA Monitor.*

Turkington, C. (1986, August). Pot and the immune system. *APA Monitor,* p. 22.

Turkington, C. (1987, September). Special talents. *Psychology Today,* pp. 42–46.

Tversky, B. (1981). Distortions in memory for maps. *Cognitive Psychology, 13,* 407–433.

Tversky, A., & Kahneman, D. (1974). Judgment under uncertainty: Heuristics and biases. *Science, 185,* 1124–1131.

Udolf, R. (1981). *Handbook of hypnosis for professionals.* New York: Van Nostrand.

Ullman, L. P., & Krasner, L. (1975). *A psychological approach to abnormal behavior* (2nd ed.). Englewood Cliffs, NJ: Prentice-Hall.

U.S. Department of Health and Human Services. (1990). *Seventh Special Report to the U.S. Congress on Alcohol and Health.* Washington, DC: U.S. Department of Health and Human Services.

Vaillant, G. E. (1984). The disadvantages of DSM-III outweigh its advantages. *American Journal of Psychiatry, 141,* 542–545.

Valenstein, E. S. (Ed.) (1980). *The psychosurgery debate: Scientific, legal, and ethical perspectives.* San Francisco: Freeman.

Veroff, J. (1982). Assertive motivations: Achievement versus power. In A. J. Steward (Ed.), *Motivation and Society.* San Francisco: Jossey-Bass.

Vonnegut, M. (1975). *The Eden express.* New York: Bantam.

Von Restorff, H. (1933). Uber die wirking von bereichsbildumgen im Spurenfeld. In W. Kohler & H. VonRestorff, *Analyse von vorgangen in Spurenfeld. I. Psychologische forschung, 18,* 299–342.

Wagner, H. L., MacDonald, C. J., & Manstead, A. S. R. (1986). Communication of individual emotions by spontaneous facial expressions. *Journal of Personality and Social Psychology, 50,* 737–743.

Waldrop, M. W. (1989, September 29). NIDA aims to fight drugs with drugs. *Science, 245,* 1443–1444.

Wall, P. D., & Melzack, R. (Eds.) (1984). *Textbook of pain.* Edinburgh, Scotland: Churchill Livingstone.

Wallace, R. K., & Benson, H. (1972, February). The physiology of meditation. *Scientific American,* pp. 84–90.

Wallis, C. (1984, June 11). Unlocking pain's secrets. *Time,* pp. 58–60.

Walster, E., & Walster, G. W. (1978). *Love.* Reading, MA: Addison-Wesley.

Warga, C. (1987, August). Pain's gatekeeper. *Psychology Today,* pp. 51–56.

Washton, A. M., & Gold, M. S. (Eds.) (1987). *Cocaine: A clinician's handbook.* New York: Guilford.

Watkins, L. R., & Mayer, D. J. (1982). Organization of endogenous opiate and nonopiate pain control systems. *Science, 216,* pp. 1185–1192.

Watson, D. (1982). The actor and the observer: How are their perceptions of causality divergent? *Psychological Bulletin, 92,* 682–700.

Watson, J. B. (1930). *Behaviorism.* New York: Norton.

Watson, J. B., & Rayner, R. (1920). Conditioned emotional reactions. *Journal of Experimental Psychology, 3,* 1–14.

Watt, N. (Ed.) (1985). *Children at risk for schizophrenia.* Cambridge, England: Cambridge University Press.

Webb, W. B. (1979). Sleep and dreams. In B. B. Wolman (Ed.), *Handbook of general psychology* (pp. 734–748). Englewood Cliffs, NJ: Prentice-Hall.

Weber, R., & Crocker, J. (1983). Cognitive processes in the revision of stereotypic beliefs. *Journal of Personality and Social Psychology, 45,* 961–977.

Wechsler, D. (1975). Intelligence defined and undefined. *American Psychologist, 30,* 135–139.

Weinberg, C. (1979). *Self-creation.* New York: Avon.

Weinberg, R. A. (1989). Intelligence and IQ: Landmark issues and great debates. *American Psychologist, 44,* 98–104.

Weiner, B. (1985). *Human motivation.* New York: Springer-Verlag.

Weiner, R. (1982). Another look at an old controversy. *Contemporary Psychiatry, 1,* 61–62.

Weitzenhoffer, A. M. (1989). *The practice of hypnotism.* New York: Wiley.

Wells, G. L., & Harvey, J. H. (1978). Naive attributors' attributions and predictions: What is informative and when is an effect an effect? *Journal of Personality and Social Psychology, 36,* 483–490.

Wells, G. L., & Loftus, E. A. (Eds.) (1984). *Eyewitness testimony: Psychological perspectives.* New York: Cambridge University Press.

Wells, G. L., & Luus, C. A. E. (1990). Police lineups as experiments: Social methodology as a framework for properly conducted lineups. *Personality and Social Psychology Bulletin, 16,* 106–117.

Wender, P. H., Kety, S. S., Rosenthal, D., Schulsinger, F., & Ortmann, J. (1986). Psychiatric disorders in the biological and adoptive families of adopted individuals with affective disorders. *Archives of General Psychiatry, 43,* 923–929.

Wender, P. H., & Klein, D. F. (1981, February). The promise of biological psychiatry. *Psychology Today,* pp. 25–41.

Wertheimer, M. (1923). Untersuchuugen zur lehre von der Gestalt. II. *Psychol. Forsch., 5,* pp. 301–350. In M. Beardsley and M. Wertheimer (Eds.) (1958), *Readings in perception.* New York: Van Nostrand.

Western, D. (1990). Psychoanalytic approaches to personality. In L. A. Pervin (Ed.), *Handbook of personality theory and research.* New York: Guilford.

Westoff, C. F. (1974). Coital frequency and contraception. *Family Planning Perspectives, 8,* 54–57.

Westover, S. A., & Lanyon, R. I. (1990). *Behavior Modification, 14,* 123–137.

Whalen, D. H., & Liberman, A. M. (1987, July 10). Speech perception takes precedence over nonspeech perception. *Science, 237,* 169–171.

Whitam, F. L. (1977). The homosexual role: A reconsideration. *Journal of Sex Research, 13,* 1–11.

Whitbourne, S. K. (1986). *Adult development* (2nd ed.). New York: Praeger.

Whorf, B. L. (1956). *Language, thought, and reality.* New York: Wiley.

Wickens, C. D. (1984). *Engineering psychology and human performance.* Columbus, OH: Merrill.

Widmeyer, W. N., & Loy, J. W. (1988). When you're hot, you're hot! Warm-cold effects in first impressions of persons and teaching effectiveness. *Journal of Educational Psychology, 80,* 118–121.

Wielkiewicz, R. M. (1985). *Behavior management in the schools: Principles and procedures.* New York: Pergamon.

Wiener, E. L., & Nagel, D. C. (1988). *Human factors in aviation.* Orlando, FL: Academic Press.

Wilkinson, A. C. (Ed.) (1983). *Classroom computers and cognitive science.* New York: Academic Press.

Willis, S. L. (1988). Cohort differences in cognitive aging: A sample case. In K. W. Schaie & C. Schooler (Eds.), *Social structure and aging: Psychological processes.* Hillsdale, NJ: Erlbaum.

Wilson, G. T., Franks, C. M., Kendall, P. C., & Foreyt, J. P. (1987). *Review of behavior therapy: Theory and practice* (Vol. 11). New York: Guilford Press.

Wilson, T. D., & Linville, P. (1982). Improving academic performance of college freshmen: Attribution therapy revisited. *Journal* *of Personality and Social Psychology, 42,* 367–376.

Wilson, T. D., & Linville, P. W. (1985). Improving the performance of college freshmen with attributional techniques. *Journal of Personality and Social Psychology, 49,* 287–293.

Winch, R. F. (1958). *Mate selection: A study of complementary needs.* New York: Harper & Row.

Winokur, G. (1983). Alcoholism and depression. *Substance and Alcohol Actions/Misuse, 4,* 111–119.

Winter, D. G. (1973). *The power motive.* New York: Free Press.

Winter, D. G. (1976, July). What makes the candidate run? *Psychology Today,* pp. 45–92.

Winter, D. G. (1988). The power motive in women—and men. *Journal of Personality and Social Psychology, 54,* 510–519.

Wolf, S. (1985). Manifest and latent influence of majorities and minorities. *Journal of Personality and Social Psychology, 48,* 899–908.

Wolozin, B. L., Pruchnicki, A., Dickson, D. W., & Davies, P. (1986). A neuronal antigen in the brains of Alzheimer patients. *Science, 232,* 648–650.

Wolpe, J. (1969). *The practice of behavior therapy.* New York: Pergamon.

Wong, D. F., Gjedde, A., Wagner, H. M., Jr., Dannals, R. F., Links, J. M., Tune, L. E., & Pearlson, G. D. (1988, February 12). Response to Zeeberg, Gibson, and Reba. *Science, 239,* 790–791.

Wong, D. F., Wagner, H. N., Jr., Tune, L. E., Dannals, R. F., Pearlson, G. D., Links, J. M., Tamminga, C. A., Broussolle, E. P., Ravert, H. T., Wilson, A. A., Toung, T., Malat, J., Williams, J. A., O'Tuama, L. A., Snyder, S. H., Kuhar, M. J., & Gjedde, A. (1986, December 19). Positron emission tomography reveals elevated D2 Dopamine receptors in drug-naive schizophrenics. *Science, 234,* 1558–1563.

Wood, J. M., & Bootzin, R. (1990). The prevalence of nightmares and their independence from anxiety. *Journal of Abnormal Psychology, 99,* 64–68.

Woodruff, R. A., Clayton, P. J., & Guze, S. B. (1975). Is everyone depressed? *American Journal of Psychiatry, 132,* 627–628.

Wu, C., & Shaffer, D. R. (1987). Susceptibility to persuasive appeals as a function of source credibility and prior experience with the attitude object. *Journal of Personality and Social Psychology, 52,* 677–688.

Wyden, B. (1971, December). Growth: 45 crucial months. *Life,* pp. 93–95.

Wynne, L. C., Singer, M. T., Bartko, J. J., & Toohey, M. L. (1975). Schizophrenics and their families: Recent research on parental communication. *Psychiatric Research: The Widening Perspective.* New York: International Universities Press.

Yamamato, T., Yuyama, N., & Kawamura, Y. (1981). Cortical neurons responding to tactile, thermal and taste stimulations of the rat's tongue. *Brain Research, 22,* 202–206.

Yates, A. J. (1980). *Biofeedback and the modification of behavior.* New York: Plenum Press.

Zajonc, R. B. (1968). The attitudinal effects of mere exposure. *Journal of Personality and Social Psychology, 9,* 1–27.

Zajonc, R. B. (1985). Emotion and facial efference: A theory reclaimed. *Science, 228,* 15–21.

Zanna, M. P., & Pack, S. J. (1974). On the self-fulfilling nature of apparent sex differences in behavior. *Journal of Experimental Social Psychology, 11,* 583–591.

Zarate, M. A., & Smith, E. R. (1990). Person categorization and stereotyping. *Social Cognition, 8,* 161–185.

Zeman, N. (1989, October 3). Fear of flying. *Newsweek,* p. 10.

Zigler, E., & Glick, M. (1988). Is paranoid schizophrenia really camouflaged depression? *American Psychologist, 43,* 284–290.

Zillman, D. (1978). *Hostility and aggression.* Hillsdale, NJ: Erlbaum.

Zillman, D., & Bryant, J. (1984). Effects of massive exposure to pornography. In N. Malamuth & E. Donnerstein (Eds.), *Pornography and sexual aggression.* Orlando, FL: Academic Press.

Zimmer, J. (1984). Courting the Gods of sport: Athletes use superstition to ward off the devils of injury and bad luck. *Psychology Today, 18,* 36–39.

Zivin, G. (Ed.) (1985). *The development of expressive behavior: Biology-environmental interactions.* New York: Academic Press.

Zubin, J., & Spring, B. (1977). Vulnerability: New view of schizophrenia. *Journal of Abnormal Psychology, 86,* 103–126.

Zuckerman, M., Kuhlman, D. M., & Camac, C. (1988). What lies beyond E and N? Factor analyses of scales believed to measure basic dimensions of personality. *Journal of Personality and Social Psychology, 54,* 96–107.

Credits

❖

Meister/Staatliche Kunstammlungen Kassel; bottom right, National Galleries of Scotland/Duke of Sutherland; bottom left, © Scala Art Resource, 1986, p. 342; James Kamp/Black Star, p. 346

Chapter 9 Joel Gordon, p. 356; George Gardner/The Image Works, p. 360; UPI/Bettmann Newsphotos, p. 372; Eugenia Clark/American Museum of Natural History, p. 383; Bettman Archive, p. 385; Joe Connor/Stock, Boston, p. 394; Richard Hutchings/Science Source/Photo Researchers, p. 395

Chapter 10 Chester Higgins, Jr./The New York Times, p. 405; Bonnie Freer/Photo Researchers, p. 409; Bettmann Archive, p. 414; James Wilson/Woodfin Camp & Assoc., p. 424; Photo Fest, p. 428; Susan Greenwood/Liaison Agency, p. 430; Richard Choy/Peter Arnold, Inc., p. 431; Bettmann Archive, p. 433; Wide World Photos, p. 436

Chapter 11 Innervisions, p. 452; Lester Sloan/Woodfin Camp & Assoc., p. 455; Courtesy of Albert Ellis, p. 459; Alex Webb/Magnum, p. 465; Kenneth Karp, p. 473; Will McIntyre/Photo Researchers, p. 476

Chapter 12 Left, James Hamilton/Sygma; right, Sygma, p. 483; Comstock, Inc., p. 487

Chapter 13 Andy Levin, p. 514; Innervisions, p. 516; Courtesy of Albert Bandura, Stanford University, p. 528; Erika Stone/Peter Arnold, Inc., p. 534; J. L. BarKan/The Picture Cube, p. 542; John Griffin/The Image Works, p. 544

Name Index

Subject Index

Acknowledgments

❖

Figure 1-1 from Stapp, J., Tucker, A. M., & VandenBos, G. R., Census of Psychology personnel. *American Psychologist, 40,* 1324. Copyright 1985 by the American Psychological Association. Reprinted by permission of the publisher.

Figure 2-7 adapted from Nanta, W. J. H., & Feirtag, M., The organization of the brain. *Scientific American.* Copyright 1979 by Scientific American, Inc. All rights reserved.

Figure 2-8b adapted from Geschevird, N., Specializations of the human brain. *Scientific American.* Copyright 1979 by Scientific American, Inc. All rights reserved.

Figure 3-3 from Coren, S., Porac, C., & Ward, L. M., *Sensation and Perception* (2nd ed.), 1984. Orlando, FL: Harcourt Brace Jovanovich.

Figure 3-4 from Lindsey, P. H., & Norman, D. A., *Human Information Processing* (2nd ed.), 1977. Orlando, FL: Harcourt Brace Jovanovich.

Figure 3-10 from Boring, E. G., Langfeld, H. S., & Weld, H. P., *Foundations of Psychology.* Copyright 1948 by John Wiley and Sons, Inc. Reprinted by permission of the publisher and Mednick, S. A., Higgins, J., & Kirschbaum, J., *Psychology: Explorations in Behavior and Experiences.* 1974. NY: John Wiley and Sons, Inc.

Figure 3-13 from James, Ronald C., from Carraher, R. G., & Thurson, J. B., *Optical Illusions in the Visual Arts.* 1966. NY: Von Nostrand Reinhold.

Figures 3-12, 3-17, & 3-18a from Coren, S., Porac, C., & Ward, L. M., *Sensation and Perception* (2nd ed.), 1984. Orlando, FL: Harcourt Brace Jovanovich.

Figure 4-2 from Thorndike, 1932; Sepp/Seitz/Woodfin Camp. & Assoc.

Figure 4-7b from Tolman, E. C., & Henzik, C. H. *University of California Publications in Psychology, 4,* 257–275. Copyright 1930 by University of California Press. Reprinted by permission of the publisher.

Figure 5-1 adapted from Atkinson, R. C., & Shiffrin, R. M., Human memory: A proposed system and its control processes. In K. W. Spence & J. T. Spencer (eds.), *The Psychology of Learning and Motivation: Advances in Research and Theory* (vol. 2), 1968. Orlando, FL: Harcourt Brace Jovanovich.

Figure 5-2 from Kleinmuntz, B., *Problem Solving: Research Method and Theory,* 1966. NY: John Wiley and Sons, Inc.

Figure 5-3 from Rubin, D. C., September 1985. The subtle deceiver: Recalling our past. *Psychology Today, 19,* 39–46.

Figure 5-4 based on Allport, G. W., & Postman, L. J., The basic psychology of rumor. In E. E. Maccoby, T. M. Newcomb, & E. T. Hartley (eds.), *Readings in Social Psychology* (3rd ed.), Copyright 1958 by Holt, Rinehart, Winston. Reprinted by permission.

Figure 5-8 from Bourne, L. E., Dominowski, R. L., Loftus, E. F., & Healy, A. F., *Cognitive Processes* (2nd ed.), 1986, pp. 239, 271. Reprinted by permission of Prentice-Hall, Inc., Englewood Cliffs, NJ.

Figure 5-9 from Anderson, Barry F., *The Complete Thinker,* 1980. Reprinted by permission of Prentice-Hall, Inc., Englewood Cliffs, NJ.

Figure 6-2 from Maslow, Abraham H., *Motivation and Personality,* Copyright 1954, 1987 by Harper & Row, Publishers, Inc. Copyright 1970 by Abraham H. Maslow. Reprinted by permission of Harper & Row Publishers, Inc., NY.

Figure 6-4 from Sue, D., 1979. Erotic fantasies of college students during coitus. *Journal of Sex Research, 15,* 299–305.

Figure 6-7 courtesy of Paul Ekman.

Quotation in Chapter 7 on p. 284 from Milloy, C., *Washington Post,* June 22, 1986, p. A1. Crack users, highs, lows. Reprinted by permission.

Figure 7-2 from Hartmann, E., 1967. *The Biology of Dreaming*. Springfield, IL: Thomas.

Figure 8-5 from Schikendanz, Schikendanz, & Forsythe, 1982.

Figure 8-6 from Tanner, J. M., *Education and Physical Growth* (2nd ed.), 1978. Madison, CT: International University Press.

Table 8-3 from Kohlberg, L., Stage and sequence: The cognitive developmental approach to specialization. In *Handbook of Socialization Theory and Research*, David A. Goslin (ed.), Copyright 1969 by Houghton Mifflin Company. Reprinted with permission.

Figure 9-2 adapted from Catell, Eber, & Tatsuoka. Copyright 1970 by the Institute for Personality and Ability Testing. Reproduced by permission.

Figure 9-3 from Eysenck, H. J., *Eysenck on Extraversion*, 1973. Collins Professional and Technical Books, Ltd.

Figure 9-8 from Sternberg, R. J., Reasoning, problem solving, and intelligence. In R. J. Sternberg (ed.), *Handbook of Human Intelligence*. Copyright 1982 by Cambridge University Press. Reprinted by permission of the publisher and the author.

Quotation in Chapter 10 from Kraines, S. H., *The Therapy of the Neuroses and Psychoses* (3rd ed.), 1948. Philadelphia, PA: Lea and Febinger.

Quotation in Chapter 10 from Spitzer, R. L., Skodol, A. E., Gibbon, M., & Williams, J. B. W. *Psychopathology: A Case Book*, 1983. NY: McGraw-Hill Book Co.

Figure 10-3 from Zubin, J., & Spring B., A new view of schizophrenia. *Journal of Abnormal Psychology, 86*, 103. Copyright 1977 by the American Psychological Association. Reprinted with permission.

Quotation on pp. 440–441 from Duke, M. & Nowicki, S., *Abnormal Psychology: Perspectives on Being Different*, 1979, pp. 309–310, Monterey, CA: Brooks Cole.

Quotation in Chapter 11 from Goldfried, M. R., & Davison, G. C., *Clinical Behavior Therapy*. Copyright 1976 by Holt, Rinehart, and Winston.

Table 11-2 from Benson, Herbert, *The Relaxation Response*. Copyright 1975 by William Morrow and Company, Inc., NY.

Figure 13-1 from Parlee, M. B. The friendship bond. *Psychology Today*, October 3, 1979. Reprinted with permission from *Psychology Today Magazine*. Copyright 1979 (PT Partners, L.P.).

Table 13-1 excerpted from Rubin, Zick, *Liking and Loving: An Invitation to Social Psychology*. Copyright 1973 by Holt, Rinehart, and Winston, Inc. Reprinted by permission by the publisher.

Table 13-2 from Sternberg, R. J., Triangular theory of love. *Psychological Review, 93*, 119. Copyright 1986 by the American Psychological Association. Reprinted by permission of the publisher and the author.

Table 13-3 from Laver, J., & Laver, R., Marriages made to last. *Psychology Today, 19*, (16), 22–26. Reprinted with permission from *Psychology Today Magazine*. Copyright 1985 (PT Partners, L.P.).

Table 13-4 from Kanner, A. D., Coyne, J. C., Schaefer, C., & Lazarus, R. S., Comparison of two modes of stress measurements: Daily hassles and uplifts versus major life events. *Journal of Behavioral Medicine, 4*, 14. Copyright 1981 by Plenum Publishing Corp. Reprinted with permission.